MAINTENANCE IN MEDIEV

This is the first book covering those who abused and misused the legal system in medieval England and the initial attempts of the Anglo-American legal system to deal with these forms of legal corruption. Maintenance, in the sense of intermeddling in another person's litigation, was a source of repeated complaint in medieval England. This book reveals for the first time what actually transpired in the resultant litigation. Extensive study of the primary sources shows that the statutes prohibiting maintenance did not achieve their objectives because legal proceedings were rarely brought against those targeted by the statutes: the great and the powerful. Illegal maintenance was less extensive than frequently asserted because medieval judges recognized a number of valid justifications for intermeddling in litigation. Further, the book casts doubt on the effectiveness of the statutory regulation of livery. In fact litigants used maintenance litigation to harass and burden their opponents. This book is a treasure trove for legal historians, literature scholars, lawyers, and academic libraries.

JONATHAN ROSE is Professor of Law and Willard H. Pedrick Distinguished Research Scholar Emeritus, Sandra Day O'Connor College of Law, Arizona State University; Faculty Affiliate, Arizona Center for Medieval and Renaissance Studies, Arizona State University; Affiliated Faculty Member, Department of History, Arizona State University. He has taught Legal History, Contracts, Professional Responsibility, and Antitrust. He has received several awards for outstanding teaching. Professor Rose is the author of numerous articles and other works on legal history, antitrust, economic regulation, and legal ethics.

CAMBRIDGE STUDIES IN ENGLISH LEGAL HISTORY

Edited by
J. H. Baker

Fellow of St Catharine's College, Cambridge

Recent Series Titles Include

MAINTENANCE IN MEDIEVAL ENGLAND

JONATHAN ROSE

Sandra Day O'Connor College of Law
Arizona State University

CAMBRIDGE
UNIVERSITY PRESS

CAMBRIDGE
UNIVERSITY PRESS

University Printing House, Cambridge CB2 8BS, United Kingdom

One Liberty Plaza, 20th Floor, New York, NY 10006, USA

477 Williamstown Road, Port Melbourne, VIC 3207, Australia

314-321, 3rd Floor, Plot 3, Splendor Forum, Jasola District Centre, New Delhi - 110025, India

79 Anson Road, #06-04/06, Singapore 079906

Cambridge University Press is part of the University of Cambridge.

It furthers the University's mission by disseminating knowledge in the pursuit of
education, learning and research at the highest international levels of excellence.

www.cambridge.org
Information on this title: www.cambridge.org/9781107619791
DOI: 10.1017/9781107358324

First published 2017
First paperback edition 2018

A catalogue record for this publication is available from the British Library

Library of Congress Cataloging in Publication data
Names: Rose, Jonathan, 1938- author.
Title: Maintenance in medieval England / Jonathan Rose, Arizona State University.
Description: New York, NY : Cambridge University Press, 2017. | Series: Cambridge studies in
english legal history | Includes bibliographical references and index.
Identifiers: LCCN 2016046126 | ISBN 9781107043985 (hardback : alk. paper)
Subjects: LCSH: Public interest law–Great Britain–History–To 1500. |
Judicial corruption–England–History–To 1500. | Actions and defenses–England–History–
To 1500. | Law–England–History–To 1500. | Law, Medieval.
Classification: LCC KD667.P83 R67 2017 | DDC 347.42/05–dc23 LC record available
at https://lccn.loc.gov/2016046126

ISBN 978-1-107-04398-5 Hardback
ISBN 978-1-107-61979-1 Paperback

To Wendy
For her support, endurance, and love

CONTENTS

FIGURES

TABLES

PREFACE AND ACKNOWLEDGMENTS

This book has a serendipitous origin. My interest in English legal history grew out of a sabbatical project on the ethical rules governing the American legal profession. As part of that effort, I studied the origins of the legal profession and its regulation in medieval England. That inquiry resulted in an article that changed my scholarly career.[1] After three decades of focusing on other legal subjects, I decided to change my primary scholarly interest to English legal history. Learning the necessary language and paleographic skills and developing an intellectual foundation from the scholarly literature were arduous and time-consuming tasks.[2] In pursuing this new undertaking, my earlier interests in the legal profession influenced my research topics.

One of my earliest efforts was an article on conflicts of interest by medieval lawyers.[3] This research introduced me to Sir John Fastolf and led me to the first of many visits to the Archives of Magdalen College, University of Oxford, and The National Archives, Public Record Office in Kew. As I made my way through the Fastolf Papers and the plea rolls recording the litigation of Fastolf and his servants, I encountered the medieval actions of conspiracy, maintenance, and attaint, which was the first step on the path to this book. Initially, this research produced a draft article on lordship, maintenance, and fifteenth-century social and legal norms with Fastolf's maintenance and related litigation as illustrative. Readers of the draft suggested that more plea roll research would enrich the article and that a book rather than an article might be feasible and appropriate. Thus, I began many hours of research in the plea rolls and

---

[1] Jonathan Rose, "The Legal Profession in Medieval England: A History of Regulation," *Syracuse Law Review* 48 (1998), pp. 1–137.
[2] Jonathan Rose, "Learning to Be a Legal Historian: Reflections of a Non-Traditional Student," *Journal of Legal Education* 51 (2001), pp. 294–304.
[3] Jonathan Rose, "The Ambidextrous Lawyer: Conflict of Interest and the Medieval Legal Profession," *The University of Chicago Law School Roundtable* 7 (2000), pp. 136–203.

Year Books collecting maintenance and related actions and cases as well as perusing the petitions to the king, his council, and parliament complaining about maintenance and abuse by powerful individuals and officials. In the process, many relevant primary sources were found, which suggested some interesting conclusions about the law of maintenance in medieval England. This research and its results were the basis of a book proposal to Cambridge University Press.

Over time, the scope of the book expanded. The initial proposal focused on maintenance and litigation in late medieval England, 1377–1485. But the statutes and other legal mechanisms directed at maintenance and other forms of legal corruption and the complaints of petitioners emerged at the beginning of the reign of Edward I (1272–1307). As a result, the temporal and substantive scope of the book expanded to include the various legal measures and litigation involving maintenance, champerty, conspiracy, and abuse of legal procedure in the period 1272–1377. In addition, chapters on earlier social norms regarding assisting persons with their problems and litigation, livery, and medieval literature were added. These changes resulted in a more comprehensive study of maintenance and other forms of abuse of legal procedure in medieval England.

In the course of my work on this book, numerous people provided me with valuable assistance, for which I am very grateful. I am indebted to them in ways too numerous to mention in complete detail. Five persons deserve special mention. John Baker and Paul Brand have provided substantial and extensive assistance over several years. They read drafts of many chapters and made detailed comments. They gave me useful primary sources and references to relevant secondary literature. They helped me understand medieval legal institutions, concepts, and primary sources. They have been mentors as well as friends, who have guided me and unselfishly provided their time, assistance, and support to me on this book and as a newcomer to English legal history. Initially, I was a novice in the use of medieval primary sources, but my language and paleographic skills developed over time. Nevertheless, I still needed assistance from time to time in understanding and transcribing primary sources. Christopher Whittick was my "go to" person on these matters. We have exchanged hundreds of e-mails, in which he provided invaluable help in these tasks. His extensive assistance gave me the benefit of his substantial skills and the unselfish commitment of his time. Susanne Jenks also assisted me in understanding primary sources and provided me with many primary sources. I was fortunate to have her nearby in the Map

Room at The National Archives early in the project on those occasions in which I encountered difficulty in going through the plea rolls. She was always willing to help me. Finally, my wife, Wendy Rose, has read every word of the book and proofread all the chapters. She also endured the impact on our personal life of my numerous trips to The National Archives and Cambridge to do research and my constant need to work on the book over the years.

In addition (I hope I have not omitted anyone), Neil Andrews, Paul Booth, Karen Bradshaw, Jeroan Chorus, Peter Coss, David Crook, Edwin DeWindt, Gwillym Dodd, Charlie Donahue, Paul Eckstein, Chris Given-Wilson, Ralph Griffiths, Richard Helmholz, Michael Hicks, Rosemary Horrox, John Hudson, Lindsey Hunter, Paul Hyams, David Ibbetson, Nicholas Le Poidevin, Gordon McKelvie, Mark Ormrod, Robert Palmer, Ryan Rowberry, Simon Stern, and Henry Summerson have provided assistance in reading and commenting on drafts, identifying relevant primary and secondary sources, and answering my queries on various aspects of medieval English legal history and other matters. Since I am not an expert on medieval literature, I particularly needed help with that chapter in identifying both primary and secondary sources and understanding Middle English. Richard Beadle and Robert Sturges gave me substantial assistance on those matters and also read and commented on that chapter. Diane Facinelli, Robert Meindl, Wendy Scase, and Robert Yeager provided similar assistance. I have presented portions of this book at legal history and medieval conferences in the United States, the United Kingdom, and several other European countries. I want to thank the organizers of those conferences and those who attended my presentations for their interest and comments. Further, significant gratitude is owed to Robert Palmer and those who assisted him in developing the online resource *The Anglo-American Legal Tradition*, for access to the The National Archives, Public Record Office records, and to David Seipp and his website, *Legal History: The Year Books*. It would have been very difficult to do the research necessary to write this book without access to these websites.

I also want to acknowledge several institutional debts. I am grateful for the support that the Sandra Day O'Connor College of Law, Arizona State University, provided for my research and the assistance of the College of Law Library Staff, especially Marianne Alcorn, who sadly passed away before the book was completed. I also want to thank the President and Fellows of Magdalen College, University of Oxford, especially Fellow librarian Christine Ferdinand and archivist Robin Darwell-Smith, for their assistance. I similarly want to express my gratitude to the academic, administrative, and library staff of the Faculty of Law and Clare Hall, University of Cambridge. Finally, I want to thank Cambridge University Press for undertaking this book and Finola O'Sullivan and the others involved for their assistance. For those who want further information on the sources and have comments, I can be contacted at jonathan. rose@asu.edu.

ABBREVIATIONS

A. 3d	Atlantic Law Reports Third
A.C.	Law Reports Appeal Cases
All E.R.	All England Law Reports
CJ	Chief Justice
CJCP	Chief Justice Common Pleas
CJKB	Chief Justice King's Bench
Eng. Rep.	English Report Full Reprint
Img.	Image
J	Judge or Justice
JCP	Justice Common Pleas
JKB	Justice King's Bench
MS	Manuscript
No.	Number
Oxford History	*The Oxford History of the Laws of England*, 11 vols. (Oxford, various dates)
PROME	*Parliament Rolls of Medieval England* C. Given-Wilson, Paul Brand, Seymour Phillips, Mark Ormrod, Geoffrey Martin, Anne Curry, and Rosemary Horrox, eds. (online version)
Q.B.	Law Reports Queen's Bench
Q.B.D.	Law Reports Queen's Bench Division
Co. Rep.	Coke's Reports
S.R.	Statutes of the Realm
TNA: PRO	The National Archives: Public Record Office
tr.	Translation into English by the author. In general, all the descriptions or summaries of the records in the plea rolls and the Year Book cases are my translations.
WL	West Law
W.L.R.	Weekly Law Reports
Y.B.	Year Book

STATUTES AND OTHER LEGISLATION

1

Introduction

A 1315 Commons' Petition complained that

> Because where a great lord, or a man of power, wishes to disgrace a man, he fabricates a trespass against him or he commits himself to maintaining another to whom a trespass has been made and obtains commissions of oyer et terminer from people biased in his favour, and suspect to the opposing party who will commit themselves to doing all that he wishes . . . Also in a plea of land, and in all other pleas, the great lords of the land and those who are powerful, too often undertake to maintaining parties, so that those who have less power, even if they have a right, are not sufficiently able to sue to obtain their right, but they are put thereby in the situation of losing their right forever.[1]

As this petition illustrates, the legal institutions in medieval England designed for dispute settlement created opportunities for misuse of the legal system. Several scholars have suggested that this manipulation and perversion of the machinery of justice was to some extent a product of the decline of violence in settling disputes and was prompted by a desire to advance self-interest.[2] By the thirteenth century, individuals began to petition the crown and parliament to complain about these abuses and these complaints became common. They sometimes used the word "maintenance" to describe various types of wrongdoing, which were often related to litigation or legal issues and undermined the complainants' legal rights and security of property.

---

[1] Edward II: Parliament of January 1315, no. 10 (8) in C. Given-Wilson, Paul Brand, Seymour Phillips, Mark Ormrod, Geoffrey Martin, Anne Curry, and Rosemary Horrox, eds. *British History Online, The Parliament Rolls of Medieval England* (hereafter referred to as *PROME*).

[2] W.S. Holdsworth, *A History of English Law*, 17 vols. (London, 1936–66), vol. III, pp. 394–95. He said that this was a "phenomenon which recurs in many nations in many periods." Ibid., p. 395. McFarlane expressed a similar view, stating that "disorder was obliged to assume subtler forms" as it was "no longer possible . . . to settle a dispute out of court by open violence" and it "was necessary to have recourse to a legal guide." K.B. McFarlane, *The Nobility of Later Medieval England: The Ford Lectures for 1953 and Related Studies* (Oxford, 1973), pp. 102–21.

Moreover, these petitions often alleged the use of power and influence by powerful individuals and officials to pervert the justice system.[3]

By the later thirteenth century, contemporaries considered mainten-ance a significant social and legal problem. Prompted by these concerns and complaints, the king and parliament responded. Beginning in the reign of Edward I (1272–1307), parliament began to enact statutes to deal with the maintenance problem.[4] Starting with the Statute of Westminster I 1275 and continuing through the medieval period, parliament enacted numerous statutes directed at conduct that threatened the proper oper-ation of the legal system.[5] Several of them prohibited maintenance and champerty.[6] Maintenance was assisting and supporting another person's litigation. Champerty[7] was a form of maintenance in which

---

[3] Hyams said that the degeneration of good lordship into abuse was a fascinating story that merited detailed study. Paul Hyams, *Rancor and Reconciliation* (Ithaca, 2003), p. 263.

[4] Misuse of legal procedure as a general phenomenon was not limited to maintenance. As Hudson insightfully pointed out, "Legal norms became detached from social norms. This development allowed those skilled in law to play with legal norms in order to achieve their party's aims, even contrary to the intention of those norms, and in turn new rules had to be devised." John Hudson, "*The Making of English Law* and the Varieties of Legal History," in Stephen Baxter, Catherine Karkov, Janet L. Nelson, and David Pelteret, eds., *Early Medieval Studies in Memory of Patrick Wormald* (Farnham, 2009), p. 431.

[5] McFarlane said that the theory of these statutes was that "lordship should not be so strong as to affect the impartial administration of justice," which in the late thirteenth century was a "novel one, at first not generally accepted, at any rate in practice, and hard to enforce." K.B. McFarlane, "Lords and Retainers," (unpublished manuscript in the Magdalen College Archives, University of Oxford), Lecture III, p. 13). These lectures were delivered in 1966 and were a revision of lectures given in a 1959 course, "Livery and Maintenance." G.L. Harriss "Introduction," in K.B. McFarlane, *England in the Fifteenth Century: Collected Essays* (London, 1981), p. x, n. 2. Gratitude is expressed to the Fellows of Magdalen College and Robin Darwall-Smith, College Archivist, for giving me access to these manuscripts.

[6] More than fifteen statutes were enacted between 1275 and 1542. The primary enactments were: Statute of Westminster I, cc. 25, 28, 33, 3 Edw. I (1275), *Statutes of the Realm*, A. Luders, T. Tomlins, J. France, W. Tauton and J. Raithby, eds., 11 vols. (London, 1810–28), vol. 1, pp. 33–34; Statute of Westminster II, 13 Edw. I, c. 49, *Statutes of the Realm*, vol. 1, p. 95; *Articuli Super Cartas*, 28 Edw. I, st. 3, c. 11, *Statutes of the Realm*, vol. 1, p. 139; Ordinance of Conspirators 1293, Edward I Parliaments: Roll 6, no. 14, *PROME*; 4 Edw. III, c. 11, *Statutes of the Realm*, vol. 1, p. 264; 20 Edw. III, cc. 4, 5, and 6, *Statutes of the Realm*, vol. 1, pp. 304–5; I Rich. II, c. 4, *Statutes of the Realm*, vol. 2, pp. 2–3.

[7] "Champerty" is a Middle English word, deriving from the French, *champart*, referring to a form of tenure in which the landlord received a portion of the produce of the land, and the Latin *campipars* and *cambipars*, part of the field. Max Radin, "Maintenance by Champerty," *California Law Review* 24 (1935), pp. 61–62. *Oxford English Dictionary Online, s.v.* "cham-perty" and "champart." Blackstone associated the word with the Latin, *campum partire*, meaning "to divide the land." William Blackstone, 4 vols., *Commentaries on the Laws of England* (London, 1765–69; facsimile of the first edition, Chicago, 1979), vol. IV, p. 314.

the maintainer entered a covenant with a party to the action to receive all or part of the money or land in dispute if the action were successful in exchange for assisting the litigant.[8] Other statutes with related objectives focused on additional forms of conduct such as embracery, livery, bribery of jurors, extortion, deception, and other misconduct by royal officials as well as deceit and misconduct by members of the legal profession.[9]

"Maintenance" was a word that commonly appeared in several contexts in medieval records and other documents. The ordinary meaning was the provision of support or assistance.[10] Its use in this sense appears in several medieval contexts.[11] But in this period the word "maintenance" also acquired additional meanings. It became a term

---

[8] Blackstone thought that this offense had its roots in Roman law and cited Justinian's Digest. Blackstone, *Commentaries*, vol. IV, pp. 134–35. The provision, which he cited, Dig. 48.7.6, states that "in accordance with the *senatus consultum Volusianum*, persons are liable under the *Lex Julia* on *vis privata* who dishonestly combine in a third party's action with the intention of sharing out between them whatever shall be recovered for his property after his [opponent's] condemnation." Alan Watson, ed., *The Digest of Justinian*, 4 vols. (Philadelphia, 1998), vol. IV, p. 332.

[9] In discussing these statutes, Stephen said that "the offence of maintenance . . . was neither more nor less than chronic organized anarchy, striking at all law and government whatever." James Fitzjames Stephen, *A History of the Criminal Law of England*, 3 vols. (London, 1883), vol. III, p. 238.

[10] *Manutenere* was one of several Latin words used to mean support. Other words included *alere, adjurvare, assistere, favere, fovere,* and *sustinere*.

[11] Medieval arrangements, which modern scholars have labeled "maintenance contracts," provided support during old age to persons who were no longer able to perform labor services and other obligations for the lord and wanted to "retire." These contracts involved transfers of land by villein tenants, often by first surrendering it to the lord, their children, or some other younger person. They frequently obligated the new tenant to provide a place to live and various other types of support to the former tenant or other beneficiary during the latter's life. Richard Firth Green, *A Crisis in Truth* (Philadelphia, 1999), pp. 161–63; L.R. Poos and Lloyd Bonfield, eds., *Select Cases in Manorial Courts 1250–1500* (London, 1998), 114 Selden Society, pp. cxv–cxxvii; R.M. Smith, "The Manorial Court and the Elderly Tenant in Late Medieval England," in Margaret Pelling and Richard Smith, eds., *Life, Death, and the Elderly: Historical Perspectives* (London, 1991), pp. 41–48; Barbara Hanawalt, *The Ties That Bound* (New York, 1986), pp. 229–33; 71–74, 220–22; Elaine Clark, "Some Aspects of Social Security in Medieval England," *Journal of Family Law* 7 (1982); J. Ambrose Raftis, *Tenure and Mobility* (Toronto, 1964), pp. 42–46. The register of the abbeys of Ramsey contained fifty-five such records for the period 1398–1458. *Registrum Abbatiae Ramesiensis*, British Library MS Harley 445; Edwin DeWindt, The *Liber Gersumarum* of Ramsey Abbey: A Calendar and Index of B.L. Harley MS 445 (Toronto, 1976). Poos and Bonfield, who discussed the legal aspects of the agreements and their significance for legal historians, included thirty such records in their volume. Although commentators called them maintenance contracts and sometimes

used to describe abusive conduct that corrupted the justice system, including the maintenance of felons, a form of accessorial criminal liability.[12] By the end of the thirteenth century, maintenance became a specific legal term used to designate a distinct form of unlawful abuse of legal procedure.[13] It meant supporting or assisting a party in litigation, in which one was not a party.[14] In addition, maintenance was a

    used the word "maintain" in translating the records, none of records that were viewed used the word *manutenere*. In these records, the word *sustinere* appeared several times and *adjuvare* once. Most often the agreements said that a room or other form of support was reserved (*reservare*) to the beneficiary, that he or she would have an easement (*aisiamentum*) to or have (*habere*) the room or other form of support or that the new tenant would provide (*invenire*) land or other support. Some agreements also obligated the new tenant to repair and maintain the buildings on the land and used the words *reparare, sustinere,* and *manutenere*.

[12] McFarlane defined its nature in Lancastrian England as "meed, dread, and favor." McFarlane, "Lords and Retainers," Lecture III, pp. 2–3.

[13] Discussions with legal historians outside the Anglo-American tradition suggest that this notion of maintenance was unique to that tradition. However, Stephen asserted that an analogue to medieval England statutes on maintenance and livery existed in Roman law by the incorporation in Justinian's Digest of the *Lex Julia* on *Vis Publica*. Stephen, *History of the Criminal Law*, vol. I, p. 17. That provision was directed, *inter alia,* at "anyone who does something with malicious intent to hinder the safe exercise of justice or hinder judges in the proper giving of judgment ..." Alan Watson, ed., *The Digest of Justinian* (Philadelphia, 1998), vol. IV, p. 331. Blackstone also saw a similarity to the Digest. Blackstone, *Commentaries*, vol. IV, pp. 134–35. There was also a provision in Canon Law called the *juramentum perhorrescentiae*, which entitled a plaintiff to invoke a special jurisdiction of the papal curia to hear a case in which "he could not expect to be able to obtain justice in the provinces because the power of his adversary" (*non sperat in partibus posse consequi iustitiae complementum propter potentiam adversarii*)." Richard Perruso, "The *Iuramentum Perhorrescentiae* under Canon Law: An Influence on the Development of Early Chancery Jurisdiction," *Comparative Legal History* 3 (2014), pp. 2–37. Others have suggested that Justinian's Code contains provisions that might be seen as related. One provision stated "That influential persons shall not be permitted to lend aid to litigants or transfer actions to themselves." Book II, Title XIII, 2.13.1. Another "Concern [ed] those who put placards on their landed estates in the name of dignitaries, or use their name as a pretense in a lawsuit." Ibid., Book II, Title XIV, 2.14.1., Online, uwacadweb. uwyo.edu/blume&justinian/. I am grateful to Jeroen Chorus, Retired Vice-President, Amsterdam Court of Appeal in the Netherlands, for these references and insight. However, these provisions in the Codex are somewhat different from the English maintenance provisions since the focus is on the person who requests the assistance of the powerful man rather than on the activity of the powerful man himself.

[14] Holdsworth stated that maintenance did not acquire this technical meaning until it was made illegal by statutes during the reign of Edward I. Holdsworth, *History English Law*, vol. III, p. 396. Radin stated that there were notions in both Athenian and Roman law dealing with excessive intervention on behalf of a litigant, instituting baseless litigation, and perversion of justice that resembled this meaning of maintenance. In Athenian law, it was known as *syncophancy*; in Roman law, it was a form of *calumninia* and its practioners

social concept, as reflected in the broad use of the word in the petitions and medieval literature. Thus, contemporary sources revealed three different usages or meanings of the word "maintenance," as reflected in the *Oxford English Dictionary*,[15] the *Middle English Dictionary*,[16] and the *Anglo-Norman Dictionary*.[17]

Although maintenance was a common type of wrongdoing in medieval England, and medieval sources such as petitions, plea rolls, the Year Books, and other documents are replete with references to maintenance, scholars have not thoroughly explored this topic. Legal historians have largely ignored it, with a few notable exceptions. Sir Percy Winfield's seminal study traced the development of the maintenance and related statutes, but he did not make a detailed examination of the cases in the plea rolls and Year Books.[18] Holdsworth discussed maintenance in

---

were called *syncophants* and *calumniators*. Radin, "Maintenance by Champerty," pp. 48–57.

[15] The Oxford English Dictionary defines maintenance, maintain, and maintainer. It has multiple definitions of each word. Most of those definitions are included in the sense relating to support or assistance, one of which is the category of law. The definition of maintenance in the legal definition is "wrongfully aiding and abetting litigation; *spec.* support of a suit or suitor by a party who has no legally recognized interest in the proceedings." The more general meaning of "action of giving aid, countenance, or support to a person in a course of action" is marked as obsolete. *Oxford English Dictionary Online, s.v.* "maintenance."

[16] In the *Middle English Dictionary* most of the definitions focus on the broad usages of supporting wrongdoing of various types with numerous examples from medieval sources. Several definitions mention abuse of lordship and retaining. Two of the words, *maintenuance* and *maintainour*, have legal definitions containing examples of the narrow definition, but also including examples of the broad usage. *Medieval Dictonary Online, s. v.* "mainten," "maintenen," "maintenuance," and "maintenour." The glossary of the fifteenth-century *Paston Letters* defines maintenance as used in those letters in a manner very similar to the narrower, legal definition. Norman Davis, Richard Beadle, and Colin Richmond, eds., *Paston Letters and Papers of the Fifteenth Century*, 3 vols. (Early English Text Society, Supplementary Series 20–22) (Oxford, 2004–5), vol. III, p. 220.

[17] The *Anglo-Norman Dictionary* defines *maintenir*, *maintenaunce*, and *maintenour*, all of which have several variant spellings. Although there is a legal definition with an example of that usage, examples of both the broad and narrow usages seem to be included within several of the definitions. *Anglo-Norman Dictionary Online, s.v.* "maintenir," "maintenaunce," and "maintenour."

[18] P.H. Winfield, *The History of Conspiracy and Abuse of Legal Procedure* (Cambridge, 1921). He traced the history of maintenance. Ibid., pp. 131–60. In the same year, Winfield wrote another book, which he characterized as "supplementary" to the first book. P.H. Winfield, *The Present Law of Abuse of Legal Procedure* (Cambridge, 1921), p. v. The latter book focuses on cases from the late seventeenth century to the first two decades of the twentieth century. It does refer to some medieval Year Book actions and statutes, but not to official plea roll records.

several places in his treatise.[19] He said that "maintenance [was] one of the most crying evils of the later medieval period."[20] Two more recent works provided valuable insights regarding maintenance, but studied it in a more limited fashion.[21] Social historians, particularly those of the late medieval period, have frequently written about maintenance and that literature contains numerous references to it. In the debate over bastard feudalism, historians took different views of the fifteenth century and the problem of maintenance. Some historians have viewed that century as more lawless and corrupt than earlier centuries and believed that wide-spread maintenance was part of the problem.[22] Those historians seemed to use maintenance in the broader sense to describe various types of wrongdoing by influential and powerful persons.[23] K.B. McFarlane, a renowned scholar who provided new insights into the study of late

---

[19] He discussed its development chronologically, starting with the medieval period. Holds-worth, *History English Law*, vol. III, pp. 394–400, vol. V, pp. 201–3, vol. VIII, pp. 397–402. Tapp studied its relation to contracts. William Tapp, *An Inquiry into the Current State of Law of Maintenance and Champerty Principally as Affecting Contracts* (London, 1861). Bodkin reviewed the history and development of maintenance and the state of the law in the early decades of the twentieth century. Edmund Bodkin, *The Law of Maintenance and Champerty and the Lawful Financing of Actions by Solicitors, Legal Aid and Trade Protection Societies and Others* (London, 1934).

[20] Holdsworth, *History of English Law*, vol. III, p. 398.

[21] J.H. Baker, "Solicitors and the Law of Maintenance 1590-1640," in *The Legal Profession and the Common Law* (London, 1986), pp. 125–50; David Seipp, "Jurors, Evidences and the Tempest of 1499," in John Cairns and Grant McLeod, eds., *The Dearest Birth Right of the People of England: The Jury in the History of the Common Law* (Oxford, 2002), pp. 75–92.

[22] E.g., Ralph Griffiths, *The Reign of Henry VI*, 2nd ed. (Stroud, 1998), pp. 128–53, 562–609; Michael Hicks, *Bastard Feudalism* (London, 1995); J.G. Bellamy, *Bastard Feudalism and the Law* (Portland, 1989), pp. 79–101; J.G. Bellamy, *Crime and Public Order in England in the Middle Ages* (London, 1973) (numerous references to maintenance); R.L. Storey, *The End of the House of Lancaster* (Guildford, 1966), pp. 1-28. When these books use the word "maintenance," it is not always clear what they mean or the types of conduct to which they are referring. In general, they use it broadly and to include maintenance of felons and false causes as well as livery. Hicks said that "it could involve violence, the threat of violence, blackmail, influence or bribery." Hicks, *Bastard Feudalism*, p. 119. Bellamy defined it as "giving favor and support to felons and trespassers." Bellamy, *Crime and Public Order*, p. 6. The sources of these definitions are not clear.

[23] Griffiths said "equally skillful was the use of maintenance by influential men to bend the legal process in their favor and, perhaps, to insure for themselves immunity from the consequences of their deeds." Griffiths, *Henry VI*, p. 133. Bellamy saw maintenance as the greatest threat to public order and described it as "tampering with juries of indictment and of trial or with some of the justices, and that it was accomplished through the agency of someone with greater weight in society than the party himself." Bellamy, *Bastard Feudalism*, p. 80.

medieval history,[24] took a more charitable view of the fifteenth century and the conduct of powerful persons.[25] In particular, he did not agree that maintenance was a significant problem.[26] He said it was an ancient practice.[27] "Maintenance was after all no novelty. But the novelty lay in its being more talked about, denounced, and legislated against."[28] He asserted that it did not involve "new threats to the administration of justice" and that the laws against maintenance were an attempt to reject "practices as old as the law itself," originating in the Anglo-Saxon period and involving conduct that was not subject to "disapproval, but veneration." In his view, "what had once been, and was still thought by most to be, a solemn obligation was now to become an offence against the law."[29] But the contemporary sources show that McFarlane's fears that preferred conduct was being made illegal were unfounded.[30] His views, however, influenced many others who took a similar view.[31]

---

[24] Karl Leyser, "Kenneth Bruce McFarlane: A Memoir," and Gerald Harriss, "Introduction to the Letters," in Gerald Harriss, ed., *K.B. McFarlane: Letters to Friends 1940–1966* (Oxford, 1997), pp. ix–xxxii.

[25] McFarlane, *Nobility*, pp. 102–21; K.B. McFarlane, *England in the Fifteenth Century*, pp. 23–43. His protégé, Gerald Harriss, said that he "attacked the prevailing orthodoxy that late middle ages witnessed the spread corruption and disorder ..." G.L. Harriss, "Introduction," ibid., p. xix.

[26] McFarlane defined "simple maintenance" as the "attempts to overawe the court by the present of armed men," which he said was unusual. McFarlane, *Nobility*, p. 115. Further, he believed that "the emergence of maintenance in its broadest sense was an undoubted improvement on more direct forms self-help ..." Christine Carpenter, "Law, Justice, and Landowners in Late Medieval England," *Law and History* Review 1 (1983), p. 215.

[27] McFarlane traced maintenance back to the Anglo-Saxon oath helpers and to the mainpast of the Angevin kings. Harris, "Introduction," pp. x, xix–xx.

[28] He continued by saying that "being men of their time they believed that the evils with which they contended showed a contemporary falling-off from a more perfect past. In thinking so, they were usually wrong." McFarlane, *Fifteenth Century*, p. 42.

[29] McFarlane, "Lords and Retainers," Lecture III, pp. 5–6, 10–12. But he recognized the longstanding problem of abuse of legal procedure, its causes, and the initial attempts to deal with it. Ibid., Lecture II, pp. 6–12.

[30] Relying on McFarlane, Carpenter asserted that "a very thin and not altogether logical line between legitimate and illegitimate manoeuvres developed" and that certain forms of common conduct "were certainly maintenance" or "could be construed" as such. Carpenter, "Law, Justice, and Landowners," p. 215. Richard Firth Green, a law and literature scholar, made a similar assertion. He said that "the communal protection afforded by the earlier notions of warranty and good lordship was redefined by such offenses as maintenance and champerty to appear like reprehensible partisanship." Richard Firth Green, *A Crisis of Truth: Literature and Law in Ricardian England* (Philadelphia, 1998), p. 163.

[31] E.g., Christine Carpenter, *The Wars of the Roses: Politics and the Constitution in England, c. 1437–1509* (Cambridge, 1997); John Watts, *Henry VI and the Politics of Kingship* (Cambridge, 1996).

A problem with the work of these historians is that it made almost no use of the plea rolls and Year Books, sources that do not support some of their assertions about the nature of illegal maintenance. Thus, as a result of inattention of legal historians and failure of other historians to explore the primary sources, there is a gap in the scholarship. This book proposes to fill that gap by a thorough and comprehensive study of maintenance in medieval England.

Despite the numerous statutes enacted at the end of the thirteenth and during the fourteenth centuries, maintenance actions, other than those alleging champerty and conspiracies to maintain, were uncommon in the first 100 years after the initial prohibitions in the Statute of Westminster I 1275. From 1272 to 1377, conspiracy cases were most common. The litigation was primarily criminal and the civil litigation consisted of actions for champerty and procuring false appeals and indictments. There were no civil maintenance actions. But by end of the fourteenth century, likely as result of a 1377 statute, civil maintenance actions began to appear and by the fifteenth century they were extensive. An examination of the primary sources from 1272 to 1485 identified more than 3,000 entries regarding maintenance and related actions in the plea rolls, comprising just under 2,000 individual actions.[32] An examination of the Year Books during the same period revealed 150 cases involving or discussing maintenance. This litigation has previously never been studied. The present research has revealed, for the first time, the nature of the conduct complained of in actual cases and the manner in which the statutes were actually used by litigants.[33]

---

[32] This total included private maintenance, champerty, and conspiracy actions; criminal indictments; and crown maintenance actions as well as actions to enforce the livery statutes. This number is smaller than the total entries as the latter includes multiple entries of the same case as well as nonmaintenance and other cases that are relevant to various discussions. Appendix A summarizes this data.

[33] This research used two primary sources: the records of the King's Bench (KB 27) and Common Bench (CP 40) contained in the plea rolls of The National Archives, Public Record Office, and the cases in the printed versions of the Year Books and Abridgements. References to the National Archives' series CP 40 and KB 27 refer to the digital archive assembled by Robert C. Palmer and Elspeth K. Palmer, *The Anglo-American Legal Tradition*, available at aalt.law.uh.edu/ (hereafter AALT). Individual citations will provide the AALT Image number. The Year Book cases are also available in digital format in Boston University School of Law, *Legal History: The Year Books*, compiled by David Seipp and available at www.bu.edu/phpbin/lawyearbooks/search.php. Individual citations will provide the Seipp number.

Based on this research, the book has two major findings. First, as the relevant statutes did not define illegal maintenance or indicate what particular types of conduct were illegal,[34] medieval judges needed to draw the line between lawful and unlawful conduct. In developing the law, judges limited the offense of maintenance by recognizing several valid justifications for involvement in the litigation of another person. But sometimes assistance was inappropriate either because a justification was lacking or because the conduct exceeded the bounds of propriety.

The second finding is that the statutes prohibiting maintenance in all likelihood did not achieve their objectives. These statutes were directed primarily at controlling the abuse of the legal procedure by powerful individuals and officials. The status and occupation of the parties to litigation, however, show that maintenance actions were not in fact used to control abuse by such persons. Instead, the litigation reveals a more complex and significantly different picture. Another possible objective of the statutes may have been to reduce specious litigation. But an examination of the actual litigation casts doubt on whether the statutory prohibitions actually had that effect. Although some maintenance actions may have involved legitimate actions against abusive conduct that increased litigation, many did not. In fact, it is quite possible that the maintenance actions actually resulted in more litigation rather than reducing it and that the actions were used abusively. In a number of instances, the sources suggest the parties brought maintenance actions to harass and burden personal adversaries.

In addition, the maintenance litigation demonstrates that the common definition of maintenance by legal dictionaries and commentators over the centuries is likely overbroad or incomplete. Early law dictionaries broadly defined maintenance as any support or assistance of another's legal action. For example, Rastell's *Les Termes de la Ley* said that "Maintenance is, where any Man gives or deliver[s] to another, that is Plaintiff or Defendant in any Action, any Sum of Money or other Thing, to maintain his plea, or takes great Pains for

---

[34] There was one exception. The statute prohibiting champerty identified three forms of permissible assistance. *Articuli Super Cartas*, 28 Edw I, st. 3, c. 11 (1300), *Statutes of the Realm*, vol. I, p. 139.

him when hath Nothing therewith to do."[35] Modern legal dictionaries provide essentially the same definition.[36]

Seventeenth- and eighteenth-century commentators defined maintenance similarly, but also identified defenses or exceptions to the statutory prohibitions. Coke divided maintenance into lawful and unlawful and general and special. He said that illegal maintenance was "an upholding of the demandant or plaintiff, tenant, or defendant in a cause depending in suit, by word, action, writing, countenance, or deed."[37] Hawkins discussed maintenance extensively.[38] He stated that "maintenance is commonly taken in an ill sense, and in general seemeth to signify an unlawful taking in hand or upholding of quarrels or sides to the disturbance or hindrance of the common right." It consisted of officious intermeddling in a suit pending in court, to which he was not a party, by assisting either party with money or otherwise in prosecuting or defending the suit.[39] Like Coke, Hawkins divided the conduct into that which was a violation of the statute and that which may be justified, identifying numerous examples in each category.[40] Blackstone defined maintenance as "an officious intermeddling in a suit that no way belongs to one, by maintaining or assisting either party with money or otherwise,

---

[35] William Rastell, *Les Termes de la Ley*, p. 433 (London, 1721). This work, likely the first law dictionary, was initially published in 1527 as *Exposionciones Terminorum Legum Anglorum*. The next law dictionary, initially published in 1607, defined maintenance as "an upholding of a cause or person ... him that secondeth a cause depending in suite between others, either by lending money, or making friends for either partie, toward his help." John Cowell, *The Interpreter* (Cambridge, 1637). Cowell said that the word was "metaphorically drawn from the succoring of a young child, that learned to goe, by ones hand. In our common lawe, it is used in the euill part ..." Ibid.

[36] *Black's Law Dictionary*, 6th ed. (St. Paul, 1990), p. 954; William Edward Baldwin, ed., *Bouvier's Law Dictionary, Baldwin's Edition* (Cleveland, 1934).

[37] He asserted that maintenance was *malum in se* and against the common law. He said that it was *duplex*. He denoted one type as *curialis*, providing support or assistance in a plea pending in court, and the other type as *rurialis*, stirring up litigation. Edward Coke, *The Second Part of the Institutes of the Laws of England*, 2 vols. (London, 1797; reprint, 1986), vol. I, 212. The latter sounds more like barratry, which he discussed separately. Ibid., p. 225.

[38] William Hawkins, *A Treatise of the Pleas of the Crown*, 5th ed. (London, 1771), Book I, ch. 83, pp. 249–56.

[39] Ibid., p. 249.

[40] He identified ten general categories of conduct that may be justified. In his discussion, he included numerous references to the Year Books and abridgments. Ibid., pp. 249–54. A dictionary published one year later had definitions and justifications very similar to those of Hawkins. Giles Jacob, *A New Law Dictionary*, 9th ed. (London, 1772).

to prosecute or defend it." He also gave examples of permissible forms of maintenance.[41]

Later commentators also explored the nature of maintenance. Stephen thought maintenance had both a general meaning and a technical narrower meaning, which was "exceeding vague." The first was "interfering in the due course of justice," and the second, "the act of assisting the plaintiff in any legal proceeding in which the person giving the assistance has no valuable interest, or in which he acts from any improper motive."[42] Thus, he recognized that not all assistance was unlawful.[43] Stubbs viewed maintenance as "the strong man upholding the cause of the weak" and was subject to "gross perversion" and the support of false pleas.[44] Winfield viewed Coke's definition of unlawful maintenance as an accurate statement of law found in the Year Books.[45] Holdsworth agreed with Coke's and Winfield's definition of illegal maintenance. He identified some instances of lawful maintenance and said that there was a good deal of authority on the question of what was unlawful upholding.[46]

The book proceeds chronologically. Chapters 2 through 6 discuss the evolution of medieval social norms and legal restrictions on providing support and protection to various persons. Chapter 2 focuses on the early development of good lordship and other norms regarding such support and the contemporary attitudes to such conduct. Chapter 3 identifies and examines the initial statutes and ordinances enacted during the reigns of Edward I and II (1272–1327) that were directed at such conduct and the petitions to the king, his council, and parliament complaining about the abuse of power and influence. Chapter 4 examines the conspiracy,

---

[41] He asserted that maintenance "was greatly encouraged by the first introduction of uses." Blackstone, *Commentaries*, vol. IV, p. 134.

[42] Stephen, *History of Criminal Law*, vol. III, p. 234. Pike defined maintenance as "the support of a suit by a person who was not a very near relative of the suitor. But it was the act of the superior toward the inferior . . ." Luke Pike, *History of Crime in England*, 2 vols. (London, 1873–76; reprint, 1983), vol. II, p. 16. He further characterized it as "the use of influence and wealth." Ibid., vol. I, p. 399.

[43] He believed that the medieval statutes were a product of the extremely litigious nature of that period and the protection by lords of their uncontrolled retainers. Stephen, *History of Criminal Law*, vol. I, pp. 236–37. Stephen reviewed statutory prohibitions, starting with those in the reign of Edward I and continuing through those in that of Henry VIII. Ibid., pp. 234–40.

[44] He noted the statutes directed at maintenance, but said that they were inadequate. William Stubbs, *Constitutional History of England*, 3 vols. (Oxford, 1897; reprint, 1967), vol. III, pp. 550–51.

[45] Winfield, *The History of Conspiracy*, p. 136.

[46] Holdsworth, *History of English Law*, vol. III, pp. 398–99.

maintenance, champerty, and related types of litigation during that period. Chapter 5 discusses additional statutes directed at maintenance and related conduct enacted during the reign of Edward III (1327–1377) and the petitions to the king, his council, and parliament about the abuse of power during that period. Chapter 6 discusses the conspiracy, maintenance, champerty, and related types of litigation in the same period. Chapter 7 explores the treatment of maintenance in medieval literature.

The next three chapters focus on maintenance litigation in late medieval England, 1377–1485. Chapter 8 identifies the changes in litigation, petitioning, and the nature of good lordship that occurred during the later period. Chapter 9 details the judicial development of the legitimate justifications for involvement in another person's litigation. Chapter 10 identifies the various forms of conduct that were illegal maintenance. Chapter 11 deals with livery, which is often viewed as part of the maintenance problem and associated with retainers and powerful men providing support to their clients. Chapter 12 analyzes whether the maintenance statutes achieved their objective of controlling the abuse of power and reducing litigation and illustrates how maintenance actions were used to harass opponents. Chapter 13 summarizes the later developments and modern legal issues involving maintenance and champerty, and offers some concluding remarks.

2

The Evolution of Social Norms Relating to the Assistance of Others

Assisting persons with their problems was a longstanding social norm deeply entrenched in medieval society. Supporting and protecting related or connected persons, groups, or institutions was a manifestation of loyalty and essential moral quality.[1] Betrayal and treason rank high on the scale of individual immorality.[2] Because the legal prohibitions on maintenance may have impacted the exercise of these social norms supporting such assistance, it is important to understand their nature.

Kinship, Community, and Charity

Accepted social and religious norms supported helping family, friends, and the poor with their legal problems and other troubles. Kinship and family were an important source of assistance.[3] Throughout medieval

---

[1] Fletcher asserted that "unbreakable loyalty [is] an ideal moral quality" and "the worst epithets are reserved for the sin of betrayal." George Fletcher, *Loyalty: An Essay on the Morality of Relationships* (Oxford, 1993), pp. 8–11, 41–60.

[2] Hyams studied the development of the meaning of treason in medieval French and English usage. He believed it was a product of the ancient "concepts of lordship and trust ... Treason ... was about breaking of faith and loyalty." Treason was not limited to the king and "the betrayed was often a lord, a vassal, sometimes a husband or master ... The betrayed person could be ... any friend, a broad category of close acquaintances to whom one was linked by bonds of loyalty most often stemming from kinship, affinity, or lordship." Moreover, the meaning of felony was resembled treason. It denoted "a serious breach of loyalty, most especially the loyalty one owed to one's lord." Paul Hyams, "Thinking English Law in French: The Angevins and the Common Law," in Belle Tuten, ed., *Feud, Violence and Practise: Essays in Medieval Studies in Honor of Stephen D. White* (Burlington, VT, 2010), pp. 190–94.

[3] Kinship and family are not necessarily equivalent notions. The former may refer to a larger group and the latter to those who actually live together and are likely to have more frequent interactions. Sam Worby, *Law and Kinship in Thirteenth Century England* (Woodbridge, 2010), pp. 1–2. Medieval documents often use terms such as "consanguinity" or "cousin" to describe relationships whose nature and proximity are ambiguous.

Europe, blood bonds were strong and kinship was important.[4] The institution of the feud and the notion of vengeance reflected their significance
and identified medieval norms of kinship.[5] "Good kinship" imposed
duties and moral obligations of mutual aid and common concern.[6] In
Anglo-Saxon England, kinship was among the strongest bonds.[7] It was
critically important for the protection of individuals.[8] Kin identified
closely with each other.[9] Medieval common and canon law took account
of kinship.[10] It played an important informal and cooperative role in
various ways. Family was instrumental in protecting rights and property
and was "an important source of alliance and loyalty and of connections
across society."[11] These actions were not limited to vengeance and dispute
settlement, as family supported and helped kinsmen on less significant
matters.[12] Thus, it was natural to turn to kin for assistance in litigation.

Community relationships were also a source of norms in medieval
society. One notion of community, *communitas*, was geographically local,

[4] Frederick Pollock and Frederic William Maitland, *The History of English Law before the
Time of Edward I*, 2 vols. (Cambridge, 1968), vol. II, pp. 240–45. There is a substantial
literature, which is outside the scope of this book, on kinship and feudalism as well as
their relationship to each other. These subjects have engendered substantial debate and
disagreement. E.g., F.L. Ganshof, *Feudalism*, 3rd ed. (Northampton, 1964); Susan
Reynolds, *Fiefs and Vassals* (Oxford, 1994); Stephen D. White, *Re-thinking Kinship
and Feudalism in Early Modern Europe* (Aldershot, 2005). White has reviewed some of
the different approaches to these subjects. Ibid., pp. vii–xvi. Different views exist as to
the nature and origins of English feudalism. Eric John, *Orbis Britanniae and Other
Studies* (Leicester, 1966), pp. 128–53. Milsom developed the classic study of the legal
aspects of English feudalism. S.F.C. Milsom, *The Legal Framework of English Feudalism*
(Cambridge, 1976).

[5] William Miller, *Bloodtaking and Peacemaking: Feud, Law and Society in Saga Iceland*
(Chicago, 1990), pp. 179–220. Paul Hyams, *Rancor and Reconciliation* (Ithaca, 2003),
pp. 3–21. Miller noted the substantial body of literature on feud. Ibid., pp. 128–81. Hyams
studied feud as one of several possible responses to wrong in the Middle Ages. Ibid.,
pp. 4–6.

[6] Miller, *Bloodtaking and Peacemaking*, p. 157. Miller stated this in his exploration of the
nature of the bonds of kinship in Icelandic society. It is likely that these norms were
general to kinship and not limited to Iceland.

[7] Pollock and Maitland, *History of English Law*, vol. I, p. 31. John Hudson said it was "a
crucial bond in Anglo-Saxon society." John Hudson, *The Oxford History of the Laws of
England*, 11 vols. (Oxford, 2012), vol. II: *871–1216*, p. 225.

[8] Anglo-Saxon laws reflected the obligation of kin to avenge another kin's death and to
enforce *wergild*. Kin also functioned as "oath helpers." Frank Stenton, *Anglo-Saxon
England*, 3rd ed. (Oxford, 1971), pp. 315–18.

[9] Lorraine Lancaster, "Kinship in Anglo-Saxon Society (7th Century to Early 11th)," in
Sylvia Thrupp, ed., *Early Medieval Society* (New York, 1967), p. 38. Lancaster discussed in
detail the nature and effect of Anglo-Saxon kinship. Ibid., pp. 17–44.

[10] Worby, *Law and Kinship*.   [11] Ibid., pp. 128, 130–31, 137–38.

[12] Stenton, *Anglo-Saxon England*, p. 316.

referring to the shires, hundreds, manors, boroughs, and vills and had important legal, social, and political characteristics.[13] Maitland said that communities were the principal governmental unit.[14] These local communities and their members had important duties, especially in the enforcement of the criminal law.[15] The tithing system and the view of frankpledge made local men responsible for the conduct of their fellow members.[16] The jury system similarly reflected this communal element. When asking for a jury trial, litigants put themselves "on the country," meaning the local area where they lived or where the events occurred. People identified closely with their "country." The "geographical contiguity" of neighbors and involvement in celebratory events created and strengthened "network bonds."[17] Hyams emphasized the importance of friendship and support groups as an extension of the institution of feud and the notion of kinship.[18] He identified their mutual expectations of friendship, including assistance in pursuing enemies and wrongdoers.[19] Given this substantial formal and informal contact that people had with each other at the local level, it is not surprising that they would turn to their neighbors and friends for help with their problems, including assistance in litigation.

Charity was a deeply entrenched religious norm and an important aspect of early English Christianity.[20] The New Testament emphasized the relation of state of perfection and the generous giving of alms. Early

---

[13] Pollock and Maitland, *History of English Law*, vol. I, pp. 494, 528, 534–35, 564–67. The village as a community in England predated the Norman Conquest. F.W. Maitland, *Doomsday Book and Beyond* (Cambridge, 1887; reprint, 1966), pp. 340–56. The bond between neighbors was initially land based. Ibid., p. 341. But Maitland stressed the importance of individuality and disagreed with those like Maine who asserted that the family was the critical unit in ancient law. Stephen White, "Maitland on Family and Kinship," in John Hudson, ed., *The History of English Law: Centenary Essays on "Pollock and Maitland"* (Oxford, 1996), pp. 91–113.

[14] Pollock and Maitland, *History of English Law*, vol. I, p. 616.

[15] The Statute of Winchester imposed law enforcement duties at the local level. 13 Edw. I (1285). *Statutes of the Realm*, A. Luders, T. Tomlins, J. France, W. Tauton, and J. Raithby, eds., 11 vols. (London, 1810–28), vol. 1, p. 96.

[16] Pollock and Maitland, *History of English Law*, vol. I, pp. 564, 570–71.

[17] Hyams, *Rancor and Reconciliation*, pp. 29–31.

[18] Ibid., pp. 21–32. He explained that their interactions could result both in friendship or hostility, *amicitia* or *inimicitia*. Ibid., pp. 22–26.

[19] Other activities included custody of valuables, standing surety, advising on marriages, warranting possession, and negotiating peace settlements. Ibid., p. 27.

[20] Bishop Aidan, having been sent to instruct the English people in Christ, urged them "by word and deed to practice almsgiving and good works" to strengthen them in their faith. Judith McClure and Roger Collins, eds., *Bede: The Ecclesiastical History of England* (Oxford, 1994), pp. 116–17; Brian Tierney, *Medieval Poor Law: A Sketch of Canonical Theory and Its Application in England* (Berkeley, 1959).

Christians were urged to give alms both during their lives and at death, although giving during life was preferred.[21] The medieval church considered helping the poor and less fortunate an important obligation.[22] Alms giving prompted land grants to religious organizations to support spiritual services, and *frankalmoin*, free alms, was a well-known form of land tenure.[23] Medieval charters granting land on such terms reflected the religious norm of giving alms for the salvation of the souls of the donor and his family.[24] This charitable norm was reinforced at a local and everyday level, as medieval canon law required parishes and their parishioners to provide alms to their poor neighbors.[25] Given these numerous formal and informal expressions of this norm, it was natural for people to assist the poor with their difficulties, whether it was for religious reasons or was morally based generosity.

In sum, assistance and support based on these well-established norms of kinship, community, and charity would not likely be considered problematic or controversial. Moreover, the persons engaging in such conduct were not necessarily powerful or influential. In medieval Europe, kinship and friendship were long associated with the preservation of peace and the provision of protection and security through mutual bonds of assistance and support.[26] Much of this conduct was voluntary and not required by law. The primary restriction on such activities was likely the prohibitions on felonies and conduct involving violence.[27]

---

[21] Michael Sheehan, *The Will in Medieval England* (Toronto, 1963), p. 11. Richard Helmholz, *The Canon Law and Ecclesiastical Jurisdiction from 597 to the 1640s, Oxford History* (Oxford, 2004), vol. 1, pp. 51–52 (hereafter referred to as *Oxford History*).

[22] Helmholz, *Oxford History*, vol. I, pp. 468–69. The medieval English kings made substantial charitable gifts to the poor. Michael Prestwich, *Plantagenet England 1225–1360* (Oxford, 2005), pp. 31, 454.

[23] Pollock and Maitland, *History of English Law*, vol. I, pp. 240–51; Hudson, *Oxford History*, vol. II, pp. 369–72, 667–70.

[24] In the mid-twelfth century, William, son of Angot, made a gift to the priory of St. John, stating that the monks should "devotedly prevail on the mercy of Christ for the salvation of my lords and myself." Such clauses were known as *pro anima* clauses. John Hudson, *Land, Law, and Lordship in Anglo-Norman England* (Oxford, 1997), p. 222.

[25] Tierney, *Medieval Poor Law*, pp. 121–29.

[26] T.L. Lambert, "Introduction," in T.B. Lambert and David Rollason, eds., *Peace and Protection in the Middle Ages* (Toronto: Pontifical Institute for Medieval Studies, 2009), pp. 5–7.

[27] White mentioned the normative constraints on conduct arising out of kinship and lordship. But it is not clear whether he was referring to norms restricting assistance or support as he may have been referring only to the obligations based on those norms. White, *Rethinking Kinship and Feudalism*, p. vii.

Good Lordship

Medieval lords were often powerful and influential. Their conduct could and did impact the operation of the justice system, particularly in the local areas in which they were dominant. These activities could be regarded as a form of maintenance. Thus, it is important to understand the evolution of norms supporting their use of power and influence as well as any norms limiting that use.

The Initial Development

Lordship was a well-established institution in medieval European society and culture. The relation of a lord and his man was important socially and politically and may have had its roots in ancient customs.[28] The relationship was one in which the lord was in a position of superior authority over the man. It created a bond between them with mutual, but unequal, obligations. The core was the fidelity that a man owed his lord and the lord's obligation of faith. This relationship created interdependent obligations and mutually beneficial bonds of loyalty.

An eleventh-century agreement between the William, count of Acquitaine, and Hugh of Lusignan[29] has been characterized as "an unequaled picture of the conditions actually governing the relationship between lord and vassal."[30] This agreement expressed the man's duty of loyalty or fealty ("*fidelitatem*") to the lord[31] and the "faith which a lord owes to help his man (*per fidem quam senior adiuvari debet homini suo*)."[32] In Hugh's

---

[28] Pollock and Maitland, *History of English Law*, vol. I, pp. 29–31. Plucknett viewed lordship as an important aspect of the criminal law enforcement beginning in the Anglo-Saxon age. He noted how Cnut and Edward the Confessor depended on the "strong right arm of the local notable" to pursue thieves, suppress disorder, and police their men. "For centuries the law had been calling on all honest men to get themselves 'lordship' with men of substance who would accept a certain responsibility for them and their behavior." T.F.T. Plucknett, *Edward I and Criminal Law* (Cambridge, 1960), p. 44.

[29] *Conventum inter Guillelmum Acquitanorum comitem et Hugonem Chiliarchum*, reprinted and translated in Jane Martindale, ed., *Status Authority and Regional Power: Acquitaine and France, 9th to 12th centuries* (Aldershot, 1997), VIIb. A commentary on the Latin text originally appeared in Jane Martindale, "*Conventum inter Guillelmum Acquitanorum comitem et Hugonem Chiliarchum*," *English Historical Review* 84 (1969), pp. 528–48.

[30] "Introduction to the *Conventum*," ibid., VIIa, pp. 528–29.

[31] *Conventum*, VIIb, pp. 543, 546, 548.

[32] Ibid., pp. 544, 547 (using *portari* rather than *adiuvari*), 548b (tr.). The count also pledged "his faith and trust." Ibid.

view, this duty of faith contemplated assistance in disputes and protection from physical harm.[33] A lord's protection of his man was the crucial aspect of personal lordship. Some medieval scholars have characterized this conduct as good lordship, an "age-old duty."[34] Protecting one's vassals was always treated as a duty that was basic to good lordship[35] as well as critical to the lord's honor.[36]

These notions were the foundation of lordship in medieval England.[37] Lordship was firmly rooted and openly acknowledged in Anglo-Saxon society.[38] Lordship was not just a royal matter,[39] as it extended to private individuals and their relationships with their men and other

[33] In a dispute over an agreement between Hugh and another man, the count said that if the other man did not keep his agreements with Hugh, "by my faith I shall come to your support (*per fidem sim tuus adiutor*). And when Hugh was threatened with attack by the man, the count told him that he had nothing to fear "as long as you are with me (*Noli hoc timere quamdiu mecum eris*) and that if Hugh were attacked, the count would put his attackers to flight and aid him (*ut venirent ego confunderer eos et tibi auxiliarem*)." Ibid., p. 545 (tr.). The lord also had a duty to give him counsel (*consilium*). Ibid.

[34] John Hudson, *Land, Law, and Lordship*, pp. 51–62; Paul Hyams, "Warranty and Good Lordship in Twelfth Century England," *Law and History Review* 5 (1987), pp. 439, 447–53. This term may have been coined by K.B. McFarlane in his discussions of the late medieval period. K.B. McFarlane, *The Nobility of Later Medieval England* (Oxford, 1973), pp. 116–20.

[35] Hyams, "Warranty and Good Lordship," p. 448.

[36] Hyams, *Rancor and Reconciliation*, p. 257. One grantor made the latter explicit. After beseeching and ordering various persons to maintain and protect the grantee, he added that they should do "as they esteem my honor" ("*sicut me diligunt honorem meum*"). F.M. Stenton, ed., *Documents Illustrative of the Social and Economic History of the Danelaw* (London, 1920), no. 333, p. 250.

[37] Sayles asserted that the obligations of lords and neighbors replaced those of kinship. G.O. Sayles, *The Medieval Foundations of England*, 2nd ed. (London, 1950), p. 109. O'Brien believed that the rise of lordship had usurped the role of kin in dispute settlement. Bruce O'Brien, "Authority and Community," in Julia Crick and Elisabeth Van Houts, eds., *A Social History of England 900–1200* (Cambridge, 2011), p. 89. Hyams viewed the comparative loyalty to lords and kin as more complicated. Hyams, *Rancor and Reconciliation*, p. 75. Some scholars have suggested that loyalty to a lord trumped kinship, but others have been skeptical. The relative importance of kinship and lordship has engendered debate. Stephen White, "Kinship and Lordship in Early Medieval England: The Story of Sigeberht, Cynewulf, and Cyneheard," *Viator* 20 (1989), pp. 1–18.

[38] Sayles, *Medieval Foundations*, p. 124. Peter Coss, *The Origins of the English Gentry* (Cambridge, 2003), pp. 30–31. Sayles discussed the development of lordship and dependency as reflected in the structure and groups in Anglo-Saxon society. Ibid., pp. 123–28. Hyams noted that it was important for each man to have a lord. Hyams, *Rancor and Reconciliation*, p. 86.

[39] Maitland stated that the king was a "general over-lord." Ibid., vol. I, p. 30. Stenton believed that the need to show a royal charter as evidence of the title to an estate was critical to the development of private lordship. Stenton, *Anglo-Saxon England*, pp. 306–7.

associates.[40] By the end of the twelfth century, homage and fealty created the tenant's obligations of fidelity, worship, and obedience; and in return the "lord [was] bound to help his man with aid and counsel in all things."[41] Lords were critical to the preservation of the structures of English society and were obligated to be responsible as sureties for their men and to protect them.[42]

Lordship and Maintenance

In Anglo-Norman England, lordship had very great importance.[43] It became a significant aspect of dependent land tenure.[44] The development of the tenurial relationship between a lord and his man in the first century of English feudalism produced interdependent obligations.[45] The oath of fealty created a solemn contract that obligated the lord to protect and maintain his man in return for the latter's obligation to serve him.[46] In an early expression of this practice, the *Leges Henrici Primi* stated that a lord must "support (*manuteneat*) his man everywhere that

---

[40] Hudson, *Oxford History*, vol. II, pp. 220–24. Commendation was an important form of pre-Conquest lordship and provided important assistance and protection to the commended men. Stephen Baxter, "Lordship and Justice in Late Anglo-Saxon England: The Judicial Functions of Soke and Commendation Revisited," in Baxter, Karkov, Nelson, and Pelteret, eds., *Early Medieval Studies* (Farnham, 2009), pp. 389–407.

[41] Pollock and Maitland, *History of English Law*, vol. I, pp. 296–307.

[42] O'Brien, "Authority and Community," pp. 85–86. In studying the development of lordship in England from the eleventh through the thirteenth centuries, Given-Wilson asserted that it had a harsh impact on the English peasantry and was more than land-lordship. Chris Given-Wilson, *The English Nobility in the Late Middle Ages* (London, 1996), pp. 19–25.

[43] Hudson, *Oxford History*, vol. II, pp. 334–36, 372–75, 431–34. It continued to be important in Angevin England, although the nature of the tenurial relationship evolved and became more complex. Ibid., pp. 630–32, 676–77. In discussing the development of the heritability of land, Hudson noted that in the early twelfth century, no clear law obligated an English lord to accept his tenant's son as his tenant on the death of the father, but that doing so was "a manifestation of good lordship, and would help to obtain loyal followers." Hudson, *Land, Law, and Lordship*, p. 65.

[44] Pollock and Maitland, *History of English Law*, vol. I, pp. 30–31, 232–40. Hudson thought that evidence of dependent land tenure in Anglo-Saxon England "was very sparse although some elements did exist." Hudson, *Oxford History*, vol. II, pp. 115–20, 148.

[45] Frank Stenton, *The First Century of English Feudalism 1066–1166* (Oxford, 1932), pp. 12–15, 122–30, 214–15.

[46] Frank Barlow, *The Feudal Kingdom of England 1042–1216*, 5th ed. (London, 1999), p. 6. Dunham said that a code and custom had existed since the tenth century that "a lord was expected 'to maintain' his man when someone had done him wrong." This obligation included supporting his right in court, and the lord would be fined if he opposed that

he should suffer no injury as a result of his protection nor any dishonor as a result of his abandonment" and that he "must in appropriate circumstances keep his man with advice as well as support (*consilio pariter et auxilio*)."[47] Good lordship's obligation of support might have included financial and other assistance to a vassal in his litigation.[48] Hyams said that the lord's obligation to maintain his vassal against harm by his adversaries was perhaps the most important attribute of good lordship.[49] Such vassals were vulnerable to the force and demands of other powerful individuals.[50] He suggested that the conduct that constituted the later medieval offenses of maintenance, champerty, and embracery had been widely understood as practices that were aspects of good lordship in the twelfth century.[51]

The emergence of the lord's obligation of warranty is informative in understanding the development of the norms related to maintenance.[52] Hyams said that "warranty came to represent the obligations of land lordship" and that "recognition of the aspiration for the protection of good lordship ... became a virtual customary tenant-right."[53] In twelfth-century England, warranty progressed from a customary practice to the

---

right and supported his man's adversary. William Dunham, *Lord Hastings' Indentured Retainers 1461–1483* (New Haven, 1955), pp. 67–68.

[47] L.J. Downer, ed., *Leges Henri Primi* (Oxford: Clarendon Press, 1972), §57.8, at 178–79, §82.4, at 256–57. The *Leges Henri Primi* is a "mixture, made up of the old traditional law, the developing feudal principles, and provisions based on royal supremacy." It was completed no later than 1118. Ibid., pp. 7, 35.

[48] Hyams, "Warranty and Good Lordship," pp. 448–52. He said the effectiveness of maintenance depended on the "promisor's physical and political clout" and may have been "an attempt to secure those oaths against some future emergency." Ibid., p. 451.

[49] Hyams, *Rancor and Reconciliation*, p. 150.

[50] Hyams, "Warranty and Good Lordship," p. 448. It was advantageous for men to enlist their lords to help them with their disputes and persuade the latter that their interests were at stake and that "good lordship" meant that the lord should "pursue his man's cause as if it were his own." Hyams, *Rancor and Reconciliation*, p. 214.

[51] Ibid., pp. 262–63.

[52] White found the obligation of warranty expressed in *The Song of Roland*. He said that the "poem presupposes recognition of a norm that a lord should be a warrantor for his men." Tracing the etymological origins of the word, he equated its use to protection "against physical attack by third parties" and compensation against any loss. A failure to warrant caused shame and loss of status to the lord. Like Hyams, he believed warranty was a characteristic of good lordship. Interestingly, he found this literary expression of warranty similar to warranty of land in the twelfth-century England. Stephen White, "Protection, Warranty, and Vengeance in *La Chanson de Roland*," in T.B. Lambert and David Rollason, *Peace and Protection*, pp. 156, 158–62, 166–67.

[53] Hyams, "Warranty and Good Lordship," pp. 453–57. He discussed the meaning of good lordship and its relationship to the development of warranty in detail. Ibid., pp. 453–74.

legal obligation of a lord to secure the tenure of his tenants against rival claimants, an obligation that was associated with good lordship.[54] It was an aspect of the bond of homage and fealty between a lord and his tenant.[55] Bracton summarized the integration of these once customary notions into the nascent common law, stating that "homage is a legal bond by which one is bound and constrained to warrant, defend, and acquit his tenant in his seisin against all persons . . ."[56] Glanvill expressed a similar view.[57] Milsom said that protection was the core notion of warranty.[58]

Many land grant charters in this period contained clauses obligating lords to warrant their grants of land.[59] One of the words used in the

[54] Hudson, *Land, Law, and Lordship*, pp. 51–58. Hyams, *Warranty and Good Lordship*, pp. 439–53. Hyams said "the age old duty of 'good lordship' lies very close to warranty," although the former term "was probably a later medieval coinage." Ibid., p. 439 and note 6. Hudson said that "services, homage, and good lordship can also be seen coming together in notions of warranty . . ." and that this obligation of lordship applied both in and out of court. Hudson denominated the failure of a lord to protect his vassals as "bad lordship," but said it was not a common occurrence. *Land, Law, and Lordship*, pp. 51, 58, 61–62. Confirmations of gifts were also a manifestation of good lordship, "reinforc[ing] the bond between lord and vassal." Ibid., p. 221.

[55] Pollock and Maitland, *History of English Law*, vol. I, pp. 301, 306–07.

[56] G. Woodbine, ed., and Samuel Thorne, ed. and trans., *Bracton de Legibus et Conseutudinibus Angliae*, 4 vols. (Cambridge, MA, 1968), vol. II, f. 78b, p. 228. Hudson said that this obligation had three aspects: to maintain his man against challenges by others, to provide equivalent land if it were lost by the tenant, and not to take back the land. If the tenant's claim was challenged, he could vouch the lord to warrant. Hudson, *Oxford History*, vol. II, pp. 345–46, 594–98.

[57] He said that "the lord owes as much to the man on account of lordship as the man owes to the lord on account of homage, save reverence." G.D.G. Hall, ed. and trans., *The Treatise on the Laws and Customs of the Realm of England Commonly Called Glanvil* (Oxford, 1993), Book IX, 4, p. 107.

[58] Milsom, *Legal Framework*, p. 42. Palmer viewed these dimensions of the obligation of maintenance as aspects of a feudal society whereby customary obligations evolved into legal ones. Robert Palmer, "The Feudal Framework of English Law, *Michigan Law Review* 79 (1980–81), pp. 1134, 1139, 1144, 1163. More generally, he asserted that the origins of English property law reflected the "inaction between law and mores." Robert Palmer, "The Origins of Property," *Law and History Review* 3 (1985), p. 47.

[59] J. M. Kaye, *Medieval English Conveyances* (Cambridge, 2010), pp. 43–59. Linsey Hunter has made an impressive and detailed study of twelfth-century charters and the language of warranty clauses. Linsey Hunter, "Charter Diplomatics and Norms of Landholding and Lordship between the Humber and Forth, c. 1066–c. 1250," unpublished PhD thesis, University of St. Andrews (2012), 2 vols., vol. I, pp. 226–79. She summarized the scholarship, examined the origins of warranty obligation and charters and their roots in the eleventh century, and described the evidence revealed by her data. Ibid., pp. 227–42. That scholarship indicates that the use of such clauses pre-dated what Stenton had suggested. Stenton, *First Century*, p. 160.

charters to describe the lord's warranty obligation was "maintain (*man-utenere*)."[60] Although this use of "maintain" may not have had a precise and fixed meaning, the charters are useful in understanding the development of the norm of maintenance. In these charters, "maintain" was used most often in conjunction with other verbs.[61] For example, grantors often obligated themselves to "maintain and warrant"[62] or to "maintain and defend."[63] One possibility is that "maintain" was synonymous with "warrant," an example of the common medieval use of multiple verbs, and that it added no further obligation.[64] The evolving charter diplomatics may tend to support that view. It is also possible that twelfth-century charters initially used the words "maintain and defend" to provide assurance for a grant and that the use of the word "warranty" was a later development.[65] Scholars agree that explicit warranty clauses

---

[60] Hunter found that 148 of these charters used the word "maintain (*manutenere*)" in describing the lord's warranty obligation. Ibid., pp. 242–46.

[61] Ibid., pp. 226–27, 242–51. In an 1140 charter, apparently the first to use this word, the lord said that "*debemus manutenere et warrantizare contra omnes homines et feminas.*" Ibid., p. 242 and note 69.

[62] Bernard de Balliol granted extensive lands to the monks of Rievaulx, stating that "*Hec omnia ego et heredes mei predictis monachis manutenebimus et warantiizabimus contra omnes homines . . .*" William Farrer, ed., *Early Yorkshire Charters*, 12 vols. (Edinburgh, 1914), vol. I, no. 562. Anschetill de Huch used the same language when granted a turbary to the nuns of Coton, as did Marmaduke Darel in his grant of land to the monks of Rievaulx. Ibid., nos. 493, 639. Numerous other charters used the same language. Ibid., vol. VI, nos. 26, 43, 58, 94; vol. IX, nos. 86, 168; vol. X, no. 111; vol. XI, nos. 192, 194; vol. XII, no. 69. A number of the Mowbray charters also used these words. D.E. Greenway, ed., *The Charters of the Honour of Mowbray* (London, 1972), nos. 35, 42, 43, 49, 53, 59, and 65.

[63] In his grant of land to the hospital of St. Peter, York, William Burhman said that he and his heirs "*warantizabimus et defendemus predictam elemosinam predicto hospitali inperpetuum contra omnes homines.*" *Early Yorkshire Charters*, vol. I, no. 259. Hugh de Lelay used similar language in his grant of the village of Baildon and its chief messuage. Ibid., no. 35. Osbert de Wanci, in his grant of land for the monks of Biddlesen, said that he and his heirs would "*defendendam et manutendam contra omnes qui ecclesie predicte aliquam calumpniam inferre temptauerint.*" Stenton, *First Century*, no. 46. Some charters used defend, maintain, and warrant. Greenway, *Mowbray Charters*, no. 55; *Early Yorkshire Charters*, vol. IX, no. 88; vol. X, no. 95; vol. XI, no. 175.

[64] Another charter with different wording also supports this conclusion. It includes an affidation and confirmation that states that the grantor, his sons, and their heirs will faithfully maintain the aforesaid gift to the aforesaid monks and without evil trickery and will warrant it to them against all men in perpetuity. *Early Yorkshire Charters*, vol. III, no. 1817.

[65] Postles had that view. David Postles, "Seeking the Language of Warranty in Twelfth-Century England," *Journal of the Society of Archivists* 20 (1999), pp. 209–22; David Postles, "Gifts in Frankalmoign, Warranty of Land and Feudal Society," *Cambridge Law Journal* 50 (1991), pp. 335–46. The earlier charters said the grantor "would stand

became more common by the 1170s.[66] Given the more specific connotation of the word "warranty," the words "maintain and defend" may have continued to be used together with the former, as is the case sometimes with evolving formulaic words.

Other evidence suggests that maintenance may have had a broader meaning as some charters do not couple the words "maintain" and "warrant" ("*manutenebimus et warrantizabimus*").[67] In one charter, the grantor said that he "will maintain all this and will warrant against all men in perpetuity."[68] In another charter, after giving a warranty, the grantor said that "he will maintain all the monks."[69] In a confirmation of a grant, the grantor said that the grantees and "all they have everywhere under my control have my peace and maintenance."[70] Some charters stated that the grantor would protect as well as maintain and warrant or defend the grantees.[71] Although the language of these documents does not clearly establish that maintenance had a broader meaning, it at least suggests that its meaning was ambiguous and may have been variable,

---

as best he could to maintain and defend their cause (*manutenendo et causam eorum defendendo secundum posse nostrum prompti defensores astabimus*)"; and by the middle of the twelfth century, charters said "we will maintain and warrant ... and will stand as defenders (*manutenebimus et warantizabimus ... defensores astabiums*)." As might be expected, the language varied and was not uniform. Postles, "Language of Warranty," pp. 209, 212–18. However, Hudson found use of the word by the earls of Chester as early as the 1140s and 1150s. But he noted that there may been an initial burst in Stephen's reign, which may have been followed by a temporary decrease. Hudson, *Land, Law, and Lordship*, pp. 55–56.

[66] Ibid., pp. 53–57.

[67] *Early Yorkshire Charters*, vol. I, no. 580; vol. III, nos. 1269, 1645, 1833, and 1840; Stenton, *Documents*, no. 426. Some of these charters confirm as well as warrant the grant. But it is possible that only warranty is being expressed.

[68] Ibid., vol. I, no. 580. Another charter also pledged to maintain the gift and warrant against all men. Greenway, *Mowbray Charters*, no. 67. In another charter, the grantor said he will support and maintain the religious house and the brothers of the house and all things that pertained to the house "wherever I shall be able to the best of my ability." Stenton, ed., *Documents*, no. 97.

[69] Ibid., no. 1680, p. 329. Another said the grantor would maintain the aforesaid monks and warrant them. Ibid., xi, no. 75, p. 73. Another variation was that the grantor would maintain the alms and warrant the monks. Ibid., no. 116, pp. 133–34. In another charter, the grantor and his heirs would warrant the monks in perpetuity and acquit and defend them for all services and keep and maintain whatever this present charter witnesses. Ibid., xi, no. 159, pp. 184–85.

[70] Kaye, *Medieval Conveyances*, p. 44.

[71] *Early Yorkshire Charters*, vol. IV, no. 91 (*servabimus, manutenebimus et warrantizabimus*); vol. XI, no. 123 ("*manuteneat et defendat et tueatur*").

constituting a more general obligation of protection that went beyond the duty to warrant.[72]

Consequently, maintenance might have had a broader meaning for contemporaries. That belief may have related to the longstanding relationship between a lord and his man. Postles stated that warranty was connected to the archaic practice of the pledge of faith,[73] as was illustrated in the agreement between the William, count of Acquitaine, and Hugh of Lusignan. The pledging of faith ("*affidavi*") by grantors in a number of charters to emphasize their commitment supports that view.[74] Although several grantors pledged their faith in charters that also expressly warranted the grant, not all did. For example, the grantor in a quitclaim of land to the monks of Rievaulx pledged his faith that he would not make any claims or challenges regarding the lands, but just as a faithful brother of their house would support and stand with them in all their causes and business.[75] Thus, regardless of whether faith was connected to the development of warranty, the notion of faith was a core element of lordship. It was likely understood to include a socially recognized, although nonlegal, obligation of support in connection with legal disputes and other problems. Hyams said that men "expected their lords to maintain them in their suits and to help them with costs when necessary."[76]

Scholars have argued that the norm of maintenance included more extensive duties of support and assistance by lords than their warranty obligation. Although Hyams focused on the evolution of the obligation of a lord to warrant the tenure of his tenants, he contrasted the use of maintenance with the use of warranty in the charters and stated that the former ranged more widely, encompassing other forms of conduct.

---

[72] The use of the word "maintenance" in other contexts reflected this obligation of protection. In one charter the grantor noted that he had given his wife certain land in exchange for land that was her marriage portion, which he had given as a marriage gift to their daughter's husband. He also specified that he had seised his wife's brother in her place so that he would maintain her and protect her from injury by everyone. J.H. Round, ed., *Ancient Charters Royal and Private Prior to A.D. 1200*, 10 *Pipe Roll Society*, vol. I (London, 1888), no. 12, pp. 20–23.

[73] Postles, "Language of Warranty," pp. 216–17.

[74] *Early Yorkshire Charters*, vol. I, no. 580; vol. VI, no. 151; vol. XI, nos. 21, 128, and 129.

[75] "*Propria manu affidavi quod numquam in posterum movebo adversos prefatos monachos de terra illa vel de illis conventionibus aliquam querelam vel calumpniam vel per me vel per aliquem alium, sed sicut frater domus illius fidelis et benevolus juvabo illos et stabo cum ipsis in eorum causis et negotiis.*" Ibid., vol. I, no. 611.

[76] Hyams, *Rancor and Reconciliation*, p. 263.

He seemed to equate maintenance and protection, noting that it described protective lordship. When a lawsuit challenged Roger de Mowbray's gift of land as part of his endowment of Byland abbey, Roger, who was in Normandy, wrote his mother, his steward, and bailiffs telling them to maintain, protect, and defend the abbot of Byland and his brother monks and their lands just as their own land.[77] Moreover, this obligation might extend to vassals who were not tenants.[78] Palmer said that the lord's duty was to protect and maintain his man, which meant proving his tenant with lifetime maintenance and support for his survivors.[79] He viewed this obligation of maintenance broadly and not limited to obligations relating to land.[80] Hudson believed that warranty included the lord's obligation to protect his man in the various ways that the latter sought. Significantly he linked this protection to notions of maintenance and said that it was not limited to the lord's tenants as "a lord might just as easily maintain a non-landed follower."[81] He noted that affinities, broader groups of beneficiaries not having a tenurial relationship with a lord, which resembled the later medieval affinities of patrons and clients, existed in the twelfth century. He said that economic considerations and competition for lordship may have prompted them.[82] Postles aptly summarized the evolution of the meaning of maintenance, asserting that the introduction of warranty in the

---

[77] "Scripsit etiam matri sue et dapifero suo, et omnibus ballivis suis in comitatu Eboracensi quod ipsi manutenerent, protegerent, et defenderent abbatem R. de Bellalandda, et monachos suos fatres, et terram eorum sicut suam propriam terram." Roger undertook a number of other measures to deal with this litigation and various problems encountered by the abbot and the monks. William Dugdale, *Monasticon Anglicanum*, 6 vols. (London, 1847), vol. V, no. VII, pp. 351–52.

[78] Hyams, "Warranty and Good Lordship," pp. 449–50.

[79] Robert Palmer, "The Origins of Property," 4–6; This obligation required a lord to provide land of equal value (*escambium*) if he were unable to provide land to an accepted tenant, whose security conflicted with that of a valid other claimant. Ibid., p. 47. He viewed this obligation of maintenance as an aspect of feudal society in which customary obligations evolved into legal ones.

[80] Palmer viewed the lord's seneschals performing suit of court on behalf of the lord's tenant as an example of this. Robert Palmer, *The County Courts of Medieval England 1150–1350* (Princeton, 1982), pp. 113–16.

[81] He specifically referred to the later medieval notion of maintenance. Hudson, *Land, Law, and Lordship*, p. 53 and note 175. Pike asserted that maintenance was a product of "those medieval ties by which man was bound to man, especially of the tie by which the lord was bound to his tenant or retainer." Lucas Owen Pike, *History of Crime in England*, 2 vols. (London, 1873–76), vol. II, p. 16.

[82] David Crouch, "Bastard Feudalism Revised," *Past and Present* 131 (1991), pp. 170–77; Hudson, *Law, Land, and Lordship*, p. 48 and note 154.

first half of the twelfth century served to augment the relationship between lord and man and that was then extended to maintaining affinities and subtenants.[83]

But, as both Hyams and Hudson noted, this broader notion of maintenance was voluntary, unlike warranty, which evolved from a social norm to a legal obligation. It was enforced by honor and shame and perhaps also by peer pressure.[84] The *Lege Henri Primi* stated that "if a lord deprives his man of his land or his fee by virtue of which he is his man, or if he deserts him without cause in his hour of mortal need, he may forfeit his lordship over him."[85] Lords who failed to protect their own men might "los[e] their authority and standing."[86] Concern for these consequences as well as further evidence of a lord's obligation of maintenance may explain why in some instances a lord ordered others to implement it. For example, Ranulf, earl of Chester, in a confirmation of the seisin of the monks of Fountain Abbey in certain of his lands, ordered his bailiffs and servants not to harm the monks but to maintain them and their men and their property.[87] In a pledge of homage and fealty to the Abbot of Glastonbury, a man "obligated himself to maintain the abbot's men at a hundred court and to be present at the abbot's pleas," and in another a forester, who held land by the gift of the abbot of Glastonbury, generally obligated himself to maintain the men

---

[83] Postles, "Gifts in Frankalmoign," p. 346.
[84] Hyams, "Warranty and Good Lordship," p. 451.
[85] *Leges Henri Primi*, §43, 8, pp. 152–53.   [86] Hyams, *Rancor and Reconciliation*, p. 107.
[87] "*Quare precipio omnibus ballivis meis et servientibus meis de Richesmund'sire ut nullum gravamen vel molestiam prefatis monachis inferant, sed eos et homines et res eorum manute[ne]ant et defendant.*" *Early Yorkshire Charters*, vol. IV, no. 86. In another charter, the earl's steward, confirming a gift by one of his men to a priory and its nuns, implored both his heirs and men to protect and maintain the nuns and their places. Ibid., vol. V, no. 174, p. 77. One grantor ordered his bailiffs and his men of the vill to protect, keep safe, and maintain the grantee monks and all their property that benefits their house. Ibid., vol. III, no. 1511. Another earl similarly commanded and ordered his officials (*mininstris*) never to disturb the grantees, the monks of Cluniac, but to favor and maintain them. Ibid., no. 399. Nor did lords limit such requests to officials and men. A lord sometimes ordered or implored all his friends to maintain and defend or support gift and the grantees. Ibid., vol. VI, no. 57; Greenway, *Mowbray Charters*, no. 351, p. 226. One grantor beseeched his lords and King Stephen to maintain his gift should any man of perverse mind cause harm or injury to the religious grantees, and he made a similar request of the dean of York regarding the same gift. *Early Yorkshire Charters*, vol. XII, nos. 74, 75. One grantor drew a distinction between those whom he could order and those whom he could only beseech. He said that he "prayed that all my friends and lords and ordered that my men and officials maintain and protect the grantee and his heirs in the land just as they esteem my honor." Stenton, *Documents*, no. 333, p. 250.

of the abbey.[88] Moreover, lords may have felt a similar obligation regarding gifts by their men. In a charter addressed to his officials confirming a gift to a priory by his barons and men, Conan, duke of Brittany and earl of Richmond, ordered several of his officials, barons, and men to maintain the nuns and all their things.[89] Although one charter did not use the word "maintenance," it explicitly obligated the grantors in a manner that resembled the later narrow and legal notion of maintenance.[90]

Determining what was considered illegitimate conduct by lords in twelfth-century England is not an easy matter. The restrictions on their use of power and influence to support their men may have been few. The *Leges Henri Primi* suggested that a lord might use any means of support "without penalty."[91] Whether that would extend to homicide or other significant wrongdoing is not clear and perhaps doubtful. But good lordship might sanction the use of force.[92] Maitland noted that a tenant might threaten his adversary with forceful retaliation by his lord.[93]

---

[88] "*Willelmus Fokerman fecit fidelitatem domino abbati et recognovit se tenere dimidiam virgatam . . . et debet manutenere homines abbattis ad hundredum de Kainesham . . . Idem debet esse ad placita domini abbatis*" and "*Moyses forestarius tenet unam virgatam . . . et debet manutenere homines de abbatia.*" N.E. Stacy, ed., Surveys of the Estates of Glastonbury Abbey c. 1135–1201 (Oxford, 2001), pp. 89, 236. Both of these documents look like a lord or a lord's predecessor passing on part of his obligation to maintain his men to someone else. Gratitude is expressed to Prof. Paul Brand for this suggestion.

[89] *Early Yorkshire Charters*, vol. IV, no. 53. Another form of words found fairly frequently in both private charters and royal ones from the early twelfth century was to tell the addressees to look after the grantee's interests as if they were the grantor's own. Gratitude is expressed to Prof. Paul Hyams for this suggestion.

[90] The charter records a grant by the priory and convent of Guisborough of its portion in the church of Hessle to the priory and convent of Watton for a certain sum, reserving certain rights and stating that the grantors will warrant and defend the grantee against all men. But the charter stated further that if the vicar of the church caused injury to the grantees on any of the foregoing or dragged them into litigation ("*in causam*") on the same, the grantors would faithfully assist them in aid against the vicar and keep them safe ("*conservabunt*") as much as possible from loss ("*indempnes*") on the claim ("*impetitionem*") of the vicar on these matters. *Early Yorkshire Charters*, vol. XII, no. 43. That the concern was narrowly focused on problems of a potentially troublesome vicar may explain why the commitment was so explicit and unusually specific and did not use the word "maintenance."

[91] *Leges Henry Primi*, §82.4, p. 257. Penalty likely meant royal monetary punishment. Gratitude is expressed to Prof. Paul Hyams for this suggstion.

[92] Hudson, *Land, Law, and Lordship*, p. 53.

[93] The tenant's lord might use "carnal weapons or let loose the thunders of the church in defence of his tenant." Pollock and Maitland, *History of English Law*, vol. I, pp. 306–07.

However, whether a lord could warrant his tenant's violence was an open question.[94] Thus, drawing a line between the permissible and illegal exercise of lordship might be difficult.[95]

The Later Development of Lordship

In the later twelfth and thirteenth centuries, the second and third centuries of English feudalism, important structural changes in the nature of the relationship between lords and tenants occurred.[96] Legal changes and inflation weakened the former tenurial lordship.[97] Its nature was altered by the substitution of rewards other than land to supplement the tenurial bond. Lordship and its "famous 'protection,'" however, remained one of the rewards provided by lords to their men.[98] The importance of loyalty and the mutual bond of obligation between lord and tenant continued.[99] As before, the lord's desire for services and the client's need for protection drove this contractual and conditionally reciprocal relationship.[100] Notwithstanding these changes, lords remained strong,[101] and good

---

[94] Pollock and F.W. Maitland, *History of English Law*, vol. I, p. 300. The question was whether a lord could defend a tenant's violence on the ground that it was done on the lord's behalf and would have been permissible if done by the lord himself.

[95] In discussing magnates and good lordship, Prestwich said that "there might be a very thin distinction between the proper exercise of patronage and support, and the unacceptable use of violence and fraud." He noted that high-ranking clerics "had a surprising involvement in criminal activity." Prestwich, *Plantagenet England*, p. 513.

[96] D.A. Carpenter, "The Second Century of English Feudalism," *Past & Present* 168 (2000); Scott Waugh, "Tenure to Contract: Lordship and Clientage in Thirteenth-Century England," *English Historical Review* 101 (1986).

[97] Waugh, "Lordship and Clientage," pp. 811–15. Waugh noted that the changes demonstrated the interdependence of legal and social change in England. Ibid., p. 832.

[98] Christopher Dyer, "The Ineffectiveness of Lordship in England, 1200–1400," in Christopher Dyer, Peter Coss, and Chris Wickham, eds., *Rodney Hilton's Middle Ages* (Oxford, 2007), p. 80; Carpenter, "Second Century," p. 35. Waugh, "Third Century," p. 50.

[99] Carpenter, "Second Century," pp. 61, 64, 66. Dyer, however, asserted that in the thirteenth century, lordship was seriously weakened, a "phase in its failure," and ceased to be benevolent, especially respecting the relationships with peasants. Dyer, "Ineffectiveness of Lordship," pp. 70, 79–82, 84–86.

[100] Ibid., pp. 817–25. In addition, "moral or psychological sentiments about loyalty ... reinforced the formal expression of social bonding in contracts and tenure." Waugh, "Lordship and Clientage," pp. 818–19. Waugh identified the important characteristics of these contracts, concluding that the contracts were the initial efforts by lords to preserve "the logic of conditional reciprocity" while mitigating the disadvantages of feudal tenure. Ibid., pp. 820–24.

[101] Coss, *Origins*, p. 40.

lordship was important and necessary to the lord's men.[102] A corollary was that lords should maintain their men. In a thirteenth-century romance depicting the life of the twelfth-century outlaw Foulke Le Fitz Waryn, he said to the king, his liege lord, that since Foulke is bound to him by fealty and holds lands of him, the king "ought to maintain [him] within reason."[103]

In sum, the early social norms of kinship, community, charity, and lordship supported, and perhaps encouraged, maintenance that consisted of supporting and assisting persons with their legal and other problems. Contemporaries viewed this conduct in a positive light.

---

[102] Waugh concluded that lords "fought to preserve their tenurial authority, so that contracts added a new dimension to lordship rather than completely altering it. They strengthened lordship by making it more supple. The development of contractual retaining in the thirteenth century thus ensured the survival of the pattern of lord/client relations that had been worked out over the two previous centuries and likewise ensured the dominance of the landed elite within those relationships and within the social hierarchy of the economy as a whole." Ibid., p. 839. David Carpenter also noted that many scholars underestimated what remained of feudalism in this period and that tenants still wanted good lordship as the lords did service. Carpenter, "Second Century," pp. 32, 34.

[103] "*[E] vous me dussez meyntenir en resoun.*" E.J. Hathaway, P.T. Ricketts, C.A. Robson, and A.D. Wilshere, eds., *Foulke Le Fitz Waryn* (Oxford: Anglo-Norman Text Society, 1975), p. 24, lines 26–29.

3

Legal Responses to the Corruption of Justice

At the end of thirteenth century, parliament enacted a number of legal measures to deal with the abuse of power and influence in the legal process. Because this conduct perverted and undermined this process, significant concerns had arisen concerning it. Aggrieved individuals began to petition the king, his council, and parliament complaining about this conduct, and legislation targeting it emerged. Although the use of power involving violence and physical threats still occurred, those types of conduct had diminished as the medieval period progressed. According to commentators, individuals often resorted to other forms of conduct such as bribery, coercion, extortion, and cronyism. Those types of conduct initially complemented these earlier methods. But they then largely replaced them as the means for lords to use their power to pursue their self-interest and to advance the interests of their clients.[1]

The Initial Statutes and Ordinances

The reign of Edward I was a critical period in the development of legal norms regarding abuse of legal procedure. Several provisions directed at such conduct were enacted: the Statute of Westminster I 1275, chapters 25, 28, and 33; the Statute of Westminster II 1285, chapters 12 and 49; the *Articuli Super Cartas* 1300, chapter 11; the Ordinance of Conspirators 1293; another conspiracy ordinance in 1305; and the Trailbaston Ordinance 1305.[2] These provisions raised two important legal questions.

---

[1] Such less tangible pressures were more common than violence. Carpenter, "Law, Justice, and Landowners in Late Medieval England," *Law and History Review* 1 (1983), pp. 205, 217; Richard Kaeuper, "Law and Order in Fourteenth-Century England: The Evidence of Special Commissions of Oyer and Terminer," *Speculum* 54 (1979), pp. 774–81; McFarlane, *The Nobility of Later Medieval England*, p. 115.

[2] In addition, the London Ordinance of 1280 prohibited maintenance and champerty by lawyers practicing in the London courts, prohibiting them from "undertak[ing] a suit to be a partner in such suit" and from "undertak[ing] a plea to partake in the demand." Henry

First, given the generality of the statutory language, the nature of the proscribed conduct required definition, and second, it was necessary to determine whether private parties as well as the crown could bring actions based on the statutes.

Maintenance and Champerty

The Statute of Westminster I included a number of these initial provisions. This statute reflected the concern with the problems of the later thirteenth-century justice system and in particular with its local administration.[3] The royal Inquests of 1274–75, known as the Hundred Rolls, produced significant evidence of abuse and may have influenced the content of the statute.[4] Chapters 25 and 28 were part of a group of sections directed at administration of justice, which dealt with maintenance, champerty, extortion, bribery, abuse of official power, and abusive litigation practiced by royal and court officials, lawyers, and individual litigants.[5]

Riley, ed., *Munimenta Gildhallae Londoniensis*, 4 vols. (Rolls Series, London, 1860–62), vol. I, part I, *Liber Custamarum*, p. 280.

[3] Michael Preswich, *Plantagenet England 1225–1360* (Oxford, 2005), p. 124; Alan Harding, *Medieval Law and the Foundations of the State* (Oxford, 2002), p. 187. Alan Harding, *England in the Thirteenth Century* (Cambridge, 1993), p. 217. Plucknett said that the problem that the criminal law faced was "getting vigorous and honest men in the lower ranks of the official hierarchy," as they "most often came in close touch with the people, and had the most opportunities of becoming petty tyrants." T.F.T Plucknett, *Edward I and Criminal Law* (Cambridge, 1960), p. 87.

[4] Cam argued that many provisions of the Statute of Westminster I were a product of these inquests. The inquests were commissioned in the fall of 1274 and occurred between November 18, 1274, and March 21, 1275. The statute was enacted in April 1275. Helen Cam, "Studies in the Hundred Rolls: Some Aspects of Thirteenth-Century Administration," in Paul Vinogradoff, ed., *Oxford Studies in Social and Legal History* (1921; reprint, New York, 1974), vol. VI, pp. 36–39; Helen M. Cam, *The Hundred and the Hundred Rolls* (London, 1930), pp. 27–51, 248–57. Prestwich, however, questioned the impact of the hundred rolls returns, indicating that the crown was well aware of the problems. Michael Prestwich, *Edward I* (New Haven, 1997), pp. 96, 106.

[5] 3 Edw. I, cc. 24–28 (1272), *Statutes of the Realm*, A. Luders, T. Tomlins, J. France, W. Tauton, and J. Raithby, eds., 11 vols. (London, 1810–28), vol. 1, pp. 33–34. Cam stated that these sections were clearly based on question twenty-one in the Articles of October 11, 1274 to the hundreds' jurors, which asked, "Again who have by the power of their office troubled any maliciously and thus have extorted lands, rents or any other contributions, and from what time" and which had elicited a wealth of information as to the various abuses and extortions of local officials. Cam, "Studies in the Hundred Rolls," p. 36; Cam, *The Hundred Rolls*, pp. 250–51.

Chapter 25 of Westminster I provided that "No officer of the king by himself nor through others, shall maintain pleas, suits or matters hanging in the king's courts, for lands, tenements or other things, for to have part or profit thereof by covenant made between them; and he that doth, shall be punished at the king's pleasure."[6] Although the statute used the word "maintain" it seems to be directed at conduct that came to be called champerty, a special form of maintenance, in which the litigant agreed to give the maintainer all or part of the subject matter of the litigation in return for his support and assistance. Holdsworth said that champerty was the first of the offenses directed at perversion of justice to be defined.[7] Coke said that of all forms of maintenance, champerty was "the worst."[8]

Although champerty had not yet become a word used commonly in legal parlance, concern with that type of conduct was longstanding. A chapter of the articles of the 1246 Yorkshire Eyre may have been the earliest manifestation.[9] Bracton said this chapter was directed at "the excesses of sheriffs and other bailiffs" and authorized inquiry into "whether they had fomented litigation for the purpose of acquiring lands or wardships or of obtaining money or other profits by which justice and truth are stifled or suffer delay."[10] By 1254, a chapter had been added to the Articles of the Eyre,[11] included with several other articles directed at

---

[6] 3 Edw. I, c. 25 (1275), *Statutes of the Realm*, vol. 1, p. 33.

[7] William Holdsworth, *A History of English Law*, 17 vols. (London, 1956–66), vol. III, pp. 394–97.

[8] Edward Coke, *The Second Part of the Institutes of the Laws of England*, 2 vols. (1642; reprint, Buffalo, 1986), vol. 1, p. 208. Although he claimed that it was an offense at common law (ibid., 208–09), recent scholars have asserted that it was unlikely that there was one. G.O. Sayles, "Introduction, XI, Conspiracy and Allied Offenses," *Select Cases in the Court of the King's Bench*, 7 vols. (London, 1939), vol. III, 58 Selden Soc., p. lv; P.H. Winfield, *The History of Conspiracy and Abuse of Legal Procedure* (Cambridge, 1921), pp. 138–42.

[9] C.A.F. Meekings, ed., *Crown Pleas of the Wiltshire Eyre 1249* (Devizes, 1961), p. 32, no. 43.

[10] S.E. Thorne and G.E. Woodbine, eds. and trans., *The Treatise Known as Bracton: De Legibus et Consuetudinibus Angliae*, 4 vols. (London and Cambridge, MA, 1977), vol. II, p. 332. The dating of the articles of the eyre contained in Bracton is problematic, as the editor noted. Ibid., p. 329, n. 3. The Bracton editors as well as Meekings have used the word "fomented (*suscitaverint*)." But a footnote indicates that some manuscripts of Bracton used "*sustentaverint*," a word commonly associated with "*manutenere*" and somewhat synonymous with it. Ibid., p. 332, n. 35. Other versions of the article said "*foverint*" and "*foverunt*," which might be understood as meaning to support or maintain. Cam, "Studies in the Hundred Rolls," p. 94, no. 43; *Statutes of the Realm*, vol. 1, p. 234, no. 41.

[11] This chapter may have manifested a longstanding concern with misconduct of sheriffs, which began with the 1170 Inquest of Sheriffs. Harding, *Medieval Law* p. 153.

administrative abuses.[12] The focus on champerty was explicit in one version of this chapter. It was directed at "the excesses of sheriffs and other bailiffs who have favored (*foverint*) any plea for any party for the purpose of having land or wardship, or acquiring money or any other profit, by which justice and truth are stifled."[13] Moreover, a 1259 statute prohibited any pleader (*causidicus*) practicing in the London courts to take part of the land in dispute as his fee (*mercedis*). If convicted, he was to be suspended from practice and lose the land.[14] Despite these earlier provisions, Westminster I, chapter 25, is notable for establishing the legal norm prohibiting this form of abuse of legal procedure.

Chapter 25 did not define what was meant by maintenance. But it seemed to prohibit only champerty but not maintenance, although that is not free from doubt.[15] Moreover, the prohibition expressly extended only to royal officials and not to private individuals.[16] As defined by the statute, champerty seemed to consist of three elements. It required an undertaking to maintain a pending plea, doing the undertaking or maintaining in exchange for all or part of the subject matter of the plea, and having an agreement with the beneficiary of the maintenance to that effect. A 1305 statute defined it similarly.[17] The penalty for a violation of chapter 25 was punishment at the king's pleasure. Sayles opined that the

[12] Cam, "Studies in the Hundred Rolls," pp. 22–25, 94. Cam thought this chapter had been added to the old chapters of the eyre, *Vetera Capitula*, in 1254. Cam said that the additions made to the articles in that year are of great interest. Ibid.

[13] *Statutes of the Realm*, vol. 1, p. 234, no. 41. This version is taken from an undated manuscript that includes both the old and new articles of the eyre. Ibid., pp. 233–38. Cam, "Studies in the Hundred Rolls," p. 89, no. 20.

[14] Thomas Stapleton, ed., *Liber de Antiquis Legibus: Cronica Maiorum et Vicecomitum Londonarium*, Camden Society, original series, 34 (1846; reprint, New York, 1968), pp. 42–43; Paul Brand, *The Origins of the English Legal Profession* (Oxford, 1992), p. 67.

[15] Brand supports a broader interpretation that includes maintenance, not just champerty. That issue is discussed below in connection with the "State Trials."

[16] Coke made clear that "minister" included judges and said that the king's ministers and the officers of his court were singled out, as they "were in place to doe more mischiefe therein to the subverting of justice and truth." Coke, *The Second Part of the Institutes*, pp. 208–09. Holdsworth thought that the statute targeted royal officials because of "the growing and widespread corruption among them," as evidenced by contemporary political songs. Holdsworth, *History of English Law*, vol. III, p. 396, n. 8. Winfield said that the statute referred to royal officials only because "they were the most conspicuous offenders" and not because of any deliberate intent to limit the prohibition to them. Winfield, *The History of Conspiracy*, p. 143.

[17] "Champertors be they who move or cause to be moved pleas; and prosecute them at their costs to have part of the land or for part of the profit." *Statutes of the Realm*, vol. 1, p. 145.

king considered it "his own special duty" to correct and punish the wrongdoing of royal officials.[18] To facilitate criminal enforcement, the 1280 Articles of the Eyre contained a chapter whose language was very similar to that of the statute.[19] Only one presentment that may have been based on this statute has been identified.[20]

Chapter 25 neither authorized nor barred actions by private parties, and enforcement may have been limited to actions by the crown. A late fifteenth-century reading on this statute took the view that before the passage of the statute aggrieved parties lacked any remedy, but as result of this prohibition, if officials violated the statute, "the party grieved shall have against them an action grounded on this statute and by it will recover his damages."[21] But there seems to be no evidence of any writ authorizing a private action pursuant to this chapter.[22] Modern scholars have concluded that this provision did not authorize a private remedy.[23]

---

[18] Sayles, "Conspiracy and Allied Offenses," p. lv.

[19] Cam, "Studies in the Hundred Rolls," pp. 100–01, no. 22. Cam provided only a partial text of the chapter, but one version of the complete language says, "Of officers of our Lord King, who have maintained, by themselves or others, the pleas or business of others, existing in the courts, concerning lands, tenements, or other things, that they might have a part thereof or any profit, by Agreement made between them concerning the same." *Statutes of the Realm*, vol. 1, p. 237, no. 20.

[20] The county coroner was accused in the 1329–30 Norhamptonshire Eyre of maintaining a plea in an assize of novel disseisin in exchange for a life estate in the land. He answered that he could not deny the accusation. TNA:PRO JUST1/635, m. 79, AALT Img. No. 832. Scrope CJKB said that since the accused, after being convicted, put himself on the grace of the king, he would not be imprisoned for three years and ransomed at the king's will, but would be treated more leniently and permitted to make a fine. Donald Sutherland, ed., *The Eyre of Northamptonshire, 3–4 Edward III, A.D. 1329–1330*, 2 vols. (London, 1983), vol. I, Selden Soc., 97, pp. 237–38.

[21] Cambridge University Library MS Ee 5.22, f. 149 (tr.).

[22] The *Registrum Omnium Brevium* contains a writ that repeated much of the language of chapter 25 and noted that section in the margin. William Rastell, ed., *Registrum Omnium Brevium tam Originalis quam Judicialium*, 3 vols. (London, 1531), vol. 2, f. 189. But that writ also contains language from a later statute. Winfield called it "a composite writ." Winfield, *The History of Conspiracy*, pp. 142, 144. The *Early Registers of Writs* does not include such a writ. Elsa de Haas and G.D.G. Hall, eds., *Register of Early Writs* (London, 1970), 87 Selden Soc. Neither Sayles nor Winfield believed such a writ existed. Sayles, "Conspiracy and Allied Offenses," p. lv; Winfield, *The History of Conspiracy*, p. 144. Moreover, no writ based on this chapter was found in the review of the unprinted Registers of Writs in the British and Cambridge University libraries.

[23] Holdsworth, *History of English Law*, vol. III, p. 397; Sayles, "Conspiracy and Allied Offenses," p. lv; Winfield, *The History of Conspiracy*, pp. 144, 150. Sayles found a case in which he said that champerty was incidental to a 1276 action by an inquest juror against a man who had contrived to impose a heavy fine on the jurors for accusing another man. The defendant had taken money from this man and jurors accused him of

Nevertheless, chapter 25 may have had some relevance to private petitions in two contexts. First, in petitions to the king and his council, some petitioners complained that conduct violated the maintenance statute. For example, Randolph of Rye complained that Walter Langton took his land and held it "against the statute" that provided "that no minister of the king should take nor maintain parties."[24] The other context involved the 1289–93 "State Trials" of the royal justices.[25] As Brand has argued, these proceedings were not really crown proceedings and were, instead, "matters of private grievance,"[26] initiated by petitions against the senior royal judges.[27] Although the fines paid by the justices to the king and their temporary removal from office have generated the most interest, some of the complainants requested and received damages and other remedies for their injuries.[28]

At least fifteen complaints were filed against the Common Bench justices and twenty against eyre justices, some of whom were the subject of multiple complaints.[29] The allegations included several types of judicial corruption, such as supporting and favoring one party to an

---

taking the other man into his protection and maintaining and defending him. TNA: PRO KB 27/21, m. 3d (1276), AALT Img. No. 7246; Sayles, "Conspiracy and Allied Offenses," p. lv. He said that this case arose from the chapter added to the Articles of Eyre based on the Statute of Westminster I, chapter 25. Ibid. But it is not clear that the defendant's conduct involved champerty, as there was no evidence that the defendant received part of anything related to the matter that was the subject of the inquisition.

[24] Interestingly, the endorsement was that he should "sue at common law." TNA: PRO SC 8/324/E621 (1295–1307) (tr.). In another petition, the abbot of Fécamp complained that he had been removed from his land by the earl of Cornwall and that the "ministers of the king still maintain all the removal." TNA: PRO SC 8/316/E217 (1302) (tr.). But it seems unlikely that "maintain" is being used in its legal sense and the petition did not allege a violation of Westminster I, c. 25.

[25] Paul Brand, "Edward I and the Judges: The 'State Trials' of 1289–93," in Paul Brand, *The Making of the Common Law* (London, 1992), pp. 103–12; T.F. Tout and Hilda Johnstone, *State Trials of the Reign of Edward the First 1289–1293* (London, 1906); Paul Brand, "Ethical Standards for Royal Justices in England, c. 1175–1307," *The University of Chicago Law School Roundtable*, 8 (2001), pp. 250–74. The record of these proceedings is in two plea rolls of The National Archives. TNA: PRO JUST1/541A and 541B. The latter roll contains the proceedings involving the judges, and many of the membranes are badly damaged.

[26] Brand, "Edward I and the Judges," pp. 111–12.

[27] Like the inquiries of 1274–75, they were a product of "another Edwardian expedient for dealing with the persistent problem of misconduct by local officials." Ibid., p. 106.

[28] Ibid., pp. 268–73.   [29] Paul Brand, "Ethical Standards," pp. 252–53.

action, personal involvement in litigation before them, altering records, intimidating parties, manipulating procedure, and tampering with juries.[30] Several complaints specifically accused the justices of maintenance. For example, Roger of Thornton complained that William of Brompton JCP maintained his adversary in violation of Westminster I, c. 25, in an action against Roger, heard before Brompton, by disallowing his exceptions to the writ.[31] The abbot of Roche complained of all the justices of the Bench, especially of William of Brompton, alleging that John of Kirkeby, bishop of Ely, had maintained the husband of John's relative in an action against the abbot's predecessor. As a result, he complained that the justices refused to accept the proof of the earlier abbot's death and entered a default against him and, without an inquiry, adjudged seisin in the husband, resulting in the abbey's loss of its lands. "Thus by error, favor, and maintenance, the justices caused this wrong to the house of Roche."[32] Henry de la Leghe and Nicholas de Cernes also accused William of Brompton of maintenance. They alleged that William maintained William, the son of the parson of Tempsford, who had been indicted for robbery, by giving him aid and counsel, procuring his acquittal, and assisting him in an action of abetment against Henry and Nicholas.[33] Ralph de Hengham CJKB was also the subject of maintenance complaints. William of Bardwell, a chaplain, accused

---

[30] The most serious charge involved Thomas Weyland CJCP, who was accused of being an accessory to a murder committed by his servants. However, the charges against him preceded the process involving the *auditores quarelarum*, who were appointed to hear the complaints against the judges. His servants were hanged and he was indicted for harboring them. After his arrest, he chose to abjure the realm rather than endure the prospect of life in prison. Paul Brand, "Chief Justice and Felon: The Career of Thomas Weyland," in Brand, *Making of the Common Law*, pp. 113–33.

[31] TNA: PRO JUST 1/541B, m. 9, AALT Img. No. 19; Tout and Johnstone, *State Trials*, pp. 18–23. Brand, "Ethical Standards," p. 256.

[32] TNA: PRO JUST 1/541B, m. 18, AALT Img. No. 37 (tr.); Tout and Johnstone, *State Trials*, pp. 1–5.

[33] The complaint also targeted Ralph de Hengham CJCP and William of Saham, eyre justice. TNA: PRO JUST 1/541B, mm. 16, 15, 16d, AALT Img. Nos. 32, 30, 132. Tout and Johnstone, *State Trials*, pp. 27–40; Brand, "Ethical Standards," pp. 255–56. John of London and Walter de la Mare, executors of Ralph Marshall, alleged that Brompton had supported the ejectment of the decedent from his land and had prevented a hearing seeking a remedy for the ejectment. TNA: PRO JUST 1/541B, m. 34d, AALT Img. No.170; Tout and Johnstone, *State Trials*, pp. 216-17. Brompton was the target of twenty-eight complaints. Ibid., pp. xxxi, 210–19. He paid £3,666 13s 4d in fines. Ibid., p. xxxviii.

him of maintaining the abbot of Bury St. Edmonds, from whose chamber Hengham had taken a fee in William's action of trespass. He alleged that Hengham, because of his favor for the abbot, led the pleaders into error by a premeditated trick and was unwilling to hear them.[34] Nicholas de Vere and Agnes, his wife, complained that they had asked Hengham for advice and assistance in claiming land, but he agreed to do so only if they gave him half of what they recovered in the action. Hengham loaned them his clerk to act as their attorney, settled the matter with their adversary, and fixed the jury to give a verdict for the adversary, who agreed to pay 200 marks. The de Veres complained that Hengham kept most of the money, paying them only 50 marks.[35] Henry de la Leghe and Nicholas de Cernes singled out Hengham in their complaint against the justices, accusing him of sealing a writ for their arrest for abetting a false indictment of William, son of the parson of Temesforde, for harboring outlaws prior to any inquiry into William's action against them and of other misconduct in taxing damages to William and for failing to hear their challenges of the jurors.[36] Solomon of Rochester, a senior eyre justice, was also the subject of complaints alleging maintenance.[37]

Brand has argued that the charges in these complaints against Brompton, Hengham, and Rochester could be characterized as "maintenance"

---

[34] William also accused Hengham of maintaining the other defendants in the trespass action. He also accused John Lovetot JCP and Thomas Weyland JCP and Richard of Boyland, an eyre justice, of maintaining the abbot by giving him counsel and aid. TNA: PRO JUST 1/541B, m. 6, AALT Img. No. 12. Tout and Johnstone, *State Trials*, pp. 49–51; Brand, "Ethical Standards," p. 256.

[35] TNA: PRO E 175/1/7, m. 4, cited in Brand, "Ethical Standards," p. 256.

[36] Hengham was found guilty and remanded to the custody of treasurer. Further process ensued involving the dispute between William and Henry and Nicholas. But the matter seemed not to have been resolved perhaps because Henry had died and Nicholas was accused of killing him. TNA: PRO JUST 1/541B, mm. 16, 16d, AALT Img. Nos. 32, 132; Tout and Johnstone, *State Trials*, pp. 27–33, 35–37; Brand, "Ethical Standards," p. 271–72. Hengham was subject of sixteen complaints, twelve solely against him. Ibid., p. 252. He paid £4,303 6s 8d in fines. Tout and Johnstone, *State Trials*, p. xxxviii.

[37] Henry, the son of Nicholas of Bury, alleged that Rochester maintained the prior of Bromholm in an advowson action against Henry and had instigated the plea at the request of his judicial colleague, Robert Fulks. TNA: PRO JUST 1/541B, m. 30d, AALT Img. No. 162; Tout and Johnstone, *State Trials*, pp. 67–70; Brand, "Ethical Standards," p. 256. Henry, son of Henry de Boys, complained that Rochester had given aid to an armed party of men who had ejected Henry from his manor and had supported the leader of the party. TNA: PRO SC 8/35/1734; Brand, "Ethical Standards," p. 255.

in violation of Westminster I, chapter 25.[38] But that conclusion is not free from doubt. First, there is a question of whether the statute targeted only champerty, as suggested above, and did not apply to maintenance. Brand argued that the statute was not so limited.[39] Resolving this inter-pretative issue turns on the word "profit." He argued that "profit" was not limited to being derived from "lands, tenements, or other things" that were the subject of the pending litigation, but meant "where a royal official stood to make any other form of gain if the litigant succeeded."[40] The French words, "to have part of that or other profit (*por aver part de ceo ou autre profit*)," strengthen his position.[41] Moreover, as Brand stated, this statute was "widely drawn" and medieval statutes were often interpreted loosely.[42] But the next words of the statute, "by agreement (*covenant*) made between them," present a bigger hurdle for Brand's broad interpretation. With the exception of the de Veres' complaint against Ralph de Hengham, none of the complaints alleged any kind of an agreement between the judge and the beneficiary of his efforts on their behalf, although there may been one or one might be implied. Finally, in some of the complaints, as Brand acknowledged,[43] the nature of the conduct alleged by the complainants to be maintenance was not known. As noted in Chapter 1, the word "maintenance" was often used broadly, especially in complaints. Arguably, only the de Veres' complaint against Ralph de Hengham was champerty in violation of Westminster I, chapter 25. But it is less clear that the other conduct alleged in the complaints against the judges violated this provision.[44]

The Statute of Westminster I contained two further relevant provisions. Chapter 28 had two prohibitions. The first one prohibited clerks of kings or justices from receiving any presentment of a church that was the subject

---

[38] Brand, "Ethical Standards," pp. 244–45, 255–65.   [39] Ibid., pp. 244–45.

[40] Ibid, p. 244.

[41] *Statutes of the Realm*, vol. 1, p. 33. The only relevant wording is that in French. Gratitude is expressed to Prof. Paul Brand for this suggestion. This English translation of these words omitted the word "other." *Statutes of the Realm*, vol. 1, p. 33. But another translation included it. David Douglas, ed., *English Historical Documents* (New York, 1975), vol. III, p. 404.

[42] T.F.T. Plucknett, *Statutes and Their Interpretation in the First Half of the Fourteen Century* (London, 1922), pp. 40–163; Jonathan Rose, "The Legal Profession in Medieval England: A History of Regulation," *Syracuse Law Review* 48 (1998), pp. 41–49.

[43] Brand, "Ethical Standards," p. 255.

[44] If the allegations, however, were true, the conduct violated the justices' oath of office. Brand, "Ethical Standards," pp. 239–44. In any event, the justices served at the pleasure of the king.

of litigation in the king's court without special license from the king. The second prohibited the clerks of the justices or sheriffs from maintaining parties or business in the king's courts or from engaging in any fraud by which the common right was delayed or disturbed.[45] This provision supplemented chapter 25 by adding the royal and judicial clerks to that chapter's prohibition.[46] Coke asserted that these clerks were added because, like the officials subject to chapter 25, they were in a position where they could "do more mischiefe."[47] Contemporaries agreed and complained to the king and his council. After reciting chapter 28, an early fourteenth-century petition said that "clerks of the justices of the Common Bench are commonly attorneys and maintainers of parties so that the right is delayed by them, which is necessary for the common profit of the people, which outrageous practice ought to be stopped and the statute be maintained and enforced by a harsher penalty."[48] A third provision, chapter 33, also reflected concern with abusive litigation and focused on maintenance by attorneys in the county courts.[49] It focused on two separate kinds of wrongdoing. It enjoined sheriffs not to permit the maintenance of cases in county courts by barretors and restricted the stewards of great lords or others from making suit of court or pronouncing judgments of the county courts unless they were attorneys for their lords.[50]

---

[45] The punishment was loss of their office or more grievous if required by the nature of the trespass. Statute of Westminster I, c. 28, 3 Edw. I (1275), *Statutes of the Realm*, vol. 1, pp. 33–34. The reference to the delay or disturbing of the "common right (*commune dreiture*)" was the basis for Coke's assertion that maintenance was an offense at common law and was *malum in se*. Coke, *The Second Part of the Institutes*, pp. 208–09.

[46] The prohibition on taking presentments that were the subject of litigation without license of the king may have expanded the notion of champerty or created an additional offense.

[47] Coke, *The Second Part of the Institutes*, p. 212.

[48] The response was that "if you wish to complain, Sir William Bereford [CJCP] will do right." TNA: PRO SC 8/100/4964 (tr.).

[49] Coke, Winfield, and Holdsworth all attributed this problem to the Statute of Merton's authorization of parties to appoint attorneys in local courts. Coke, *The Second Part of Institutes*, p. 225; Winfield, *The History of Conspiracy*, pp. 143–44; Holdsworth, *History of English Law*, vol. III, p. 396–97.

[50] Statute of Westminster I, c. 33, *Statutes of Realm*, vol. 1, p. 35. As to the latter, the stewards or others could also do so if all suitors and their attorneys were required to do so. Both the sheriff and the barretor were subject to punishment for violating the statute. The meaning of the term "barretor" is unclear in this period. It may be similar to maintainer of quarrels, but it came to mean someone who stirred up litigation. Winfield, *History of Conspiracy*, p. 200. Plucknett noted that sheriffs "from fear, or favor, or by corruption, or for affinity [did] not act vigorously when their friends ought to be arrested and kept until their trial." Plucknett, *Edward I and Criminal Law*, p. 86.

Statute of Westminster II, chapter 49, has been traditionally considered an important prohibition of champerty. This chapter was directed at the chancellor, treasurer, justices, other members of the King's Council; the clerks of the Chancery, Exchequer, justices, and other officials; and the clerical and lay members of the king's household. Unlike the prior two statutes, this provision actually used the word "champerty," rather than the more general term "maintenance," as the two prior statutes had. However, the prohibited conduct differed from the more general prohibitions on champerty for receiving a share of the subject matter of the litigation in exchange for assisting or supporting the litigant. Instead, it prohibited the targeted officials from receiving any church, advowson, land, or tenement in fee by gift or sale or by lease, whether this occurred by champerty or otherwise, if the property was the subject of a plea before the king or any of his officials, or from taking any other reward.[51] This chapter broadened the scope of the prohibited conduct in several respects. First, it increased or, at least, made explicit, the officials subject to the prohibition.[52] Second, it expanded the type of proscribed conduct to include the purchase or gratuitous acquisition of land and other property interests that were the subject of existing plea. Third, unlike chapter 25, this chapter subjected both the seller and buyer of matter in litigation to punishment.[53] Like chapter 25, this chapter also seemed limit to enforcement to the crown and did not authorize civil suits for damages by private parties.[54]

Despite not authorizing private actions, petitioners cited chapter 49 in their complaints, as they had done with Westminster I, chapter 25. In a

---

[51] Statute of Westminster II, 13 Edw. I, c. 49 (1285), *Statutes of the Realm*, vol. 1, p. 95. This provision may be the first use of the word "champerty (*chaumpartie*)" in a legal context. Holdsworth, *A History of English Law*, vol. III, p. 397; Winfield, *The History of Conspiracy*, p. 144.

[52] Coke said that there was doubt whether the chancellor, treasurer, justices, and members of the king's council were "ministers," as used in chapter 25, because they were "persons of such eminence." He opined that they were included in chapter 49 because their "countenance and places," when they became interested in land, were "apparent hindrances of the due and indifferent proceeding of law and justice." Coke, *The Second Part of the Institutes*, p. 484.

[53] The chapter provided that anyone who by himself or by another engaged, or who made any agreement to engage, in the prohibited conduct as well as anyone who purchased these interests would be punished at the king's pleasure. Statute of Westminster II, 13 Edw. I, c. 49 (1285), *Statutes of the Realm*, vol. 1, p. 95.

[54] Modern scholars have taken that view. Holdsworth, *A History of English Law*, vol. III, p. 397; Sayles, "Conspiracy and Allied Offenses," p. lv; Winfield, *The History of Conspiracy*, p. 150.

celebrated matter, John Ferrers complained of maintenance by Walter Langton, the treasurer of England.[55] He alleged that Langton purchased a manor, which was the subject of a plea brought by Ferrers in order to delay that plea, in violation of the Statute of Westminster II, chapter 49.[56] But unlike earlier cases, whether the statute authorized private actions now generated discussion. After several appearances by the parties in the proceeding, the king granted a pardon to Langton because he was unwilling that Langton be inconvenienced or troubled by this matter before the king or his justices as "such punishment belongs to the king and not to any other person."[57] Further, in a 1311 petition to parliament, Cecily Beauchamp complained that William Inge JCP had violated the champerty statute by acquiring a manor while her writ of *cui in vita* regarding the manor was pending. After the Council heard the complaint and examined the relevant statutes, they said that it seemed that "Cecily can only sue against William Inge in the king's name: and therefore William of Langley, who sued on behalf of the same Cecily, is told to acquire a writ in the king's name against the aforesaid William if he thinks that this will help him."[58] Subsequently, probably as a result of the petition, the king issued a writ, reciting Inge's violation of chapter 49 and ordering the justices of the King's Bench to summon Inge and do what needed to be done according to law and the form of the statute.[59] Langley, as the king's attorney, then sued for the king, and the sheriff was ordered to have Inge in court to respond.[60]

---

[55] Alice Beardwood, "The Trial of Walter Langton, Bishop of Lichfield, 1307–1313," *Transactions of the American Philosophical Society* 54 (1964), pp. 14–17. Ferrers had initiated the matter by a petition to the king and his council complaining of Walter's maintenance in an action John had brought against William Ferrers, his cousin. TNA: PRO SC 8/322/E528; TNA: PRO JUST 1/1344, m. 7 (1307), AALT Img. No. 14. This petition is one of a number of petitions, discussed below, complaining about Langton's maintenance, which was just one element of the numerous complaints filed against Langton. TNA: PRO JUST 1/744, m. 1 (1307).

[56] As a result of the petition, the king appointed Henry de Lacy, earl of Lincoln, to hear and adjudicate the matter and the record was sent from parliament. Langton answered that he was busy with parliamentary matters, but Ferrers said Langton was a "minister" of the king and present in court and that the statute was "binding on that treasurer, first and foremost among the other officials of the king." TNA: PRO KB 27/189, m. 1 (1307), AALT Img. No. 1377; Sayles, "Conspiracy and Allied Offenses," pp. lxvi–lxvii.

[57] TNA: PRO KB 27/189, m. 1 (1307), AALT Img. No. 1377 (tr.).

[58] "On behalf of Cecily Beauchamp," *Edward II Parliaments*: January 1315, No. 78 (64), *PROME* (tr.).

[59] TNA: PRO CP 40/211, m. 298d (1315), AALT Img. No. 592.

[60] TNA: PRO CP 40/211, m. 103d (1315), AALT Img. No. 209. Subsequently, Inge obtained letters of protection from the king permitting him to remain without day because he was in the king's service in Scotland. TNA: PRO CP 40/212A, m. 473d (1315), AALT Img.

Several proceedings on petitions in parliament also invoked Westminster II, chapter 49. John de Grey and Andrew de Jarpenville accused Ellis de Hauville, an official of the king, of champerty in violation of chapter 49.[61] He admitted the violation and was handed over to the marshal to be punished.[62] Two other complaints were against William de Vescy, lord of the liberty of Kildare. In one proceeding, the petitioner rejected William's explanation of the champerty and offered to prove the violation. But king did not want a jury inquiry since the petitioner had not lost anything.[63] In the other, William denied the charges and a jury was summoned to resolve the matter.[64] There seems to be no evidence of jury presentments or other actions based on chapter 49. Thus, petitions may have been the means of enforcing it.

The final provision enacted during the reign of Edward I that was directed at maintenance and champerty was *Articuli super Cartas*, chapter 11 (1300). Because the earlier statutes had limited the prohibition to royal officials, this chapter expanded it.[65] First, it extended the ban on champerty to all persons. To avoid adversely affecting legal representation, the chapter preserved the right of a litigant "to have counsel of

---

No. 335. The king also issued a writ of *audita querela* to the justices to determine whether there was a violation of *Articuli Super Cartas* (28 Edw. I, c. 11 (1300), *Statutes of the Realm*, vol. 1, p. 139). TNA: PRO CP 40/212A, m. 473d (1315), AALT Img. No. 335.

[61] Brand identified and discussed other misconduct by Ellis de Hauville. P.A. Brand, "Old-cotes v. d'Arcy," in R.F. Hunnisett and J.B. Post, eds., *Medieval Legal Records Edited in Memory of C.A.F. Meekings* (London, 1978), pp. 80, 96–97, 108–09.

[62] "Proceedings on complaints by John de Grey and Andrew de Jarpenville, alleging maintenance of litigants and champerty by Ellis de Hauville contrary to the statutory prohibition," Edward I Parliaments: Roll 6, no. 3, *PROME*.

[63] "Proceedings on the complaint of John FitzThomas against William de Vescy as lord of the liberty of Kildare, alleging maintenance of Gill de Cogan by agreement with Agnes de Valence," Edward I Parliaments: Roll 8, no. 5, *PROME*.

[64] "Proceedings on the complaint of Walter of Ridelesford against William de Vescy as lord of the liberty of Kildare, alleging maintenance of a land plea against him in the court of Castledermot," Edward I Parliaments: Roll 8, no. 17, *PROME*.

[65] "Moreover, because the King had previously ordained by statute that none of his officials should take any plea in champerty and by that statute no others than officials were previously bound to this, the King wills that no official nor any other, for to have part of the thing in plea, shall undertake the business that is in suit; nor none upon any such covenant grant his right to another; and if any do and be attainted thereof, he shall forfeit and lose to the King so much of his goods or lands, amounting to the value of the part of his purchase for such undertaking. To prove this, those who will sue for the king shall be received before the justices before whom the plea is pending and judgment shall be made by them." *Articuli Super Cartas*, 28 Edw. I, c. 11 (1300), *Statutes of the Realm*, vol. 1, p. 139 (tr.).

pleaders ("*countours*") or of learned ("*sage*") men for their fee or of from his kinsmen ("*parentz*") or relatives ("*procheins*"). Second, unlike the earlier statutes, this one provided that anyone could sue on behalf of the king to enforce the statute.[66]

Conspiracy

The initial responses to abuse of legal procedure also included measures against conspiracy.[67] Winfield thought that conspiracy may have had its roots in the Anglo-Saxon period.[68] Harding said that the definition of "the enormous trespass of conspiracy" had begun at the end of the thirteenth century.[69] At that time, several legal enactments made conspiracy illegal and provided criminal and civil remedies.[70] The primary measure was the Ordinance of Conspirators 1293[71] and its associated writ.[72] Winfield also asserted that there was also a 1292 Statute of

---

[66] This statute produced a number of actions, which are discussed in the next chapter.

[67] Conspiracy has received considerable scholarly attention. Sayles, "Conspiracy and Allied Offenses," pp. liv–lxxi; Holdsworth, *A History of English Law*, vol. III, pp. 400–07; Winfield, *The History of Conspiracy*, pp. 1–130; Harding, "Origins of Conspiracy," pp. 89–108; James Bryan, *The Development of the English Law of Conspiracy* (Baltimore, 1909); R.S. Wright, *Law of Criminal Conspiracies and Agreements* (London, 1873).

[68] Winfield, *The History of Conspiracy*, p. 4.

[69] Alan Harding, "Early Trailbaston Proceedings from the Lincoln Roll of 1305," in R.F. Hunnisett and J.B. Post, eds., *Medieval Legal Records*, p. 148. He said that its definition "shows best of all the nature of disorder in late medieval England and how the sense of personal wrong merged into a conception of communal harm and public responsibility ... The root meaning conspiracy in England was thus a concerted subversion of the processes of law which threatened public order." Harding, *Medieval Law*, p. 247. He viewed conspiracy as a crime against the public authority of the state, involving conduct that corrupted and obstructed administrative and legal processes. Alan Harding, "The Origins of the Crime of Conspiracy," *Transactions of the Royal Historical Society* (5th Ser.) 33 (1983), pp. 91–101, 106–07. Sayles, like Winfield, equated conspiracy with abuse of legal procedure. Sayles, "Conspiracy and Allied Offenses," p. lviii.

[70] Harding asserted that changes in English legal procedure permitting oral complaints against royal officials gave conspiracy its vigorous life in this period. He also pointed to its presence in European and canon law and its connection with oath-taking. Harding, *Origins of Conspiracy*, pp. 92–94. Bracton noted the disqualification of conspirators to prosecute the crime of *lese-majesty*, relying, as the editors pointed out, on canon law. *Bracton*, vol. II, p. 334–35. But Bracton used the word "conspirator" as a type of accessory before the fact, in connection with his discussion of outlawry of principals and accessories. He said that conspirators, like accessories, cannot be exacted until the principal has been convicted. Ibid., p. 361.

[71] *Ordinance of Conspirators*, Edward I Parliaments: Roll 6, no. 14, *PROME*.

[72] Winfield studied the nature and scope of this writ in great detail. Winfield, *The History of Conspiracy*, pp. 29–91, 118–30.

Conspirators.[73] But both Sayles and Brand disagreed and said that such a statute was not enacted.[74] A few actions, prior to the 1293 Ordinance, challenged conspiratorial conduct and used the word "conspiracy."[75]

Concern about this problem, however, had appeared earlier. Because of the Edward I's continuing concern with the corruption of justice and his desire to encourage and facilitate the making of complaints, the 1278 Gloucester parliament made important changes in the scope of the general eyre. Those changes included authorizing the eyre to hear complaints, including those against royal officials, and the addition of the new chapters (*Nova Capitula*) to the Articles of Eyre.[76] Accordingly, a new and expanded form of the king's letter patent created the eyre commissions.[77] In the following year, Edward I acted on his concern

---

[73] Ibid., pp. 22–28. The Statutes of Realm includes this provision in a section entitled, "Statutes of Uncertain Date." It was frequently called "The Statute of Champerty." *Statutes of the Realm*, vol. 1, pp. 197, 216 and note. In the second half of the fifteenth century, a Reader in an Inn of Court gave a reading on this statute and used the title, "Statute of Champerty." He said that the purpose of the statute was to expand the prohibition on champerty to anyone, not just the king's ministers, as the Statute of Westminster I, c. 25, had. He said further that any aggrieved person could have writ on the statute and recover his damages. British Library, MS Lansdowne 466, fol. 173v.

[74] Sayles consigned it to "flotsam and jetsam of legal pronouncements" included by the editors of the Statutes of the Realm. Sayles, "Conspiracy and Allied Offenses," p. lix. Brand suggested that it may have been a legislative draft copied in the statute books, but not enacted or perhaps briefly enforced and superseded by the 1293 Ordinance. Brand, *Origins*, p. 121. Gratitude is expressed to Prof. Paul Brand for his information that no copy of this statute appears in any parliamentary records, but only in private statute books. The version in the Statutes of the Realm indicated that it was from British Library, MS Harley 748, fol. 133. *Statutes of the Realm*, vol. 1, p. 216. Another version with the order of the parts reversed and with somewhat different wording is contained in Harvard Law School, MS 177, fols. 145–47.

[75] In a 1253 action, the abbot of Pershore accused Roger of Oxford for "making a conspiracy (*conspiracionem fecit*)" against the abbot that prevented him from carrying out official duties ordered by the king and causing him damage. TNA: PRO KB 26/151, m. 37d (1254), AALT Img. No. 36d. Harding said this was earliest known conspiracy action in England. Harding, *Origins of Conspiracy*, p. 94. Also in 1281, a man sued the jurors, "conspirators and confederators together," who "by their confederacy," falsely and maliciously indicted him for deaths and other trespasses because he had refused to pay them blackmail ("*tributarius*"). Sayles noted that the latter case contained many of the essentials of liability in the later writ of conspiracy, but was an isolated and unique case. Sayles, "Conspiracy and Allied Offenses," p. lviii.

[76] Cam, "Studies in the Hundred Rolls," pp. 56–62, 135–38.

[77] TNA: PRO C 66/99, m. 6 (June 16, 1278), AALT Img. No. 343; *Calendar of Patent Rolls, Edward I, A.D. 1272–81*, 4 vols. (London, 1901), vol. 1, p. 277. Cam has reprinted the letter creating eyres in Cumberland, Westmoreland, and Northumbria and compared it with the earlier letters patent reflecting a more limited scope of authority. Cam, "Studies

with the abuse of legal procedure and sent a writ to the justices in the Eyre of Kent ordering them to inquire into conspiracies to maintain pleas. He said that he understood that

> certain evil men of divers counties, for the increase of their own profit, for evil rather than good, have made detestable confederations and evil intentions, making mutual oaths to maintain and defend the sides of their friends and well-wishers in pleas and actions in which they are concerned, in their counties, such as in assizes, juries, and recognitions, and to aggrieve their enemies fraudulently and to disinherit many of them, to the extent that they can.[78]

As result of this writ, one of the new chapters added to the Articles of the Eyre was *De mutuis sacramentis*, which authorized jury presentments for conspiracy.[79] It stated, "Of those who by oaths bind themselves to support or defend the parties or pleas and businesses of their friends and well-wishers, whereby truth and justice are suffocated."[80] In addition, wrongful prosecution and false accusations were longstanding related concerns.[81] The Statute of Westminster II 1285 provided

---

in the Hundred Rolls," pp. 56–57. This new letter became the standard one used to authorize future eyres. David Crook, *Records of the General Eyre* (London, 1982), pp. 7–8; Alan Harding, "Plaints and Bills," in Daffyd Jenkins, ed., *Legal History Studies 1972* (Cardiff, 1975), p. 68.

[78] He ordered them to arrest and imprison those found guilty. TNA: PRO JUST 1/367, m. 2 (1279), AALT Img. No. 7 (tr.); *Calendar of Close Rolls, Edward I 1279–1288*, vol. 2 (London, 1902), "Close Rolls, Edward I: January, 1279," pp. 518–20, *British History Online*. Very similar writs were sent to the 1280 Somerset Eyre and the 1281–82 Devon Eyre. The record of the latter was contained in a section of the roll entitled "Of Conspirators." TNA: PRO JUST 1/759, m. 4d (1280), AALT Img. No. 3400; TNA: PRO JUST 1/181, m. 27d (1281–82), AALT Img. No. 1642.

[79] Cam stated that this chapter was added in 1279, but records of the subsequent eyres do not bear that out. *De mutuis sacramentis* first appeared in the articles used in some eyres about 1288, but it is unclear whether it was used regularly in all of the eyres after that date.

[80] Cam, "Studies in the Hundred Rolls," pp. 59, 94 no. 69, 100 no. 35; *Statutes of the Realm*, 1, p. 234, n. 12 and p. 238, n. 5. Britton (c. 1290) discussed this chapter, viewing conspiracy and confederations as causing a hindrance of justice. F.M. Nichols, ed., *Britton*, 2 vols. (Oxford, 1865), vol. I, p. 95.

[81] One concern was the negative impact they had on reputation. Various measures were adopted to deal with this problem. Winfield, *The History of Conspiracy*, pp. 4–22; Pollock and Maitland, *The History of English Law*, vol. II, p. 539. Harding, *Origins of Conspiracy*, p. 94. The 1170 Inquest of the Sheriffs and early thirteenth-century complaints about such misconduct reflected the early distress about these matters. Harding, *Medieval Law*, p. 153.

punishment for those who falsely appealed a person, who was subsequently acquitted, and authorized victims to sue for damages.[82]

The Ordinance of Conspirators 1293 was a broad provision that created a procedure for private prosecution of conspiracy and a punishment for those guilty of engaging in it. It stated

> Concerning those who wish to make complaint about conspirators arranging for pleas to be initiated maliciously in the country, as brewers of discord, maliciously maintaining and sustaining those pleas and disputes at champerty or so that they might have some other advantage from it, they are to come henceforth before the justices appointed to the lord king's pleas, and there they are to find security that they will prosecute their complaint. And the sheriffs are to be ordered by a writ of the chief justice and under his seal that they are to be attached to appear before the king on a certain day: and swift justice is to be done there. And those who are convicted of this are to be severely punished, in accordance with the discretion of the aforesaid justices, by prison and ransom; or such complainants are to wait for the eyre of the justices in their parts if they wish, and sue there.[83]

Sayles viewed the Ordinance's purpose to remedy the threat of a serious danger of collapse of the machinery of justice and the widespread lawlessness and corruption at the end of the reign of Edward I.[84] The language of the Ordinance reflected the connection between conspiracy and champerty and maintenance.[85]

---

[82] The punishment was imprisonment for a year. The statute also provided that if the appellor lacked sufficient resources to compensate the victim, the latter could sue those who abetted the appellant. Statute of Westminster II, c. 12, *Statutes of the Realm*, vol. 1, p. 81. In one action, the defendant argued that the damage action would result in "double punishment (*dupplicem penam*)," as he had already been punished by the king, and, therefore, the victim could only recover against the abettors. The court rejected that argument, pointing out abettors could only be sued, where the primary party lacked the resources to satisfy the plaintiff. TNA: PRO KB 27/130, m. 4 (1292), AALT Img. No. 884. In another action, the defendants who had been acquitted sued the abetors for £200 since the appellor had nothing. The abettors denied any false and malicious abetment. TNA:PRO CP 40/92, m. 68 (1292), AALT Img. No. 140.

[83] "Concerning conspirators: an ordinance," Edward I Parliaments: Roll 6, no. 14, *PROME*; "*De Conspiratoribus Ordinatio*," *Rotuli Parliamentorum*, 6 vols. (London, 1767), vol. 1, p. 96. Winfied asserted that this ordinance was the first legislative mention of embracery because of the Latin words "*contumelie braciatoribus*." Winfield, *History of Conspiracy*, p. 162. But Brand in his treatment of the ordinance in *PROME* translated the words as "brewers of discord."

[84] G.O. Sayles, "The Dissolution of a Gild at York in 1306," *English Historical Review* 55 (1940), pp. 84–85.

[85] Sayles said that these three offenses "were closely allied and at times shade so much into each other that it is difficult not to class them as one offence." Sayles, "Conspiracy and

The Ordinance provided that complainants should come before the king's justices and have a writ from the chief justice ordering the sheriff to attach the conspirators to appear for "swift justice to be done" and that those convicted were "to be severely punished by prison and ransom at the discretion of the justices."[86] An enrollment in the same year, likely connected to the Ordinance, provided that if anyone who wished to complain of conspirators and supporters, maintainers, and inventors of false pleas, Gilbert Thornton CJKB should cause such persons to be attached by his writ to come before the lord king to respond to the complainants.[87] Moreover, a 1293 parliamentary enrollment contained a specimen writ and provided that anyone convicted should be imprisoned until they had satisfied the aggrieved party and the king.[88]

Whether the writ was a judicial or original one has caused some confusion. What seems most likely is that the Ordinance created a judicial writ, which was the basis of the initial actions.[89] But the *Articuli*

Allied Offenses," p. liv. "The idea of conspiracy covered the spectrum of ways in which the legal process was corrupted by maintenance, embracery, and champerty." Harding, "Origins of Conspiracy," p. 96.

[86] *Ordinance of Conspirators*, Edward I Parliaments: Roll 6, no. 14, *PROME*. Coke argued that the "ordinance was but in affirmance of the common law." Coke, *The Second Part of the Institutes*, p. 561. This seems doubtful and other scholars have disagreed. Holdsworth, *The History of English Law*, vol. III, pp. 401–02; Winfield, *The History of Conspiracy*, pp. 29–37; Sayles, "Conspiracy and Allied Offenses," pp. lvii–lvix; Wright, *Criminal Conspiracies*, p. 6. In a 1298 conspiracy action, in which the conduct had occurred prior to the enactment of the Ordinance, the defendant argued that the writ could not be used. TNA: PRO KB 27/154, m. 11, AALT Img. No. 775. Sayles concluded that the action was unsuccessful. Sayles, "Conspiracy and Allied Offenses," p. lxi.

[87] TNA: PRO KB 27/137, m.12 (1293), AALT Img. No. 1841. The enrollment is an order of the king to Gilbert Rothbury, clerk of the council and parliament, to forward the information to Gilbert of Thornton.

[88] The writ provided that "If A of B give thee surety for prosecuting his claim, then put by gages and safe pledges G of C that he be before us . . . to answer the aforesaid A of plea of conspiracy and trespass according to our ordinance lately provided, as the said A can reasonably show he ought to answer to him thereof." The writ and the order to Gilbert Rothbury were included with the 1292 Statute of Conspirators, discussed above, although it belonged to the Easter Parliament of 1293. *Statutes of the Realm*, vol. 1, p. 216.

[89] There are very few such judicial writs in the registers. Winfield found only one in the registers in the Cambridge University Library and the remainders were original ones. Winfield, *The History of Conspiracy*, pp. 31–37. A British Library manuscript also contains the register with the judicial writ, which Winfield found in the Cambridge Library. British Library, MS Harley 748, fol. 52 ("conspiracy and trespass according to our ordinance"). The others in the Cambridge University Library are also original ones. E.g., Cambridge University Library, MS Additional 3469, fols. 48v–49r; Cambridge University Library, MS Hh. 2. 11, fol. 28 v; Cambridge University Library, MS Additional 3505, fol. 129v.

super Cartas 1300, chapter 10, stated that the "king had provided remedy for the plaintiffs by a writ out of the Chancery." It is unclear whether the writ was one created by the Ordinance of Conspirators or by this legislation, but the latter seems more likely.[90] A comment in a Year Book case suggested that at some point Chancery may have been prohibited from issuing conspiracy writs.[91] In an early action, the defendant argued that he should not have to answer as "the writ of conspiracy is a judicial writ or granted as it were in a special case" and not a common law writ.[92] Brand has identified the use of original writs in conspiracy actions as early as 1303.[93] Although commentators have disagreed about the nature of these writs,[94] Hall's explanation seems most convincing. He stated that the *Articuli super Cartas* referred to original writs and he thought that both judicial and original writs existed by the end of the thirteenth century and later as well.[95] As a result of this Ordinance and the associated writ, "a stream of actions started in the Michaelmas term 1293" with "a large influx of conspiracy, maintenance and champerty cases into the king's bench."[96]

---

[90] Gratitude is expressed to Prof. Paul Brand for this suggestion. Chapter 10 also authorized the justices of the Common Bench, King's Bench, and those assigned to the Assises, without the necessity of a writ, to order inquests based on complaints made to them and to "do right unto the plaintiffs without delay." *Statutes of the Realm*, vol. 1, p. 139.

[91] Y.B. Trin., 33 Edw. I, Roll Series, pp. 462–63, *Nota* (1305), Seipp No. 1305.061rs. Because this plaintiff wanted to sue the jurors, this restriction may have applied only to conspiracy writs for procuring false indictments. Gratitude is expressed to Prof. Paul Brand for this suggestion.

[92] TNA: PRO KB 27/140, m. 42 (1294), AALT Img. Nos. 2606–7.

[93] British Library, MS Additional 31826, fols. 279v, 282r. In the latter action, the defendants were found guilty of falsely procuring a man to be indicted for robberies, thefts, and other trespasses, for which the plaintiff recovered £50. TNA: PRO CP 40/148, m. 49d, AALT Img. No. 620.

[94] Winfield concluded that most of the writs were original and differed from the judicial writ created by the Ordinance. He said that the nature of writ varied at different stages, but that the judicial writ was "doubtless the parent" of the original one. Winfield, *The History of Conspiracy*, pp. 37–39. Sayles, relying on the early cases, disagreed and showed that during the reign of Edward I these writs were issued by a court of law and not by Chancery. He believed that double sealing of the writs was likely, as they were first sealed by justice in court and then taken to Chancery to receive the great seal. Sayles, "Conspiracy and Allied Offenses," p. lx.

[95] Hall found Sayles's suggestion "not an easy explanation to swallow" and rejected Winfield's parentage assertion as well. G.D.G Hall, "Introduction," *Register of Early Writs*, Selden Soc., 87, pp. cxxxiv–cxxxv and n. 1.

[96] Sayles, "Conspiracy and Allied Offenses," p. lix. He said further that "the new action met a long-felt want and was extremely popular, so much so that a single term in 1297 produced no fewer than fifty-three actions in the court of the king's bench alone." Ibid., p. lxi.

The Ordinance of Conspirators 1293 was not the end of story. Two provisions adopted in 1305 created additional weapons that strengthened the attack on these forms of abuse of legal procedure. The first involved the creation of the trailbaston commissions. The king explained the strategy in pursuing these matters. It was

> more to the honour and profit of the realm and the maintenance of the peace ... that trailbaston matters should receive attention rather than other pleas ... Therefore it is better for one to attend first and foremost to suppressing such disorder and to establishing the peace of the land, so that later one can better attend to the common pleas of the country.[97]

The king created numerous commissions, but initially, proceeded cautiously in creating them.[98] Although the commission members were experienced royal officials, the commissions only had the power to inquire, arrest, indict, and hold offenders in custody until further orders from the king.[99] Within a few months, the Ordinance of Trailbaston authorized fully empowered special commissions of *oyer et terminer* in several counties to inquire into various types of breaches of the peace and wrongdoing.[100] Pursuant to the Ordinance, the king

---

Sayles also noted that some parties attempted to manipulate the use of writ, especially to avoid using a writ of attaint. Sayles, "Conspiracy and Allied Offenses," pp. lxi–lxiii. Some commentators viewed these measures as the beginning of the modern law of conspiracy. Holdsworth, *The History of English Law*, vol. III, p. 402; Wright, *Criminal Conspiracies*, p. 6.

[97] He thought these matters were best pursued by justices who were laymen rather than those who were clerics. He considered the targeted wrongdoing as an affront to his lordship ("to the disobedience of the lordship of the king"). Sayles, "Introduction," *Select Cases*, IV, pp. lv–lvi.

[98] The king had issued the initial commission on November 23, 1304, for the counties of Lincoln, Nottingham, Derby, and York; on January 9, 1305, for the counties of Norfolk, and Suffolk; on March 12, 1305, for the county of Lancaster. *Calendar of Fine Rolls, Edward I. A.D. 1272–1307*, pp. 504–05; *Calendar of Patent Rolls, Edward I, A.D. 1272–81*, 4 vols. (London, 1898), vol. 4, p. 343.

[99] Harry Rothwell, "The Trailbaston Inquiry, 1304–05" and "The Articles of Enquiry," in Douglas, ed., *English Historical Documents*, vol. III, pp. 519–22. Phelan has discussed this process in detail. Amy Phelan, "A Study of the First Trailbaston Proceedings in England, 1304–7," unpublished PhD thesis, Cornell University (1997).

[100] The Ordinance divided wrongdoers into two groups. Those who were guilty of "enormous trespasses," who were to be tried and punished if found guilty either at the suit of a complainant or that of the king, and those who were guilty of "light and personal trespasses," who were to be released on mainprise to respond to any complainant who wished to sue. *Statutes of the Realm*, vol. 1, p. 178. It limited jurisdiction to offenses committed between June 24, 1297, and April 18, 1305, and defined procedures for trying and punishing those who presented. Phelan, "First Trailbaston Proceedings," pp. 43–44.

created commissions for the whole realm, assigning justices in particular counties to make inquiries into a series of listed transgressions.[101] The inquiries were based on articles of inquiry, which resembled the articles of the eyre.[102] They were very broad and they varied slightly from county to county.[103] One study concluded that the trailbaston proceedings, when viewed in the political context of the reign of Edward I, were a vehicle to restore royal authority and eliminate corruption. They were an aspect of the plan of royal justice in the late thirteenth and fourteenth centuries, a period of significant change in the common law.[104]

Neither the initial commission nor the Ordinance included maintenance, champerty, or conspiracy as subjects of inquiry.[105] But their absence proved to be a problem. Because one of the justices of the York

[101] This action occurred on April 6, 1305. *Calendar of Patent Rolls, Edward I, A.D. 1301–07*, vol. 4, p. 354; *Calendar of Fine Rolls, Edward I A.D. 1272–1307*, pp. 504–05. Sayles, *Select Cases*, vol. IV, 74 Selden Soc., pp. liv–lvii; Harding, "Early Trailbaston Proceedings," pp. 144–51; Cam, "Studies in the Hundred Rolls," pp. 73–77. It was apparently reissued on October 14, 1305. *Calendar of Patent Rolls, Edward I*, vol. 4, p. 404. Pursuant to this, a writ of commission was enrolled. TNA: PRO JUST 1/1107, m. 1 (1305), AALT Img. No. 8499. Sayles said that this was the first enrolled writ of commission. Sayles, "The Dissolution of a Gild," p. 85, n. 6.

[102] The 1305 Articles apparently have not survived. Phelan,"First Trailbaston Proceedings," p. 44. But versions existed in various documents, which provided details on their nature. "The Articles of Enquiry," in David Douglas, ed., *English Historical Documents*, vol. III, pp. 519–22; Cam, "Studies in the Hundred Rolls," p. 75, n. 3, p. 77; Bodleian MS, Additional A 107, fols. 136r–137r. Graitude is expressed to Paul Brand for sharing this manuscript with me.

[103] .Cam, "Studies in the Hundred Rolls," p. 77. The commissions issued for 1307 and the articles designated for inquiry differed from those issued in 1305–06. The powers were broadened to include hearing the assizes and jail delivery and the articles focused more heavily on administrative matters. Phelan, "First Trailbaston Proceedings," pp. 59–64.

[104] Phelan considered, with the benefit of hindsight, that "Edward I's trailbaston experiment marked the limits of the royal centralization of justice." She concluded that trailbaston was a success in exercising and establishing royal authority and in collecting significant amounts of money for the crown, but not in convicting and punishing felons and other lower class wrongdoers. In pursuing trailbaston, the king also alienated the knightly and gentry classes, who were punished more harshly and consistently. As a result, she felt that Edward I had gone too far in creating the 1305–06 commissions. She argued that a more limited approach, as was used in the 1307 commissions, would have been preferable. "Phelan, First Trailbaston Proceedings," pp. 6–29, 158–82.

[105] At least one of the documents reflected a concern with "those who by reason of their power and lordship have taken and take others into protection for their gifts." *Calendar of Fine Rolls, Edward I A.D. 1272–1307*, pp. 504–05.

commission had complained that they needed authority to deal with conspirators if the sessions were to be effective, the king's writ added conspiracy to the list in the articles of inquiry.[106] The expanded articles also included maintenance and champerty in many of the king's writs to the trailbaston justices, and these types of wrongdoing were prominent in the trailbaston proceedings.[107] For example, the writ to the Shropshire justices included an article directing inquiry into "those who on behalf of others move pleas or cause pleas to be moved, and sue at their own costs by champerty, or to have part of the profit, and similarly of conspirators."[108] A copy of the trailbaston articles contained an identical article and also directed inquiry "of conspirators, namely of those who make evil confederacies falsely to indict or acquit anyone or move or maintain false pleas by champerty or for the purpose of having profit."[109]

---

[106] Peter de Mauley, one of the justices, told the king that great matters were being concealed from the justices "by the procurement and alliances of men of the country." Sayles, *Select Cases*, vol. II, 57 Selden Soc., pp. cxlix–cl, "Ancient Correspondence," XXI, no. 191 (tr.). As a result, the king sent a letter to Walter Langton, the treasurer, extending the term of the York justices and empowering them to inquire into conspiracy as well as champerty. Sayles, *Select Cases*, vol. II, 57 Selden Soc., p. cl, "Ancient Correspondance," LXI, no. 36. Sayles, "The Dissolution of a Gild," p. 85.

[107] Harding, "Early Trailbaston Proceedings," pp. 148–49; Phelan, "First Trailbaston Proceedings," pp. 50–52. In the year following their complaint about the omission of conspiracy from the inquiries, a very interesting presentment was made in York Eyre. The jurors had alleged that fifty-four men of the city of York, including an alderman, who were members of the gild brethren, had confederated by oath to control many aspects of local government and undermine royal authority. Among other things, they agreed that if any of them were charged with wrongdoing, they would be tried before the alderman and not elsewhere and that they would insure that any taxes were imposed on the poorer people and not on themselves. In addition, if anyone of their fraternity sued a nonmember or was sued by such a person, they would support him, whether the claim was just or unjust. The last accusation sounded like a more charge of conspiracy to maintain each other. Seven of the defendants denied any wrongdoing. The justices adjourned the case to Westminster for judgment in which the gild was dissolved, with the seven men sent to jail until they paid substantial fines and the other defendants were arrested. As a result, a total of £120 18s 8d in fines was paid. TNA: PRO JUST 1/1107, m. 19 (1306), AALT Img. No. 8536; Sayles, "The Dissolution of a Gild," pp. 85–92.

[108] TNA: PRO JUST 1/744, m. 7 (1304–05), AALT Img. No. 2358 (tr.). The articles for Kent also had provisions directed at conspiracy and champerty. Cam, "Studies in the Hundred Rolls," p. 75 n. 3.

[109] Bodleian MS, Additional A 107, fols. 136r–137r. The manuscript also contains a writ to the justices of a commission to inquire into conspirators and confederations in nine counties.

The final measure was the Ordinance of Conspirators, also promulgated in 1305, which defined "conspirators."[110] This Ordinance, which was issued in connection with the Ordinance of Trailbaston,[111] focused on persons who made alliances or agreements by oath to support each other in their false and malicious undertakings. It also targeted procuring false indictments and acquittals. Finally, it expressed concern about the giving of livery and abuse of lordship.[112] It singled out the stewards and bailiffs of great lords who used their power to maintain pleas unconnected with their own or their lords' affairs.[113]

Several conclusions can be drawn from this legislative and other royal activity. Maintenance became a term of art describing the wrongful conduct of intermeddling in another party's litigation. Champerty emerged as a special form of maintenance, which was considered a more serious type of abuse. The primary concern was with royal and judicial officials engaging in such conduct. The primary penalties were criminal, by fines and forfeitures, as all but one of the statutes limited enforcement to the crown. But after 1300, individuals could sue on behalf of the crown for champerty. None of the statutes expressly provided a civil remedy in damages for victims. Additional concern was manifested with conspiracy and the maintenance of actions. Measures targeting conspiracy authorized criminal proceedings based on the eyre and trailbaston articles and civil actions for damages based on the writ of conspiracy. By the end of

[110] Harding said that conspiracy was the first crime defined by statute in English law. Harding "Origins of Conspiracy," p. 97. He said that was because "it perverted the means of communication between the people and their king by bills of complaint and the whole system of justice they supported." Harding, *Medieval Law*, p. 249.

[111] Cam, *The Hundred Rolls*, p. 58.

[112] "Conspirators are those who make alliances among themselves by oath, agreement, or through some other bond, that each will help and support what the other undertakes in falsely and maliciously indicting or causing to be indicted, or falsely acquitting, people, or falsely initiating or supporting pleas, and also those who have children under age appeal people of felonies, through which they are imprisoned and greatly harmed, and those who retain men of their area by robes or payments, to support their evil undertakings and to suppress the truth, both those who take and those who give, and stewards and bailiffs of great lords who through lordship, office or power undertake to maintain or uphold pleas or disputes for parties, other than those which concern the estate of their lords or themselves. This ordinance and final definition of conspirators was made and definitively agreed by the king and his council in this parliament. And it is ordained that the justices appointed to hear and determine various trespasses and felonies in each county of England are to have a transcript of it etc." "The Ordinance concerning conspirators," Edward I Parliaments: *Vetus Codex* 1305, PROME.

[113] Harding, *Origins of Conspiracy*, p. 97.

thirteenth century, the legal notions of conspiracy, champerty, and maintenance were intermingled and related. Conspiracy involved two or more
persons who combined to abuse and misuse legal procedure.[114] But as
Winfield argued, both maintenance and champerty required an agreement
with another person and were, therefore, a form of conspiracy.[115]
Nevertheless, they developed as conceptually distinct offenses.[116]

The Initial Petitions to the King, His Council, and Parliament

Edward I had encouraged his subjects to submit written petitions to
parliamentary sessions.[117] It seems to have begun in about 1275[118] and
numerous petitions were submitted during the reigns of Edward I and
Edward II. Dodd said that the period 1290–1330 was the high-water mark

[114] Later commentators adopted the definitions in 1293 and 1305 ordinances, with slight
variations in wording.: "Conspirators be they that do confeder or bind themselves by
oath, covenant or other alliance, that every of them shall aid and bear the other falsely
and maliciously to indict or cause to indict, or falsely to move and maintain pleas ... and
also to appeal men of felony, whereby that are imprisoned or soregrieved; and such as
retain men in the country with liveries or fees to maintain that malicious enterprises; ...
And stewards and bailiffs of great lords, who by their seigniory, office and power,
undertake to bearor maintain quarrels, pleas, or debates that concern other parties than
such as touch the estate of their lords or themselves." William Staunford, Les Plees del
Coron (London, 1567; 1971 ed.), ch. 12, fol. 173v; William Rastell, Termes de la Ley,
pp. 83–84 (London, 1636); William Hawkins, Pleas of the Crown, Book I, ch. LXXII,
p. 189 (London, 1739).

[115] "A champertor of the late 13th century must always have been a conspirator, for he must
always have combined with another person, and it is not intelligible how any man can
maintain another's suit without some previous agreement." Winfield, The History of
Conspiracy, p. 146.

[116] As the next chapter shows, these legal measures produced a large volume of litigation in
which these notions were frequently combined.

[117] The nature and process of medieval petitions have recently drawn considerable scholarly
attention. Linda Clark, ed., Parchment and People: Parliament in the Middle Ages (Edin-
burgh, 2004); Gwilym Dodd, Justice and Grace: Private Petitioning and English Parliament
in the Late Middle Ages (Oxford, 2007); W.M. Ormrod, Gwilym Dodd, and Anthony
Musson, eds., Medieval Peititions: Grace and Grievance (York, 2009); Gwilym Dodd,
"Henry IV's Council, 1399–1406," in Gwilym Dodd and Donald Biggs, eds., Henry IV:
The Establishment of the Regime, 1399–1406 (York, 2003), pp. 95–115; Gwilym Dodd, "The
Hidden Presence: Parliament and the Private Petition in the Fourteenth Century," in
Anthony Musson, ed., Expectations of Law in the Middle Ages (Rochester, 2001).

[118] Gratitude is expressed to Prof. Paul Brand for this suggestion. Harding viewed petitioning parliament as an important process in the emergence of the state. It was part of the
"bill revolution," which he said "marked a second beginning for the English legal
system," and that Commons' petitions were the process by which legislation was created.
Harding, Medieval Law, pp. 179–90.

of private petitioning.[119] Most of the petitions were submitted by individuals, although some were from corporate entities, groups, or communities.[120] Presenting a grievance by petition was an important method of seeking royal relief.[121] Brand stated that petitioners sought some exceptional or discretionary exercise of royal power.[122] The basis for a remedy was the king's duty to do justice and to police the misdeeds of his officials. Brand identified six categories of petitions seeking remedies for wrongdoing: (1) wrongdoing committed by the king's own officials; (2) wrongdoing committed against royal officials; (3) wrongs committed against tenants of ancient demesne manors; (4) infringement of royal rights; (5) requests for justice without any special royal interest other than the king's duty to do justice, including remedies for wrongs for which no regular remedy was available or where justice was unlikely to be done; and (6) requests seeking redress for errors and miscarriage of justice.[123] As a result, some individuals decided to seek remedies for abuse of legal procedure by petitioning rather than by, or perhaps in addition to, litigation. These petitions are significant for what they reveal about the popular attitudes about the law's attainment of justice system and the use of the word "maintenance." To the extent that the petitions produced a response, the responses reveal the official attitudes toward the adequacy of existing legal remedies for abuse and corruption.[124]

---

[119] He stated that "more private petitions were presented in this forty-year period than were submitted in all the remaining 170 years of the late medieval parliament's history." Dodd, *Justice and Grace*, p. 49. He noted the changes, patterns of petitioning, and the responses to the petitions that occurred during this period. Ibid., pp. 49–88. He also suggested that some people may have used direct petitioning to parliament to avoid the expense and time of suing at common law. Ibid., p. 81.

[120] Brand, "Petitions and Parliament," Clark, *Parchment and People*, pp. 31–32.

[121] Ibid., p. 38. Brand said that a 1280 ordinance made clear that petitioning was not yet central to the contemporary conception of parliament. Ibid. The Ordinance noted that those who came to parliament were "often delayed and disturbed to great grievance of them and the court by the multitude of petitions brought before the king ..." *Calendar of Close Rolls, Edward I 1279–1288*, vol. 2, "Close Rolls, Edward I: June 1280," pp. 56–57, *British History Online.*

[122] Brand, "Petitions and Parliament," pp. 14–16. Dodd, *Justice and Grace*, pp. 19–26.

[123] Paul Brand, "Petitions to Parliament during the Reign of Edward I," in Ormrod, Dodd, and Musson, *Medieval Petitions*, pp. 113–17. The first category would include the complaints about maintenance by royal officials and the sixth category would include maintenance by private individuals. Gratitude is expressed to Prof. Paul Brand for this suggestion.

[124] These petitions have been collected in two primary sources: The National Archives compilation known as "Ancient Petitions" (SC 8) and "Parliamentary Rolls of Medieval England" (*PROME*). Both collections are available online, the first through The National

Petitions to the King and His Council

Many petitioners in this period complained that they were victims of the perversion of justice by powerful individuals and royal officials.[125] Most of the petitions (82%) identified the status or office of the target.[126] Virtually all of them were powerful persons.[127] As Table 3.1 indicates, royal officials, including the chancellor, treasurer, justices and other judicial officials, bailiffs, and officials of the king's household, and nobles accounted for almost 60% of the petitions.

Fewer petitions (58%) revealed the status or position of the petitioner.[128] The petitioners were often not of low status or others who might be vulnerable, but frequently were of considerable status. Of the individual petitioners (80%), Table 3.2 shows the clergy and religious persons, including abbots, abbesses, priors, deans, and chaplains, accounted for the largest proportion, followed by tradesmen and merchants, royal and local officials, widows, gentry, and nobles and lords. Most of these petitioners do not seem to be those who were

Archives website and the second through the British History Online. Dodd has explored the compilation, nature, and procedures of the SC 8s. Dodd, *Justice and Grace*, pp. 1–48; Dodd, "Parlimentary Petitions? The Origins and Provenance of the 'Ancient Petititons' (SC 8) in the National Archives," in Ormrod, Dodd, and Musson, *Medieval Petitions*, pp. 12–46. Brand has examined the process and content of the *PROME* petitions. Brand, "Petitions and Parliament," pp. 14–38; Brand, "Petitions to Parliament in the Reign of Edward I," in Clark, ed., *Parchment and People*, pp. 99–119. As the commentators explain, specific dating of these petitions is problematic. Access to these two sources has been facilitated by two projects. The *PROME* project is described in "General Introduction," *PROME, British History Online*. Ormrod and Dodd have described the SC 8 project. W. Mark Ormrod, "Introduction," in Ormrod, Dodd, and Musson, *Medieval Petitions*, pp. 1–5; Dodd, *Justice and Grace*, pp. 12–15.

[125] The SC 8s contained seventy-eight such petitions, many of which were not enrolled on the rolls of parliament. The most numerous references are to power (48), followed by maintenance (27) and lordship (11), as well as a few references to champerty (4), color of office (4), and conspiracy (2). A number of the complaints about abuse of power also complain about maintenance, lordship, or champerty (11) and the complaints about maintenance also include references to power, lordship, champerty, and conspiracy (11). All the complaints about lordship were coupled with another term.

[126] Sixty-four of the seventy-eight petitions revealed the nature and status of seventy-two petition targets. Some petitions were directed at more than one individual.

[127] "The king also claimed a general jurisdiction to assist plaintiffs against defendants who were too powerful locally for justice to be obtainable against them by regular means." J.L. Barton, "Equity in Medieval Common Law," in Ralph Newman, ed., *Equity in the World's Legal Systems* (Brussels, 1973), p. 146.

[128] Thirty-six of the seventy-six relevant petitions revealed the nature and status of forty-five petitioners. Some petitions had more than one petitioner.

Table 3.1 *Petitions to the king and his council:*
Nature of the targets

Royal officials	29%
Nobles	26%
Clerical and religious officials	15%
Sheriffs and their officials	11%
Knights	11%
Bailiffs and and mayors	7%

Table 3.2 *Petitions to the king and his council:*
Nature of the individual complainants

Clergy and religious persons	42%
Tradesmen and merchants	17%
Royal and local officials	14%
Widows	14%
Gentry	8%
Nobles and lords	5%

likely to be particularly vulnerable or susceptible to pressure, except perhaps tradesmen and merchants. Widows seemed to be a mixed group as some were landowners, one the widow of a knight, but others may have been more vulnerable. In addition to the individual petitions, there were also a number of collective or group petitions (20%) by the people or communities of counties, towns, hundreds, and the commons of the realm.

The common grievance of most of the petitioners was that they could not exercise their legal rights or seek remedies for the violation of their rights because of the power, maintenance, or lordship of these officials and other individuals. Petitions alleging maintenance usually complained of champerty or maintenance of litigation. For example, a widow complained that she lost her land to earl of Hereford as result of his champerty by virtue of a covenant he entered with his groom ("*vallet*") to enfeoff the earl with the widow's land in return for his procuring the justices and jurors in the groom's assize of novel disseisin.[129] A few

---

[129] The justices disallowed the widow's exceptions, and jurors found for the groom. TNA: PRO SC 8/5/247. In another petition, the commons of the realm complained that those

petitions made explicit references to the statutory prohibitions on maintenance and champerty. Many petitions used maintenance in its broader
sense. For example, a widow complained that a felonious killing of her
husband went unpunished "because maintenance is so great in the
country."[130]

Walter Langton, treasurer of England and bishop of Coventry and
Lichfield, was involved in substantial controversy as the reign of
Edward II began. He was the target of numerous complaints regarding
champerty and maintenance. By one account, there were twenty accusations of champerty against him, characterized as the "most serious
accusations brought against" him as well as a charge of maintenance in
the manorial courts. One petitioner complained that Langton, "in the
manner of champerty against the statute," obtained a life estate in
the part of the manor "because by his lordship he had the sheriff
and ministers at will and the country in his power."[131] Several other
complaints against Langton also referred to the statute.[132] Although
financial penalties and imprisonment were imposed on Langton, he was
pardoned for many of his offenses and ultimately regained his office as
treasurer.[133]

Not surprisingly the largest number of petitions, almost 50%, involved
complaints regarding land and other property interests. In many cases,
the maintenance, which was the subject of the complaint, prevented the
aggrieved party from bringing a lawsuit. One man complained that his
mother could not recover the land of which she had been disseised and
that now he is kept out because of maintenance by the king's baker and

convicted of trespass for their fraud and maintenance removed their lands and
chattels, so that successful plaintiffs were unable to execute their judgments and obtain
damages. TNA: PRO SC 8/323/E558. Another petitioner alleged that the king's bailiffs
disturbed his use of his land and disinherited him by their great power. TNA: PRO SC
8/329/E903.

[130] TNA: PRO SC 8/49/2423 (tr.).

[131] He also accused Langton of champerty regarding another manor. TNA: PRO SC 8/322/
E528 (tr.). Beardwood, "The Trial of Walter Langton, Bishop of Lichfield," 3, 14–20,
23–24, 31–32, 36–38; "Walter Langton," *Dictionary of National Biography*, online.

[132] A late thirteenth-century petition also directed at Langton referred to the statutory
prohibition on maintenance by the king's ministers. Another petitioner, who had sued
a writ of novel disseisin, also accused Walter of champerty in violation of the statute.
TNA: PRO SC 8/324/E621. The complaints by John de Ferrers against Walter were
among the most notorious.

[133] Beardwood, "The Trial of Walter Langton, Bishop of Lichfield," 3, 14–20, 23–24, 31–32,
36–38; "Walter Langton," *Dictionary of National Biography*, online.

because of the great gifts given to the justices and bailiffs.[134] Other complaints were related to goods, assaults, money, and a variety of other matters.[135] The dean of the church of St. John of Chester complained that a castle constable took his corn without paying for it and by the power of his office prevented the petitioner from profitably selling it.[136] One man complained that he was assaulted, but could never have a remedy because of a clerk's "great power and high status (*magna potentia et excellencia*).[137] Two men complained that because of their opposition to a lord who held leets without a franchise to do so, he maliciously pursued them and maintained his parson, who excommunicated them.[138] A widow sued for debt by an executor on a "suspicious" deed sought a remedy "because she was old and powerless."[139]

The great majority of petitions contained a response (79%).[140] Most of them were positive in the sense that they said that the matter warranted further inquiry or action, but not necessarily that they were meritorious.[141] In more than half of the responses, the king and council seemed to believe that the law provided an adequate remedy. Those responses directed the petitioner to sue at common law, obtain a writ from the Chancery, or seek relief in Chancery or at the Exchequer. But these endorsements did not necessarily mean that the king and his council believed that the petitioner would or should prevail. As the king had encouraged petitioning and had the obligation to exercise grace for his subjects, such responses may have been the most politically and practically convenient.

---

[134] He alleged further that, as a result, his mother "and her children were and are beggars." TNA: PRO SC 8/339/15960 (tr.).

[135] E.g., abduction, imprisonment, marriage, franchises, excommunication, and trespasses and felonies in general.

[136] TNA: PRO SC 8/55/2739.   [137] TNA: PRO SC 8/123/6144 (tr.).

[138] TNA: PRO SC 8/41/2019.   [139] TNA: PRO SC 8/33/1623 (tr.).

[140] All petitioners likely received some response, even if it is no longer to be found endorsed on the petition, as all petitions that were presented had to be dealt with for administrative and political reasons. Gratitude is expressed to Prof. Paul Brand for this suggestion.

[141] But only three responses rejected a petition, most likely for technical reasons. One said it was unjust for a woman, who held land jointly with her husband, to petition while her husband was still alive. TNA: PRO SC 8/6/299. In another, the endorsement said, "For this petition, nothing," in response to a complaint that the earl of Arundel used his lordship corruptly to gain possession of a manor. TNA: PRO SC 8/14/665. A third said the "action was void," perhaps because it complained of a wrong to a person who was now dead. TNA: PRO SC 8/6/269A.

Table 3.3 *Enrolled petitions: Nature of the targets*

Nobles and lords	42%
Knights	16%
Sheriffs	16%
Clergy	11%
Justices	5%
Bailiffs	5%
Jurors	5%

Enrolled Petitions

The number of petitions regarding legal corruption found in the rolls of parliament was far fewer than the petitions discussed above.[142] However, Brand believes that most of the enrolled petitions were likely to have been presented to the king and his council.[143] Most of these enrolled petitions (73%) indicated the status or position of the target.[144] Again, like those petitions addressed to the king and his council, almost all of the complaints were against powerful officials and individuals. As indicated by Table 3.3, nobles and lords accounted for the largest proportion, followed by knights, sheriffs, clergy, justices, bailiffs, and jurors.[145] But the nature of the parliamentary petitions differed from those addressed to the king and his council. First, the great majority of these petitions specifically complained of maintenance (74%). Some of them also included champerty, and others also alleged conspiracy, collusion, or procurement. Almost all these petitions used the word "maintenance" in the narrower legal sense. Several complained of conspiracy, independent of maintenance. Only one petition complained about abuse of power.

---

[142] There were only fifteen relevant petitions located by searching *PROME*. There were also four proceedings enrolled. Since they resemble legal actions in the plea rolls, they are discussed with the litigation.

[143] He further noted that "there are more surviving individual petitions than surviving petitions enrolled in the rolls of parliament but others were undoubtedly so enrolled but the rolls do not survive . . . They are not therefore two different categories of petition, but two different archival sources of a similar document type." Gratitude is expressed to Prof. Paul Brand for this suggestion.

[144] Eleven of the fifteen relevant petitions revealed the nature and status of nineteen petition targets. Some petitions were directed at more than one individual.

[145] Of the nineteen, the absolute numbers were nobles and lords (8), knights (3), sheriffs (3), clergy (3), justices (1), bailiffs (1), and jurors (1). The lower numbers make it more difficult to draw meaningful conclusions.

Like those to the king and his council, many of these petitions involved land (40%). For example, Cecily de Beauchamp alleged champerty in violation of *Articuli super Cartas*. She accused Sir William Inge JCP and the sheriff of Surrey of colluding with the man whom she had sued in a writ of *cui in vita*, and of altering her writ and fabricating and substituting a false writ "in alienation and disinheritance of Cecily" and "in deception" of the king's court.[146] In another action, Reginald of Berwick and Peter Sarnel sought the return of land as rightful heirs, which they claimed their ancestor had granted to the king when he was not of a sound mind. But Stephen of Penchester, who acquired the land on behalf of king, said that the ancestor was of sound mind and that the petitioners had lied. Since it was also attested that Stephen of Pope's Hall had maintained and abetted the complaint, further inquiry was required.[147]

One petition is particularly interesting, as the adversaries accused each other of maintenance. Also a knight, who was not a litigant but whose power was a critical influence in the matter, switched sides. In addition, there are important differences between the language of the enrolled petition and that of the original petition.[148] Richard, the son of William Gykel, alleged he had been seised as heir until he was expelled by Robert, his bastard brother, "with the assistance of Sir John de Grey" ["came and made an agreement with Sir John de Grey and gave him ten marks to eject the aforesaid Richard from his inheritance and maintain the aforesaid Robert in his land so that the aforesaid Richard was ousted from the said tenements by the power and force of the aforesaid Sir John de

---

[146] "On behalf of Cecily Beauchamp," Edward II Parliaments: January 1315, No. 78 (64), *PROME* (tr.). The petition resulted in litigation, which is discussed in the next chapter.

[147] "Petition of Reginald of Berwick and Peter Sarnel," Edward I Parliaments: Roll 1, no. 15, *PROME*. On further inquiry, it was found that the grantor was of sound mind and that Stephen had composed and written the petition for a fee of only four pence. But it was also found that the "real mover" of the false allegation was Solomon of Burne, who would have received Reginald's share for his effort. Ibid., "Appendix: Additional Information and Related Material for Roll 1," No. 15 (ii). Solomon's conduct was champerty. There was also a related petition. "Petition of Reginald of Berwick and Peter of Cerley claiming the lands of William of Clamberk of Langdon, in the king's possession," Edward I Parliaments: Roll 2, no. 201, *PROME*.

[148] "Petition Richard, son of William Gykel," Edward I Parliaments: Roll 12, no. 187, *PROME*. The language of the original petition, TNA: PRO SC 8/266/13274, is included in the Parliamentary Roll in the appendix, both in Law French and English. Ibid., Appendix to Roll 12: Original Petitions and related materials, No. 187. Where significant, the language of the original petition has been inserted in brackets. Neither the enrolled nor the original petition explained how the petitioner "allied himself by marriage" to Richard Clerk.

Grey"]. Richard then "allied himself" to Richard Clerk "by marriage," who "persuaded the said John de Grey to expel the said Robert and have the same Richard, the son of William, reseised" ["Richard saw that he needed to have aid to maintain himself and arranged with Richard Clerk ... and allied himself with him through marriage and so ... Richard Clerk approached Sir John de Grey and gave him fifteen marks to oust this Robert, the elder brother and bastard, whom he had maintained at the start, and reinstate Richard the younger and legitimate brother who was the rightful heir to the tenements, whom he had previously ejected by power and force"]. "Robert, finding that ... John de Grey had abandoned him, went to lord Reginald de Grey ["the father of ... Sir John Grey"] and sold all the right which he had in the aforesaid tenements to him and his heirs, through collusion between ... lord Reginald and John de Grey and the aforesaid bastard; whereupon, the said lord Reginald expelled the same Richard the son of William ["who was legitimate and the rightful heir to the said tenements by power and force"]," who brought an assize of novel disseisin against Reginald, and "on account of the threats of, and fear of ... Reginald that assize went against the same Richard the son of William." Although Richard, the petitioner, and Richard Clerk seem to have been guilty of maintenance and champerty, the petitioner apparently prevailed, as he was to have remedy in Chancery by a writ of champerty or otherwise from Chancery, "if it seemed expedient to him." Perhaps his sins were considered the lesser as he was "fighting fire with fire" and because of the power and importance of Sir Reginald, Baron Grey of Wilton, and John, his son, a knight and an ambidextrous maintainer.

Another group of petitions concerned wrongful conduct and the dysfunctional operation of the justice system.[149] All of them contained allegations of conspiracy. A few alleged only the conduct, but others also included allegations of maintenance, power, or procurement. In a number of these petitions both the petitioners and target were groups. For example, "the community of England" complained in parliament about conspirators who were "linked by oath to maintain and procure false parties" and who "boast that a man can plead in the king's court, but in the end it will go on their word of mouth at their will." They also complained that they threaten the king's attorneys and beat those who

---

[149] Some of these may have been connected to disorder in the reign of Edward II. One of these enrollments is the articles charging the Despensers. Edward II Parliaments: July 1321, no. 2, *PROME*.

sue for their clients against those whom they support.[150] In addition, "the entire community of the realm" complained of the perpetration of felonies and trespasses and of illegal leagues and confederacies entered into by trespassers and disturbers of the peace.[151] Further they complained that great lords fabricated trespasses to destroy a man or maintained others to do so. They also alleged that those lords purchased *oyer et terminer* commissions and because of their great power, their adversaries do not dare to appear in court.[152] Thus, another vehicle for corrupting the legal system involved manipulating the crown's investigatory procedures by procuring commissions.[153] It became "a new and powerful legal device" used by country society against their adversaries.[154]

Again the responses to the petitions often indicated that further inquiry was merited. One-third of responses suggested that the law provided adequate remedies, telling the petitioners to sue at common law or seek a remedy in Chancery. Almost half of the responses (47%) stated that further action by the council, an *oyer et terminer* commission, or a judicial official was appropriate. In the remaining responses the council took direct action to stop the wronging. In one petition, the trailbaston jurors complained that those whom they had indicted paid to be put on juries so they could take revenge against the jurors. To remedy the problem, the

---

[150] "A petition against conspirators," Edward II Parliaments: January 1315, no. 3, *PROME* (tr.).

[151] "The complaint of the entire community of the realm concerning trespasses and felonies perpetrated in the realm," Edward II Parliaments: October 20: SC 9/23, no. 8, *PROME*. On March 10, a commission of *oyer et terminer* was issued regarding violation of this proclamation in the counties of Norfolk and Suffolk. *Calendar of Patent Rolls, Edward II 1315–17*, 4 vols.(London, 1898), vol. 2, p. 262.

[152] "On behalf of the community of England, that writs of *oyer et terminer* are not to be granted," Edward II Parliaments: January 1315, no. 10, *PROME*. Phelan's study of the *Berkeley v. Bristol* dispute over Redclif showed that litigants also misused trailbaston to prosecute their opponents. Phelan, "First Trailbaston Procedings," pp. 118–57, 172–78.

[153] Harding, *Medieval Law*, pp. 183–84; Kaeuper, "Special Commissions of Oyer and Terminer," pp. 734–84. The frequency of these special commissions, which began to appear in the 1270s, quickly caused concern and prompted a parliamentary effort to control their use. Statute of Westminster II, c. 29, *Statutes of the Realm*, vol. 1, p. 85. Although a substantial decrease in their use soon occurred, their frequency quickly began to increase again, reaching peaks about 1320 and 1330. Kaeuper, "Special Commissions of Oyer and Terminer," pp. 740–42.

[154] The gentry were responsible for obtaining the greatest number of these commissions. But powerful individuals did so as well. Ibid., pp. 749–51. "Lords invent trespasses on the part of their enemies and secure commissions of oyer and terminer for justices who are favorable to them." J.E.A. Jolliffe, *The Constitutional History of Medieval England* (London, 1961), p. 410.

council promulgated an ordinance prohibiting conspirators from serving on juries if they had been convicted or admitted of making false alliances to maintain falsehoods, had procured themselves to be placed on juries for profit, or had taken bribes from both parties.[155] In response to another petition complaining about the abuse of *oyer et terminer* commissions, the granting of them was limited to "great trespasses."[156] Only the petition by Cecily de Beauchamp against William Maire, sheriff of Surrey, and Sir William Inge, a Common Bench justice, discussed above, produced a different kind of response. First, the council said that no remedy could be had against Inge, who was accused of conspiring with the sheriff and Cecily's adversary, until it was determined whether the sheriff had fabricated a fraudulent writ as alleged, perhaps treating Inge as an accessory to the sheriff's offense. Second, if the allegations against the sheriff were true, the council said Cecily could only sue in the king's name and that her attorney should acquire a writ in the king's name.[157]

These petitions to the king and his council and Parliament were further evidence of the concern about maintenance, champerty, and conspiracy. Why complainants chose to petition rather than sue is not completely clear. Perhaps, as their petitions often alleged, they were or would be unable to get justice through the litigation process and, therefore, thought that petitioning would be more effective in producing a remedy. But complainants may have had less evident motivations. They may have favored petitioning because they thought it would be less costly or quicker. They would not have to hire pleaders or attorneys or pay for writs and for other litigation costs or undergo the commonly lengthy delays attendant to litigation. Even if the matter ended up in litigation, they may have thought that the petition's endorsement would strengthen

---

[155] "Petition of the members of juries at trailbaston sessions, complaining about those whom they have indicted subsequently serving on juries and taking their revenge against them," Edward I Parliaments: *Vetus Codex*, 1307, no. 84, *PROME*. As a result of this legislation, a mandate was issued soon afterward to the justices of trailbaston in Devon and the sheriff of Devon for its application; see *Calendar of Close Rolls*, Edward I, 1302–1307 (London, 1908), vol. 5, p. 531, Close Rolls: Edward I: 1307, *British History Online*. In the Staffordshire Trailbaston, a man procured himself to be put on a jury and falsely indicted a man, who was subsequently acquitted. TNA: PRO JUST 1/809, m. 12, AALT Img. No. 3120. Two others also did so to facilitate taking bribes and took them from both parties. Ibid., m. 4d, AALT Img. No. 3150.

[156] "On behalf of the community of England, that writs of oyer et terminer are not to be granted etc.," Edward II: January 1315, no. 10, *PROME*.

[157] "On behalf of Cecily Beauchamp," Edward II Parliaments: January 1315, No. 78 (64), *PROME*.

their case. That the endorsement frequently suggested that there was an adequate remedy at law or from Chancery is interesting, given the rather limited availability of private actions prior to the 1293 Ordinance of Conspirators. But the responders may have thought that the trespass or land actions that they identified would suffice. Also, some petitions were a product of political turmoil, and petitioners may have thought that political considerations would produce a favorable result.[158]

These petitions were an important component of the responses to the abuse of legal procedure and the corruption of justice. Much of the conduct that was the subject of the complaints was similar to that in the litigation, which is discussed in the next chapter. In addition, the petitions provide information about the attitudes toward the operation of the legal system. More generally, petitioning played a significant legal and political role in the relationship between the king and his subjects.

---

[158] A number of the petitions seem to be a product of the disorder during the reign of Edward II and the revolt of barons during that period. There are several petitions against Thomas, earl of Lancaster, and the Despensers.

4

The Early Litigation, 1272–1327

As a result of the enactments discussed in the previous chapter, victims of abusive litigation began to seek legal redress in the courts. In addition, wrongdoers were prosecuted criminally. The legal actions targeted various forms of abuse of legal procedure and its corruption of justice. Sayles said that "the plea rolls are soon to be covered with illustrations of the multifarious and subtle means adopted to make the law itself become an instrument of injustice."[1]

During this period, there was a substantial volume of litigation involving conspiracy, maintenance, champerty, and ambidexterity.[2] Criminal cases (73%) greatly outnumbered civil actions (27%), and conspiracy cases were by far the most common type of action (68%). Although the various statutes and ordinances began with the Statute of Westminster I 1275, the litigation regarding the abuse of legal procedure, except for the 1289 "state trials" of judges discussed in Chapter 3, did not begin for two decades. The period 1293–1307 was clearly the most litigious, with about 75% of this type of litigation occurring in these years. This litigation included the cases that arose as a result of the enactment of the Ordinance of Conspirators of 1293 and the *Articuli super Cartas* of 1300, chapter 11, and the numerous presentments made in the eyres[3] and in

---

[1] G.O. Sayles, "Introduction, XI, "Conspiracy and Allied Offenses," *Select Cases in the Court of the King's Bench*, 7 vols. (London, 1939), vol. III, 58 Selden Soc., p. liv.

[2] In the period 1272–1327, there were 317 separate criminal presentments and civil actions that involved conspiracy, maintenance, champerty, and ambidexterity, and related subjects. Some of the conspiracy presentments involved both ambidexterity and maintenance, which were counted in each category. If multiple persons were the subject of a single presentment, that was treated as only one case.

[3] The basis for the presentments in the eyres is unclear. Some may have been based on the Articles' chapter *de mutuis sacramentis*, but, as indicated in Chapter 3, there is no evidence that that chapter was used regularly in the eyres. In most of the eyres, there is specific language preceding the presentments that explained why the justices were inquiring about conspiracy and maintenance. The authority for doing so may have been based on the commissions creating the eyres. In addition, there may have been a separate general

Table 4.1 *Different types of criminal cases and civil actions, 1272-1327*

	Criminal	Civil	Total
Conspiracy	146	68	214 (68%)
Maintenance	32	0	32 (10%)
Ambidexterity	20	0	20 (6%)
Champerty	5	19	24 (8%)
Misconduct involving jurors and juries	14	0	14 (4%)
Procure false indictment or appeal	0	0	0
Aid or abet false indictment or appeal	0	0	0
Procure false civil plea	0	0	0
Other abuse of legal procedure	13	0	13 (4%)
Totals	230 (73%)	87 (27%)	317

the trailbaston sessions as a result of the Trailbaston Ordinance of 1305. This litigation revealed the widespread perceived corruption and the development of the different types of legal devices to deal with it. Table 4.1 identifies the various types of criminal and civil actions that were initiated.

Criminal Litigation

Most of these criminal prosecutions in the eyres and trailbaston sessions involved charges of conspiracy and maintenance (78%).[4] Many individual presentments involved large numbers of accused as well as several different offenses. Special jurors, known as triers (*triatores*) and who represented the whole county, made most of the presentments. In those presentments, the record stated that jurors of various hundreds or similar places or knights made the presentment.[5] The eyre presentments began slowly. On January 13, 1279, the king sent a writ to the eyre justices in

instruction issued to the eyre justices in the early 1280s. Gratitude is expressed to Prof. Paul Brand for these suggestions.

[4] The records of thirteen eyres and five trailbaston sessions were reviewed. Seven of the eyres and all the trailbaston sessions occurred between 1292 and 1307. Four of the eyres was earlier and two were during the reign of Edward II. Selected presentments in additional eyres were also examined.

[5] Triers were used in place of the usual twelve men of the various hundreds, cities, vills, or other locations. Their first use occurred in the 1281–82 Devon Eyre and they became a regular feature of the general eyre. They were also used later in the trailbaston and peace sessions. Presumably they were used to minimize the impact of local influence that might

diverse counties directing them to inquire into conspiracy and maintenance. Although it produced no presentments in the 1279 Kent Eyre,[6] several presentments were returned in the 1280 Somerset and 1281–82 Devon Eyres[7] as well as the 1288 Dorset and Sussex Eyres.[8] There was a deluge of activity, however, in 1292 and 1293. Sayles argued that this activity was related to the decline of the rule of law during Edward I's reign.[9] He said that when Hugh de Cressingham, a 1293 Yorkshire Eyre justice, commented on the prevalence of maintenance, champerty, and conspiracy, he was "reporting to his master the root cause of the social malaise."[10]

Eyre Proceedings

In authorizing the eyres, the king's writ indicated a specific concern with conspiracy and maintenance. For example, he ordered the itinerant justices in the 1292 Lancashire Eyre to come because he had

cause corruption and intimidation and also because it was thought they were less susceptible to bribes and threats. However, the form of their presentments did not differ from those made by ordinary local presenting juries. Anthony Musson, *Public Order and Law Enforcement: The Local Administration of Criminal Justice, 1294–1350* (Woodbridge, 1996), pp. 181–84, 186, 220; David Crook, *Records of the General Eyre* (London, 1982), p. 32; Amy Phelan, "A Study of the First Trailbaston Proceedings in England, 1304–7," unpublished PhD thesis, Cornell University (1997), pp. 17–18; David Crook, "Triers and the Origin of the Grand Jury," *Journal of Legal History* 12 (1991), pp. 103–16.

[6] TNA: PRO JUST 1/367 (1279), AALT Img. No. 7 (Kent).

[7] In Somerset Eyre, the writ resulted in five men being presented as conspirators, and in Devon, the writ, which was contained in a portion of the roll entitled "Of Conspirators," resulted in eleven men and one woman being presented as conspirators. In the former eyre, all were found not guilty and in the latter the result was similar except two defendants did not appear. TNA: PRO JUST 1/759, m. 4d (1280), AALT Img. No. 3400; TNA: PRO JUST 1/181, m. 27d (1281–82), AALT Img. No. 1642.

[8] In Dorset, the jury found an attorney pleading pleas in the county and elsewhere guilty of being a maintainer of false pleas and of taking money from a plaintiff in a land action and from several others. TNA: PRO JUST 1/213 m. 31d (1288) AALT Img. No. 5446. In Sussex, the jury found nine men were bound together by mutual oaths to maintain actions and pleas and procuring the indictment of men and then taking ransom to deliver them. TNA: PRO JUST 1/924, m. 72 (1288), AALT Img. No. 4014.

[9] Sayles, *Select Cases*, IV, 74 Selden Soc., pp. liii–lv.

[10] Ibid., p. liv. Cressingham said that "Whereas a serious complaint came to the justices immediately on their arrival here to the effect that there were so many and so influential maintainers of false pleas and upholders of champerty and conspirators joined together to maintain any kinds of business whatsoever in this county that justice and truth are suffocated, the justices here have made a most careful investigation into the matter." TNA: PRO JUST 1/1095, m 1 (1293), AALT Img. No. 6558 (tr.).

learned from both the faithful lieges and the clamor of the poor community that the men of the country frequently summoned on assizes and
juries are conspirators and confederators and joined together in several
counties. So that when one of them undertakes or maintains any plea for
profit, bribe, or other means, that one maintains all his fellows . . . and the
poor and others who are unwilling to give such bribes or money or
champerty in their plea or action are often defrauded of the right, because
of which the justices have come here to guard against this danger.[11]

As result, the jurors presented forty men, including an attorney and
several bailiffs, for maintaining false pleas, champerty, bribing sheriffs
and bailiffs to have their friendship to unjustly accuse their neighbors,
influencing the selection of jurors, and similar offenses. For example,
they charged that Alan le Noreys, Robert le Noreys, and Gilbert de
Halsale were conspirators and confederated together to maintain each
other's pleas and often by champerty to divide the profit among
themselves.[12] Table 4.2 shows the different types of criminal cases that
were prosecuted.

The experience in Lancashire was not unique. The record of
1293 Yorkshire Eyre contained a section entitled "Roll of Conspirators
and Maintainers of False Pleas at York." The jurors charged more than
100 separate individuals in at least sixty presentments, some of whom
were the subject of multiple presentments.[13] The individuals charged
included many royal officials such as sheriffs, undersheriffs, bailiffs,
underbailiffs, coroners, and the clerks of these officials, as well as local
lawyers. The offenses included conspiracy, maintenance of false pleas,
ambidexterity, champerty, tampering with the composition of juries to
favor one party to an action, procuring indictments and acquittals of
felons, procuring false writs and altering writs, and demanding money

---

[11] TNA: PRO JUST 1/409, m. 2 (1292), AALT Img. No. 6 (tr.).

[12] The jury found them guilty and said that they were magnates in the country, to whom all
others attached themselves and shared their friendship, favor, and profit. Gilbert successfully challenged some of the jurors and a new panel was arraigned. All three men were
taken into custody. There was no indication that the others indicted had appeared yet to
respond. TNA: PRO JUST 1/409, mm. 2–2d (1292), AALT Img. Nos. 6, 107.

[13] Because the jurors presented some persons multiple times, at least 230 names appear in
these presentments. The roll consists of two membranes, both of which are damaged,
which makes it impossible to calculate accurately the number of individuals presented
and the total presentments and to know whether there were any jury verdicts. At the end
of m. 1d, thirty-one individuals appeared and pleaded not guilty and put themselves on a
jury. Another sixty-three individuals failed to appear and were amerced for their defaults.
TNA: PRO JUST 1/1095, m. 1d (1293), AALT Img. No. 6565.

Table 4.2 *Types of criminal cases, 1272–1327*

Conspiracy cases	146 (63.5%)
Maintenance and champerty	65 (28.3%)
Ambidexterity	34 (14.8%)
Procure false appeal or indictment	10 (4.3%)
Misconduct involving jurors and juries	8 (3.5%)
Procure false civil plea	1 (.4%)
Other conspiracy actions	14 (6.1%
Eyre prohibition	4 (1.7%)
No details	10 (4.3%)
Total	146
Other types of cases	84 (36.5%)
Maintenance	32 (13.9%)
Ambidexterity	20 (8.7%)
Misconduct involving jurors and juries	14 (6.1%)
Champerty	5 (2.2%)
Procure false appeal or indictment	0
Procure false civil plea	0
Other abuse of legal procedure	13 (5.7%)
Total	84
Total criminal cases	230

for the exercise of offices. In many presentments, it was alleged that an official engaged in this conduct for profit and reward. For example, Richard de Lacy, former bailiff of the East Riding, Yorkshire, was accused of being a maintainer of false pleas, joining in a conspiracy in his bailiwick, and commonly changing jury panels at the will of a party procuring him by gift and profit.[14] Jurors were similarly charged. Robert of Holme was said to be a veteran and common assize juror, taking profit and reward from all parties, and saying his verdict for the side who gave him more.[15] Lawyers were among those charged.[16] The jurors said that Little Michael of Layton was a pleader ("*narrator*") and took from each

---

[14] TNA: PRO JUST 1/1095, m. 1 (1293), AALT Img. No. 6558 (tr.).

[15] Seven others similarly were charged. TNA: PRO JUST 1/1095, m. 1 (1293), AALT Img. No. 6559 (tr.).

[16] There is an extended discussion of maintenance and other wrongdoing in litigation by a lawyer, Hugh Tyrel, in the discussion of the 1306 Norfolk Trailbaston session at pp. 78-80, *infra*.

party for doing his office.[17] In some cases, numerous defendants were accused of being sworn together to engage in maintenance and champerty.[18] This Yorkshire Eyre produced "an appalling list of evildoers,"[19] whose abuses of legal procedure had corrupted the administration of justice at the local level.[20] Similarly, in the 1293 Eyre of Kent, the jurors presented that fifty named individuals "were conspirators and maintainers of parties ... and by mutual oaths confederated together ..." Two were found guilty and the others said that they could not deny the charges.[21]

Multiple guilty verdicts were not uncommon. In the 1299 Cambridgeshire-Ely Eyre, four men were charged with confederating together to maintain false pleas and all were found guilty.[22] Another group of twenty-four other men were charged with the same offense and twenty-two said that they could not deny the charges.[23] In the 1292 Herefordshire Eyre, a group of seventeen men was charged with supporting false parties, taking money from both sides, and procuring the delivery of felons at gaol delivery.[24] Two lawyers were among those presented.

---

[17] TNA: PRO JUST 1/1095, m. 2d (1293), AALT Img. No. 6567.

[18] Fourteen men were charged as "having sworn together to maintain all the business that any of them undertook, indifferent to whether it was just or unjust, for reward and profit and some for champerty." TNA: PRO JUST 1/1095, m. 1 (1293), AALT Img. No. 6558 (tr.).

[19] Sayles, *Select Cases*, IV, 74 Selden Soc., p. liv.

[20] A few were acquitted. Two presentments said that eight named men were acquitted. In another, the jurors said that three men were unknown to them. In some cases the jurors reported mitigating factors. They said that Nicholas de Meynell was a cruel neighbor, but was quit of other charges. Alexander of Leeds and Robert, his clerk, took money to do his office and to make favorable inquisitions, but the jurors said that they were more faithful than all the other coroners in the country. Thomas of Poynton, a coroner there, took sometimes, but infrequently. Hugh of Bilton was found guilty of champerty, but was acquitted on other charges. Nicholas of Leicester was neither a conspirator nor maintainer of false pleas, but assisted his clients and friends.

[21] TNA: PRO JUST 1/376, m. 69d (1293), AALT Img. No. 3479 (tr.).

[22] TNA: PRO JUST 1/96, m. 49d (1299), AALT Img. No. 2898. In the 1293–94 Middlesex Eyre, eighteen men were presented as conspirators and common maintainers of false parties. Ten said that they were unable to deny the charges; seven were found guilty; and one did not appear. TNA: PRO JUST 1/544, m. 66d (1293–94), AALT Img. No. 4674.

[23] Two were found not guilty. TNA: PRO JUST 1/96, m. 54d (1299), AALT Img. No. 2908. All but two of nine Ely men, who were similarly charged, were found not guilty. TNA: PRO JUST 1/96, m. 78 (1299), AALT Img. No. 2795.

[24] Ten were found guilty, two of conspiracy and eight of maintaining parties and taking money from both sides. Four were found not guilty and there was no finding on three others. In another case, the jurors presented thirty-five individuals for conspiracy. TNA: PRO JUST 1/303, m. 67 (1292), AALT Img. No. 8780.

William de la Haye took 40s from John Ragon to maintain his side and afterward he counseled the adverse party and showed how John's writ could be quashed, so that John lost his plea.[25] John Lightfoot was found guilty of maintaining his own clients both justly and unjustly.[26] But not all those charged were found guilty.[27]

There were two eyres during the reign of Edward II. In the first one, the 1313–14 Kent Eyre, there were more than twenty presentments of over forty men, several of whom appear to be local lawyers. The great bulk of the presentments were for conspiracy, maintenance of false pleas, champerty, and ambidexterity.[28] Some presentments charged defendants with several of these types of conduct.[29] One group of seven presentments in this eyre is particularly interesting as it involved an

---

[25] The jury said William acted similarly on other occasions. Ibid. Brand thought that William was probably a local professional lawyer. Brand, *Origins of the English Legal Profession* (Oxford, 1992), p. 140.

[26] Brand has suggested that he may have been charged because local jurors felt that it was not acceptable for a lawyer to give professional assistance to clients when justice did not support their side. Ibid., p. 141. But that does not explain why maintaining clients justly was illegal. Perhaps this language was just formulaic as it appears in numerous presentments. The use of the word "maintenance" in this context may mean only that the lawyer was engaged in representational activity.

[27] In one presentment in this eyre, only five of the eighteen men charged were found guilty. Similarly, in the 1293 Staffordshire Eyre, twenty men were presented as maintainers of false parties and as ambidexters. Ten were found not guilty and ten guilty. TNA: PRO JUST 1/806, m. 34, AALT Img. No. 2931.

[28] Several men, previously convicted of conspiracy, were indicted for living in the city of Canterbury or coming to the Great Hall there in violation of the eyre justices' prohibition on doing so. E.g., TNA: PRO JUST 1/383, m. 108d, AALT Img. No. 1897; Y.B. Trin. 6 Edw. II, Kent Eyre, pl. Corone 6 (1313), Seipp No. 1313.162ss. Several also involved extortion. E.g., TNA: PRO JUST 1/383, m. 108, AALT Img. No. 1684 (John at Feld and Bertam of Goatley); TNA: PRO JUST 1/383, m. 110, AALT Img. No. 1688 (Thomas Geg, undersheriff for use of his lord, the sheriff).

[29] Walter Turet was found to be a maintainer of false pleas and to have taken 20s and three quarters of wheat to maintain Walter at Hall in an assize and then took a robe from Robert le Sauser, Walter's adversary. TNA: PRO JUST 1/383, m. 108, AALT Img. No. 1684. Two other men were charged with conspiring to maintain each other as well as for ambidexterity. TNA: PRO JUST 1/383, m. 108d, AALT Img. No. 1897. In a more devious scheme, John le Palmere took 40d to maintain Thomas Reynauld in a plea in a hundred court against Adam Knotte, the underbailiff of the hundred, and then switched sides to represent Adam, so that he falsely recovered 1/2 mark against Thomas, of which John had half. John then levied 20d from Thomas because he had not paid Adam the half mark within four days. He was also indicted for another instance of ambidexterity, in which he took 1/2 mark to maintain one party in a trespass action and afterwards opposed that party, taking one pipe of cider, worth 1/2 mark from his adversary. TNA: PRO JUST 1/383, m. 108, AALT Img. No. 1685.

extensive scheme by a group of clergy. The conspiracy began when John of Hucking, vicar of Chart, convened a group of clergy. The jurors presented that

> immediately after death of the archbishop[30] when the coming of the itinerant justices was noted,[31] John of Hucking, parson of Chart, made a certain feast at Chart, next to Sutton Valance, and assembled Thomas le White, parson of Harrietsham, William Fleming, vicar of Thornham, together with others indicted, and there made an oath that John of Hucking and the others bound themselves together on the gospels that each of them would maintain the pleas and actions which anyone of them began or undertook, whether justly or falsely, and that none of them would fail the other even if they should die together. And that for long time they were bound as conspirators and united by oath and they were and are maintainers of unjust pleas and actions and so that by their conspiracy through the greatest part of the whole county of Kent, truth and justice are suffocated.[32]

What followed were six presentments of these men and others for conspiracy, maintenance, ambidexterity, and procuring false indictments and acquittals. In one case, John of Hucking unsuccessfully tried to assert a royal pardon regarding his indictment for being mutually bound with William Fleming and Thomas Somery, a local parson, to maintain each other.[33] But the same jurors subsequently said that John had not withdrawn from the previous confederacy and conspiracy, but by the same malice undertook to maintain William Fleming, to whom he was still bound and "did not permit that confederacy and conspiracy to be extinguished or expire," thus removing himself from the king's grace.[34]

---

[30] Presumably, this was the death of Robert Winchelsey, archbishop of Canterbury, who died on May 11, 1313.

[31] Edward II's notice creating the commission for this eyre was sent on July 1, 1313, "the Octave of the Nativity of St. John the Baptist, Towards the Close of the Sixth Year of the Reign of Edward II." F.W. Maitland, L.W.V. Harcourt, and W.C. Bolland, eds., "The Eyre of Kent, 6 & 7 Edward II, A.D. 1313–1314," 2 vols., *Year Books of Edward II*, vol. I, 24 Selden Soc. (London, 1909), p. 1. The regnal year 6 Edw. II ended on July 7, 1313.

[32] TNA: PRO JUST 1/383, m. 109, AALT Img. No. 1686 (tr.).

[33] In addition, the jury presented John for two instances of ambidexterity for taking money to give aid and counsel to the parson of Maidstone and from the former parson and then giving counsel to their adversaries and for procuring that three men not be indicted for theft and burglary. Ibid.

[34] John continued conspiring by confederating with two other men, both wearing his livery, to procure the jury to conceal William's indictment for trespass. TNA: PRO JUST 1/383, m. 109, AALT Img. Nos. 1686–87 (tr.). John of Lykyng, another parson, was also indicted for conspiracy with others to maintain each other after he had been pardoned for

Thomas le White, another of the clerical conspirators, was accused in a quite complicated matter involving maintenance, ambidexterity, defamation, and extortion in both the secular and ecclesiastical courts.[35]

In second eyre in the reign, the 1321 London Eyre, the king ordered the justices to inquire into

> the confederacies made amongst citizens of London by covenants, oaths, and other unlawful means against the eyre, as the king understands that many of the citizens have made such confederacies to help, maintain, and sustain each other in their suits, just and unjust, and in other matters, and to punish all those whom they shall find guilty of such confederacies, so that the punishment shall strike terror into others in the city or elsewhere in the realm committing such evils.[36]

The inquiry produced twenty-two presentments, charging more than fifty men with conspiracy, confederacy, and being bound together by mutual oaths.[37] Of these, fourteen (64%) involved conspiracy to maintain false pleas and three others involved ambidexterity. A number of these presentments were of John de Wengrave, the former mayor of London (1316–18) and those allied with him.[38] He was charged with being bound

previously conspiring. The subsequent indictment involved his conspiracy with John of Hocking and others to conceal the indictment of William Fleming for his trespass. "The Eyre of Kent," *Year Books of Edward II*, vol. 1, 24 Selden Soc., pp. 145–46.

[35] Thomas was bound by oath to John and William to maintain parties and maintained two plaintiffs in a nuisance action and then switched sides to represent Simon, the defendant, who was indebted by a bond to Thomas's valet. But Simon complained to his friends since Thomas declined to assist him and return the bond, and William sued him in an ecclesiastical court for defamation. Although Thomas promised to withdraw his action and release Simon if the latter would admit before an official that he had spoken falsely, which Simon did, Thomas sued him again for defamation and made a fine with him for £20. TNA: PRO JUST 1/383, m. 109d, AALT Img. No. 1899 (tr.).

[36] "Close Rolls, Edward II: January 1321," *Calendar of Close Rolls, Edward II*, vol. III: *1318-23* (London, 1895), pp. 284–88. The justices set aside a day to do so. Helen Cam, ed., "The Eyre of London, 14 Edward II, A.D. 1321," 2 vols. (London, 1968), *Year Books of Edward II*, vol. I, 85 Selden Soc., p. 27. They issued a proclamation that "no one attainted of the crime of false conspiracy, of champerty, and the defence of false plaints should come into that Eyre." It provided further that "he should remain in his lodging, unless he had any plea to make, and for this he should pray license from the justices for that purpose." Ibid., p. 17.

[37] Two different documents were the sources for these presentments. The official record of the eyre contained fifteen actions. TNA: PRO JUST 1/547A. A Corpus Christi College, Cambridge, manuscript contained seven more. Cam said that manuscript was "an early and seemingly accurate account of the proceedings of the Eyre of 1321." Cam, "The Eyre of London," pp. xii–xiv. She discussed the conspiracy presentments. Ibid., pp. cxi–cxvi.

[38] The jury also charged that when he was clerk to the London sheriff, he maintained a man accused of homicide and took 26 marks to deliver him from prison. TNA: PRO JUST 1/

by mutual oaths to Robert de Kelsey, William de Leyre, John of the Chamber, and others to maintain and foment false actions in the city of London.[39] The jurors also accused John de Wengrave with ambidexterity and cited four instances of him switching sides in the same litigation while he was the mayor. In what appeared to be a dispute between two craft guilds over the scope of their trades, the jurors said that he took £9 from the hatters of Fleet Street to maintain them in their pleas in the Guildhall and afterward took £20 from the haberdashers to maintain them "in one and the same plea."[40]

The Eyres of Kent and of London both had numerous conspiracy and maintenance presentments. Those in the 1313–14 Kent Eyre seem similar to those during the reign of Edward I. But the nature of those in the London Eyre seems different, which may be due to its context. In London, both national and local politics were an important influence. London was a highly privileged corporation that had not been subjected to scrutiny since 1276.[41] In addition, Cam argued that a number of the London presentments were the product of municipal rivalries.[42] She said that the presentments "reflect[ed] the antagonisms of the two main factions in the City which had been competing for power ever since 1310."[43] This hostility was apparent in one case, in which Robert de

---

547A, m. 60, AALT Img. No. 5771. Five other presentments were conspiracies between him and several of his allies for wrongdoing in the collection of royal monies and three others involved other types of conspiracies such as rigging elections and a scheme to enroll an indicted felon as a freeman of city so he would qualify for mainprise.

[39] TNA: PRO JUST 1/547A, m. 60, AALT Img. No. 5770. The other three men and a fourth, together with numerous others, were similarly charged. TNA: PRO JUST 1/547A, m. 61, AALT Img. No. 5772. The presentment also charged that these men, as collectors of tallages and other royal moneys, collected more than was due, retaining the balance for their own use. They were all found guilty.

[40] TNA: PRO JUST 1/547A, m. 60, AALT Img. No. 5770. Robert of Kelsey was also charged with ambidexterity. TNA: PRO JUST 1/547A, m. 63d, AALT Img. No. 5931.

[41] The eyre provided an opportunity for "the detailed attentions of justices and royal advocates imbued with a questioning outlook and with a concept of a unified common law" that viewed some cities' practices unacceptable. David Crook, "The Later Eyres," *English Historical Review* 97 (1982), p. 260. In addition, Cam demonstrated how the Despensers had played a critical role in its initiation to punish the city for its sympathy toward the supporters of Thomas of Lancaster, their adversary. Cam, "The Eyre of London," pp. xv–xvii.

[42] Ibid., pp. xviii–xix, cxiii.

[43] One faction was led by John of Wengrave, mayor 1313–19, an opponent of the reform movement that had begun in 1310 and the opposition by Hamo Chigwell, mayor, 1319–20, 1321–22, 1323–25, 1327, with members of each faction being indicted for conspiracy. Ibid., cxiii–cxv.

Kelsey said that he had been expelled as an alderman and "did not dare to put himself on an inquisition of the city because he says his rivals have such great power in the city that the whole commonalty is led by their will in these days."[44] Morever, the eyre articles posed questions that were unique to London.[45] Also, unlike the Eyre of Kent where convictions were common, two-thirds of those charged with conspiracy in the London cases were acquitted.[46] Perhaps the political context was a factor in the high rate of acquittals.

Trailbaston Sessions

Several trailbaston sessions were held in the first decade of the fourteenth century. They targeted conspiracy, maintenance, champerty, and ambi-dexterity as the eyres had.[47] Some of the sessions had sections of the rolls specifically devoted to conspiracy.[48] In the 1304–05 Shropshire sessions, there were nine such presentments.[49] Many defendants, some of whom may have been local lawyers, were accused of multiple offenses. Walter, son of Reginald de Playssh de Edgerton, was indicted for conspiracy, maintenance, ambidexterity, and champerty. One indictment said that he was a conspirator who maintained Margery le Harpe against her sisters, suing that plea at his own cost to have part of the land. Also he maintained the side of Simon Oldacre against William the Bastard and

---

[44] He sought to be admitted to the king's grace, but the justices said such action was not within their power and told Robert to respond if it seemed expedient. When he failed to do so or to deny confederacy, he was taken into custody. TNA: PRO JUST 1/547A, m. 63d, AALT Img. No. 5932.

[45] David Crook, "The Later Eyres," *English Historical Review* 97 (1982), p. 259.

[46] Not all the jury verdicts were recorded. They were recorded for forty-five of the men indicted, of whom thirty were acquitted.

[47] The primary object was to punish offenses that were committed in the prior decade. The sessions were a temporary measure, intended to be followed by an eyre, which never occurred. Edward II did not order a resumption of trailbaston. Phelan has explored these sessions in detail. Phelan, "A Study of the First Trailbaston Proceedings," pp. 30–66.

[48] Lincoln, *"Northr' et Southr' de Conspiratoribus*, TNA: PRO JUST 1/509, m. 18 (1305), AALT Img. No. 306; Nottingham, *Rotulus conspiratorum de Notingham*, TNA: PRO JUST 1/675, m. 2 (1306), AALT Img. No. 4699; Suffolk, *Placita de conspiratoribus apud Hennowe*, TNA: PRO JUST 1/843, m. 35 (1306); Norfolk, *Placita de conspiratoribus*, TNA: PRO JUST 1/1334, m. 48 (1306), AALT Img. No. 2640.

[49] At this session, the king sent a writ to the justices that instructed to them to inquire, *inter alia*, into "those who for others move or cause to be moved the pleas and sue at their own costs to have by champerty or part of the profit and similarly of conspirators." TNA: PRO JUST 1/744, m. 7 (1304–05), AALT Img. No. 2358 (tr.).

afterward took 20s from William and was a "common conspirator and champertor of pleas."[50] He was similarly indicted for taking two oxen to be of counsel to Roger Kaleback in a plea against the bishop of Hereford. Afterward he abandoned Roger to represent the bishop, causing Roger to lose his action "by Walter's default and his conspiracy."[51]

In the 1304–06 Herefordshire sessions, there were nineteen indictments for these offenses. Ten men were indicted for conspiracy and ambidexterity. Among them was Miles Pichard, the former sheriff and perhaps a local lawyer, who was indicted twice for ambidexterity, abandoning his initial clients to favor a woman who was the adversary in both actions.[52] Both indictments concluded by stating that "thus by his conspiracy, he took from both sides." John Monnington, "a common conspirator," was indicted twice for conspiracy and champerty.[53] Other lawyers were similarly charged.[54] Of the seven indictments in the 1305 Lincolnshire trailbaston session, most of them dealt with procuring appeals or indictments or tampering with the jurors. But two indictments accused Randoph of Friskney, a knight and justice of the peace, of maintaining parties in litigation.[55]

---

[50] TNA: PRO JUST 1/744, m. 5d (1304–05), AALT Img. No. 2376. Brand believed Walter may have been a local lawyer. Brand, *Origins*, p. 140.

[51] TNA: PRO JUST 1/744, m. 5d (1304–05), AALT Img. No. 2376. Nor was he the only one indicted for such offenses. Fremond de Roed, Robert de Buckenhale, and Roger, son of Roger de Wigwick, were also indicted for conspiracy and ambidexterity. TNA: PRO JUST 1/744, m. 3d (1304–5), AALT Img. No. 2373; TNA: PRO JUST 1/744, m. 5d (1304–5), AALT Img. No. 2376.

[52] Having taken robes and fees from year to year to counsel Robert Tony, he abetted and counseled Robert to implead Katherine of Audley for her manor and he maintained him in that plea and then left Robert and "adhered to and maintained" Katherine in the same plea for a robe and 100s. He took 40s to maintain another woman against Katherine and again deserted his first client to maintain Katherine, receiving 100s from her. TNA: PRO JUST 1/306, m. 6 (1304–06), AALT Img. No. 9060.

[53] He abetted Agnes, daughter of Richard de Badeschawe, falsely and maliciously to implead John Smith, to whom Agnes had previously sold the land, at his own cost to have the land, in exchange for which John gave him land of lesser value. As attorney for John de Willenhale, he not only maintained the side of his client at his own cost and in champerty, but bound his client by a statute of merchant, so that the client could not settle with the defendants without John's counsel and assent. Ibid. Brand was not entirely certain that John was a professional lawyer. Brand, *Origins*, p. 140.

[54] John Lightfoot was also indicted for taking from both sides. Brand thought he was a local lawyer. Ibid.

[55] In one case, the jurors found that he was a common maintainer and supporter of pleas and actions and that he threatened jurors to find for those he favored, so that they feared coming to his court. In the other, he maintained and supported those indicted before him, who were wearing his livery, and he supported and maintained two such men whom

Other trailbaston sessions revealed a similar picture. The Staffordshire sessions in 1305–06 and 1307 produced 625 presentments.[56] Most of the presentments were for felonies.[57] But there were also a significant number for nonfelonious wrongs.[58] Among the latter were thirty-six indictments for conspiracy and maintenance.[59] Nineteen indictments were for maintenance or bringing false pleas, which was the largest category of conspiracy cases.[60] The maintenance presentments included seven for champerty and five for ambidexterity.[61] The 1305 Kent and 1307 Shropshire sessions generated very few indictments.[62] But one in the Kent session was interesting, as it showed a broad view of what constituted maintenance. In response to the trailbaston article, "Of those

the jury had found to be common wrongdoers at fairs and markets and who by the support and maintenance of Randolph often beat people there, both before and after the inquisition. He was committed to jail for both offenses TNA: PRO JUST 1/509, m. 15 (1305), AALT Img. No. 300. He was also the subject of several other indictments.

[56] Phelan examined and discussed in detail all of the indictments in the several visitations to this county. Phelan, "The First Traibaston Proceedings," pp. 67–117.

[57] Phelan noted that "overall profile and individual cases generally resemble[d] felonies presented in eyre." Homicide cases were the most common and constituted 30.6% of the presentments. Ibid., pp. 74–75.

[58] Phelan said that nonfelonious "wrongs" accounted for 27%. She divided these cases into five categories: violent offenses against the person including extortion, conspiracies, offenses against property, official corruption, and complicity in committing such offenses. Ibid., pp. 75–85. According to Phelan's analysis, conspiracy presentments, in which she included maintenance, champerty, and procuring false indictments and pleas, accounted for 7.4% in the 1305–05 visitations, which also included a category she labeled "common conspirator" and 21% in the 1307 visitation. Ibid., pp. 75, 106. She said conspiracy presentments were the second most common of those for wrongs. Ibid., pp. 81–82. All but two of those charged with conspiracy and appeared were fined, although fines were relatively modest. Ibid., pp. 91, 96–97, 106. Those charged with conspiracy had a relatively high appearance rate and generally were individuals with middling to high status, including knights, sheriffs, bailiffs, constables, court suitors, and jail custodians. Ibid., p. 94.

[59] TNA: PRO JUST 1/809 (1305–7).

[60] This number does not include thirteen presentments for procuring false indictments and appeals, which was the second largest category of conspiracy presentments. Of the remaining four presentments, two were accusations of conspiracies to beat others and two involved other misconduct by jurors.

[61] One juror was also charged with ambidexterity. TNA: PRO JUST 1/809, m. 4d, AALT Img. No. 3150. A few of those charged with such offenses were accused of being common conspirators, although that term was used most often for those involved in procuring false indictments and appeals.

[62] Several groups of the Kent jurors answered that they knew of none who maintained pleas or maintained for money or champerty. TNA: PRO JUST 1/396, mm. 1, 7, 11, 15, 17, AALT Img. Nos. 2603, 2622, 2630, 2640, 2646. The 1307 Shropshire jurors indicted one man for ambidexterity. TNA: PRO JUST 1/746, m. 2.

who maintain pleas," they said that Richard, the vicar of Putham and lessee of that manor from the archbishop, "supported (*sustinet*) pleas in the hundred of Putham and elsewhere to the grave damage of the people." In explaining what he had done, they said "and especially (*hoc maxime*)" that when Richard had received the goods of a deceased servant of the archbishop, who had died with his account in arrears, he not only had refused to make restitution, but had caused the poor tenants of that manor, who were free men and not villeins, to pay the arrearages, although he lacked any authority to do so.[63] Thus, he was indicted for maintenance even though his conduct, which was unjust and reprehensible, involved neither bringing an action nor supporting another's plea.

At least one of the trailbaston sessions, the 1306 Norfolk session, departed from the usual profile of indictments as a single individual, Hugh Tyrel, a local lawyer and steward accounted for over one-third of the cases.[64] Hugh's sins were manifold.[65] Most of them involved wrong-doing in litigation in the local courts and in his activities as a lawyer and steward there.[66] He was charged numerous times with conspiracy, maintenance, and maliciously moving false pleas as well as champerty.[67]

---

[63] TNA: PRO JUST 1/396, m. 14, AALT Img. No. 2638 (tr.).

[64] TNA: PRO JUST 1/1334. There were about 100 total presentments, with slightly over thirty presentments of Hugh as well as at least six independent private actions against him as well. TNA: PRO JUST 1/1334, mm. 48–48d, 49d, 51–51d, 52–52d, 53, 54 and 55d, AALT Img. Nos. 2640–42, 2762–64, 2766, 2647–48, 2768–69, 2649–51, 2770–71, 2652–54, 2776–77.

[65] Brand has discussed all of Hugh's wrongdoing in detail and carefully analyzed its nature. He used Hugh's activities to illustrate the existence of local lawyers as an unstudied aspect of the emerging English legal profession. Although these lawyers were not professional in the sense that they were formally admitted to practice or could be disciplined for unethical behavior, as was the case with those who practiced in the royal and major courts, they used their legal knowledge and skill to engage in various activities in the local courts. Hugh's case, although atypical as Brand acknowledged, provided an opportunity to explore the nature of local legal practice. Paul Brand, "Stewards, Bailiffs, and the Emerging Legal Profession," in Ralph Evans, ed., *Lordship and Learning: Studies in Memory of Trevor Austin* (Woodbridge, 2004), pp. 139–53.

[66] Hugh Tyrel was a member of the minor local gentry. He was steward of John Engayne and among other things presided over his court. Hugh held a half of a knight's fee in several Staffordshire vills and had his own manorial court with his own stewards, bailiffs, and clerks. Ibid., pp. 142, 147, 149–52.

[67] TNA: PRO JUST 1/1334, m. 52d, AALT Img. No. 2770. He also brought such actions in his own name when, as it was alleged, he had no right to vindicate. TNA: PRO JUST 1/1334, m. 52, AALT Img. No. 2649. He brought actions in the names of other persons who sometimes had no underlying right and sometimes without their knowledge. TNA: PRO JUST 1/1334, m. 51, AALT Img. No. 2647.

He maintained the actions of others at his own cost.[68] He conspired with eight men as his confederates and supporters in all of his false business.[69] He was an ambidexter, taking money to represent one client and acting for the adverse party after he knew the confidential information of the first client.[70]

Dubious motives often seemed to prompt his litigation. For example, he instigated litigation against the abbot of Bury St. Edmunds because the abbot refused to retain him and give him livery.[71] Because he was displeased with the verdict of the suitors of the Aylesham court in a writ of right, he punished them by suing an action of false judgment against them until they made a fine.[72] He engaged in extortion by using his position as a steward to institute an action in his own name in the court in which he presided.[73] He was found guilty of many of the charges.[74]

---

[68] TNA: PRO JUST 1/1334, m. 51, AALT Img. No. 2647; TNA: PRO JUST 1/1334, m. 53, AALT Img. No. 2652. He advised clients on litigation and on obtaining appropriate writs and purchased them himself from Chancery at his own cost. TNA: PRO JUST 1/1334, m. 48, AALT Img. No. 2640.

[69] Six of the others appeared and were found not guilty. TNA: PRO JUST 1/1334, m. 49d, AALT Img. No. 2766.

[70] TNA: PRO JUST 1/1334, m. 55d, AALT Img. No. 2777.

[71] TNA: PRO JUST 1/1334, mm. 48–48d, AALT Img. Nos. 2640–42, 2762. He formerly had acted as steward for the abbot in his court in Aylesham (Norfolk). While in that position, he counseled a man to bring a writ of right in that court, taking 100s to be of counsel to him and sued the writ at his own costs and then secretly supported the adverse parties, who gave him a horse worth 40s. Even though the plaintiff recovered the land, Hugh bought the land for himself after judgment was entered and ordered the bailiffs of the court not to deliver seisin to the successful plaintiff. TNA: PRO JUST 1/1334, m. 48, AALT Img. Nos. 2640–41. The plaintiff then sued Hugh for his false, malicious, and conspiratorial actions, alleging 10 marks' damages. Hugh denied the allegations and the matter and the parties put themselves on the jury.

[72] TNA: PRO JUST 1/1334, mm. 51–51d, AALT Img. Nos. 2647–48, 2768–69.

[73] TNA: PRO JUST 1/1334, m. 52, AALT Img. Nos. 2649; TNA: PRO JUST 1/1334, m. 53, AALT Img. No. 2652.

[74] The King had instructed all the trailbaston justices to refer the wealthiest of the offenders to the council to decide on an appropriate fine. Phelan, First Trailbaston Proceedings," p. 56. As a result, William Ormesby, chief justice of the Norfolk and Suffolk sessions, wrote to William Carleton, a baron of the Exchequer, telling him that Hugh had been attainted before him and his fellow justices "for diverse conspiracies and false moving of pleas and of false maintenance and that he is a common conspirator" and that he had £30 worth of land and £20 in chattels. The council replied that Hugh and the others convicted should be sent to the Tower and imprisoned there until the king decided otherwise. TNA: PRO E159/79, m. 30, AALT Img. No. 73. Subsequently, on April 25, 1306, the king sent a writ to Ormesby saying that he wanted the Treasurer and Barons to be informed of the record and process involving Hugh and three other men, who were imprisoned in the Tower, and ordering that the record and process together with their counsel and wisdom

No wonder Hugh was called a "common instigator both of false quarrels and a maintainer of others."[75]

Civil Litigation

Although criminal cases substantially outnumbered civil ones, there were still a significant number of the latter. These civil actions consisted of conspiracy actions pursuant to the 1293 writ of conspiracy and champerty actions based on the 1300 *Articuli super Cartas*, chapter 11.[76] As with criminal actions, conspiracy actions were much more common and there were three times as many of them as there were champerty actions.

Conspiracy Cases

Although there were various types of conspiracy actions, the most common were those alleging the procurement of false indictments and appeals.[77] Given the longstanding concern with false and malicious criminal prosecution, that should not be surprising.[78] Although the 1293 Ordinance provided for both criminal and civil remedies, private actions for such conduct were by far more common.[79] Of these

---

on the level of fines taken from them to be sent to the Treasurer and Barons of the Exchequer, which it was. TNA: PRO JUST 1/1334, m. 53, AALT Img. No. 2653.

[75] Also he retained other men by livery to maintain his false quarrels by conspiracy and confederation between them. TNA: PRO JUST 1/1334, m. 48, AALT Img. No. 2640 (tr.).

[76] There were a total of eighty-seven civil actions, of which 78% were for conspiracy and 22% for champerty. A majority of them were brought in the King's Bench (53%), with 28% in the Common Bench, 6% in the eyres, 5% proceedings on parliamentary complaints, and 1% before a Commission of *Oyer et Terminer*.

[77] Winfield identified five types of conspiracy actions involving procuring indictments and appeals and maintaining false pleas as well as actions involving civil proceedings and other malicious conduct involving legal proceedings. Winfield, *History of Conspiracy*, pp. 51–59.

[78] Although the Statute of Westminster II, chapter 12, provided a remedy for those falsely appealed and subsequently acquitted, the Ordinance of Conspirators also provided a remedy for such conduct, which had certain advantages over the earlier provision that made it preferable to victims. Winfield, *History of Conspiracy*, pp. 39–51. Also it provided a remedy for those who were falsely indicted.

[79] Several defendants argued that the plaintiff had no action since he had not been acquitted since the appellor had been nonsuited, but uncertainty existed as to whether the writ was available in such circumstances. Y.B. Mich. 17 Edw. II, fols. 509–10, pl. 40 (1323), Seipp No. 1323.074; Y.B. East. 17 Edw. II, fol. 544, pl. 43 (1324), Seipp No. 1324.089. But in the reign of Edward III, the writ seemed to lie in such circumstances. Winfield, *History of*

proceedings, civil actions for damages constituted 70% and criminal cases 30%.[80] Table 4.3 identifies the different types of civil actions initiated.

The allegations in the civil actions followed a common form, but the litigation contexts varied.[81] Many actions involved the misuse of the standard criminal process.[82] For example, Robert atte Ok' complained that Nicholas de Ichene and Adam de Ripling, by a conspiracy previously made between them, maliciously and falsely procured Robert to be detained and indicted for homicide, resulting in his arrest and imprisonment until he was delivered from jail by the justices according to the law and custom of the realm. He said he was wronged in violation of the ordinance of the king and his council.[83] In a more unusual and colorful action, Henry Pentel was angry with Matilda, the widow with whom he lived, because she brought a dower action against him. He retaliated by procuring Matilda's dogs to be taken into the king's forest at Nottingham and then led out of it for wrongfully hunting in the royal forest and by procuring the verderers and foresters to indict Matilda for trespass. After she was acquitted by an inquisition in the forest court, she sued Henry in a plea of conspiracy and trespass.[84]

Conspiracy, pp. 42–44. Defendants also argued that damages should be available for their imprisonment if the writ omitted their acquittal. Y.B. Mich. 19 Edw. II, fols. 638–39, pl. 48 (1325), Seipp No. 1325.149.

[80] There were a total of 33 proceedings, 23 of which were civil actions and 10 were criminal cases. There were jury verdicts in 27% of these proceedings, resulting in 14 defendants being found guilty and 2 not guilty. The criminal actions all occurred in the eyres and trailbaston sessions. E.g., TNA: PRO JUST 1/744, m. 3d (1305), AALT Img. No. 2373; TNA: PRO JUST 1/509, m. 18 (1305), AALT Img. Nos. 306–7; TNA: PRO JUST 1/383, m. 110 (1313–14), AALT Img. No. 1688. In addition, the pleas of the crown for the King's Bench's perambulation to Wigan included an article directing inquiry into such conduct. TNA: PRO KB 27/254, m. 40 rex (1323), AALT Img. Nos. 326–27.

[81] In a plea of conspiracy and trespass, Adam of Whytine complained that a vicar and another man conspired and confederated maliciously to present and defame his wife before the archbishop of York's visitor on the ground that she had committed adultery with a monk. She successfully purged herself of that crime, but at a cost of £20. The jury found the defendants guilty, stating that they caused her to be cited by malice and not for the salvation of her soul. She recovered 60s in damages and the defendants made a fine with the king for 40s. TNA: PRO KB 27/161, m. 25 (1300), AALT Img. No. 2365.

[82] Shanks and Milsom included counts for such actions in the collection of new counts. Elsie Shanks and S.F.C. Milsom, eds. *Novae Narrationes* (London, 1963), 80 Selden Soc., pp. 126–27, 328–29.

[83] The defendant denied the charges. TNA: PRO CP 40/155, m. 21d (1305), AALT Img. No. 612.

[84] The jury found Henry guilty and Matilda recovered 100s. TNA: PRO KB 27/144, m. 27 (1295), AALT Img. No. 58.

Table 4.3 *Types of civil cases, 1272–1327*

Conspiracy	68 (78%)
Procure indictment-appeal	23 (26.4%)
Procure civil plea	14 (16.1%)
Maintenance	6 (6.9%)
Ambidexterity	3 (3.5%)
Other types	18 (20.7%)
Mesne process, no details	4 (4.6%)
Total	68
Other types of cases	19 (22%)
Champerty	19 (21.8%)
Maintenance	0
Procure false indictment or appeal	0
Procure false civil plea	0
Other abuse of legal procedure	0
Total civil cases	87

Although not as serious as criminal charges in terms of deprivation of liberty and injury to reputation, procuring false civil proceedings also involved corruption of legal process.[85] Several of these actions involved land and in particular procuring assizes of novel disseisin. For example, Henry Wastel brought a conspiracy action against four men, alleging that they falsely and maliciously procured him to be impleaded by a writ of novel disseisin and procured the jurors to be suborned and Henry to be harassed by multiple hardships and expenses until he went quit.[86]

Several conspiracy actions for falsely and maliciously indicting innocent persons were brought against members of the inquest that had indicted the plaintiff. Determining whether a writ of conspiracy could

---

[85] In one action, the plaintiff sued a writ of conspiracy, alleging false allegations in a writ of entry that they had agreed to arbitrate, but pending the arbitration the defendant recovered the land by judgment of the court. The court held that the recovery of the land negated the deceit essential to a writ of conspiracy and ordered that the plaintiff take nothing by the writ, but suggested the possible use of the writ of right. TNA: PRO KB 27/208, m. 6d (1312), AALT Img. No. 11; Y.B. Trin. 5 Edw. II, fol. 172, pl. 22, Seipp No. 1312.141ss.

[86] The defendants denied the charges and the parties put themselves on the jury. TNA: PRO KB 27/180, m. 79 (1305), AALT Img. No. 529.

be brought against them posed a dilemma.[87] On one hand, jury corruption was a common and serious problem. In his writ to the 1279 Kent Eyre justices, which was also sent to other eyres, the king expressed his concern about those who made mutual oaths to maintain and defend their friends and well-wishers in pleas and actions in assizes, juries, and recognitions.[88] But criminal prosecution would be undermined if jurors refrained from indicting those who should have been indicted because they feared being sued for doing so.[89] By end of the thirteenth century, jurors of presentment began to demur in actions against them, saying that they should not have to answer as they were members of an inquest. For example, in 1281, a man sued twelve jurors whom he claimed conspired and confederated to falsely indict him for the death of man who died a natural death because he refused to pay them blackmail ("*tributarius esse*").[90] To resolve this problem, the king issued an order in 1304 prohibiting Chancery from issuing conspiracy writs to persons to sue those who had indicted them, without special command from him. He said that otherwise "many people would fear to be put on inquests and indict no man however guilty, and evildoers would be free to do wrong."[91]

---

[87] Winfield, *History of Conspiracy*, pp. 267–71; Sayles, "Conspiracy and Allied Offenses," pp. lviii, lxiv; Harding, "Origins of Conspiracy," pp. 95, 98–99.

[88] The writ ordered the justices to arrest and imprison the offenders. TNA: PRO JUST 1/367, m. 2 (1279), AALT Img. No. 7. Jurors were often indicted for their corrupt conduct. One common charge was that they had taken money from one or both of the parties to the inquisition to say their verdict or that they had procured themselves to be on the inquisition in order to return a false indictment. TNA: PRO Just 1/809, mm. 4d, 12 (1305–6, 1307 Staffordshire Eyre), AALT Imgs. 3120, 3150.

[89] Harding said that the king and parliament "could not remain indifferent to the wholesale corruption of jurors." But that "it was quickly realised that the threat of a charge of conspiracy was itself the best way of coercing jurors." Harding, "Origin of Conspiracy," pp. 95, 99. Sayles said that there was "a confusion of the innocent with the guilty and it is little wonder that they began to refuse to indict influential wrongdoers so that the criminal law was in danger of completely breaking down." Sayles, "Conspiracy and Allied Offenses," p. lxiv.

[90] TNA: PRO KB27/60, m. 2 (1281), AALT Img. No. 4. In another case, defendants, who were sued for conspiracy for procuring two men to present a man for a trespass at the sheriff's tourn, responded that they should not have to answer as the presentment was true and remained unchanged and they prevailed. Since the plaintiff could not deny their plea, the defendants were quit without day and the plaintiff amerced for a false claim. TNA: PRO KB 27/152, m. 27 (1297), AALT Img. 387.

[91] *Calendar of Chancery Warrants, A.D. 1244–1326* (London, 1927), vol. 1, pp. 241–42 (November 24, 1304). Harding said that Edward I's initiation of the trailbaston inquests required this order. A comment in a Year Book case, which suggested that at some point Chancery may have been prohibited from issuing conspiracy writs, may have been

This rule "soon became settled law"[92] and it appeared in writ registers.[93] Nevertheless, actions continued to be brought against jurors for procuring false indictments.[94] In 1312, defendants, who were sued for falsely indicting a man for burglary and carrying off goods, said that the writ did not lie against the jurors and that "no man could procure himself."[95] At the urging of Bereford CJCP, the plaintiff said that the defendants were not jurors and the parties joined issue and put themselves on the country.[96] In another case, the defendants' plea was that they need not answer "because they were jurors on a certain inquest with others ... with whom they said their verdict according to their understanding by their oath, and they seek judgment since they were indictors." They said the plaintiff could only sue them for conspiracy as procurers. Thus the plaintiff said that they were procurers not indictors and the issue was for the country.[97] Contemporary thinking was that one could not be both.

What happened in these cases is interesting. The defendant had raised an issue of law by his demurrer to the plaintiff's plea on the ground that he was one of the indictors. Because of the legal rule against charging indictors, the plaintiff would want to avoid a ruling on the demurrer and get the matter to the jury. By denying that the defendants were members of

---

referring to writs against indictors for falsely procuring indictments. Y.B. Trin. 33 Edw. I, Roll Series, pp. 462–63, *Nota* (1305), Seipp No. 1305.061rs.

[92] Harding, "Origins of Conspiracy," p. 99.

[93] "Note that the writ of conspiracy does not lie against indictors." CUL MS Ff. 5.19, fol. 95r (fifteenth century); CUL MS Gg.5.19, fol. 85v (fifteenth century); CUL MS Additional. 6854, fols. 121r (fifteenth century). Winfield also found one example from the reign of Edward I. Winfield, *History of Conspiracy*, p. 67 n. 5.

[94] In one case, in which one of the defendants said he was a juror in the inquest that made the indictment, the plaintiff said that he was not one of the indictors, but by conspiracy procured his indictment. TNA: PRO 27/231, m. 54 (1318), AALT Img. No. 114.

[95] *Goscelyn v. Kempe*, TNA: PRO CP 40/190, m. 95d (1312), Seipp No. 1312.024ss, reprinted in W.C. Bolland, ed., "5 Edward II, A.D. 1311–1312," *Year Books of Edward II*, vol. I, 31 Selden Soc (London, 1915), pp. 114–16.

[96] Although a number of the defendants admitted that they were members of the inquest, not all did. Two, who were reeves of the vill, said that they presented the plaintiff "because it was common fame and notorious throughout the countryside, and so they did it not by conspiracy, either of malice." The plaintiff said that "even though they be indicators, which we do not admit, yet he can indict them for conspiracy." But when Bereford CJ asked whether they were on the inquest, the plaintiff said they were not and issue was joined. There was a suggestion that if some were found not to have been on the inquest that process against the other would abate as all of them were charged with conspiring. Ibid.

[97] TNA: PRO KB 27/238, m. 23d (1319, AALT Img. 45; *Bartaille v. Blampayn*, Y.B. Mich. 13 Edw. II, fol. 401, pl. 22 (1319), Seipp No. 1319.191 (tr.). The Year Book case is a copy of the enrollment, which likely erroneously transcribed *indictatores* as *judicatatores*.

the inquisition, the plaintiff evaded the question of the law and created one of fact.[98] Now the country will decide the case and the jurors will likely be influenced by their view of whether the defendants acted as honest or corrupt jurors. Perhaps this was the best approach, as the indicting jurors could be either.[99] Nevertheless, the rule precluding conspiracy actions against indictors posed a risk that it would protect indictors who were in fact corrupt, that is, "procurers." Scrope CJKB was concerned about that problem in a later case, in which the defendant alleged he was a member of the inquest and could not be indicted.[100] Scrope said that

> it would be hardship if this writ did not lie against the indictors, because when someone wanted to indict another he would procure the sheriff to put him on a panel so that he could indict him, so that although he were acquitted, he would never have a writ of Conspiracy against him because he was on the inquest.[101]

But the defendant thought that legal process and the jurors' oath resolved that dilemma because he was compelled by law to be on the panel and by his oath to say the truth. Thus, if the writ lay against the indictors, the law would suppose that they had spoken falsely. It would follow then that attaint was the legal action in such instances. That would not bode well for defendants as attaints were time consuming and plaintiffs rarely prevailed. But Scrope finally decided that making the writ of conspiracy

---

[98] One wonders why the defendants did not vouch the record to show that they were members of the inquest. That seemed to be the practice in later cases. TNA: PRO KB 27/411, m. 22d rex (1363), AALT Img. No. 400; TNA: PRO KB 27/416, m. 13 rex (1364), AALT Img. No. 184; TNA: PRO KB 27/416, m. 33 rex (1364), AALT Img. No. 224. But it seems unlikely that there was any real doubt about whether the defendants were indictors. The plaintiff's denial likely pleased the judge, given the judicial aversion to demurrers.

[99] But it does not eliminate all problems as the jurors in the conspiracy case could also be corrupt and a general verdict would preclude knowing the basis of their decision.

[100] The defendant said that "it could not be understood by law that a man could be a procurer and an indictor, that one could not procure himself. The plaintiff replied that although the defendant was an indictor, he could still procure the other jurors to indict the plaintiff. The defendant replied that the indictment was by all the jurors and the "verdict in itself was one" and none could make the indictment without all, "so he could not procure anyone to indict if he did not procure himself." Y.B. East. 17 Edw. II, fol. 547, pl. 2 (1324), Seipp No. 1324.100, TNA: PRO KB 27/257, m. 55d, AALT Img. 108 (tr.).

[101] Ibid. (tr.). Jurors in fact were indicted for procuring themselves to be on a jury in order falsely to indict a particular person for robbery. TNA: PRO Just 1/809, m.12 (1305–06 1307 Staffordshire Eyre, AALT Img. 3120; TNA: PRO Just 1/809, m. 4d (1305–06 1307 Staffordshire Eyre, AALT Img. 3150 (two cases).

available against indictors was not the preferred alternative. He said that, if so, jurors "would more often avoid indicting anyone for fear of being troubled." Thus, the court adjudged that the plaintiff take nothing by the writ and be amerced him for a false claim and that the defendant should go without day. Perhaps, in light of these cases, it is understandable why, despite the formal rule, courts continued to hear and struggle with these actions.

Some confusion arises in these conspiracy actions against jurors, as some of the actions were not against presenting jurors but against trial jurors who said that they were members of an inquest and could not be sued for conspiracy. For example, in a 1294 action, the plaintiff alleged that a man who sued him for trespass conspired with the trial jurors to find for the trespass plaintiff and amerce him £10, which he would share with the jurors. The defendant jurors responded that they were on the inquisition and had made a good and lawful oath, which still stood. They said that if there were perjury, the plaintiff could have recovery by writ of attaint. The court agreed, saying that plea did not sound in conspiracy.[102]

In sum, neither presenting jurors nor trial jurors could be sued in an action of conspiracy, although the legal rationale differed. An action of attaint lay against trial jurors for a false oath, and, therefore, conspiracy did not lie. As to presenting jurors, a specific legal rule precluded an action of conspiracy against them. Perhaps a criminal indictment was the only remedy against them for returning a false indictment.

Champerty Cases

The *Articuli super Cartas*, c. 11, which prohibited champerty, provided that "whosoever will, shall be received to sue for the king before the justices before whom the plea hangeth and judgment shall be given by them."[103] Contemporaries believed that this language did not authorize a private damage action. In a 1332 champerty action based on this statute,

---

[102] TNA: PRO KB 27/141, m. 8 (1294), AALT Img. Nos. 2762–63. In another action, a man sued a local lawyer and two bailiffs for conspiring to procure a man to bring a writ of novel disseisin against the conspiracy plaintiff. One of the bailiffs was a recognitor and procured the other jurors to find for the plaintiff in the assize. The defendants responded that the conspiracy plaintiff had brought a writ of attaint against them, which was still pending, and, therefore, they should not have to respond to the conspiracy action. The plaintiff could not deny this and he was amerced for a false claim. TNA: PRO KB 27/151, m. 22 (1297), AALT Img. No. 217.

[103] 28 Edw. I, c. 11 (1300), *Statutes of the Realm*, vol. 1, p. 139.

Herle CJCP said that "the suit belonged to the king, for the party could not have his suit."[104] In the 1321 London Eyre, Justices Stanton and Herle said that "an action for champerty nor suit concerning this is given or reserved by any statute except to the king."[105] In response to a complaint made in the 1329–30 Northamptonshire Eyre alleging champerty, Scrope stated that "champarty may be punished only at the king's suit. On that account therefore, we award that you take nothing by your bill."[106] Modern scholars also opined that this provision did not create a private remedy.[107] Although these views are not inaccurate, they are incomplete. An examination of the plea rolls reveals a more complex and somewhat different picture.

Several civil champerty actions based on this provision were brought during this period.[108] The king's writ of *audita querela* initiated the action.[109] The writ recited the words of the statute and recounted a violation of the statute, of which the king had learned from the victim's complaint ("*sicut ex querela predicti Johannis accepimus*"). The writ

---

[104] Shardelow JCP made similar comments, stating that "by statute it was ordained that they be punished, and another than the king could not have the suit." Y.B. Trin. 6 Edw. III, fol. 33, pl. 19 (1332), Seipp No. 1332.122.

[105] Y.B. Mich. 14 Edw. II, *Nota* (1320), Seipp No. 1320.062ss; S.J. Stolar and L.J. Downer, eds., *The Yearbooks of Edward II, 14 Edward II, Michaelmas 1320*, 27 vols. (London, 1988), 104 Selden Soc., p. 141 (tr.). The justices may have been referring to all the champerty statutes enacted during the reign of Edward I.

[106] Donald Sutherland, ed., *The Eyre of Northampton Shire, 3-4 Edward III, A.D. 1329–1330*, 2 vols. (London, 1983), vol. I, 97 Selden Soc., pp. 221–22; Seipp No. 1330.434ss. In that case, the defendant's lawyer argued that such an action was available to a tenant, but not a demandant. Ibid. Another report of this action stated that Scrope said that "the action for champarty belongs only to the king, by presentment." Ibid. The second version of Scrope's statement is consistent with Westminster I, c. 25, and Westminster II, c. 49, but inconsistent with *Articuli super Cartas*, c. 11.

[107] Holdsworth, *A History of English Law*, III, p. 397; G.O. Sayles, "Conspiracy and Allied Offenses," p. lv; Winfield, *The History of Conspiracy*, pp. 148, 150.

[108] There were nineteen such actions. Ten were based on *Articuli super Cartas*, c. 11. Of the remaining nine, four were proceedings before the king's council arising from parliamentary petitions and involved Westminster I, c. 25; three others involved Westminster II, c. 49, arising also from private petitions; one appeared in a British Library manuscript; and the other was a product of an assize of novel disseisin in which the jurors found that a man, who was not a party to the assize, was guilty of champerty.

[109] Of these ten actions based on *Articuli super Cartas*, c. 11, nine of them were brought by victims and the other one was brought by William Ganet, a Common Bench attorney suing for the king although not as the king's attorney. He appeared numerous times in the 1311 and 1312 Year Books of Edw. II, Selden Society volumes, and in the Norhamptonshire Eyre volumes, where he also appeared as a bailiff and guardian.

ordered the justices, who having heard the complaint ("*audita querela*"),
should do what was necessary according to the law and the form of the
ordinance.[110] The writ registers contain many such writs.[111] With one
exception, the records of all the civil champerty actions during this
period either included a writ from the king to his justices or there was
other pleading such as an attachment or a mesne process entry that
indicated that such a writ had been previously sent to the justices.[112]
What happened in these cases as result of the king's writ of *audita
querela* is interesting. The records show that a victim's action on behalf
the king not only was a vehicle for the imposition of punishment by
crown, but it became a basis for the recovery of damages by the
1. First, the *venire facias* in the king's writ usually instructed
sheriff to have the defendant in court to respond to both the king

*impert'. Rex justiciariis suis de Banco salutem. Cum inter ceteros articulos quos ad
acionem status populi de regno nostro de gracia nostra speciali duximus conceden-
linavimus quod nullus minister noster nec aliquis alius [pro] parte rei que est in
habendi negocia que sunt in placito assumat manutenenda nec aliquis jus suum
tsmodi convencione alteri dimittat ac Ricardus Huberd de Rypoun loquelam que
ria nostra per breve nostrum inter Johannem de Carleton' petentem et Agnetam
uxor Johannis Prest de Ripon' tenentem de uno mesuagio cum pertinenciis in
i pro parte mesuagii habenda jam [manutenenda] in ipsius Johannis dampnum
cum et periculum exheredacionis manifestum et contra formam ordinacionis
licte, sicut ex querela predicti Johannis accepimus, nos ordinacionem illam
violabiliter observare vobis mandamus quod audita querela ejusdem Johannis
 inspectoque tenore ordinacionis predicte ulterius inde fieri faciatis quod de
idum formam ordinacionis predicte fuerint faciendum. Teste me ipso apud
die Julii anno regni nostri xxx." Bodleian MS Hatton 28, f. 85r. This writ
the litigation pursuant to this statute may have begun in 1302. Gratitude is
'rof. Paul Brand for sharing his copy of this writ with me. The one writ that
\qquad ich was based on a violation of Westminster II, c. 49, contained neither
\qquad rela nor audita querela language. TNA: PRO CP 40/211, m. 103d (1315),
\qquad . 209.
\qquad nted registers contain examples of this writ. De Haas and Hall, eds.,
\qquad Writs, 87 Selden Soc., p. 311, no. R. 886; Registrum Omnium Brevium, 3
\qquad 1531), vol. II, fol. 183r. The former is from the early fourteenth century
\qquad rom the reign of Edward III, as the writ recited that it was sent by the
\qquad the statute ordained by "Edward, former king of England, our grand-
\qquad us examples were also found in unprinted fourteenth-century registers.
\qquad University Library, MS Additional 3469, fol. 49r; Cambridge University
\qquad ditional 3506, fol. 45r; Cambridge University Library, MS Additional
\qquad ', 146r; British Library, MS Harley 961, fol. 60v; British Library, MS
\qquad 59, fol. 62v; British Library, MS Harley 1118, vol. 155r.
\qquad 40/149, m. 213d (1304), AALT Img. No. 1369; TNA: PRO KB 27/180,
\qquad ALT Img. No. 529.

and the victim.[113] Second, in the notice of attachment, the defendant was attached to respond to both the king and the plaintiff.[114] Third, in almost all the mesne process entries involving victims as plaintiffs, the plaintiff sued both for the king and himself. The basis for the notice of attachment and the mesne process seems to have been an original writ that the plaintiff had obtained from Chancery.[115] Finally, in the pleaded actions, the plaintiffs claimed damages and the matter went to a jury.

One of the earliest champerty actions based on this provision illustrated this procedure. In Easter Term, 32 Edw. I (1304), the king sent a writ to the Common Bench justices based on a complaint from Baldwin of Panton. Baldwin alleged that the bailiff of the hundred of Blything in Suffolk, his wife, and the underbailiff had undertaken to maintain Roger, the son of Geoffrey Kempe, and Isabel and Agnes, the daughters of William of Sotherton, in exchange for part of the land in Baldwin's writ of entry against them, in violation of *Articuli super Cartas*, c. 11. The king noted Baldwin's pending action and sent a writ of *audita querela* ordering the justices to do what was necessary according to the law and the form of the ordinance.[116] Baldwin then came into court and sought a writ from the coroners against the defendants in the champerty action, and the court ordered the coroners to have them in court to answer both to the king and to Baldwin.[117] Two terms later, the champerty defendants and two of three defendants in the underlying action, the beneficiaries of the champerty, were attached to respond to both the king and Baldwin for this violation of *Articuli super Cartas*, c. 11. Baldwin, suing for both himself and the king, alleged the illegal conduct and claimed damages of £200.[118] In the same term, Baldwin instituted mesne process against

---

[113] TNA: PRO CP 40/149, m. 213d (1304), AALT Img. No. 1370.

[114] TNA: PRO CP 40/149, m. 63 (1304), AALT Img. No. 133; TNA: PRO KB 27/180, m. 27 (1305), AALT Img. No. 422; TNA: PRO CP 40/180 (1310), AALT Img. No. 606.

[115] A notice of attachment for champerty in a fourteenth-century register of writs containing writs "*temp* Edw. I and II" is in the standard trespass *ostensurus quare* form, "*Si Johannes fecerit, etc, tunc pone, etc.*" British Library MS Harley 961, fol. 86v.

[116] Baldwin had brought two prior actions in this dispute. TNA: PRO CP 40/144, m. 220d (1302), AALT Img. No. 1263; TNA: PRO CP 40/145, m. 154 (1303), AALT Img. No. 321_1.

[117] TNA: PRO CP 40/151, m. 108d (1304), AALT Img. No. 750.

[118] Two of the defendants admitted purchasing the land, but said no plea was pending, and the third denied any purchase. Baldwin's replication repeated his allegations and the parties put themselves on a jury. TNA: PRO CP 40/149, m. 63 (1304), AALT Img. No. 133.

the third defendant in the underlying action, suing for himself and the king and referring to the earlier writ sent by the king to the justices.[119]

In one particularly interesting action, another plaintiff, who had brought a writ of entry, alleged a violation of *Articuli super Cartas*, chapter 11, because the defendant had demised his right to a third party in return for maintaining and defending the defendant in the pending plea. The defendant denied the champerty and the jurors found him not guilty. They said that the defendant had sold the land for 60 marks to have money for food and not for maintenance and also on the condition that he would repay the money if he later lost the land. The jury found further that the plaintiff had suffered no injury by the sale of the land because of his failure to prosecute the action, which had been continued after the death of Edward I.[120]

To the extent that the statements by the justices in the Year Books only meant that in this period a writ from the king to his justices was necessary to initiate an action based on the *Articuli super Cartas*, they were correct. But their accounts, as well as those of modern scholars, noted above, are incomplete, for they fail to reveal what occurred subsequent to those writs. Herle's statements in Peter of Saltmarsh's action were in response to the defendant's argument that the king had not been informed of the action and not that the plaintiff could not bring the action. In saying that the action belonged to the king and the party could not have his suit, he continued by saying that the "king had recited all in the writ and had said as we understand from the aforesaid Peter of S."[121] Thus, Herle indicated that the king had previously sent his writ to the justices, and, as was the standard procedure, Peter's action resulted from that writ. Scrope's comments in the Northamptonshire Eyre are less clear. He acted correctly in dismissing the plaintiff's bill as there had been no prior writ from the king. But if saying that champerty "may be punished only at the king's suit" meant that a victim could sue only to

---

[119] TNA: PRO CP 40/149, m. 213d (1304), AALT Img. No. 1369. His pleading included the language *ut accepit Rex*. When this language or *sicut ex querela accepimus* appeared in a pleading, it would indicate that there had been a writ from the king to the justices prior to the notice of attachment or the mesne process.

[120] TNA: PRO CP40/180, m. 301d (1310), AALT Img. No. 606. It is curious that the plaintiff did not sue the third party, who was the champertor. Moreover, the jury's explanation of the transaction is unusual, as none of this information is in the defendant's plea and the justification is one that could be made in many cases that had the potential of undermining the statute. Also the plaintiff dropped the action based on the writ of entry although he pursued the champerty claim.

[121] Y.B. Trin. 6 Edw. III, fol. 33, pl. 19 (1332), Seipp No. 1332.122. Winfield relied on these statements in asserting his view. Winfield, *The History of Conspiracy*, pp. 148–49.

obtain punishment by the king and not also for damages, that statement is contrary to what actually occurred in the cases. In sum, at the end of this period, a victim could not independently bring a champerty action, and the king's writ of *audita querela* was a prerequisite to initiating an action, but ultimately could recover damages if the statute had been violated.

Conclusion

The examination of the criminal and civil litigation in the period 1272–1327 prompts several conclusions. First, conspiracy and maintenance corrupted justice and were considered significant legal problems. Criminal prosecution as the predominant method of dealing (73%) with this conduct underscored the significance of this abuse. Second, conspiracy prosecutions were the primary weapon against maintenance and ambidexterity. There were twice as many criminal prosecutions for conspiracy to maintain pleas as there were other forms of criminal maintenance prosecutions. There were no civil maintenance actions, and of the civil actions (27%), the most common were conspiracy to procure false appeals, indictments, and civil pleas (43%) and champterty (22%).[122] In addition, the conduct of lawyers, who were commonly accused of ambidexterity, was a considerable aspect of this litigation and corruption.[123] Further, in both types of criminal maintenance prosecutions, the gravamen of the offense appears to be the falsity of the pleas and not support of another's plea. In these cases, the word "maintenance" is being used to denote instituting proceedings and not just providing support to someone else's litigation.

This litigation also provides significant insight into the nature of the conspiracy offense. The varied forms of conduct that were the subject of conspiracy actions suggest that conspiracy was a rather flexible notion and, perhaps, at least initially, not well defined.[124] With regard to civil

---

[122] "Other" civil conspiracy actions, those few not involving conspiracies to procure false appeal, indictments, or civil pleas, was the only other significant category of civil actions (21%),

[123] Although lawyers were charged with conspiracy for being ambidexters, that conduct was also a violation of the Statute of Westminster I. 3 Edw. I, c. 29 (1275), *Statutes of the Realm*, vol. 1, p. 34. Amibidexterity was probably the most common form of unethical and illegal wrongdoing by lawyers in medieval England. Jonathan Rose, "The Ambidextrous Lawyer: Conflict of Interest and the Medieval Legal Profession," *The University of Chicago Law School Roundtable*, 7 (2000), pp. 136–203.

[124] It was not clear that alleging a false statute merchant was an action within the scope of the statute. A case raising that issue did not resolve it as it was dismissed because of a pleading defect. TNA: PRO CP40/182, m. 123 (1310), AALT Img. No. 248, Y.B. Trin. 3

actions, the scope of the conspiracy action was broader in its early stage than in its later development. Modern commentators have asserted that, by the early fourteenth century, the civil conspiracy actions focused substantially on procurement of false criminal charges. "In time, the burden of the writ lay usually in an agreement to procure a false appeal or a false indictment of a felony," but trespass was covered as well.[125] Winfield and Holdsworth attributed this narrowing of the scope to the 1305 Ordinance's definition of conspirators.[126]

Conspiracy by its nature involved multiple persons. In 1321 London Eyre, Stanton, chief justice of the Eyre, said, "Note that fewer than two cannot conspire or organize conspiracy."[127] But the civil action of conspiracy did not require two or more defendants. The 1293 writ permitted an action against one defendant and an agreement between two or more persons was not specifically alleged.[128] By the second decade of the fourteenth century, it was less clear that that was true, and perhaps an agreement to conspire needed to be alleged and at least two or more persons had to be sued.

As the presentments and indictments in the eyres and trailbaston sessions show, the nature of the criminal offense of conspiracy remained

---

Edw. II, fol. 81, pl. 27, Seipp No. 1310.111ss; F.W. Maitland, ed., *Yearbooks of Edward II*, 27 vols., vol. III, 20 Selden Society, pp. 194–97 (1905); ibid., William Boland, ed., vol. XI, 31 Selden Society, pp. 42–46 (1915) (longer version).

[125] Sayles, "Conspiracy and Allied Offenses," p. lxiii. A 1609 treatise limited its discussion to the procurement of criminal charges. "A Writ of Conspiracy," *De Pace Regis et Regni* (London, 1609; reprint, 2007), pp. 245–48.

[126] Holdsworth, *The History of English Law*, vol. III, pp. 404–7. Winfield also included the moving and maintenance of false pleas as the most common actions subsequent to this definition. Winfield, *The History of Conspiracy*, pp. 52–54.

[127] He said further that "a man ought not to be called a conspirator (when acting) in his own cause." Cam, ed., "The Eyre of London," vol. II, 86 Selden Soc., (London, 1969), p. 357. Although this note is included after a civil conspiracy action, it is not clear whether his comment was limited to such actions. Holdsworth said that the later writs describing the alleged conspiracy "always supposed at least two defendants." Holdsworth, *The History of English Law*, III, p. 404. A 1609 treatise also stated the conspiracy required two or more persons as did one written in 1873. "A Writ of Conspiracy," *De Pace Regis et Regni*, p. 245; R.S. Wright, *The Law of Criminal Conspiracies and Agreements* (London, 1873), p. 20.

[128] Sayles stated that "this suggests the emphatic feature of the action was the question of damages rather than the act of conspiring and noted an action against three defendants in which the jury acquitted two of them and convicted the third." Sayles, "Conspiracy and Allied Offenses," pp. lxii–lxiii. Winfield said that the writ was good against one person until the 1305 Ordinance of Conspirators. Winfield, *The History of Conspiracy*, p. 60.

murky. The chapter in the Articles of the Eyre, the comparable trailbaston article, and the definition of conspirators in the 1305 Ordinance all expressly contemplated multiple conspirators, as was inherent in the nature of conspiracy. In her discussion of the 1321 London Eyre, Cam said the eyre chapter, *de confederatoribus et conspiratoribus*, defined the essence of conspiracy as "the sworn association of two or more persons ... to manipulate or defeat justice, but also for other purposes ..."[129] Although many of the criminal cases during this period were directed at defendants who were bound by mutual oaths, tied together, or conspiring with one or more other persons, there were numerous charges of conspiracy against single defendants. There were nine such presentments in the 1293 Yorkshire Eyre, seven in the 1304–05 Shropshire Trailbaston session, ten in the 1304–06 Hereford Trailbaston session, and twenty in the 1305–07 Staffordshire Trailbaston session. In some of these actions, the defendant was simply accused of being a "conspirator" or "common conspirator." In the Yorkshire Eyre, the jurors presented that "Master William de Towthorpe is a common conspirator," with no indication of what his conduct had been.[130] Moreover, the presentments distinguished between single and multiple conspirators. In the Yorkshire Eyre, one presentment charged eighteen men with conspiracy, of which eight were charged as single conspirators and ten as conspirators bound together.[131] In addition, although a number of those presented in this eyre were charged with conspiracy and maintenance of false pleas, a few were found guilty of the latter charge, but not of conspiracy.[132] Thus, although conspiracy by definition involved two or more persons, it was common practice to accuse a single person or for a jury to convict only one person although multiple individuals had been charged as conspirators. But neither the 1313–14 Kent Eyre nor the 1321 London Eyre appears to have produced presentments against single conspirators. Perhaps by that time, conspiracy required two defendants in criminal actions, as it apparently did then in civil actions, or at least, it was becoming more common to charge multiple persons.

---

[129] She said that words *convenciones* and *juramenta illicita* in the king's writ to justices manifested the requirement of multiple persons. As examples of "other purposes," she said they included conduct that "concern[ed] the eyre justices" and listed manipulating the election of City officials and fixing prices as examples. Cam, "The Eyre of London," vol. I, 85 Selden Soc., pp. cxii–cxiii.

[130] TNA: PRO JUST 1/1095, m. 1, AALT Img. No. 6559.

[131] TNA: PRO JUST 1/1095, m. 1d, AALT Img. No. 6564.

[132] TNA: PRO JUST 1/1095, m. 2d, AALT Img. No. 6567.

These actions against single conspirators also shed light on the nature of the conduct that constituted conspiracy. In nine presentments in the 1304–05 Shropshire and 1304–06 Hereford trailbaston sessions, the conspiracy consisted of individual ambidexterity. An indictment in the Shropshire proceedings charged that "Robert de Buckenhale is a conspirator because he took one mark" from a woman to be of counsel to her in a plea and afterward abandoned her and took 40s from her adversary and was with him in the action.[133] Several other indictments in both sessions used the same language. Other presentments seemed to suggest that conspiracy might also have consisted of one individual maintaining false pleas.[134] In the Yorkshire Eyre, the jurors presented fourteen men as single conspirators who also "maintained false pleas" and were false assize jurors "taking from all parties"; one of them was also a champertor.[135] Thus, it seems clear that as late as the early fourteenth century, a single individual who was an ambidexter could be charged as a conspirator and perhaps also if he were a maintainer of false pleas. More generally, the accusation of many defendants for the multiple charges of conspiracy, maintenance, and ambidexterity showed the continuing interrelationship between these offenses and that they were still evolving into distinct, separate legal notions of abusive conduct.

[133] TNA: PRO JUST 1/744, m. 5d, AALT Img. No. 2376.
[134] "Maintaining," "maintenance," or a "maintainer" of false pleas are common phrases in the presentments during this period. It seems likely that it means that the defendant is knowingly supporting a claim lacking merit. When the defendant is a lawyer, it probably means that he is engaging in his role as a professional representative. When the defendant is not a lawyer, maintenance would mean that his conduct is the type of support prohibited by statute.
[135] TNA: PRO JUST 1/1095, m. 1d, AALT Img. No. 6564.

5

Efforts to Deal with Corruption of Justice
in the Reign of Edward III

Statutes Directed at Legal Abuse

Maintenance continued to be a problem as the fourteenth century progressed. Despite the substantial legislative activity regarding conspiracy, maintenance, and champerty during the reign of Edward I, further provisions were enacted during the reign of Edward III. Many of these statutes were a product of the Commons' petitions.[1] In his first parliament in January 1327, the turmoil of Edward II's reign and his deposition produced numerous complaints.[2] The conduct of the Despensers was fresh in the minds of many persons. The opposition to Queen Isabella and Sir Roger Mortimer compounded the unrest. A number of petitions presented to the January 1327 session reflected these concerns and grievances.[3] Complainants viewed the activities of the men, who surrounded and advised the king, as particularly problematic and also expressed concern about the conduct of magnates who misused the law to pursue their self-interest.[4] The petitions sought a new and different regime.[5]

---

[1] Richardson and Sayles pointed that the parliaments of Edward III were different from the earlier ones because of the development of the commons' petition and its role in producing legislation. H.G. Richardson and G.O. Sayles, "Parliaments and Great Councils in Medieval England – I," *Law Quarterly Review* 77 (1961), pp. 227–28. Many of these petitions were enrolled in the parliamentary rolls. There were also four individual petitions enrolled, one of which was actually put forth by the Commons on behalf of the individual.

[2] W. Mark Ormrod, *The Reign of Edward III: Crown and Political Society in England 1327–1377* (New Haven, 1990), pp. 97–99.

[3] In Edward III's first parliament, shortly after his coronation, the community of the realm presented forty-two petitions to the king and his council. Edward III Parliaments: January 1327: C 65/1, *PROME*.

[4] Seymour Phillips, "Introduction January 1327," Edward III Parliaments: January 1327, *PROME*; Ormrod, *The Reign of Edward III*, p. 98.

[5] "The items in the commune petition deal with matters of general interest and were clearly intended to make the 1327 parliament a means of cementing the change of regime by settling causes of concern and grievance inherited from the previous reign." Phillips, "Introduction."

As a result, Edward III's initial parliament "was preoccupied with efforts to undo the evils of the previous reign."[6] Among those evils were conspiracy and maintenance. Ormrod asserted that maintenance was by far the most serious problem of Edward II's reign.[7]

Conspiracy and Maintenance

Several parliamentary petitions and statutes confirmed that conspiracy, maintenance, and their interrelationship continued as primary concerns during the reign of Edward III. One of the petitions in the new king's first parliament said:

> Also, the community prays: that suitable and wise men be placed around the king, who will counsel him well, and that they be chosen by the magnates, and that none of them, nor any other great man of the land, nor anyone from the king's household, neither great nor small, nor any official who shall be under the authority of the king, shall maintain by him nor by another person nor by the sending of letters, parties or disputes by which the common right be disturbed. And if it can be found that anyone has done this let it be shown at the next parliament, and let him be dismissed from the king's council. And that the injured party shall recover his damages against him.[8]

The king responded positively, saying that "as regards the petition concerning wise men remaining close to the king, and the maintenance of suits etc., it is agreed that it be done. It pleases the king."[9] As a result, that parliament enacted a statute directed at maintenance.[10] It provided that

> none of the [king's] counsellors, nor any of his household, nor any other of his officers nor any magnate of the land by himself, nor by other, by sending of letters, nor in any manner, nor none other in the realm, small

---

[6] Ormrod, *The Reign of Edward III*, p. 3.

[7] Ibid, p. 98 One of the charges against Hugh Despenser, the Younger, was that he, his father, and Robert Baldock, the chancellor, had compelled men to swear and guarantee to maintain them in false quarrels against all the people without having regard that such confederations were false and traitorous and against the king's statute and the loyalty owed him. Reprinted in G.A. Holmes, "Judgement of the Younger Despenser, 1326," *English Historical Review* 70 (1955), p. 266.

[8] Edward III Parliaments: January 1327, no. 33, *PROME*.   [9] Ibid.

[10] This statute echoed the concerns about royal officials expressed in Edward I's first statute directed at legal corruption. Westminster I, c. 25, 3 Edw. I (1275), *Statutes of the Realm*, vol. 1, p. 33.

nor great, shall undertake to maintain disputes or parties in the country to
the disturbance of the common law.[11]

In addition, in the next parliament, the Statute of Northampton recited
that the king and great men of the realm had taken an oath, *inter alia*, not
to maintain wrongdoers privately or openly.[12] Although the petition
requested punishment of the offender and recovery of damages by the
injured party, the statute provided no remedy, which prompted another
petition two decades later. It said that "no penalty was ordained definitely
in respect of those who act contrary to the said statute," and, thus, it
requested that "a certain penalty should be ordained in this matter
according to the advice of parliament."[13] The response asserted there
already was a penalty ordained for some of the conduct and that for
the other conduct, "a fine and ransom to the king was intended,
according to the degree of the trespass."[14] As to the former conduct,
the answer likely was referring to one or more of the statutes prohibiting
maintenance enacted during the reign of Edward I. As to the latter
conduct, perhaps the crown was suggesting that any statutory violation
could be punished by fine and ransom without the need of explicit
statutory authority. No evidence of either criminal cases or civil actions
based on this statute has been discovered nor have any writs based on it
been found in the registers. These petitions prompted an eyre in the
following year. At opening day of the 1329–30 Eyre of Northamptonshire, Chief Justice Scrope explained that the eyre was being held
because of complaints in the 1328 Northampton parliament about
the suffering caused by the "manifold oppressions of the magnates and
from the extortions of the maintainers," other wrongdoing, and the

---

[11] I Edw. III, st. 2, c. 14 (1327), *Statutes of the Realm*, vol. 1, p. 256. Another provision of the
same statute prohibited maintainors of evil or barretors from serving as keepers of the
peace. Ibid., c. 16, pp. 256–57.

[12] 2 Edw. III, c. 7 (1328), *Statutes of the Realm*, vol. 1, p. 259. A 1366 statute ordered the
imprisonment of maintainers of felons and other wrongdoers. 10 Edw. III, st. 2, c. 3,
Statutes of the Realm, vol. 1, p. 277.

[13] "Also, because there was a statute made in the first year of the present king, in which it is
contained that none of the king's councillors nor any of his other officers shall maintain
pleas or disputes that are pending in the king's court or elsewhere within the realm, in
which statute no penalty was ordained definitely with respect to those who act contrary to
the said statute. Wherefore the said community prays that a certain penalty should be
ordained in this matter according to the advice of the parliament." Edward III Parliaments: January 1348, no. 14, *PROME*.

[14] Ibid.

failure to keep the peace. He ordered the gathered magnates, "the leading men of the country," not to support any "maintainers of false suits" or "persons of evil reputation."[15]

The next year parliament visited the subjects of maintenance and conspiracy again. A 1330 statute granted authority to royal and assize justices to inquire, hear, and determine at the suit of the king or an injured party complaints regarding maintainers, embracers of enterprises, conspirators, and champertors.[16] The preamble to this provision underscored the persistent concern with these types of conduct. It stated that

> in times past divers people of the realm, as well great men as other, have made alliances, confederacies, and conspiracies, to maintain parties, pleas, and disputes, whereby divers parties have been wrongfully disinherited; and some ransomed and destroyed; and some, for fear to be maimed and beaten, dare not sue for their right, nor complain, nor the jurors of the inquests give their verdicts, to the great injury to the people, and detriment of the law and of the common right.[17]

As Chapter 6 will show, there were many jury presentments in the reign of Edward III accusing numerous individuals of conspiracy and maintenance. Unlike the maintenance statutes of the earlier reigns, the language of the 1330 statute, "suit of the party," seemed to authorize a civil damage action.[18] Both Winfield and Holdsworth took that position.[19]

---

[15] "The Eyre of Northamptonshire, Opened by Geoffrey Scrope, CJ, on Monday, 6 November 1329," Donald Sutherland, ed., *Eyre of Northampshire, 3–4 Edward III*, 2 vols. (London, 1983), vol. I, 97 Selden Soc., pp. 2, 5–6.

[16] 4 Edw. III, c. 11 (1330), *Statutes of the Realm*, vol. 1, p. 264.

[17] Ibid. Winfield asserted that this statute was enacted to deal with the failure of 28 Edw. I, c. 10, to eliminate conspiracies, confederacies, and maintenance. Winfield, *History of Conspiracy*, p. 96.

[18] It said that "the justices of one bench or of the other, and the justices of assises ... shall enquire, hear, and determine as well as at the king's suit as at the suit of the party of such maintainers, bearers and conspirators, and also of them that commit champerty, and all other things contained in the foresaid Article, as well as justices in eyre should do if they were in the same county." 4 Edw. III, c. 11 (1330), *Statutes of the Realm*, vol. 1, p. 264.

[19] After noting the absence of such a remedy prior to this statute, Winfield said that "an undoubted civil remedy is conferred on persons injured." Ibid., pp. 149–51. He also asserted that the statute would support a writ for conspiracy actions and perhaps for maintenance ones as well. Ibid., pp. 147, 153. Holdsworth said that this statute created "a civil as well as a criminal remedy for the first time." Holdsworth, *History of English Law*, vol. III, p. 397. However, no writ based on the statute was found in the registers that were examined.

But it was quite uncommon for maintenance actions to be based on this statute. None was found during the reign of Edward III, although there were a few in the early fifteenth century.[20]

As in the earlier reigns, multiple legislative attacks were made on these types of legal corruption. In the April 1343 parliament, the chancellor told the prelates, earls, barons, and other great men of the realm that the king, who had recently returned from Brittany, was troubled by his discovery that the law was not being upheld "because of various impediments and maintenances" and sought their counsel and advice "as to how such impediments and wrongful maintenance could best be removed and the law better kept and upheld." The magnates replied that justices should be commissioned "to hear and determine felonies, trespasses, conspiracies, confederacies and evil maintenance." Asked to be more specific, they provided a detailed list of matters, one of which said that inquiry should be made "into all manner of conspiracies, confederacies, champerties, ambidexters, maintainers of wrongdoers and false disputes and of all other corruption in deception of the law."[21]

The conduct of royal justices caused a particular concern because private litigants were retaining them as counsel.[22] In 1346, an ordinance dealing with this problem was enacted and sent to the sheriffs.[23] Its initial

[20] There were two actions in Hilary Term, 6 Hen. IV, and another that year in Easter term. TNA: PRO KB 27/575, m. 2d (1405), AALT Img. No. b194; ibid., m. 53d (1405), AALT Img. No. c32; TNA: PRO KB 27/577, m. 35 (1405), AALT Img. No. 78. But these cases constituted less than 1% of the fifteenth-century civil maintenance actions.

[21] Another item on the list targeted maintenance of wrongdoers. Edward III Parliaments: April 1343, nos. 10, 11, and 12, *PROME*. In the following months, numerous *oyer et terminer* commissions were authorized, but nothing explicitly tied any of them to this petition and many were special ones. *Calendar of Patent Rolls, Edward III, A.D. 1343–45* (London, 1902), pp. 93–100.

[22] J.R. Maddicott, *Law and Lordship: Royal Justices as Retainers in Thirteenth- and Fourteenth-Century England, Past and Present*, Supp. (1978), pp. 4, 13–81. In 1340–41, Edward III undertook an inquiry into the conduct of royal justices. The Common Pleas chief justice and six other justices were dismissed and tried before a special commission. N.M. Frye, "Edward III's Removal of His Ministers and Justices, 1340–1," *Bulletin of the Institute of Historical Research* 48 (1975), p. 157; Maddicott, *Law and Lordship*, pp. 43–44. Further, in 1350, Edward III dismissed William Thorpe CJKB for maintenance. Although sentenced to hang, he was pardoned and subsequently appointed as a baron of the Exchequer. Maddicott, *Law and Lordship*, pp. 48–53. Richard Kaeuper, "Sir William Thorp," *Oxford Dictionary of National Biography Online*; Anthony Musson and W. Mark Ormrod, *The Evolution of English Justice* (Basingstoke, 1999), p. 38.

[23] King said that he had learned from many complaints that the execution of the law had been "disturbed many times by maintenance and procurement." The ordinance said that

provision, the "Ordinance of Justices," required that all royal justices take an oath to do right to all persons and to take no fees, robes, gifts, or rewards from anyone other than the king.[24] Maddicott concluded that this Ordinance was ignored and ineffective.[25] Another chapter prohibited any of the king's household, prelates, earls, barons, or any great or other man to maintain quarrels other than their own "for gift, promise, amity, favour, doubt or fear or any other cause" and required the earls, barons, and great men to insure that the ordinance was kept.[26] It recited the prevalence of "maintainers of disputes and parties in the country," singled out the lords, and noted the harms caused by such "covin, procurement, and maintenance." The statute ordered the exclusion of maintainers from the retinues of the great men and the examination and charging of the maintainers.[27] Finally the statute reiterated the *oyer et terminer* authority of the assize justices regarding maintenance and other abuses of legal procedure and the power to punish guilty parties at both the king's suit and that of the parties.[28]

---

it was ordained "by the assent of the great men and other wise men of our council." It also had numerous provisions directed at maintenance and other abusive conduct. 20 Edw. III, cc. 1–6 (1346), *Statutes of the Realm*, vol. 1, pp. 303–06. This enactment, unlike much of the other Edward III legislation, was not a product of a parliamentary petition. Moreover, it was not enacted when parliament was in session. But it responded to various constituencies and pressures. Maddicott, *Law and Lordship*, pp. 40–48.

[24] The justices were also prohibited from giving counsel to anyone if the king were party to matter. Justices were permitted to take meat and drink if it was of small value and their fees were increased. Ibid., c. 1, pp. 303–06 (Oath of the Justices). The barons of the Exchequer were also ordered to do right to all persons, and those assigned as *oyer et terminer* and assize justices were also required to take an oath. *Statutes of the Realm*, vol. 1, cc. 2, 3, p. 304. The oath had been drafted with the advice of "prelates, earls, barons, magnates, and *proceres*." Maddicott, *Law and Lordship*, p. 42. The community of the realm subsequently expressed their gratitude for the imposition of the oath to show no favor and to observe the king's laws and for impartial judging and justice. They also requested that any of the royal officials who had not yet taken the oath should do so. The king answered that he would consider which other officials should be sworn and would "ordain what will be best to do." Edward III Parliaments: January 1348, no. 7, *PROME*.

[25] Maddicott, *Law and Lordship*, pp. 48–59.   [26] *Statutes of the Realm*, vol. 1, c. 4, p. 304.

[27] Ibid., c. 5, pp. 304–05. The preamble associated this conduct with the magnates' retaining of such wrongdoers by fees and robes, which may have been the first statutory link between maintenance and livery.

[28] It further charged the chancellor and treasurer to hear all complaints and "to ordain that speedy remedy be thereof made." Ibid., c. 6, p. 305. Winfield said that "this comprehensive prohibition of maintenance," providing "both criminal and civil remedies," was "little more than a dead letter" due to "the invertebrate administration of the law." Winfield, *History of Conspiracy*, p. 151.

Apparently the Commons was not satisfied, for despite the enactment of this statute, it petitioned the next year for the enactment of another ordinance against maintenance. It requested that

> it should be prohibited on a certain penalty that no magnate of the land, or other, should maintain or give support to traitors, felons, robbers, trespassers against the peace, barrators, maintainers of disputes and strife, embracers of legal actions, conspirators, confederators, champertors or other such men, by whose fraud and false deceit the peace is troubled and disturbed everywhere, and the laws hindered and nearly destroyed.[29]

In response, the king said that he "will consult the great men, and propound this article to them, and having had their advice he will ordain such remedy as will please God and man."[30] But no further maintenance statute was enacted.[31] The Commons persisted, complaining again in the next parliament about maintenance of felons by the great men of the country and requesting that commissions of *oyer et terminer* be ordained for this.[32] The king said that this matter had been answered in the last parliament.[33]

Concern, however, about maintenance continued. It was cited as one of the reasons for summoning parliaments in February 1351 and January 1352. In the former session, the king was again troubled that "the peace of the realm was not as well kept as it should be" and that "maintenance of parties" was one of the causes. He encouraged his subjects to complain to obtain redress.[34] In the latter session, the king expressed his concern about keeping the peace and upholding the law, citing "maintenance of disputes" as a reason.[35] Another petition in that parliament

---

[29] Edward III Parliaments: January 1348, no. 6, *PROME*.   [30] Ibid., no. 7, *PROME*.

[31] However, as discussed above, another petition in that parliament requested that a penalty be supplied for violation of the maintenance statute enacted in Edward III's first parliament in January 1327, and the king responded that for some of the conduct a remedy already existed and he provided a remedy where none existed. Edward III Parliaments: January 1348, no. 14, *PROME*.

[32] Ibid., no. 6, *PROME*.

[33] Ibid. In that parliament, two petitions objected to the pardoning of felons and their maintainers, and the king said such charters would be issued only when it was honorable and profitable. Ibid., nos. 53, 62, *PROME*. Despite this repeated concern with maintenance by magnates, it did not reappear during the next two decades. Ormrod, *The Reign of Edward III*, p. 112.

[34] Edward III Parliaments: February 1351, no. 4, *PROME*. The Commons also requested enforcement of the statutes regarding maintenance of wrongdoers and disturbers of the peace, and the king agreed that it should be done. Ibid., no. 15, *PROME*.

[35] In addition, the failure to execute judgments of the courts properly was attributed to maintenance and favor. Edward III Parliaments: January 1352, no. 7, *PROME*.

recommended a new system for appointing and using justices of the peace. The complaint was that they had not properly executed the law "because they have not had the opportunity on account of the great maintenance to their office."[36] Petitions in both Edward III's 1327 initial parliament and his penultimate parliament, the 1376 "Good Parliament," again expressed concern about justices of the peace and maintenance. The earlier petition requested that "good and loyal men be assigned" and that they "not be maintainers of false litigation."[37] The latter petition said that justices are "often assigned by the procurement (*brocage*) of maintainers of the country who do great damage by their maintenance to the poor people of the country, and are commonly maintainers of wrongdoers." It requested that the justices should be appointed by the lords and knights of the shire, sworn before the king's council like others, and paid suitably.[38]

There were also complaints about the impact of maintenance on parliamentary elections. The writs summoning parliament in 1351–1355 stated that those elected must not be "persistent litigators, maintainers of plaints or persons living by that sort of trade."[39] Similarly, in the 1376 "Good Parliament" concern was expressed about influence

---

[36] The answer was that he would assign suitable justices and deploy them where it was most necessary. Ibid., no. 13, *PROME*.

[37] Parliaments of Edward III: January 1327, no. 40, *PROME*.

[38] The king said that the justices would be named by the king and his council and that he would be advised as to wages. Edward III Parliaments: April 1376, no. 67, *PROME*. The Commons also petitioned regarding false claims by religious officials. The petition said that abbots, priors, and other religious people made claims without right or title or other false assertions tried by inquests. But as a result of their favors, bribes, and promises made to sheriffs and maintainers of quarrels, the inquests are impaneled by the sheriffs at the will of those taking favor and the jurors "are wickedly informed by their maintainers," so that the inquests pass falsely. The Commons requested that a writ of *jus quale* be available to ascertain the existence of the right and to prevent collusion and evasion of the Statute of Mortmain. Parliaments of Edward III: April 1376, no. 192, CXXXIIII, *PROME*.

[39] The writs said that the men to be elected "must not be '*placitatores querelarum manutentores aut ex huiusmodi questi viventenes.*'" Herman Cohen, *A History of the English Bar and Attornatus to 1450* (London, 1929), p. 458. K.L. Wood-Legh, "Sheriffs, Lawyers, and Belted Knights in the Parliaments of Edward III," *English Historical Review* 46 (1931), p. 377; J.R. Maddicott, "Parliament and the Constituencies 1272–1377," in R.G. Davies and J.H. Denton, eds., *The English Parliament in the Middle Ages* (Manchester, 1981), p. 77. This concern was not new, as the king's writ to the sheriff of Lancaster for the November 1330 parliament directed the selection of "two of the most loyal and sufficient knights and serjeants ... who not be suspected of evil covin, nor common maintenours of parties (*qui soient mie suspicionous de male coveigne, ne communes meintenours des parties*)." William Stubbs, *The Constitutional History of England*, 5th ed., 3 vols. (New York, 1967), vol. III, p. 411; Maddicott, "Parliament and the Constituencies," p. 77; Cohen, *History of the Bar*, p. 467.

of maintenance on the elections of the knights of the shire and the sheriffs.[40] Finally, in the king's last parliament, the Commons repeated, yet again, its concern about maintenance by royal officials, singling out this time those of the Exchequer. They requested that any "great officer in the king's exchequer who maintained a dispute should lose his office and pay double damages to any aggrieved party."[41]

Despite all these Commons' complaints about maintenance, no new provisions regarding maintenance, except for one rather odd exception, were enacted after the 1346 statute.[42] Overall, parliament adopted only a few statutes dealing with maintenance during the reign of Edward III. These measures did not seem to have a significant impact on litigation directed at maintenance. What may have been the most important legislation was the explicit grant of *oyer et terminer* authority to the royal justices and commissions.[43]

Other Forms of Abuse of Legal Procedure

Although conspiracy and maintenance were the prime subjects of legislative attention in the reign of Edward III, they were not the only ones. Concern with false appeals and indictments, which was first manifested

---

[40] As to the knights, the Commons requested that they be chosen by common election and not by sheriffs and the sheriffs chosen in the same manner and not appointed by bribery or "by the procurement of the maintainers of the region, to sustain their deceits and evils and their false quarrels" as was common in the past. The king responded that existing statutes and ordinances ought be observed and upheld. Parliaments of Edward III: April 1376, no. 186, CXXVIII, *PROME*.

[41] The petition said that these remedies were necessary because "the sheriffs were so much in their power that they dared not to act against them in such disputes." The petition also requested that the same penalty be ordained for all other royal officers. The king answered that he would forbid his officials from doing this as had been done previously and that justice would be done to anyone who felt aggrieved and complained individually. Edward III Parliaments: January 1377, no. 42, *PROME*. Although several existing statutes would have prohibited maintenance by Exchequer officials, these specific penalties would have been new. But it would seem that the king could have removed officials who violated a statute without explicit authorization.

[42] The antipathy toward the notorious Alice Perrers provoked the exception. An ordinance issued in the April 1376 parliament forbade any woman from maintaining, bribing, or influencing parties in matters in the king's courts because of a complaint about women pursuing business and disputes in such courts. Although the ordinance forbade any woman from such conduct, it said, "and specifically Alice Perrers, on penalty of whatever the said Alice can forfeit and of being banished from the realm." "Alice Perrers," Edward III Parliaments: April 1376, no. 45, *PROME*; George Holmes, *The Good Parliament* (Oxford, 1975), pp. 136–37.

[43] Mark Ormrod, *Edward III* (New Haven, 2011), pp. 73, 269.

during the reign of Edward I and a prime target of the writ of conspiracy, appeared again. In the first parliament of the reign, a statute was enacted directing royal justices and commissions to inquire of sheriffs, jailers, and keepers of prisons "who have by punishment of prison and by other evil means compelled and procured [prisoners] to become appealors and appeal people who are not guilty" for the purpose of extracting fines from them.[44] A later statute added death as a punishment for keepers of the jails and their deputies who "by very great constraint of imprisonment and by punishment make any prisoner who is in his custody become an appellor against his will."[45]

The final form of this type of wrongdoing that attracted attention during this reign was juror misconduct. The most common form was "the actual or attempted corrupt or forcible influencing of jurors," which contemporaries called embracery.[46] In the criminal presentments of jurors for taking money from litigants to say their verdicts and others for giving such bribes discussed in Chapter 4, that conduct was treated as a form of conspiracy or maintenance. The conduct of jurors who took money from both sides as ambidexters was regarded similarly. However, during the reign of Edward III, embracery emerged as a separate and distinct offense.[47]

Four statutes were enacted to deal with jury bribery. Early in the reign, a statute focused on the offending jurors. It provided that a person on a jury, assize, or inquest who took from one party or the other should be attainted and precluded from being a juror in the future, imprisoned, and ransomed at the king's will.[48] Fifteen years later, embracery was also

---

[44] The statute authorized the justices to hear and determine complaints at the suit of the king and the aggrieved party. 1 Edw. III, stat. 1, c. 7 (1327), *Statutes of the Realm*, vol. 1, pp. 253–54.

[45] The statute put the jails back in the custody of the sheriffs and authorized them to install keepers, for whose conduct they were responsible. 14 Edw. III, stat. 1, c. 10 (1340), *Statutes of the Realm*, vol. 1, p. 284.

[46] Winfield, *History of Conspiracy*, p. 161. Fitzherbert defined an embraceor as "he who cometh to the bar with the party, and taketh in the cause, or standeth there to survey the jury, or to put them in fear." Anthony Fitzhberbert, *The New Natura Brevium*, 9th ed. (Dublin, 1793), fol. 171, p. 397.

[47] Winfield noted the close relationship between embracery and conspiracy, maintenance, and champerty. Winfield, *History of Conspiracy*, p. 162. Holdsworth said that embracery and maintenance were similar, but "clearly distinct." Holdsworth, *The History of English Law*, vol. III, p. 399.

[48] The justices before whom the bribery had occurred were given the power to inquire and determine the matter. 5 Edw. III, c. 10 (1331), *Statutes of the Realm*, vol. 1, p. 267. In 1334, the Commons requested that the king ordain regarding false jurors. The response

targeted as part of a statute directed at maintenance and bribery of justices. Assize justices were authorized to inquire into the "gifts, rewards, and other profits" that officials took for putting "suspect jurors and of evil fame" on the panels of array and into the "maintainors, embraceors, and jurors taking gifts and rewards of the parties."[49] Several years later, another statute directed at jury bribery created incentives for private actions. It provided for private parties to sue any juror who had taken money from either him or his adversary and recover his damages. It also authorized nonparties to sue and recover half of any fine imposed on a guilty juror.[50] Only a few years later, another statute adding stronger penalties to the prior statute was adopted.[51] The statute required jurors who were found guilty of taking anything from either party to say their verdict to pay ten times as much as they had taken. To enforce the statute, a party for himself or the king or any other person could sue a writ of *decies tantum*,[52] with half of the fine paid to the plaintiff and other half to the king.[53] The statute also provided the same penalty for "embraceors that bring or procure such inquests in the country to take gain or profit."[54] Unlike most of the statutes regarding legal corruption

---

authorized the justices of both Benches, assize justices, and those assigned to the county court to hear and determine such matters at the suit of the king or other persons without the need for a special commission. Parliaments of Edward III: February 1334, no. 6, *PROME*.

[49] The guilty were to be punished "according to law and reason at the king's suit or that of the parties." The chancellor and treasurer were ordered to hear complaints and the provisions were to be published to facilitate aggrieved parties seeking a remedy. 20 Edw. III, c. 6 (1346), *Statutes of the Realm*, vol. 1, p. 305. In the following year, the Commons petitioned again for a statute that included embraceors among its many targets, but no legislation resulted. Edward III Parliaments: January 1348, no. 6, *PROME*.

[50] Guilty jurors were to be imprisoned for a year and not subject to a pardon in exchange for a fine. 34 Edw. III, c. 8 (1360–61), *Statutes of the Realm*, vol. 1, p. 366.

[51] This statute explicitly was "assented and joined" to the prior statute and guilt was determined "by the process contained in the same Article." 38 Edw. III, st. 1, c. 12 (1363–64), *Statutes of the Realm*, vol. 1, pp. 384–85.

[52] The fifteenth-century registers contain a number of these writs. Cambridge University Library, MS Additional 6854, fol. 167r. A fourteenth-century register table of contents erroneously identified a writ as one of *decies tantum*, but it was actually based on 5 Edw. III, c. 10 (1331). British Library, MS Harley 1118, fol. 116v.

[53] The statute prohibited any justice or official from inquiring into violations of the statute and specifically limited enforcement to a suit by a party or other person. 38 Edw. III, st. 1, c. 12 (1363–64), *Statutes of the Realm*, vol. 1, pp. 384–85.

[54] If a juror or embraceor were unable to pay ten times the amount taken, the punishment was a year in prison. Ibid.

passed during this reign, this statute produced substantial litigation, which began soon and continued throughout the fourteenth and fifteenth centuries.[55]

Individual Petitions to the King and His Council

Petitioning about legal corruption continued during the reign of Edward III.[56] Aggrieved parties again complained about being victims of the maintenance, abuse of power, and other wrongdoing of powerful officials and individuals.[57] Almost all of the petitions (89%) either revealed the status or office of the target or has been ascertained from extrinsic sources.[58] As in the early period, the great majority of the targets were powerful persons. As Table 5.1 shows, they included high royal officials such as the chancellor, treasurer, and justices; the nobility; knights; local officials such as sheriffs and coroners; and senior clerics such as bishops and abbots.[59] The nobility and knights accounted for two-thirds of the petitions' targets.

Almost two-thirds of the petitioners' status or position was revealed or otherwise determined. As in the earlier period, various types of clergy or religious persons such as abbots, deans, chaplains, and parsons were the most frequent complainants. Others included the nobility,[60] knights and their widows, royal officials, and merchants.[61] Some, but not all, were

---

[55]   TNA: PRO KB 27/422, m. 35 (1366), AALT Img. No. 73 (earliest one found). There were about twenty such actions during the remainder of the Edward III's reign.

[56]   Seventy-two of these individual petitions were found in the SC 8s. In addition, there were twenty-three such petitions enrolled on the rolls of parliament. Two of the petitions in the SC 8s were also enrolled.

[57]   The most common complaints were about maintenance (36) and power (29). Others targeted corruption and procurement (13), lordship (8), conspiracy (6), and champerty (2). A number of the complaints used more than one of these terms. Complaints about maintenance often referred to power, conspiracy, or procurement as well. Similarly, complaints about power were frequently coupled with maintenance, lordship, and procurement.

[58]   Some petitions were directed at multiple persons. One complained about thirty-two individuals. TNA: PRO SC 8/13/607 (1348).

[59]   Some of the targets were generic, such as "great men" or the petitioner's adversaries. TNA: PRO SC 8/54/2681 (1327); TNA: PRO SC 8/47/2308 (1327); TNA: PRO SC 8/88/4380 (1342?).

[60]   One of those was Edward III's son, Edmund of Langley.

[61]   There were also complaints that the "great men of the land" maintained thieves and robbers when instead they "should help arrest and capture such evil people." Parliaments of Edward III: March 1348, no. 6, *PROME*.

Table 5.1 *Petitions to the king and his council: Nature of the targets*

Nobility	37%
Knights	30%
Clerical officials	24%
Royal officials	11%
Sheriffs and local officials	10%

Table 5.2 *Petitions to the king and his council: Nature of the individual complainants*

Clergy or religions persons	34%
Nobility	13%
Royal officials	11%
Knights and their widows	6%
Other widows	6%
Others	13%

likely powerful individuals. There were also several petitions by groups of people or communities of cities or towns (17%). Table 5.2 reveals the nature of the petitioners.

The gist of most of the complaints was that the target's wrongdoing prevented or impeded the complainant's ability to exercise his or her legal rights or obtain justice. When the complaint was about maintenance, that word seemed to have been used most often in its broader social sense, which included various types of wrongdoing rather than in its narrower legal sense, which was limited to supporting another's plea.[62] Several petitions used it in the latter sense, complaining about maintainers of false litigation or quarrels.[63] As might be expected, by far

---

[62] The two petitions complaining about champerty were related and both referred to the champerty statute. Roger Dautre, who may have been the king's serjeant-at-arms, complained against Lord Neville, likely John Neville, Third Baron Neville de Raby, royal official and Knight of the Garter. TNA: PRO SC 8/41/2049 (1372); SC 8/169/8427 (1372).

[63] Parliaments of Edward III: January 1327, no. 40, *PROME*; Parliaments of Edward III: February 1334, no. 6, *PROME*. In his response, the king said to request all the archbishops and bishops that "every Sunday in every parish church they shall pronounce sentence on

the greatest number of complaints involved rights in land (46%). For example, John Scot complained that Ralph Weedon, knight, and four other men by their conspiracy and false plotting sued John, and by their false testimony and process, John lost his land. But he was unable to undertake an action because of the "great maintenance" that Ralph had from "the great men at court, namely from Sir Hugh le Despenser and Master Robert Baldock, the chancellor, to whom he was an adherent."[64] In another petition, Oliver, Lord Ingham, requested that he be restored to two manors that he was forced to lease to Walter Stapledon, bishop of Exeter, and Richard Stapledon, knight, by the "mastery and great power" of Walter.[65] Most of the remaining petitions were divided equally between those regarding the complainants' goods and money and those involving their legal actions (15% each). In one petition, William of Ownby, chaplain, complained that six people took and imprisoned him and took his chattels. Although he purchased a writ against them, he did not dare to sue them because of the maintenance of the abbot of Ramsey and because of the letters that the abbot sent to the king's justices and to other great lords.[66] In another one, John of Monmouth, defendant in an assize of novel disseisin that passed against him, brought a writ of error before Sir Henry Scrope CJKB and his fellow justices. He complained that because of the procurement and maintenance of Sir Robert Wodehouse, former treasurer of England, who "was sitting in the Bench with Sir Henry," Scrope delayed in acting for over two years and then ruled against John, as advised by Wodehouse, "contrary to law and right."[67]

---

felons, maintainers of felons, conspirators, false jurors, and disturbers of the peace and their maintainers, and the maintainers and instigators of false quarrels" and that the sentence be pronounced also. Ibid.

[64] He also complained that his livestock were seized and that he was imprisoned until he made a release to Ralph of all the rights he had (manuscript damaged here). The response was that he should sue at common law. TNA: PRO SC 8/71/3536 (1327).

[65] He said that he had not been able to sue as he was sent to Gascony soon afterward. The response was to sue at common law. TNA: PRO SC 8/159/7942 (1327). Oliver, who was a house knight of Edward II, was the steward of Aquitaine. He held several other royal offices and fought in the Hundred Years War and was an advisor to the earl of Kent, Edward II's half-brother and his lieutenant in Aquitaine. Malcolm Vale, "Oliver Ingham," *Oxford Dictionary of National Biography Online.*

[66] He requested a commission of justices, who were not of the abbot's affinity. TNA: PRO SC 8/194/9692 (1332). Although there was no response, a commission of *oyer et terminer* was granted. *Calendar of Patent Rolls, Edward III, A.D. 1330–1334* (London, 1893), p. 351.

[67] The petition also stated that Wodehouse "undertook at his peril to save Sir Henry without damages." TNA: PRO SC 8/61/3021 (1332). This event likely occurred when

Most of the petitions prompted a response (81%).[68] The majority of them told the petitioners to sue at common law or to obtain a writ or take other action in Chancery (70%). These responses do not necessarily imply that the council believed that the petitions had merit. Nor is it clear that legal remedies for these petitioners were available. But the responses may have engendered good will for the crown by appearing to indicate its sensitivity to the plight of the complainants.

Although there were numerous petitions to the king and his council in this period, there were fewer than in the earlier period.[69] In addition the volume of petitioning relative to the volume of litigation regarding abuse of legal procedure declined in comparison with that during the reigns of Edward I and II.[70] The turmoil of the reign of Edward II and its aftermath likely influenced the timing and volume of these complaints.[71] Over 60% occurred in the first decade of the reign, with 80% of those during the first three years and many in the first year.[72] In addition,

Scrope was chief justice of the King's Bench, October 28, 1329, to December 19, 1330. Sir John Sainty, *The Judges of England 1272–1990* (London, 1993), p. 7. Wodehouse was treasurer of England, September 16, 1329, to November 30, 1330, and March 10 to December 30, 1338. From December 17, 1330, to October 16, 1331, he was chancellor of the Exchequer. J.L. Kirby, "Robert Wodehouse," *Oxford Dictionary of National Biography Online*. The petition stated that Wodehouse sat with Scrope during the most recent quindene of Michaelmas, which would have been October 13–19, 1330, given the dates of their offices.

[68] Three responses were illegible and another was on an attached schedule that was not included with the petition.

[69] Gwilym Dodd, *Justice and Grace* (Oxford, 2007), pp. 115–55. Dodd said that "far reaching changes to the place of private petitioning in parliament" occurred in the fourteenth century, as it ceased to have "the same priority in parliament" that it had under his predecessors. Ibid., pp. 108–16, 124.

[70] During the reign of Edward III, there were seventy-two petitions regarding abuse of legal procedure and 561 actions and cases regarding that type of conduct. During the reigns of Edward I and II, there were 81 such petitions and 298 actions and cases.

[71] The problems did not end with the deposition of Edward II and the ascent to the throne by Edward III in 1327. Roger Mortimer continued as a powerful and leading force and perhaps the de facto ruler, as did Queen Isabella. During the "informal regency" of the young king, Edward III struggled to take control of the country from them. In 1330, Edward III defeated Mortimer, who was executed. At that point, Edward III, now seventeen with a pregnant wife, emerged in control and full enjoyment of his royal powers. Ormrod, "Tutelage, 1327–1330," *Edward III*, pp. 55–89.

[72] The distribution of the petitions was as follows: 1327–36: 45; 1337–46: 8; 1347–56: 8; 1357–66: 3; and 1367–77: 8. The dating of the petitions is often difficult and is approximate as they often do not reveal their dates. Harris has analyzed all of the private petitions in this period of crisis. Simon Harris, "Taking Your Chances: Petitioning in the Last Years of Edward II and the First Years of Edward III," in W.M. Ormrod, Gwilym Dodd, and Anthony Musson, eds., *Medieval Petitions: Grace and Grievance* (York, 2009), pp. 173–92. He found that a significant number (38.5%) related to the baronial revolt

many of the complaints in that decade involved the leading figures in this disorder. They frequently targeted one or both of the Despensers (44%),[73] Roger Mortimer, the earl of March and Queen Isabella's companion, and Walter Stapledon, bishop of Exeter and treasurer of England.[74] Ormrod noted that among the most pressing business facing the young king and his council were the "huge numbers of private petitions" that required resolution and the forty-two Commons' petitions at the top of the agenda.[75] This new political environment increased the likelihood that the new king and his council would be sympathetic to petitioners' plight and perhaps more amenable to granting some relief.[76] In addition to the surge in the first three years of the reign, there were a significant number of petitions at the end of Edward III's reign. The turmoil and political strife in this period likely accounted for large volume then.[77] The chronology and context of petitioning during the reign of Edward III may indicate that it played a diminished role in dealing with legal corruption.

and its aftermath. He also found that petitions between 1322 and 1326 produced a more positive response than those from 1327 to 1330. Finally, he said that "a complex series of motives that encompassed opportunism, malice, spite, and retribution" likely induced the petitions. Ibid., pp. 184–91.

[73] Harris found that 23% of all the petitions were directly related to the Despensers and that 64% of those involved extortion by them and their associates. Ibid., p. 192.

[74] All of the complaints against these individuals occurred in the first decade of the reign.

[75] He said that the private petitions "flooded in from the farthest corners of the realm, recounting the unscrupulous activities of the Despenser regime and expressing high hopes that the new king would redress the wrongs thus sustained." Ormrod, *Edward III*, pp. 58–60.

[76] In discussing private petitions, Ormrod stated that "this public campaign of vindication was an important opportunity to express committment to the new regime," and he said that the Commons' petitions "marked a defining moment in the evolution of the 'community of the realm' away from a sworn league of barons and toward the representative element in the parliament, the commons." Ibid., pp. 59–60.

[77] About 10% of the petitions in the SC 8s were presented in the final five years of Edward III's reign. But 35% of the enrolled petitions were in the penultimate parliament, the 1376 "Good Parliament." Two of those were individual petitions, one by the prior of Ecclesfield, presented by the Commons on his behalf, complaining that he had been ousted from his church by Sir Henry Melbourne, clerk of William, Lord Latimer, and another by Henry le Despenser complaining that he had been disseised of the advowson of the archdeaconry of Norwich "by the great maintenance of some intimates close to the king." Parliaments of Edward III: April 1376, no. 46, *PROME*; ibid., no. 48. Both Lord Latimer and Richard Lyons were impeached in that parliament for financial wrongdoing and corruption and the proceedings regarding Lyons referred to champerty and maintenance. Parliaments of Edward III: April 1376, nos. 17–30, *PROME*.

6

Criminal and Civil Litigation in the Reign of Edward III

In this period, legal corruption prompted a substantial volume of criminal presentments and civil actions. As Figure 6.1 indicates, this type of litigation was heaviest at the beginning of the reign and, with the exception of one early period, slowly declined over the lengthy period of the reign. The turmoil during the reign of Edward II, his deposition, and its aftermath likely accounted for the large number of cases in the first years of Edward III's reign.[1] The lull of 1337–45 is perplexing, perhaps resulting from an intensive, troublesome period in the wars. The increase in 1347–56 may have been due to the 1346 legislation, the Ordinance of the Justices, and parliamentary concerns in 1348.[2] The drop in cases in the last decade of the reign may have occurred because the King's Bench stayed at Westminster for eighteen of the twenty terms in the last five years of the reign.[3] As in the reigns of Edward I and II, the bulk of this type of litigation in this reign involved conspiracy, maintenance, champerty, and ambidexterity.[4] Conspiracy cases were the most common,

---

[1] The eyres during this period impacted the volume of litigation and reflected this disorder. Further evidence of latter was the substantial number of special commissions of *oyet et terminer*, which peaked in 1327. This volume may represent not only legitimate investigations of wrongdoing but the misuse of the commissions as an abuse of legal procedure, as the involvement of the Despensers suggests. "The two Despensers ... were probably the masters in malicious prosecution through oyer and terminer." Richard Kaeuper, "Law and Order in Fourteenth-Century England: The Evidence of Special Commissions of Oyer and Terminer," *Speculum* 54 (1979), pp. 741, 745–46, 778.

[2] Gratitude is expressed to Prof. Mark Ormrod for this suggestion.

[3] There were 42 cases in the last decade and 39 of them came from 4 terms in 1368–1372, none of which occurred at Westminster. Criminal presentments were more numerous when the court perambulated outside Westminster. For example, one term when the King's Bench sat at Lincoln produced 51 cases, in another term there 40 cases, and in one term at York 42 cases. TNA: PRO KB 27/285 (Trin.1331); TNA: PRO KB 27/294 (Mich.1333) TNA: PRO KB 27/296 (Hil. 1334).

[4] After eliminating duplicate and irrelevant entries, 464 separate criminal and civil records were found in the plea rolls. Some cases contained accusations of multiple offenses or different types of conduct by the same individual, and some conspiracy presentments

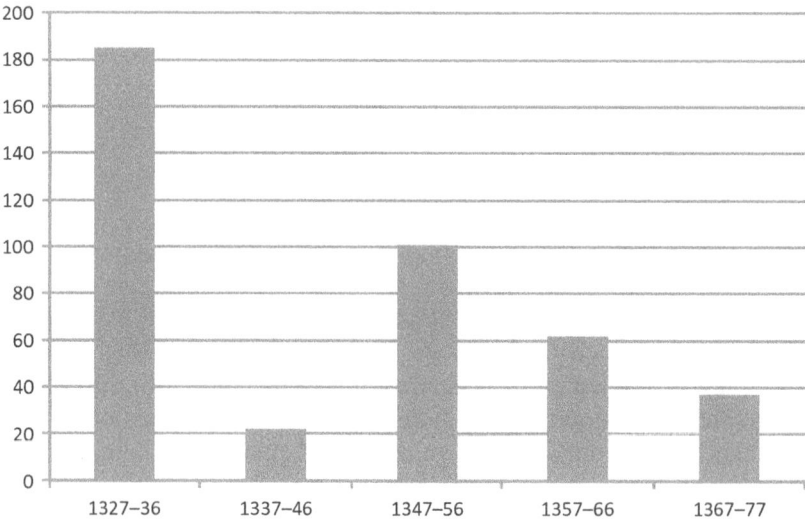

Figure 6.1   Litigation in the reign of Edward III.

constituting 61% of total litigation. Again criminal cases predominated, accounting for 76% of the total. Table 6.1 identifies the different types of criminal cases and civil actions in this period.

Criminal Litigation

There were several types of criminal cases in this period and conspiracy presentments were again the most common, as revealed by Table 6.2. There were 285 conspiracy presentments, constituting 62% of the total presentments.[5] There were 178 other criminal cases (38%).[6]

---

   involved both ambidexterity and maintenance, which were counted in each category, which produced a total of 612 criminal presentments and civil actions. If multiple persons were the subject of a single presentment, that was treated as only one case.

[5] Only 252 contained sufficient information to identify the specific conduct involved. Of entries of the criminal conspiracy presentments, 33 (11.6%) were mesne process records, which revealed only the names of the parties and the nature of the case as conspiracy, but not the specific details of the conduct that had been undertaken.

[6] There were also 57 presentments involving maintenance of felons. Despite the use of the word "maintenance," these cases were not included in the statistics because they were not a form of abuse of legal procedure. This accessorial liability was expressed in various ways. Most common were those charging the accused with receiving felons, but some charged maintenance of felons or both receiving and maintenance of them. Also some presentments used other words as well such as procurement, counsel, assistance, and assent of

Table 6.1 *Different types of criminal and civil cases, 1327–77*

	Criminal	Civil	Total
Conspiracy	285	91	376 (61.4%)
Maintenance	82	0	82 (13.4%)
Ambidexterity	41	0	41 (6.7%)
Champerty	19	10	29 (4.7%)
Procure false indictment or appeal	21	0	21 (3.4%)
Procure false civil plea	6	0	6 (1%)
Misconduct involving jurors and juries	4	0	4 (.7%)
Aid-abet false indictment or appeal	0	44	44 (7.2%)
Other abuse of legal procedure	5	4	9 (1.5%)
Total	463 (75.7%)	149 (24.3%)	612

Table 6.2 *Types of criminal cases, 1327–77*

Conspiracy actions		285 (62%)
Maintenance and champerty	71 (15.3%)	
Procure indictment or appeal	52 (11.2%)	
Against an individual	42 (9.1%)	
Procure civil plea	25 (5.4%)	
Misconduct involving jurors and juries	18 (3.9%)	
Against a vill	6 (1.3%)	
Ambidexterity	5 (1.1%)	
Eyre prohibition of conspirators	3 (.7%)	
Other conspiracy actions	30 (6.5%)	
Mesne process – no information	33 (7.1%)	
Total	285	
Other types of criminal cases		178 (38%)
Maintenance	82 (17.7%)	
Ambidexterity	41 (8.9%)	
Procure false indictment or appeal	21 (4.5%)	
Champerty	19 (4.1%)	
Procure false civil plea	6 (1.3%)	
Misconduct involving jurors and juries	4 (.9%)	
Other abuse of legal procedure	5 (1.1%)	
Total	178	
Total criminal cases		463

After conspiracy, maintenance presentments were the next most numerous, followed by ambidexterity, procuring of indictments and appeals
and civil actions, champerty, and other forms of abuse of legal procedure.

Conspiracy Cases

The conspiracy presentments reveal widespread group wrongdoing
during the reign of Edward III as in the earlier reigns. However, in this
period, their nature was somewhat different. The nature of conspiracy as
a criminal offense was developing and the conduct at which it was
directed was expanding.[7] Conspiracy cases in this period sometimes
involved increased and broader forms of group wrongdoing. The criminal litigation that targeted such conduct was not limited to that involving abuse of legal process. Almost all of these presentments of
conspiracies to maintain each other also included additional accusations
of a wide variety of additional illegal activity.[8]

Conspiracies to Maintain

Conspiracies to engage in maintenance were the most common type of
conspiracy case (25%), and defendants were often called "common
conspirators."[9] Over 70% of those presentments included an accusation

---

felons in their felonies. It was not clear what different conduct distinguished the use of
these various accessorial terms. In many of the cases, those accused of accessorial conduct
asserted the rule that they were not required to answer until the resolution of the charge
against the principal felon.

[7] In one case, a man brought a conspiracy action against an abbot and two others for
bringing an assize of novel dissseisin in his name, in which one of the defendants was
procured to be the plaintiff's attorney and plead at the will of the abbot. The defendant
argued that nothing was put into operation in the county where the writ was brought, as
only a conversation had occurred. But Fyncheden JCP thought the writ was good. Y.B.
East. 42 Edw. III, fols. 14–15, pl. 27 (1368), Seipp No. 1368.064. Charlemagne propounded
a similar rule that conspirators could be punished even though no evil was perpetrated.
Alan Harding, "The Origins of the Crime of Conspiracy," *Transactions of the Royal
Historical Society* (5th Ser.), 33 (1983), p. 92. Thus, it is not clear whether medieval
conspiracy required an overt act as modern law does. R.S. Wright, *The Law of Criminal
Conspiracies and Agreements* (London, 1873), p. 68.

[8] Only five of such presentments (7%) did not contain accusations of other illegal conduct.

[9] For example, jurors charged that a father and his son were "common conspirators,
confederated together and maintainers of pleas and actions between parties in their parts,
maintaining one against the other for his gift." TNA: PRO JUST 1/166, m. 49d (1330–31),
AALT Img. No. 9781.

that the defendants had conspired or confederated together to maintain each other's actions or enterprises, often by oath, and "for good or bad" or "just or unjust." For example, the jurors charged that two men "were joined together by oath of each of them to maintain the other's enterprises."[10] In some instances, these groups of conspirators were quite large.[11] Other presentments charged persons with conspiracy to maintain other parties or maintain false pleas, often in exchange for money.[12]

One type of conspiracy to maintain involved conspiring to procure false indictments, appeals, or civil actions. In one case, four men, sworn by oath to maintain each other, "by false conspiracy" procured a woman to bring a false appeal against a man who had sued an associate of the conspirators, and they maintained her so that "he would not dare sue."[13] In the 1330–31 Derbyshire Eyre, two conspirators, bound by oath to support and maintain each other, were charged with falsely procuring an assize of novel disseisin, by which one of the conspirators recovered the land.[14]

Extortion was another type of wrongdoing alleged in presentments for conspiracy to maintain. In a number of instances, defendants engaged in beatings, imprisonment, and threats to coerce the payment of fines. The mayor of York and others, who were confederated together to maintain each other's pleas, were also accused of denying all rights in the city to any person unless they made a fine with their members of their

---

[10] TNA: PRO KB 27/273, m. 26 rex (1328), AALT Img. No. 321 (tr.). In a 1353 list of articles for the King's Bench to inquire by inquest of office, it said, "And note, that two were indicted of confederacy, each of them of maintaining the other, whether their matter was true or false, and notwithstanding that nothing was supposed to be put into effect, the parties were put to answer, because this matter was prohibited in the law." Y.B. 27 Edw. III, Lib. Ass. 138, pl. 44 (1353), Seipp No. 1353.169ass (tr.).

[11] The jurors in the 1330–31 Derbyshire Eyre said that 35 men were and still are confederated together by conspiracy and by oath that each of them is bound to sustain and support the other in all his pleas and business. TNA: PRO JUST 1/166, m. 55 (1330–31), AALT Img. No. 9672.

[12] TNA: PRO KB 27/285, m. 14 rex (1331), AALT Img. No. 461; TNA: PRO KB 27/354, m. 71d (1348), AALT Img. No. 7449; TNA: PRO KB 27/422, m. 15 rex (1366), AALT Img. Nos. 155–56.

[13] When the man appeared, the woman did not wish to prosecute her appeal. TNA: PRO KB 27/369, m. 55d rex (1352), AALT Img. No. 9775 (tr.).

[14] One of the defendants was found guilty. He was ordered not to come within twelve miles of the eyre and he made a 40s fine. TNA: PRO JUST 1/166, m. 50 (1330–31), AALT Img. No. 9662. The other defendant, who was the one who had recovered the land, was indicted several other times for conspiracy and maintenance and found guilty. TNA: PRO JUST 1/166, m. 49d (1330–31), AALT Img. No. 9781.

confederacy and of fabricating trespass actions against the men as a basis for demanding the money. They were also accused of assaulting and imprisoning one man until he made a fine with them for £60 and another until he made a fine of £200.[15] Some of those charged with conspiracy to maintain each other were charged with further conduct corrupting the legal system.[16] These other offenses included procuring or engaging in jury misconduct,[17] maintenance of other parties and false pleas,[18] interfering with the choice of local officials,[19] ambidexterity by counsel and jurors,[20] unauthorized assessment of taxes,[21] maintenance of felons,[22] concealing felonies and wrongdoing,[23] disseising and coercing persons from their lawful possession of land,[24] and fixing the price of corn and victuals.[25]

In addition, in over one-third of these presentments of those who were joined together by oath to maintain each other or other persons, the accused were also charged with violent or forcible conduct and accused in over half of these cases of being "common wrongdoers and disturbers."[26]

---

[15] Both victims were found guilty of the trespasses and imprisoned until they paid the demanded money. In addition, in order to be delivered from prison, each of them was required to obligate himself to five men for £100 if the victims sued them for the extortionate conduct. The accused obtained a pardon for their offenses, and as to some the mayor was deemed immune from prosecution since he was acting in a judicial capacity. He was also a member of parliament for York. TNA: PRO KB 27/407, m. 37 rex (1362), AALT Img. Nos. 198–201, 412–15.

[16] Five men bound by mutual oath, conspiracy, and covenant to maintain each other's false enterprises threatened men to prevent them from suing and jurors to prevent from saying the truth. They also threatened the life of a man and twice extorted fines and crops from him and were "common ransomers of men, taking fines from them." TNA: PRO KB 27/310, m. 42 rex (1337), AALT Img. No. 417.

[17] TNA: PRO KB 27/285, m. 12 (1331), AALT Img. No. 457; TNA: PRO KB 27/294, m. 21 rex (1333), AALT Img. No. 395.

[18] TNA: PRO KB 27/369, m. 4 rex (1352), AALT Img. Nos. 9292–93, 9674; TNA: PRO KB 27/381, m. 30 rex (1355), AALT Img. Nos. 5720–21, 6035–36.

[19] TNA: PRO JUST 1/24, m. 50 (1330–31), AALT Img. No. 116; TNA: PRO JUST 1/26, m. 13 (1330–31), AALT Img. No. 781.

[20] TNA: PRO KB 27/407, m. 37 rex (1362), AALT Img. No. 198; TNA: PRO KB 27/294, m. 21 rex (1333), AALT Img. No. 395.

[21] TNA: PRO JUST 1/166, m. 55 (1330–31), AALT Img. No. 9672.

[22] TNA: PRO KB 27/354, m. 124d (1348), AALT Img. No. 7552.

[23] TNA: PRO KB 27/374, m. 35 rex (1354), AALT Img. No. 2209.

[24] TNA: PRO KB 27/285, m. 14 rex (1331), AALT Img. No. 461; TNA: PRO KB 27/374, m. 35 rex (1354), AALT Img. Nos. 2449, 2211.

[25] George Holmes, The Good Parliament (Oxford, 1975), p. 117.

[26] Eleven such men were said to have been armed and to have wandered day and night and by force, threats, and duress caused many of the vill to be part of their covin as well as rescuing one of their "society of wrongdoers," who had been arrested for assault, and permitting him to go free. TNA: PRO KB 27/275, m. 13d rex (1329), AALT Img. No. 248 (tr.).

Their conduct included assaults, beatings, threats to kill or maim, duress, coercion, imprisonment, carrying off goods, breaking into land, and being armed in a warlike manner and as insurgents. As a result, those targeted feared approaching their homes, vills, markets, and fairs; were reluctant to initiate litigation or say the truth in inquests; were coerced into joining the confederacy against their will; and were induced to make fines. For example, in addition to conspiring to maintain, two men were accused of assaulting a man in the market, following him to his house, and threatening to kill and maim him so that he did not dare to stay in the area for six months. In addition they agreed that, after the king left the country, they would kill "some of the better and more powerful men of Essex."[27]

Conspiracies Directed at Individuals

Another type of conspiracy case[28] that reflected its expanding nature was schemes targeting individuals.[29] Many of the presentments spoke of conspiring to destroy or disinherit a person. The steward of the earl of Hereford, a common maintainer of pleas, and others conspired together to destroy Martin Rook and falsely charged that he held by service certain lands of earl at three times the actual annual rent, for which they distrained and detained his livestock until he made a fine with

---

[27] TNA: PRO KB 27/313, m. 14d rex (1338), AALT Img. Nos. 236–37. In another case, men were accused of breaking into the house of the vill's vicar and taking, beating, and wounding a chaplain and holding him against his will until he made a fine with them, of beating and wounding three other men at a fair, and of assaulting another chaplain and detaining him in the church until he made a fine with them. The accused said that they were unable to deny the confederation or trespass. TNA: PRO KB 27/285, m. 10d (1331), AALT Img. No. 443 (tr.).

[28] Conspiracy presentments for procuring false indictments, appeals, and civil actions also targeted individuals, but those cases are treated as a separate category of cases.

[29] There was also a small number of conspiracy presentments that were directed at a vill rather than a person. Several of these cases charged a conspiracy to exert authority and oppress a vill by controlling the choice of mayors and bailiffs. TNA: PRO JUST 1/24, m. 50 (1330–31), AALT Img. No. 116 (8 men and others; Bedford); TNA: PRO JUST 1/26, m. 13 (1330–31), AALT Img. No. 781 (35 men and others; Bedford); TNA: PRO JUST 1/166, m. 55 (1330–31), AALT Img. No. 9672 (35 men, Derby). In one case, the conspirators were charged with demanding that all the members of the vill of Pinchbeck in Lincolnshire support and contribute to their confederation on the penalty of imprisonment. Resorting to violence, they took and detained two men until they agreed to do their will and threw another man in a pit and almost drowned him because he refused to swear to support them. TNA: PRO KB 27/285, m. 8 rex (1331), AALT Img. No. 448 (tr.).

them for marks.[30] Ten Lincoln men contrived to disinherit a man of his lands by falsely alleging that he had escaped from prison, causing him to be outlawed and enabling his chief lords to enter his lands and keep them for eighteen years.[31] Obtaining the victim's land was a frequent objective[32] and sometimes it involved ejecting the lawful possessors.[33] In one case, seventeen Norfolk men conspired with a husband and wife, who prevailed in an assize of novel disseisin, by contriving a rather macabre and sacrilegious scheme to thwart the losers in their action of attaint.[34] In other instances, the conspirators sought the money rather the land of their victims. John fitz Wauter, the often indicted Essex knight, and others falsely plotted as to how they could be enriched by Henry Basset's silver, and they chased him by threats and distraints to such an extent that he bound himself to John for £40 out of fear of losing his land and life.[35]

[30] TNA: PRO KB 27/366, m. 19 rex (1352), AALT Img. No. 8035. In another case, conspirators maintained a man to sue and recover another's land, which he held until the victim paid them 11 marks. TNA: PRO KB 27/436, m. 12 rex (1370), AALT Img. No. 144.

[31] TNA: PRO KB 27/285, m. 12 rex (1331), AALT Img. No. 456. In another case, John Fermer, an Essex knight and coroner who was presented numerous times, conspired with another man to disinherit an heir by counterfeiting a deed by which the deceased enfeoffed another man, who then enfeoffed John Fermer. TNA: PRO KB 27/367, m. 35 rex (1352), AALT Img. Nos. 8550–51.

[32] John fitz Wauter, an Essex knight, conspired with others as to "how and in what manner they could deprive" three men of their land. To do this, they caused a man to make an unfounded claim for the land, promised to maintain him, and put him in seisin, disseizing the others and afterward causing him to enfeoff John. In addition, the next day, John sent men to the land, who cut down and took away the grain growing there. TNA: PRO KB 27/366, m. 30 rex (1352). AALT Img. No. 8061 (tr.).

[33] TNA: PRO KB 27/285, m. 13 rex (1331), AALT Img. No. 458; TNA: PRO KB 27/285, m. 13 rex (1331), AALT Img. No. 461 (two cases); TNA: PRO KB 27/367, m. 35 rex (1352), AALT Img. Nos. 8318–19.

[34] They pretended falsely that the husband had died, and they caused masses to be celebrated for his soul and an empty coffin to be buried. Fearing that the coroners might make an inquiry into the death, they brought the body of a dead man from elsewhere and put it in the coffin. As a result, the writ of attaint was quashed. The conspirators also took and carried away £100 worth of the goods and chattels of the attaint plaintiffs and committed other crimes. TNA: PRO KB 27/349, m. 49 rex (1347), AALT Img. Nos. 3043–44 (tr.).

[35] TNA: PRO KB 27/366, m. 30 rex (1352), AALT Img. No. 7801 (tr.). The abbot of Malmesbury and a fellow monk conspired to procure the death of a man, killed another man, and beat and wounded others. TNA: PRO KB 27/352, m. 130 (1348), AALT Img. Nos. 2674–75. The king had appointed a special commission to arrest them and many others after their indictment for "perpetrating very many damages and crimes." *Calendar of Patent Rolls, Edward III, A.D. 1343–45* (London, 1902), pp. 78–79. But the king

The conspirators in these cases often used violence or force to achieve their objectives.[36]

The different tactics used by the accused in these cases also illustrated the expansive nature of conspiracy. One strategy was to exert leverage over the targeted individuals by detaining them or their goods. In two of the numerous Essex conspiracies, the conspirators falsified a tenant's service obligation and distrained his animals until he made a fine with them[37] and retained another man's animals until he enfeoffed their designee with his land.[38] Another means of exerting leverage was to bring false claims against the targeted individual.[39] Another tactic was falsely impersonating litigants. The lawyer for the defendants in an assize of novel disseisin, perceiving that his client would likely lose, enlisted John Fermer, the Essex knight who was indicted numerous times, in a conspiracy to prevent recovery by the plaintiff. They clothed a man in clerical vestments, who took the plaintiff's name and fled to a church as a felon. In response to questioning by John Fermer, then the Essex coroner, the fugitive responded in the plaintiff's name, saying he was in the church because he feloniously killed a man and prayed to abjure the realm. When the real plaintiff appeared in court, the defendants, by the maintenance and counsel of John Fermer, put forward the record of the abjuration and the plaintiff was imprisoned and barred from his action.[40]

---

determined that the charges against them were made maliciously and pardoned the defendants. The *oyer et terminer* justices refused to allow the pardons and the defendants continued to be "disturbed" before the justices appointed to continue the processes. After the abbot made a fine of £500, the king ratified his pardons, which had been "impeached by the justices," and further granted a general pardon to the defendants. Ibid., p. 131. Despite the pardon, the abbot feared being accused by his enemies of firing certain houses and he obtained a further special pardon for the firings. *Calendar of Patent Rolls, Edward III, A.D. 1345–48* (London, 1902), p. 558.

[36] Nine Kent men together with others conspired to destroy and kill a man, assaulted him, and chased him out of the church where he sought refuge, but men responding to his hue and cry rescued him. TNA: PRO KB 27/310, m. 39d rex (1337), AALT Img. Nos. 397–98.

[37] TNA: PRO KB 27/366, m. 19 rex (1352), AALT Img. No. 8035.

[38] TNA: PRO KB 27/366, m. 19 rex (1352), AALT Img. No. 7778. In another instance, John fitz Wauter and some of the same conspirators, plotting the seizure of a man to prevent his recovery against them, harassed him to such an extent that he failed to prosecute his action against them and was amerced for his failure by a jury stacked with men of John's affinity. TNA: PRO KB 27/366, m. 19 rex (1352), AALT Img. No. 7779.

[39] The earl of Hereford's steward and other Essex conspirators took the timber of a man and then sued him falsely until he agreed to release his trespass action against them for the taking. TNA: PRO KB 27/366, m. 19 rex (1352), AALT Img. No. 8036.

[40] Later, John Fermer took 40s from the plaintiff to come to court and record that the plaintiff was not the same person who had abjured. TNA: PRO KB 27/367, m. 35 rex

Conspiracies to Procure False Appeals, Indictments, and Civil Actions

The final type of conspiracy case was actions for procuring false indictments, which was the initial notion of conspiracy, false appeals, and false civil pleas. These cases accounted for slightly more than a quarter of the criminal conspiracy cases (27%). Procuring false indictments was alleged three times more often than procuring false appeals. Almost two-thirds of the actions were for false acccusations of felonies and those for causing death were the most common although there were also a number for theft or robbery. In this type of conspiracy case, allegations of violence or forceful conduct were less common than with the other types of conspiracy cases.

In a significant number of these cases, extortion appears to have been the purpose of these false accusations and threats.[41] Several men "by conspiracy and confederation between them to gain money by extortion" caused the indictment of several men for a death at a presentation of frankpledge without a jury inquest. The conspirators took fines either to remove them from the indictment or not to indict them.[42] Those who resisted the threats suffered retaliation. Four jurors conspired by threatening to indict a parson for diverse felonies and trespasses unless he gave them 10 marks. When he refused, they procured a prostitute to prosecute him for trespass and so he paid them 9 marks not to be indicted.[43] Personal animus was another motive for making or threatening false accusations. Several men, conspiring to "destroy and annihilate [a man] . . . on account of the malevolent will which they had toward him without cause," falsely procured his indictment for breaking into a rectory and stealing goods there.[44]

(1352), AALT Img. No. 8319 (tr.). In another case, several Essex conspirators "falsely plotted to exclude" a man from his action of mort d'ancestor by procuring a groom to pose as the plaintiff, seek sanctuary, confess to killing a man, and abjure the realm. TNA: PRO KB 27/316, m. 13d rex (1339), AALT Img. No. 265.

[41] False accusations to extort were also made in the church courts. Several ecclesiastical judges and church officials falsely imposed usury and other crimes to extort money from innocent people. TNA: PRO KB 27/355, m. 3d (1349). AALT Img. No. 8089. The chaplain and other commissaries of the bishop of Lincoln wrongfully summoned men to the ecclesiastical courts, falsely alleging that they were indicted of perjury and refusing to permit them to make purgation until they made a fine, "so that no juror hardly dared to indict such commissaries or clerks of any extortions perpetrated by them." TNA: PRO KB 27/295, m. 16d rex (1334), AALT Img. No. 286 (tr.).

[42] TNA: PRO JUST 1/166, m. 49d (1330–31), AALT Img. No. 9781.

[43] TNA: PRO KB 27/415, m. 11d rex (1364), AALT Img. No. 406.

[44] They also falsely accused him of another theft and "tied his hands so tight that the blood came out by the nails of his fingers." They sent him to the Hertford jail because they

A number of these presentments (25%) followed the standard formula, charging that conspirators procured a false indictment or appeal and that the defendant had been acquitted, delivered, or was not guilty.[45] But some were more detailed and complex. In Norfolk, several men conspired to destroy a clerk, the returner of writs for Norfolk and Suffolk, and replace him with one of their own. After obtaining a commission in the name of the sheriff, without his knowledge, they indicted the clerk for making false money so he could not intermeddle in that office, and then the office could be exercised by one of the conspirators. But the sheriff caused the seal of the office to be returned and prevented that, so the conspirators procured themselves to be impaneled on an inquest and indicted the sheriff for several felonies.[46] In several of these cases, they were indicted and said that they were members of an inquest lawfully carrying out their legal duties with their fellow jurors and could not be charged.[47] The justices agreed. "It is not possible by the law of England to adjudge any conspiracy of any indictors presented by whomsoever jurors."[48]

Procuring false civil pleas most frequently involved land actions.[49] In one case, an abbot and knight at the cost of the former procured a man to bring an assize of novel disseisin against the rightful tenants and agreed that if the man recovered the tenements, which he did, that the abbot

believed that if he were sent to Colchester castle, he would have assistance there. They also sent the jailer there certain gifts to kill him by hunger and other punishments, and the jailer, while he had custody of the prisoner, put him naked on a hurdle and threw a full jar of water on him. TNA: PRO KB 27/418, m. 20d rex (1365), AALT Img. No. 408 (tr.).

[45] In two instances, women who were procured to file false appeals failed to prosecute them. TNA: PRO KB 27/315, m. 10d rex (1339), AALT Img. No. 255 (rape); TNA: PRO KB 27/369, m. 55d rex (1352), AALT Img. No. 9775 (husband's death).

[46] Also the new custodian of the office and its seal made false returns and orders to attach several men without an original writ. They also falsely indicted others and coerced a man to provide financial assistance in these matters by threatening to indict him TNA: PRO KB 27/415, m. 11d rex (1364), AALT Img. No. 407 (tr.).

[47] TNA: PRO KB 27/411, m. 22d rex (1363), AALT Img. No. 400; TNA: PRO KB 27/416, m. 13 rex (1364), AALT Img. No. 184; TNA: PRO KB 27/416, m. 33 rex (1364), AALT Img. No. 224. In these cases, the defendants vouched the record to prove that they were the indictors.

[48] TNA: PRO KB 27/411, m. 22d rex (1363), AALT Img. No. 400.

[49] False pleas also occurred in the church courts. Pursuant to a plan to extort money from people, the chaplain and other commissaries of the bishop of Lincoln improperly summoned and harassed numerous people to appear in the ecclesiastical courts, including in matters outside their jurisdiction. TNA: PRO KB 27/295, m. 16d rex (1334), AALT Img. No. 286.

would have them for his benefit.[50] As was true with false indictments and appeals, money was often the object of the conspiracy. Conspiring how "to oppress and have the money" of executors of a will, the steward of the earl of Hereford and others procured and promised to maintain a man to sue the executors in the earl's court for a fabricated £10 debt. When the executors brought a writ to remove to the plea, the steward refused to accept the writ and obey the king's order, condemned the executors in £10, and took the money for himself.[51] Personal hostility also seemed to motivate some of these false civil pleas.[52]

Other Types of Conspiracy Cases

A residual category of cases further reflected the broad nature of group wrongdoing and the use of conspiracy as the legal mechanism to deal with it. Some cases in this category involved misconduct regarding jurors and juries (6%), such as procuring false acquittals;[53] procuring, rewarding, and threatening jurors;[54] procuring a substitute jury panel by a counterfeit seal and suborning it;[55] revealing the confidential counsel of the jurors;[56] choosing men of the affinity of one of the parties;[57]

---

[50] The tenants, after losing the assize, brought an attaint, and the abbot gave them 400 marks to drop that action. TNA: PRO KB 27/285, m. 11d (1331), AALT Img. No. 444. In another case, conspirators fabricated a testament. TNA: PRO KB 27/429, m. 18d rex (1368), AALT Img. No. 321.

[51] TNA: PRO KB 27/366, m. 37 rex (1352), AALT Img. Nos. 7776–77. In another case, the conspirators fabricated a recognizance under the Statute of Merchant and successfully sued to enforce it, collecting a portion of the money claimed. TNA: PRO KB 27/392, m. 17 rex (1358), AALT Img. Nos. 1605, 1854.

[52] The chief bailiff of a Lincoln wapentake sued a writ of account against his underbailiff, falsely stating that the latter could not be found and had nothing by which he could be distrained. As a result, the defendant was imprisoned, and, by confederation between the chief bailiff and custodian of the jail, the latter subjected him to punishment that caused his death. TNA: PRO KB 27/285, m. 6d rex (1331), AALT Img. No. 436.

[53] TNA: PRO KB 27/273, m. 26 rex (1328), AALT Img. No. 321.

[54] TNA: PRO KB 27/285, m. 12d rex (1331), AALT Img. No. 446; TNA: PRO KB 27/411, m. 17d rex (1363), AALT Img. No. 390; TNA: PRO KB 27/436, m. 13 rex (1370), AALT Img. No. 145. A cleric, councilor of the abbot of Cirencester and a proctor, conspired with others and threatened to destroy those who spoke against the defendant, whom the cleric was maintaining, in an action of *scire facias*. The cleric also wrote letters to several vicars, telling them to pronounce in their churches that no one summoned in action should come to Gloucester unless they would speak for the defendant. TNA: PRO KB 27/411, m. 17 rex (1363), AALT Img. No. 178.

[55] TNA: PRO KB 27/352, m. 32 rex (1348), AALT Img. Nos. 2745-46.

[56] TNA: PRO KB 27/355, m. 3 (1349), AALT Img. No.7781.

[57] TNA: PRO KB 27/366, m. (1352), AALT Img. Nos. 7805, 8060.

and falsifying and concealing indictments.[58] Other conspiracy cases involved litigation misconduct, such as making false pleas,[59] fabricating documents,[60] engaging in false pleading,[61] unethical lawyer conduct,[62] and other forms of deceit.[63] Conspirators also undertook actions to protect guilty parties, including themselves, from the consequences of their criminal conduct by means of false acquittals,[64] preventing

[58] A clerk sworn to the jurors, without their knowledge, falsely wrote in the indictment that the defendant had committed felonies when he had been indicted for trespasses. TNA: PRO KB 27/354, m. 15 rex (1351), AALT Img. No. 6657.

[59] Conspirators procured a false plea based on a nonexistent trespass. TNA: PRO KB 27/285, m. 16d rex (1331), AALT Img. No. 455. In a rather striking case, the conspirators plotted to put pig blood on a man and to bind his legs and arms with splints and linen cloths and procured him to file a trespass action. They then brought him in a cart to Westminster to give the impression that he had been beaten and wounded, although he was sound and had no wounds. The jury found them not guilty. TNA: PRO KB 27/385, m. 14 rex (1356), AALT Img. No. 7326 (tr.).

[60] A lord who was a defendant in several actions brought by both the king and private parties colluded with others to fabricate a deed of enfeoffment granting all his lands in Essex to two lords and other people, although he remained in possession and took all the profits. TNA: PRO KB 27/367, m. 36 rex (1352), AALT Img. No. 8321. In the 1351 Essex sessions of the peace, the executors of a will fabricated a nuncupative will to get the decedent's goods, but in the probate proceedings the will was ultimately proven false because the true will was produced. The executors appealed to the Court of Arches, but failed to prosecute it. TNA: PRO KB JUST 1/266, m. 9, AALT Img. No. 3375 (tr.).

[61] In one case, as a result of the conspirators procuring a man wrongfully to present a cleric to a moiety, the rightful owner of the advowson brought an action of *quare impedit* against the presenter and one of the conspirators. The former appeared and admitted that he had no right, so the conspirator falsely answered that a nonexistent person occupied the moiety, and the rightful occupier was disinherited TNA: PRO KB 27/285, m. 16d rex (1331), AALT Img. No. 455.

[62] In one conspiracy, an attorney falsely represented that he was a tenant's lawyer and stated in court that he could not deny the plaintiff's action, so that the tenant lost his land. TNA: PRO KB 27/354, m. 33 rex (1348), AALT Img. No. 7200. In another case, ecclesiastical judges acted as counsel for parties pleading or being impleaded before them to the prejudice of the opposing party. TNA: PRO KB 27/355, m. 3d (1355), AALT Img. No. 8089.

[63] In one case, Robert Baker and John Causey were parties in a trespass action and agreed to concord on a day of love and release all actions. But John deceived Robert by delaying to make the release until the next day and then committing another trespass to Robert, which was unknown to Robert. Afterward they made a waiver of all actions, and John alleged the waiver in an action by Robert based on the later trespass. TNA: PRO KB 27/392, m. 17 rex (1358), AALT Img. No. 1604. Two Dorset conspirators made a false release and quitclaim, which caused a man to be disseized of his lands. TNA: PRO KB 27/392, m. 22 rex (1358), AALT Img. No. 1614.

[64] Two York conspirators took money to acquit a vicar guilty of causing a death as well as falsely indicting another vicar and others, who were innocent. TNA: PRO KB 27/273, m. 26 rex (1328), AALT Img. No. 321. In a complicated case, nine conspirators devised an elaborate scheme to indict and falsely acquit Lionel of Bradenham by misleading a justice of the peace to inquire of a robbery by him without the participation of his fellow justices.

indictments,[65] precluding punishment for wrongdoing,[66] and concealing offenses.[67] Other cases in this residual category involved commercial matters such as forestalling and preventing purchases by others, fabricating tithing obligations, and price fixing,[68] fraudulent assessments and levies,[69] and violations of eyre and court prohibitions regarding conspirators.[70] In one rather striking case, ten Surrey men dressed in borrowed clerical vestments of monks and in robes with fur-lined hoods to simulate high officials. They then presented various grievances and trespasses to the king, saying that there were no keepers of the peace nor justices in their areas and praying that he appoint three of the conspirators as peace keepers and put them on commissions to investigate the wrongdoing, which the king did. They then held sessions causing great harm, subjecting poor men to them, and falsely telling the king that they had generated more than £1,000 for him.[71]

One of the conspirators posed as sheriff's deputy to return a jury panel, which included some of the conspirators, to indict and acquit Lionel, and fabricated documents to produce a sealed record of acquittal. TNA: PRO KB 27/416, m. 25 rex (1364), AALT Img. Nos. 208–09 479 (tr.); TNA: PRO KB 27/416, m. 48 rex (1364), AALT Img. Nos. 528, 255–56, 529–32 (tr.).

[65] A Surrey jury indicted twenty men for conspiring to prevent their indictment and to cause their delivery if any of them were indicted. TNA: PRO KB 27/374, m. 35 rex (1354), AALT Img. Nos. 2210, 445. York conspirators took 11 marks from a chaplain to prevent his indictment for a death, although he was ultimately indicted. TNA: PRO KB 27/273, m. 26 rex (1328), AALT Img. No. 322.

[66] A Lincoln prior and others conspired to cause the delivery of woman indicted for the death of her husband and to prevent punishment of her for that felony, for which the prior received 200 marks and two casks of wine. TNA: PRO KB 27/285, m. 14 rex (1331), AALT Img. No. 461. A group of Essex conspirators obtained and destroyed the coroner's arrest record of a man jailed for theft, as a result of which he was not arrested and went at large. TNA: PRO KB 27/367, m. 36 rex (1352), AALT Img. No. 8321.

[67] Two men conspired to procure a bailiff to put them on a jury "to conceal wickedness and trespasses by themselves and others of their confederation." TNA: PRO KB 27/285, m. 14d rex (1331), AALT Img. No. 450.

[68] TNA: PRO KB 27/285, m. 16d rex (1331), AALT Img. No. 454; TNA: PRO KB 27/315, m. 23d rex (1339), AALT Img. Nos. 283, 454; TNA: PRO JUST 1/266, m. 9 (1351), AALT Img. No. 3375.

[69] Three Lincoln men conspired to assess and levy from the vill of Pinchbeck £36 for the arms and stipends of men in the king's service against the Scots and kept all but 40s for themselves. TNA: PRO KB 27/285, m. 14d rex (1331), AALT Img. No. 450.

[70] Those convicted of conspiracy were prohibited from being present at the eyre or some courts, unless they were pleading or impleaded and then to make an attorney, and to come no closer than twelve miles. TNA: PRO JUST 1/166, m. 52 (1330–31), AALT Img. No. 9665; TNA: PRO KB 27/391, m. 28 rex (1358), AALT Img. Nos. 1158–59, 1400; TNA: PRO KB 27/391, m. 1d rex (1358), AALT Img. No. 1347.

[71] But "they were utter liars because they did nothing except destroy loyalty and justice and maintain thieves, murderers, and malefactors." TNA: PRO KB 27/374, m. 35 rex (1354), AALT Img. No. 2209 (tr.).

The Changing Concept of Conspiracy

Although the conspiracy presentations were the predominant type of criminal case in the reign of Edward III as in the earlier period, there were some noteworthy differences in those in the later period. First, the factual natures of the later conspiracies seem more diverse. Also there is more evidence that conspirators are targeting specific individuals. Finally, these presentations more commonly involved violence. Almost 20% of the presentments either targeted conspiracies that themselves involved violence or force or accused the conspirators of other criminal activity involving such conduct.

Second, the frequency of some types of the cases was different. During the reign of Edward III, conspiracies involving maintenance were again the most common type, but they occurred almost half as often as in the earlier period. In addition, conspiracies involving ambidexterity declined substantially and were one-third less than in the earlier reigns. In contrast, conspiracies involving procuring false indictments and appeals increased substantially and were twice as common in the later period. In addition, there were a number of conspiracies involving the procuring of false civil pleas, which were infrequent in the earlier period. As to these types of legal corruption, there seems to have been a shift to more frequent criminal cases as compared with more common use of civil actions in the earlier period. These differences suggest that the nature of group wrongdoing and the use of conspiracy as legal remedy had both expanded. Also Commons seemed to have been concerned that the crime of conspiracy had been restricted.[72]

The development of a larger vocabulary to characterize group wrong-doing in the reign of Edward III reinforces these conclusions. As was true in the earlier period, presentments commonly charged that individuals had conspired or confederated together, sometimes using both words, and often that they were sworn by oath to engage in some form of antisocial behavior. In 1330–31 Derbyshire Eyre the jurors presented that two men were "common conspirators" who had "confederated together" and were

[72] In 1355, they complained that the justices in their inquiries into confederacies, conspiracies, and maintenances "judge very strictly to the detriment of the commons" and requested that matters of inquiry be more specifically defined. The king's response was puzzling, as he said that "no one shall be judged or punished for confederacy except in cases where the statute made thereon expressly declares upon the points contained in the same statute." Parliaments of Edward III: November 1355, no. 21.X, *PROME*. Presumably, he was referring to the 1305 Ordinance of Conspirators, which defined conspirators. *Statutes of the Realm*, vol. 1, p. 145. But numerous presentments for conspiracy during his reign involved conduct that was not described in that Ordinance.

"maintainers of pleas and actions." By their conspiracy they devised a plan in which a woman should fabricate an appeal of homicide against seventeen innocent men for the death of her husband. They also "by conspiracy and confederation" determined to indict several men in order to extort money from them.[73] In another case, the jurors presented that five men were "confederated together, bound by mutual oath by a false covenant and conspiracy" to maintain each other's false enterprises.[74]

But other words were also used to characterize group wrongdoing, both in conjunction with conspiracy and confederation and without those words. "Covin" was probably the most frequent additional word used to describe illicit collective activity.[75] It was used repeatedly in some records and in different contexts.[76] "By false covin made between them" was a common accusatory phrase.[77] In some cases, covin was used in conjunction with conspiracy.[78] But in others, it seemed to have been

---

[73] The jury found them guilty of all the articles. TNA: PRO JUST 1/166, m. 49d (1330–31), AALT Img. No. 9781 (tr.).

[74] In addition, the jurors said that they threatened men so that the latter did not dare to sue or defend their right or say the truth in assizes or juries and that they were "common ransomers of men, taking fines from them" as well as "common wrongdoers and disturbers of the peace at fairs, markets, and other places." TNA: PRO KB 27/310 m. 42 rex (1337), AALT Img. Nos. 417, 401 (dorse) (tr.).

[75] The Oxford English Dictionary gives several meanings, all marked obsolete, with medieval examples, all of which involve confederation, conspiracy, collusion, compact, or agreement involving wrongful or prejudicial conduct such as deceit, fraud, treachery, or injury to another. *Oxford English Dictionary Online*, s.v. "Covin," definitions 1–4. According to one commentator, fourteenth-century contemporaries equated it with a group of corrupt persons "banded together for mutual profit and protections." Paul Booth, "The Last Week of the Life of Edward the Black Prince," in Hannah Skoda, Patrick Lantschner, and R.J. Shaw, *Contract and Exchange in Later Medieval Europe: Essays in Honor of Malcolm Vale* (Woodbridge, 2012), p. 226.

[76] In two very long records, each containing numerous presentments charging John fitz Wauter, an Essex knight, and others with conspiratorial conduct and multiple kinds of offenses, "covin" was used eighteen times. TNA: PRO KB 27/366, m. 19 rex (1352), AALT Img. Nos. 7776–79, 8035–38; TNA: PRO KB 27/366, m. 30 rex (1352), AALT Img. Nos. 7801–13, 8058–67. Covin was also to identify defendants. TNA: PRO KB 27/436, m. 13 rex (1370), AALT Img. No. 145 ("Thomas of Swaffham and others who are of the covin of Roger of Harleston") (tr.). There was one civil conspiracy action that used covin. PRO KB 27/295, m. 120 (1334), AALT Img. No. 248.

[77] E.g., TNA: PRO KB 27/367, m. 10d rex (1352), AALT Img. No. 8499; TNA: PRO KB 27/368, m. 7 rex (1352), AALT Img. No. 8728; TNA: PRO KB 27/369, m. 4 rex (1352), AALT Img. No. 9292. Another presentment used language very similar to the standard formulaic words used with conspiracy. TNA: PRO KB 27/374, m. 35 rex (1354), AALT Img. 2210 ("covin previously arranged between them").

[78] Four related presentments charged that a large group of men in Surrey "by false covin and conspiracy" destroyed another man by disseising and disinheriting him of his land and

used instead of conspired or confederated, but with the same intended meaning.[79] In the 1330–31 Befordshire Eyre, the jurors found that Hugh de Cressey asked Roger the marshal "to be of his covin" and that he would support him to procure a woman to appeal two men, who were enemies of Hugh, of rape and "by covin made between them," abetted her to falsely and maliciously appeal the men.[80]

Another word commonly used to describe the association of persons to do wrongdoing was *alligancia*.[81] John Fermer, an Essex knight, "*per falsas conspiracores, alligancias, et falsas confederaciones*," was alleged to be a maintainer of all false pleas and others for the fifteen years in Essex.[82] Covin and *alligantia* were also used together.[83] "Collusion" was also used in several cases to express the notion of wrongful collective activity.[84] The use

other property interests. TNA: PRO KB 27/374, m. 35 rex (1354), AALT Img. Nos. 2210–11, 2448–51. In one of the cases, one of the defendants was a justice of the peace and was accused of refusing to release a man acquitted of a felony until he swore on the Holy Gospels that he would not prosecute any of the conspirators and would quitclaim certain actions to those nominated by the justice. The justice successfully claimed that he could not be indicted for anything that he did as the king's justice. TNA: PRO KB 27/374, m. 35 rex (1354), AALT Img. Nos. 2214, 2448. A justice of the commission in the session in which the plaintiff was indicted for receiving a felon said that he was bound by his office to inform the people on behalf of the king as best he could in this capacity. He put himself on the king's grace, but was not wholly excused for the entire time while he was the indictor Y.B. 27 Edw. III, Lib. Ass. 134, pl. 12 (1353), Seipp No. 1353.137ass.

[79] Latham defined it as an illegal compact or association. R.E. Latham, *Revised Medieval Latin Word-List* (Oxford, 1980), p. 120. In a civil case, "conspiracy and false alliance" were used to characterize the defendant's conduct, and in another record of the same action, "false covin" was used instead. TNA: PRO KB 27/294, m. 133d (1333), AALT Img. No. 275; TNA: PRO KB 27/295, m. 120 (1334), AALT Img. No. 248.

[80] Roger was found guilty and Hugh had died. The presentment also charged them and others as being confederated together by oath and that they were common abettors and maintainers of false appeals. The jury found Roger not guilty of those charges. TNA: PRO JUST 1/24, m. 47 (1330–31), AALT Img. Nos. 110, 231 (tr.).

[81] Latham gives several meanings, including compact, bond, conspiracy, maintenance, confederate, and alliance. Latham, *Medieval Latin Word-List*, p. 15.

[82] TNA: PRO KB 27/367, m. 35d rex (1352), AALT Img. No. 8551. In another presentment, a jury presented that a knight and fifteen other men of "*se alligaverunt per convencione*" to maintain each other's pleas, to conceal their felonies and wrongdoing, and to destroy a man because he refused "to consent to their *alligancia*." TNA: PRO KB 27/374, m. 35 rex (1354), AALT Img. No. 2210.

[83] TNA: PRO KB 27/366, m. 30 rex (1352), AALT Img. No. 8061 ("by false covin and *alliganciam* between themselves"); TNA: PRO KB 27/367, m. 35 rex (1352), AALT Img. No. 8319 ("by false covin and *alliganciam* between them, they conspired among themselves").

[84] E.g., TNA: PRO KB 27/324, m. 107 (1338), AALT Img. No. 227 ("Adam by prior collusion with William wickedly scheming to trick the court …"); TNA: PRO KB

of these various words to present persons for group wrongdoing, often coupled with existence of an oath or a covenant to engage in multiple types of conduct, may be more than verbal variation and may suggest something more substantive, reflecting a more expansive notion of conspiracy.

The differing factual and legal nature of the conspiracies and the use of a larger vocabulary to characterize it in the reign of Edward III may indicate an increase in the variety of wrongful collective activity and a broadening of the notion of criminal conspiracy to deal with it. In the earlier period, conspiracy and confederation were used almost exclusively to designate wrongdoing by two or more persons and were usually directed at conduct abusing the machinery of justice. To some extent, this transformation in the nature of conspiracy may be a product of the changing dynamics of retaining that had begun in the late thirteenth century.[85] Although the objectives of assembling these aristocratic bands were varied and not always directed at the manipulation of justice, they contributed to a rise in corruption, disorder, and violence.[86] Returning soldiers who had been pardoned to fight in the war may also have caused a rise in violence.[87] In addition, gang activity increased in the fourteenth century,[88] including the infamous Folville and Coterel gangs,[89] whose

27/367, m. 36 rex (1352), AALT Img. No. 8321 ("They contrived and made between them by collusion a certain deed ..."); TNA: PRO KB 27/411, m. 25 rex (1363), AALT Img. No. 227 ("by collusion made between them to enfeoff . . .").

[85] Scott Waugh, "The Third Century of English Feudalism," in Michael Prestwich, Richard Britnell, and Robin Frame, eds., *Thirteenth Century England VII* (Woodbridge, 1999), pp. 49–51.

[86] Ibid., p. 58. Waugh was reacting to the debate over "bastard feudalism" and asserting an alternative approach. He argued that the role of magnates in causing corruption by retaining had been exaggerated. Ibid., p. 53. "The phenomena of corruption and disorder during the third century of English feudalism were too complex to be encompassed by the terms 'bastard feudalism.'" Ibid., p. 58.

[87] Scott Waugh, *England in the Reign of Edward III* (Cambridge, 1991), p. 139.

[88] Waugh linked retaining and crime to "activities of professional, or habitual, criminal gangs," which was a problem that had worsened in the fourteenth century. Ibid., pp. 161–62; J.G. Bellamy, *Crime and Public Order in England in the Later Middle Ages* (Toronto, 1973), pp. 68–88. Edward III had recognized this problem during the reign, as evident from the Statute of Northampton 1328. One of the several provisions dealing with the administration of criminal law prohibited riding armed, bringing force and arms in a disturbance, or coming before the king's justices or other ministers with force and arms. Statute of Northampton, c. 3 (1328), *Statutes of the Realm*, vol. 1, p. 258. Moreover, the initial statutes dealing with riot appeared late in the reign. J.G. Bellamy, *Criminal Law and Society in Late Medieval and Tudor England* (New York, 1984), pp. 54–56.

[89] These two gangs seem to have been connected. E.L.G. Stones, "The Folvilles of Ashby-Folville, Leicestershire and Their Associates in Crime, 1326–1347," *Transactions of the*

members were the subject of several of the presentments.[90] All these influences and factors were likely responsible for the expansion of conspiracy as a legal concept and its increased use as a legal weapon.[91]

Other Criminal Cases

The other criminal litigation involving abuse of legal procedure (38%) consisted of five types of cases and a residual category. The bulk of these cases involved presentments for maintenance and ambidexterity (26%) and the remainder dealt with champerty; procurement of false appeals, indictments, and civil pleas; and other abuses of legal procedure.

Maintenance

Maintenance cases were the most common type of the nonconspiratorial criminal cases, accounting for 45% of them and 17% of the total number of the criminal cases. A number of the persons charged with maintaining pleas were officials acting under the color of their offices such as bailiffs, sheriffs,[92] escheators, stewards, and their clerks.[93] More than half of the

---

Royal Historical Society, Fifth Series, 7 (1957), pp. 117–36; J.G. Bellamy, "The Coterel Gang: An Anatomy of a Band of Fourteenth-Century Criminals," *English Historical Review*, 79 (1964), pp. 698–717.

[90] Five presentments found in this research were of various members of the Folville family, including Eustace, their leader. TNA: PRO KB 27/285, m. 15d rex (1331), AALT Img. No. 452; TNA: PRO KB 27/294, m. 12d rex (1333), AALT Img. No. 377; TNA: PRO KB 27/294, m. 8d rex (1333), AALT Img. No. 360; TNA: PRO KB 27/295, m. 12d rex (1334), AALT Img. No. 278; TNA: PRO KB 27/366, m. 13 rex (1352), AALT Img. Nos. 7762–63. In 1332, the Folvilles abducted Sir Richard Willoughby, King Bench justice. TNA: PRO KB 27/294, m. 8d rex (1333), AALT Img. No. 360.

[91] Waugh asserted that maintenance and conspiracy were a significant cause of lawlessness in the reign of Edward III and that gang violence involved the confluence of retaining and crime. Waugh, *Edward III*, pp. 160–62. Similar disorder occurred in the latter half of the fourteenth century in Cheshire, prompting a trailbaston session in 1353. Paul Booth, "Taxation and Public Order: Cheshire in 1353," *Northern History* 12 (1976), pp. 16–25.

[92] Maintenance and other forms of corruption by sheriffs were common. Richard Gorski, *The Fourteenth-Century Sheriff* (Woodbridge, 2003), pp. 102–25.

[93] The earl of Leicester's bailiff was a common maintainer of pleas before him in his lord's court, for which he took money. TNA: PRO JUST 1/635, m. 46d (1329–30), AALT Img. No. 963 (Northamptonshire Eyre). The earl of Richmond's bailiff, who was presented multiple times, was "a champertor and maintainer of all pleas pleaded in the court of his lord and he made juries to pass for his side justly and unjustly." TNA: PRO KB 27/285 m. 10 rex (1331), AALT Img. Nos. 452–53 (tr.).

cases charged the accused with maintenance of false pleas.[94] In a number
of these cases, the accused received money from the beneficiaries of their
efforts and were often described as "common maintainers." For example,
the prior of Chicksands and a fellow monk made a false acquittance to
Lucca merchants, which the court nevertheless treated as valid, and they
paid the steward of Lord Grey 100s to maintain them in that "false plea,
who did so knowing it to be false"[95] Some of those charged were accused
of undertaking to do so in multiple pleas or for the life of the beneficiary.
Four men were charged with maintaining all pleas in Middlesex for three
years and were "common undertakers and maintainers of false pleas . . .
furthering the business of those who will give or promise them the most
gold or silver."[96] The sheriff of Northamptonshire was said to have taken
fees from a man to maintain him for his life.[97]

What seems noteworthy about these maintenance cases is the
expansion of this concept. The presentments were not limited to
maintenance of pleas, but included other kinds of maintenance. Such
conduct included wrongfully entering or using land,[98] ejecting lawful

---

[94] One case involved bringing bills under the names of plaintiffs without their
knowledge. TNA: PRO JUST 1/632, m. 54d (1329–30), AALT Img. No. 953
(Northamptonshire Eyre).

[95] TNA: PRO JUST 1/24, m. 48d (1330–31), AALT Img. No. 233 (Bedfordshire Eyre) (tr.).
In finding Lord Grey's steward guilty of several other instances of maintenance, the jurors
found that he was "a common maintainer of pleas and false actions." They also found that
he was "accustomed to maintain and support pleas and actions in the county against the
form of the statute," perhaps the Statute of Westminster I, c. 25. TNA: PRO JUST 1/24,
m. 47 (1330–31), AALT Img. Nos. 109–10 (Bedfordshire Eyre) (tr.).

[96] They said that they were unable to deny the charges. TNA: PRO KB 27/381, m. 30 rex
(1355), AALT Img. No. 5720 (tr.). Occasionally, those accused took money to maintain
others, but then failed to do so. An Essex man, presented for several types of legal
corruption, took over 10 marks from several men to maintain their suits, but "he influenced nothing for them and he is a common maintainer of false pleas." TNA: PRO KB
27/418, m. 27 rex (1365), AALT Img. No. 208 (tr.).

[97] TNA: PRO JUST 1/632, m. 89d (1329–30), AALT Img. No. 1022 (Northamptonshire
Eyre). A Warwick man was charged with taking 12d annually to maintain him for his life
against all men and also maintained a man, who was a common beater of men at fairs and
markets, in all things and in his pleas. TNA: PRO KB 27/369, m. 4d rex (1352), AALT
Img. Nos. 9292–93, 9674. In the Essex sessions of the peace, a man was charged with
taking an annual pension of 20s to maintain a man to prevent a debt action against him.
TNA: PRO JUST 1/266, m. 8d (1351), AALT Img. No. 3387.

[98] The steward of John, Lord Grey, procured a man wrongfully to enter land and, for
money, promised that he would maintain him "both by plea and by power of the arms
[and] trust of his stewardship," and "by which maintenance and abetting and the color of
office and lordship." TNA: PRO JUST 1/24, m. 47 (1330–31), AALT Img. No. 109
(Bedfordshire Eyre) (tr.). An Essex knight, presented for multiple offenses, maintained

tenants,[99] coercing sheriffs in jury selection,[100] forceful and wrongful detention,[101] and fabrication of documents.[102] In another type of non-plea-related maintenance, several bailiffs were charged with maintaining guilty persons by protecting them from the consequences of their criminal behavior.[103] Another form of protecting the guilty involved maintaining false enterprises and assizes, and threatening jurors to prevent them from returning truthful verdicts.[104] Some cases also charged those who were hired to maintain wrongdoers.[105]

---

his villeins to unjustly burden the common pasture of the king and burgesses of Colchester with their sheep and animals. TNA: PRO KB 27/366, m. 30 rex (1352), AALT Img. No. 8064.

[99] TNA: PRO KB 27/285, m. 13 rex (1331), AALT Img. No. 458; TNA: PRO KB 27/366, m. 19 rex (1352), AALT Img. No. 7778; TNA: PRO KB 27/367, m. 35 rex (1352), AALT Img. No. 8318.

[100] TNA: PRO KB 27/366, m. 19 rex (1352), AALT Img. Nos. 7779, 8037; TNA: PRO KB 27/366, m. 30 rex (1352), AALT Img. Nos. 7805–6, 8060.

[101] Lord Robert Marny maintained a parson and others who took a man against his will and detained him until he made a fine with them. TNA: PRO KB 27/367, m. 36 rex (1352), AALT Img. No. 8321

[102] A Leicester man complained to the king that another man maintained the making of a false charter that disinherited the complainant of his lands. TNA: PRO KB 27/369, m. 32 rex (1352), AALT Img. No. 9358. In some of the cases, those accused of maintenance obtained possession of the land. Lincoln jurors presented that Alan of Leicester granted twelve acres of land to John Rogger under the condition that John would reenfeoff Alan, and William Sewal agreed to block Alan from all actions in exchange for five of the twelve acres. "And thus by the threats and maintenance of William, Alan did not dare to demand the land nor sue according to the law of the realm." An interesting aspect of this presentment is that it seems to treat the maintenance agreement between William and John as a conspiracy. TNA: PRO KB 27/285, m. 14d rex (1331), AALT Img. No. 450 (tr.).

[103] In the Northamptonshire Eyre, the jurors accused John le Keu, the longstanding bailiff of Daventry, of maintaining the purse cutters, whom he often arrested, because he promised that they would go unpunished and took the money found with them for his own use. TNA: PRO JUST 1/632, m. 89d (1329–30), AALT Img. No. 1023. Similarly, Roger of Glentworth, a Lincolnshire bailiff, "annually took robes and fees ... to save from indictment several guilty persons who by law ought to have been indicted" and was "a common maintainer of parties who are indicted or appealed for their gift." TNA: PRO KB 27/285, m. 9d rex (1331), AALT Img. No. 441 (tr.).

[104] TNA: PRO KB 27/311, m. 5 rex (1338), AALT Img. No. 268; TNA: PRO KB 27/436, m. 13 rex (1370), AALT Img. No. 145.

[105] Two Yorkshire men were charged as "common malefactors" violently threatening people at fairs and markets, "taking seisins," and maintaining people, who hired them, "against the peace." TNA: PRO KB 27/310, m. 7d rex (1337), AALT Img. No. 335. Peter de Maulay, lord of Mulgrave and "a maintainer of all false pleas in the East and North Ridings of Yorkshire where he resides," had several common wrongdoers in his household, whom "he maintained to the greatest terror of the people." TNA: PRO KB 27/354, m. 143 (1348), AALT Img. No. 7096.

As with conspiracy presentments, a number of the presentments for maintenance involved extortion and violence. Extortion was present in about 20% of these maintenance cases.[106] One type of case consisted of coercing money from those falsely sued or indicted.[107] Another type involved maintaining officials to use their office as a means of extortion.[108] Also officials maintained pleas to extort fines from the adverse party, sharing the money with the plaintiff.[109] Violence was a common element in these actions (18%). Instances included maintaining men to beat and wound others or forcibly to take their goods[110] and the accused themselves engaging in violence or threatening to do so or doing both.[111] In addition to being charged with taking money for maintaining wrongdoing, Peter de Maulay, lord of Musgrave, led a large group of armed men and engaged in violence.[112]

[106] The leader of a group of vagabonds extorted over £40 in a three-year period by procurement and maintenance. By such conduct, he also prevented himself from being charged with wrongdoing. TNA: PRO KB 27/436, m. 13 rex (1370), AALT Img. No. 145.

[107] TNA: PRO JUST 1/632, m. 54d (1329–30), AALT Img. No. 953 (Northampshire Eyre); TNA: PRO KB 27/285, m. 9d rex (1331), AALT Img. No. 441.

[108] The steward of the earl of Hereford maintained bailiffs to oppress and extort people at fairs and markets, and they took money from several men. TNA: PRO KB 27/366, m. 19 rex (1352), AALT Img. No. 8036.

[109] Ralph of Middleney, escheator for Somerset, was accused of such maintenance. He also took money from various men to support them and was the leader and maintainer of a society of wrongdoers, who "ruled" various vills and markets. TNA: PRO KB 27/392, m. 9 rex (1358), AALT Img. Nos. 1586–90, 1837–40.

[110] The steward of John, Lord Grey, maintained several men to beat and wound another man. When presenters in the leet wished to charge the men, the steward threatened to harm them, and out of fear they presented that the victim himself caused the shedding of his blood, for which he was amerced. TNA: PRO JUST 1/24, m. 47 (1330–31), AALT Img. Nos. 109–10 (Bedfordshire Eyre). In another case, the same lord sent more than 100 armed men to take the animals of a man who refused to discontinue his assize of novel dissesin against the lord. TNA: PRO KB 27/366, m. 30 rex (1352), AALT Img. No. 7804.

[111] TNA: PRO KB 27/294, m. 1 rex (1333), AALT Img. No. 354; TNA: PRO KB 27/310, m. 7d rex (1337), AALT Img. No. 335; TNA: PRO KB 27/353, m. 52d rex (1348), AALT Img. No. 6592.

[112] He took and carried off the goods of a parson, worth £100, forcibly entered the land of several tenants, took the animals within his lordship without paying for them, and struck a Bench attorney for suing him for debt on behalf of a merchant. He also came with sixty armed men to the vill of Routh and took a standing image of the Blessed Virgin Mary and extorted fines from numerous people. He made a fine with king for his wrongdoing and provided a surety of peace against future maintenance and trespasses under penalty of 3,000 marks. TNA: PRO KB 27/354, m. 143 (1348), AALT Img. Nos. 7096–97.

Ambidexterity

Ambidexterity presentments accounted for 9% of all criminal cases and 23% of the nonconspiracy ones. Most of these cases recited that the accused had undertaken to maintain or counsel one party to a plea and then had switched sides to the adverse party and took money from both parties. In some cases, it just said that the defendant was an ambidexter. Some presentments alleged that the accused knew the "counsel" of the initial party when they switched their allegiance to the adverse party.[113] Sometimes they were also charged with being common maintainers of pleas or common ambidexters.[114] William Seymour, when he was sheriff of Northamptonshire, took fees for life from one party in a land action and, after he learned that party's counsel, promised to maintain the adverse party in the same plea in return for a gift, and "was a common maintainer of pleas in the whole county."[115] Unlike in conspiracy and maintenance cases, extortion and violence were uncommon allegations in ambidexterity cases.

Although some of the accused were jurors and officials, such as sheriffs and bailiffs, many of the defendants seemed to be engaging in legal representation. But only three presentments specifically identified the defendant as a lawyer.[116] In a majority of the cases, they were identified as "counsel" and may have been lawyers. When a person was charged with maintaining a plea, it may mean that he was engaged in legal representation and the nature of the fee may also indicate that.

---

[113] Peter of Scremby, a Lincoln knight, was counsel for plaintiffs in an assize of novel disseisin, and after learning all their counsel, he abandoned them because of their poverty, and was counsel to the defendant. TNA: PRO KB 27/285, m. 13d rex (1331), AALT Img. No. 448.

[114] One defendant was charged with being both a common maintainer and a common ambidexter. TNA: PRO KB 27/355, m. 6 (1349), AALT Img. No. 7788.

[115] The jury found him guilty. TNA: PRO JUST 1/635, m. 79 (1329–30), AALT Img. No. 832 (Northamptonshire Eyre) (tr.). Ambidexterity also occurred in the ecclesiastical courts. E.g., TNA: PRO JUST 1/24, m. 47d (1330–31), AALT Img. No. 231 (Bedfordshire Eyre); TNA: PRO KB 27/313, m. 4 rex (1338), AALT Img. No. 230.

[116] One is identified as an attorney and another as a proctor, who took from both parties in two different pleas and was called "a common ambidexter." TNA: PRO JUST 1, m. 49d (1330–31), AALT Img. No. 236; TNA: PRO KB 27/354, m. 35 rex (1348), AALT Img. No. 7204. The third was a man who was acting as an attorney, but was apparently not authorized to do so. William Sewal was counsel to John of Rye, assisting him to obtain a writ of account against Richard le Skinner, John's receiver, to whom he was also counsel. But Richard swore on the gospels that he had no knowledge that William "was admitted as an attorney on the rolls of the justices." TNA: PRO KB 27/285, m. 14 rex (1331), AALT Img. No. 450.

Over 75% of the ambidexterity cases specified the fees taken from each party, with the amounts varing from a 1/2 mark to £40.[117] Many fees were for a particular occasion, but others were for the life of the litigant or annually and some included the giving of robes as well as money. For example, Roger the marshal was counsel to a man in an action of waste against a widow, taking robes and fees from the plaintiff for a year and, after knowing his counsel, took 6 marks and a robe annually from the widow for her life to be her counsel in the matter.[118] In another case, John Fermer, the Essex knight frequently charged with ambidexterity, was counsel to Ralph Stratford, bishop of London, in a writ of ejection against Lady Joan de Baud. So John would remain with Ralph, as his "good friend," Ralph granted him a 100s annual pension for his life. But afterward "in deception of the bishop," John took 10 marks from Lady Joan to delay the matter.[119] These longer retainers seem more likely to indicate that the accused was a person with some legal knowledge or experience. Thus, many of those charged with ambidexterity probably were lawyers, although some may have been local ones and not necessarily professional ones admitted in the royal courts.

Champerty

The champerty cases accounted for 11% of the nonconspiracy ones and 4% of all the criminal cases. In about half of them, the person charged

---

[117] Although money was the most common fee, in one case the former sheriff of Nottingham took a palfrey worth 6 marks from a parson and 40s from his adversary. TNA: PRO KB JUST 1, m. 59d (1330–31), AALT Img. Nos. 9784–85. In another case, John Frere of Doncaster, bailiff of the vill and collector of royal taxes, took three pigs to support a plaintiff suing a man who stole his oxen and then took 1 mark not to attach the defendant, and "thus he took from both sides." John was also charged with a number of instances of extortion. TNA: PRO KB 27/356, m. 5 (1349), AALT Img. No. 8391. He was also appointed as a justice to make inquiries regarding the Statute of Labourers. *Calendar of Close Rolls, Edward III 1354–1360*, vol. 10 (London, 1908), "Close Rolls, Edward III: April 1358," *British History Online*.

[118] Roger's plea, which resulted in him being found not guilty, was interesting. He said that when he undertook the representation of the widow, he refused to be her counsel in this matter and expressly excluded it from his representation and that he successfully caused the parties to settle that matter. His success is puzzling because he knew the plaintiff's confidences and still seemed to be representing both of them in arranging the settlement. TNA: PRO JUST 1/24, m. 49d (1330–31), AALT Img. No. 235 (Bedfordshire Eyre).

[119] TNA: PRO KB 27/367, m. 35 rex (1352), AALT Img. No. 8550. In another case in the Befordshire Eyre, Nicholas of Stukeley was of counsel to a knight, taking robes and fees for a year, and afterward, when he knew the knight's counsel, he switched sides to the adverse party for 1 mark a year for his life. TNA: PRO JUST 1/24, m. 50 (1330–31), AALT Img. No. 117.

was an official or a lawyer.[120] In many respects, these cases are puzzling. Very few of these presentments were limited to accusations of champerty, but included other types of criminal conduct, which makes it difficult to determine the impact of champerty on the presentment. But one-third of the presentments were likely for champerty, as they described champertous conduct and explicitly said that it was against the statute, although they used the word "maintenance."[121] Other cases used the word "champerty" but did not provide much insight into its relevance.[122] In several cases, the word was used generically, labeling the defendant a "champertor" or a "common champertor," without describing any champertous or other conduct. After presenting the earl of Richmond's bailiff for conspiracy to maintain, procuring inquests, and extortion, the presentment said that he was "a champertor and maintainer of all pleas in the court of his lord."[123] In another case, jurors accused the defendant of several instances of ambidexterity and then charged that he was "a common ambidexter" and "a common mover and maintainer of false pleas" and that he "commonly took for champerty in several pleas."[124]

Finally, champerty was not charged in several cases that seemed to involve champerty. In one case, the accused maintained the defendant in a land plea while the plea was pending, in exchange for enfeoffing him of the land.[125] In another variation, the defendants caused a man to bring

---

[120] The officials included a coroner, a lord's steward, an earl's bailiff, and two royal tax collectors. One was a clearly a lawyer, a proctor, and official of an abbot. The others seemed to have been acting as lawyers, but again it is not always possible to be certain, as some were described as "counsel."

[121] Half of these cases said that the conduct was "against the form of the statute." It is likely that the statute was the 1300 *Articuli Super Cartas*, c. 11. The other half refer to the acquisition of land while a plea was pending, which may then be referring to the Statute of Westminster II, c. 49. One presentment did both. TNA: PRO KB 27/285, m. 13d rex (1331), AALT Img. No. 448.

[122] One of these instances is in a note in the report of the case and not in the plea roll record. Donald Sutherland, ed., *Eyre of Northamptonshire, 3–4 Edward III*, 2 vols. (London, 1983), vol. I, 97 Selden Soc., p. 237. Seipp No. 1330.443ss.

[123] TNA: PRO KB 27/285, m. 10 rex (1331), AALT Img. Nos. 452–53. Another presentment charged a tax collector with extortion, and then said he was "a common champertor with another man of all pleas in the vill." TNA: PRO KB 27/355, m. 4 (1349), AALT Img. No. 7783.

[124] TNA: PRO KB 27/355, m. 6 (1349), AALT Img. No. 7788. Another case charged John Fermer, the Essex lawyer, with ambidexterity and maintaining the false delivery of an indicted man, concluding that "thus John Fermer is a champertor." TNA: PRO KB 27/367, m. 35 rex (1352), AALT Img. No. 8317.

[125] The plaintiff prevailed in the Common Bench by default and brought a writ to have seisin. The defendant prevented execution of the writ and continued to hold the land by force and lordship. TNA: PRO KB 27/369, m. 4 rex (1352), AALT Img. No. 9292. In

an action, in which he recovered the land and sold it for 40 marks and the defendants kept most of the money from the sale.[126] None of these cases makes any reference to the champerty statutes nor uses the word "champerty," although all these defendants were presented for various other offenses.

Other Criminal Cases Regarding Abuse of Legal Procedure

The remaining criminal cases require little discussion. One group involved presentments for procuring, aiding and abetting, or threatening a false appeal or indictment, which accounted for 4.5% of all criminal cases and 12% of the nonconspiracy ones.[127] Over half of these cases involved extortion or other wrongful conduct and all the accused were officials.[128] In one case, the former sheriff of Nottingham coerced fines from several men by falsely telling them they had been indicted for theft.[129] A bailiff, who was also a tax collector, threatened to indict a knight until he made a fine with him.[130] A smaller group of cases involved procuring false civil

---

  another instance, the plaintiff's attorney caused his client to implead a man and his wife of their land and, with the plea pending, agreed with the parties that the land would remain with the attorney because of the plea, and he enfeoffed his brother of the land. The record said that the attorney still held the land. TNA: PRO KB 27/354, m. (1348), AALT Img. No. 7205.

[126] The defendants gave the plaintiff 40s, a tunic, and a cloak and gave the plaintiff's attorney 40s. TNA: PRO KB 27/356, m. 5 (1349), AALT Img. No. 8391.

[127] Some of them only alleged that defendant procured or abetted a false criminal accusation. For example, two men falsely and maliciously procured another for the theft of four pigs, and he was subsequently acquitted. TNA: PRO JUST 1/24, m. 52 (1330–31), AALT Img. No. 121 (Bedfordshire Eyre).

[128] Although violence was uncommon in these cases, one instance is noteworthy. John fitz Wauter, the frequently indicted Essex knight, wrongfully had a coroner sit in the liberty of Colchester. But a juror impaneled before the coroner refused to indict falsely the bailiff of Colchester and other men of the town, enemies of John, for a death of which they were not guilty. As a result, John had his men go to the juror's house and beat and wound him, which caused his death. TNA: PRO JUST 1/266, m. 4d (1351), AALT Img. No. 3379 (Essex sessions of the peace).

[129] He also took money to grant bail to those indicted, although they were repleviable and took money to execute a writ of novel disseisin, in which his undersheriff took a reward from the defendant to delay execution of the writ and was indicted for extortion and other types of wrongdoing involving prisoners and approvers. He was found guilty on some of the charges and not guilty on others. TNA: PRO JUST 1/166, m. 50d (1330–31), AALT Img. Nos. 9784–85.

[130] TNA: PRO KB 27/356, m. 5 (1349), AALT Img. No. 8391. In another case, a juror was presented for threatening to indict a man falsely unless the latter, who was already in prison, enfeoffed the juror's son of a toft and delivered the charters to them, which he did as a result of his fear. TNA: PRO KB 27/295, m. 8 rex (1334), AALT Img. No. 283.

pleas.[131] A few others involved the misconduct of jurors, juries, and inquests. A few residual criminal cases involved various types of conduct, such as biased and manipulated arbitration,[132] falsification of jury documents,[133] giving food and drink to jurors,[134] and bribery of jurors by counsel to obtain the defendant's release at jail delivery.[135]

Changes in Criminal Litigation Dealing with Abuse of Legal Procedure

The criminal litigation involving legal corruption during the reign of Edward III was quite similar at a global level to that of the earlier reigns. In both periods, the criminal litigation regarding abuse of legal procedure was substantially greater (75% and 73%) than the civil litigation involving this conduct and conspiracy cases predominated in both periods (62% and 64%). But a more detailed examination reveals interesting differences regarding the nature of the conspiracy cases and the relationship of conspiracy to maintenance, ambidexterity, champerty, and the other forms of abuse.[136] As suggested above, the factual and legal nature of

[131] A Dorset parson "commonly falsely and maliciously impleaded and oppressed to have gain falsely." TNA: PRO KB 27/392, m. 25 rex (1358), AALT Img. No. 1619. In one case, a Wiltshire clerk caused two men to plead another in a land matter and then took an ox worth 15s from the defendant, "so that by his deceit both parties were harmed." TNA: PRO KB 27/352, m. 35 (1348), AALT Img. No. 2472.

[132] In an arbitration of a plea before the archbishop of York, the plaintiff's proctor and two of his associates were made the arbitrators and were advised by the archbishop's clerk to condemn the defendant for £30 with the money divided between the plaintiff, the arbitrators, and the clerks. TNA: PRO KB 27/355, m. 10d (1349), AALT Img. No. 8103.

[133] The jury clerk, unknown to the jurors, wrote an indictment that falsely stated that the defendant had committed felonies when he had been indicted for trespasses. TNA: PRO KB 27/364, m. 15 rex (1351), AALT Img. No. 6657.

[134] In a case in which John fitz Wauter was the plaintiff, his steward gave the jurors, who had not been able to agree, food and drink. The panel was quashed and the sheriff ordered to make "a new jury of wealthier men and men nearer the view, who were not suspect to either side." TNA: PRO KB 27/366, m. 30 rex (1352), AALT Img. No. 7807.

[135] But the defendant was not released and was condemned because his counsel bribed two men to say the defendant was guilty after he had told the defendant that "he could be absolutely sure about being acquitted and released" if two men were on the jury and not challenged by the defendant. TNA: PRO KB 27/374, m. 35 rex (1354), AALT Img. No. 2451 (tr.).

[136] Stubbs said that the law viewed maintenance and champerty as they related to the support of pleas "as a description of conspiracy," but when it was connected with the giving of livery and the "gathering around the lord's household of a swarm of armed retainers," the law viewed it "as an organization of robbers and rioters." William Stubbs, Constitutional History of England, 3 vols. (Oxford, 1897; reprint, 1967), vol. III, pp. 551–52.

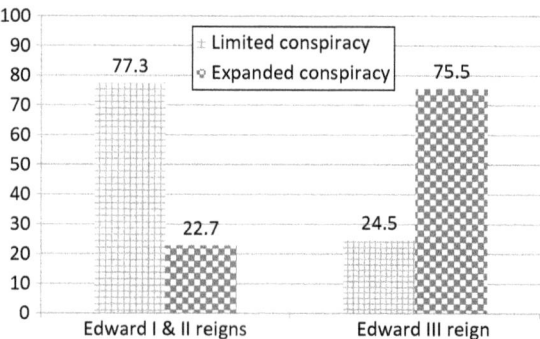

Figure 6.2 Comparison of conspiracy cases in the reigns of Edward I, Edward II, and Edward III (in percentages).

conspiracy seems to have expanded during the reign of Edward III. Further, it is possible to divide conspiracy cases into two categories: limited conspiracy, in which the presentments involved only allegations such as maintenance, ambidexterity, champerty, and procuring false criminal accusations and civil pleas, and expanded conspiracy, in which the presentment included other allegations, frequently ones involving extortion or violence. As Figure 6.2 reveals, separating the cases into these two categories shows the different nature of the conspiracy litigation in the two periods.[137] In this comparison, the different nature of conspiracy in each of the two periods seems to be a mirror image of each other. In both periods, conspiracies involving maintenance remained the predominant type of criminal conspiracy case, accounting for 44% of those cases in the reigns of Edward I and II and 42% in the reign of Edward III. However, an examination of the different types of nonconspiracy criminal cases suggests that maintenance, ambidexterity , champerty, and procuring false indictments, appeals, and civil pleas were becoming more established as criminal offenses independent of

---

[137] In dividing the cases into these two categories for each of the two periods, those cases that revealed no details of the conspiracy, usually because the presentment only charges that the defendants are conspirators or because they involve mesne process entries that do not reveal any information about the conspiracy, were eliminated not included. Further, the few cases that charged only a violation of eyre prohibition on the presence of those convicted of conspiracy were also eliminated. This reduced the total number of conspiracy cases during the reigns of Edward I and II from 146 to 132 and those during the reign of Edward III from 285 to 249.

Table 6.3 *Criminal abuse of legal procedure cases compared*

	1272–1327	1327–77
Maintenance	14.8%	19.2%
Ambidexterity	9.3%	9.6%
Champerty	2.3%	4.5%
Procure indictment of appeal	0	4.9%
Procure civil plea	0	1.4%

conspiracy. Prosecution of all of these forms of legal corruption increased during the reign of Edward III. Further, ambidexterity cases, which accounted for almost 25% of the conspiracy cases in the earlier period, largely disappeared as a type of conspiracy case in the latter period. In addition, conspiracy as a criminal offense not only had expanded, but its interrelationship with maintenance and other forms of legal corruption, so common in the earlier period, had diminished.[138] Table 6.3 compares the criminal prosecutions in these two periods and their changing nature.

As discussed in Chapter 4, conspiracy was a crime that required two or more persons to engage in the prohibited conduct. Nevertheless, during the reign of Edward III, jurors continued to present only one individual for conspiracy, but not as frequently as was done during earlier period. The presentment usually accused one named person "and others" as having conspired.[139] A few cases charged one individual with being "a common conspirator."[140] In one case, this practice was challenged. Thomas Southover was the only defendant named as conspiring with unnamed others and was found guilty by the jury. He brought a writ of

---

[138] Musson and Ormrod asserted that the offense of conspiracy became "a generic term covering threats to the community, to political liberty, and to the workings of the state ... The meaning of conspiracy therefore expanded beyond the simple the simple obstruction of legal processes to encapsulate any form of sworn alliance or confederation ..." Anthony Musson and W. Mark Ormrod, *The Evolution of English Justice* (Basingstoke, 1999), p. 185.

[139] E.g., TNA: PRO KB 27/315, m. 10d rex (1339), AALT Img. No. 255; TNA: PRO KB 27/366, m. 3 (1352), AALT Img. Nos. 7741–42, 8003; TNA: PRO KB 27/369, m. 5 rex (1352), AALT Img. Nos. 9294–95, 9675–76. Occasionally, the presentment named just one individual as having conspired. TNA: PRO KB 27/352, m. 31d rex (1348), AALT Img. No. 3100.

[140] E.g., TNA: PRO KB 27/354, m. 71d (1348), AALT Img. No. 7449; TNA: PRO KB 27/355, m. (1349), AALT Img. No. 7785.

error in the King's Bench, alleging that it was error for the justices to put him alone to answer the charge of conspiracy because

> no one else was named as a conspirator in the presentment and no one else previously or at the time was put to answer with him, for conspiracy especially must be the doing of two men at least and they ought to be arraigned and judged together and not separately.[141]

The King's Bench justices agreed and annulled the judgment, holding that it was erroneous because

> the justices passed judgment in this way upon Thomas as a conspirator on his own without anyone else being convicted for aforesaid conspiracy, although this must be the work of at least two persons and cannot be done by one alone.[142]

This decision was an important clarification of the law of conspiracy.[143] Requiring two defendants to be charged was likely a change from that of the earlier period, even though it was not consistently followed.

Civil Litigation

The civil cases during the period 1327–77 constituted 24% of the litigation regarding legal corruption, a similar proportion to that in 1272–1327. But for the civil litigation in the later period, it would have been much less except for the large number of actions for aiding and abetting false indictments or appeals, which was by far the most common

---

[141] He also said that it was error because the justices "adjudged him to be a conspirator, whereas the record does not mention anyone else who had been previously or at the same time convicted with him of the said conspiracy." TNA: PRO KB 27/337, m. 111 (1344), AALT Img. Nos. 237–38, 225, reprinted in G.O. Sayles, ed., *Select Cases in the Court of the King's Bench*, 7 vols. (London, 1965), vol. VI, 58 Selden Soc., pp. 33–36.

[142] Ibid., m. 111d, AALT Img. No. 225. In one case, several individuals were indicted for conspiracy, and all but one were acquitted. Therefore, the remaining defendant said that he could not be adjudged a conspirator or confederator. Y.B. East. 28 Edw. III, Lib. Ass. 146, pl. 12 (1354), Seipp No. 1354.106ass.

[143] The court said in one case that a man, who engaged in malice and falsehood and for which he paid a fine, could not be indicted as a conspirator in his own dispute. Y.B. Hil. 22 Edw. III, fol. 1, pl. 4 (1348), Seipp No. 1348.004. Similarly, a husband and wife argued that they could not be charged with conspiracy for a matter in their own right. Y.B. East. 40 Edw. III, fol. 19, pl. 10 (1366), Seipp No. 1366.042. The defendant later excepted on the ground that writ could not be brought against a *feme covert* as she could not conspire with her husband because she was at his will, and, therefore, it was only the act of husband. TNA: PRO KB 27/342, m. 78 (1345), AALT Img. No. 158; Y.B. Mich. 19 Edw. III, Roll Series fols. 346–49, pl. 24 (1345), Seipp No. 1345.188rs.

civil action in this reign (30%).[144] As in the earlier period, conspiracy actions were still the most common type of civil action (60%), but there was a significant decrease from the earlier period (78%). In addition, there was a substantial decrease in each of the various types of conspiracy cases.[145] There is, however, less information available about the nature of the civil conspiracy actions since many of the records (60%) were only entries of mesne process.[146] Table 6.4 identifies the different types of civil actions and their frequency.

During this period as in the prior one, the most common civil conspiracy actions were for procuring false indictments or appeals (23%), although they were less common than in the earlier period (38%).[147] Similarly, there was a significant decrease in conspiracy actions alleging the procurement of false civil pleas.[148] As was typical in cases regarding false criminal accusations, the plaintiff alleged that the defendants falsely and maliciously procured the plaintiff to be indicted or appealed and afterward he was acquitted to his damage and against the form of the ordinance.[149] Almost all the actions were against multiple defendants.[150]

Similar legal issues arose in these actions as had arisen in civil actions in the earlier reigns. Plaintiffs continued to bring conspiracy actions

---

[144] All of them were mesne process entries. When added to the civil conspiracy mesne process entries, such entries constituted 67% of the civil actions in this period.

[145] The procurement of false indictments and appeals decreased from 26.4% of the civil cases to 14.1%, procuring false civil pleas from 16.1% to 0.7%, maintenance from 6.9% to 1.3%, ambidexterity from 3.5% to 0, and other types of civil conspiracy cases from 20.7% to 3.4%.

[146] During the earlier period, mesne process entries were only 5.9% of the civil conspiracy actions.

[147] In one case, the defendant argued that an action was available only when there was a false indictment for felony. The court rejected the argument because a person was damaged by imprisonment for trespass as well as felony. Although the peril and mischief were less, the availability of remedy did not depend on the quantity of damage. Y.B. East., 3 Edw. III, fol. 19, pl. 34 (1329), Seipp No. 1329.073.

[148] During the earlier period, they were 20% of such actions, but in the later period they constituted only 2% of the civil conspiracy actions. In one such action, the plaintiff alleged the defendants conspired to impersonate him and make a release of the right he had in tenements, for which he had brought an assize of novel disseisin against one of the defendants. Y.B. Mich. 6 Edw. III, fol. 41, pl. 21 (1332), Seipp No. 1332.151.

[149] Over half of these actions were mesne process entries, but their allegations did not differ from those in pleaded cases.

[150] There were twenty-one of these actions and in only two was there a single defendant, who was the same person being sued by different plaintiffs. In two of these actions there were nine defendants. TNA: PRO KB 27/369, m. 72d (1352), AALT Img. No. 9598; TNA: PRO KB 27/421, m. 59 (1366), AALT Img. No. 120.

Table 6.4 *Types of civil actions, 1327–77*

Conspiracy		91 (61%)
Procure false indictment or appeal	21 (14.1%)	
Against individual	6 (4%)	
Procure false civil plea	1 (1.3%)	
Maintenance	2 (.7%)	
Ambidexterity	0	
Other types	5 (3.4%)	
Mesne process, no details	56 (37.6%)	
Total	91	
Other types of actions		58 (39%)
Aid or abet false indictment or appeal	44 (29.5%)	
Champerty	10 (6.7%)	
Maintenance	0	
Procure false indictment or appeal	0	
Procure false civil plea	0	
Other abuse of legal procedure	4 (2.6%)	
Total	58	
Total civil cases		149

against the jurors who had indicted them.[151] In some actions, the plaintiffs attempted to evade the rule precluding the writ of conspiracy against indictors by arguing that the conspiracy had occurred prior to the indictment, but this tactic was not successful. In one case, the plaintiff argued that the conspiracy occurred first, followed by the defendants procuring themselves to be on the inquest, and then the defendant jurors not doing what their office required by violating their oath to say the truth.[152] But Thorp CJKB said that when the defendants swore to tell the truth, it was by their oath and not by conspiracy and that "it was not reason to attaint a man by conspiracy where he did nothing except that which the law willed." In a later case, Shareshull CJKB also asserted

---

[151] TNA: PRO KB 27/392, m. 28d (1358), AALT Img. No. 1731. The court ordered the sheriff to provide the names of the indictors. In other cases, the defendant jurors vouched the record to prove their role. TNA: PRO KB 27/421, m. 59 (1366), AALT Img. No. 120; Y.B. 27 Edw. III, Lib. Ass. 134, pl. 13 (1353), Seipp No. 1353.138ass; Y.B. 30 Edw. III, Lib. Ass. 177, pl. 21 (1356), Seipp No. 1356.136ass.

[152] The defendant argued that as an indictor, he could not procure himself. Y.B. East. 21 Edw. III, fol. 17, pl. 19 (1347), Seipp No. 1347.064.

that the oath eliminated any conspiracy between the indictors. He said that "it could not at any time be adjudged conspiracy against them, of that which they affirmed by their oath."[153] The justices seemed to treat this issue as settled. At the end of this period, when the court rejected the plaintiff's argument that the conspiracy had preceded the indictment, Cavendish CJKB said that "we must support the ancient judgments of our predecessors, as if to say, that conspiracy cannot be in such a case."[154] Although such actions continued to come before the courts,[155] the rule denying a writ of conspiracy against the indictors was restated in broad and definitive terms by Chief Justices Popham and Coke, Chief Baron Tanfield, and Lord Chancellor Egerton in a later Star Chamber case. Citing these earlier Year Book cases, they said:

> No conspiracy lies for him who is acquitted against the indictors, for that they are returned by the sheriff by process of law to make inquiry of the offences upon their oath, and it is for the service of the king and the commonwealth ... [T]hey are compellable by law to service the law, and the court: and their indictment or verdict is a matter of record ... and shall not be avoided by surmise or supposal, and no attaint lies. And for this reason they shall not be impeached for any conspiracy or practice, before the indictment: for the law will not suppose any unindifferent, when he is sworn to serve the king: and with this agrees the books.[156]

Actions accusing a single conspirator arose in civil cases, as they had in criminal ones in this period. In 1348, the Common Bench acquitted a conspiracy defendant, agreeing with the defendant that he could not be indicted as a single conspirator where the other conspirator was an indictor.[157] But in a writ of error by a man convicted of conspiracy for procuring another to be appealed of robbery, it was argued that the judgment should be reversed because none of the other conspirators

---

[153] Y.B. 27 Edw. III, Lib. Ass. 134, pl. 12 (1353), Seipp No. 1353.137ass.

[154] Y.B. Mich. 47 Edw. III, fols. 16–17, pl. 30 (1373), Seipp No. 1373.043 (tr.).

[155] Winfield, *History of Conspiracy*, pp. 68–71.

[156] Floyd and Barker (1608), 12 Co. Rep. 23, 77 Eng. Rep. 1305–6.

[157] The other defendant, alleged to have been falsely procured for the death of another, admitted causing the death, but was acquitted by force of law as acting in self-defense. Y.B. 22 Edw. III, Lib. Ass. 102, pl. 77 (1348), Seipp No. 1348.285ass. In another case, two defendants were sued for fabricating a false deed of excommunication. One defendant was acquitted and other found guilty. The latter demanded judgment "in as much as conspiracy cannot be by fewer than two." Willoughby JKB said that "the inquest was taken of one, whereas the conspiracy was alleged by the two. And then they were adjourned." Y.B. Hil. 8 Edw. III, fols. 17–18, pl. 50 (1334), Seipp No. 1334.049 (tr.).

had not yet been attainted or subjected to process.[158] But the finding of guilt was affirmed. Shareshull CJKB said that because defendant had conspired "in a conspiracy made beforehand and procured him to be appealed ... Thus it seemed that, since the evil, namely the procurement that followed after the conspiracy, is alleged only in [the defendant], the judgment of damages was perfectly good enough, and in accordance with the law."[159] Pursuing the same legal point, defendants also argued that a husband and wife could not conspire with each other. In one case, the court seemed to agree, although it was not completely clear.[160] In addition, the courts continued to deal with issues involving the impact of a nonsuit.[161] A woman, who had been procured by a man and his wife to appeal the plaintiff for the death of her husband, was nonsuited and the plaintiff was quit. The defendant demanded judgment as the plaintiff could still be convicted by indictment, but the writ was adjudged good.[162] The impact of a nonsuit would be negated if the king continued to pursue the prosecution and the conspiracy plaintiff was acquitted.[163]

Conspiracies against individuals were the only other type of conspiracy actions that occurred with any frequency (6.6%). Two cases involving

---

[158] In a writ of error in another conspiracy case, one of the plaintiffs had died and Thorp CJKB said that a reversal for error would have to be for him as well as the plaintiff bringing the writ of error because one person could not conspire. Shareshull JCP said that "it would be harsh if the death of his neighbor or his companion would deprive him of the action." The writ was annulled, however, because of the absence of required details of the conspiracy. Y.B. Mich. Edw. III, fols. 75–76, pl. 99 (1350), Seipp No. 1350.212 (tr.).

[159] Y.B. Mich. 24 Edw. III, fol. 34, pl. 34 (1350), Seipp No. 1350.203 (tr.). Several other defendants alleged the same defense. Y.B. Mich. Trin. 27 Edw. III, fol. 4, pl. 6 (1353), Seipp No. 1353.032. In another case, the defendant excepted on the ground that writ could not be brought against a *feme covert* as she could not conspire with her husband because she was at his will and, therefore, it was only the act of husband. TNA: PRO KB 27/342, m. 78 (1345), AALT Img. No. 158; Y.B. Mich. 19 Edw. III, Roll Series fols. 346–49, pl. 24 (1345), Seipp No.1345.188rs.

[160] Thorp CJCP said that the case of his action "could not be said to a conspiracy, for then each man of law would be said a conspirator. For I give you counsel to sue an action, and the action is not maintainable in the cause, that one could not be called a conspirator." Y.B. Hil. 38 Edw. III, fol. 3, pl. 12 (1364), Seipp No. 1364.012 (tr.).

[161] Winfield, *History of Conspiracy*, pp. 43–44.

[162] TNA: PRO KB 27/342, m. 78 (1345), AALT Img. No. 158; Y.B. Mich. 19 Edw. III, Roll Series fols. 346–49, pl. 24 (1345), Seipp No.1345.188rs. Eustace de Folville was the plaintiff. Other defendants made the same argument. Y.B. Mich. 41 Edw. III, fol. 1, pl. 40 (1367), Seipp No. 1367.080. TNA: PRO CP 40/341, m. 424 (1345), AALT Img. No. 872; Y.B. Hil. 19 Edw. III, Roll Series fols. 567–69, pl. 53 (1345), Seipp No. 1345.053rs.

[163] TNA: PRO CP 40/341, m. 424 (1345), AALT Img. No. 872; Y.B. Hil. 19 Edw. III, Roll Series fols. 567–69, pl. 53 (1345), Seipp No. 1345.053rs.

villeins were perhaps the most interesting ones. In one case, two Lincoln men conspired with the abbot of Selby's villeins to rise up against the abbot, promising them that they would attain free status and counseling them to engage in various litigation tactics to wear out the abbot and cause him to make significant expenditures.[164] In the other, a villein sued his lord for trespass and conspired with a clerk to devise a complex scheme to prevent the lord from averring the villein's status in order to avoid answering the villein's action.[165]

Perhaps the champerty cases were the most significant civil ones in this period. Although not that numerous (6.7%), they were important because they completed the development of civil champerty actions based on *Articuli super Cartas*, c. 11. As explained in Chapter 4, these actions were initiated by a king's writ of *audita querela*, which caused the defendant to be ordered to appear to answer both the king and the complainant, and the latter pursued the matter to recover damages. But since the justices had said the action belonged to the king, parties could not obtain original writs to bring champerty actions. This same procedure continued through the first decades of the latter period.[166] Consequently, private civil actions still could not be initiated by an original writ.[167]

---

[164] They instructed the villeins to bring multiple, successive assizes of novel disseisin, essoin themselves at each, and not prosecute their writs until the abbot conformed to their will. The abbot recovered 200 marks against the two men, who were ordered to answer the king for their conspiracy. TNA: PRO KB 27/285, m. 97d (1331), AALT Img. No. 208.

[165] In the scheme, the villein brought another trespass action against the lord, unknown to the latter, and the conspirators procured a man to appear in that action to impersonate the lord, so that neither the lord nor his attorney appeared. In that action, the villein sought to establish his free status and recover £200. While the action was pending and after the villein had counted, the lord complained to the king, who sent a writ to King's Bench justices, and the lord obtained a writ against the two conspirators, who were ordered to come and answer. TNA: PRO KB 27/369, m. 51 (1352), AALT Img. No. 9158.

[166] There were several such champerty actions. TNA: PRO KB 27/280, m. 53d (1330), AALT Img. No. 105; TNA: PRO CP 40/313, m. 14d (1339), AALT Img. No. 28. Similarly in 1347 and 1348 mesne process entries based on the statute the inclusion of the words "as the King learned (*ut accepit Rex*)" indicated that action was originally initiated by the king's writ of *audita querela*. TNA: PRO KB 27/350, m. 78 (1347), AALT Img. No. 3640; TNA: PRO CP 40/353, m. 298 (1348), AALT Img. No. 6526.

[167] A 1348 action was begun by the king's writ, although the writ omitted the *audita querela*, saying instead that the king wished the ordinance "to be observed imperishably" and that the "justices should further inspect the tenor of the ordinance." TNA: PRO CP 40/353, m. 298 (1348), AALT Img. No. 7185.

However, the procedure seemed to have changed after the middle of the century as actions initiated by original writs began to appear. In champerty actions in 1352 and 1366, there is no evidence of a prior writ of *audita querela* by the king, and, therefore, it seems that they were initiated by an original writ.[168] In the April 1376 parliament, the Commons requested that the statute prohibiting champerty be "better explained and confirmed" and that the Chancellor order granting writs "at the suit of the party so that he might recover his damages."[169] By the end of the fourteenth century, there were numerous civil champerty actions, all of which seem to have been initiated by original writ without a prior royal writ.[170] The fifteenth-century writ registers contain a number of original writs founded on *Articulas Super Cartas*, c. 11.[171]

Conclusion

Overall, the reign of Edward III, like the earlier ones, was quite litigious in terms of prosecutions and actions targeting legal corruption. Although the litigation in these two periods may appear generally similar, there were noteworthy differences. During the later period, there is a modest increase in criminal cases and modest decline in civil actions. In both instances, the cause seems to have been a pronounced decline in civil conspiracy actions and in civil actions not alleging

---

[168] The 1352 action is in *qui tam* form and the defendants were attached to answer for champerty that occurred in a trespass action before the steward and marshal of the king's household. TNA: PRO KB 27/367, m. (1352), AALT Img. No. 8421. The 1362 action was a mesne process entry for champerty in a debt action in the Common Bench. TNA: PRO KB 27/423, m. 58 (1366), AALT Img. No. 495. No other records in either of these actions were found.

[169] Edward III Parliaments: April 1376, No. 89, XXXIX, *PROME*.

[170] TNA: PRO KB 27/522, m. 50 (1391), AALT Img. No. 116; TNA: PRO CP 40/536, m. 107 (1395), AALT Img. No. 243; TNA: PRO CP 40/536, m. 171d (1395), AALT Img. No. 393; TNA: PRO CP 40/536, m. 248d (1395), AALT Img. No. 555; TNA: PRO CP 40/536, m. 349d (1395), AALT Img. No. 769; TNA: PRO CP 40/536, m. 435d (1395), AALT Img. No. 951; TNA: PRO KB 27/543, m. 24d (1397), AALT Img. No. 237; TNA: PRO KB 27/543, m. 60d (1397), AALT Img. No. 317; TNA: PRO KB 27/544, m. 32d (1397), AALT Img. No. 285; TNA: PRO KB 27/546, m. 81d (1397), AALT Img. No. 421; TNA: PRO CP 40/544, m. 408 (1399), AALT Img. No. 822; TNA: PRO CP 40/559, m. 68d (1400), AALT Img. No. 1556; TNA: PRO CP 40/559, m. 401(1400), AALT Img. No. 871; TNA: PRO CP 40/559, m. 68d (1400), AALT Img. Nos. 1106–7.

[171] Cambridge University Library Add. MS 6854, f. 270r; ibid., Gg. 5.19, f. 111v; ibid., Ff. 1.32, f. 190v; British Library Harley MS 4701, f. 127r; ibid., Ff. 5.5, f. 199v; British Library Harley MS 4021, f. 107r–107v.

conspiracy.[172] These data seem to reinforce the suggestions made above that conspiracy as a legal device for attacking abuse of legal procedure was declining and that the substantive notions of maintenance, champerty, and procuring of false indictments and appeals were becoming more established as legal weapons against this type of conduct. And as also suggested earlier, the legal concept of conspiracy seemed to be expanding during this period. Table 6.5 reflects the changing nature of this litigation in these two periods.

One final noteworthy development is that there was some evidence / that legal weapons developed to attack legal corruption were being used to harass litigation opponents. For example, early in the reign of Edward III, there were four lawsuits between William of Wendlebury and his wife, Maud, and John, the son of William Bost. John brought two trespass actions against William and Maud.[173] John and his wife Margaret also brought an assize of novel disseisin against William and Maud.[174] Perhaps in retaliation, William and Maud complained to the king that John had engaged in champerty in violation of *Articuli super Cartas*, c. 11, by maintaining John Baret, who had arraigned an assize of novel disseisin against William and Maud regarding the same land.[175] All of these actions were brought within a short period of time.[176]

---

[172] Moreover, because of the substantial and increased number of mesne process criminal and civil conspiracy entries in the latter period, there were far fewer conspiracy cases that provided any information regarding the nature of the conduct. The mesne process records in civil conspiracy actions may have indicated that these matters were more likely to be settled in the latter period.

[173] One for taking and imprisoning him and the other for taking and carrying away his timber, wood, hay, thatch, and straw. William and Maud were convicted in both actions and John recovered his damages. TNA: PRO KB 27/281, m. 93 (1330), AALT Img. No. 191. TNA: PRO KB 27/281, m. 93 (1330), AALT Img. No. 198.

[174] The jury found for John and Margaret, who recovered their seisin and damages, although they were amerced for a false claim against two other defendants. TNA: PRO KB 27/281, m. 97d (1330), AALT Img. No. 196.

[175] The king sent a writ of *audita querela* to the King's Bench justices to proceed with the matter. John sought judgment whether he had to respond to the writ since it varied from the words of the statute. TNA: PRO KB 27/280, m. 53d (1330), AALT Img. No. 105.

[176] From the records, it is not really possible to fix the order of these actions. The trespasses occurred on May 26, 1330, and October 2, 1329. John's assize of novel disseisin was arraigned on May 7, 1330, but because of failures of mayor and bailiff of the liberty of Oxford, he requested and obtained a writ to reattach the defendants, returnable on June 18, 1330. It is unknown when William and Matilda complained to the king, but his writ was on May 1, 1330, and, after John's plea, a day was given to the parties on June 11, 1330. All of John's actions were enrolled in Trinity Term, 4 Edw. III, and the king's writ in Easter Term, 4 Edw. III.

Table 6.5 *Abuse of legal procedure litigation, 1272–1327 and 1327–77, compared*

	1272–1377	1327–77
Criminal cases	72.6%	75.7%
Conspiracy	46.1%	46.6%
Other types	26.5%	29.1%
Civil actions	27.4%	24.3%
Conspiracy	21.4%	14.9%
Other types	6 %	9.5%

Conspiracy actions also may have been used as a tool of abuse. In 1352, Robert de Bilkemore and four other Wiltshire men were presented for conspiring to extort money from Robert Hoppegras and William Waryn by threatening to indict them for conspiring to eject the former Robert from his manor. Although they claimed that they were not guilty, each made a fine for £20 with Robert. Nevertheless, after receiving the money, they procured Robert Hoppegras and William to be indicted for conspiracy, of which they were acquitted.[177] In a dispute in the royal manor of Havering, the jurors in the Essex sessions of peace indicted eleven wealthy, senior men of Havering for conspiracy to indict a number of prominent Havering tenants, including some of the jurors. A number of those targeted made fines, hoping to avoid being indicted. Then the eleven, who were initially indicted, threatened to indict the jurors in revenge and nine of them made fines. The king intervened and sent the matter to the King's Bench and the eleven men were acquitted.[178] Kaeuper described how the commissions of *oyer et terminer*,

---

[177] Robert Bilkemore pleaded not guilty and claimed he took the money from the two men, at the behest of his friends, to dismiss his conspiracy action, but he was found guilty by the jury. He argued, however, that judgment ought not be entered against him because of parliamentary action quashing and annulling commissions for new acquisitions and that a writ of *supersedeas* should be granted. Also he put forth a writ of *non molestando*. After two further writs from the king supporting Robert's position, the justices, although initially saying that they were "not yet advised," decided that Robert should go without day. TNA: PRO KB 27/368, m. 8 rex (1352), AALT Img. Nos. 8729–30, 8983–84.

[178] TNA: PRO KB 27/366, m. 35 rex (1352), AALT Img. Nos. 7824, 8077. Many of the details of the conflict, including some of those recited in the text, are recounted in Marjorie McIntosh, *Autonomy and Community: The Royal Manor of Havering, 1200–1500* (Cambridge, 1986), pp. 60–62.

although an instrument to control disorder, became a new and powerful legal device for less salutary purposes. Powerful and influential lords, the gentry, and others obtained them to harass their opponents and make false criminal accusations.[179] He said this procedure "must be counted a negative force in fourteenth century English law" that "actually magnified the problem of disorder by providing a mechanism easily used for malicious prosecution."[180] These perverse abuses of the legal procedures enacted to punish legal corruption undermined the genuine efforts to deal with these problems.

---

[179] They also influenced the selection of the justices, which facilitated the plaintiffs' ability to influence the commissions. Kaeuper, "Special Commissions of Oyer and Terminer," pp. 749–74.

[180] He said further that these commissions were "near the top of the list" of the devices for the abuse of legal procedure and were "convenient and powerful weapons" in the contemporary local disputes. Kaeuper, "Special Commissions of Oyer and Terminer," pp. 775–77, 771, 784. Walker identified numerous examples of the manipulation of these commissions in late fourteenth-century Sussex. Simon Walker, *The Lancastrian Affinity 1361–1399* (Oxford, 1990), pp. 127–41.

7

Maintenance and Medieval Literature

Medieval English literature provides another source for understanding social attitudes toward the legal system and the meaning of the word "maintenance."Leading scholars have called this literature the most impressive association of law and literature and its ubiquity a feast.[1] They have attributed this heavy literary emphasis on law to a "profound faith" in law as an ordering principle.[2] These medieval works were frequently directed at "the sorry state of law in the middle ages," drawing on estate and venality satire[3] as well as nostalgia for the old law.[4]

---

[1] John Alford, "Literature and Law in Medieval England," *PMLA* 92 (1977), p. 941; Richard Firth Green, "Medieval Literature and Law," in David Wallace, ed., *The Cambridge History of Medieval Literature* (Cambridge, 2002), pp. 410–31. Although English legal historians have not devoted substantial attention to medieval literature, they have not totally ignored it. Cohen's book on the history of the legal profession has a section on literature, which discusses the work of Chaucer, Gower, and Hoccleve. Hermann J. Cohen, *History of English Bar and Attornatus to 1450* (London, 1929), pp. 474–97; Jonathan Rose, "Of Ambidexters and Daffidowndillies: Defamation of Lawyers, Legal Ethics and Professional Reputation," *University of Chicago Law School Roundtable* 8 (2001), pp. 448–51. Pollack and Maitland noted that "law and literature grew up together in the court of Henry II." Frederick Pollock and F.W. Maitland, *The History of English Law before the Time of Edward I*, 2nd ed., 2 vols. (Cambridge, 1968), vol. I, p. 161.

[2] Alford, *Literature and Law*, pp. 942–49; Green, *Medieval Literature*, pp. 410–11.

[3] Wendy Scase, *Literature and Complaint in England, 1272–1553* (Oxford, 2007); John Yunck, *The Lineage of Lady Meed: The Development of Medieval Venality Satire* (Notre Dame, 1963); J.R. Maddicott, "Poems of Social Protest in Early Fourteenth-Century England," in W.M. Ormrod, ed., *England in the Fourteenth Century: Proceedings of the 1985 Harlaxton Symposium* (Bury St. Edmunds, 1986), p. 140.

[4] Green, "Medieval Literature," pp. 418–31. These literary works have been a popular topic for modern literature scholars. John Alford and Dennis Seniff, *Literature and Law in the Middle Ages* (New York, 1984). This bibliography identified over 900 scholarly works, and many more have been produced in the twenty years since this book was written.

Traditional Forms of Literature

Complaint literature began to appear in England in the early thirteenth century and continued at least through the end of the fifteenth century.[5] The initial literature, beginning in the thirteenth century and continuing through the reigns of Edward I and II, included relatively short poems, traditionally called "political songs," that voiced complaints about many aspects of medieval society and institutions, including law and the legal profession.[6] Some of the poems bemoaned the general failure of the legal system and the pervasiveness of injustice. A poem written during the reign of Edward I said that "right and law lie as it were asleep,"[7] and another in the same period said that "law is destroyed."[8] A number of poems targeted the criminal justice system.[9] A second source of complaint was the corruption of the legal system, bribery, and the focus on money. One poem complained that "The cause is money, to which almost every court has now wedded itself . . . There are judges, whom partiality and bribes seduce from justice."[10] Judges, lawyers, and other legal and royal officials were often targeted. One poem complained that lawyers were deceivers, did nothing for their fees, and stirred up litigation. The word "maintenance" in its wrongful sense does not, however, appear in these early poems.

---

[5] There are several collections of this literature. Isabel Aspin, ed., *Anglo-Norman Political Songs* (Oxford, 1953); Thomas Wright, *Political Songs of England* (London, Camden Society, 1839); Rossell Hope Robbins, *Historical Poems of the XIVth and XVth Centuries* (New York, 1959). The latter collection contains 100 works from 1300 to 1499. In discussing literary treatments of lawyers in the canon law profession, Brundage said that such literature had ancient origins with respect to Roman lawyers and suddenly reappeared in both Latin and the vernacular in Western literature in the middle of the twelfth century. James Brundage, "Vultures, Whores, and Hypocrites: Images of Lawyers in Medieval Literature," *Roman Legal Tradition* 1 (2002), p. 66.

[6] Owst has traced the history of this literature. G.R. Owst, *Literature and Pulpit in Medieval England* (New York, 1966), pp. 210–26.

[7] "A Song on the Times," Wright, *Political Songs*, p. 133. Another says "Every eye is blind to justice; every mind is large to injustice." *Song on Corruptions of the Time*, ibid., p. 28.

[8] "Song of the Husbandman," ibid., p. 150.

[9] Scase, *Literature and Complaint*, pp. 42–82. She noted that by the mid-fourteenth century, the notion of *clamour*, which denoted widespread complaint rather than individual ones, had emerged. Ibid., p. 43. She has an extended discussion of the literature of clamour. Ibid., pp. 83–136.

[10] "Song on the Venality of the Judges," ibid., p. 225. Similar accusations were made against the ecclesiastical courts and judges. "Song on Corruptions of the Time," ibid., p. 31; "A Satyre on the Consistory Courts," ibid., p. 156. Yunck noted that the venality of judges had been a target of satire "since the days of ancient Israel" but that attacks on lawyers for their venality were the product of the emergence of the profession in the twelfth century. Yunck, *Lady Meed*, pp. 139–59.

By the middle of the fourteenth century, medieval literature, responding to "new social tendencies," evinced concerns about the abusive
conduct and collusion of unscrupulous lords made possible by "a new
syntax of personal relationships."[11] This may explain why the word
"maintenance" began to appear in these works.[12] Although sometimes
used to mean support in its normal, benign sense, it was commonly used
to describe a constellation of practices of wrongful and corrupt conduct.[13] Its first literary usage may have been in William of Shoreham's
poem *De Decem Preceptis* (*The Ten Commandments*) (1350).[14] In discussing the eighth commandment's prohibition on bearing false witness,
the poem complained that no man obeys the commandment; they all lie;
and "along with that comes their great maintenance that causes them to
be well supported."[15] The most extensive discussion of maintenance was
in the work of Langland and Gower, leading poets of this period.[16]

[11] Paul Strohm, *Hochon's Arrow: The Social Imagination of Fourteenth-Century Texts*
(Princeton, 1992), pp. 57–63.

[12] Kathleen Kennedy has produced the most extensive work on maintenance in medieval
literature. Kennedy, *Maintenance, Meed, and Marriage* (New York, 2009); "Retaining
Men (and a Retaining Woman) in *Piers Plowman*," *Yearbook of Langland Studies* 20
(2006), pp. 191–214; "Maintaining Injustice: Literary Representations of the Legal System
c. 1400," unpublished PhD thesis, Ohio State University (2004). Her book and disserta-
tion are replete with references to maintenance. She uses the term in a wider sense to
denote a social institution consisting of "an entire field of relationships that medieval
English people discussed in broadly the same cultural terms." Kennedy, "Retaining Men,"
pp. 193–94. She also uses the term "maintenance-at-law" to denote the narrow, legal
meaning. Kennedy, *Maintenance*, p. 68.

[13] Kennedy, "Retaining Men," p. 192.

[14] M. Konrath, ed. *The Poems of William of Shoreham* (Early English Text Society, Extra
Series, LXXXVI) (London, 1902). Editors have dated this poem as ranging from the
beginning of the reign of Edward III to the last quarter of the fourteenth century. Both the
Middle English Dictionary's and the Oxford English Dictionary's definitions of mainten-
ance date it at 1350, using the date indicated by F.J. Furnvall, director of Early English
Text Society. Ibid., xi.

[15] Konrath, *Poems of William Shoreham*, p. 96, ll. 317–18.

[16] The word "maintenance" or its variants appears about a dozen times in Chaucer's works.
But all of its usages are in its normal sense of support or similar meanings and it is not
used to describe any wrongful conduct. John Tatlock and Arthur Kennedy,
A Concordance to the Complete Works of Geoffrey Chaucer (Gloucester, MA, 1963),
564. Chaucer also used the word "champerty" in the *Knight's Tale*. "The Knight's Tale,"
Larry Benson ed., *The Riverside Chaucer*, 3rd ed. (Dallas, 1987), p. 51, l. 1949. But its
meaning there was different from the use of word as a form of maintenance and is an
obsolete one. "Champerty," 1.a., *Oxford English Dictionary Online*. The description of the
Serjeant of the Lawe in the Prologue to *The Canterbury Tales* says that he had "many fees
and robes" as compensation from the clients who had retained him. "Prologue," Benson,
The Riverside Chaucer, p. 28, l. 317.

William Langland

Langland's *Piers Plowman* (c. 1362–85) may be the first medieval work to use the word "maintenance" extensively. It has been called the greatest English poem of the Middle Ages[17] and, together with the poem *The Pearl*, the "most successful integration of literature and law."[18] According to a leading scholar, "knowledge of law [was] the common property of poets," and *Piers Plowman* "stands out as the most saturated in legal concepts and terminology."[19] This allegorical satire, written in a dream vision form, makes numerous references to maintenance, associating it with various forms of wrongful conduct.[20] For example, the king wants revenge on Fals, Favel, and their criminal partners for their vicious conduct. He wants to hang them and "all that maintain them."[21] In Peace's plea against Wrong, he accuses the latter of many forms of misconduct, including that Wrong "maintains his men to murder my servants."[22]

---

[17] William Langland, *The Vision of Piers Plowman*, A.V.C. Schmidt, ed. (New York, 1978), xi–xvi. Schmidt has reproduced the multiple texts of the poem in parallel fashion. William Langland, *Piers Plowman: A Parallel-Text Edition of the A, B, C, and Z Versions*, A.V.C. Schmidt, ed., 2nd ed., 3 vols. (Kalamazoo, 2011). Maddicott linked *Piers Plowman* and earlier protest poems in the "traditions of satire, protest, and social comment," finding *Piers Plowman* "a far more eloquent expression" in that tradition. Maddicott, "Poems of Social Protest," p. 144.

[18] Alford, "Literature and Law," p. 942. The poem's involvement with medieval law was "pervasive, complex and potentially illuminating." Andrew Galloway, "Piers Plowman and the Subject of the Law," *Yearbook of Langland Studies* 15 (2001), p. 117. *Piers Plowman* has attracted substantial attention from medieval law and literature scholars. Kennedy, *Maintenance*; Matthew Giancarlo, *Parliament and Literature* (Cambridge, 2007); John Yunck, *The Lineage of Lady Meed*; John Alford, ed., *A Companion to Piers Plowman* (Berkeley, 1988); Kennedy, "Retaining Men"; J.A. Burrow, "Lady Meed and the Power of Money," *Medium Aevum* 74.1 (2005), pp. 113–18; Andrew Galloway, "Piers Plowman and the Subject of the Law," pp. 117–40; D. Vance Smith, "The Labors of Reward: Meed, Mercede, and the Beginning of Salvation," *Yearbook of Langland Studies* 8 (1995), pp. 127–54; Gerald Morgan, "The Status and Meaning of Meed in the First Version of Piers Plowman." *Neophilologus* 72.3 (1988), pp. 449–63.

[19] John Alford, *Piers Plowman: A Glossary of Legal Diction* (Cambridge, 1988), p. ix.

[20] All textual references are to the B text unless otherwise indicated. Schmidt, ed., *Parallel-Text Edition*. Some of the references use maintenance in its ordinary, nonwrongful, sense of support. Passus B II, ll. 36–37, ibid., p. 58. In some cases, the nature of its use is ambiguous, perhaps intentionally so. Two such examples involve Lady Meed's request that the mayor take silver from regraters who harm the poor by sales at inflated prices and her support of prebends, parsons, and priests to have mistresses and concubines. Passus B III, ll. 87–90 , 149–52, ibid., p. 98, 108.

[21] Passus B II, ll. 193–97, ibid., p. 80.

[22] Passus B IV, l. 55, ibid., p. 148. Schmidt thought that the use of maintenance in this passage was ambiguous. Schmidt, *Piers Plowman*, p. 317.

Other passages connect maintenance to the abuse of lordship. In condemning venality, the poet asserts that powerful men "accept reward to maintain wrongdoers."[23] Similarly, Covetous seems to acknowledge that he has lent money to lords to have their maintenance.[24] At the end of the poem, Langland presents maintenance as inconsistent with justice. In Will's dream regarding the distribution of seeds representing the four cardinal virtues, the poem states that judges, who ate the seed of justice, "did not do the law for present or for prayer or for prince's letters."[25] In this context, "prayer (*preiere*)" refers to maintenance in the legal sense, meaning the judges rejected the lords' attempts to use their influence in supporting quarrels.[26] Many of these passages are from the poem's trial of Lady Meed,[27] whose name symbolizes the corruptive influence of money.[28] Lady Meed's "episode is a vivid allegorical dramatization of power of money ... and venality in blunting justice."[29] Conscience charges that she corrupted the king's justices with her jewels, told lies against the law, and led the law as she likes.[30]

In several passages, Langland may have characterized Lady Meed as a powerful person with a retinue, a classic context of medieval maintenance.[31]

---

[23] Passus B III, ll. 246–47, Schmidt, *Parallel Text Edition*, 122.

[24] Passus B V, ll. 249–50, ibid., p. 210.   [25] Passus B XVIX, ll. 299–311, ibid., p. 706.

[26] Alford, *Glossary*, 119.

[27] Her trial involves her proposed marriage to False Fikel tongue, which angers Theology because he says God has given Meed to Truth. They all agree to settle the matter by law and proceed to "London to find out if the Law would judge jointly in joy forever." The king rejects this marriage and attempts to marry her to Conscience, who rejects her because of her wrongful nature and deeds. The king summons Reason to judge the dispute between Conscience and Meed and he sides with the former. Passus B II ll. 115–20, 156–57; Passus B III, ll. 114–69, Passus B IV, ll. 171–95, Schmidt, *Parallel Text Edition*, pp. 66–68, 74, 102–10, 164–66.

[28] Meed (Mede) is an ambiguous Middle English word meaning reward or payment, but associated with bribery and venality. Lady Meed has been characterized as "barratry, simony, bribery, human venality." Yunck, *Lineage of Lade Mede*, 290. Some commentators have identified Lady Meed with Alice Perrers, Edward III's notorious mistress. E.g., Giancarlo, *Parliament and Literature*, 184; Anna Baldwin, "The Historical Context," in Alford, *Companion*, p. 80.

[29] Yunck, *Lady Mede*, p. 6.

[30] Passus B III, ll. 155–58, Schmidt, *Parallel Text Edition*, pp. 108, 110. All those who work at Westminster worship Lade Meed and the justices hasten to her bedroom. Passus B III, ll. 12–14, ibid., pp. 86–88. As Yunck has noted, she has seduced those in the legal system who should have been dealing with her wrongdoing. Yunck, *Lady Meed*, 297.

[31] One commentator said that the language of retainership suffuses Langland's entire account of Meed. He said further that "Meed identifies herself with those 'gifts' that bind all retinues, royal as well as magnatial." Ralph Hanna, *London Literature, 1300–1380* (Cambridge, 2005), pp. 264–66.

The poet accuses Lady Meed of maintaining her retainers.[32] Her conduct has been identified with maintenance because she failed to know or willfully ignored "the boundaries of one's own legal interest."[33] Some passages in a legal action described in the poem seem to indicate some instances of maintenance by her.[34] Peace has brought a bill in parliament accusing Wrong of numerous trespasses and felonies, which have resulted in prolonged litigation.[35] Wisdom and Wit, from whom Wrong has sought advice on settling the matter, warned Wrong that Meed should help in resolving the matter, and they persuaded Meed to assist in dealing with both the king and Peace. Although the king rejected their attempts to "overcome him with wealth," Wisdom argued that if Wrong makes amends, he should be released on mainprise.[36] Then, Meed asked for mercy and offered to pay Peace for his injuries on behalf of Wrong. She further says that she will guarantee that Wrong will not injure Peace in the future. Peace, following Wisdom's counsel, then prayed that the king have mercy on Wrong, stating that he has been well paid. "For Meed has compensated me – I ask no more."[37] Others appeal to Reason to counsel the king and Conscience to permit Meed to be Wrong's mainpernor. But Reason refuses and the king says, "Meed shall not mainprise you" because the king has lost property rights due to Meed's overcoming law and impeding truth.[38]

In this story, three types of conduct, two in which Meed engaged and another proposed for her but rejected, raise issues regarding illegal maintenance and resemble the conduct that was the subject of actual maintenance actions.[39] First, Meed paid Peace's damages, which Wrong

---

[32] Passus B III, ll. 166–67, Schmidt, *Parallel Text Edition*, p. 110.

[33] Hanna noted the mention of maintenance in the poem and discussed the parliamentary and social concern with it. He said that a maintainer violated "the most basic rules of Langland's communal foundation." He said Meed "ignores the fine line that divided "confederacy, social bonding, from conspiracy, fellowships pledged to an extra-legal act." Hanna, *London Literature*, pp. 265–68.

[34] Passus B IV, ll. 47–195, Schmidt, *Parallel Text Edition*, pp. 148–66. The C Text has a longer version of Peace's bill. Ibid., p. 149. Galloway stated that the passages regarding Peace's bill are "a presentation of the quintessential 'subject of law'" and presented a radical shift in the subject of law. Galloway "Piers Plowman and the Subject of Law," pp. 121, 126–28.

[35] Peace and his supporters complained against him forever. Passus IV B, l. 66, Schmidt, *Parallel Text Edition*, p. 150.

[36] Ibid., ll. 62–86.   [37] Ibid., ll. 94–103.   [38] Ibid., l. 176.

[39] In another passage, it is possible that Conscience and Reason may have engaged in illegal maintenance. They went with Wisdom and Wit to assist in discharging the actions against them in the Exchequer and in Chancery. Passus IV B, ll. 27–31, Schmidt, *Parallel Text Edition*, p. 144.

inflicted. Second, she agreed to act as surety of peace for Wrong, which would subject her to a financial penalty if Wrong acted wrongfully again. Third, she was willing to act as his mainpernor, so Wrong would not have to remain in prison pending the satisfaction of both Peace and the king. Paying the damages on behalf of Wrong was probably a violation of the maintenance statute. As to the other conduct, although some lawyers argued that it was illegal for a person to volunteer to act as a surety or a mainpernor, it was probably legitimate, especially if requested by the defendant.[40]

John Gower

John Gower, "moral philosopher and friend of Chaucer,"[41] has been called the "moral voice of his age."[42] A recurring theme of his work is the disparity between law and justice.[43] His three major poems, *Mirour de l'Omme* (c. 1376–1379), *Vox Clamantis* (c. 1377–1381), and *Confessio Amantis* (c. 1386–93), all deal with law.[44] *Mirour* targets the abusive and corrupt conduct of judges and lawyers as well as sheriffs, bailiffs, and jurors.[45] "Justice is now in the balance of gold," and the "law has lost its charity by force of money."[46] Pleaders, judges, apprentices, and attorneys "have perverted law in trickery and subtlety," and the estate of law is

---

[40] Jonathan Rose, "The Law of Maintenance and the Obligations of Lordship: A Case Study," in Per Andersen, Kirsi Salonen, Helle Møller Sigh, and Helle Vogt, eds., *Law and Disputing in the Middle Ages. Proceedings of the Ninth Carlsberg Academy Conference on Medieval Legal History 2012* (Copenhagen, 2013), pp. 111–21. These issues are discussed later in Chapters 9 and 10.

[41] John Fisher, *John Gower, Moral Philosopher and Friend of Chaucer* (New York, 1964).

[42] Winthrop Wetherbee, "John Gower," in David Wallace, ed., *The Cambridge History of Medieval Literature* (Cambridge, 2002), p. 598.

[43] Van Dijk argued that this disjunction "explains his constant focus on the limits of law." Conrad van Dijk, *John Gower and the Limits of Law* (Woodbridge, 2013), p. 6. The justice and law theme is especially evident in *Mirour de l'Omme*. Maria Wickert, *Studies in John Gower*, trans. Robert Meindl (Washington, DC, 1981), pp. 134–45.

[44] A leading Gower authority suggested that Gower may have been a lawyer. Fischer, *John Gower*, pp. 54–58, 154. Van Dijk has recently reviewed all the evidence and concluded that it is "circumstantial," "tantalizingly elusive," and "ambiguous." He does, however, acknowledge, as have others, that Gower had extensive knowledge of legal terminology and judicial business. Van Dijk, *John Gower*, pp. 1–5.

[45] *Mirour de l'Omme*, ll. 24625–816 (judges), ll. 24181–624 (lawyers), ll. 24817–5176 (sheriffs, bailiffs, jurors). The references to Gower's poems, unless otherwise stated, are to G.C. Macaulay, ed., *The Complete Works of John Gower*, 4 vols. (Oxford, 1899).

[46] *Mirour de l'Omme*, ll. 24629–30, 24803–4, pp. 272, 274.

the worst of all secular estates.[47] Lawyers are venal and avaricious, "so emboldened by lucre," pervert the law, are deceitful, and enrich themselves by extortion.[48] "O what sorrow the law brings us."[49] *Vox Clamantis* also bemoans the failure of law to achieve justice. "Injustice is accustomed to being done under the name of justice."[50] "Thus the law is governed by the heavy reins of gold so that now it is not able to go in just ways."[51] Book VI targets judges and lawyers. Its introductory passage says that the author will discuss "ministers of justice, however much they nevertheless confound all justice by their tricks and repeatedly weaken it for worldly profit."[52] Lawyers are not worthy of being called men of law. Their numerous tricks and deceit overwhelm and conquer law.[53] Venality prevails, for "if you give him gold, you can have his body."[54] When a man is a victim of their malpractice, he cannot retain a lawyer because they refuse to sue one another.[55] Aiming his pen at judges, Gower says that when lawyers ascend to judicial office, they are the "struck with the blindness of avarice" and are "the guiltiest of all."[56] "Gold blinds the eyes of judges and his reason is contaminated by gain."[57] Bribery, friendship, and fear confuse law and deny justice.[58] Concluding with a letter to the judges, who sell law by fraud, the poet says, "Judge, is not the brightness of your gold sufficient so that your blind mind can dispel its shadows[?] . . . Why do you seek silver for yourself, why do you put hope in gold?" and he warns them of their future punishment by God.[59]

[47] *Mirour de l'Omme*, ll. 24794–808, p. 274.
[48] *Mirour de l'Omme*, ll. 24181–216, 24292–93, 24337–41, 24409–624, vol. I, pp. 267, 268, 269–72.
[49] *Mirour de l'Omme*, l. 25165, vol. I, p. 278.
[50] *Vox Clamantis*, Book VI, ll. 169, 189, pp. 234–35. "Lawyers are clouds that darken the skies so that no one can see the light of the sun: indeed they obfuscate the clearest rights of law." Ibid., ll. 25–27, p. 236.
[51] Ibid., ll. 252–54, p. 237. [52] Ibid., chapter I introduction, p. 230.
[53] *Vox Clamantis*, Book VI, ll. 1–4, 15–40, pp. 230–31.
[54] Ibid., l. 46, p. 231. Book VI includes several characterizations of lawyers as spiders, hawks, bats, night owls, Scylla, hounds, wolves, and foxes, who prey on their victims. Ibid., ll. 69–104, p. 232; ibid., chap. 2, ll. 105–52, pp. 233–34; ibid., chap. 3, ll. 207–8, p. 235.
[55] The poem says that "lawyers know that conspiracies are illegal, but nevertheless they do not do what the law teaches because if the law requires me to act against a pleader and I seek to have legal counsel, then they all say they will not oppose their colleagues." Ibid., ll. 239–43, p. 236.
[56] Ibid., introduction, chap. 4, p. 237; l. 252, p. 237. [57] Ibid., ll. 269–70, p. 237
[58] Ibid., ll. 265–70, p. 237.
[59] Ibid., l. 312, p. 238; ll. 351–52, 359, pp. 239, 240; ll. 399–418, p. 241.

Confessio Amantis, using a confession by Amans, an aging lover, to Genius, the chaplain of Venus, as a framework,[60] focuses on courtly love and like his other poems laments the departure from the "ancient course of things" and the "decline from the blessed life of the past."[61] Although Gower does not deal as extensively with law as in the other two poems, he does not ignore it altogether.[62] Book VII focuses on the relationship between the law and royal authority.[63] As a *speculum principis*, it advises rulers on their important obligation to keep the law and abide by it.[64] A section entitled "Justice" has several tales that emphasize the important relationship between law and justice. Divorcing justice from law will prevent the people from seeing the right path.[65] Judges must be learned, true, and wise to promote justice, and covetous judges will cause misery to the people of the land.[66] Gower then uses several tales to illustrate these notions.[67]

---

[60] Wetherbee, "John Gower," pp. 598–609.

[61] *Confessio Amantis*, prologue, ii, ll. 1–2, p. 6.

[62] Two commentators have focused on the legal aspects of *Confessio Amantis*: Van Dijk, *John Gower*, and Elliot Kendall, *Lordship and Literature: John Gower and the Politics of the Great Household* (Oxford, 2008). Van Dijk noted that often its connection to law was not explicit. "Law is central to the *Confessio*, both structurally and thematically, despite frequently appearing merely in the margins." *John Gower*, p. 87. But he concludes that "Gower's writings, like those by so many contemporaries, are suffused with legal themes and preoccupations." Ibid., p. 191. Kendall focused on the impact on justice of the great households and their affinities and the role of legitimate lordship. Kendall, *Lordship and Literature*, pp. 173–241. Drawing on Green's work on the replacement of "trouthe" with "truth," he viewed the poem's nostalgic lament as contrasting the earlier age that "shone, one-hued (*unicolor*)" and a "justice of law" with the laws of a current period of loss and decay, as manifested in the "king's law." Ibid., pp. 183–87, 211, 214, 230.

[63] Van Dijk asserted that many of the tales in *Confessio Amantis* are narratives in the form of an exemplum that can be viewed as a legal case. But such metaphorical depictions of law are quite different from specifically raising questions about justice and the legal system as his other poems do. Van Dijk, *John Gower*, pp. 15–48.

[64] *Confessio Amantis*, Book VII, ll. 2694–3102, pp. 306–17. Both Kendall and van Dijk analyzed the poem's treatment of kingship. Kendall, *Literature and Law*, pp. 248–65; van Dijk, *John Gower*, pp. 89–138.

[65] *Confessio Amantis*, Book VII, ll. 2694–708, pp. 306–07.

[66] Ibid., ll. 2748–57, pp. 308. "If the law stand with the right, the populace is glad and stands upright. Wherever the law is reasonable, the common people can be led. And if the law turn amiss, the populace is also misguided." Ibid., ll. 2759–64, pp. 308.

[67] Van Dijk discussed these tales in van Dijk, *John Gower*, pp. 125–33. In the most graphic tale, King Cambyses slew and flayed a lawless judge and upholstered the judicial bench with the judge's skin. The king then appointed the judge's son to succeed him and sit on the bench. *Confessio Amantis*, Book VII, ibid., ll. 2833–916, pp. 310–13.

In these three poems, Gower dealt with maintenance in a variety of ways. In the final book of *Confessio Amantis*,[68] Gower condemned maintenance outright, using the word broadly to denote wrongful conduct. He focuses on the nobility, whom he says are to be commended to some extent, but also need to correct their large retinues because

> the land is full of maintenance, which causes the common right in few countries to stand upright. Extortion, dissension, robbery are retained by that conspiracy, all day men hear great complaint of the trouble, of the compulsion whereof the people are grievously oppressed.[69]

In *Mirour*, Gower targeted the abuse of lordship, specifically accusing lords of both champerty and maintenance in the legal sense of the words. He says that misguided lords by their tyranny use

> the power of their lordship to support common barrators in return for a small part of their profit and thus injustice comes to us. For when so many lords are maintainors, the law loses its course, by which wrong justifies itself, whereby justice is reversed.[70]

Vox Clamantis seemed to charge lawyers with champerty by suggesting that they took contingent fees. "He profits from what you lose, and if you should profit, he seeks his part from this with you."[71] In one passage in *Mirour*, Gower seems to exploit the multiple meanings of the word "maintenance" by suggesting that lawyers are engaging in maintenance in their ordinary representation of clients. "But they conspire with the rich, and to maintain their case they put a price on justice and law."[72]

Nor were lords and lawyers the only ones accused of maintenance in these poems. Knights were accused of causing disorder in inquests when they order and threaten poor people by maintenance to their dismay and striving by the wrong of maintenance to ransom poor people.[73] Moreover, *Mirour* describes the manner in which lords engaged in maintenance and the judges' receptivity to their efforts:

---

[68] It ends with a prayer for England and the king and notes "the evil of division in the land," *Confessio Amantis*, Book VIII, ll. 2970–3053, pp. 468–72.

[69] Ibid., ll. 3012–19, p. 470. Commenting on this passage, Kendall said that "in the 'complaint poetry' of the *Confessio*, Gower joins a mainstream of late fourteenth-century complaint attacking lords and their household retinues for illegitimately 'maintaining' their friends' causes." Kendall, *Literature and Lordship*, p. 175.

[70] *Mirour de l'Omme*, ll. 23317–28, p. 257.

[71] *Vox Clamantis*, Book VI, ll. 125–26, p. 233.   [72] *Mirour de l'Omme*, ll. 24202–04, p. 267.

[73] Ibid., ll. 23732–39, p. 262.

> Thus, if my case be wrong, but great lords bring their letters to pray for me, the judge, who has a vain heart, ... will undertake my case when it comes to the king's court and cause the law to be turned, so that justice is not upheld, but my wrong advances against good faith; and thus I see that the [great lord's] prayer is stronger than law.[74]

Vox Clamantis contains a similar passage. "When a great man's letter beats a judge's ears, his pen's strength destroys the obligation to follow the law."[75] Just judges should be immune to such efforts. As the poem illustrated by the Latin gloss to the exemplum of "rightful" Emperor Conrad, "in whose time, the statutes of the laws could by no means be commuted or bought by respect for any person, by any intervention of petitions, or by the payment of money."[76] Thus, Gower, like Langland, has asserted that maintenance in the sense of general wrongdoing has perverted law and thwarted justice. More specifically, his poems portray the abuse of power by lords to influence litigation and undermine justice by supporting the quarrels of their retainers and others and undermining the rights of their adversaries.[77]

Other Poems and Plays

An early fifteenth-century poem, *Richard the Redeless*, "an alliterative poem of admonition,"[78] focused on the reign of Richard II. Drawing on the implications of its title, "Richard without Counsel," the poem argued that "Richard has been poorly advised, his kingdom mismanaged [and] his subjects ill-served."[79] Among the king's failings was the harm caused

---

[74] Ibid., ll. 24637–48, p. 272.   [75] *Vox Clamantis,* Book VI, ll. 277–78, p. 237.

[76] *Confessio Amantis,* Book VII, l. 2933, p. 310. Van Dijk asserts that the Tale of Virginia illustrates how King Appius and his brother were engaged in "maintenance in abusing the legal system." Van Dijk, *John Gower,* p. 134.

[77] Kendall focused on *Confessio Amantis* and on retaining, maintenance, and livery. *Literature and Lordship,* pp. 175–93, 210–41. Despite these passages, he took a more charitable interpretation of Gower's views toward these practices. He argued that Gower does not view local power as perverting justice and does not view all maintenance nor retaining as bad. He argues that Gower rejects royal authority and law as a solution to the maintenance and livery problem in favor of legitimate lordship and a properly constituted household. Ibid., pp. 176–77, 224, 262–65.

[78] Strohm, *Hochon's Arrow,* p. 183.

[79] James Dean, ed., "Richard the Redeless: Introduction," Teams Middle English Text Series, www.d.lib.rochester.edu/teams/text/dean-richard-the-redeless-and-mum-and-the-soth segger-richard-the-redeless-introduction. All references are to "Richard the Redeless," METS TEXTS, Teams, Middle English Texts Series, www.lib.rochester.edu/camelot/teams/richtext.htm.

by retaining, maintenance, and livery. In several passages, the poem dealt with these topics and their interrelationship. In linking livery and maintenance, the poet said that "no type of maintainor should wear badges nor have the lord's livery," which damages the law, and "let no lordship sustain the law." Instead, he asserted, with a touch of irony, that lords who avoid this harmful and undesirable conduct "should have a badge and annual salary for keeping his country in quiet and at rest."[80] Later, the poet linked abuse of lordship and maintenance. He attacked clerks, who "seek bribes before pleadings are summoned and cancel all the accusations of those who bring them nothing; and whosoever grumbles or groans about their powerful wills." "Thus is the law brought low through mighty lords' wills" and because they "maintain miscreants more than other people for maintenance many days – more's the pity."[81] The poet advised the king "to strike the maintainors with maces [rather than give them badges] and to ruin arrogant men who acted against right."[82]

In another passage, the poet expressed concern with the harmful effects of the king's extensive giving of livery to his affinity:[83]

> He marked his lieges ... with badges that swarmed so thick throughout his land in length and in breadth ... harassing the country, serving curses, speaking to the common people as the king's spokesmen, or with the lords with whom they dwelt so that no man could show reason. They plucked the plumage from the skins of the poor and showed their badges so men should dread to demand any redress for their misdeeds ... and they thrust out their chests [with the badges] and oppressed the poor lieges who loved you less because of their [the retainers'] evil deeds.[84]

The poem singled out the "chyders (brawlers) of Chester," a special group of Richard's personal liveried retainers, because of their abusive conduct and their perversion of justice by their false pleading.[85] It said

[80] Ibid., Passus II, ll. 77–90. [81] Ibid., Passus III, ll. 305–12.
[82] Ibid., Passus III, ll. 268–69.
[83] Ibid., Passus II, ll. 1–4. The poem "emphasizes Richard's failings as a guardian of good justice and local order and, particularly his abusive and puzzling overreliance on the livery of the White Hart." Strohm, *Hochon's Arrow*, 183. The lollards took a more positive view of Richard's livery, preferring it to that of bishops, who gave out "crowns," which was the "livery of the antichrist" rather than giving Richard's livery of the "white heart." Scase, *Literature and Complaint*, p. 90.
[84] "Richard the Redeless," passus ll. 21–22, 28–34, 38–40.
[85] "The Chester guard constituted Richard's personal army of archers who were noted for their arrogance and brutality. The chronicler Adam Usk regarded them as a ruthless gang who unwittingly contributed to Richard's downfall: 'The king, meanwhile, ever hastening

that they were "chosen many days to be of counsel for causes that pended in court and pleaded all manner of pleas in the piepowder courts and pled at piepowder courts all manner of complaints." They did not wear coifs like other pleaders, But they "moved many matters, of which man never thought, and concocted falsehood, until they obtained a settlement although they understood no legal pleading, as the Commons reported."[86] Further, "they contrived quarrels to squelch the people, and pleaded their cases with poleaxes and points of swords and at the judgement drew out their blades and allowed men to experience their long clubs."[87] As a result, "there was no noble of the realm that dared rebuke them, nor judge nor justice that dared deem judgment against them for anything they stole or trespass they did against the people."[88]

Mum and the Sothsegger, a fifteenth-century poem frequently linked to *Richard the Redeless*, also advised a king, this time Henry IV, It voiced many of the same concerns as other complaint literature.[89] The poem is "a meditation on statecraft and an often satirical anatomy of the contemporary institutions, especially the estates and the courts of law."[90] In exploring the problems of Henry IV's administration, the poem is in the form of a debate, which contrasts the harmful influence of silence (Mum) with the beneficial effect of truth-telling (Sothsegger). The object of the poet's travels among various individuals and groups was to "truly know

---

to his fall, among the many burdens which he inflicted upon his realm also kept about him in his following four hundred supernumeraries from the county of Cheshire, men of the utmost depravity who went about doing as they wished, assaulting, beating, and plundering his subjects with impunity; wherever the king went, night and day, they stood guard over him, armed as if for war, committing adulteries, murders, and countless other crimes; yet so inordinately did the king favour them that he would not listen to anyone who complained about them, indeed he regarded such people with loathing; and this was the chief cause of his ruin.'" Ibid., Passus Tercius, l. 317 Note, p. 49.

[86] Ibid., passus III, ll. 317–24. The crimes and harms suffered by the people of Chester, which were inflicted by these wrongdoers, were among the items in the Articles of Depositions of Richard II. Henry IV: Parliament of October 1399, Nos. 20, 22 in *PROME*, III *Rotuli Parliamentorum*, p. 418.

[87] "Richard the Redeless," passus III, ll. 327–30. They "allegedly packed rural courts to discourage witnesses." Dean, *Richard the Redeless*, "Introduction."

[88] "Richard the Redeless," passus III, ll. 340–42.

[89] Because of the knowledge of law, legal terms, and the courts that the poems reveal, some have suggested that authors were law clerks. James Dean, ed., "*Mum and the Sothsegger*: Introduction," Teams Middle English Text Series, www.d.lib.rochester.edu/teams/text/dean-richard-the-redeless-and-mum-and-the-sothsegger-richard-the-redeless-introduction.

[90] Ibid. All references are to *Mum and the Sothsegger*, METS TEXTS, Teams, Middle English Texts Series, www.lib.rochester.edu/camelot/teams/richtext.htm.

who should have the mastery, Mum or the Sothesigger."[91] In this contest between modes of self-expression, not surprisingly, truth is victorious.

As with the other poems, the poet casts aspersion on maintenance. At the beginning of the poem, he advises the king that he should "have pity on the poor and listen to their complaints ... and for God's sake and with good cheer grant them legal writs and wax seals and they will love you as liege men ought to more than for the maintenance."[92] The poet showed his awareness of the harmful impact of maintenance in the legal sense, saying, "There is a "raggeman roll made by the devil of the maintenance and people's litigation and how they shove about at the assizes and sessions."[93] He continued by condemning the abuse of lordship. The poem recited that the "if poor man complain, though he plead ever and litigate with his superior, it happens often that he works all in vain and wins little" and that "it will not benefit a poor man a great man for to plead, for the law lieth much in lordship since loyalty was exiled and poor men's complaints conclude penniless."[94] The poet also accused Mum of maintaining his retainers. The poem depicted Mum as lord of the town mayors, who wear Mum's livery, and Mum maintains their income in return for a year-end gift.[95] Moreover, the poem linked venality and maintenance. Covetise, portrayed as a knight, prevails in jousting by greed and "wins new spurs at Westminster ... multiplies his money in the council chamber more for his maintenance and menacing words than for drawing his sword or deeds of arms."[96] The clergy are equally guilty. They are more interested in benefices than the Bible, loving "Mum and money ... for maintenance and reward have been their two mates."[97]

Thomas Hoccleve, writing again for a king, Henry V, elaborated on vices and virtues in his fifteenth-century "didactic and political" poem, *The Regiment of Princes*.[98] Like the earlier poets, he was concerned about

---

[91] Ibid., ll. 574–75. [92] Ibid., ll. 21–27.
[93] Ibid., ll. 1565–68. A ragman roll is a compilation of wrongdoing by various individuals or types of persons. The poem's editor explained its use here as follows. "raggeman rolle. A legal document, with ragged edges, containing accusations. The term 'rigmarole' or 'rigamarole' derives from the alleged petty legalisms of these rolled-up parchment documents. *Ragenelle* is the name of a devil or demon."
[94] Ibid., ll. 1577–84.
[95] Ibid., ll. 818–20. It is unclear what Mum did to benefit the mayors' incomes. Perhaps it was for maintaining the mayors' litigation.
[96] Ibid., ll. 481–86. [97] Ibid., ll. 669–773.
[98] Charles Blyth, ed., "Thomas Hoccleve, *The Regiment of Princes*: Introduction," www.d.lib.rochester.edu/teams/text/blyth-hoccleve-regiment-of-princes-introduction.

justice and the importance of observing the law, and the poem has sections on both subjects.[99] He explained the nature of justice and the obligation of the king "to keep and maintain justice."[100] The king should hold his laws precious and "observe them and not offend them in any way ... Law is both the lock and key of stability."[101] But then he noted the problem of lawlessness and its harmful effects. Felons are not brought to justice and "law has been banished out of the country." People take matters into their own hands and do not attempt to sue wrongdoers at common law. Since this undermined security and caused destruction, the poet asked, "Is there no law to remedy this?" But he concluded that the problem was maintenance and abuse of lordship. "And all such maintenance, as men well know, is not caused by people of low station, but great lords sustain this disorder."[102]

Other fifteenth-century literary works also dealt with maintenance, although less extensively. The Wakefield *Second Shepherds' Pageant* portrayed contemporary society and its abuses through the optic of a manor court. As it begins, the shepherds complain about the way that the "gentry men" oppress them, as they "hold us under and bring us to grief, so that is a great wonder that we should ever thrive."[103] Their problem was that these gentry were the retainers of a lord, whose livery ("painted sleeve or a brooch") they wore. They derived their power from that relationship, which permitted them to act in the outrageous ways the play described. The shepherds were at their mercy, as "all is through maintenance of men that are greater."[104] Another fifteenth-century poem on lovedays[105] focused on the duties of lords who acted as arbitrators in

---

[99] All references are Thomas Hoccleve, *The Regiment of Princes*, METS TEXTS, Teams, Middle English Texts Series, http://d.lib.rochester.edu/teams/text/blyth-hoccleve-regiment-of-princes. *Regiment of Princes*, *De justitia*, ll. 2465–772; ibid., *De legum observatione*, ll. 2773–996. The latter title is contained in a marginal Latin gloss. Note, l. 2773.

[100] Ibid., ll. 2514–15.   [101] Ibid., ll. 2774–78.   [102] Ibid., ll. 2782–806.

[103] *Second Shepherd's Play*, in A.C. Cawley, ed., in *The Wakefield Pageants in the Towneley Cycle* (Manchester, 1958), p. 43, ll. 22–27.

[104] Ibid., ll. 28–36. Strohm argued that this passage showed that at the end of the fifteenth century "maintenance was more a fact of life than it had ever been – and all the more eligible to serve in this play as one of several emblems of rural privation and subjection in a world unknowingly awaiting a new spiritual dispensation." Strohm, *Hochon's Arrow*, 184. Nisse linked this assertion to the "Bills of Complaint" associated with Jack Cade's 1450 rebellion. Ruth Nisse, *Defining Acts: Drama and the Politics of Interpretation in Late Medieval England* (Notre Dame, 2005), pp. 78–79.

[105] Lovedays were days designated for dispute resolution. Michael Clanchy, "Law and Love in the Middle Ages," in John Bossy, ed., *Disputes and Settlements: Law and Human Relations in the West* (Cambridge, 1983), pp. 47–67; Stephen White, "'Pactum . . . Legem*

this process. It advised them to "confound all falseness" and "to uphold righteousness" and "not to work according to their will." It counselled the arbitrator to avoid bias based on friendship. The poet said, "Is it good right and reason that because this man is my friend I will maintain him and all his business also? No, for truth and reason why forever more at the last end, be he false or true, I prove myself false."[106] Finally, a mid-fifteenth-century political poem targeted William Booth, bishop of Coventry and Lichfield.[107] The poem depicted Booth, a protégé of the disgraced Duke of Suffolk, as "a grasping figure who has obtained wealth and position by corrupt means."[108] It charged that Booth exerted himself to lead and speak for the powerful and assisted them to get off when they had been accused, provoking complaints by the oppressed. His conduct "is contrary to virtue and it is a grievous [crime] to provide maintentance in a case of such wickedness."[109]

Some quite interesting literary instances of maintenance appear in the Carpenters' Pageant of *The Resurrection* in the *York Corpus Christi Plays* (1463–1477).[110] The play explored "the matter of bearing true and false witness to a specific event."[111] Maintenance appeared in several passages dealing with the conspiracy between Pilate, Annas, and Caiphas

---

Vincit et Amor Judicium': The Settlement of Disputes by Compromise in Eleventh-Century Western France," *American Journal of Legal History* 22 (1979), pp. 291–309.

[106] Thomas Heffernan, "A Middle English Poem on Lovedays," *Chaucer Review* 10 (1975), p. 175. The author has reproduced the text of the poem. Ibid., pp. 177–82, which has been quoted above. Ibid., p. 177, ll. 5–7, 11–14.

[107] Thomas Wright, "On Bishop Booth," in Wright, *Political Poems and Songs Relating to English History, Composed during the Period from the Accession of Edw. III. to That of Ric. III.*, 2 vols. (London, 1861), vol. II, pp. 225–29, reprinted in *Rerum Britannicarum Medii Aevi Scriptores, on Chronicles and Memorials of Great Britain and Ireland during the Middle Ages*. Booth studied common law at Gray's Inn and was the only fifteenth-century bishop to do so. A.C. Reeves, "Booth [Bothe] William," *Oxford Dictionary of National Biography Online*.

[108] Scase, *Literature and Complaint in England*, p. 131. The preceding poem in the collection is "On the Arrest of the Duke of Suffolk."

[109] Wright, "On Bishop Booth," p. 227. Gratitude is expressed to Prof. Wendy Scase for her translation of this passage.

[110] *The Carpenters: The Resurrection*, in Richard Beadle, ed., *The York Plays: A Critical Edition of the York Corpus Christi Play as Recorded in British Library MS Additional 35290*, 2 vols. (Early English Text Society, Supplementary Series 23) (Oxford, 2009), vol. I, pp. 366–80.

[111] Ibid., vol. II, p. 365. Horner explored the play through the notion of witnessing actions and the different ways in which modern and medieval audiences would have understood the events. Olga Horner, "'Us must make lies': Witness, Evidence and Proof in the York Resurrection," *Medieval English Theatre* 20 (1998), pp. 24–76.

wrongfully to convict Jesus and to deny the resurrection.[112] The initial maintenance reinforced the three conspirators' agreement to support each other in their collusion regarding the death of Jesus. Pilate commands Caiphas to support the crucifixion of Jesus. He said that "since by your assent we did put to death Jesus this day, that you maintain and stand thereby that work always." Caiphas responded, "Yes sir, that deed shall we maintain that by law it was done all indeed, you know as well yourself as well as we."[113]

The next instances deal with Pilate's anger with the Centurion, who told him "truly without deception" that he has slain a "righteous man." Pilate told him to "stop such talk, thou are a man learned in the law and if we should call upon any witness to excuse, you always ought to maintain us and not refuse." But in a reversal of the prior use of maintenance to connote wrongdoing, the Centurion used it in a positive sense. He said that "to maintain truth is well worthy."[114] Although the Centurion persisted in asserting his belief in the truth, Annas told the Centurion to stop his talk and that they did not fear his words. As they have disregarded what the Centurion has said, he bid them farewell, but asserted, "God grant the grace that you may always know the truth." Reasserting the conspiracy, Annas told him to depart quickly and said, "for we shall well maintain our deeds."[115] As the play ends, Pilate enlisted the soldiers to support the conspiracy. He told the soldiers that in whatever country he sends them,

> Do that no man the wiser be nor ask questions ... For we shall always maintain you, and to the people we shall say it is greatly against our law to believe such thing. So shall they deem both night and day, all is lies.[116]

---

[112] Horner discussed how medieval audiences would have understood the play's use of legal terms. She asserted that maintenance included variety of types of criminal activity, including bribery, perjury, and conspiracy, and that these types of conduct would have violated several of the statutes prohibiting maintenance. Ibid., pp. 36–47. Medieval audiences would likely have understood the word in a similar broad manner.

[113] *The Resurrection*, p. 366, ll. 9–16. As Horner pointed out, maintenance was used in a similar way in another one of the York Plays, the Cutlers' *The Conspiracy*. Horner, "Witness, Evidence, and Proof," p. 37. In that play, Cayphas says to Pilate, "Why sir, for he would overthrow our law, we firmly hate him as we ought to, and thereto should you maintain our might." *The Conspiracy*, p. 226, ll. 96–98.

[114] He continued by telling Pilate that he saw Christ die and that he "God's son almighty that was recently hanged." *The Resurrection*, p. 368, ll. 63–76.

[115] *The Resurrection*, p. 369, ll. 107–8, 113–22.   [116] Ibid., p. 379, ll. 437–48.

Medieval audiences might well have understood that Pilate, as a lord, would maintain the soldiers as his retainers, as lords generally did.[117]

Another very interesting literary connection to maintenance occurred in the fifteenth-century morality play *Wisdom*.[118] In dealing with the "fallen condition of humanity [and its] being subject to time and change," the trinity of the soul, Mind, Will, and Understanding become, respectively, Maintenance, Perjury, and Gentle Fornication.[119] In describing his condition, Mind acknowledges his "worship," and that he serves "mighty lordship." He says that many folk dread him and that men are attracted to his friendship "for maintenance of their wrong-doing" and that he supports them by lordship.[120] He then stated that "law proceeds not for maintenance."[121]Mind, Will and Understanding then have an exchange. Mind says that "maintenance is now so mighty, and all for mede." Understanding responds that "the law is so colored falsely by trickery and perjury, bribes be so greedy" and Will adds that "maintenance and perjury now stand. They were never flourishing so much since God was born." A new footnote will have to be added after born & it should say: Ibid., p. 136, ll. 671-80. Shortly thereafter, he announced that he is Maintenance and introduces six dancers, adorned in his livery, who perform the "dance of maintenance."[122] In another passage, livery was associated with maintenance as the jurors in a lawsuit wore "hoods about their necks" and "hats of maintenance."[123] Later, Will

---

[117] Horner asserted that Pilate has bribed the soldiers to lie. Horner, "Witness, Evidence, and Proof," p. 38. Although bribery, embracery as it was known, was illegal, whether it was illegal maintenance would depend on knowing the facts of a particular incident.

[118] In Mark Eccles, ed., *The Macro Plays* (London, 1969), pp. 113–52. *Wisdom* was written in about 1460. Ibid., xxx. Gratitude is expressed to Prof. Richard Beadle, University of Cambridge, for bringing this work to my attention.

[119] The play "draws on a tradition in which the soul is multifaceted and the object of contemplative exploration." Pamela King, "Morality Plays," in Richard Beadle and Alan Fletcher, eds., *The Cambridge Companion to Medieval English Theatre*, 2nd ed. (Cambridge, 2008), pp. 247–52. It may be a satire of William de la Pole, duke of Suffolk, his wife, Alice Chaucer, and the Suffolk affinity, drawing on the Suffolk reputation for engaging in maintenance and other wrongdoing. John Marshall, "'Fortune in the Worldys Worschyppe': The Satirising of the Suffolks in *Wisdom*," *Medieval English Theatre* 14 (1992), pp. 37–66.

[120] *Wisdom*, p. 134, ll. 630–35.

[121] In modern English, this means that the law does not proceed because of maintenance. Ibid., p. 135, l. 653.

[122] Ibid., pp. 136–36, ll. 691–708; Marshall, "Satirising the Suffolks," pp. 41–48.

[123] *Wisdom*, p. 138, preceding l. 725. A recent article examined the drawings of the Folger Library manuscript of this play and found a crude sketch of a hat and suggested that it might be "a costume parody of a hat of maintenance." The article also noted the hat of

linked maintenance and perjury, and Mind told those assembled that "you may not endure without my maintenance." Understanding responded, "This is bought with a bribe of our substance."[124] An exchange between Mind and Understanding showed the connection between maintenance and other wrongdoing:

> *Mind.* Wrong is born up boldly
> Though all the world know it openly
> Maintenance is now so mighty
>   And all for reward (mede).
> *Understanding.* This is so colored falsely
> By tricks and perjury,
> Bribes be so greedy
>   That to the poor truth is taken right not ahead.[125]

Thus, this play used maintenance to illustrate "the psychology of the fall into sin."[126]

Other Types of Medieval Literature

Although not products of literary imagination, like the works discussed above, other types of medieval literature such as religious works and letters also dealt with these subjects.

Religious Works

Medieval sermons involved preaching that commonly consisted of satire and complaint.[127] These sermons dealt with many of the same topics as the plays and poems. "The voice of the preacher" echoed these

> widely distributed criticism of abuses ... These very complaints are sown broadcast over the whole field of medieval English sermon-literature. Not

maintenance appeared later in the crest of Magdalene College, University of Cambridge, based on the arms of Thomas Audley, Lord Chancellor 1533–1544, who founded Magdalene College in 1542. Gail Gibson, "Doodles and Dragons," in Folger Shakespeare Library, *The Collation: Research and Exploration at the Folger* (November 12, 2015), http://collation.folger.edu/2015/11/doodles-and-dragons/.
[124] *Wisdom*, pp. 138–39, ll. 745–46, 761.   [125] Ibid., p. 136, ll. 669–76.
[126] King, *Morality Plays*, p. 247.
[127] In his seminal study of medieval sermons, Owst devoted three chapters to this topic, tracing its evolution and its use with regard to the vices of the church and its ministers, those of the secular estates and various professions and occupations, and the vices of domestic life. G.R. Owst, *Literature and Pulpit*, pp. 210–470.

merely the general tone of condemnation in the poems, but the very phrases of satire or invective used are characteristic of the pulpit, which employs them with ceaseless reiteration.[128]

Owst argued that the literary works discussed above were one of the influences on the sermons' use of complaint and satire and that religious works had also influenced the literary ones.[129] He illustrated the similarity of the sermons to the plays and poems by comparing language of the latter in the work of Chaucer, Gower, and Langland with similar language in the sermons and in particular with the portions in *Piers Plowman* dealing with Lady Meed.[130]

Although some of the sermons' complaints were directed at the Church and its officials,[131] their sharp and persistent reproach of the sins of secular society are the most relevant to this chapter. Many sermons indicted the rich and powerful, the nobility, the lawyers, and the judges.[132] Prominent in these rebukes was the work of John Bromyard, the Dominican friar and "a venomous and effective critic of abuses and vanities in all areas of ecclesiastical and secular life."[133] Owst characterized his *Summa Praedicantium* as a masterpiece of satire and complaint, full of "passion and suspense" and "intensity of feeling" and having an appeal of "majestic terror."[134] Bromyard attacked the rich and powerful for using legal devices to oppress the poor.[135] Standing before the "supreme Judge's throne" were "the harsh lords, who plundered the people of God with grievous fines, amercements and exactions."[136] In heaping scorn on them, he condemned "the evil princes of the world, the kings, earls, and other lords of estates ... who used to keep many hounds and a numerous and evil retinue." He indicted them as evil lords and criticized their abuse of lordship and retaining. On the relationship with their retainers, he said that the latter cried, "I am wholly at your service, always ready to do your will and favor."[137] He also

---

[128] Ibid., p. 224.

[129] Ibid., pp. 214, 226–41. He noted that sermons also used verse. Ibid., pp. 226–27. He viewed the medieval preacher as competing with the lay minstrel on his own ground for the popular ear. Ibid., pp. 218–19. Scase also illustrated the relationship between sermons and complaint poems and judicial complaints. Scase, *Literature and Complaint*, pp. 5–11.

[130] Owst, *Literature and Pulpit*, pp. 232–36, 316–18, 339–41, 345–49.

[131] Ibid., pp. 242–86.

[132] The lesser nobility were also subjected to criticism. Ibid., pp. 331–38.

[133] Peter Brinkley, "John Bromyard," *Oxford Dictionary of National Biography Online*.

[134] Owst, *Literature and Pulpit*, p. 302.   [135] Ibid., pp. 292–307.

[136] John Bromyard, *Summa Praedicantium*, as quoted in Owst, *Literature and Pulpit*, pp. 316–17.

[137] Ibid., p. 321.

condemned the rich and powerful for their avarice.[138] "To money all hearts and deeds alike of evil men are obedient ... Money conquers: money rules."[139] He argued that avarice caused "strife, discords, and law-suits."[140]

Nor was Bromyard alone in his criticism of the powerful and mighty. Others also attacked them, targeting their avarice and pride, "this wicked pride among lords and knights."[141] Bishop Brunton excoriated them as "*magnati* ... extortioners, destroyers of their tenants ..."[142] Master Robert Rypon characterized them as "proud and greedy exactors and oppressors of the poor ... the greatest deceivers of their neighbors with falsities, lies, and subtleties."[143] Another preacher noted that the "Devil has whispered in their ear, 'Thou are a lord of great power.'"[144] The powerful were indifferent to the complaints of the poor, and "[w]icked lords cultivated evil laws and evil customs, which were seldom either undone or revoked after they are begun" and in other ways manipulated the law to favor their interests.[145] The law favored the powerful to the detriment of the poor, who were unlikely to get relief from the courts. One sermon said, "For if he go to law, there is no help; for truly law goes as lordship bidded him."[146]

The criticism of nobles, lords, and other powerful persons specifically targeted maintenance and its partners, livery and retaining. In attacking their "swarm of unruly retainers," Bromyard said that "no hounds were ever readier for the chace, no hungry falcon for the bird it has spied than are these to do whatever their great lord bids them, if they should want to

---

[138] Ibid., pp. 307–19.   [139] Ibid., pp. 316–17.   [140] Ibid., pp. 319.

[141] As quoted in ibid., p. 320. Owst noted the "clamor raised against the great nobility of England" and that "every sermon-book that we handle seems to tell a similar tale. An exceeding bitter cry goes up from the pulpits of the land against those who are here pictured as monsters of cruelty and extortion." Ibid.

[142] As quoted in ibid., p. 321. Thomas Brunton (Brinton) was a Benedictine monk and bishop of Rochester from 1373 to 1389. He was active in parliamentary and political activities. His 105 sermons were his most important legacy and in them he outspokenly denounced the wealthy and powerful for their irresponsibility, pride, greed, and sloth. Henry Summerson, "Thomas Brinton," *Oxford Dictionary of National Biography Online*.

[143] He said this in a sermon at Paul's Cross, as quoted in Owst, *Literature and Pulpit*, p. 321. Paul's Cross was "the most famous pulpit in England." Ibid., p. 305. Rypon was a Benedictine monk and subprior of Durham for two decades. Most of his preaching was in the first decade of the fifteenth century; he was "an important preacher in an important period." Siegfried Wenzel, *Latin Sermon Collections from Later Medieval England: Orthodox Preaching in the Age of Wyclif* (Cambridge, 2009), pp. 66–73.

[144] Owst, *Literature and Pulpit*, p. 310.   [145] As quoted in ibid., pp. 328–29.

[146] Ibid., p. 329.

beat or spoil or kill anyone."[147] Moreover, their livery would protect them from being punished in the courts for their wrongdoing.[148] In a sermon at Paul's Cross, Rypon, speaking of the "temporal lords, knights, and squires," faulted "how the lords oppressed the poor ... how they promote and maintain quarrels with their neighbors, yea and protect the most abandoned of their officials in causes the most unjust, through their pride defending them."[149] One preacher said that "there be many secret robbers, and maintained by their masters, as false bedels and bailiffs, false haywards and jailers."[150] Sermons repeatedly subjected livery to the fiercest denunciation, and they said that "Officers of great men that wear their livery; the which by color of law and against law rob and despoil the poor people."[151] Some criticism linked their conduct to the sin of pride. A sermon said that such men cultivated worship and were "proud of their office, proud of lordship and maintenance, of might and of great reputation."[152] Another sermon connected avarice to conduct that seemed to resemble maintenance, saying that a "covetous man ... will be an intermeddler (*entremettoure*) in every man's legal action; and thereby he hopes, within process, to lead and rule all the country."[153]

One of the more interesting religious texts directed at maintenance was a tract of the Lollard reformer John Wyclif. This work makes extensive use of the word "maintenance." In attacking legal abuses and injustice, it stated:

> Also all that take and maintain false causes have been cursed grievously, as they have been worthy both of God and man. Their worldly clerks with their abettors run fully in this curse; for they maintain their worldly life against the true teaching of Christ and his law ... Also lords holding great lovedays and by there lordship maintain the false side, for money, friendship or favor, fallen openly in this curse, and so do men of law, with all false witnesses that maintain falseness against truth, wittingly or unwittingly. For in all this false maintaining they hold with the opponents against God, and as much as is in them ... Clerks that do evil and maintain it by subtlety of word have been sly or subtle heretics, but these lords of priests, that have bishops, and other officials that maintain other men in sin, have subtle masters of errour and heretics ... And commonly

---

[147] Bromyard, *Summa Praedicantium*, as quoted in Owst, *Literature and Pulpit*, p. 325.
[148] Ibid., p. 325.
[149] As quoted in G.R. Owst, *Preaching in Medieval England: An Introduction to Sermon Manuscripts of the Period c. 1350–1450* (New York, 1965), p. 182.
[150] As quoted in Owst, *Literature and Pulpit*, p. 324.   [151] Ibid.   [152] Ibid., p. 309.
[153] As quoted in ibid., p. 319.

all misdoers fall into this curse for they maintain a false quarrel against
God and his saints.[154]

In attacking the abuse of lovedays, a day set aside for dispute settlement,
the tract used maintenance broadly to characterize wrongful conduct by
those who acted as arbiters of the disputes and those "who take and
maintain false causes" and "falseness against truth" for "money friendship or favor." It also pronounced a curse on abusive lordship and
lawyers for this misconduct. By stating that "they maintain a false
quarrel" and "maintain false causes," the tract may suggest an awareness
of the narrower legal definition of maintenance. The author has used a
legal word and concept metaphorically to make religious accusations.[155]

   As the poems and plays indicate, the legal system was a common target,
and medieval sermons also had harsh words for it and its officials.[156]
Bishop Brunton railed against the deficiencies of the English system of
justice. He compared it with the treatment of Jesus by Pilate and Judas.
"Come, let us oppress the just man who is contrary to our doings, so also
is it with the powerful men of the world today and the leaders of our
realm." The just man who will not consent to their plans or publicly
rebukes them is oppressed as their enemy by slander, reproof, and
persecution. They free the murderer or thief from the legal punishment
and the imposition of justice. "And in the realm of England, so many
laws abound, and yet there is not utterance or observance of the laws."
The realm will be destroyed "unless these injuries, injustices, and wrongs
are quickly reformed by execution of the laws."[157] Bromyard noted the
"hatreds and cursings engendered" by the legal system's injustice.[158] He
said England enjoyed "an evil name among foreign nations for her lack of
justice, for the reign of perjury and false-witness," and for its flourishing
crimes and unpunished criminals.[159] The *Gesta Romanorum*, used by
writers such as Chaucer, Gower, and Shakespeare, spoke of England's
"mighty judges," saying that they on "the day of doom were worth no

---

[154] John Wyclif, "The Grete Sentence of Curse Expounded," in Thomas Arnold, ed., *Selected
English Works of John Wyclif*, 3 vols. (Oxford, 1871) (republished in Liberty Fund
Online), vol. III, no. XXII, pp. 322–23. This tract was composed in 1383. Ibid., p. 267.

[155] Whether Wyclif actually wrote this is unclear. Arnold, ed., *Wyclif Works*, vol. III, p. 267.

[156] Owst, *Literature and Pulpit*, pp. 339–49. Owst identified the similarities between the
sermons and the poems, particularly between the former and Langland's *Piers Plowman*
and the portions involving Lady Meed. Ibid., pp. 339–41, 344, 347.

[157] As quoted in ibid., pp. 339–40.

[158] Bromyard, *Summa Praedicantium*, as quoted in Owst, *Literature and Pulpit*, p. 329.

[159] Ibid., p. 340.

more than worms, or else worse."[160] It noted that poor and middling men were at the mercy of great power of "the cunning (*wytty*) men of this world, as justices, advocates and men of law."[161]

Preachers complained about the avarice and greed of judges, lawyers, and jurors, which made them amenable to bribery. In his scornful reflections on the mighty who had died, Bromyard indicted those involved in the legal system, "the false wise men of the world, the judges, assessors, advocates, swearers and perjurers" for taking bribes.[162] "Like weathercocks, they will turn automatically at every wind of silver."[163] In his attribution of judicial vices, Bromyard identified bribes (*munera*) as the first, followed by love, favor, and hate.[164] He said that the belt of justice, rather than properly positioned "mid-way," sagged "toward the heavier purse" when justice was dispensed by judges, lawyers, and jurors. Money is the "only key" to admission "to the courts of false men of law," and "as reapers" with their "sickle," they "collect mede." Being a judge was a fast and effective route to wealth.[165] One preacher said that "for both Christian courts and secular courts … they go for gold and gifts and truth is forsaken."[166] Another sermon said that "but truly gifts so blind the judges again, that they had not seen the fair, right way in the balance."[167]

Lawyers were also targeted for their misconduct in litigation and abuse of the justice system, conduct reminiscent of that for which they were indicted in the Edward I eyres and trailbaston sessions.[168] A sermon in the first half of the fifteenth century complained about ambidextrous

---

[160] As quoted in ibid., p. 340.   [161] Ibid., p. 341.   [162] Ibid., pp. 293–94.

[163] Ibid., p. 317.

[164] Ibid., pp. 340–41. Owst said that in complaining of these vices, "English medieval preaching against the law [did] little else than ring the changes on these unhappy themes." Ibid., p. 341.

[165] Bromyard, *Summa Praedicantium*, as quoted in ibid., pp. 345–47. Jurors were similarly condemned. False men will bribe judges to be on juries for the opportunity for enrichment. Ibid., p. 346.

[166] As quoted in ibid., p. 341.   [167] Ibid., p. 342.

[168] There are a variety of literary sources regarding trailbaston. Amy Phelan, "A Study of the First Trailbaston Proceedings in England, 1304–7," unpublished PhD thesis, Cornell University (1997), p. xvii. The best known one is the "Outlaw's Song of Trailbaston." The author complained about the misuse of these sessions, in which "deceit mouths" caused him to be victim of false accusations of "wicked thefts and other misdeeds." Thus, he will hide in the woods "where there is no deceit nor any bad law." He advised others to do the same because "the common law is too uncertain." He was "indicted out of spite" as a result of "what bad laws [did] to him by so great abuse." Aspin, *Anglo-Norman Political Songs*, pp. 67–78.

lawyers, saying that "many pleaders and advocates set all their hearts so much on winning that some of them have taken from both sides sometimes."[169] Another sermon, from perhaps the mid-fifteenth century, said, "For a little money, they initiate false, unjust actions (*"quest-mongers"*), or else for a dinner will save a thief and condemn a true man."[170] In attacking the vices caused by the law, one sermon singled unjust legal actions, "especially now a days by false quarrels to get a man's goods." The preacher continued by noting the perversity of the legal system because when common people attempted to vindicate their rights in court, they failed "for gold or silver or some other gift will turn the law anon and make the wrong as it were very right and of the right the wrong."[171] The legal profession was "a craft of knowing the virtue of lying."[172] According to Bromyard, although other professions and crafts would not undertake unsuitable or impossible tasks, it is only the lawyer and advocate who will do so, for "no case is too palpably unjust for them. Indeed, some prefer to undertake false cases rather than the true, because they can make more money out of them."[173] To sum, Bromyard's strong denunciation of the legal system said that

> in every direction truth and justice perish, and injustice reigns. For, not he who shall do more justly, but he who gives and takes more, is set in offices and juries. He, who can bring in his train more thieves and murderers is master of all.[174]

Letters

Letters were another form of medieval literature. The *Paston Letters* are a notable example. These letters are the largest surviving collection of English medieval family letters and the greater part of the entire corpus. In them, there are numerous uses of the word "maintenance."[175] It was

---

[169] As quoted in Owst, *Literature and Pulpit*, p. 343. Bromyard leveled similar charges against serjeants-at-law. Ibid., n. 1.

[170] Ibid.   [171] Ibid.   [172] Ibid.

[173] As paraphrased in ibid., pp. 347–48. He also attacked their high fees, which were beyond what their clients could afford; their threats to compel their payment; their exaggeration of the risks regarding the cases and their unnecessary prolongation of them; their conspiracies with other lawyers; and their skill in procuring favorable judges and juries. Ibid., p. 348

[174] Bromyard, *Summa Praedicantium*, as quoted in ibid., pp. 346–47.

[175] It was present in ten letters, although four of them just referred to maintenance actions. The other six actions describe conduct of maintenance and maintainers. Norman Davis, Richard Beadle, and Colin Richmond, eds., *Paston Letters and Papers of the Fifteenth*

used to label individuals as wrongdoers and to describe their conduct. They were called "extortioners" and "false maintainors,"[176] "one of the greatest maintainors,"[177] and "a maintainor of the king's enemy."[178] A member of Sir John Fastolf's household said that the chancellor would not have been made executor of Fastolf's will "but for maintenance."[179] Fastolf himself complained about maintenance. He asserted that a bailiff of Hickling had "maintained the Prior in his wrong against me ... as a maintainor he may be put up."[180] Also, he complained that Thomas, Lord Scales, "will maintain [Thomas] Tuddenham and [John] Heydon [Fastolf's adversaries] in all he can or may" at the *oyer et terminer* proceedings at Lynn.[181]

A more detailed letter provided insight into the exercise of lordship and its relation to maintenance. Elizabeth Clere, a wealthy widow and landowner,[182] seeking advice from John Paston, recounted a dispute between William Stewardson, a servant of Thomas, Lord Scales, a powerful East Anglian lord,[183] and Elizabeth and her attempt to distrain William for rent he owed her.[184] Although he confessed that his allegations of being beaten in the process were untrue, she refused his attempt to submit to her mastery and to be in her good graces. Maintenance was the problem. She told William that "his master should stop his maintenance" and "for his maintenance he shall fare the worse."[185] Her first allegation

---

Century, 3 vols. (Early English Text Society, Supplementary Series 20–22) (Oxford, 2004–5), part II, no. 579, p. 181; part III, nos. 989, 995, 996, 1006, 1009, pp. 99, 109, 111, 126, 134.

[176] Ibid., vol. II, no. 460, p. 48.   [177] Ibid., II, no. 579, p. 181.

[178] Ibid., II, no. 665, p. 275.   [179] Ibid., II, no. 584, p. 187.

[180] Ibid., III, no. 991, p. 103.   [181] Ibid., III, no. 996, p. 111.

[182] Colin Richmond, "Elizabeth Clere: Friend of the Pastons," in Jocelyn Wogan-Browne, Rosalynn Voaden, Arlyn Diamond, Ann Hutchison, Carol Meale, and Leslie Johnson, eds., *Medieval Women: Texts and Contexts in Late Medieval Britain: Essays for Felicity Riddy* (Brepols, 2000), 259–73.

[183] Scales became the leader of the Suffolk affinity, the controlling power in East Anglia, in its reemergence after the death of the Duke in 1450, and Scales was closely connected with Queen Margaret of Anjou in opposition to the Yorkist forces. Helen Castor, "Thomas Scales," *Oxford Dictionary of National Biography Online*.

[184] There had been conflict between Elizabeth and the Stewardson family for almost a decade regarding land to which they both claimed right. The Stewardsons had kidnapped the seller and forced him to sell to them. This dispute prompted substantial litigation. Richmond, "Elizabeth Clere," pp. 257–59. The distraint may have involved other land that William held of Elizabeth, but trouble arising out of the distraint may have been part of the larger conflict and its settlement part of the settlement of the latter. Ibid., p. 259, n. 20.

[185] Davis, Beadle, and Richmond, *Paston Letters and Papers*, II, no. 600, p. 199.

seemed to be voicing her displeasure with Scales's support for William in the dispute. But it is not clear that Scales had acted wrongfully. He wrote John Paston asking him to "labor and entreat" Elizabeth to accept a proposed agreement in dispute ("variance") and to "do your true diligence in this matter as Scales would do for him."[186] Although Scales's action was probably a legitimate exercise of "good lordship," Elizabeth deemed it maintenance, as she felt that it disadvantaged her in her dispute with William. Scales also brought an action against Elizabeth and her men for the alleged assault on William. But Scales was exercising his legal right, as a master had a trespass action for an assault or abduction of his servant based on his loss of services. Since the allegations, however, were untrue, Elizabeth viewed the action as wrongful and, therefore, called it maintenance, as it increased the pressure on her and her expenditures.

Conclusion

These medieval poems, plays, sermons, and letters showed a widespread concern with contemporary abuses and in particular with the failure of the law to achieve justice; the vices of judges, lawyers, and others instrumental in its administration; and the negative impact on the middling and poor people. Like the petitions, the literature complained of maintenance by great powerful men. Undoubtedly some of the portrayals and complaints were intentionally exaggerated for effect and were not always factually accurate. Nonetheless all this literature revealed actual discontent. In addition, the complaints were consonant with allegations in the legal actions and petitions. Thus, the literary portrayals likely reflected some level of genuine social attitudes about law and litigation and those who abused and perverted it.

Exploring the purpose and audience of these works would perhaps enhance the understanding of their impact. Although a detailed study of this subject is one for experts in medieval literature, some preliminary observations might be made. Middleton has studied this impact

---

[186] The nature of the proposed agreement is unclear. Scales says the person delivering his letter to Paston will inform him. Scales's request of Paston is interesting. The Suffolk affinity, which Scales now headed, and its members such as Thomas Tuddenham and John Heydon, were generally adverse to the Pastons and Sir John Fastolf. The latter had hoped Scales would support them in their effort to curtail the local power of the Suffolk affinity after the Duke's death. But instead Scales aligned his lordship with the Suffolk forces and became their leader. Castor, "Thomas Scales."

with reference to *Piers Plowman.*[187] Although that poem may be distinct-ive,[188] much of her general argument on purpose and audience would seem to be applicable to the other poems and plays as well. Other than the letters, which were a matter of private correspondence, it would seem that the works of literary imagination were didactic. They were con-cerned with contemporary abuses and directed at achieving social reform. Middleton argued that they were "to fill some perceived gap in discourse," combining "wholly familiar uses in partly new ways" and to have a social utility, "a margin of culturally practical interpretability." As such, the poems identified "the foundations of social virtue, of legitimate authority, and of spiritual renewal."[189]

The religious literature also pertained to the contemporary abuses and the connection between religion and social reform and argued that reli-gious duty compelled social reform. Through their moral complaint and "rebuke of the sins of secular society," the sermons aspired to effectuate the moral improvement of the laity.[190] The task of the preacher was "to pre-pare the minds and stir the hearts again to combat old evils, to revive old courage and open vision toward duly authorized reforms."[191] With regard to the sermons' attack on the abuses of the legal system and the vices of its officials, Owst said that "in long history of Christian oratory, it is not often that we can point to achievements in practical politics, and hail them as the fruit of faithful pulpit denunciation." Moreover, the "unrelenting exposure by our medieval homilists" contributed significantly "to call attention to false indictments at law, perjury and other abuses which bore down upon the poor, and to secure their suppression."[192]

[187] Anne Middleton, "The Audience and Public of 'Piers Plowman,'" in David Lawton, ed., *Middle English Alliterature Poetry and Its Literary Background* (Bury St. Edmunds, 1982), pp. 101–23.

[188] It was distinctive because of the widespread distribution, transmission, and reception of its texts soon after its composition. Ibid., pp. 102–10. Moreover, it was more "insouciant and enigmatic" as compared with the explicit, intentional nature of Gower's work. Ibid., pp. 112–13. Middleton attributed its "social power and its wholly *ad hoc* authority" to its "heteroclitic nature." Ibid., p. 123.

[189] Ibid., pp. 102–04.

[190] Owst, *Literature and Pulpit*, p. 287. The pre-reformation preachers aimed "to break down man's natural ordinate attachment to the world and created goods." J.W. Blench, *Preaching in England in the Late Fifteenth and Sixteenth Centuries: A Study of English Sermons 1450–c. 1600* (New York, 1964), p. 232.

[191] Owst, *Preaching in Medieval England*, p. 248.

[192] Owst, *Literature and Pulpit*, pp. 348–49.

In terms of the audience, it seems the different genres require separate consideration. The plays were likely designed for public consumption.[193] They were a visual and aural experience. Beadle's study of the York Plays suggested that this was true with those plays. Their production involved the various craft guilds and was part of a pageant held on Corpus Christi day. The performance was a well-known civic event.[194] Although other plays may not have been as celebrated, it would still seem that they were aimed at the local citizenry. Sermons likewise were aural. But the venues of the sermons varied, which might affect the nature of the audience. Some sermons occurred in the church or other religious building as part of the mass (*inter missarum sollemnia*), but others were more public, occurring "at the cross" and "procession."[195] The type of sermon might also have determined the audience. Some sermons, those given on Sundays or feast days (*sermones de tempore*), would seem to be directed at the general laity. But others were for those of a particular status (*sermones ad status*), such as the clergy, nobility, merchants, and other lay groups and professions.[196]

The poems were different because they required a literate audience. Understanding them required literacy, as the poems were written in all three contemporary languages, Middle English, Latin, and French. In her study of *Piers Plowman*, Middleton noted the various ways in which its audience had been characterized. One way involved dividing it into an old audience of clerks and a new audience of "prosperous literate laymen." Another distinguished between national and local or regional readership. But she was skeptical of those characterizations in favor of an audience "interested, by virtue of social location and experience, in the foundations of Christian authority." That audience was both ecclesiastical and lay, consisting of those who by "their customary activities [were involved] in counsel, policy, education, administration, pastoral care – in those tasks and offices, where spiritual and temporal

---

[193] Some scholars have argued that the plays were initially intended for public performance, but later compiled for reading. Peter Happe, *Cyclic Form and the English Mystery Plays: A Comparative Study of the English Biblical Cycles and Their Continental and Iconographic Counterparts* (New York, 2004), p. 37.

[194] Beadle, *The York Plays*, vol. II, pp. xvii–xxxiii. These plays were performed, almost without exception, annually from about the 1370s onward on Corpus Christi Day for more than 200 years to a large audience, which sometimes included royalty and local magnates. Gratitude is expressed to Prof. Richard Beadle for this suggestion.

[195] Owst, *Preaching in Medieval England*, pp. 144–221.   [196] Ibid., pp. 234–71.

governance meet."[197] Her thesis is that *Piers Plowman* was a literary work "received by a heterogeneous and attentive readership."[198] It is unclear whether the same could be said for all the other poems. But the difference may be one of degree and not of kind. Arguably, the audience for the other poems was more or less the same and was also a diverse one, consisting of the same types of literate ecclesiastics and laymen. In any event, these observations on the purposes for which these various forms of literature were written reinforce the existence of the concern with injustice and the inadequacies of the legal system. With regard to the audiences, they included those both guilty of the various vices and those in a position to effectuate reform.

These works also show the widespread depiction of maintenance in nonlegal medieval literature. It is used in all three senses of the word identified in Chapter 1. Most commonly it was used in its broadest sense, connoting various forms of wrongful conduct. But it was occasionally used in the narrow legal sense to describe conduct that violated the statutory prohibitions. Its use in these literary works showed a public understanding of the word and a contemporary concern with the harmful effect of maintenance, livery, and retaining.[199] These activities were viewed not separately, but as part of a larger problem involving the abuse of lordship. Richard II's reign, in particular, was viewed as one where the evils of maintenance and livery were rampant. Given the political climate as well as the legal developments of the late fourteenth and fifteen centuries, it was not surprising that this literature singled out this conduct for harsh treatment. The later years of Edward III's reign were troublesome and the political turmoil of Richard's rule are well known, highlighted by the appellants, the Peasants' Revolt,[200] and his ultimate deposition.

Moreover, this literature is interesting for additional reasons. First, the literature's use of poetry, allegory, and satire as modes of complaint reflect an interesting juxtaposition with the petitions' use of formal,

---

[197] Middleton, "Audience and Public," pp. 103–4.   [198] Ibid., p. 101.

[199] In her essay on the York Resurrection Play, Horner discussed in detail the audience's understanding of these legal notions and how they impacted their witnessing of the play. Horner, "Witness, Evidence, and Proof," 27–67.

[200] Abuse of lordship was one of the complaints of Wat Tyler and his followers. When asked by the king what his complaints were, one of those he listed was that "no one should have lordship except proportionally among all the people, except only the lordship of the king." V.H. Galbraith ed., *The Anonimalle Chronicle 1333 to 1381* (New York, 1970), 147, fol. 348v.

official, and legal language.[201] These literary complaints and the manner in which they were expressed were quite similar to the petitions to the king, his council, and parliament complaining about the same types of conduct.[202] Second, this literature enhances insight into public attitudes toward law and the operation of the legal system. It confirms the legal nature of medieval English society and the widespread knowledge of law. Further, it provides a broader context for the study of legal issues and illustrates how the use of nonlegal sources can provide a richer understanding of legal history.

---

[201] Scase has studied the notion and use of complaint in detail in Scase, *Literature and Complaint*. She views this literature as a distinct genre, manifested in both literary and legal contexts. Her thesis is that "the judicial institutions of written complaint which emerged dramatically in the reign of Edward I came into dialogue with literary production, becoming part of, and centrally informing a wider literature of complaint." What developed were common "theories of complaint." Ibid., p. 1.

[202] Scase showed the similarity between several poems of complaint and judicial complaint. Ibid., pp. 5–41.

8

Changes in the Late Medieval Period

Maintenance litigation changed significantly in the late medieval era, 1377–1485. There were substantial differences in the nature and extent of litigation regarding abuse of legal procedure. Petitioning continued much in the same manner as in the prior reigns, with only a few differences. Finally, there was a transformation in the social context in which this litigation and petitioning occurred.

Maintenance and Related Litigation in the Late Medieval Period

The nature of the maintenance and related litigation in this period is almost the exact opposite of that during the period 1272–1377.[1] In the earlier period, the predominant types of this kind of litigation were criminal indictments (75%) and conspiracy cases and actions (66%), as compared with 25% and 13%, respectively, in the later period. In further contrast, the most common types of this litigation in this later period were civil actions (51%) and the predominance of private maintenance and champerty actions (45%),[2] as compared with 25% and 3%, all of which were champerty actions, respectively in the earlier period. Finally, the use of conspiracy actions as a weapon against maintenance declined from15% of all litigation in the earlier period to less than 1% in the later period. All of these changes in litigation reflected a trend that had begun in the reign of Edward III.

The most important change was the substantial number of civil maintenance actions that were brought in the later period. Other changes included the decline of both criminal and conspiracy actions, and the

---

[1] Both periods covered a similar time span, 95 years and 108 years, and produced a similar amount of this type of litigation, 929 and 1,028 cases and actions. Appendix A contains a detailed computation of the different types of actions in each period.

[2] There were 420 maintenance actions (41%) and 38 champerty actions (4%).

continued attenuation of the connection between conspiracy and main-tenance. These changes demonstrated that in dealing with abuse of legal procedure, maintenance actions had emerged as the primary type of litigation, and the conspiracy cases had declined concomitantly. As was true in the period 1327–77, most of the criminal conspiracy actions in this later period targeted conduct involving force and violence (85%).[3] All the civil conspiracy cases involved the procurement of false appeals and indictments.[4] The proportion of civil conspiracy actions decreased from 67% of all civil actions relating to abuse of legal procedure in the earlier period to 9% in the later period. In the period 1377–1485, maintenance and champerty action accounted for 45% of all litigation, of which 95% were civil actions.[5] Table 8.1 identifies the different types of litigation and their frequency in this period.

The explosion of civil maintenance actions is striking since there were no such actions in the earlier period. In addition, the substantial number of crown maintenance actions was a new development, as there were no such actions in the earlier period. The combined private and crown maintenance actions constituted 65% of all litigation concerning abuse of legal procedure in this period. However, one must be cautious in assessing complaints about maintenance. Charges of maintenance were easily made, especially against one's adversaries. Many who complained about maintenance were its clearest beneficiaries.[6] Maintenance, like justice, was often in the eye of the beholder.

The onset of private civil maintenance actions was the result of a 1377 statute.[7] In Richard II's first parliament in October 1377, the Commons

---

[3] Some of these criminal cases involved procuring false appeals or indictments and were not always presented as conspiracies. Criminal conspiracies to maintain accounted for the remainder of the criminal conspiracy cases.

[4] Nine of the 45 civil conspiracy actions (20%) specifically mentioned such procurement, but the remainder (80%) were all mesne process entries with no further details. But since all the actions were brought by private plaintiffs, no other type of civil conspiracy action appeared. Since these were the most common type of civil conspiracy actions in the earlier period, it seems likely that these mesne process entries involved similar conduct.

[5] The principal action maintained was identified in 43% of the actions and involved 41 different types. The most common were common law trespass actions (40%) and debt actions (17%). The court in which the maintenance occurred was identified in 60% of the actions. The most actions were in the King's Bench (38%), in the Common Bench (29%), and in London and other local courts (17%).

[6] Harriss, "Introduction," in McFarlane, England in Fifteenth Century, xxii; Carpenter, "Law, Justice, and Landowners in Late Medieval England," Law and History Review 1 (1983), pp. 226–31.

[7] Although this study focused on parliamentary statutes and litigation in the royal courts, almost all towns also adopted ordinances in the mid-fifteenth century against livery and

Table 8.1 *All cases, 1377–1485*

	Criminal	Civil	Other	Total
Private maintenance actions	0	420	0	420 (41%)
Maintenance indictments	24	0	0	24 (2%)
Crown maintenance actions	0	0	253	253 (25%)
Conspiracy and false appeals/indictments	86	45	0	131 (13%)
Champerty	0	38	0	38 (4%)
Livery	142	20	0	162 (16%)
Totals	252 (25%)	523 (51%)	253 (24%)	1028

submitted three petitions complaining about maintenance. One complained about the king's unsuitable councilors and requested that they be prohibited from engaging in maintenance.[8] Another petition complained about defendants in lawsuits granting their lands and goods to lords and great men in return for aid and maintenance in their wrongdoing.[9] The third petition linked maintenance and livery. It complained about small landholders who engaged in maintenance and gave livery to their retainers and affinities in exchange for supporting their legal actions.[10]

All these petitions produced legislation.[11] The king's response to the first petition and was broader than the request and it produced the above

maintenance. The objective was to preserve their autonomy and limit the influence of outsiders. The chief concern was interference in local elections and threats to public order. Rosemary Horrox, "Urban Patronage and Patrons in the Fifteenth Century," in Ralph Griffiths, ed., *Patronage, the Crown and the Provinces in Later Medieval England* (Gloucester, 1981), pp. 156–61.

[8] Parliaments of Richard II: October 1377, no. 49, *PROME*. Another petition in the same parliament requested the appointment of worthy counselors. In response, the king restricted gifts to the counselors and prohibited them from engaging in maintenance. Ibid., no. 23.

[9] Ibid., no. 83. Another petition with a similar complaint was submitted to the next parliament also. The king responded that the statute made in the prior parliament should be upheld. Parliaments of Richard II: October 1378, no. 43, *PROME*.

[10] Parliaments of Richard II: October 1377, no. 92, *PROME*.

[11] I Rich II, cc. 4, 7, 9, *Statutes of the Realm*, vol. 2, pp. 2–4. The second and third petitions resulted in a prohibition on gifts of land or goods by fraud or maintenance. Ibid., c. 9, vol. 2, pp. 3–4. The response to the final petition confirmed the statutes prohibiting maintenance and prohibited giving livery for maintenance or other confederacies. Ibid.,

statute, on which the civil maintenance actions were based. It prohibited any of his officials "or any other person ... of whatsoever estate or condition they be" from engaging in maintenance and prescribed a penalty of imprisonment and ransom to the king.[12] But, as was true with almost all of the earlier statutes, it did not explicitly authorize a civil remedy. Nevertheless, as the actions show, Chancery began to issue writs based on the 1377 statute.[13] The Register of All Writs contains three writs of maintenance authorizing private parties to bring civil trespass actions.[14] Fifteenth-century registers contain several similar writs.[15] During the next several years, parties began to bring civil damage actions using these writs, suing on behalf of themselves and the king. A prerequisite for actionability was that the plea, which was alleged to have been maintained, was pending at the time of the alleged maintenance. In a 1425 case, Martin JCP said that there can be no maintenance unless there is some plea pending at that time.[16] In another action, Babington CJCP said the court needed to see the record to make this determination.[17] But this requirement was not commonly challenged. The writs in the maintenance actions, as well as the count if the action was pleaded, routinely contained an allegation of a pending plea and its details.

---

c. 7, vol. 2, p. 3. This statute is likely the first one to deal with livery, a subject that is dealt with in Chapter 11.

[12] 1 Rich II, c. 4, *Statutes of the Realm*, vol. 2, p. 2 (1377); Winfield, *History of Conspiracy*, pp. 150–54; Holdsworth, *History of English Law*, vol. III, pp. 397–98.

[13] Several 1405 maintenance actions were based on the 1331 statute, discussed in Chapter 5, rather than the 1377 one. E.g., TNA: PRO KB 27/575, m. 2d, Hil. 6 Hen. IV (1405), AALT Img. 194. But no evidence was found of a writ that was based on the 1331 statute or of an action that was based on that statute prior to 1377.

[14] *Registrum Omnium Brevium*, 2 vols. (London, 1531), vol. II, fol. 182. The first one used language quite similar to that of the statute. Winfield believed these writs were based on the 1377 statute. Winfield, *History of Conspiracy*, p. 153.

[15] E.g., Cambridge University Library, MS Additional 6854, fol. 270r; MS Ff. 1.32, fol. 119v.

[16] "*Un maintenance ne purroit estre sinon que il avoit ascun ple pend a celle temps.*" Y.B. Trin. 3 Hen. VI, fol. 53, pl. 24 (1425), Seipp No. 1425.086. This requirement was explicit in the early statutes. Statute of Westminster I, 3 Edw. I, cc. 25, 28 (1275), *Statutes of the Realm*, vol. I, pp. 33–34; Statute of Westminster II, 13 Edw. I, c. 49 (1285), *Statutes of the Realm*, vol. I, p. 95; *Articuli Super Cartas*, 28 Edw. I, st. 3, c. 11 (1300), *Statutes of the Realm*, vol. I, p. 139. Champerty actions, which were based on the 1300 statute, reiterated this requirement. E.g., Y.B. Hil. 15 Hen. VII, fol. 2, pl. 3 (1500), Seipp No. 1500.03. Although not explicit in the later statutes, the use of the word "quarrel" may have incorporated this notion. In any event, as the early law dictionaries and Year Book cases show, it was commonly understood to be a requirement in action for maintenance.

[17] Y.B. Hil. 9 H6 fol. 64, pl. 17 (1431), Seipp No. 1431.017.

The first maintenance action based on the 1377 statute, an entry of mesne process,[18] did not appear until 1391.[19] In the next year, in a pleaded action, the plaintiff alleged that the defendant had maintained a trespass action in the Court of the Steward and Marshal of the King's Household.[20] The defendants' answer, a special traverse, alleged that a trespass defendant had been imprisoned and had asked them and other neighbors to be his mainpernors, and they agreed, but did not otherwise maintain him.[21] By the end of the century, several additional maintenance actions appeared.[22] Actions were sporadic during the reign of Richard II. But by beginning of the fifteenth century, during the reigns of Henry IV and V, these civil actions rose steadily, increasing substantially in the second half of Henry VI's reign and declining significantly in the reigns of Edward IV and Richard III.[23]

The pleading in these actions followed the standard pattern of common law pleading. The plaintiff by original writ or bill brought a *qui tam* action,[24] alleging that the defendant had maintained a plea in violation of the 1377 statute and sought damages for the harm caused

[18] In that action, an attempt to compel the defendant's appearance was enrolled. TNA: PRO KB27/522, m. 19d (1391), AALT Img. No. 284.

[19] A number of champerty actions appeared in the years following enactment of the 1377 statute. Most of them were based on *Articuli super Cartas*, c. 11. E.g., TNA: PRO KB 27/522, m. 50 (1391), AALT Img. No. 116; TNA: PRO CP 40/536, m. 107 (1395), AALT Img. No. 243. Some, however, were based on 1 Rich. II, c. 4. TNA: PRO KB27/499, m. 5d (1391), AALT Img. No. 198; TNA: PRO KB27/521, m. 76d (1391), AALT Img. No. 384.

[20] TNA: PRO KB 27/524, m. 49d, AALT Img. No. 271. These initial actions used the first writ in *Registrum Omnium Brevium*, noted above, although two of them had an interesting variance. They used the word *manucepit* instead of *manutenuit*, reflecting perhaps the newness of writ's use.

[21] The first writ of maintenance seeking damages in the Year Books appeared in 1405. Y.B. Mich. 7 Hen. IV, fol. 30b, pl. 8, Seipp No. 1405.084. The plea involved an objection to the form of the writ and not a substantive issue.

[22] TNA: PRO KB27/543, m. 65 (1397), AALT Img. No. 140; TNA: PRO CP 40/553, m. 406 (1399), AALT Img. No. 198; TNA: PRO CP 40/553, m. 406 (1399), AALT Img. No. 802 (two actions); TNA: PRO CP 40/553, m. 475d (1399), AALT Img. No. 1916; TNA: PRO CP 40/554, m. 250 (1399), AALT Img. No. 505.

[23] The Year Book evidence shows that maintenance cases were common in the fifteenth century. In his Year Book database, Seipp found 47 maintenance cases in the period 1399–1465 and none from 1302 to 1345. David Seipp, "Patterns and Problems in Fifteenth-Century Litigation: A View from the Year Books," unpublished paper, American Society for Legal History Annual Conference, Austin, TX, 2004.

[24] A *qui tam* action is one in which a private plaintiff sues for both the king and himself (*qui tam pro domino rege quam se ipso sequitur*) to enforce a statute. The plaintiff may seek damages or a portion of the statutory penalty, depending on the language of the statute and that of writ.

him. In most actions, the defendant answered, and in some cases the plaintiff replied to the answer. In discussing the pleading in these main-tenance actions, the justices distinguished between general maintenance, where the plaintiff generally alleged maintenance, and special mainten-ance, where he alleged more specific details.[25] For example, in discussing bribery of a jury by a lawyer, Martin JCP said that if he gave his own goods to a juror, it went beyond the appropriate conduct of a lawyer and was maintenance. Because of the details alleged, Babington CJCP responded by saying that such bribery was "special maintenance."[26] Figure 8.1 indicates the frequency of these maintenance actions during several periods between 1377 and 1485.

In addition to criminal indictments, the crown also brought numerous actions to enforce the maintenance statute. These actions were instituted by the king's attorney in the *qui tam* form asserting a plea of trespass and contempt for a violation of the maintenance statute. The substantial number of such actions contrasted sharply with their complete absence prior to this period. A very substantial portion of them (82%) were mesne process entries of the crown's action (*optulit se quarto die*).[27] But the defendant appeared in a significant number of the records of these entries and prayed that the king count against him in the action (30%). In such instances, the court would issue a proclamation, stating that "if anyone knew or wished to inform the king's justices, serjeants or attorneys in the matter, they should come and be heard."[28] In none of these instances did anyone appear, and, therefore, the defendants went without day.

---

[25] This procedural distinction had important implications concerning a defendant's rejoin-der, its plea in response. Winfield, *History of Conspiracy*, pp. 136–37. Coke also used the term "special maintenance," but did not make clear what he meant by it use. Ibid., p. 136.

[26] "*Coment que il ne done ses propres biens, eins des biens son maistre: uncore ceo est un speciale maintenance, et il fait autrement que partient a luy a faire.*" Y.B. Mich., 11 Hen. VI, fol. 10, pl. 24 (1432), Seipp No. 1432.024. The defendant had argued that the plaintiff's replication was double, but the judges thought that all the conduct alleged constituted one special maintenance. Gratitude is expressed to Prof. John Baker for clarifying this case. Lawyers also used these terms. *Pomeroy v. Abbot of Buckfast*, Y.B. Mich., 21 Hen. VI, fol. 15, pl. 30 (1442), Seipp No. 1442.126, CP 40/729, m. 301 (East. 1443), AALT Img. No. 594 (Serjeant Markham); Y.B. East., 18 Edw. IV fol. 2, pl. 8 (1478), Seipp No. 1478.014 (Serjeant Pygot); Y.B. Mich.,19 Edw. IV, fol. 3, pl. 9 (1479), Seipp No. 1479.038 (Serjeant Vavasour).

[27] In the other 18%, the defendant appeared and responded only in a small number of them (7%). The remainder (11%) were mesne process entries ordering the sheriff to take various steps to cause the defendant to appear.

[28] E.g., TNA: PRO KB 27/626, m. 12d (1417), AALT Img. No. 564. In this typical action, Thomas Covele, the king's attorney, initiated action on behalf of the king and himself for

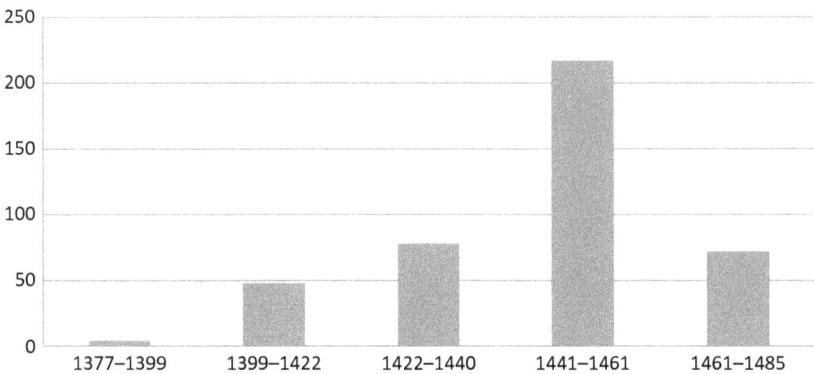

Figure 8.1   Private maintenance actions, 1377–1485.

What was likely occurring was that the crown was instituting an enforcement action as the result of a complaint by an aggrieved individual and pursuing the normal efforts to get the defendant into court, but dropping the action if the aggrieved individual or someone else did not appear in response to the proclamation. At the same time, the crown had largely abandoned the use of indictments as a means of attacking maintenance. Moreover, the proportion of criminal conspiracy to maintain cases dropped from 20% of all criminal cases in the earlier period, 1272–1377, to 5% in the later period, and criminal maintenance cases decreased from 17% to 10% of all criminal cases. As Figure 8.2 shows, the frequency pattern of these crown maintenance actions was very similar to that for the civil maintenance actions, although they started somewhat later than private actions.[29]

This approach seems to be very different from the crown's policy during the reigns of Edward I, Edward II, and Edward III. Perhaps this change was the basis of the criticism voiced in 1485 by William Hussey CJKB and Edward IV's former attorney general. He told an after-dinner gathering of justices that the maintenance and other statutes intended to prevent wrongdoing would

> never be well executed until the lords spiritual and temporal are of one mind, for love and dread that they have of God, or of the king, or of both,

a violation of the maintenance statute against four cordwainers and a chandler for maintaining a trespass action in the London sheriff's court.

[29] The first one was in 1412. Only three crown maintenance actions were found that seem to be against the same defendants in a private maintenance action.

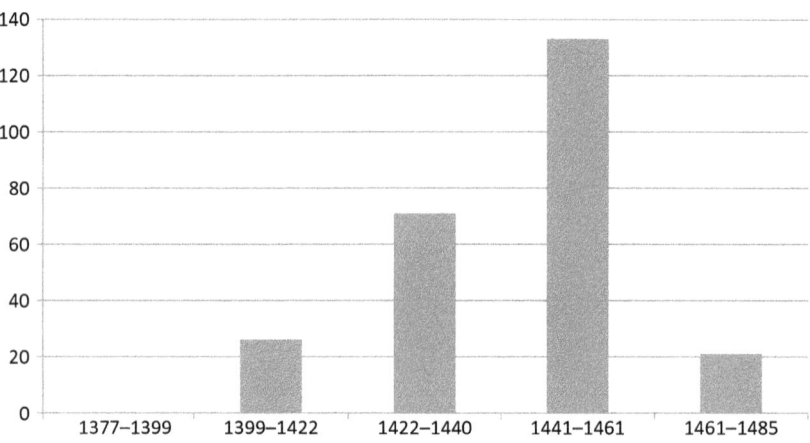

Figure 8.2   Crown maintenance actions, 1377–1485.

to execute them effectively ... For he said that, when he was the king's attorney, all the lords swore to keep the statutes which they with others had then compiled together, by order of the same king, and diligently to execute them, and he saw that within an hour, while they were in the Star Chamber, several of the lords made retainers by oath and swearing, and did other things that were directly contrary to their said sureties and oaths ... And he told this to the king.[30]

Nevertheless, these crown maintenance actions, likely prompted by individual complaints, coupled with the very large number of private actions reflected a dramatic change in the nature of maintenance litigation in late medieval England.

[30] "*Et le Chief Justice disoit, que le ley ne sera onques bien execute tanque touts les seigniors espirituels et temporels sont d'un confirment pur l'amour que ils ad de Dieu, ou de roy, ou d'ambideux effectuelment de eux executer ... Car il dit que il veist en temps E .4 quand il fuit son atturney, touts les seigniors jures a garder les statuts, queux ils ove autres avoit adonq compile ensemble par commandement de mesme le roy, & eux diligentment executent: et il veiast deins un heure tanque ils furent en le Star Chambre divers de les seigniors faire retainments par oath & serement, et autres choses, que furent directement contraries a lour dits suretes, et oathes ... et disoit que il disoit ceo au roy mesme.* " Y.B. Mich. 1 Hen. VII, f. 3, pl. 3 (1485), Seipp No. 1485.003. His comment was made with regard to the statutes regarding "robberies and other felonies, riots, routs, and forcible entries, labourers and vagabonds, liveries, maintenance, and embracery." Ibid. William Hussey was attorney general from June 16, 1471, to July 7, 1478. John Sainty, *A List of English Law Officers, King's Counsel and Holders of Patents of Precedence* (London, 1987), p. 44.

The reasons for this change are not obvious. A critical step facilitating this new litigation was that Chancery began to issue writs based on the 1377 statute. This change is rather perplexing, as Chancery clerks did not do so with earlier statutes, even when the statutes appeared to authorize private remedies.[31] The decision to create a writ based on this statute may have involved senior officials of the Chancery or consultation with the King's council.[32] The only evidence touching on this issue appeared in the chancellor's opening remarks in the November 1384 parliament. He said:

> And that maintenance, diffused almost throughout the entire kingdom, be crushed and entirely destroyed. And that those who wished to complain of such maintenance, or of any other matter in which the common law did not suffice, should submit and show their petitions to certain chancery clerks assigned thereto, whose names were to be read out by the clerk of parliament, that they might thereby find a suitable remedy, God willing.[33]

His remarks would seem to provide sufficient authority and incentive for the chancery clerks to create a new writ based on the 1377 statute for aggrieved individuals who requested one. They would profit by doing so, and it was not their problem if the court rejected a plaintiff's action.[34]

Maintenance, livery, and retaining had become significant issues in the reign of Richard II.[35] That concern was evident in the 1377 statute itself

---

[31] Most of the maintenance statutes prior to the 1377 statute also did not do so. There were two possible exceptions in the reign of Edw. III, 4 Edw. III, c. 11 (1330) that authorized royal and assize justices to hear and determine maintenance and other complaints at the suit of the king or an injured party, and 20 Edw. III, cc. 4 and 6 (1346), which prohibited maintenance by royal officials, barons, and any great or other man, reiterated the authority of the *oyer et terminer* justices to hear complaints and punish guilty parties at the suit of the king or parties, and charged the chancellor and treasurer to ordain a speedy remedy.

[32] Sayles doubted whether Chancery officials had much discretion and normally refrained from creating a novel writ without consulting the council for approval. G.O. Sayles, "Introduction," *Select Cases in the Court of the King's Bench*, 7 vols. (London, 1939), vol. V, 76 Selden Soc., p. lxvii. But he was discussing a much earlier period in the development of the writ system. Also, although the writ based on 1 Rich. II, c. 4 (1377), was new, it was not necessarily novel.

[33] Parliaments of Richard II: November 1384, no. 5, *PROME*.

[34] There are examples of Chancery clerks issuing mesne process where the legal right was unclear at best. Baker cites instances where they issued mesne process on writs of *assumpsit* for nonfeasance actions before the law recognized such actions. J.H. Baker, *Introduction to English Legal History*, 4th ed. (London, 2002), pp. 334–35.

[35] This included concern with Richard's royal affinity and his distribution of livery. Nigel Saul, *Richard II* (New Haven, 1997), pp. 81–82; J.G. Bellamy, *Crime and Public Order in*

since the three chapters of that statute linked maintenance, livery, retaining, and affinities. The availability of the newly created writ was critical. A heightened concern with these matters may be the factor that most likely motivated the requests of aggrieved parties for such writs and the willingness of chancery clerks to respond. As the experience with trespass on the case, bills of Middlesex, and defamation has illustrated, new remedies often prompted an increased volume of litigation. Moreover, the chancellor's remarks at the opening of the 1384 Parliament encouraged aggrieved parties to complain, and he had the names of the clerks assigned to handle these complaints read out in parliament. It is certainly possible that the knights and burgesses in attendance would convey this information to their local constituents. Moreover, the failure of the crown's maintenance actions[36] and diminished criminal enforcement may have prompted aggrieved individuals to bring their own actions. Losing parties may have felt that the assistance or support that their adversaries had received was an unfair advantage that had contributed to the latter's victory or diminished their own chance of prevailing. Also they may have been looking for ways to retaliate against the victor or to diminish the impact of their own loss. With the writ now clearly available, aggrieved individuals or their attorneys began to exploit this opportunity in increasing numbers. Also the general increase in civil litigation at the end of the fourteenth century may have also influenced the volume of maintenance actions.[37]

In addition to the three petitions submitted in Richard II's first parliament, the Commons submitted eight more petitions complaining

---

England in the Later Middle Ages (London, 1973), p. 7; Simon Walker, "Lordship and Lawlessness in the Palatinate of Lancaster 1370–1400," in *Political Culture in Later Medieval England* (Manchester, 2006), pp. 18, 25, 32; ibid., "Communities of the Country in Later Medieval England," p. 69. Ormrod and Musson characterized these efforts regarding the corruption of justice by maintenance and livery during this reign as a campaign against maintenance. Anthony Musson and W. Mark Ormrod, *The Evolution of English Justice: Law, Politics and Society in the Fourteenth Century* (Basingstoke, 1999), pp. 109–10.

[36] As explained above, the crown abandoned these actions when no one appeared to complain against the defendants. See p. 186.

[37] Palmer analyzed the volume of litigation in the Common Pleas Trinity terms from 1200 to 1607. His analysis revealed a significant increase in litigation from 1370 to 1417. He also found that even though the Black Death caused a 40% decline in population, litigation nevertheless increased. Robert Palmer, "Volume of Litigation," in *AALT, A Statistical Overview of English Legal History*, http://aalt.law.uh.edu/ELHOv/ Enrollments.html; Robert Palmer, "England: Law, Society and the State," in S.G. Rigby, ed., *A Companion to Britain in the Later Middle Ages* (Oxford, 2003), pp. 249–51.

about maintenance and livery in the next parliaments.[38] Further, in the November 1381 parliament, it was agreed that the Chancery clerks, justices, serjeants, barons, Exchequer officials, and great apprentices of the law "should be charged on oath and on the strength of their allegiance" to inform themselves of the wrongdoing in the offices and in the royal courts, "especially of the said maintainers and extortioners in the county, and of their misdeeds."[39] Finally, the "advice of the lords touching good government of the king and of the realm" given to Richard II stated that all those who will be around the king should "cease and utterly abstain for the time being and henceforth from doing any maintenance, or from undertaking or advancing any quarrel of another person of any matter which touches a party before our lord the king."[40]

This increased concern with maintenance was an aspect of the broader context of the disorder during the reign of Richard II. In addition to the 1381 Peasant's Revolt, there was the rebellion of the Lords Appellant, beginning in 1386 and culminating in the February 1388 Merciless Parliament, the subsequent return to power of Richard II, and his ultimate deposition in 1399.[41] The king created a commission in 1386 "to conduct a wholesale and radical review of all offices of government, redress faults, and punish offences."[42] Among its concerns were

---

[38] Parliaments of Richard II: October 1378, nos. 43, 44, 49, 50, *PROME*; Parliaments of Richard II: January 1380, nos. 38, 40, *PROME*; Parliaments of Richard II: November 1384, nos. 17, 18, *PROME*. In addition there were two individual petitions complaining about maintenance and another by the mayor, aldermen, and common of London; Parliaments of Richard II: November 1381, no. 61, *PROME*; Parliaments of Richard II: October 1382, no. 55, *PROME*; Parliaments of Richard II: November 1284, no. 12, *PROME*. Commentators have disagreed about the nature of these petitions. Some have regarded that taking them at face value is oversimplified. They have argued that the complexity of the legal system and the resulting opportunities for manipulation and collusion may have been a greater cause rather than the deliberate lawlessness of the nobility. Walker, "Lordship and Lawlessness," pp. 18–19.

[39] Parliaments of Richard II: November 1381, no. 28, *PROME*.

[40] S.B. Chrimes and A.L. Brown, eds., *Select Documents of English Constitutional History 1307–1485* (London, 1961), pp. 160–62 (tr.). The date of when this advice was given is unclear. Chrimes and Brown cited sources putting it between 1386 and 1392. Ibid., p. 160. Given-Wilson dated it as October 20, 1385. Parliaments of Richard II: October 1385, appendix 1385, Westminster, October 20, 1385, no. 1, *PROME*.

[41] Gerald Harriss, *Shaping the Nation* (Oxford, 2005), pp. 458–91; Michael Bennett, *Richard II and the Revolution of 1399* (Gloucester, 1999), pp. 27–55, 82–135, 170–91; Saul, *Richard II*, pp. 157–204, 366–434.

[42] Harriss, *Shaping the Nation*, p. 459.

"maintainers and undertakers of quarrels and embracers of inquests."[43] In February 1388, the Merciless Parliament was summoned to deal with the dissension in the realm and to promote better governance, peace, and the observation and execution of law. It articulated the need to destroy "extortion, fraud and false maintenance" and to punish malefactors and maintainers.[44] The Lord Appellants were in control and took revenge against the king, who was their prisoner, and his leading supporters.[45] A major item was their appeal of treason against Alexander Neville, archbishop of York; Robert de Vere, duke of Ireland; Michael de la Pole, earl of Suffolk; Robert Tresilian, Chief Justice; Nicholas Brembre, knight; and others.[46] One of the thirty-nine articles of the appeal, article 13, charged that the archbishop, duke, earl, and Nicholas, were "traitors to the king and kingdom, [who] have often taken large gifts in the king's name from various parties for the maintenance of causes, and sometimes from both parties."[47]

Given the failure of the Merciless Parliament to achieve much reform, the Commons requested another parliament, which the council approved. It met in Cambridge in September 1388.[48] Maintenance and livery were again a significant issue. At this parliament,

> the Commons complained bitterly about the badges issued by the lords, since those who wear them are, by reason of the power of their masters, flown with such insolent arrogance that they do not shrink from practising various form of extortion ... [and] do not allow right to go hand

---

[43] *Statutes of the Realm*, vol. 2, pp. 45; L.C. Hector and Barbara Harvey, eds., *The Westminster Chronicle 1381–1394* (Oxford, 1982), p. 173.

[44] Parliaments of Richard II: February 1388, part 1, no. 1, *PROME*.

[45] Harriss, *Shaping the Nation*, pp. 461–69.   [46] Ibid., pp. 464–66.

[47] Parliaments of Richard II: February 1388, part 2, article 13, m. 6, *PROME*. The Commons also accused Simon Burley, knight, constable of Dover and Windsor, and chamberlain of the king, of being an abettor, maintainer, and sustainer of the treacherous purpose of Robert de Vere, duke of Ireland, to procure armed men and archers. Parliaments of Richard II: February 1388, part 3, article 6, m. 10, *PROME*.

[48] Parliaments of Richard II: February 1388, part 1, no. 22, *PROME*; Harriss, *Shaping the Nation*, p. 466; Chris Given-Wilson, "Introduction," Parliaments of Richard II: September 1388, *PROME*. No roll for this parliament survives, but the petitions were preserved in the *Westminster Chronicle*, pp. 354–70, which is reprinted in "Introduction," appendix, item 1, *PROME*. Given-Wilson said that "the after-shocks of the Merciless Parliament seem to have been little felt at Cambridge, at least not in a direct and personal way. What this parliament is generally remembered for is its legislation – or, more precisely, for the labour laws which it passed, and for the debate on the question of liveries which served as the prelude to the famous livery legislation of 1390." Given-Wilson, "Introduction."

in hand with justice along the paths of reason; and it is certainly the boldness inspired by their badges that makes them unafraid to do these things and more besides.[49]

In response, the lords invited them to identify individual cases in order to punish the offenders and deter others. In addition to a prohibition on livery, they requested that the king authorize the assize justices and justices of the peace to hear and determine "all manner of maintenance, extortions, and oppressions" at both the king's suit and that of a party and to ordain a statute against maintenance requiring guilty parties to pay a fine to the king and double damages to complainants.[50] Neither request was successful.[51] This "campaign against maintenance"[52] during the first troubled decade of Richard II's reign produced twenty-one Commons' petitions or other parliamentary matters regarding maintenance and related conduct and six legislative enactments directed at this conduct.[53]

Concern with maintenance persisted during the remainder of Richard II's reign. The Commons continued to complain about maintenance and its causal relation to livery.[54] Also, one of the reasons given by the king for summoning parliament in November 1391 was "to decide how the peace and tranquility of the land, which previously have been greatly

---

[49] *Winchester Chronicle*, pp. 354–55.   [50] Ibid., pp. 355–57.

[51] 12 Rich. II, cc. 1–16 (1388), *Statutes of the Realm*, vol. 2, pp. 55–60. Tuck made a tabular comparison of the petitions and the statute, which showed that most of the items in petition, including those dealing with maintenance and livery, did not produce a legislative response. He attributed the basis of their failure to the self-interest of the lords. J.A. Tuck, "The Cambridge Parliament 1388," *English Historical Review* 84 (1968), pp. 227–29, 234–35. Harriss agreed. Harriss, *Shaping the Nation*, p. 467.

[52] Anthony Musson and W. Mark Ormrod, *The Evolution of English Justice* (Basingstoke, 1999), p. 109.

[53] A related problem was the retention of royal justices as advisors by private litigants. J.R. Maddicott, *Law and Lordship: Royal Justices as Retainers in Thirteenth- and Fourteenth-Century England, Past and Present*, Supp. (1978). There was also concern about the alliances between justices and lords and the former as members of the latter's affinities and retinues. Two Commons' petitions complained about justices taking fees and robes from lords. Parliaments of Rich. II: November 1384, nos. 17–18, *PROME*. As a result, statutes were enacted prohibiting lawyers from sitting as assize justices in their own counties and prohibiting justices of both benches and barons of the Exchequer from accepting fees or rewards from anyone other than the king and giving counsel to any man in any plea before them or in any of the royal courts. 8 Rich. II, cc. 2, 3 (1384), *Statutes of the Realm*, vol. 2, pp. 36–37.

[54] Parliaments of Rich. II: January 1390, no. 45. *PROME*; Parliaments of Rich. II: January 1393, no. 31, *PROME*; Parliaments of Rich. II: January 1397, no. 13, *PROME*.

impaired and hindered, both by detraction and maintenance and other-wise, might best be upheld and kept."[55] During this reign, parliament enacted three further statutes dealing with this conduct.[56]

These same concerns continued to be manifested throughout the late medieval period, although not as frequently as they had during the reign of Richard II. During the remainder of the later period, the Commons submitted about fifteen petitions to parliament complain-ing about maintenance and livery, almost all of which were during the reigns of Henry IV and Henry VI. During the first three years of the former's reign, they complained about maintenance and its connection to livery, bribery, enfeoffments of land, and forcible entries as well as the failure to enforce existing statutes.[57] Most of these petitions did not concern new subjects of complaint, and some were based on conduct during the reign of Richard II. They produced either the enactment of new legislation[58] or responses that existing statutes should be enforced. The complaints in the petitions during the reign of Henry VI were similar.[59] Finally, petitions were not the only parliamentary evidence of the concern with maintenance. Articles put forth by the lords in the September 1429 parliament of Henry VI prohibited maintenance and livery by the lords of the council and required an oath to that effect.[60] Also, statements made at the opening parliament and in explaining

---

[55] Parliaments of Rich. II: November 1391, no. 2, *PROME*.

[56] 13 Rich. II, st. 3(1390), *Statutes of the Realm*, vol. 2, pp. 74–75; 16 Rich. II c. 4 (1393), *Statutes of the Realm*, vol. 2, p. 84; 20 Rich. II, cc. 1–2 (1396–97), *Statutes of the Realm*, vol. 2, p. 93.

[57] Parliaments of Hen. IV: October 1399, no. 84, *PROME*; Parliaments of Hen. IV: October 1399, no. 161, *PROME*; Parliaments of Hen. IV: September 1402, nos. 40, 43, *PROME*.

[58] 1 Hen. IV c. 7 (1399), *Statutes of the Realm*, vol. 2, pp. 113–14; 2 Hen. IV, c. 21 (1400–1401), *Statutes of the Realm*, vol. 2, pp. 129–30; 4 Hen. IV, c. 8 (1402), *Statutes of the Realm*, vol. 2, pp. 134–35; 7 Hen. IV, c. 14 (1405–6), *Statutes of the Realm*, vol. 2, pp. 155; 13 Hen. IV, c. 3 (1411), *Statutes of the Realm*, vol. 2, p. 167. The new statutes commonly began by confirming the prior ones.

[59] Parliaments of Hen. VI: October 1427, no. 34; *PROME*; Parliaments of Hen. VI: Septem-ber 1429, nos. 35, 49; *PROME*.

[60] Parliaments of Hen. VI: September 1429, no. 27, XVI, *PROME*. The members of the council had also taken an oath that "neither you nor any go between shall receive or accept any gift, bribe, or benefit, or promise of benefit for promotion, favouring or for declaring, preventing, of hindering any matter or thing to be dealt with or done in the said council." Parliaments of Hen. VI: April 1425, appendix no. 1, *PROME*. This prohib-ition and oath regarding maintenance and livery were repeated several years later in the reign and again by Edward IV. Parliaments of Hen. VI: January 1433, no. 14, *PROME*. Parliaments of Edw. IV: November 1461, nos. 38, 39, *PROME*.

the reasons for proroguing it mentioned the prevalence and negative impact of maintenance and the desire to eliminate it.[61] In sum, all these statutes, petitions, and other activities reflected the persistent concern with maintenance, livery, and related activities and provided the foundation for the substantial maintenance litigation that emerged in the late medieval period.

Individual Petitions in the Late Medieval Period

Individuals continued to submit petitions during this period complaining about maintenance and the corruption of justice.[62] But there were changes in this activity as well. The most significant change was the emergence of Chancery as a recipient for the submission of petitions complaining about the impairment of legal rights. Complainants now had an additional option for seeking a remedy, petitioning the chancellor.[63]

---

[61] Parliaments of Hen. VI: January 1431, no. 4, *PROME*; Parliaments of Hen. VI: July 1433, no. 11, *PROME*; Parliaments of Hen. VI: March 1453, no. 20, *PROME*; Parliaments of Edw. IV: October 1472, no. 10, *PROME*. Parliament also dealt with maintenance in its judicial capacity. In Henry IV's first parliament, the pleas of the crown against the dukes and earls who had been advisors of Richard II included maintenance of quarrels. Parliaments of Hen. IV: October 1399, no. 1, *PROME*. The articles presented against William de la Pole, duke of Suffolk, in the November 1449 parliament of Henry VI included accusations of maintenance. Parliaments of Hen. VI: November 1449, no. 45 and appendix no. 1; *PROME*.

[62] Wright cautioned that allegations in actions and petitions might exaggerate allegations of force and damage to increase the opportunity for redress and, therefore, must be viewed with a degree of skepticism. Susan Wright, *The Derbyshire Gentry in the Fifteenth Century* (Chesterfield, 1983), pp. 121–22.

[63] These two options had a historical relationship. Petitioning the chancellor had its roots in the petitions to the king and his council. The chancellor had participated in the latter, and, in some cases, the council gave the petitions to the chancellor. It had been difficult to distinguish between council and chancery jurisdiction. At some point, the volume of petitions became too voluminous for the council to handle and the process was formally delegated to the chancellor. In light of these developments, the petitioning of the king and his council has been regarded as the source of the Chancery's equitable jurisdiction. Baker, *Introduction to English Legal History*, pp. 101–3; Holdsworth, *History of English Law*, vol. I, pp. 395–409; J.F. Baldwin, *The King's Council in England during the Middle Ages* (Gloucester, MA, 1913; reprint, 1965), pp. 241–54; William Baildon, "Introduction," *Select Cases in Chancery* (London, 1896), 10 Selden Soc., pp. xvi–xxi, xlv; J.B. Post, "Equitable Resorts before 1450," in E.W. Ives and A.H. Manchester, eds., *Law, Litigants, and the Legal Profession* (London, 1979), p. 69; Margaret Avery, "The History of the Equitable Jurisdiction of Chancery before 1460," *Bulletin of the Institute of Historical Research* 42 (1969), pp. 141–44.

Individual Parliamentary and Conciliar Petitions

Some individuals seemed to prefer a parliamentary forum and submitted petitions to the king, his council, and parliament.[64] In total, individuals or the Commons on their behalf submitted 144 petitions complaining about legal corruption during the late medieval period.[65] Many characteristics of these petitions were similar to those during the period 1272–1377. Most of petitioners complained again about maintenance, the power of their adversaries, or their own lack of power (82%).[66] The next leading type of complaint concerned various forms of corruption, such as procurement, extortion, conspiracy, and embracery (11%). Although the subject matter of the complaints varied, most petitioners still complained about being disseised of their land or the loss of other property rights (42%). A number also complained about legal corruption involving litigation such as false pleas, indictments or accusations, and wrongful convictions (19%). Overall, these individual petitions occurred disproportionately at the beginning of this period, declining significantly during the reign of Henry VI (1422–1461) and rising at the end of this later period, as indicated by Figure 8.3.

As Tables 8.2 and 8.3 illustrate, there were significant differences between the petitioners and targets in the petitions to the king and his council, most of which were not enrolled, and those in the individual petitions that were enrolled on the rolls of parliament.[67] The petitioners

---

[64] These petitions are included in *PROME* and the SC 8s, some of which are enrolled and many others not. The nature of the process of composing and submitting these petitions changed during the fifteenth century, as commentators have noted and discussed. Gwilym Dodd, *Justice and Grace* (Oxford, 2007), pp. 156–96; W.M. Ormrod, Gwilym Dodd, and Anthony Musson, eds., *Medieval Petitions: Grace and Grievance* (York, 2009), pp. 222–41; Alec R. Myers, "Parliamentary Petitions in the Fifteenth Century. Part I: Petitions from Individuals and Groups," 52 *English Historical Review* 52 (1937), pp. 385–404; Alec R. Myers, "Parliamentary Petitions in the Fifteenth Century. Part II: Petitions of the Commons and Commons Petitions," *English Historical Review* 52 (1937), pp. 590–613.

[65] Most of these were to the king and council in the SC 8s (71%), only a few of which were enrolled on the rolls of parliament (9%). Most of the enrolled petitions were those of the Commons or involved some other parliamentary matter (62%). In the period 1272–1377, petitions to the king and council constituted a larger proportion of the individual petitions (88%) and the Commons' petitions were about the same proportion (65%) of the enrolled petitions as in the later period.

[66] Some petitions complained both about power and maintenance and, in some cases, some other forms of corruption as well.

[67] The natures of the petitioners and their targets were not stated or known in some instances. These individual petitions include those by groups.

Table 8.2 *Petitions to the king and his council: Nature of the petitioners (61)*

Widows and other women	26%
Clergy	21%
Group	13%
Esquires and gentlemen	12%
Occupations and trades	10%
Knights	8%
Local officials	3%
Royal officials	2%
Nobility	0%
Other	5%

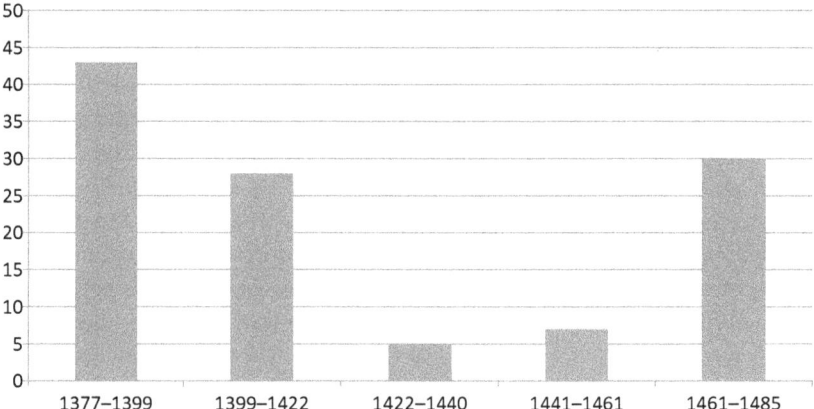

Figure 8.3   Individual parliamentary and conciliar petitions in late medieval England.

in enrolled petitions were of a higher social status or importance and those to the king and council of a more "middling status." Table 8.2 shows the nature and distribution of the latter petitioners.

Table 8.3 shows the distribution of the petitioners in the enrolled petitions. The gentry – knights, esquires, and gentlemen – constituted 26% of the individuals whose petitions were enrolled, and 20% of the other petitions. Also, petitioners who were local officials were twice as common among enrolled petitions. Conversely, tradesmen, widows and other women, and clergy were frequent petitioners to the king and council, constituting 57% of those petitions. There were no women

Table 8.3 *Enrolled petitions: Nature of the petitioners (34)*

Group	41%
Esquires and gentlemen	15%
Knights	11%
Clergy	11%
Occupations and trades	7%
Local officials	7%
Nobility	7%
Royal officials	0%
Widows and other women	0%
Other	0%

petitioners among the enrolled petitions, and clergy and tradesmen made up 18% of those petitions.[68] Although groups were an important type of petitioners to the king and his council (13%), they were the overwhelming leader among enrolled petitions (41%). Also the nature of the groups differed. In the case of enrolled petitions, the groups were the "commons" of several counties, cities and their officials, and gilds. Although some of these types of groups petitioned the king and council, the groups in those petitions were largely religious ones. Moreover, individual religious petitioners were almost twice as numerous among these petitions. These differences may explain why some petitions were enrolled and others were not. The Commons and the lords may have considered the petitions of those of higher social status and those of local officials more important. The most significant difference between the two groups of petitions was the responses to them, which seemed to confirm this importance. All but one of the enrolled petitions, which called for a response, received one. In contrast, only 25% of the petitions to the king and his council did so. The nature of the responses differed also. In the enrolled petitions, many of the petitioners received the substantive relief that they requested, but in the other petitions, the response was only to

---

[68] The nature of only two of the women (12.5%) indicated a possible higher status. One was a widow and "dame" and the other the widow of an esquire. Among religious petitioners to the king and his council, almost all were priors, parsons, and clerks. Only two (15%), a warden petitioning for himself and his college and an abbot for himself and his convent, indicated a higher status.

Table 8.4 *Nature of the targets:*
Petitions to the king and council (78)

Knights	24%
Sheriffs and local officials	22%
Esquires and gentlemen	17%
Nobility	9%
Royal officials	8%
Clergy	6 %
Other	14%

Table 8.5 *Nature of the targets:*
Enrolled petitions (31)

Knights	19%
Royal officials	19%
Esquires and gentlemen	16%
Nobility	16%
Sheriffs and local officials	10%
Clergy	0%
Other	19%

require the target to appear before the council to explain his complaint or to be examined on it.[69]

As Tables 8.4 and 8.5 show, there were also differences between the nature of the targets in the enrolled and other petitions, although they do not seem as significant as they were with petitioners. In both groups, knights top the list of targets, and when esquires and gentlemen are added, the gentry together with the nobility account for about 50% in both groups. There is a switching of rankings of royal officials and sheriffs and other local officials in the two groups. There are more than twice as many royal officials as targets in those enrolled positions as in

---

[69] This low response rate also differs substantially from those in the reigns of Edward I and Edward II (79%) and that of Edward III (81%). In addition, in those earlier reigns, the most common response was to sue at common law or obtain a remedy in Chancery, whereas in the later period there was only one such response (1%). In the reigns of Edward I and Edward II, those responses accounted for more than half, and in the reign of Edward III it was 70%.

those to king and council and also more than twice as many sheriffs and other local officials as targets in petitions to the king and council as in enrolled petitions. In addition, clergy disappear as targets in enrolled petitions. In both the earlier and the later periods, the nobility and gentry were dominant targets, although the percentages vary.[70]

Chancery Petitions

Most commentators agree that Chancery's equitable jurisdiction,[71] later known as the "English Side," emerged initially in the late fourteenth century.[72] During this period, individuals began to petition the chancellor seeking relief.[73] Included among these petitioners were those seeking

[70] In the reigns of Edward I and Edward II, they constituted 46% of the targets, in the reign of Edward III 67 %, and in the later period 51%, although that proportion is somewhat understated, as the "Other" category included several that likely were of higher status such as "great men," "the great men of London," and "wealthy citizen of London."

[71] Baildon said that this petitioning should properly be known as "Chancery Proceedings," to distinguish these petitions from the ones that had been made to the chancellor earlier in the medieval period. He defined a Chancery proceeding as having four essential elements: a petition to the chancellor, an alleged wrong by a specified person or persons, a request that the wrongdoer be ordered to appear to answer the complaint, and a prayer for a remedy. He said that it was "difficult to draw a hard and fast line" between the administrative and judicial functions of the Chancery, but asking the defendant to appear to answer involved the judicial function. Baildon, "Introduction," pp. xii–xv.

[72] There has been, however, substantial disagreement as to when the development of this jurisdiction occurred, the types of cases involved, and the reasons for the growth of this petitioning. P. Tucker, "The Early History of the Court of Chancery: A Comparative Study," *English Historical Review* 115 (2000), pp. 791–811; Post, "Equitable Resorts," pp. 68–79; J. A. Guy, "The Development of Equitable Jurisdiction," in E.W. Ives and A.H. Manchester, eds., *Law, Litigants, and the Legal Profession* (London, 1979), pp. 80–86; Nicholas Pronay, "The Chancellor, the Chancery, and the Council at the End of the Fifteenth Century," in H. Hearder and H.R. Loyn, *British Government and Administration* (Cardiff, 1974), pp. 87–103; Avery, "History," pp. 129–44.

[73] The Commons objected to this exercise of Chancery jurisdiction and to the potential for abuse of the writ of *subpoena*. They petitioned parliament to empower the chancellor to assess costs and damages against petitioners who made false allegations and to insure that no free tenement or other action that may be tried by the common law could be dealt with in Chancery. The king ordained that the chancellor "for the time being" shall have the power to award damages at his discretion. Parliaments of Richard II: January 1394, no. 52, *PROME*. Parliament enacted a statute empowering the chancellor to do so, but it said nothing about interfering with the common law. 17 Rich. II c. 6, (1394), *Statutes of the Realm*, vol. 2, p. 88 (1393–94). Baker, *Introduction to English Legal History*, p. 103 and note 30. Spence stated that the passing of the earlier statute established the Court of Chancery as a distinct and permanent court, with separate jurisdiction and procedures.

remedies for maintenance and other forms of corrupt legal practice.[74] Although these petitions are difficult to date, several complaining of these types of wrongdoing were submitted during the reign of Richard II and a few it seems in the next two reigns, but more during the reign of Henry VI, and an increasing number during the reign of Edward IV.[75] In most instances (64%), the petitioners sought a writ of *subpoena* or other order requiring the wrongdoer to appear before the chancellor to be examined.[76] Usually the petitioners made a request for an appropriate remedy, often concluding "for love of God and by way of charity."[77] But some petitioners made more specific remedial requests, such as compensation, restoration of goods, or requiring the wrongdoer to give a surety of the peace. In seeking relief, most petitioners did not allege the unavailability or ineffectiveness of a remedy at common law (73%). However, some petitions did allege that they were unable to sue a remedy at common law because of the wrongdoer's conduct or their own lack of power or poverty (24%). In most instances, the petition lacked a response (70%).[78] The few that did so ordered the wrongdoer to appear before the king in Chancery (16%).[79]

George Spence, *The Equitable Jurisdiction of the Court of Chancery*, 2 vols. (London, 1846), vol. I, p. 345.

[74] Eighty-three such petitions were found for the period 1377–1485.

[75] The pattern of these petitions involving legal corruption seems consistent with the pattern of Chancery petitions generally. Baker, noting the above disagreement, stated that there was general agreement that the volume of petitions steadily increased toward the end of the fifteenth century. J.H. Baker, *Introduction to English Legal History*, p. 104.

[76] Writs of *subpoena* were requested in the great majority of petitions to the chancellor. Baildon, "Introduction," pp. xiv–xv. Some petitioners requested other types of writs such as *habeas corpus cum causa* (12%) and *certiorari* (10%). Tucker included these writs in the main types of writs issued in response to petitions. Tucker, "Early History," p. 798. Other writs requested included *oyer et terminer, dedimus potestatem*, and *supplicavit*.

[77] Baildon said that most petitioners just asked for a remedy in general terms, as they may not have known what remedy to ask for and left it entirely to the chancellor's superior wisdom and good graces. He said further that these concluding words were the almost invariable expression in the older cases. Ibid., pp. xv, xxv.

[78] Avery said that in these early proceedings, recorded judgments were extremely rare and the remedies granted in cases involving poverty or maintenance rarely known. Avery, "History," pp. 129, 130.

[79] Sibyl, the widow of Robert Darcy, knight, petitioned against John of Skipwith, former sheriff of Lincoln, and the response indicated that an inquisition was held before the assize justices and that the jury found that Sibyl's allegations to be true. TNA: PRO C 1/3/55, 60–61 (1385–96), AALT Img. Nos. 438, 449–50, reprinted in Baildon, ed., *Select Cases in Chancery*, 10 Selden Soc., no. 24, pp. 29–30. Skipworth was the target of several other petitions. Ibid., nos. 25–30, pp. 30–34.

Many of the types of wrongdoing targeted in these Chancery petitions were similar to those to the king and his council in both this and the earlier periods. In their petitions to the chancellor, many petitioners complained about maintenance that adversely affected the exercise of their rights to their land or goods (48%). For example, John Everly, a priest, complained that Robert Somer maintained a false trespass action by William Somer against him, alleging that John had abducted William's wife and goods. As a result, John was imprisoned and Robert extorted his goods and money, which prevented John's delivery from prison.[80] A number of petitioners alleged that they could not sue or obtain a remedy at common law because of maintenance. As in the earlier period, numerous petitions complained about fraudulent or deceitful conduct with similar adverse effects on their rights. John Oremesby alleged that Laurence Pikemonger by his "false plotting and covin" assisted John's debtor, John Hervey, to bring an action in debt in the name of a third person, without the latter's knowledge. As a result, the third person recovered the debtor's goods, which prevented John from having execution on those goods to satisfy his debt.[81] Quite a few petitions complained of maintenance and fraud as well as various other types of corruption.

In addition to these similarities to the other petitions, there were also a number of differences between these Chancery petitions and those to the king and his council regarding maintenance and legal corruption. One significant difference was the larger number of Chancery petitions alleging that the petitioner was the victim of a fabricated or baseless legal action (43%). Also numerous petitions alleged that maintenance actions had been wrongfully brought against them (53%).[82] Many of these petitioners requested writs of *corpus cum causa* and *certiorari*. In one petition, a servant complained that he had wrongfully been sued for maintenance for attending to his master's debt action in his master's absence.[83] Two petitioners complained about maintenance actions

---

[80] John alleged that he had no remedy at common law and requested a writ of *subpoena* directed to Robert. TNA: PRO C 1/45/229 (1467–72), AALT Img. No. 186.

[81] John Oremesby asked that the chancellor consider how the debtor had entered Westminster by the false plotting of Laurence and to grant a writ of *subpoena* directed to Laurence. TNA: PRO C 1/9/41(1386–1411), AALT Img. No. 48.

[82] This total includes two petitions alleging wrongful conspiracy actions. Trespass were the next most common kind of wrongful action alleged in these petitions (25%).

[83] He requested a writ of *certiorari*. TNA: PRO C 1/31/74 (1465–71 or 1480–83), AALT Img. No. 101.

against them for being sureties for a litigant, one for his son-in-law and another for his neighbor.[84] In a more complicated matter involving multiple maintenance actions, a London chaplain, a member of the orders of St. Charity and St. John the Evangelist, complained that he had been wrongfully sued for maintenance for his "labor" in Chancery regarding a testament demising lands to the use of those orders and for his assistance in obtaining a writ of *subpoena* to the feoffees to perform the will.[85]

The Chancery petitions also differed from those to the king and his council in that they were a form of litigation. Like common law legal actions, Chancery petitions referred to the statutes of maintenance, champerty, staple, false deeds and muniments, and to various writs. Five petitions contained endorsements that the petitioner had obtained mainpernors in Chancery to satisfy the defendant's costs and damages in the event that petitioner was unable to prove the truth of his allegations.[86] In addition, almost 25% contained pledges of prosecution.[87] But there was no evidence of why pledges of prosecution and mainpernors had been used in these cases.[88]

---

[84] Both petitioners requested writs of *corpus cum causa*. TNA: PRO C 1/48/75 (1473–75), AALT Img. Nos. 165–66; TNA: PRO C 1/64/155 (1475–80 or 1483–85), AALT Img. Nos. 298–99.

[85] These orders were founded for the relief and support of poor priests. He was also involved in other litigation regarding the land. He was arrested and imprisoned in the maintenance action and obtained a writ of *corpus cum causa*, which was pending, so the defendant brought a new maintenance action based on the same conduct and he was arrested for the same cause. He then requested a writ of *subpoena* to the plaintiffs in the maintenance actions. TNA: PRO C 1/19/265 (1452–54), AALT Img. No. 365.

[86] Two of which said it was required by statute and another by ordinance. TNA: PRO C 1/3/125 (1399–1401), AALT Img. No. 537; TNA: PRO C 1/9/433 (1432–33), AALT Img. No. 570; TNA: PRO C 1/9/473 (1432–33), AALT Img. No. 633; TNA: PRO C 1/9/478 (1432–33), AALT Img. Nos. 638–40; TNA: PRO C 1/68/192 (1386–1486), AALT Img. No. 222.

[87] Baildon said that the inclusion of pledges of prosecution was just the "short form" of the "longer form" using mainpernors. Baildon, "Introduction," p. xxvi.

[88] The authority for the use of mainpernors and pledges of prosecution is not entirely clear. Spence argued that the use of mainpernors was a product of the 1394 statute enacted in response to the objections to the exercise of Chancery jurisdiction. 17 Rich. II c. 6 (1394). Spence, *Equitable Jurisdiction*, vol. I, pp. 341–46. He relied on cases where it was used at about the time of the statute's enactment. *Calendars of the Proceedings in Chancery in the Reign of Queen Elizabeth*, 2 vols. (London, 1827), vol. I, pp. vi, xi, xii. But this seems unlikely. The statute did not require the petitioner to provide security, but authorized the chancellor to award damages for allegations found to be false. Moreover, as Baildon noted and Coke had pointed out much earlier, that power arose only after proof of the allegations'

Three petitions seemed very similar to bill litigation. Two of them had answers by the defendant,[89] and another had four pleadings: a petition, an answer, a replication, and a rejoinder.[90] Moreover, the language in these pleadings was identical to that seen in common law actions, except it was in English. One answer began with a demurrer ("not sufficient in law") in the protestation form and concluded with a special traverse ("without that"). Another answer was a demurrer ("not sufficient in law to put him to answer"), a special traverse ("without that"), and an offer to prove his allegations.[91] In another matter, the petitioner's replication joined issue on the demurrer ("true and sufficient in every point"), an offer to prove his allegations, and a prayer for damages, and the defendant's rejoinder joined issue and prayed judgment of dismissal with costs and damages.[92] It seems likely that the petitioners in a number of these petitions had legal assistance.[93] Given the terminology and pleading, it was probably from common lawyers, even though the matters involved Chancery proceedings.

Finally, there also seems to be some difference in the nature of the individuals involved in the petitions to Chancery from those to the king and his council.[94] As Table 8.6 shows, the number of petitioners in

---

falsity, but these requirements were imposed on the submission of the petition. Further, Baildon found several instances of pledges of prosecution earlier in the reign of Richard II before the enactment of the statute. Thus, he suggested that the requirement may have been a product of an ordinance by the Council or chancellor, although he did not completely rule out the 1394 statute. Baildon, "Introduction," pp. xxv–xxvi. A later statute required that writs of *subpoena* could not be granted without surety. 15 Hen. VI, c. 4 (1436–37), *Statutes of the Realm*, vol. 2, p. 296. One of these five petitions was before the later statute, but the other four could have been after that statute.

[89] TNA: PRO C 1/17/7–8 (1407–56), AALT Img. Nos. 13–14; TNA: PRO C 1/32/89 (1465–71), AALT Img. Nos. 142–41. Baildon said that for a long time, the defendant's answer was not recorded in writing, beginning perhaps in the mid-fifteenth century. Baildon, "Introduction," p. xxvii.

[90] TNA: PRO C 1/47/193 (1472–73 or 1475), AALT Img. Nos. 361–64. Post said that the bill, answer, replication, and rejoinder became the ever more popular trend of Chancery procedure. Post, "Equitable Resorts," p. 68.

[91] TNA: PRO C 1/17/8 (1407–56), AALT Img. No. 13.

[92] TNA: PRO C 1/47/193 (1472–73 or 1475), AALT Img. Nos. 361–64.

[93] Baildon believed that the early bills were prepared by lawyers although not signed by them until the reign of Edward VI. Baildon. "Introduction," p. xxviii.

[94] Far fewer of the Chancery petitions revealed the status of the targets, and there was some decline in the identification of the petitioners' status as well. In petitions to the king and his council in the period 1272–1485, the status of the targets was identified in 85% of the petitions, but only in 52% of those to the Chancery in the period 1377–1485. With regard to petitioners, it was 68% in petitions to the king and his council and 57% in those to Chancery in comparable periods.

Table 8.6 *Petitions to chancery:*
Nature of the petitioners

Occupations and trades	32%
Clergy	30%
Esquires and gentlemen	13%
Knights	6%
Officials	6%
Widows and other women	4%
Group	2%
Nobility	0%
Sheriffs	0%
Other	11%

Table 8.7 *Petitions to chancery:*
Nature of the targets

Officials	28%
Sheriffs	23%
Clergy	15%
Esquires and gentlemen	15%
Occupations and trades	11%
Knights	6%
Nobility	6%
Widows and other women	0%
Other	13%

occupations or trades in the petitions to Chancery in the period 1377–1485 was three times greater than those to the king and his council in the same period, and the clerical petitioners increased by half.

Moreover, as Table 8.7 indicates, members of occupations and trades appeared as targets in petitions to Chancery, although not in those to the king and his council. Finally, officials and sheriffs increased as targets of Chancery petitions and powerful individuals decreased, as compared with those of the king and his council. In sum, there seems to have been a greater diversity of individuals in Chancery petitions than in those to the king and his council.

Overall, these Chancery petitions alleging maintenance and other forms of legal corruption illustrated a common theme of early Chancery equitable jurisdiction. Baker noted that the typical petitions in this period involved complaints of "weakness or poverty, or the abuse of position by an opponent" and were different from those in later equity litigation.[95] Harding said that these early petitions complained about "violence, maintenance and corruption of justice by the overmighty."[96] Moreover, the substantial number of petitions alleging fabricated or baseless maintenance or other legal actions illustrated the use of litigation as a mechanism to pervert the justice system. Although not all of them alleged that they had no remedy at common law, it is unlikely that they did.[97] A remedy through the writ of conspiracy existed for those who had been acquitted of false appeals and indictments.[98] But it is unlikely that it was available for those falsely sued for maintenance, trespass, or other actions. Attaint was available in such cases, but prevailing in such an action was unlikely.

In these Chancery petitions, maintenance was the dominant form of the alleged wrongdoing, confirming again that it was perceived as a

---

[95] He provided an example of a defendant's use of local influence "to prevent a just remedy" in a common tort action. Baker, *Introduction to English Legal History*, p. 104. Baildon described an early inquiry that determined that most of these petitions involved assaults and trespasses and other outrages, for which there were common law remedies, but in which the petitioner "was unable to obtain redress because of the maintenance or protections afforded to his adversary by some powerful baron, or by the sheriff, or some other officer of the county in which they occurred." He also provided examples from the cases that he collected. Baildon, "Introduction," pp. xvi, xxi–xiv.

[96] Alan Harding, *The Law Courts of Medieval England* (London, 1973), p. 100. Avery noted that complaints often were directed at "abuse of the common law by the rich, powerful, and violent" and the "helplessness of the ordinary machinery of justice in the face of local power." Avery, "History," pp. 132, 133. Similar cases continued to appear in the late fifteenth century. Pronay, "The Chancellor, the Chancery, and the Council," p. 92.

[97] The substantial requests for writs of *corpus cum causa* and *certiorari* in these cases may have implied the inadequacy of a remedy at common law.

[98] One case is interesting because of the defendant's attempt to preclude the petitioner's use of a writ of conspiracy for a false appeal and indictment. The defendant appealed the petitioner for the same felony for which he had been indicted, fearing he would be acquitted on the indictment. By permitting himself to be nonsuited on the appeal, on which the petitioner had been arraigned, the petitioner could not sue a writ of conspiracy because the indictment had been found. This use of an appeal was another example of the perverted use of legal remedies. TNA: PRO C 1/47/193–96 (1472–73 or 1475), AALT Img. Nos. 161–64; Christopher Whittick, "The Role of the Criminal Appeal in the Fifteenth Century," in J.A. Guy and H.G. Neale, *Law and Social Change in British History* (London, 1981), p. 71. In another case involving a conspiracy action against an accessory, Danby JCP stated that conspiracy did not lie if one was indicted and then appealed and arraigned and acquitted on the latter. But Danvers said that conspiracy did lie if the appellant was nonsuited before the count. Y.B. Hil. 33 Hen. VI, fol. 1, pl. 6 (1455), Seipp No. 1455.006.

significant social and legal problem.[99] Although these petitioners might have sued for damages based on the 1377 statute, as many aggrieved parties did, they chose not to do so.[100] Instead they petitioned the chancellor for relief. Perhaps they preferred the more flexible and informal procedure in that forum.[101] They also may have feared that the power and influence of their adversaries would have been an obstacle to relief in such an action. In petitioning the chancellor, they found an individual and institution that were amenable to exercise this new jurisdiction. Petitioning the chancellor grew during the fifteenth century "in order to deal with the crippling tendency to pervert the machinery of justice."[102] Although the legal corruption during the reign of Richard II may have been the catalyst for its emergence, it drew on longstanding notions of royal grace.[103]

Good Lordship Revisited

During the late medieval period, there was a change in social context in which maintenance and other forms of legal corruption occurred, which had the potential to affect their legal treatment.[104] This change in

[99] The complaints about maintenance combined with the allegations of baseless maintenance actions accounted for a great majority of the Chancery petitions (69%).

[100] Avery said that the common law remedies against maintenance and similar corrupt practices were limited in scope and of doubtful effectiveness. Avery, "History," p. 133.

[101] Post said that the emergence of Chancery was not development of a new type of court of justice but the formalization of "a tribunal whose uniqueness lay in its central bureaucratic power and not in the quality of justice it dispensed ... Such cases might have remedies at common law, or they might not; ... What mattered to litigants or – at least to plaintiffs – was the advantage of Chancery's legal freedom and administrative power." Post, *Equitable Resorts*, pp. 68, 70–71. Avery asserted that the greatest appeal of Chancery procedure to those who complained about violent trespasses, maintenance, and embracery was that it was "speedier, cheaper, and less susceptible to local influence than the common law courts." Avery, "History," p. 134.

[102] Pronay, "The Chancellor, the Chancery, and the Council," p. 96. He argued that there was a growing recognition that the council was either not able or not best suited to deal with this problem. Ibid.

[103] As to the reign of Richard II, Spence said that the various remedial statutes "were rendered in a great degree ineffectual by the lawless spirit of the times ... In this state of things the middle and lower orders of society were almost out of the protection of the law ... The chancellor, therefore, at the very outset of Richard's reign ... with the sanction no doubt of the council, exercised an authority especially in favor of the weak, for repressing disorderly obstructions to the course of law." Spence, *Equitable Jurisdiction of Chancery*, pp. 342–43.

[104] Since the middle of the twentieth century, there has been a large volume of scholarship by social and political historians regarding the nature of lordship in the fifteenth century, particularly the question of lawlessness and wrongdoing by powerful individuals and

normative attitudes focused on the nature of good lordship, the practice of retaining, and the development of affinities.[105] Likely beginning in the fourteenth century, aristocratic retinues were the product of an adaption "to the general change in the structure of society . . . [and were] traditionally regarded as a retrograde step in social organization."[106]

K.B. McFarlane's insights provided the basis for reexamining the political and social institutions of this period.[107] McFarlane and his followers viewed lordship and the lord's affinities as the dominant political and social structure and a source of order and stability.[108]

---

officials. Substantial disagreement has arisen over these issues. Much of it concerns the controversy and debate regarding "bastard feudalism."

[105] Like other scholars, Davies pointed out that these retinues extended far beyond those men retained by a formal indenture and included not only those also who received an annuity or livery from the lord but "a less distinct group of men who had no formal link . . . but who nevertheless moved in his orbit of power and were thereby amenable to his summons." R.R. Davies, *Lords and Lordship in the British Isles in the Late Middle Ages* (Oxford, 2009), p. 121.

[106] These retinues lacked the stability of the tenurial relationship and facilitated the breakup of late medieval society by loosening types of traditional loyalty and obedience. Moreover, they created opportunities for violent seizing of disputed property and for civil war. N.B. Lewis, "The Organisation of Indentured Retinues in Fourteenth-Century England," *Transactions of the Royal Historical Society* (4th Ser.), 27 (1945), p. 29. Waugh viewed these developments as a continuous process, with the techniques and uses of lordship varying in different periods. He noted the astonishing forms that retaining took throughout medieval Europe. He argued that a new phase of retaining began in the late thirteenth century. Scott Waugh, "The Third Century of English Feudalism," in Michael Prestwich, Richard Britnell, and Robin Frame, eds., *Thirteenth Century England VII* (Woodbridge, 1999), pp. 48–53.

[107] McFarlane was the most important scholar in studying the social and political nature of the fifteenth century. His work influenced many other scholars and was the basis of a revisionist view of the late medieval period. It was also a catalyst for the explosion of scholarship by those who both agreed and disagreed with him. Coss has summarized his influence. Peter Coss, "Hilton, Lordship and the Culture of the Gentry," in Christopher Dyer, Peter Coss, and Chris Wickham, eds., *Rodney Hilton's Middle Ages: An Exploration of Historical Theories, Past and Present*, Supplement 2 (Oxford, 2007), pp. 40–45.

[108] They have challenged other historians for not taking account of these contemporary phenomena. They have alleged that the view of the fifteenth century as more lawless than other centuries has misinterpreted the evidence. K.B. McFarlane, *The Nobility of Later Medieval England* (Oxford, 1973), pp. 114–15, 118; McFarlane, "Lords and Retainers," III, pp. 2–4; G.L. Harriss, "The Dimensions of Politics," in R.H. Britnell and A.J. Pollard, eds., *The McFarlane Legacy: Studies in Late Medieval Politics and Society* (New York, 1995), pp. 4–5; Helen Castor, *The King, the Crown, and the Duchy of Lancaster* (Oxford, 2000), pp. 128–55; Edward Powell, "Law and Justice," in Rosemary Horrox, ed., *Fifteenth-Century Attitudes* (Cambridge, 1994), p. 34. McFarlane said that "conditions in the 1450s were exceptional." McFarlane, *Nobility*, p. 118; Carpenter, "Law, Justice, and Landowners in Late Medieval England," *Law and History Review* 1 (1983), pp. 205, 206–09, 226–31.

Local officials, especially sheriffs, were also part of the local power structure.[109] McFarlane asserted that the notion of lordship had changed in the late medieval period from how it was understood in the earlier medieval period.[110] He said:

> Late medieval lordship, indeed, has not much in common with feudal *dominium*. When a man asked another to be his "good lord," he was not commending himself and his land; nor did he become anything remotely like a vassal. Rather he was acquiring a temporary patron. In this loosely-knit and shamelessly competitive society, it was the ambition of every thrusting gentleman – and also of anyone who aspired to gentility – to attach himself for as long as it suited him to such as were in a position to further his interests. For those who wished to rise in this world, good lordship was essential. A successful man, therefore, gathered about him what was sometimes called his "affinity"; those who staked their hopes on a share of his good fortune.[111]

In his study of the relationship between a lord and his man, Bean expressed a view of this change that was different from McFarlane's. He focused on indentures of retinue, annuities, and livery and discussed how they had evolved and operated from the end of the thirteenth century into late medieval England as aspects of lordship and good lordship. He said that there was a trend in the evolution of lordship that began in Anglo-Saxon England and continued into the modern period. He stated that it made more sense to think of it as from lord to patron, "a phrase that encapsulates the constant tendency of lordship to adjust

---

[109] Richard Gorski, *The Fourteenth Century Sheriff* (Woodbridge, 2003), pp. 11–32, 102–25; Harriss, "The Dimensions of Politics," pp. 5–7; Pamela Nightingale, "The Intervention of the Crown and the Effectiveness of the Sheriff in the Execution of Judicial Writs, c. 1355–1530," *English Historical Review*, 123 (2008), pp. 1–34; Roger Virgoe, "The Crown, Magnates, and Local Government in Fifteenth-Century East Anglia," in J.R.L. Highfield and Robin Jeffs, eds., *The Crown and Local Communities in England and France in the Fifteenth Century* (Gloucester, 1981), pp. 72–87.

[110] The discussion of lordship in this context is in a social and political sense and not in the legal sense, which is predicated on tenure of land.

[111] K.B. McFarlane, "Parliament and 'Bastard Feudalism,'" in G.L. Harriss, ed., *England in the Fifteenth Century* (London, 1981), pp. 17–18. This essay was a seminal work in the debate over bastard feudalism. In it and in his other work, he discussed maintenance. McFarlane, *Nobility*, pp. 115–18. Many historians writing about bastard feudalism also did so. E.g., Gerald Harriss, "Introduction," in ibid.; J.G. Bellamy, *Bastard Feudalism and the Law* (Portland, 1989); John Watts, *Henry VI and the Politics of Kingship* (Cambridge, 1996); Michael Hicks, *Bastard Feudalism* (London, 1995); Simon Walker, *The Lancastrian Affinity 1361–1399* (Oxford, 1990), pp. 235–61; Phillippa C. Maddern, *Violence and Social Order: East Anglia 1422–1442* (Oxford, 1992); P.R. Coss, "Bastard Feudalism Revised," *Past & Present* 125 (1989), pp. 54–55.

to its environment and the fundamental tensions that were created by the process of adjustment in the contexts of medieval England."[112]

Although some scholars were critical of the influence of over-mighty lords,[113] McFarlane and his adherents viewed lordship in a positive light. Since lords were supposed to protect and support clients, there was a possibility that in some cases obligations of lordship might conflict with the law of maintenance. Davies, a student of McFarlane, said that good lordship's legitimacy derived from its claim that it afforded maintenance and protection.[114] He, like others influenced by McFarlane, believed that the lord's support of his clients' quarrels was "the residual legatee of an age-old expectation . . . an obligation of honour," an "obligation of good lordship and good clientship," and that the concern about maintenance was an exaggerated part of a contemporary polemic.[115] Criticizing the assumptions of the modern outlook, Davies took a rather benign view of maintenance. He said that it was "recognized that mechanisms of 'maintenance' worked alongside the normal process of litigation, seeking no doubt to accelerate and influence them, but not working directly against them or challenging their authority." Maintenance was not necessarily viewed as covert and reprehensible activity. Contemporaries understood "how the system was 'played' . . . in the legal and social context in which it operated."[116] In prohibiting maintenance, McFarlane feared that the law would make beneficial conduct unlawful.[117] He also believed that

---

[112] J.M.W. Bean, *From Lord to Patron* (Pittsburgh, 1989), pp. 235–36.

[113] Maddicott noted that the key social unit was the "sustained lordship, the great estate . . . [M]embership in a lord's connection rather than the possession of a stake in the country . . . gave men security and nourished their aspirations." He asserted that "forces of lordship . . . the territorial power of the overmighty lords" contributed to causing the Wars of the Roses. J.R. Maddicott, "The County Community and the Making of Public Opinion in Fourteenth Century England," *Transactions of the Royal Historical Society* (5th Ser.), 28 (1978), p. 27.

[114] His comments dealt in part with a period earlier than the late medieval one, and some of them dealt with the earlier notions of lordship that McFarlane distinguished. R.R. Davies, *Lords and Lordship,* p. 15. His study focused on the period 1272–1422. Ibid., p. 7.

[115] In discussing the use of the word "maintenance," he stressed that it should be understood as improper and excessive support. He warned against taking at face value the "crude claims about the nature and vicissitudes of 'maintenance.'" Ibid., pp. 213–14.

[116] Ibid., pp. 213–14.

[117] K.B. McFarlane, "Lords and Retainers," unpublished manuscript in the Magdalen College Archives, University of Oxford, Lecture III, pp. 5–6, 10–12. But he also recognized that the evidence of corrupt practices was "overwhelming." McFarlane, *Nobility,* p. 118.

maintenance was less frequent than contemporary complaints would suggest.[118] Not all scholars have agreed with McFarlane. Coss disagreed and believed that control of the local justice system and its officials, maintenance and retaining, and affinities "all stemmed from a single impulse – that which sought the survival of magnate power." He found the intrusion of private power into the public courts unsettling.[119] Other commentators shared this view.[120] Thus, determining how the late medieval society viewed obligations of good lordship is critical to understanding their relationship to the developing law of maintenance.[121]

Lordship was a longstanding concept, deeply entrenched in medieval institutions.[122] The good lordship of the fifteenth century was not well defined.[123] Horrox has noted that the lord–retainer relationship was at

[118] He stated that it was difficult to find many actual examples prior to 1422 "of simple maintenance, by which I mean attempts to overawe the court by presence of armed men." McFarlane, *Nobility*, p. 115. This statement is inconsistent with the plea roll evidence during the reigns of Edward I, Edward II, and Edward III, discussed in prior chapters. Also it is an odd definition of maintenance and differs from that which has been deduced from the primary sources.

[119] Coss, "Bastard Feudalism Revised," pp. 54–55. The basis of the development of networks and affinities was "the understanding that the legal system could be accelerated, impeded, deflected, and manipulated in ways that were either detrimental or beneficial to particular members of the gentry and aristocracy." Richard Gorski, *The Fourteenth-Century Sheriff: English Local Administration in the Late Middle Ages* (Woodbridge, 2003), pp. 14–17.

[120] For example, in discussing Langland's *Piers Plowman*, Hanna said that "'good lordship,' now re-emergent in the 1370's , cut both ways and expressed itself as proliferating social discord." Ralph Hanna, *London Literature, 1300–1380* (Cambridge, 2005), p. 267.

[121] An earlier essay studied the relationship between good lordship and Sir John Fastolf's support of the litigation of two of his servants. Jonathan Rose, "The Law of Maintenance and the Obligations of Lordship: A Case Study," in Per Andersen, Kirsi Salonen, Helle Møller Sigh, and Helle Vogt, eds., *Law and Disputing in the Middle Ages. Proceedings of the Ninth Carlsberg Academy Conference on Medieval Legal History 2012* (Copenhagen, 2013), pp. 111–21.

[122] Peter Coss, *The Origins of the English Gentry* (Cambridge, 2003), pp. 30–31, 40; Bean, *From Lord to Patron*, pp. 231–37.

[123] The parties felt no need to do so. Rosemary Horrox, "Service," in Rosemary Horrox, ed., *Fifteenth-Century Attitudes* (Cambridge, 1994), p. 66; Rosemary Horrox, *Richard III: A Study in Service* (Cambridge, 1986), p. 2. Davies said that it was "ultimately more than exploitation or power, even if it was most certainly that also," and it was "much more than land-lordship" and was a "lordship over men." Davies, *Lords and Lordship*, pp. 15, 159, 201. Lander said that the quality of good lordship was well understood by contemporaries, but modern historians have found it difficult to define its exact essence with any degree of precision. J.R. Lander, "Family, 'Friends' and Politics in Fifteenth-Century England," in Ralph Griffiths and James Sherborne, *Kings and Nobles in the Later Middle Ages: A Tribute to Charles Ross* (Gloucester, 1986), pp. 28–29.

the heart of medieval politics.[124] Coss said that it was the essence of feudal society, at the very heart of feudal dynamics, and a complex phenomenon. "Its power was at once customary, economic, and coercive."[125] Good lordship was the real cement between lord and retainer.[126] Good lordship could be manifested in ways that were endless, and the relationship was personal and essentially open-ended.[127] The relationship was a complex one and the benefits to each party were not simply produced by a traditional exchange. Lordship was a set of abstract commitments, and its foundation was the concepts of dependence and service.[128] A core notion was that the lord ought to use his influence to support his client when assistance was required.[129] In return, the latter had an obligation of loyalty and owed service induced not primarily by

---

[124] Horrox, *Richard III*, p. 25; Virgoe, "The Crown, Magnates, and Local Government," p. 83. Lordship was not limited to the peers but was exercised by the gentry as well, although its nature and extent were diminished in the case of the latter.

[125] He stated further that "it required force, economic stability and consent. It was always essentially exploitive, so that any deterioration in the vigour, reputation or economic viability which served to sustain it could adversely affect its quality and even, ultimately undermine it. At the same time its complex nature invested it, quite often with a considerable capacity to adapt and survive." Peter Coss, *Lordship, Knighthood and Locality* (Cambridge, 1991), pp. 159–60.

[126] Walker, "Lordship and Lawlessness," p. 18. Pollard said that retaining was the most formalized element of good lordship. A.J. Pollard, *Late Medieval England 1399–1509* (Harlow, 2000), p. 247.

[127] Horrox, *Richard III*, p. 227. Walker said that in the case of John of Gaunt's affinity, the obligations of the retainers were specified, and the duke's patronage included material goods, countenance, support, and protection and an expectation that he would "sponsor the petitions of his clients, to obtain for them favours from the king and to provide a bulwark against the schemes of their enemies." He stated that "protection, whether physical or legal, was one of the attributes of lordship that the country gentry most valued in a patron." Walker, *The Lancastrian Affinity*, pp. 81–94, 227.

[128] Davies, *Lords and Lordship*, pp. 198, 200.

[129] Davies said that the lord's dependents formed a series of concentric circles, which included his affinity. Ibid., pp. 201, 205–06. Pollard described various types of groups, which consisted of fluctuating circles around a lord. Pollard, *Late Medieval England*, p. 247. Wright explained that there was a permanent core around which temporary elements were grouped. The core consisted of those in the household and the lord's administrative personnel and nonresident adherents, which could include a variety of different types of individuals. "On the periphery was an extremely amorphous group whose relationship with the lord was sporadic." She discussed the various factors that affected the nature and operation of the affinity and the influence of the lord's power. Wright, *The Derbyshire Gentry*, pp. 62–66. Walker made a detailed study of John of Gaunt's affinity, one of the largest and best known ones. He concluded that it was composed of three major categories: household attendants, indentured retainers, and estate officials. Walker, *The Lancastrian Affinity*, pp. 8–18, 24–38.

money but by the lord's protection, patronage, and prestige. But there was no precise correlation between service and patronage.[130]

Although a lord's support for the client was an important aspect of the relationship, the client was not the only beneficiary of this relationship. It also generated intangible benefits for both parties, such as honor and prestige, including the important quality of worship for the lord.[131] Worship was a product of a lord's effectiveness in using his influence to benefit his clients.[132] Loss of worship resulted in shame and rebuke.[133] Davies argued that lords were scrupulous in exercising their lordship, as misrule was dangerous and would damage the lord's reputation.[134] In addition, retaining clients was critical to the viability of lordship and the preservation of each party's "lyvelode."[135] In some instances these benefits were mutually interdependent.[136] For example, an attack on the clients was an attack on the lord's honor, and the ethics of good lordship required a response.[137] A defeat would have a negative impact on the lord's reputation. His retainers' support endowed him with the influence that facilitated promoting both their reputations.[138] Thus, it was desirable both to possess lordship and to be its beneficiary.[139] "The association between them was one of mutual convenience and profit."[140] But, as McFarlane made clear, "lordship lasted only as long as it was found to be *good* lordship or until it was ousted by a better [one]."[141]

---

[130] Harriss, "Introduction," in McFarlane, *England in the Fifteenth Century*, xii. A lord could offer his tenant support, prestige, and security, which determined the strength of his lordship, and the client's loyalty was built on mutual self-interest and seignorial strength. Coss, *Lordship, Knighthood and Locality*, p. 158.

[131] Horrox, "Service," pp. 68, 72; Horrox, *Richard III*, pp. 1–12; Coss, "Hilton, Lordship and the Culture of the Gentry," 46; Phillipa Maddern, "Honour among the Pastons: Gender and Integrity in Fifteenth-Century English Provincial Society," *Journal of Medieval History* 14 (1988), pp. 357–71.

[132] Pollard, *Late Medieval England*, p. 247.

[133] McFarlane, *Nobility*, p. 113; Virgoe, "The Crown, Magnates, and Local Government," p. 72.

[134] He cited an example of John of Gaunt punishing a retainer for maintenance. Davies, *Lords and Lordship*, pp. 214–25.

[135] Coss, "Hilton, Lordship and the Culture of the Gentry," pp. 46, 49.

[136] Davies illustrated this mutuality by recounting a vignette involving Thomas of Lancaster and the men of Bromfield and Yale. Davies, *Lords and Lordship*, p. 15.

[137] Horrox, "Service," p. 68; Paul Hyams, *Rancor and Reconciliation* (London, 2003), pp. 256–57.

[138] "The world ... was full of patrons seeking clients and clients in need of patronage." McFarlane, *Nobility*, p. 113.

[139] Horrox, *Richard III*, pp. 3–4.   [140] McFarlane, *Nobility*, p. 113.

[141] McFarlane, "Parliament and 'Bastard Feudalism,'" p. 18.

Lordship had its roots in the household, which was regularly exempted from the prohibitions on livery and retaining.[142] A good lord was expected to look after his servants' interests.[143] Good lordship was especially import-ant in helping clients resolve their disputes.[144] Good lords were expected to uphold their servants' litigation.[145] In 1455, Sir John Fastolf requested the Duke of Norfolk "to continue your good lordship and support" in the litigation involving the duke's servant, who had been in Fastolf's service.[146] Such assistance might involve arbitrating among conflicting retainers of the same affinity or using the patron's power, prestige, and resources to insure the client's success in conflicts with outsiders.[147] In this dimension, it could operate to ease tensions and "lubricate relationships."[148] But good lordship also had the potential for expanding and exacerbating local conflict.[149]

---

[142] Bean, *From Lord to Patron*, pp. 72–153, 203–04, 206, 211–13, 225, 231–37. McFarlane said that a man's duty to family and friends overrode any public duty. McFarlane, *Nobility*, p. 114; Edward Powell, *Kingship, Law and Society* (Oxford, 1989), p. 110.

[143] Horrox, "Service," p. 66. On occasion, it was specifically included in their indentures. In 1356, the earl of Ormond "granted and undertook to help, favor, and maintain Sir Richard [de Burgh] in all his just quarrels, just as a lord was held to favor, help, and maintain his knight or his vassal." Michael Jones and Simon Walker, eds., "Private Indentures for Life Service in Peace and War 1278–1476," in XXII *Camden Misc.* (5th ser.), 3 (London, 1994), no. 44, p. 76.

[144] Harriss, *Shaping the Nation*, p. 194; Powell, *Kingship, Law and Society*, p. 90.

[145] Horrox, "Service," p. 65. Support could be both legal and extralegal. Walker, "Lordship and Lawlessness," p. 18. As Horrox has pointed out, this support was viewed as a means of containing conflict, but the efforts of each side to prevail could cause it to be transformed into over trials of strength. "Service," p. 77. The latter seems to have occurred in the Fastolf–Suffolk disputes. Powell has identified the numerous ways in which the legal system and powerful individuals could resolve conflict. Powell, "Law and Justice," pp. 35–36. Wright said that the expectation of protection by the lord extended to any subsequent action, violent or legal. Hereditary tenants often were the nucleus of the affinity. Wright, *The Derbyshire Gentry*, p. 144.

[146] N. Davis, R. Beadle, and C. Richmond, eds., *Paston Letters and Papers of the Fifteenth Century*, 3 parts, Early English Text Society, Supplementary Series 20–22 (Oxford: 2004–2005), part III, no. 1021, p. 151.

[147] Stevens cited many supporting case studies. Matthew Stevens, "Failed Arbitrations before the Court of Common Pleas: Cases Relating to London and Londoners, 1400–1468," *Journal of Legal History* 31 (2010), p. 24 and note 15. Wright discussed the operation of settlement and arbitration of disputes in Derbyshire. Wright, *The Derbyshire Gentry*, pp. 122–27. Payling identified formal litigation and informal dispute settlement as a means of control-ling violence in fifteenth-century Nottinghamshire. He found that it had both positive and negative effects. Simon Payling, *Political Society in Lancastrian England: The Greater Gentry of Nottinghamshire* (Oxford, 1991), pp. 186–215. But arbitration could also be impacted by the illegitimate influence of lordship. Walker, *The Lancastrian Affinity*, p. 119.

[148] Davies, *Lords and Lordship*, p. 175.

[149] The challenge was the "ill-defined line between self-help and lawful 'good lordship.'" Ibid., p. 127. Payling cited examples where competitive maintenance between lords caused an arbitration to fail and a riot to ensue. Payling, *Political Society*, pp. 112, 114.

Harriss, a leading protégé of McFarlane, recognized that lordship could be both a stabilizing, disruptive, and ambivalent force.[150] But however it was manifested, good lordship was critical to the protection of gentry interests[151] and necessary to their worldly advancement.[152]

But good lordship did not sanction all conduct in support of clients, and it could be abused.[153] In the view of some contemporaries, it was supposed to be exercised only "as far as law and conscience required."[154] Good lordship, retaining, and affinities could be causes of disorder, including violence, and operate as instruments of injustice.[155]

---

[150] G.L. Harriss, "The Dimensions of Politics," in R.H. Britnell and A.J. Pollard, *The McFarlane Legacy* (New York, 1995), pp. 4–5.

[151] Carpenter, *Locality and Polity: A Study of Warwickshire Landed Society, 1401–1499* (Cambridge, 1992), pp. 288–89. In 1450, when Thomas Tuddenham and John Heydon fell out of favor because of the duke of Suffolk's death, they were apparently willing to spend £2,000 to have the lordship of Sir William Oldham, speaker of the Commons. Davis et al., *Paston Letters*, part II, no. 460, p. 47. In order to thwart their willingness to spend thousands of pounds, King's Bench Justice William Yelverton gave similar advice to John Paston ("spend somewhat of your goods now and get your lordship and friendship there"). Ibid., no. 463, p.53.

[152] McFarlane, *Nobility*, p. 113. He noted that the advice frequently given men was to "get you lordship." McFarlane, *Nobility*, p. 116. Davies said that protection was one of the most treasured facets of lordship. Davies, *Lords and Lordship*, p. 200.

[153] Walker argued that "local violence was an inevitable reaction to abuse of lordship," but abuse was not that of the lords, but resulted from their inability to eliminate corruption and to control the abuse by the men in their retinues and to discipline them. Walker, *The Lancastrian Affinity*, pp. 166–69, 221–22, 226–28, 232–34.

[154] Jones and Walker, "Private Indentures for Life Service," p. 25 (quoting language in an indenture of Lord Hastings). In his indenture with John Libburn, gentleman, Thomas Sandforth agreed "in all his power to assist and maintain the said John of Clebburn as his man in that as right or conscience may require." Ibid., no. 150, pp. 174–75. In indentures, the promise of lordship was not commonly made explicit, as it was "an assumption so central to the relationshiip." Ibid., p. 25. John of Gaunt's support of his clients' petitions contained similar language limiting the favor to be shown the latter. Walker, *The Lancastrian Affinity*, p. 85. In his study of William, Lord Hastings's indentured retainers, Dunham found that a common aspect of most of the agreements was that the extent of the lord's obligation was in all things reasonable and only if required by right, law, and conscience. William Dunham, *Lord Hastings' Indentured Retainers 1461–1483* (New Haven, 1955), pp. 48, 50, 66.

[155] Wright detailed numerous conflicts and disorders, many involving murder, violence, and assemblies of hundreds of persons that occurred among the aristocratic Derbyshire families and leading gentry, starting in 1434 and extending more three decades. "'Official' crime was in reality no more than a form of local self-help on the part of the gentry," which was reinforced by magnate interference. These activities caused Derbyshire to be identified as example in a 1440 parliamentary complaint against the national decay of law and order. Wright, *The Derbyshire Gentry*, pp. 128–42. Bean viewed the antipathy toward retaining as driven by the concern with maintenance. Bean, *From Lordship to Patron*, pp. 200–230.

In particular, good lordship was a primary means for the control and manipulation of the legal system, which was critical for survival.[156] Walker observed that an examination of royal justice showed the ease with which the course of law could be diverted.[157] Bean believed that creation of the justice of peace system lay at the heart of the problem.[158] Powell asserted, "There can be little doubt then that the realities of wealth and political power in late medieval England invariably influenced, and sometimes distorted, the workings of the law."[159] Contemporaries were well aware of this, as indicated by the common complaint that "law goeth as lordship willeth"[160] and Sir John Fastolf's statement to John Paston that "for nowadays ye know well that law goeth as it is favored."[161] As Harriss noted, "lordship likewise pervaded the whole system of local justice."[162] But there were limits on its exercise and effect.[163]

---

[156] Powell, *Kingship, Law and Society*, p. 90. McFarlane and other scholars have questioned the extent to which lordship contributed to lawlessness. Walker, "Lordship and Lawlessness," pp. 18–19.

[157] Walker, *The Lancastrian Affinity*, p. 156.

[158] Bean, *From Lord to Patron*, pp. 201–2. In his study of aristocratic violence and the regulation of local conflict in fifteenth-century Nottinghamshire, Payling identified many examples of violence and lawlessness. Although wrongdoers were indicted, he found that royal efforts failed to impose good order. A particular problem was the aristocratic domination of the local judicial system, which gave them the opportunity to abuse royal power in furtherance of their own interests. But that informal reconciliation of disputes was sometimes successful. He found, however, that arbitration had both positive and negative effects. It had flaws and could be a means of abuse. He concluded that although local communities and magnates achieved some success in controlling disorder, the impact was limited because it depended on good will rather than coercion. Payling, *Political Society*, pp. 186–215.

[159] Powell, "Law and Justice," p. 40.

[160] Harris, *Shaping the Nation*, p. 135; Powell, "Law and Justice," p. 40.

[161] Davis et al., *Paston Letters*, part II, no. 520.

[162] Harriss, *Shaping the Nation*, 55. Waugh argued that aristocratic retinues and lordship had a long history before and after the thirteenth century in their "tendency to influence, manipulate, or overawe the legitimate agencies of government." Waugh, "The Third Century of English Feudalism," p. 53. One concern regarding disorder implicated magnate participation in the peace commissions, and they were excluded for several years. Walker, "Lordship and Lawlessness," p. 83.

[163] In fourteenth-century Lancaster, "this influence was formalized, legitimate, and open." These comments were made in the context of discussing the conduct of John of Gaunt, duke of Lancaster, to shield members of his affinity from the legal consequences of their violent and conspiratorial conduct. In some cases, "he instructed his justices to proceed with a case, but to come to no judgment without his assent." Nevertheless, his power was not absolute, but his "influence on the course of justice … while appreciable, appears neither excessive in its extent nor baleful in its consequences." Walker, "Lordship and Lawlessness," pp. 20–24.

Since McFarlane's initial revisionist views of lordship in the late medieval periods, a substantial debate has emerged among scholars, some supporting his views and others criticizing them. Some scholars have taken a less benign view of the conduct of powerful and influential individuals. Perhaps it is fair to say that there is a consensus that lordship could have both positive and negative effects and the disagreement is about the frequency of these effects and the effect of particular forms of conduct. But whatever view one takes on these matters, both the exercise of good lordship and maintenance could involve supporting the litigation of another person. The notions of good lordship that emerged in this period likely increased both the frequency of support and assistance and the number of clients, who were the beneficiaries. As will be seen, a number of maintenance actions involved supporting servants, tenants, and others with whom those providing assistance had a relationship. Thus, the potential conflict between these social and legal norms required resolution. Whether the exercise of good lordship and this support were lawful or illegal depended on the manner in which the justices developed the law of maintenance and how they drew the line between lawful and unlawful conduct.

9

The Development of the Law of Maintenance

Legitimate Maintenance

Permissible Justifications for Intermeddling

The 1377 statute, which was the basis of the onset and explosion of civil maintenance actions in the late medieval period, like the others prohibiting maintenance, did not define maintenance. In 1388, the Commons suggested a definition. They said:

> And because there are different opinions about the cases in which maintenance ought or ought not to be adjudged, the definition follows: that is to say when any lord, spiritual or temporal, lady, woman of religion, or any other of whatsoever estate or condition he be, takes up or supports another's quarrel to which he is not a party by reason of blood or marriage, in order to have the whole or a part of that which is claimed, or instigates or procures for reward, gift, or promise the passing of inquests in quarrels to which he is not a party; and when any gather together in great routs and multitudes of people in excess of their degree and condition in fairs, markets, sessions of justices, courts, love-days, and elsewhere and maintain and support false provisors or others in their churches or prebends with great power, to the disturbance of the law or to the intimidation of the people; or feign sundry quarrels by the agency of others in collusion with them against many lieges of the realm and practise against them assault, menaces, and battery or oust them from their lands contrary to right and process of law and occupy those lands with great power so that the said lieges dare not pursue the law or defend their right for fear of death; and when any maintain or retain about them any persons indicted or outlawed for felony or any common thieves, murderers, or other felons, so that the king's officers, such as sheriffs, bailiffs, and other officers, dare not perform their offices, as of right they ought, for fear of their maintenance and support; and let it be understood that in the cases abovesaid it shall be adjudged maintenance.[1]

---

[1] L.C. Hector and Barbara Harvey, eds., *The Westminster Chronicle 1381–1394* (Oxford, 1982), pp. 358–59.

This definition produced no response or legislative recognition.[2] It was both broader and narrower than the legal definition developed by the justices. The Commons' definition included four separate offenses: champerty, embracery or bribery, conspiracy, and the accessorial offense of knowingly assisting or supporting felons. The legal definition that had evolved by this date would have included the first two, but not the second two. The Commons' definition also omitted other kinds of support of another's litigation, which was or might have been maintenance. Although it identified specific forms of conduct as maintenance, it did not indicate what made some of them lawful and others unlawful. The definition also required guilty persons to pay double damages to complainants, which was neither authorized by the statutes nor applied in the actions.

In the course of addressing the issues raised in pleading, the judges developed an interpretation that provided the meaning of the statute. The plaintiff's count, like the writ, alleged only that the defendant had "maintained and upheld" (*manutenuit et sustentavit*) a particular plea pending in a particular court for the side of the adverse party, but did not specify what it was that the defendant had done.[3] If the defendant appeared, he would deny the maintenance and put himself on the country, ask to imparl, or justify what he had done in supporting or assisting the party in the principal action.[4] Significantly, the justices made it clear that not all support or assistance violated the maintenance statute.

---

[2] 12 Rich. II, cc. 1–16 (1388), *Statutes of the Realm*, vol. 2, pp. 55–60; J.A. Tuck, "The Cambridge Parliament 1388," *English Historical Review* 84 (1968), pp. 227–29, 234–35.

[3] *Thurstan v. Scott*, TNA: PRO KB 27/580, m. 30 (1406), AALT Img. No. 66; *Stok v. Dogge*, TNA: PRO KB 27/673, m. 75d (1429), AALT Img. No. 534–35; *Clement v. Mader*, TNA: PRO CP 40/756, m. 104 (1450); *Mitchell v. Coutesham*, TNA: PRO CP 40/771, m. 114 (1453). In a few cases, the complaint supplied more detail as to alleged illegal behavior. In a 1405 action, for example, the plaintiff alleged that the defendant in assize of novel disseisin bribed the jurors and threatened the plaintiff. Although the defendant had been attached, no plea appeared in the enrollment. *Creyk v. Senelle*, TNA: PRO KB27/578, m. 52d (1405), AALT Img. No. 381; Paul Brand, "Ethical Standards for Royal Justices in England, c. 1175–1307," *The University of Chicago Law School Roundtable* 8 (2001), pp. 239, 244–45, 254–55.

[4] The defendants appeared in 49% of the actions. When they appeared, they pleaded a general denial and put themselves on the country in 35% of the actions and denied and imparled in 31%. Defendants alleged an affirmative plea in 30% of the actions in which they appeared, of which 88% were an affirmative justification for their involvement and conduct and 12% alleged the action was invalid because it was mispleaded or there was a settlement or arbitration. The remainder of the actions where the defendant appeared involved fines, default, inability to deny, demurrers, and writs of *supersedeas* (4%).

In a 1431 case, Martin JCP said that "when a man has cause or sufficient color to maintain, he can maintain well enough."[5] In contemporary parlance, the question was whether one had cause to intermeddle. Prysot CJCP said, "for everyone who has cause to intermeddle can well justify the maintenance."[6] When such cause was lacking, the justices often characterized the maintainer as a "stranger," whose support was considered impermissible.[7] Having a justification for intermeddling was necessary but not sufficient to a successful defense. The defendant also had to assert that his conduct in supporting the adverse party of the plaintiff was legitimate. Thus, if the defendant justified his conduct, medieval judges and juries had to determine whether the justification was acceptable and the alleged conduct permissible.[8]

But the defendant's allegations were only one side of the story, and the plaintiff often had a different view. In their replications, plaintiffs would often deny the veracity of the defendant's plea and assert that the defendant's conduct was not that alleged in the plea, but that which was more egregious.[9] The acceptance or rejection of the defendants' justifications and the plaintiffs' replications provided the most important basis for understanding the development of the law of maintenance and identifying what type of conduct violated the statute.[10]

---

[5] *"Quand un home ad cause ou sufficient colour de maintenir, il peut maintenir assez bien."* *Rothwell v. Pewer*, Y.B. Hil., 9 Hen. VI, fol. 64, pl. 17 (1431), Seipp No. 1431.017.

[6] *"Car chescun qe ad cause de mesler poit bien justifier le maintenaunce."* *Horne v. Forster*, Y.B. Hil., 34 Hen. VI, fol. 30, pl. 15 (1456), Seipp No. 1456.016, CP 40/780, m. 124, AALT Img. No. 250.

[7] *Pomeroy v. Abbot of Buckfast*, Y.B. Mich., 21 Hen. VI, fol. 15, pl. 30 (1442), Seipp No. 1442.126, CP 40/729, m. 301(1443), AALT Img. No. 594 (Newton CJCP and Paston JCP *"Purque en estranger il est un maintenaunce"*); *Rothwell v. Pewer*, Y.B. Hil., 9 Hen. VI, fol. 64, pl. 17 (1431), Seipp No. 1431.017 (Strange JCP *"mes sans attournment il n'est fosque come un estrange person"*); Y.B. Mich., 22 Hen. VI, fol. 35, pl. 54 (1443), Seipp No. 1443.113 (Newton CJCP *"en estrange person un choce torcious et maintenaunce"*).

[8] Later abridgements structured their discussion of maintenance according to the justifications and their nature. Charles Viner, *Abridgement*, 2nd ed. (London, 1793), vol. 15, pp. 160–65.

[9] When the defendant alleged a justification, the plaintiff almost always replied. In those replies, the plaintiff denied the factual accuracy or legal sufficiency of the justification 40% of the time and alleged different, more egregious conduct in 60% of those actions.

[10] As was typical in medieval litigation, the parties in most pleaded maintenance actions put themselves on the country and no further information appeared in the record. But the records in 114 of the maintenance actions (16%) contained the following further information. There were jury verdicts in 41 actions, 26 guilty verdicts, and 15 not guilty ones; 6 in which defendants paid a fine for violating the statute; 2 in which they defaulted; 1 in which the defendant was not able to deny the plaintiff's allegations; 2 writs of error;

Justifications and Conduct

In these actions, the defendants alleged five types of justifications for their involvement in another person's litigation.[11] The justifications were that the defendant had been retained as a lawyer in the principal action; was acting on behalf of a servant; was assisting a family member, friend or poor person; had an interest in the subject matter of the principal litigation; or had engaged in legitimate participation in the process of litigation. As Table 9.1 shows, having an interest in the subject matter of the principal litigation was the most common justification for providing support and assistance.

These justifications were associated with several types of conduct, which constituted the assistance or support. As Table 9.2 shows, the most common activity alleged by the nonlawyer defendants was that they were helping the parties in the principal actions find a lawyer to represent them in the matter.[12] Medieval judges seemed sympathetic to this justification, saying in one case that it would be "against reason" not to permit someone to assist a party in finding counsel and it was "an act of charity to assist someone who could not help himself."[13] The justices viewed many of these justifications alleged by defendants as legitimate grounds for their involvement in principal litigation.[14]

Acting as Lawyer

Lawyers were targets of a number of maintenance actions. Interestingly, the 1377 maintenance statute did not expressly exempt lawyers, as the

pardons were granted in 18 actions; plaintiffs failed to prosecute 13 actions; defendants were granted a writ of *supersedeas* in 22 actions; there were jurisdictional challenges in 7 actions; and jury challenges in 2 actions, both successful.

[11] Justifications were alleged in 142 actions, 99 were found in the plea rolls, and additional 43 in the Year Books.

[12] The pleas alleging legitimate conduct constituted 88% of the affirmative pleas by defendants. The other 12% alleged that the maintenance action was invalid because it had been mispleaded or because the principal dispute had been settled or arbitrated.

[13] In a 1500 case, the court said, "*il sera enconter reason que il ne aura un de luy amesner a Conseil et ce fait un fait de charitie de aider et succourir un que ne poit aider luy mesme.*" Y.B. Hil. 15 Hen. VII fol. 2, pl. 3 (1500), Seipp No. 1500.003 (tr.).

[14] Holdsworth asserted different view, stating that the courts interpreted the maintenance statutes strictly as "an expression of the censure of the common law." Holdsworth, *A History of English Law* (London, 1966), vol. II, p. 416. He said that "the courts were inclined to hold many kinds of 'upholding' as unlawful," although he recognized some forms of maintenance were lawful. Ibid., vol. III, p. 398.

Table 9.1 *Justifications for involvement in the litigation*

Interest in the subject matter of the litigation	28%
Master assisting servant and vice versa	22%
Legitimate participation in the process of litigation	19%
Assisting family, friends, and the poor	18%
Retained as a lawyer	13%

Table 9.2 *Conduct alleged by defendants as legitimate*

Finding a lawyer to act as counsel in the principal litigation	31%
Providing evidence, information, or otherwise in the litigation	25%
Paying money for a legitimate reason	20%
Providing services as retained counsel or attorney	16%
Acting as a mainpernor or surety of peace	8%

champerty and livery statutes did.[15] This omission is somewhat puzzling, since champerty was a form of maintenance, and livery and maintenance were often associated with each other as indicated by the statutory provisions that combined their prohibition.[16] Despite the absence of an explicit statutory exemption, it was, nevertheless, clearly understood that the traditional representational activities of lawyers did not violate of the statute. In a 1432 case, Martin JCP said, "As, if one of the law be with a matter, it excuses him of maintenance for this cause . . ."[17] In fact this view of the law was asserted as early as 1297. Thomas le Mareschall, a conspiracy defendant, justified an accusation of maintenance on the ground that he was a common serjeant counter ("*communis serviens*

---

[15] *Articuli super Cartas*, 28 Edw. I, c. 11 (1300), *Statutes of the Realm*, vol. 1. p. 139 (champerty); 1 Hen. IV, c. 7 (1399) (livery). The former said it did not prohibit persons from having counsel of pleaders, or of learned men in the law for their fees ("*ne puet aver consail de contours, et des sages gentz, par du soen donant*"). The latter said livery could be given to them who were of his counsel, spiritual as well as temporal, learned in the one law or the other ("*ceux qi sont de son conseil sibien espirituelx come temporelx aprisez de lune ou lautre ley*") (tr.).

[16] 1 Rich. II, cc. 4, 7, 9 (1377), *Statutes of the Realm*, vol. 2, p. 3 (1377); 13 Rich. II, st. 3 (1389–90), ibid., pp. 74–75. Modern scholars have viewed them as related and connected to the use of retainers. J.M.W. Bean, *From Lord to Patron* (Pittsburgh, 1989), pp. 143–46, 200–211; J.R. Maddicott, "Law and Lordship: Royal Justices as Retainers in Thirteenth- and Fourteenth-Century England," *Past and Present*, Suppl. 4 (1978), p. 66.

[17] "*Come si un de Ley soit ove un mattere, il luy excuser de maintenaunce par cest cause.*" Y.B. Mich., 11 Hen. VI, fol. 10, pl. 24 (1432), Seipp No. 1432.024.

narrator") "before the justices and elsewhere, where he will be better able to be of assistance in the matter" and that he "stood" with his client in an assize and "was of his counsel." He said further that "he was able to assist him as his serjeant as is it permitted to such serjeants in like cases."[18] Even the plaintiffs' lawyers in these cases acknowledged that a lawyer's representation of a client was permissible as long as no other conduct was involved.[19] The plaintiff's replication in these cases often alleged further conduct such as bribing jurors.[20]

These maintenance actions were brought against counsel, apprentices, and attorneys.[21] In the actions, the defendants normally alleged that they were learned in the law of the land (*homo in lege terre eruditus*) and a member of an Inn of Court or Chancery and that they had been retained as counsel by one of the parties in the principal action.[22] But the plaintiff might challenge these allegations. In one aspect of a Devon dispute, Nicholas Radford, a lawyer, city judge, and member of parliament, sued

---

[18] "*[C]oram justiciarios et alibi ubi melius ad hoc conduci poterit. Et quod ipse in placito prefate assise ... stetit cum predicto Johanne et de consilio suo fuit. Et in hoc ei in quantum potuit auxiliatus fuit tanquam serviens suus et sicut in talibus servientibus hujusmodi casibus bene licet.*" The plaintiff acknowledged that Thomas was a *narrator* in the Oxford court and often sat on the bench with bailiffs of Oxford, but charged that he had procured and abetted the bringing of an *assise of novel disseisin* against the plaintiff and had procured others to falsely maintain the assize. *Thomas, son of Thomas of Oxford v. Thomas the Marshal*, TNA: PRO KB 27/151, m. 22 (1297), AALT Img. No. 217 (tr.).

[19] Y.B. Mich. 22 Hen. VI, fol. 35, pl. 54 (1443), Seipp No. 1443.113. Baker has also opined that lawyers were exempt from maintenance. J.H. Baker, *The Order of Serjeants at Law* (London, 1984), p. 26; J.H. Baker, "Counsellors and Barristers," in *The Legal Profession and the Common Law* (London, 1986), pp. 60, 76–77, 112–14 (numerous cases cited); J.H. Baker, "Solicitors and the Law of Maintenance 1590–1640," in ibid., pp. 125–50 (numerous cases cited).

[20] *Smythe v. Paslewe*, TNA: PRO KB 27/543, m. 65 (1397), AALT Img. No. 140; *Norton v. Mitchell*, TNA: PRO KB 27/609, m. 35 (1413), AALT Img. No. 78; *Mitchell v. ClHoutesham*, TNA: PRO CP 40/771, m. 114 (1453), AALT Img. Nos. 227–29, 1616–17.

[21] E.g., *Tewe v. Catesby*, TNA: PRO KB 27/750, m. 105 (1453), AALT Img. No. 210 (counsel and Inn member); *Clement v. Mader*, TNA: PRO CP 40/756, m. 104 (1450), AALT Img. No. 209, Trin. Y.B. 28 Hen. VI, fol. 7, pl. 1, fol. 12, pl. 28, Seipp Nos. 1450.011, 1450.038 (apprentice); *Mitchell v. ClHoutesham*, TNA: PRO CP 40/771, m. 114 (1453), AALT Img. Nos. 227–29, 1616–17 (attorney). Many of the same kinds of issues arose in champerty actions brought pursuant to the 1300 *Articuli Super Cartas*, c. 11. *Martel v. de Sallowe*, TNA: PRO KB 27/522, m. 50 (1391), AALT Img. No. 116 (apprentice loaning money to a client to prosecute an action); *Forster v. Penros*, TNA: PRO CP 40/565, m. 236 (1402), AALT Img. No. 464 (serjeant retained as legal counsel for client's life for annual fee).

[22] Moile JCP said that one who was a general attorney even though not learned in law could maintain on behalf of his client. *Horne's Case*, Y.B. Hil., 34 Hen. VI, fol. 25, pl. 3 (1456), Seipp No. 1456.003.

Sir John Speke for maintaining a conspiracy action against Nicholas in the Exeter city court.[23] John responded that he was a fellow of Lincoln's Inn, an apprentice, learned in law, learning and studying law of the land of England, and had been retained by the conspiracy plaintiffs as counsel and had counseled them in that action. But Nicholas said John was "a lay man and inexpert in the law of the land" and in addition he procured the earl of Devon to assist the conspiracy plaintiffs.[24] In a 1457 action, the defendant, an attorney of the Common Bench, alleged that he was learned in law and a member of Staple Inn and that he had been retained by the plaintiff to be of counsel in a trespass action against the mainten-ance plaintiff. He said he was paid 3s 4d for counseling his client. In his replication, the plaintiff denied that the attorney was learned in the law.[25] It is interesting to consider how these plaintiffs would make good their denials of the defendant's status as a lawyer. If, indeed, the defendants were, as alleged, a member of an inn of court as an apprentice or a member of an inn of Chancery as an attorney of the Bench, they would seem to have a strong, if not conclusive, case, unless they engaged in conduct other than normal representational activity.[26] In another case in which a lawyer was sued for maintaining a trespass action in the King's Bench, the plaintiff alleged not only that lawyer had received 10 marks for his maintenance but that he made a bond with his client that the latter would not concord nor make a fine without the assent of the lawyer. In justification, the lawyer pleaded that he was learned in the law and that the trespass defendant asked him to be counsel because of

---

[23] *Radford v. Speke*, TNA: PRO CP 40/714, m. 320 (1439) (not in AALT); Hannes Kleineke, *The Chancery Case between Nicholas Radford and Thomas Tremayne: The Exeter Depos-itions of 1439* (Exeter 2013), 55 Devon and Cornwall Record Society, New Series, pp. 56–62.

[24] Nicholas also alleged that John had offered the earl £10 to have his assistance, which the earl had refused. He also said that John had procured a goldsmith to counterfeit a signet of Nicholas Tremayne for sealing a false charter enfeoffing land. In response, John alleged a detailed story involving arbitration between Nicholas Radford and the conspiracy plaintiffs, which the earl would undertake and that John, as counsel for the conspiracy plaintiffs, at their request, informed the earl of their willingness to abide by the earl's judgment and to pay him £10 for his services.

[25] *Clon v. Kellowe*, TNA: PRO CP 40/786, m. 403 (1457), AALT Img. No. 800. It was common for attorneys, like Kellowe, to allege that they were learned in law and members of an inn of Chancery.

[26] Baker said that such membership "was *ipso facto* evidence that a man was learned in the law and exempt from maintenance" and that membership meant that he would have spent time there in learning exercises. Baker, *The Legal Profession and the Common Law*, pp. 60 and n. 47, 76–77 and n. 8.

his knowledge and retained him for 40s. In his replication, the plaintiff alleged that the lawyer "on his own motion put himself forward to be retained ... and, in so far as he could, urged" the trespass defendant to retain him. He further alleged that the lawyer told the latter that he was counsel to the sheriff, who would not act without the counsel of the lawyer.[27]

Some of these actions raised interesting questions about the nature of a lawyer's role. In a 1454 action, the defendant, Richard Alfray, alleged that he was a member of Gray's Inn and a man learned in law and that he was retained by Thomas Wode, plaintiff in a trespass action, for 40d to be his counsel in the action. He further stated that he gave Thomas counsel according to the law of the land ("*dedit predicto Thome consilium secundum legem terre*").[28] But the plaintiff did not allege anything further and joined issue, stating that nothing alleged should preclude him having his action. In this case, it seems clear that the defendant barrister ought to have prevailed. Giving legal advice to a client was (and still is) an aspect of the lawyer's duty and, therefore, appropriate.[29] When Richard Chalderon, servant of William Bompstead, was sued

---

[27] The plaintiff alleged further that the lawyer told his client that the sheriff would not return a writ of *venire facias* and if coerced by law to do so, the lawyer would prepare a schedule of names that the client wished to be impaneled, which he in fact did, and he also bribed two of them to say their verdict for his client as well as several more instances of similar wrongdoing. The lawyer repeated his justification and the parties put themselves on the jury. *Daynard v. Sumpter*, TNA: PRO KB 27/619, m. 74 (1416), AALT Img. Nos. 172–73 (tr.).

[28] *Forster v. Alfray*, TNA: PRO CP 40/774, m. 313 (1454). AALT Img. Nos. 623–24 (tr.). Defendants in other actions alleged that they were learned in law, retained as counsel, and permissibly advised their clients. In one action, the defendant said he advised his client on the manner of prosecuting his action according to the law. *Welfore v. Gloucestre*, TNA: PRO KB 27/817, m. 100 (1465), AALT Img. No. 222. In another, the defendant said his client asked whether his bill of trespass in the King's Bench was good and he replied that based on his knowledge, it was good and sufficient. *Grey v. Jenney*, TNA: PRO KB 27/847, m. 35 (1473), AALT Img. No. 76. In the latter action, which involved two well-known Norfolk personages and families, Jenney abandoned the verification of his initial plea and then pleaded a detailed concord, which Grey denied.

[29] Baker said that Alfray had a basis for claiming protection. Baker, *The Legal Profession and the Common Law*, pp. 60 and n. 47, 76–77 and n. 6. An earlier conspiracy action indicated that pleading that an act was done by reason of an office was a sufficient defense. It illustrated that principle by reference to a maintenance action against a lawyer, stating that "as if a man learned in the law maintain a quarrel, a writ of maintenance is brought against him, and he pleads that he is a man of law, and was of counsel to the party, and did his duty for his client ..." *Conington's Case*, Y.B. Mich., 8 Hen IV, fol. 6, pl. 8 (1406), Seipp No. 1406.107 (tr.).

for maintenance by a man whom William had sued for debt, he alleged that William gave him 3s 4d to give to Thomas Luyt, counsel and learned in law. William told Richard to tell Thomas to attend to the plea and "to do what he was able to do lawfully to expedite the plea," which Thomas said he did.[30] In several actions, lawyers alleged that they were retained as counsel and assisted their client in dealing with other counsel in the litigation. In one action, an attorney alleged that he had retained a lawyer to be counsel to his client and paid him with the client's money to do so.[31] In another, a lawyer alleged he was of counsel and informed a serjeant, also counsel to the same client, of the facts of the matter.[32] Engaging in these types of assistance would seem to be an appropriate role for an attorney to engage in for his client and, therefore, not unlawful.[33] Explaining the evidence in an action to the jury, as one attorney alleged by way of justification, may also have been appropriate.[34] The import of the opinion of Paston JCP was that it was permissible for a person, who had justification to intermeddle and was learned in law, to show a party, his counsel, or the jury the truth of the matter and to bring evidence of the matter to the trial, but if he did otherwise, it

---

[30] The plaintiff reiterated his original allegations of maintenance. *Hethenesse v. Chalderton*, TNA: PRO KB 27/860, m. 71 (1476), AALT Img. Nos. 157–58.

[31] William Couper, alleging his membership in New Inn and that he was learned in law and the attorney of Walter, then approached Thomas Yonge, a man learned in law, informed him of the matter, and asked him to be counsel to Walter and paid him 6s 8d of Walter's money to do so, as a result of which Thomas was counsel to Walter. Walter's action alleged that by false procurement he had been indicted for his involvement in Jack Cade's rebellion and the battle with the king at Mile End. *Heron v. Couper*, TNA: PRO CP 40/784, m. 380 (1457), AALT Img. No. 747 (tr.).

[32] William Clouwesham alleged that he lived for many years at an inn called The Strand to learn the law and was learned in the law when a widow requested him to be counsel in an appeal of homicide for the death of her husband and retained him for 40d. William said he then went to Walter Moile, a serjeant at law and counsel to the widow, and informed him of the facts and circumstances of the appeal. *Mitchell v. Clouwesham*, TNA: PRO CP 40/771, m. 114 (1453), AALT Img. No. 227 (tr.). Although William was living at an Inn of Chancery, his status is unclear. His name has not been found in the warrants of attorney and he may have been an apprentice.

[33] In both of the cases noted, the plaintiffs alleged further conduct in their replications.

[34] John Norton, defendant in assize of fresh force in the London Sheriffs' Court, brought a maintenance action against John Mitchell, a London grocer, and another man. Mitchell alleged that the assize plaintiffs retained him as their attorney and that he explained the evidence of the plaintiffs' tenements to the jurors and informed the jurors of the plaintiffs' rights according to the form of the law. But Norton alleged replied that Mitchell gave food and drink to the jurors and bribed them to say their verdict for his clients and that he also threatened the plaintiffs. *Norton v. Mitchell*, TNA: PRO KB 27/609, m. 35 (1413), AALT Img. No. 78 (tr.).

was maintenance.[35] More difficult questions were raised by a lawyer using his own money to assist a client in litigation.[36]

Master Assisting a Servant

Masters were frequently sued for maintaining their servants, and this issue prompted substantial discussion.[37] Both the justices and lawyers frequently asserted that a master could lawfully maintain his servant's actions.[38] In many cases, the defendants alleged that they had assisted their servant in retaining counsel, which was often said to be permissible.[39] In the leading case, *Pomeroy v. Abbot of Buckfast* (1442), the

---

[35] He said, "*Car si celuy que rien ad a meler ove le mater, et que nest erudite de ley veut monstrer al' jurours ou al party mesme, ou son counsel le verity de mater, et apporte evidence de le mater, et ceo sibien et circumstancialment come un que fuit erudite de ley scavoit; uncore ceo est maintenaunce en son person.*" *Pomeroy v. Abbot of Buckfast*, Y.B. Mich., 22 Hen. VI, fol. 5, pl. 7 (1443), Seipp No. 1443.066 (motion in arrest of judgment); Y.B. Mich. 21 Hen. VI, fol. 15, pl. 30 (1442), Seipp No. 1442.126, TNA: PRO CP 40/729, m. 301 (1443), AALT Img. No. 594.

[36] *Tewe v. Catesby*, TNA: PRO KB 27/750, m. 105 (1448), AALT Img. No. 210; *Leukenor v. Alfray*, TNA: PRO KB 27/826, m. 118 (1467), AALT Img. No. 271. These actions will be discussed below in the broader context of payment of money by a maintenance defendant. See Chapter 10, pp. 256–63.

[37] This issue arose in champerty actions as well as maintenance actions. E.g., *Courtenay v. Bryt*, TNA: PRO CP 40/560, m. 385d (1401), AALT Img. No. 1998; *Martell v. Sallowe*, TNA: PRO KB 27/522, m. 50 (1391), AALT Img. No. 116.

[38] *Rothwell v. Pewer*, Y.B. Hil. 9 Hen. VI, fol. 64, pl. 17 (1431), Seipp No. 1431.017; Y.B. Mich., 22 Hen. VI, fol. 35, pl. 54 (1443), Seipp No. 1443.113; *Clement v. Mader*, Trin., Y.B. 28 Hen. VI, fol. 7, pl. 1, fol. 12, pl. 28 (1450), Seipp Nos. 1450.011, 1450.038; TNA: PRO CP 40/756, m. 104, AALT Img. No. 209; *John Doket's Case*, Y.B. Hil. 32 Hen. VI, fol. 24, pl. 11 (1454), Seipp No. 1454.011; *Horne's Case*, Y.B. Hil., 34 Hen. VI, fol. 25, pl. 3 (1456), Seipp No. 1456.003; William Rastell, *A Collection of Entrees* (London, 1670), fol. 428, pls. 8 and 9.

[39] Y.B. Mich., 19 Hen. VI fol. 30, pl. 56 (1440), Seipp No. 1440.074; *Clement v. Mader*, Y.B. Trin. 28 Hen. VI fol. 12, pl. 28 (1450), Seipp No. 1450.038; TNA: PRO CP 40/756, m. 104, AALT Img. No. 209; *Horne's Case*, Y.B. Hil. 34 Hen. VI, fol. 25, pl. 3 (1456), Seipp No. 1456.003; Y.B. Mich., 19 Edw. IV, fol. 3, pl. 9 (1479), Seipp No. 1479.038. As in other actions involving assistance in finding a lawyer, the legitimacy of the justification required a relationship with the party maintained. The justices were reluctant to bless helping a stranger find a lawyer. *Pomeroy v. Abbot of Buckfast*, Y.B. Mich. 21 Hen. VI, fol. 15, pl. 30 (1442), Seipp No. 1442.126; TNA: PRO CP 40/ 729, m. 301 (1443), AALT Img. No. 594; Y.B. Mich., 22 Hen. VI, fol. 35, pl. 54 (1443), Seipp No. 1443.113. A statement by Prysot CJCP may raise some doubt about these assertions. He said that "if a man come with any man (*ascun home*) and request a man learned in the law to be of counsel with this man who comes with him, that this is maintenance." Anthony Fitzherbert, *La Grande Abridgement* (London, 1577), *Maintenaunce* 21, fol. 65 (Trin., 35 Hen. VI, 1457), Seipp No. 1457.043abr. But in the context of all the other discussions of this issue, arguably

defendant justified the maintenance, alleging that he had sought several men to be counsel to a man retained as his carver.[40] Newton CJCP and Paston JCP had no doubt that the plea was a good justification. They said:

> And so in a stranger it is maintenance, but in the abbot who is his master, it is not: and so it seems the bar is good ... For it is lawful for a master to maintain his servant, as to be with him at the bar, standing there with him give him counsel, and by bringing his own counsel with him to give counsel to his servant ...[41]

In a 1479 case, Bryan CJ said, "I understand this case has been adjudged in our books ... that a master can maintain his servant's suit."[42]

Some argued that the rationale for this justification did not focus on the servant's interest but on that of the master. In *Horne's Case*, the defendant in a maintenance action justified on the ground that he was the master of a man, who requested him to speak to a man of law to be the servant's counsel.[43] The defendant's lawyer explained that "the master can

---

"any man" means "not just any man," but means one with whom the defendant did not have a relationship.

[40] *Pomeroy v. Abbot of Buckfast*, Y.B. Mich., 21 Hen. VI, fol. 15, pl. 30 (1442), Seipp No. 1442.126; 22 Hen. VI fol. 5, pl. 7 (1443), Seipp No. 1443.066, (motion in arrest of judgment); TNA: PRO CP 40/729, m. 301, AALT Img. No. 594. The plaintiff did not traverse that plea, but, as was common, alleged other conduct. He said that abbot had paid his own money to a person to labor the jury on his behalf. In addition to these two lengthy discussions, the case was discussed again at length as part of the initial action and prior to the writ of error. Y.B. Mich., 22 Hen. VI, fol. 5, pl. 7 (1443), Seipp No. 1443.006.

[41] "*Purque en estranger it est un maintenaunce, et en l'abbe que est son master, nemy: purque semble le barre bon ... Car il est loial [al'] master de maintenir le servant, come d'estre ove luy al barre, et la estoir ove luy, et doner a luy counsel; et port son counsel demense ove luy a doner counsel a son servant.*" *Pomeroy v. Abbot of Buckfast*, Y.B. Mich., 21 Hen. VI, fol. 16, pl. 30 (1442), Seipp No. 1442.126 (tr.). Subsequent cases discussing this issue referred to this case. Y.B. East., 22 Hen. VI, fol. 49, pl. 10 (1444), Seipp No. 1444.047; *Clement v. Mader*, Y.B. Trin., 28 Hen. VI, fol. 7, pl. 1, fol. 12, pl. 28 (1450), Seipp Nos. 1450.011, 1450.038; TNA: PRO CP 40/756, m. 104, AALT Img. No. 209; *Horne's Case*, Hil., 34 Hen. VI, fol. 25, pl. 3 (1456), Seipp No. 1456.003.

[42] "*Jeo entend cest case ad estre judge en nostre livres, que ... le mastre poit maintenir le querele son servant.*" Y.B. Mich. 19 Edw. IV, fol. 3, pl. 9 (1479), Seipp No. 1479.038. Other cases referred to this case. Y.B. East. 22 Hen. VI, fol. 49, pl. 10 (1444), Seipp No. 1444.047; *Clement v. Mader*, Y.B. Trin., 28 Hen. VI, fol. 7, pl. 1, fol. 12, pl. 28 (1450), Seipp Nos. 1450.011, 1450.038; TNA: PRO CP 40/756, m. 104, AALT Img. No. 209; *Horne's Case*, Hil. 34 Hen. VI, fol. 25, pl. 3 (1456), Seipp No. 1456.003.

[43] *Horne's Case*, Hil., 34 Hen. VI, fol. 25, pl. 3 (1456), Seipp No. 1456.003. Prysot CJCP, as often seemed to be the case, expressed a narrower view of the lawfulness of this kind of maintenance than the other justices. He said that whether a master can maintain for a servant depended on the legality of the servant's conduct and whether the master had a

intermeddle for his servant: for he is to have the loss of his service, for that it is expedient that he speak to counsel learned in the law to aid his servant."[44] He stated that the intermeddling was for the master's "ease," "profit," and "advantage" and "not the advantage of the servant."[45] Another of the defendant's lawyers went further, stating that "the master is obliged by true right to find his servant his necessaries, or otherwise he does him wrong: and so he can have the writ of covenant against him, if he has indentures of covenants."[46] The defendant's lawyer in another case argued that assistance in finding counsel enabled the servant "to hasten his cause so that he was more hastily able to return to his service."[47] A 1401 champerty action vividly illustrated the connection between maintenance and loss of service. A master's reeve brought a writ of *de homine replegiando* against a knight who detained and imprisoned the reeve, claiming him as his villein. The master loaned money to the reeve to proceed against the detention in Chancery and was his pledge of prosecution for the writ.[48]

---

legitimate interest in the litigation. (This is a different justification that is discussed next.) He said that "in your case of breaking the close, if the issue be taken and the soil, where freehold of his master is, [is] in dispute; in this case it appears that the master has an interest in the matter. For if I order my servant to enter your land, and the entry be lawful; in this case I must help him: but if the entry be not lawful, which he is in a position to know, and he still enters by my order; in this case he has done ill, and the master cannot intermeddle nor aid him in this case ... but if he be arrested for his own debt or his own trespass, I cannot intermeddle for him; for it is my foolishness to have such a servant (*mes si soit arreste pur son det demesne, ou son transgressioun demesne, jeo ne purrai mesler pur luy, car cest ma foly d'aver tiel servant*)." Ibid., fol. 26 (tr.). A few years earlier Prysot referred to the maintenance statute as a "strong law" (*Cest fort ley*). *John Doket's Case*, Y.B. Hil. 32 Hen. VI fol. 24, pl. 11 (1454), Seipp No. 1454.011.

[44] "*Le maistre poit mesler pur le servant: car il est de aver perdue son service et pur ceo il est expedient que il parler al' counsele appris de Ley pur aider le servant.*" *Horne's Case*, Hil., 34 Hen. VI, fol. 25, pl. 3 (1456), Seipp No. 1456.003. Littleton, the plaintiff's lawyer, rejected this analysis. He argued that it was maintenance for the master to ask of his own authority ("*prie de son auctoritie demensne*"), but not so if he asked at the request of the servant.

[45] "*Mon ease et profit auxi ... que ceo est pur mon ease et avantage, et nemy pur avantage de mon servant.*" Ibid., fol. 26.

[46] "*Mes le maistre est oblige pur vray droit de trouver son servant ses necessaries, ou autrement il fait tort a luy: purque il poit aver brefe de covenant envers luy, s'il avoit endentures de covenants.*" Ibid., fol. 26.

[47] "*Pur ceo il a luy notifia quex il prenda de son conseille a haster la cause; issint qe il peut hastimnent revenir a sa service.*" Y.B. Mich., 19 Hen. VI, fol. 30, pl. 56 (1440), Seipp No. 1440.074.

[48] The plaintiff alleged that the master was paid £20 for his assistance. The jury found for the plaintiff and assessed damages of £38. Judgment was entered for the plaintiff and the defendant obtained a writ of error. *Courtenay v. Bryt*, TNA: PRO CP 40/560, m. 385d (1401), AALT Img. No. 1998.

A century later, Fineux CJKB seemed to consider that a master could
maintain his servant only if he risked losing the latter's service. This view
would distinguish between maintaining servants in principal actions where
the servant would be arrested and those where he would not be.[49]

In addition to alleging different and more egregious conduct, the
plaintiffs' replies pursued several additional lines of attack. In some
actions, they alleged that the servant had not been retained in service[50]
or had been discharged.[51] These allegations raised interesting questions as
to what was necessary to qualify as a servant. Although some actions said
only that the party maintained was a servant, other actions identified a
wide variety of servants: carver, valet, chaplain, groom, hosier, bailiff, and
a person to go and ride with his master ("*ad eundum et equitandum cum
eodem*"). The discussions seem to suggest that the justification was not
limited to those retained as household servants or in the defendant's trade,
but might depend on some formalized relationship such as by indenture,
charter, or contract.[52] In one action, the justification was upheld as to a
chaplain because he was retained.[53] But in another action, the plaintiff
traversed the justification for a priest who said divine service and who
asked the defendant to be his counselor, because it was not alleged that he
was retained as a servant by the defendant, the vicar of the vill.[54] In one

---

[49] He said, "*Si mon servant soit arreste pur dette, ou autre chose en Londres, ou en tiel ville
    privilegee, jeo puis maintenir mon servant, et expend de mes propres deniers pur luy aider,
    et cest pur le perde de ses services; mes si mon servant soit empled par praecipe quod reddat
    de terre, jeo ne puis luy maintenir, car jeo n'ay perte de sa service par ce.*" Nota, Y.B. Mich.,
    21 Hen. VII, fol. 40, pl. 61 (1505), Seipp No. 1505.062.

[50] *Hertwell v. Nicoll*, TNA: PRO KB 27/744, m. 80d (1447), AALT Img. No. 416; *Jenney v.
    Selot*, TNA: PRO KB 27/793, m. 105d (1459), AALT Img. No. 683; *Leukenor v. Alfray*,
    TNA: PRO KB 27/826, m. 111 (1467), AALT Img. No. 253.

[51] Y.B. Mich., 19 Hen. VI fol. 30, pl. 56 (1440), Seipp No. 1440.074; *Dee v. Dene*, TNA: PRO
    KB 27/748, m. 39 (1448), AALT Img. No. 82 (plaintiff servant chancellor Exchequer).

[52] In a number of actions, the defendants alleged the term of the retention or the salary or
    both. *Stok v. Dogge*, TNA: PRO KB 27/673, m. 75d (1429), AALT Img. No. 534; *Dee v.
    Dene*, TNA: PRO KB 27/748, m. 39 (1448), AALT Img. No. 82; *Clement v. Mader*, TNA:
    PRO CP 40/756, m. 104 (1450), AALT Img. No. 209; *Hathewick v. Peytowe*, TNA: PRO
    KB 27/762, m. 35 (1451), AALT Img. No. 75; *Crowe v. Foken*, TNA: PRO KB 27/778,
    m. 99 (1455), AALT Img. No. 191; *Horton v. Blackhorn*, TNA: PRO CP 40/780, m. 316
    (1456); *Jenney v. Selot*, TNA: PRO KB 27/793, m. 105d (1459), AALT Img. No. 683;
    Alfray v. Leukenour, TNA: PRO KB 27/826, m. 111 (1467), AALT Img. No. 271;
    Beauchamp v. Monyngton, TNA: PRO KB 27/833, m. 113 (1469), AALT Img. No. 295.

[53] Y.B. Mich., 19 Hen. VI, fol. 30, pl. 56 (1440), Seipp No. 1440.074.

[54] The plaintiff said, "*Et auxi n'est surmis que le dit prestre fuit servant retenu ove le
    defendant, mes solement que il fuist en le dit Eglise fesant Divine Service.*" The mainten-
    ance conduct alleged was that the vicar had given legal advice to the priest. The plaintiff

action, the defendant, a servant of the marshal of the Marshalsea prison, alleged that a man, who was detained in prison, was unable to do the things necessary for his personal business and retained him for a quart of red wine to ask a man expert in law to be of counsel with the prisoner.[55] The plaintiff demurred.[56]

In some instances, servants were sued for maintaining their masters. In one action, the defendant alleged that he was the servant of the bishop of London, a defendant in a *quare impedit* action, and of another person claiming the right of presentation to the church and that at their order he carried the evidences concerning the right of advowson to the vill where the church was located and stood with them in the action.[57] As was the case with masters charged with maintenance, the actions against servants in some cases also involved dealing with counsel. For example, a factor alleged that he used the money that he collected on behalf of the merchants who retained him to pay for their counsel.[58] In another case,

---

also alleged that he should recover, as the defendant had not alleged that he was learned. Y.B. Mich., 22 Hen. VI, fol. 35, pl. 54 (1443), Seipp No. 1443.113.

[55] *Illingworth v. Heyward*, TNA: PRO KB 27/782, m. 101 (1456), AALT Img. No. 207. The maintenance plaintiff had sued the imprisoned man for a violation of the statute dealing with false deeds and muniments.

[56] The court delayed several times because it was not yet advised in how judgment should be rendered and no further entry was located. In another action, the defendant alleged that he retained the party in the principal action as a brewer and retained a man expert in law as counsel to the latter. The plaintiff demurred. Again the court delayed several times, not yet being advised regarding judgment. *Bonde v. Kirkeby*, TNA: PRO KB 27/740, m. 85 (1446), AALT Img. No. 178. The court succeeded in avoiding the demurrer, as the plaintiff pleaded in the next term that the alleged servant was not in service. The jury agreed and he recovered 8 marks in damages and costs. *Bonde v. Kirkeby*, TNA: PRO KB 27/741, m. 83 (1446), AALT Img. No. 167.

[57] The plaintiff denied that the defendant was a servant of the parties. *Doreward v. Barners*, TNA: PRO KB 27/750, m. 29 (1450), AALT Img. No. 61. The plaintiff brought three further maintenance actions regarding this dispute. *Doreward v. Roo*, TNA: PRO KB 27/750, m. 27 (1450), AALT Img. No. 57; *Doreward v. Hodelston*, TNA: PRO KB 27/750, m. 27d (1450), AALT Img. No. 398; *Doreward v. Ferthyng*, TNA: PRO KB 27/750, m. 31d (1450), AALT Img. No. 406; *Doreward's Case*, Y.B. East., 28 Hen. VI, fol. 6, pl. 1 (1450), Seipp No. 1450.002. In another case, the defendant claimed he was a servant assisting his master in procuring a writ from Chancery to sue an appeal of mayhem. The plaintiff denied that the defendant was a servant. *Hull v. Daucomb*, Y.B. Trin., 3 Hen. VI, fol. 53, pl. 24 (1425), Seipp No. 1425.086.

[58] He alleged that he was retained as a general factor for four years by foreign merchants for an annual salary of 100s. The plaintiff did not challenge his status as a servant, but alleged different conduct. *Crowe v. Foken*, TNA: PRO KB 27/778, m. 99 (1455), AALT Img. No. 191.

a prior alleged that he gave muniments to his servant, who showed them
to the prior's counsel.[59]

There seemed to be a consensus that a servant could maintain for his
master, just as a master for his servant, and statements by lawyers said
both were permissible.[60] But a plaintiff could deny that the defendant was
a servant.[61] Moreover, the scope of the retainer affected the permissibility
of the servant's maintenance. If the servant were retained generally, the
legality to maintain was broad, but it was restricted if the retainer of the
servant were more limited. In a case where the servant was retained only
to ride to London with his master, Markham JKB said that then he could
do nothing to help his master in this case "because he was not retained
except to do special acts and moreover he could not justify any intermeddling; but if he were to be retained generally to be with his master to
do every manner of services ... he might well help and maintain him in
all things, namely to ride with him and to be with him at the bar and to
proffer to men of the law for him, and so it is of a servant."[62] Thus, it
was important for defendants to make the nature of the retainer clear in
their plea.[63]

---

[59] The plaintiff did not deny that the defendant was a servant, but alleged that he had
engaged in other conduct. Y.B. Mich., 19 Hen. VI, fol. 31, pl. 60 (1440), Seipp
No. 1440.078. In another case, the defendant claimed he was a servant assisting his
master in procuring a writ from Chancery to sue an appeal of mayhem. The plaintiff
denied that the defendant was a servant. Y.B. Trin., 3 Hen. VI, fol. 53, pl. 24 (1425), Seipp
No. 1425.086.

[60] E.g., Y.B. Hil., 32 Hen. VI, fol. 24, pl. 11 (1454), Seipp No. 1454.011; Y.B. Mich., 19 Edw.
IV, fol. 3, pl. 9 (1479), Seipp No. 1479.038; *Horne's Case*, Y.B. Hil., 34 Hen. VI, fol. 25,
pl. 3 (1456), Seipp No. 1456.003.

[61] *Bonde v. Kirkeby*, TNA: PRO KB 27/741, m. 83 (1446), AALT Img. No. 167; *Doreward v.
Barners*, TNA: PRO KB 27/750, m. 29 (1450), AALT Img. No. 61.

[62] "*Car quand il fuit son servant, il fuit solement a chevaucher ove luy vers Londres: donque
n'ad il rien a faire a eider son maistre ciens, pur ceo que il ne fuit retenu sinon pur especial
actes a faire et oustre ceo il ne puit justifier ascun mesler: mes s'il ussoit estre retenu
generalment estre ove son maistre a faire chescun maner des services ... il bien list a luy
adier et maintenir en toutes chose, scilicet a chevaucher ove luy, et a estre ove luy al' barre,
et a profere a's homez de ley pur luy, et issint est del servant.*" Y.B. Mich., 39 Hen. VI, fol. 5,
pl. 8 (1460), Seipp No. 1460.036 (tr.).

[63] In one action, seven defendants alleged that they were retained to ride with a widow, who
brought an appeal of homicide, and to provide her with other services ("*ad eundum et
equitandum cum eadem Anna et circa materias et occupaniones ejusdem Anne ad
faciendum eidem Anne alia servicia ad valectum pertinencia*") and, at her request, had
asked her counsel to attend the appeal. The plaintiff replied *de injuria*. *Beauchamp v.
Monyngton*, TNA: PRO KB 27/833, m. 113 (1469), AALT Img. No. 295 (tr.).

Some lawyers also expressed a different rationale to justify intermeddling by servants. They stated that the servant was obliged to follow his master's orders and thus doing so was not maintenance.[64] In a 1479 case, a lawyer argued that the covenant between the servant and his master required the former to do diligent service for the latter.[65] Arguments in these cases stressed that the servant could act not on his own authority or in his own name, but only on behalf of his master.[66] Based on this notion, some lawyers seemed to think that the servant had a stronger position for maintaining his master than vice versa.

Interest in the Subject Matter in Dispute

In a number of actions, the defendant based his justification for intermeddling on having a legal interest in the subject matter of litigation. The most common one alleged was having an interest in the land involved in the principal action. If a lord was assisting a tenant, it was cause to meddle in the litigation. Babington CJCP said in a 1431 case that "a lord can maintain his tenant,"[67] a view that was expressed in numerous other actions.[68] In one case, a widow said her tenant, who had been sued by the maintenance plaintiff in a trespass action, asked her for aid and counsel and to find counsel sufficiently learned in the law to represent him, which she did.[69]

[64] In a 1456 case, Littleton argued that. He said that "*mes le servant poit [maintenir] pur son maistre, pur ceo que il est oblige de faire son comandement.*" Horne's Case, Y.B. Hil., 34 Hen. VI, fol. 25, pl. 3 (1456), Seipp No. 1456.003.

[65] "*Car il est tenus et oblige per son covenant de faire a son master son diligent service.*" Y.B. Mich., 19 Edw. IV, fol. 3, pl. 9 (1479), Seipp No. 1479.038.

[66] Y.B. Mich., 19 Edw. IV, fol. 3, pl. 9 (1479), Seipp No. 1479.038; Horne's Case, Y.B. Hil., 34 Hen. VI, fol. 25, pl. 3 (1456), Seipp No. 1456.003.

[67] "*Car un Seignior peut maintenir son tenant.*" Martin JCP agreed, stating that it gave the defendant cause or sufficient color ("*cause ou sufficient colour*") to maintain. Rothewell v. Pewer, Y.B. Hil., 9 Hen. VI, fol. 64, pl. 17 (1431), Seipp No. 1431.017.

[68] Y.B. East., 11 Hen. VI, fol. 41, pl. 36 (1433), Seipp No. 1433.058; Chein v. Hertwell, Y.B. Trin., 11 Hen. VI, fol. 39, pl. 33 (1433), Seipp No. 1433.055; Fitzherbert, Le Graunde Abridgement, Maintenaunce, 25, fol. 65 (Mich., 27 Hen. VI, 1448), Seipp No. 1448.103abr; Horne v. Forster, Y.B. Hil., 34 Hen. VI, fol. 30, pl. 15 (Mich., 27 Hen. VI, 1456), Seipp No. 1456.016; TNA: PRO CP 40/780, m. 124, AALT Img. No. 250; Y.B. Mich., 19 Edw. IV, fol. 3, pl. 9 (1479), Seipp No. 1479.038; Y.B. Mich., 14 Hen. VII, fol. 2, pl. 6 (1498), Seipp No. 1498.046.

[69] The plaintiff alleged other conduct, claiming that the widow had paid the tenant's counsel with her own money. The defendant replied that she had paid the money to the same lawyer for her own counsel in another action in which the maintenance plaintiff had sued her for the unjust taking and detention of her beasts. Briggeman v. Waldern, TNA: PRO KB 27/817, m. 78d (1465), AALT Img. No. 492.

In another action, the defendant alleged that he found counsel at the request of his tenant, a prior, in an action of fresh force.[70] In some actions, the maintenance action was a by-product of an underlying land dispute. In one matter involving two men both claiming seisin of property in London, one of the men sued the other man and his tenant for trespass and also sued the other man for maintenance. The other man justified his action claiming that, as requested by his tenant, he found counsel for the tenant who had been wrongfully ousted from the property.[71]

Defendants' justifications also involved other interests in land.[72] Moile JCP said that a feoffor could support his feoffee, who was enfeoffed to his use and who had been disseised.[73] Similarly a feoffee could maintain his feoffor.[74] A feoffee also could assist a party if the dispute would affect the former's rights in the land. In addition, the beneficial interest of a *cestuy que use*, whose feoffees held in use for his benefit, had a sufficient interest in land held in use for his benefit if the land were in dispute.[75] Further, a lessor could maintain his termor or

---

[70] The plaintiff alleged other conduct, claiming that the defendant had given his own food and drink to the lawyers who were representing the prior. The defendant replied that he had retained those same lawyers to represent him in another action between him and the plaintiff and had asked them to come to his home and discuss that action. *Jenney v. Selot*, TNA: PRO KB 27/793, m. 103 (1459), AALT Img. No. 263.

[71] The maintenance action was successful, probably because it had been determined that the maintenance defendant did not have a legitimate interest in the property that he said that he had granted to the trespass defendant. *Lounde v. Arnold*, TNA: PRO KB 27/750, m. 131 (1448), AALT Img. No. 254; *Lounde v. Arnold*, TNA: PRO KB 27/750, m. 134 (1448), AALT Img. No. 263.

[72] *Inglose v. Stapelton*, TNA: PRO KB 27/734, m. 93 (1444), AALT Img. No. 223 (reversion, grantee); *Huberd v. Brosyngham*, TNA: PRO KB 27/738, m. 31 (1445), AALT Img. No. 70 (life tenant's lessee); *William v. Nicoll*, TNA: PRO KB 27/756, m. 22 (1450), AALT Img. No. 46 (lessor–lessee); *Jenney v. Selot*, TNA: PRO KB 27/793, m. 105d (1459), AALT Img. No. 683 (lessor–lessee); *Payn v. Bygge*, TNA: PRO KB 27/832, m. 40 (1469), AALT Img. No. 97 (feoffee–feoffor); *Wyndsore v. Frome*, TNA: PRO KB 27/848, m. 51 (1473), AALT Img. No. 110 (feoffor–feoffee).

[73] He said, "*si jeo enfeffe un home a mon use et il est disseisi, et porte an assise, jeo labore le matter, et le disseisor porta briefe de maintenaunce envers moy, jeo dire que il fuit mon feffee, et labore le matter, et jeo pay monoye pur ceo, (Jugement, si action) ceo est assets bon ple.*" Y.B. Mich., 35 Hen. VI, fol. 15, pl. 25 (1456), Seipp No. 1456.079. The same view was expressed in other cases. *Horne v. Forster*, Y.B. Hil., 34 Hen. VI, fol. 30, pl. 15 (1456), Seipp No. 1456.016; TNA: PRO CP 40/780, m. 124, AALT Img. No. 250; Y.B. Pasch., 2 Edw. IV, fol. 2, pl. 6 (1462), Seipp No. 1462.006 (Serjeant Littleton).

[74] Y.B., 14 Hen. VI, fol. 7, pl. 32 (1436), Seipp No. 1436.032.

[75] Prysot CJCP said that "*si divers homes soient enfeoffes en terr a mon use et jeo vende la terre a un estranger, et nous sumus accreez (?), et accorde que memes les premiers feoffes estoient avant seisi en la terre a l'us l'estranger; cest cas si les feoffees soient empledes, est*

lessee.[76] Nor was permissible support limited to these types of relationship, as it could extend to a person who had an interest by
remainder, reversion, or descent.[77] But some justices asserted that if
the person's interest was as an heir apparent, he might not become the
actual heir, and, therefore, sufficient cause was lacking. Rede JKB said
that "if someone has married his kinswoman, who can inherit my land,
it is lawful for him to maintain and aid me in any action against me:
but if his wife, who is my kinswoman, dies so that none of his issue
remain living, and he helps me in the suit, this is maintenance by
him."[78]

In addition to a legal relationship between the defendant and the
party in the principal action, a sufficient justification based on an
interest in the land also required that the land underlying the relationship be in dispute in the principal case. A 1448 case noted that "a man
cannot maintain his tenant for any reason other than something that
relates to his land."[79] Similarly, Prysot CJCP said that "so it is if someone
is enfeoffed of land to my use, it is lawful for me to sue any manner of
suit that touches that land, in the name of the feoffees or if they are

---

loial pur l'estranger a mesler pur son interest demesne." Horne v. Forster, Y.B. Hil., 34 Hen.
VI, fol. 30, pl. 15 (1456), Seipp No. 1456.016; TNA: PRO CP 40/780, m. 124, AALT Img.
No. 250.

[76] Danby JCP said, "*Vostre termor ou lessee pur terme dans puit aver aid de vous, et pur ceo il
est loial a maintenir en le querele.*" Mich., 39 Hen. VI, fol. 19, pl. 29 (1460), Seipp
No. 1460.057.

[77] Y.B. Mich., 19 Edw. IV, fol. 3, pl. 9 (1479), Seipp No. 1479.038. In this case, the defendant
was married to the daughter of the party that he had allegedly maintained in the principal
action.

[78] "*Si un ad marie mon cousin, que poit inheriter ma terre, il est loyal a luy a maintenir et
aider moy in ascune accion vers moy: mes si sa femme que est ma cousin devy, issint que
nul issue de luy remain in vie, si il me aidra in ma suite, ceo est maintenaunce in luy.*" Y.B.
Mich., 14 Hen. VII, fol. 2, pl. 6 (1498), Seipp No. 1498.046 (tr.). In another case, the
defendant had married the sister of the party in the principal action and had retained
counsel for his brother-in-law. But the sister, who had a life estate, had died. The
plaintiff's lawyer said that "he did not show that his wife was alive at the time of the
maintenance, therefore, his plea is not good." Markham CJKB agreed: "*Vous dits voier,
car il ne poet maintain forsque durant sa vie.*" Y.B. Mich., 6 Edw IV, fol. 5, pl. 15 (1466),
Seipp No. 1466.017 (tr.).

[79] "*Home ne peut maintener son tenant pur autre cause sinon pur chose que appent a son
terre.*" The defendant showed that he leased an acre of land for a term of a year to the one
that the plaintiff alledgedly maintained and that the plaintiff brought a writ of trespass to
the same land and he maintained him. The plaintiff said that the trespass was brought for
a trespass to another acre of land. Fitzherbert, *Le Graunde Abridgement, Maintenaunce*
25, fol. 65 (Mich., 27 Hen. VI, 1448), Seipp No. 1448.103abr (tr.).

impleaded to intermeddle."[80] The fact that the tenant could vouch the
lord to warranty might give the lord sufficient cause to maintain. In one
case the defendant, who had granted a rent with a warranty clause,
justified his maintenance in an assize of rent brought against his grantee
on ground that he did so "in discharge of his warranty of the rent (*en
discharge de son garrante del' dit rente fait al' plaintif*)."[81] Cheyne CJKB
said, "And I say if one has a warranty against another, and he is
impleaded, the one who bound to the warranty can well stand with
him without any voucher in a writ of warranty of charters and deliver
charters and muniments to him to bar the demandant from [his] action
in discharge of his warranty."[82] Moreover, the necessary interest in the
land was not limited to actions where the land itself was in dispute. For
example, in a case involving the defendant's support of a plaintiff in a
detinue action regarding a box containing charters and deeds, Babington
CJCP said, "since he had the rent, which the said deeds concerned, he
had cause to maintain."[83]

In addition to the common reply that the defendant had engaged in
conduct different from that alleged in his plea, plaintiffs also replied to
the defendants' justifications in other ways. For example, they denied the
existence of an interest in the land, attacking the rights of both the
defendant and the party in the principal action. In a forcible entry action,
the defendant justified on the ground that he was the feoffee of the
defendant in the principal action. The plaintiff replied that the latter
was not seised of land because it was not granted to him as alleged.[84] In
one action, the plaintiff alleged that the defendant lacked seisin as he had

---

[80] "*Issint est si ascun soit enfeoffe de terre a mon use, est loial pur moy a suir ascun manner
suite que touche cest terre, en le nom des feoffees. ou s'ils soient empledes a mesler.*" Horne
v. Forster, Y.B. Hil., 34 Hen. VI, fol. 30, pl. 15 (1456), Seipp No. 1456.016; TNA: PRO CP
40/780, m. 124, AALT Img. No. 250.

[81] The grantee told the defendant that he had been impleaded and asked the defendant to
come to the assize with the evidence regarding the grant of rent to him and the defendant
did so. Y.B. East., 11 Hen. VI, fol. 41, pl. 36 (1433), Seipp No. 1433.058.

[82] He continued by saying he did not have to wait to be vouched to warranty to do so. "*Et
jeo die que si on [un] ad un garranty vers un auter, et il est emplede, cestuy que est tenu al'
garranty peut bien ester ove luy sans ascune voucher en bref de garrante de chartres, et
deliverer chartres et muniments a luy a barrer le demandant d'accion en discharge de sa
garrante, pluis tost que estre vexe par voucher a garrante en brefe de garrrante de chartres.*"
Ibid., fol. 4.

[83] "*Car esteant que il avoit la rent, quel les dits faits furent concernants, it avoit cause a
maintenir.*" Martin JCP agreed, but Paston JCP did not. Rothewell v. Pewer, Y.B. Hil., 9
Hen. VI, fol. 64, pl. 17 (1431), Seipp No. 1431.017.

[84] Payn v. Bygge, TNA: PRO KB 27/832, m. 40 (1469), AALT Img. No. 97.

been enfeoffed in exchange for laboring the jurors in the feoffor's trespass suit against the maintenance plaintiff.[85] In another action, the defendant said the dispute involved different land.[86] In some actions, the defendant's need to allege a complicated series of transactions to establish an interest in the land made these challenges more likely. For example, in a 1445 action, the maintenance defendant justified finding counsel for a plaintiff who had brought a trespass action against a prior lessee, who entered on the plaintiff's possession, on the ground that the plaintiff held a messuage in fee tail for the defendant's use and benefit. The maintenance plaintiff replied that the defendant had no interest in the messuage or any other parcel of land. To establish his interest, the defendant alleged an interest based on that of his grandmother, who held the messuage in demesne as of fee and had demised it to her son in male tail, who died with two male heirs.[87]

Although justifications involving an interest in the subject matter more commonly involved land, some of them involved an interest in the goods at issue in the principal action. In these instances, the same justifications that were recognized as when the interest was in land ought to have been applicable on similar reasoning when goods were involved. For example, in one case the defendant justified his helping the defendant in a *scire*

---

[85] Y.B., 14 Hen. VI, fol. 7, pl. 32 (1436), Seipp No. 1436.032. Although the plaintiff brought a writ of maintenance, the action sounded more like champerty. In another case, a writ of champerty was sued for enfeoffment in exchange for the land. Before the writ was brought, the defendant said he would maintain, but after the action was brought, he did nothing. Thus the court upheld the defendant's plea on the ground that such agreement was not maintenance if he did not act while the plea was pending. Y.B. Hil., 9 Hen. VII, fol. 18 pl. 12 (1494), Seipp No. 1494.012.

[86] Fitzherbert, *La Graunde Abridgement, Maintenaunce*, 25, fol. 65 (Mich., 27 Hen. VI, 1448), Seipp No. 1448.103abr.

[87] He alleged further that the elder son leased the land to the trespass defendant for twenty years and died without heirs. The younger son, the trespass plaintiff, entered on the possession of the lessee, claiming the fee tail, and made an agreement with the maintenance defendant that he would sell the messuage to the defendant, who paid part of the purchase price, and as part of the agreement would hold it for the defendant's use and profit until the full price was paid. *Bray v. Bray*, TNA: PRO KB 27/754, m. 67 (1449), AALT Img. Nos. 141–42, 455. In a 1444 action, the defendant's interest in the moiety of a manor derived from a feoffor, James Jenney, who instructed several feoffees, holding to his use, to enfeoff him and several others to hold to his use, but with two of them holding in demense as of fee and the other two in free tenancy. He then made a will naming two executors and giving a life estate to one of them. After he died, the defendant purchased the reversionary interest from the executors and the life tenant's interest, which had not yet been granted to him. *Inglose v. Stapelton*, TNA: PRO KB 27/734, m. 93 (1444), AALT Img. No. 223.

facias action to find counsel on the ground that the "property in the goods was in him (*le property de les dits biens furent a luy*)." Moile JCP agreed that this justified the maintenance, comparing it to maintenance of a bailee of charters or of a lessee.[88]

But in some actions, the defendant's alleged interest was more removed. In one action, the defendant justified on the basis of an interest in an intangible chose in action. Although the plaintiff argued that the right to sue was nonassignable, Prysot CJCP said the defendant had an interest that gave him the right to intermeddle.[89] But in a champerty action, a master justified his agreement to obtain a portion of a staple debt sued against his servant because, if the servant prevailed, the master needed to protect his interest in wine that the servant had purchased with the master's money, as the goods were those of the servant. This kind of an interest seems more remote and less clearly a legitimate justification.[90] In sum, intervening in another person's litigation to protect a legal interest was a strong justification.

Assisting Family, Friends, and the Poor

In a number of actions, defendants alleged that they were assisting a family member who was a party in the principal action. For example, in a 1458 action, the defendant alleged that his brother, a defendant in a *scire facias* action who claimed ownership of the goods that were the subject of the action, requested him to ask Thomas More, learned in the law of the land, to be counsel to him in the action and explain the brother's ownership, which he did.[91] Assisting members of one's immediate family would seem to have been permissible.

---

[88] He also said that the fact that the judgment in the *scire facias* action did not bind the defendant and was not relevant: "*Comment que le jugement ne liere luy, encore purle property de les biens que il list a luy maintenir le querele.*" Y.B. Mich., 39 Hen. VI, fol. 19, pl. 29 (1460), Seipp No. 1460.057.

[89] The administrators of a Genoese merchant, who had died intestate, sued the maintenance plaintiff on his obligation to the merchant, who had assigned the debt, and delivered the obligation to the maintenance defendant in satisfaction of the merchant's debt in the same sum to the defendant and ordered him to sue in the merchant's name if the maintenance plaintiff refused to pay. The defendant delivered the obligation to his attorney and asked him to sue the obligation in the name of the administrators, to which they agreed. *Horne v. Forster*, Y.B. Hil., 34 Hen. VI, fol. 30, pl. 15 (1456), Seipp No. 1456.016; TNA: PRO CP 40/780, m. 124 (1456), AALT Img. No. 250.

[90] *Spenser v. Mokkyng*, TNA: PRO KB27/521, m. 76d (1391), AALT Img. No. 384.

[91] The maintenance plaintiff prosecuted the *scire facias* action by reason of a foreign attachment of linen cloths of a Genoese merchant. The defendant alleged that the goods

Given the acceptability of this justification, the issue would be what types of kinship relationships sufficed. In some actions, the defendant would specify the details of a relationship that went well beyond his immediate family, but in other actions, he would allege only that he was a kinsman ("*consanguinens*") of the party in the principal action. Despite the literal meaning of *consanguinitas*, these relationships were not limited to blood relatives. In several actions, the defendant alleged that he was assisting his wife's kin, but not always specifying the precise relationship.[92] In one action involving assistance to his wife's kin, the defendant alleged that his wife's mother was sister to the father of the party in the principal action.[93] But in some actions, the relationship might be much more distant. In justifying his assistance to a widow in an appeal of homicide for the death of her husband, the defendant alleged his kinship by tracing it back through four generations showing that his great-grandmother was the sister of the widow's great-great-grandfather.[94] Nevertheless, despite the remote nature of some of these relationships, the justices seemed generally sympathetic to justifications based on kinship. The common use of the word *cosin* seemed to indicate that the justices took a broad view of kinship. Given the importance of family in medieval society, it is not surprising that the justices took a broad and favorable view of justifications based on assisting kin.[95]

were the property of his brother, who, before attachment, delivered them to the Genoese merchant to keep them safely for his use, and the merchant, before the attachment, delivered the goods to the *scire facias* defendant to keep them safely for the use of the brother, who requested the assistance of the maintenance defendant after the attachment was made and *scire facias* action had been initiated. The plaintiff did not challenge the defendant's support, but denied the brother's ownership of the goods, saying that they belonged to the merchant. *Gyll v. Catayn*, TNA: PRO KB 27/790, m. 103 (1458), AALT Img. No. 211.

[92] In one action, the defendant alleged that the deceased wife of the party he assisted in the principal action was "kin" of his wife, but there was a blank space in the record where the relationship was intended to be specified. *Pole v. Cok*, TNA: PRO KB 27/577, m. 38 (1405), AALT Img. No. 78. This action was unusual as it was brought under 4 Edw. III, c. 11 (1331), rather than the much more common 1377 Richard II statute. In a champerty action, the defendant alleged that he had loaned money to the plaintiffs in a land action, a husband and wife, the latter being "kin" to his wife, which they promised to repay if they recovered the tenement. *Tollere v. Fletesmonth*, TNA: PRO CP 40/536, m. 107 (1395), AALT Img. No. 243.

[93] *Dent v. Magot*, TNA: PRO KB 27/818, m. 76 (1465), AALT Img. No. 173.

[94] He said that "he was kin to Anne (the widow), viz. son of Hugh, son of Hugh, son of Elizabeth, sister of Richard, father of Ralph, father of Richard, father of Ralph, father of Anne." *Beauchamp v. Monyngton*, TNA: PRO KB 27/833, m. 113 (1469), AALT Img. No. 295.

[95] In contrast to most other actions, the plaintiffs in these actions involving kinship often did not challenge the justification nor deny the existence of the kinship. The most

Some justices saw kinship as a justification comparable to those for supporting servants and tenants. Cheyne CJKB said that "if he has shown a cause of maintenance, for which cause the law presumes that it is permissible to be with him, then it will not be adjudged a maintenance, as it was with his kin (*cosin*) or that he came with him because he was his servant or his tenant."[96] Similarly, Newton CJCP noted that what was maintenance or tortious in a stranger was lawful if done for servants or kinsmen.[97]

In addition to kinship, affinity – a relationship arising from marriage or sexual intercourse outside of marriage[98] – justified maintenance. Martin JCP said that "one can maintain his blood, and a person who is of his affinity."[99] Several actions involved the relation between godparents and their godchildren, a form of spiritual affinity. The court said that pleading such a relationship was a good plea in a maintenance action

common replies were that the defendant had engaged in other conduct or lacked an interest that justified assistance. Several replies attacked the sufficiency of the plea. Only two plaintiffs replied by reasserting the maintenance, which would have put the kinship justification to the jury.

[96] "*Mes s'il ust monstre une cause de maintenaunce, pour quel cause le ley presume que il est lye a estre ove luy pur ceo cause, donques ceo ne sera adjudge un maintenaunce. Come fuit ove son cosin, ou que il vient ove luy. Pur ceo que il suit son servant ou son tenant.*" Y.B. East., 11 Hen. VI, fol. 41, pl. 36 (1433), Seipp No. 1433.058. Moile JCP thought the justification was stronger in the case of a master for a servant, as the former was bound to provide the servant with food and drink and could be sued in covenant for failing to do so, but that a father was not similarly obligated to his son. *Horne's Case*, Y.B. Hil., 34 Hen. VI, fol. 25, pl. 3 (1456), Seipp No. 1456.003.

[97] "*Come si le maistre justifia per son servant, ou per son 'kinsman' a luy, et 'similia,' en lour person poet estre tiel que il est loial, et nul maintenaunce, et en estrange person un choce torcious et maintenaunce.*" Y.B. Mich., 22 Hen. VI, fol. 35, pl. 54 (1443), Seipp No. 1443.113. Other statements by justices and lawyers viewed supporting kin in their litigation as lawful. E.g., Y.B., 19 Hen. VI, fol. 14, pl. 34 (1460), Seipp No. 1440.052 ("*frere*"); Y.B., 39 Hen. VI, fol. 5, pl. 8 (1440), Seipp No. 1460.036 ("*come frere, cosin*"); Y.B., Mich., 9 Edw. IV, fol. 31, pl. 4 (1469), Seipp No. 1469.093 ("*son frere ou cosin*"); Rastell, *A Collection of Entrees* , fol. 431v, pl. 16 and 17.

[98] *Oxford English Dictionary Online, s.v.* "Affinity," definitions I .1.a. and b.

[99] "*On peut maintenir son sang, et celui que est de son alliance.*" Y.B. Hil., 9 Hen. VI, fol. 64, pl. 17 (1431), Seipp No. 1431.017. The justices rejected justifications based on assisting a brother-in-law in one case and a father-in-law in another. But it was not because they rejected the relationship as a justification for maintenance. It was because in each case the defendant was claiming an interest in the land in dispute in the principal action and the justices said he had no interest. In the action involving the brother-in-law, the defendant's deceased wife had held a life estate; and in the action involving the father-in-law, the land could not come to the defendant by remainder, reversion, or descent. Y.B. Mich., 6 Edw. IV, fol. 5, pl. 15 (1466), Seipp No. 1466.017; Y.B. Mich., 19 Edw. IV, fol. 3, pl. 9 (1479), Seipp No. 1479.038.

because of the affinity between them.[100] In two actions, the justification involved support by a godfather ("*compater*"). In one action, the defendant in a plea of account had raised the maintenance defendant's daughter, and in the other, the defendants, who were sued for procuring a false appeal, had raised the sons of the maintenance defendants.[101]

Several cases also suggested a person might lawfully assist his neighbors and friends.[102] In particular, the justices said that helping them find lawyers was not maintenance. In a 1479 case, Bryan CJCP said, "I understand this case has been adjudged in our books, that a neighbor can go with another neighbor to seek out a man knowledgeable in the law"[103] and also that a friend could advise a person needing a lawyer who the best one was.[104] The court said it was not maintenance for a vicar, not learned in law, to give legal advice to a priest, "for it would follow that no friend could counsel another."[105] The justices also asserted that it was not

---

[100] "*Et auxy uit dit il fuit bon plee adire que il est gossop al cestuy pur que le maintenaunce est suppose, etc par le affinitie que est enter eux, etc.* " Y.B. Mich., 6 Edw. IV, fol. 5, pl. 15 (1466), Seipp No. 1466.017.

[101] In both actions, the defendants alleged that they had retained counsel for the parties in the principal actions as requested, since the parties said that they knew no experts in law. *Anderby v. Plesyngton*, TNA: PRO KB 27/778, m. (1455), AALT Img. No. 104; *Couper v. Pake*, TNA: PRO KB 27/785, m. 87 (1457), AALT Img. No. 180. In the latter action, the plaintiffs denied the existence of the godfather relationship.

[102] As early as 1294, a parson, who was a defendant in a conspiracy action, had advised two men regarding their disputes with the plaintiffs. As to one, whom he advised to bring an *assize of novel disseisin*, he said that his advice was lawful, as the man was his parishioner. As to the other, he said that he advised him to defend his right according to the custom of realm, "just as everyone in the kingdom is allowed (*prout unicuique de Regno licet*)." He prayed judgment whether he needed to answer the plaintiffs "since everyone in the kingdom is allowed to help or advise his friends in their right in the court of the lord king (*unicuique de Regno liceat amicis suis in jure in curia domini Regis adjuvare, etc sive consulere*)." *Lewknor v. John, parson of the church of Souldern*, TNA: PRO KB 27/140, m. 42 (1294), AALT Img. No. 2606 (tr.).

[103] "*Jeo entend cest case ad estre judge en nostre livres, que un neighbor poit aler ove un autre neighbor a enquerer pur un home sachant del ley.*" Y.B. Mich.,19 Edw. IV, fol. 3, pl. 9 (1479), Seipp No. 1479.038. Again, Prysot CJCP may have taken a narrow view. In a note, he said, "*si home vient ove ascun home et request un home appris en ley deste de counseile ove cety home que il vient ove luy que cest maintenaunce.*" Fitzherbert, *Le Grand Abridgement, Maintenaunce*, 21, fol. 65 (Trin., 35 Hen. VI, Trin., 1457), Seipp No. 1457.043abr.

[104] "*Si un del company de Lumbards veigne icy a London, et un de son company ala ove luy a un home sachant del ley, et il dit a luy que de eux est melior, cest ne poit estre dit ascun maintenaunce.*" Y.B. Mich., 19 Edw. IV, fol. 3, pl. 9 (1479), Seipp No. 1479.038.

[105] "*A que il fuit dit par le court que ceo ne poet estre ajuge asacun maintenaunce: car adonques ensuere qu nul amy counsellera autre.*" There was a *capias* against the priest and the defendant advised him to go to London and purchase a writ of *supersedeas*. Y.B. Mich., 22 Hen. VI, fol. 35, pl. 54 (1443), Seipp No. 1443.113.

maintenance for inhabitants of the defendant's vill to assist the latter at his request to provide evidence.[106]

In some actions, defendants justified their support because of the poverty of the party in the principal action[107] or because he did not know how to speak English.[108] The justices seemed to accept the justification with regard to both poverty[109] and inability to speak English.[110] Some viewed such support as a permissible act of charity.[111]

Legitimate Participation in the Process of Litigation

The actions revealed two primary categories of this assistance: supporting the party by acting as a mainpernor or pledge of prosecution and providing evidentiary support to a party.[112] In several actions, the defendants justified by alleging that they had been asked by the principal

---

[106] Some justices also believed that the lord of the vill, even though not one of the inhabitants, could provide support because he was the lord. Y.B. East., 18 Edw. IV, fol. 2, pl. 11, fol. 4, pl. 23 (1478), Seipp Nos. 1478.017, 1478.029.

[107] *Martell v. Sallowe*, TNA: PRO KB 27/522, m. 50 (1391), AALT Img. No. 116; *Courtenay v. Bryt*, TNA: PRO CP 40/560, m. 385d (1401), AALT Img. No. 1998; *Tewe v. Catesby*, TNA: PRO KB 27/750, m. 105 (1448), AALT Img. No. 210. Sergeant Prysot, counsel for a plaintiff in an action, acknowledged that helping a poor man was not maintenance. Y.B. Mich., 22 Hen. VI, fol. 35, pl. 54 (1443), Seipp No. 1443.113.

[108] *Horne's Case*, Y.B. Hil., 34 Hen. VI, fol. 25, pl. 3 (1456), Seipp No. 1456.003.

[109] Martin JCP said, "*jeo di que jeo puis done or ou argent a un home que est pauvre pur maintenir son plee, s'il mesme ne puit pur pauvrete, et ceo n'est maintenaunce encontre ley.* " Y.B. Hil., 9 Hen. VI, fol. 64, pl. 17 (1431), Seipp No. 1431.017.

[110] The court said, "*issint quand cest home ne scavoit parler 'ut supra,' il sera enconter reason que il ne aura un de luy amesner a conseil et cest fait est un fait de charite de aider et succourir un que ne poet aider luy mesme.*" Y.B. Hil., 15 Hen. VII, fol. 2, pl. 3 (1500), Seipp No. 1500.03. In another action, the defendant justified helping a party find a lawyer, as he was a foreigner, a merchant of the German Hanse, born in Germany, and on only a brief stay in England, with no knowledge of men experienced in the law of the land of England. *Payn v. Van Bleken*, TNA: PRO KB 27/739, m. 94d (1446), AALT Img. No. 462 (tr.).

[111] *Pomeroy v. Abbot of Buckfast*, Y.B. Mich., 21 Hen. VI, fol. 15, pl. 30 (1442), Seipp No. 1442.126; TNA: PRO CP 40/ 729, m. 301 (1443), AALT Img. No. 594; *Horne's Case*, Y.B. Hil., 34 Hen. VI, fol. 25, pl. 3 (1456), Seipp No. 1456.003.

[112] While these two categories of cases comprised the most common instances of assisting in the process of litigation, a few actions involved other types of support. In one action, the defendant's justification was that he came to Westminster and stood with his servants and provided support. *Hertwell v. Nicoll*, TNA: PRO KB 27/744, m. 80d (1447), AALT Img. No. 416. In another action, the defendant alleged that a trespass defendant had suggested to a justice of the peace that certain men held a messuage by force and that the constable, whom the justice of the peace had ordered to arrest the wrongdoers and take sufficient force of men, had requested the defendant to come to the messuage, which was on the land of the plaintiff in the trespass and maintenance actions, and aid in the arrest and removal

party to act as a mainpernor.[113] Such defendants often claimed that they were neighbors or friends of the party in the principal action. In one action, the defendant alleged that he and other neighbors had been asked by a trespass defendant to be his mainpernors in an action in the Court of the Steward and Marshal of the King's household,[114] and in another action the defendant said that he was mainpernor for his kinsman ("*cosin*") who was arrested in a debt action.[115] In two other actions, the party in the principal action asked the defendant to come with him to court to be a mainpernor because of his fear of being arrested and needing to provide surety of peace.[116] Serving as a mainpernor was a common and essential official action. Thus, one might find it surprising that a person might be sued for maintenance for performing this function.

Nevertheless, the Year Book discussions and plea roll evidence in the records do not provide a clear answer regarding its legality. In *John Doket's Case*, in which the maintenance defendant alleged he was a mainpernor for a man whom Doket sued, Danby JCP said that a mainpernor "can well justify the matter; for if the one for whom he is mainpernor be attainted, and not be found, the mainpernor will be charged of all."[117] But in a 1456 case, Prysot CJCP said that a mainpernor for a surety of the peace could not meddle in a *scire facias* action against the principal, who had broken the peace, even though the mainpernor

---

of one of the wrongdoers. *Thurstan v. Scot*, TNA: PRO KB 27/580, m. 30 (1406), AALT Img. No. 66 (tr.).

[113] *Horbury v. Langeley*, TNA: PRO KB 27/524, m. 49d (1392), AALT Img. No. 271; *Hore v. Hatfield*, TNA: PRO KB 27/661, m. 101d (1425), AALT Img. Nos. 533–34; *Lude v. Fydelow*, TNA: PRO KB 27/669, m. 51 (1428), AALT Img. No. 138; *Becket v. Greth*, TNA: PRO KB 27/737, m. 69 (1445), AALT Img. No. 145; *Fitz v. Rede*, TNA: PRO KB 27/739, m. 85 (1446), AALT Img. No. 170.

[114] *Horbury v. Langeley*, TNA: PRO KB 27/524, m. 49d (1392), AALT Img. No. 271.

[115] The plaintiff argued that the defendant could not justify without admitting the maintenance. But the court held that the plea was good. "The Apprentices who were around Common Pleas marvelled (*marvellent*) greatly at this." The plaintiff then said that the defendant had given money to the jurors to say their verdict for the debt defendant, which the maintenance defendant denied. The plaintiff argued that the defendant must deny the maintenance generally and not the special maintenance, but the court disagreed. Y.B. Trin., 14 Hen. VI, fol. 6, pl. 30 (1436), Seipp No. 1436.030.

[116] *Hore v. Hatfield*, TNA: PRO KB 27/661, m. 101d (1425), AALT Img. No. 533–34; *Lude v. Fydelow*, TNA: PRO KB 27/669, m. 51 (1428), AALT Img. No. 138.

[117] "*Et a l'autre entent me semble que mainpernor en cest case poit bien justifier le matter; car si cestuy pur quel il est mainpernor soit attaint, et ne soit trove le mainpernor sera charge de tout.*" Prisot CJCP seemed to disagree. *John Doket's Case*, Y.B. Hil., 32 Hen. VI, fol. 24, pl. 11 (1454), Seipp No. 1454.011.

would be bound to pay. He concluded by saying that "it was his foolishness that he would be his mainpernor."[118] Further, rejecting a case put by Serjeant Choke, the defendant's lawyer, Prysot, said that a pledge of prosecution could not intermeddle for the party, "for no law compelled him to be a pledge, but of his own will."[119] This reasoning is puzzling, as almost all, if not all, justifications of maintenance that were acceptable, as discussed above, involved acts that were voluntary and not those that were mandated by law.

But there may be another way to interpret these speeches by justices in these actions. In one case the defendant's justification was that he asked a man learned in the law to be of counsel to his servant, who had been sued by the plaintiff. The issue was whether the relationship with the party in the principal case justified intervention on his behalf. Thus, these judicial statements may be read narrowly to mean that neither a mainpernor nor a pledge of prosecution had the type of relationship with the party in the principal action or a sufficient interest in the principal action to justify intermeddling and not that simply performing those functions was maintenance. This interpretation is consistent with the views of Brian CJCP and Serjeant Bridges, who said it was lawful for someone to be a mainpernor as long as nothing further was done.[120]

But other actions may create doubts as to the permissibility of participating in litigation in those ways. In one action, the two maintenance defendants justified their presence in court, alleging that they were mainpernors for a man whom the maintenance plaintiff had sued for trespass.[121] Similarly, a man sued for maintenance said that a widow, who was sued by man and his wife for trespass to the wife, asked him to

---

[118] "*Et posito, que un home soit mainpernor pur un auter icy en cest Court pur suertie de paix, et un scire facias soit agarde envers le principal supposant que il ad enfreint l' paix, en cest cas le mainpernor ne poit my mesler nienobstant que soit trove pur l' roy, il sera charge de s' summe: car seroit dit sa foly que il voilet estre son mainpernor ...*" *Horne's Case*, Y.B. Hil. 34 Hen. VI, fol. 25, pl. 3 (1456), Seipp No. 1456.003.

[119] "*Et en le cas que est mis per Sjt Choke, si un home soit plege de pursuer pur moy, que en c'est cas il poit mesler pur moy, ceo n'est issint: car nul ley coarcte luy estre plege, mes de son volonte demesne.*" Although Prysot, as noted previously, took a narrower view on permissible justifications, both Danby JCP and Aysshton JCP agreed with him. Ibid.

[120] They said, "*il est bon plee en action de maintenaunce adire que il fuit un que prist le defendant en le primer action en mainpris, le quel est mesme le maintenaunce, et ceo est loyal pur chescun home, etc. issint que il ne medle pluis in le matter.*" Y.B. Mich., 18 Edw. IV, fol. 12, pl. 7 (1478), Seipp No. 1478.078.

[121] The defendants said that the trespass defendant had asked them and other neighbors to be his mainpernors, which they had done. *Horbury v. Langeley*, TNA: PRO KB 27/524, m. 7d (1392), AALT Img. No. 271.

come to court with her to be her mainpernor in case a surety of peace was demanded.[122] But the plaintiffs in these two cases did not allege other conduct, as often was the case in response to the justifications, and just reasserted the initial allegation of maintenance, leaving it up to the jury.[123] Also one action seemed to suggest there was a distinction between volunteering to undertake these types of tasks, which was unlawful, and being requested to do so, which was permissible.[124] In a 1446 maintenance action, the defendant's plea alleged he and other neighbors were mainpernors for an imprisoned trespass defendant, as the latter had requested, so he could go at large until his court date.[125] The plaintiff demurred to the defendant's plea and the court upheld the demurrer and entered judgment for the plaintiff.[126] In sum, although the law is not entirely clear, it difficult to believe that lawyers and justices considered that the huge number of people who served as mainpernors and pledges of prosecution had engaged in illegal activity. A few other cases raised similar issues regarding serving as a compurgator.[127]

---

[122] *Lude v. Fydelow*, TNA: PRO KB 27/669, m. 51 (1428), AALT Img. No. 138.

[123] There is no evidence of the jury decision.

[124] Prysot CJCP would draw this distinction since he believed volunteering to be a mainpernor was maintenance. *Horne's Case*, Y.B. Hil., 34 Hen. VI, fol. 25, pl. 3 (1456), Seipp No. 1456.003.

[125] The defendant agreed to do so, "not refusing neighborly charity (*caritatem vicinam renuentes*)." The relationship as a neighbor and the charitable motive, while influential in other contexts, apparently had no impact here. The sheriff had told the trespass defendant that he could go at large if he found sufficient security.

[126] The jury assessed damages of £36 13s 4d. *Fitz v. Rede*, TNA: PRO KB 27/739, m. 85 (1446), AALT Img. Nos. 170–71, 444. Fitz sued William Rede for maintaining Thomas Hamelyn and several others, whom Fitz had sued for trespass. Rede alleged that pursuant to Hamelyn's request, Rede and the others mainprised Hamelyn until his court date, the octave of Trinity (June 15–18, 1444). But he said that they did this on June 20, 1444 ("the same day as the supposed maintenance"), but Hamelyn had appeared in the trespass action no later than June 18. Thus, the court granted the demurrer because Rede's explanation did not match the dates and the mainprise had expired on June 18. These dates make the case puzzling. Rede's allegation of mainprise on June 20 implies that Hamelyn was in jail from June 1 to 19, although he had already appeared in the trespass case. The parties either had the dates confused or it implied that Rede was not telling the truth and some other maintenance had occurred on June 20, which was outside the time frame of the mainprise.

[127] *Sewall v. Martyn*, TNA: PRO KB 27/770, m. 61 (1453), AALT Img. Nos. 133–34, 517; *Copley v. Went*, TNA: PRO CP40/799, m. 313 (1460), AALT Img. No. 613. In *Sewall*, the defendant said that a woman, who sued for trespass in the London Guildhall and wanted to wage her law, as was permitted by the custom of the city, showed him evidence of her innocence and asked him to be a compurgator, which he was. But the plaintiff said that the defendant did so of his own accord and will prior to any request and procured others

Moreover, the great bulk of such individuals do not appear to have been sued for maintenance. Indeed it would be surprising if these maintenance defendants were actually sued for these types of conduct, making one wonder whether those few cases where they were charged involved more than is evident in the record.

Another group of actions involving assistance in the process of litigation involved defendants who had provided evidence on behalf of one of the parties in the principal action.[128] For example, the defendant alleged in one action that he told the jurors the truth regarding the taking of goods with the permission of plaintiff and at the wish of Babington CJCP.[129] But most instances did not involve the permission of the adverse party or a justice, and the defendants acted in response to a request of the party in the principal action.[130] Four actions brought by the same plaintiff for maintaining a *quare impedit* action prompted the most extensive discussion of this type of conduct. The defendants, jurors charged by the bishop's commissioner general to investigate the right of patronage, told one of the defendants in the action that he should come before the commissioner and show his evidence proving his right of patronage if he wished, which he did.[131] Serjeant Littleton, the defendant's lawyer, argued that what "a man does by coercion of the law cannot be said to be maintenance, as where a juror who finds for me against you," and Fortescue CJKB agreed.[132] But Fortescue went on to discuss

---

to be compurgators. The jury found that defendant neither offered to do so nor procured others and acquitted him.

[128] This type of activity should be distinguished from "laboring the jury," which is discussed in the next chapter. Admittedly, in some actions, it may be difficult to draw a line between these two types of conduct.

[129] The truth was that the maintenance plaintiff, who was the trespass defendant, had taken the goods as the defendant alleged. The plaintiff replied that he had given the defendant license to inform the jurors on May 11, 1434, not July 3, 1434, as alleged by the defendant. *Shopman v. Waryn*, TNA: PRO KB 27/734, m. 42 (1444), AALT Img. No. 108.

[130] In a 1430 action, the defendant alleged that a defendant in an appeal of felony, as requested by the party, gave "witness" to the jurors and a sealed testimonial letter that he had seen the appellee at a place different from the place alleged as the place of felony at the time of the alleged felony. The plaintiff replied that the defendant had incited and procured the appeal jurors to say their verdict for the defendant. *Daby v. Chalkhill*, TNA: PRO KB 27/677, m. 77 (1430), AALT Img. No. 180.

[131] *Doreward v. Barners*, TNA: PRO KB 27/750, m. 29 (1450), AALT Img. No. 61; *Doreward v. Roo*, TNA: PRO KB 27/750, m. 27 (1450), AALT Img. No. 57; *Doreward v. Hodelston*, TNA: PRO KB 27/750, m. 27d (1450), AALT Img. No. 398; *Doreward v. Ferthyng*, TNA: PRO KB 27/750, m. 31d (1450), AALT Img. No. 406.

[132] "*Et auxi cest que un home fait per cohercion de ley ne poet estre dit maintenaunce come un juror que passa pur moy encontre vous, vous n'aura accion de maintenaunce de cest*

those much more common instances not involving legal coercion. He said:

> And if a man was at the bar and it is said for the defendant or plaintiff to the court, that the man knew the truth of the issue, and prayed that he might be examined by the court to say the truth to the jury and the court asked him to speak the truth, and he at the request of the court said that what he knew in the matter, it is justifiable maintenance, but if he has come to the bar on his own account and speaks on behalf of one or the other, it is maintenance and he will be punished for this.[133]

Although drawing a line between acting in response to a request to provide evidentiary support and doing so on one's own initiative seems to make sense[134] and is consistent with a distinction articulated in other maintenance actions, it is a murky line in terms of proof. Moreover, some justices did not explicitly state that a request was required in all cases.[135] In contrast, not all the justices seemed to agree that providing evidence in response to a request was lawful. In an action where Hals JKB expressed the same view as Fortescue,[136] Cheyne CJKB disagreed. He said:

---

envers luy." Littleton also argued that the court had no jurisdiction because it was a spiritual matter. *Doreward v. Ferthyng*, Y.B. East., 28 Hen. VI, fol. 6, pl. 1 (1450), Seipp No. 1450.002; TNA: PRO KB 27/750, m. 31d (1450), AALT Img. No. 406.

[133] "*Et si un home soit al' barre et dit est pur le defendant ou plaintif al' Court, que le dit home conut le verite del'issue, et pria que il poit estre examine par le Court adire le verite al' jury, et le Court luy demanda adire le verite, et il al' request del' Court dit cest que il seit en matter, il est maintenaunce justifiable: mes s'il ust venu al' barre de son test demesne et dit pur l'un ou pur l'auter, il est maintenaunce, et il sera puni pur ceo.*" Ibid. In a later case, the justices agreed that the inhabitants of the defendant's vill could provide evidence if requested to do so by the latter. Y.B. East., 18 Edw. IV, fol. 2, pl. 11, fol. 4, pl. 23 (1478), Seipp Nos. 1478.017, 1478.029.

[134] The conduct in some actions was both less and more egregious. In one action, the defendant alleged that he came to the assize, at the request of the party in the principal action, to hear the evidence that the party would show the jury and offered to assist in arranging a concord in the action. The plaintiff alleged other conduct. *Hore v. Hatfield*, TNA: PRO KB 27/661, m. 101d (1425), AALT Img. No. 533. In another action, the plaintiff alleged that the defendant agreed to show evidence in return for being enfeoffed, which would seem to be champerty. Y.B. 14 Hen VI, fol. 7, pl. 32 (1436), Seipp No. 1436.032.

[135] In a debt case, Newton CJCB said that "for in a writ of maintenance sued against me, I say well that the one for whom you supposed that I maintained, was my brother and that I showed evidence at the inquest … it is a good justification of a special maintenance which is lawful, the plea is good." Y.B. 19 Hen. VI, fol. 14, pl. 34 (1460), Seipp No. 1440.052.

[136] "For in the writ of maintenance it is a good plea to say for the one that he ought to maintain, come with him and ask us, inasmuch as we had a former man of the country, and have knowledge of the title of the land for which he was impleaded, that we wished

> It will be adjudged a maintenance in your cases, because he had no more
> cause nor privity to maintain the quarrel than the greatest stranger in the
> world unless that the other has cause to warrant against him. And to this
> you say that it is a good plea in a writ of maintenance, that he is an old
> man of the region, and has better knowledge of the right and title of the
> said rent, and he came with the defendant to declare his right in the said
> rent, I say that that is a true maintenance: [for] by such cause anyone
> could justify a maintenance;[137]

More clearly permissible, it would seem, was being paid to deliver a
party's evidence to his lawyers, as one defendant alleged in a 1440
action.[138] Thus, in certain instances it was not maintenance to provide
evidentiary support to one of the parties in the principal action, although
it was not totally free from doubt and a person doing so risked being sued
for maintenance.[139]

In conclusion, it is clear that many forms of support and assistance to a
party in a pending action were lawful. The above discussion shows that
the justices recognized a number of justifications for intermeddling in
another person's litigation. Given the extent of these justifications, the
scope of permitted support and assistance to litigants was broad and the
extent of illegal activity was much less than alleged by contemporaries
and asserted by modern commentators.

---

to stand with him to inform the jury of the title to the said land." Y.B. East., 11 Hen. VI,
fol. 41 pl. 36 (1433), Seipp No. 1433.058.

[137] "*Il sera adjuge un maintenaunce in voz cases, pour ceo que il n y ad nul cause ne privity
pur maintenir le quarele plus que le plus estranger del' monde sinon que l'auter avoit
cause d' garrante envers luy. Et a ceo vous dits que il est bon ple in [un] breve de
maintenaunce, que il est un ancien home del' pays, et ad le meliour conusance del droit
et title de ceste rente, et il vient ove le defendant a declarer son droit en le dit rent. Jeo di
que ceo est un vray maintenaunce, car tiel cause peut chescun justifier un maintenaunce.*
Ibid. (tr.).

[138] The defendant, a draper, alleged that Richard, earl of Salisbury, had paid 6s 8d to his
lawyers, Nicholas Gyrlington and Robert Danby. *Matany v. Edolf*, TNA: PRO KB 27/
718, m. 85d (1440), AALT Img. No. 542.

[139] Holdsworth believed that concern with perjury caused courts to enlarge the definitions
of maintenance and conspiracy, so "that it was very dangerous to come forward as a
witness." Holdsworth, *History English Law*, vol. 1, pp. 334–35. Modern scholars have
opined that the subsequent Elizabethan Statute of Perjury (5 Eliz. I, c. 9, § 6 (1563),
Statutes of the Realm, vol. 4, p. 438) likely eliminated that risk. Langbein, Lerner, and
Smith, *The History of the Common Law* (New York, 2009), p. 247.

The Development of the Law of Maintenance

Illegal Maintenance

Plaintiffs frequently rejected the defendants' justifications. Their replications told a different story and often claimed that defendants had engaged in different, more egregious, and unlawful conduct.[1] The conduct that they alleged can be grouped into two categories. The first category included types of conduct that were illegal because they violated another statute or were otherwise manifestly improper such as bribery, threatening or influencing jurors, falsifying evidence or releases, or falsely procuring indictments. The second category involved allegations that masters, friends, or others paid their own money to retain counsel or to pay other litigation expenses on behalf of the party in the principal action.[2] Despite the plaintiffs' view that such conduct was illegal, its judicial treatment was more complicated and less clear.[3]

Illegal Conduct

Bribery

The most common kind of illegal maintenance alleged by plaintiffs was bribery of the jurors.[4] Many of the allegations of jury bribery involved

---

[1] Plaintiffs alleged such conduct in 60% of the actions where the defendant alleged a justification.

[2] Actions involving the first type constituted 61% of the illegal maintenance, and the second type, 39%.

[3] In addition to the various types of conduct that were illegal maintenance, Newton CJCP said that maintenance could be based on intent in the absence of actual conduct. He said that if "one who is of great power in the county wills in the presence of the jury and of the people clearly that he would spend on the matter £20, and shows it; or that he wishes to give £20 to labor the jury; although he has not given any money, nor made any labor, and never acted further in the matter, this is a maintenance; for perhaps for the reason that his intent is made known, those who ought to pass on the inquest will not dare to find against his intent." *Pomeroy v. Abbot of Buckfast*, Y.B. Mich., Hen. VI, fol. 5, pl. 7 (1443), Seipp No. 1443.066 (motion in arrest of judgment).

[4] *Norton v. Mitchell*, TNA: PRO KB27/609, m. 35 (1413), AALT Img. No. 78; *Mitchell v. Cloutesham*, TNA: PRO CP40/771, m. 114 (1453), AALT Img. No. 227; *Grey v. Emmesley*,

249

defendants who were lawyers. In one action, eight men whom Joan Beauchamp, Lady of Bergavenny, had sued for trespass charged William Bekke with maintaining the trespass action for the plaintiffs. William responded that for a long time he had been retained by Joan, taking fees and robes of her livery to be her counsel and that he had acted as her counsel in the plea and declared the evidence to the impaneled jurors. But the maintenance plaintiffs said that William went beyond that conduct, giving money and food and drink to four jurors and threatening all the jurors with "severe and violent words (*grandia verba et austera*)" if they said their verdict for the trespass plaintiffs.[5] In some cases, it was alleged that the defendant had hired a third party to commit the bribery.[6] Nor was bribery limited to gifts of money. One plaintiff alleged that the defendant, a goldsmith, gave "gold, silver, and silk stockings" to the jurors in an assize of novel disseisin.[7]

There is no doubt that the justices and lawyers considered bribery a form of illegal maintenance.[8] In a 1412 action, the plaintiff alleged that the defendant, an attorney, gave food (fish) to the jurors, and Thirning CJCP said that "all the justices were clearly of the opinion that it is not

---

TNA: PRO KB 27/769, m. 119 (1453), AALT Img. No. 229; *Heron v. Couper*, TNA: PRO CP 40/784, m. 380 (1457), AALT Img. No. 747; *Grey v. Jenney*, TNA: PRO KB 27/847, m. 35 (1473), AALT Img. No. 76.

[5] Gerald Usflete and his wife, Elizabeth, duchess of Norfolk, were also plaintiffs in the trespass action. *Usflete v Bekke*, TNA: PRO KB 27/638, m. 87 (1420), AALT Img. Nos. 212, 511. In another action where the defendant had alleged that he was learned in the law and acting as the attorney of the party in the principal action, the plaintiff replied that the defendant had given 6s 8d of his own money to one of jurors impaneled in the action to say his verdict for his client. *Heron v. Couper*, TNA: PRO CP 40/784, m. 380 (1457), AALT Img. No. 747.

[6] In one action, the plaintiff alleged that the defendant had given his own money to a woman to procure her husband to incite a juror to say his verdict for Richard, earl of Salisbury. The defendant denied the allegation. *Matany v. Edolf*, TNA: PRO KB 27/718, m. 85d (1440), AALT Img. No. 542.

[7] *Creyk v. Senelle*, TNA: PRO KB 27/578, m. 52d (1405), AALT Img. No. 381.

[8] E.g., Y.B. Hil., 13 Hen. IV, fol. 16, pl. 12 (1412), Seipp No. 1412.012; *Pomeroy v. Abbot of Buckfast*, Y.B. Mich., 22 Hen. VI, fol. 5, pl. 7 (1443), Seipp No. 1443.066 (motion in arrest of judgment); Y.B. Mich., 21 Hen. VI, fol. 15, pl. 30 (1442), Seipp No. 1442.126; TNA: PRO CP 40/729, m. 301, AALT Img. No. 594; *W.H. v. W.C.*, in William Rastell, *A Collection of Entries* (London, 1670), fol. 431, pl. 17 (1457); Y.B. East., 18 Edw. IV, fol. 4, pl. 23 (1478), Seipp No. 1478.29; Y.B. Mich., 19 Edw. IV, fol. 3, pl. 9 (1479), Seipp No. 1479.038; Rastell, *A Collection of Entries*, fol. 428, pl. 9; ibid., fol. 429, pl. 10. David Seipp, "Jurors, Evidences and the Tempest of 1499," in John W. Cairns and Grant McLeod, eds., *"The Dearest Birth Right of the People of England": The Jury in the History of the Common Law* (Oxford, 2002), p. 83.

permissible for an attorney to promise or to give a reward to the jurors; if he does, he is punishable for this just as a stranger will be."[9] In *Pomeroy v. Abbot of Buckfast*, Newton CJCP and Paston JCP said that it was unlawful maintenance "when a master gives any money for his servant to [give] to a juror to say his verdict because it is not lawful in that case for the juror to accept it."[10] Such payments may have also violated the statute prohibiting bribery of jurors, who were subject to penalty by a writ of *decies tantum*.[11] In some cases, bribery was coupled with allegations that the defendants threatened jurors.[12] That was also illegal conduct.[13] Newton CJCP stated that a threat by a lawyer would cause the prior

---

[9] "*Et touts les justices fuerent clerement d'opinion que ne list a un attorney a promitter ne doner regard as jurours, et s'il face, il est punishable pur icel, come ascun estraunge person sera.*" The defendant claimed that he had only showed his client's evidence to the jurors. Thirning CJCP rejected the plaintiff's argument that the defendant's speaking "great words (*parlance des graund parolx*)" was maintenance. *Oliver Becket's Case*, Y.B. Hil., 13 Hen. IV, fol. 16 and 17, pl. 12 (1412), Seipp No. 1412.012 (tr.). It was also maintenance for a juror to give money to a fellow juror although permissible to exhort fellow jurors to give a verdict for one party or the other. Y.B. Mich., 17 Edw. IV, fol. 5, pl. 2 (1477), Seipp No. 1477.23.

[10] "*Car il est loial al'apprentice de prendre pur son conselle. Autre est ou le master dona ascun argent pur son servant [doner] a un juror adire son verdit: car en cele n='est loial al' juror a prendre, etc.*" *Pomeroy v. Abbot of Buckfast*, Y.B. Mich., 21 Hen. VI, fol. 16b, pl. 30 (1442), Seipp No. 1442.126; TNA: PRO CP 40/729, m. 301 (1443), AALT Img. No. 594 (tr.).

[11] The writ was so named as the penalty was ten times the amount of the bribe, with half to be paid to the plaintiff and the other half to the crown. 38 Edw. III, st. 1, c. 12 (1364), *Statutes of the Realm*, vol. 1, p. 384; Anthony Fitzherbert, *The New Natura Brevium* (Dublin, 1793), pp. 396–98. One action distinguished maintenance and embracery, bribery of jurors. It stated that the person who gave the money committed maintenance, and the one who took it was an embraceror. *Oliver Becket's Case*, Y.B. Hil., 13 Hen. IV, fols. 16 and 17, pl. 12 (1412), Seipp No. 1412.012. Another action said that if the third party gave his own money to the juror, it was maintenance, and otherwise embracery. Y.B. Mich., 11 Hen. VI, fol. 10, pl. 24 (1432). Both Hawkins and Coke treated embracery as a form of maintenance. Edward Coke, *The First Part of the Institutes of the Laws of England or a Commentary on Littleton* (London, 1832), fol. 369; Hawkins, *Pleas of the Crown*, 3rd ed. (London, 1739), Book I, c. 83, p. 249.

[12] *Norton v. Mitchell*, TNA: PRO KB27/609, m. 35 (1413), AALT Img. No. 78. In one action, the jury presented that three men promised the jurors in a writ of villeinage that they could share the recovery if they found for the villein, and, after they failed to do so, they threatened the jurors and said they were false. *Rex v. Drayton*, TNA: PRO KB 27/548, m. 22 rex (1398), AALT Img. No. 141.

[13] In one case, the plaintiff alleged that the defendant, a servant of a prior, who had brought a trespass action, threatened the jurors that "they should not be so brave as to live in their own house if they did not give a verdict for the prior." Y.B. Mich. 19 Hen. VI, fol. 31, pl. 60 (1440), Seipp No. 1440.078. Seipp discussed threatening jurors. Seipp, "Jurors, Evidences and the Tempest of 1499," p. 83.

representation of the client, which was otherwise lawful, to be unlawful maintenance.[14] In one action, the defendants were charged with influencing the jury by multiple types of conduct. The plaintiff alleged that they had given money and promised gifts to three jurors, given them food and drink, and threatened and insulted three other jurors with bodily and other harm if they refused to say their verdict for the plaintiff's adversary. Since the defendants were already subject to a prior writ of prohibition ordering them not to maintain a land action of the plaintiff's adversary or any other person in violation of the maintenance statute, the plaintiff alleged that they violated both the maintenance statute and the writ of prohibition.[15]

Bribery was not limited to jurors. In one action, the plaintiff alleged that the defendant, again a lawyer, bribed the sheriff, giving him 40s to arrange a jury in the assize to the devotion of his client,[16] and in another action it was alleged that a defendant, also a lawyer, had paid the coroners 5 marks to return a favorable jury panel.[17] Such payments to sheriffs, coroners, and other officials were also illegal maintenance.[18] In a 1412 action, all the justices said it was illegal for anyone "to give a reward to . . . a sheriff and bailiff of the liberty and other officials in this

---

[14] He said, "*Mes le ley est, si un serjeant ou apprentice ministre le ley al' barre pur son client, a or ceo que ils font est loial; si en apres pendant mesme le ple le serjeant or apprentice vient a un que est enpanelle, et dit a luy, que s'il ne voit passer pur son client, il serra batu, or il sera adjuge pur un maintenor a tout temps pendant le ple, et ce que fuit dit loialment fait avant serra ajudge or pur un maintenaunce.*"*Pomeroy v. Abbot of Buckfast*, Y.B. Mich. 22 Hen. VI, fol. 5, pl. 7 (1443), Seipp No. 1443.066 (motion in arrest of judgment), TNA: PRO CP 40/729, m. 301, AALT Img. No. 594.

[15] *Lyvot v. Thomelyn*, TNA: PRO KB 27/621, m. 28d (1416), AALT Img. 293.

[16] *Smythe v. Paslewe*, TNA: PRO KB 27/543, m. 65 (1397), AALT Img. No. 140. Plaintiffs were not the only ones alleging that juries were biased, as in several actions defendants alleged that jury panels were arraigned to the devotion and favor of the plaintiff. E.g., *Spenser v. Mokkyng*, TNA: PRO KB27/521, m. 76d (1391), AALT Img. No. 384; *Lyster v. Slaper*, TNA: PRO KB 27/753, m. 20d (1449), AALT Img. No. 256.

[17] The plaintiff also alleged that the defendant had given 6s 8d to the defendant's attorney and 40d to his counsel. *Dynham v. Gylbert*, TNA: PRO CP 40/866, m. 158 (1478), AALT Img. No. 300; Y.B. East., 18 Edw. IV, fol. 4, pl. 23, Seipp No. 1478.029.

[18] Y.B. Hil., 13 Hen. IV, fol. 16, pl. 12 (1412), Seipp No. 1412.012; Y.B. Mich., 12 Edw. IV, fol. 14, pl. 15 (1472), Seipp No. 1472.053; Y.B. East. 18 Edw. IV, fol. 4, pl. 23 (1478), Seipp No. 1478.029; *Dynham v. Gylbert*, TNA: PRO CP 40/866, m. 158 (1478), AALT Img. No. 300; Rastell, *A Collection of Entrees*, fol. 428, pl. 9. In another case, the plaintiff alleged that, as soon after the verdict had been given, the defendant, one of the jurors, required ("*require*") the steward of the court to give judgment for the plaintiff. Y.B. East., 18 Edw. IV, fol. 2, pl. 8 (1478), Seipp No. 1478.014.

case and similar ones," as it was for an attorney to promise one to the jurors.[19]

Laboring the Jury

Laboring the jury was another way to influence a jury verdict. Laboring was a common medieval word, whose contemporary meaning was "to advocate strenuously" or "to endeavor to influence or persuade."[20] It was used in a variety of contexts, not limited to attempts to influence juries. In the context of the maintenance actions, it would seem to connote efforts by someone, not a party in the principal action, to convince the jury that one side's story and evidence should prevail. But it is necessary to distinguish such advocacy from legitimately providing evidence, which has been previously discussed,[21] as well as providing the information requested by jury in the process of informing itself.[22] Although it would likely be illegal for anyone outside the legitimate participation in a judicial proceeding to attempt to influence the jury after it was sworn, any advocacy directed at jurors by someone other than the litigant or his representative before or after they were sworn was likely illegal maintenance.[23]

This type of conduct prompted substantial discussion. Some actions contain statements that laboring a jury by a nonparty violated the maintenance statute.[24] In *Pomeroy v. Abbot of Buckfast*, the justices said that giving

---

[19] "*Et touts les Justices fuerent clerement d'opinion que il ne list a un attorney a promitter ne doner regard as jurours . . . et simile est de visconte et bailli de liberte et autres officials in hoc casu et similibus.*" Y.B. Hil. 13 Hen. IV, fol. 16, pl. 12 (1412), Seipp No. 1412.012.

[20] *Oxford English Dictionary Online*, s.v. "labour/labor," definitions 5a and 5c. Both these definitions are indicated as being obsolete.

[21] Chapter 9, pp. 246–48.

[22] McFarlane, who took a skeptical view of the prohibitions on maintenance, used laboring the jury to illustrate his view that the extent of illegal conduct had been exaggerated. He linked laboring or informing the jury to the self-informing jury and said it was lawful. Although that could be true, he failed to distinguish between laboring by the litigant, which was lawful if the jury had not been sworn, and that by a third party. K.B. McFarlane, *The Nobility of Later Medieval England* (Oxford, 1973), pp. 116–17.

[23] Seipp has discussed communicating with jurors. "Jurors and Evidences and the Tempest of 1449," pp. 80–85. In that connection, he said, "Before trial they were fair game for all sorts of communications of evidence and arguments by the parties and their counsel." Ibid., p. 82. The Year Book discussions do not identify the timing of the laboring.

[24] *Horne's Case*, Y.B. Hil., 34 Hen. VI, fol. 25, pl. 3 (1456), Seipp No. 1456.003 (Prysot CJCP); *John Doke's Case*, Y.B. Hil., 32 Hen. VI, fol. 24, pl. 11 (1454), Seipp No. 1454.011 (Prysot CJCP).

money to a third party to do so was also maintenance.[25] In that case, they stated their views on the limits of permissible conduct regarding jurors:

> And then the opinion of Paston, Newton and all the others was that it was a maintenance: for the record is, that he gave W.E. 40s of his own goods to labor the jury to say their verdict for the said side of the said M and it was not lawful for the abbot to do so, nor for any other: for although it is lawful for one who has [cause] to intermeddle with the matter to show evidence to the inquest, to ask them to say their verdict; nevertheless it is not lawful to labor the inquest to say their verdict for one party specially, although the truth be on that side.[26]

Other justices seem to go further, saying it was maintenance simply to labor them to say the truth.[27] Contemporary commentators also asserted that laboring the jury was illegal.[28] But the justices distinguished illegal laboring of a jury from informing the jury at its request. Fortescue CJKB said that

> if the jurors come to a man where he lives in the country to have knowledge of the truth of the matter, and he informs them, it is justifiable: but if he comes to the jurors or labors to inform them of the truth, it is maintenance and he will be punished ... And this was admitted by the Court.[29]

---

[25] *Pomeroy v. Abbot of Buckfast*, Y.B. Mich., 22 Hen. VI, fol. 5, pl. 7 (1443), Seipp No. 1443.066; Y.B. Mich., 21 Hen. VI, fol. 15, pl. 30 (1442), Seipp No. 1442.126; TNA: PRO CP 40/729, m. 301 (East. 1443), AALT Img. No. 594. The jury found that the abbot had engaged in unlawful maintenance. Another case noted that the abbot obtained a writ of error, but that the verdict for the plaintiff was affirmed. *Horne's Case*, Y.B. Hil. 34 Hen. VI, fol. 25, pl. 3 (1456), Seipp No. 1456.003.

[26] "Et puis l'opinion de Paston et Newton, et touts les autres fuit que ceo fuit un maintenaunce: car le record est, quod dedit W.E. xl s. de bonis suis propriis ad laborandum juratoribus pro verdicto suo dicendo pro parte dicti M et ceo ne fuit loial affaire pur le dit abbe, ne pur nul autre: car tout soit que il est loial a celuy que ad [cause] a mesler ove le matter pur monstre evidence al'enquest, et eux enquere adire lour verdit; uncore il n'est loyal a luy de laborer l'enquest adire lour verdit pur l'un party specialment, tout soit le veritie de cele party." *Pomeroy v. Abbot of Buckfast*, Y.B. Mich., 22 Hen. VI, fol. 5, pl. 7 (1443), Seipp No. 1443.066 (motion in arrest of judgment) (tr.).

[27] Y.B. Mich., 20 Hen. VII, fol. 11, pl. 21 (1504), Seipp No. 1504.021 (Rede JKB). But it was lawful for an attorney or other person learned in law and of counsel to ask the jurors to appear on the day to say the truth. *Horne's Case*, Hil., 34 Hen. VI, fol. 25, pl. 3 (1456), Seipp No. 1456.003 (Serjeant Choke).

[28] Fitzherbert and Coke both treated such laboring of the jury as illegal. Fitzherbert, *New Natura Brevium*, p. 396; *Coke on Littleton*, fol. 369. Seipp has asserted the same view. Seipp, "Jurors and Evidences and the Tempest of 1449," pp. 80–85. Hawkins treated laboring the jury as a form of embracery. Hawkins, *Pleas of the Crown*, Book II, c. 83, p. 249.

[29] "Et si les jurors venent a un home ou il demurre en le pais pur aver le conusance del' verite del' matter, et il eux enforme, il est justifiable: mes si vient a les jurors ou laboure a eux

Similarly, Rede JKB said that laboring the jury was maintenance, "but if the jury comes into my house to be informed of the truth and I inform them, this is not maintenance, inasmuch as I do not labor them."[30]

Abuse of Process

Some actions suggested that initiating legal proceedings could be illegal maintenance if it involved the abuse of legal processes. In *Pomeroy v. Abbot of Buckfast*, Newton CJCP said that "if someone labors to indict me, by force of which I am indicted, I will have a writ of maintenance against him, and yet that is not a suit, but the reason is in my view, it is the king's action between him and the party."[31] In *Radford v. Speke*, Radford, the maintenance plaintiff, alleged abusive procuring as maintenance. He said that Speke had procured Thomas Courtenay, the earl of Devon, to assist and support Radford's adversaries in the principal action. He also accused Speke of procuring a goldsmith fraudulently to counterfeit a signet for use in sealing a false charter of enfeoffment.[32] Instigating other kinds of legal proceedings such as inquisitions may raise similar issues. To the extent that the inquisitions resulted from third-party pressure, that might also be

---

enformer del' verite, il est maintenaunce, et sera puny pur cest, come Fortescue *disoit. Et ceo fuit admis par le Court."* Doreward v. Ferthyng, Y.B. East., 28 Hen. VI, fol. 6, pl. 1 (1450), Seipp No. 1450.002; TNA: PRO KB 27/750, m. 31d, AALT Img. No. 406 (tr.).

[30] "*Et en maintenance il dira quel fuit jure adire la verite: mes s'il labeure le jure adire la verite, c'est maintenance. Mes si le jure vient en ma meason d'estre informe de la verite, et jeo eux informe, ceo n'est maintenance, entant que je ne labeure eux.*" Y.B. Mich., 20 Hen. VII, fol. 11, pl. 21 (1504), Seipp No. 1504.021 (tr.).

[31] He continued that "the statute is general, that it does not lie to anyone to maintain in any quarrel or action between him and the party." Paston JCP apparently did not agree. "*Nota, que Newton tient pur opinion; si un fait un labour a moy endite, par force de quel jeo suis endite, jeo averay brefe de maintenaunce envers luy, et uncore ceo n'est nul querele, mes le case est a ma entent, c'est l'accion le Roy perenter luy et le party, et le statut est general, que ne list a ascun de maintenir en ascun quarel ou accion perenter luy et le party. Paston tient le contrary.* " Pomeroy v. Abbot of Buckfast, Mich., 22 Hen. VI, fol. 6, pl. 7 (1443), Seipp No. 1443.066 (motion in arrest of judgment). Writs of conspiracy were also used against those who procured indictments. Conington v. Eglister, Y.B. Mich., 8 Hen. IV, fol. 6, pl. 8 (1406), Seipp No. 1406.107.

[32] Speke alleged that he had been retained as counsel in the principal conspiracy action. In responding to Radford's allegations, he claimed that it was all part of an agreed mediation of a dispute between Radford and him. The parties put themselves on the jury. Radford v. Speke, TNA: PRO CP 40/714, m. 320 (1439) (reprinted in Hannes Kleineke, "The Chancery Case between Nicholas Radford and Thomas Tremayne: The Exeter Depositions of 1439," Devon and Cornwall Record Society 55 (Exeter 2013) New Series, pp. 56–62) (not in AALT).

illegal maintenance by reasoning analogous to Newton's arguments regarding procuring an indictment. However, the findings of fact in such an inquisition were not binding in other proceedings and were more easily reversed, suggesting perhaps a contrary conclusion.[33] In addition to violating the statute prohibiting maintenance, all of these types of conduct frequently violated some other statute as well.[34]

Payment of Money

Commentators over the years have asserted that the payment of money to support a litigant was illegal maintenance.[35] Plaintiffs' lawyers often took that position.[36] Some justices made similar statements. Bryan CJCP said a companion could help a party identify the best man of law, but his delivery of money to pay for counsel was maintenance.[37] Although the payment of money for a share of the recovery was champerty,[38] the

---

[33] Gratitude is expressed to Prof. Paul Brand for pointing this out to me. Nevertheless, the return of some of these types of inquisitions may have violated a 1429 statute enacted to guard against abusive escheators. 8 Hen. VI, c. 16 (1429), *Statutes of the Realm*, vol. II, pp. 252–53.

[34] In another action, the plaintiff alleged that the defendant's illegal maintenance was contriving, fabricating, and delivering to defendants' counsel a waiver in the plaintiff's name to release the defendants in a debt action brought against them by the plaintiff. *William v. Nicoll*, TNA: PRO KB 27/756, m. 22, (1450), AALT Img. No. 46.

[35] Edward Coke, *The Second Part of the Institutes of the Law of England*, 2 vols. (London, 1642, 1797; reprint, Buffalo, 1986), vol. I, p. 212; John Rastell, *Les Termes del Ley* (London, 1636), p. 433; William Blackstone, *Commentaries on the Law of England*, 4 vols. (Oxford, 1765–1769; Chicago, 1979, facsimile of the 1st edition), vol. 4, p. 134; Henry John Stephen, *New Commentaries on the Laws of England*, 21st ed., 4 vols. (1841–45; London, 1950), vol. IV, p. 154; Percy H. Winfield, *The Present Law of Abuse of Legal Procedure* (Cambridge, 1921), p. 19; *Black's Law Dictionary*, 6th ed. (St. Paul, 1990), 954; John Langbein, Rene Leetow Lerner, and Bruce Smith, *History of the Common Law* (New York, 2009), p. 1053, citing *Slywright v. Page*, 1 Leonard 166, 167, 74 Eng. Reps. 153, 154 (C.P. 1589).

[36] *Pomeroy v. Abbot of Buckfast*, Y.B. Mich., 21 Hen. VI, fol. 15, pl. 30 (1443), Seipp No. 1442.126; TNA: PRO CP 40/729, m. 301, AALT Img. No. 594 (Serjeant Markham); *Clement v. Mader*, Y.B. Trin., 28 Hen. VI, fol. 7, pl. 1 (1450), Seipp Nos. 1450.011, 1450.038; TNA: PRO CP 40/756, m. 104, AALT Img. No. 209 (Serjeant Pole).

[37] He said, "*Si un del company de Lumbards veigne icy a London, et un de son company ala ove luy a un home sachant del ley, et il dit a luy que de eux est melior, etc. cest ne poit estre dit ascun maintenaunce, mes s'il delivera ascun argent pur son compaignon al dit home del ley, etc. adonques cest serra dit maintenaunce.*" Y.B. Mich., 19 Edw. IV, fol. 3, pl. 9 (1479), Seipp No. 1479.038.

[38] In one action, the defendant alleged that the plaintiff in a debt action was an alien born in Burgundy, who did not know how to speak English or Latin, and he requested that the defendant, who could speak his language, bring him to a man knowledgeable in law. He further alleged that the dept plaintiff promised to pay him for his assistance if the party

assertion that all such payments were illegal maintenance was likely overbroad. An examination of the actions demonstrates that a judicial consensus regarding the legality of the payment of money on behalf of a litigant did not exist.[39] Various judges took different positions. But not all aspects of the law regarding this matter were unclear. Illegality required that the payment be made after an action had been initiated, so money paid beforehand was not maintenance.[40] But in those actions where the action had been instituted, it was not always clear whether the defendant had paid his own money to assist the party. Moreover, even if he had, the legality of the payment of money could depend on the relationship between the maintenance defendant and the party in the principal action as well as on other circumstances.

Whose Money Was Paid?

Although there were some instances where a plaintiff alleged that the defendant had paid litigation expenses such as clerical fees[41] or paying the sheriff to arrest the plaintiff,[42] the most common situation in which this issue arose was in those actions in which the plaintiff replied that the defendant had paid for the party's counsel with his own money. In some of these actions, the defendant denied that allegation.[43] But more often,

---

recovered. The court held that the covenant was lawful, as it gave the defendant a legitimate interest in the debt, which was the subject of the principal action. Y.B. Hil., 15 Hen. VII, fol. 2, pl. 3 (1500), Seipp No. 1500.003.

[39] About fifty plea roll actions and Year Book cases that involved the payment of money by a maintenance defendant were identified.

[40] In an action where the plaintiff alleged that a master had procured his servant to sue an appeal against the maintenance plaintiff and gave him 4 marks to aid him in his costs, Martin JCP said that the plaintiff must allege that the money was given after the writ was sued because otherwise no plea was pending. *Hull v. Daucombe*, Y.B. Trin., 3 Hen. VI, fol. 53, pl. 24 (1425), Seipp No. 1425.086.

[41] *Hathewyk v. Peytowe*, TNA: PRO KB 27/762, m. 35 (1451), AALT Img. No. 75 (knight paid for valet's *corpus cum causa* writ); *Welford v. Gloucestre*, TNA: PRO KB 27/817, m. 100 (1465), AALT Img. No. 222 (lawyer paid Exchequer clerk for entry of client's plea).

[42] *Abson v. Darlyngton*, TNA: PRO KB 27/787, m. 76 (1458), AALT Img. No. 164 (defendant paid serjeants at mace to arrest plaintiff sued in trespass in London's sheriff's court); Y.B. Mich., 12 Edw. IV, fol. 14, pl. 15 (1472), Seipp No. 1472.053 (defendant paid undersheriff to arrest plaintiff).

[43] *Dent v. Magot*, TNA: PRO KB 27/818, m. 76 (1465), AALT Img. No. 173; *Chadirton v. Senester*, TNA: PRO KB 27/821, m. 88d (1466), AALT Img. No. 469; *Leukenor v. Alfray*, TNA: PRO KB 27/826, m. 118 (1467), AALT Img. No. 271; *Beauchamp v. Monyngton*, TNA: PRO KB 27/833, m. 113 (1469), AALT Img. No. 295; *Dynham v. Gylbert*, TNA: PRO CP 40/866, m. 158 (1478), AALT Img. No. 300.

the defendant provided a detailed explanation of why the money paid was not his own money. For example, one defendant alleged that he owed the plaintiff in a conspiracy action £8 for the purchase of sheep and that the plaintiff as his creditor requested him to deliver the money in the plaintiff's name to his counsel for distribution by the latter to other lawyers representing the creditor in the conspiracy action.[44] In several other actions, defendants alleged similarly that they had delivered money, which they owed the party in the principal action, to his lawyers, as he requested.[45] Defendants also alleged that they delivered money that they held as a receiver or factor of the party in the principal action to the latter or his lawyer, as the party requested.[46] Two defendants alleged that the delivery of money involved fulfilling their duties as testamentary executors.[47] In several actions, defendants alleged that they delivered money of their masters or clients, as instructed by them.[48] In two actions, the defendants

---

[44] The plaintiff replied that the defendant paid 20s of his own money in addition to the £8. *Grove v. Okeborn*, TNA: PRO KB 27/754, m. 106 (1449), AALT Img. No. 216.

[45] In another action, the defendant-lessee alleged that he was requested by his lessor, a trespass defendant, to pay rent arrears to the latter's attorney. *Rex v. Custe*, TNA: PRO KB 27/738, m. 28d rex (1445), AALT Img. No. 762. Further, a defendant alleged that a trespass defendant, who owed him 6s 8d for the purchase of a gold ring and twelve elm boards, requested that he pay the money in the party's name to his attorney or the attorney's servant. *Golding v. Clerk*, TNA: PRO KB 27/845, m. 36 (1472), AALT Img. No. 94. A knight sued for maintenance alleged that he paid 2s 6d to a chancery clerk for his valet's writ of *corpus cum causa* from the 6s 8d that he owed his valet for a portion of his annual salary. *Hathewyk v. Peytowe*, TNA: PRO KB 27/762, m. 35 (1451), AALT Img. No. 75.

[46] In *Broke v. Delamare*, the defendant alleged that he was the receiver of the defendant in a debt action and had delivered money that he had received from the debtor's lessee to the debtor's apprentice for counsel, as he requested. *Brook v. Felyce*, TNA: PRO KB 27/789, m. 57d (1458), AALT Img. No. 154. In another action, the defendant alleged that he was the factor for foreign merchants and paid some of the money collected on their behalf to their counsel, as they requested. *Crowe v. Foken*, TNA: PRO KB 27/778, m. 99 (1455), AALT Img. No. 191.

[47] In one action, the defendant said he was executing a gift as provided in the testator's will by delivering money from the sale of land to the donee. The plaintiff demurred, and the court said it wished to be advised further. *Becket v. Greth*, TNA: PRO KB 27/737, m. 69 (1445), AALT Img. No. 14. In another action, the defendant, one of the executors who had custody of the testator's chest, delivered a portion of the money contained in the chest to counsel, retained in a trespass action against a man who tried to steal the chest and its contents, on behalf of one of the other executors, to whom the custodial executor had promised the money. *Hethman v. Dreff*, TNA: PRO KB 27/747, m. 88 (Hil. 1448), AALT Img. No. 184.

[48] In one action, the defendant, a draper, alleged that Richard, earl of Salisbury, and others retained him for 6s 8d, had given him security of 20d, and instructed him to deliver it to their counsel. *Matany v. Edolf*, TNA: PRO KB 27/718, m. 85d (Mich. 1440), AALT Img.

acknowledged paying or giving their own property to counsel, but alleged it was their own counsel and not that of the party.[49] Some of these actions regarding the payment of money could be rather complicated and involve multiple transactions and the use of bonds as well as money for payment of counsel and other litigation expenses.[50]

If defendants' allegations in these maintenance actions were true, which the plaintiffs often denied, it would seem that the allegations should have constituted successful defenses. In principle, if the money delivered to the party was owed to him by the defendant, it belonged legally to the former and not the latter. As will be discussed below in the master–servant actions, the justices said it was permissible for a master to pay for a servant's counsel with money owed to the servant.[51] In addition, if a person instructed another person to deliver that person's money to another person, it was permissible to do so. Prysot CJCP said that "for it is no kind of cause for maintenance, for it is lawful for any

No. 542. In two actions, defendants, who were attorneys, alleged that they had delivered their client's money to the client's counsel, as he requested. *Heron v. Couper*, TNA: PRO CP 40/784, m. 380 (1457), AALT Img. No. 747; Y.B., 36 Hen. VI, fol. 27, pl. 28, (1457–58), Seipp No. 1458.028.

[49] In one action, the defendant alleged that she helped her tenant find counsel, whom tenant paid 40s and that she paid the same lawyer 40s to represent her in the maintenance action. *Briggeman v. Waldern*, TNA: PRO KB 27/817, m. 78d (1465), AALT Img. No. 492. In another action, the defendant alleged that he helped his tenant find and retain counsel. He denied paying counsel with his own money, but alleged that he retained two men learned in the law, one of whom was the tenant's counsel, to counsel him in the maintenance action, and they gave him counsel at his house, where he gave them food and drink, during their discussion of the matter. *Jenney v. Selot*, TNA: PRO KB 27/793, m. 103 (1459), AALT Img. No. 263.

[50] In *Serle v. Songer*, the defendant, counsel for an abbot in a debt action, alleged he counseled the abbot to deliver a bond, on which the debt action was based, to his attorney for representation in the debt action. In response, the plaintiff said that the defendant gave 13s 4d to the abbot for suing the action. The defendant responded that the bond was made the benefit of a third party, who earlier delivered 13s 4d to the defendant for delivery to the abbot for the prosecution of the action, which the defendant did. *Serle v. Songer*, TNA: PRO KB 27/861 m. 28 (1476), AALT Img. No. 65 (tr.). In *Flemmyng v. Thelwall*, the baron of Slane alleged that the defendant, a clerk, had maintained the plaintiffs in a debt action on a bond of 100 marks, which they brought against the baron. In justification, the clerk asserted that the baron delivered the bond to the debt plaintiffs for the use of the clerk, who paid 6s 8d of it to an expert in law to be counsel to the debt plaintiffs in their action against the baron. The baron demurred and the court said it was not yet advised in how to rule on the matter. TNA: PRO KB 27/778, m. 98 (1455), AALT Img. No. 190.

[51] Baker stated that the payment of money owed was not maintenance. He cited *John Doke's Case* (Y.B., Hil., 32 Hen. VI, fol. 24, pl. 11 (1454), Seipp No. 1454.011), as analogous authority. Baker, *Legal Profession and the Common Law* (London, 1986), p. 135, n. 49.

man to bring money to any man of law, or to another man as a messenger."[52]

Payments by Masters for Servants

Masters were often accused of maintenance in retaining and paying for counsel for their servants.[53] Whether the master could pay for the servant's counsel prompted substantial discussion among the justices.[54] The relationship that justified intermeddling in the first place might also permit the payment of the master's own money. The resolution of this issue was not clear. At least three different views appeared in the Year Book cases.

One view was that the payment by the master of his own money was permitted as an aspect of his right to support his servant. In *Pomeroy v. Abbot of Buckfast*, Newton CJCP and Paston JCP expressed this view and identified numerous means of legitimate support. They said:

> For it is lawful for a master to maintain his servant, as by being with him at the bar and standing there with him and giving him counsel, and by bringing his own counsel with him to give counsel to his servant and, just as it is lawful for him to counsel his servant and bring his own counsel to counsel his servant, so too he can give his own money to an apprentice to give him counsel. For it is lawful for the apprentice to take [money] for his counsel. It is otherwise where the master give any money for his servant to [give] to a juror to give his verdict because it is not lawful in that case for the juror to accept it. And even though his counsel and he himself pays on behalf of the servant his fees to the court in discharge of the servant for his

---

[52] He said, "*Car il est loyal a chescun home de porter monoie a chescun home de ley, ou a un auter home par voye de message.*" *Horne's Case*, Hil., 34 Hen. VI, fol. 25, pl. 3 (1456), Seipp No. 1456.003.

[53] *Stok v. Dogge*, TNA: PRO KB 27/673, m. 75d (1429), AALT Img. No. 534; *Bonde v. Kirkeby*, TNA: PRO KB 27/741, m. 83 (1446), AALT Img. No. 167; *Dee v. Dene*, TNA: PRO KB 27/748, m. 39 (1448), AALT Img. No. 82; *Jenney v. Selot*, TNA: PRO KB 27/793, m. 103 (1459), AALT Img. No. 263; *Jenney v. Selot*, TNA: PRO KB 27/793, m. 105d (1459), AALT Img. No. 683; *Alfray v. Leukenour*, TNA: PRO KB 27/826, m. 111 (1467), AALT Img. No. 271. Actions were not limited to retaining counsel, but also involved a master paying a servant's litigation expenses. *Hathewyk v. Peytowe*, TNA: PRO KB 27/762, m. 35 (1451), AALT Img. No. 75 (knight paid for valet's *corpus cum causa* writ).

[54] There were also actions against servants for paying a master's counsel with their own money. *Horton v. Blackhorn*, TNA: PRO CP 40/780, m. 316 (1456), AALT Img. No. 624; *Crowe v. Foken*, TNA: PRO KB 27/778, m. 99 (1455), AALT Img. No. 191; *Heron v. Couper*, TNA: PRO CP 40/784, m. 380 (1457), AALT Img. No. 747; Y.B., 36 Hen. VI, fol. 27, pl. 28 (1457–58), Seipp No. 1458.028.

counsel and he himself pay it for the servant to the advantage of his servant or otherwise give or loan his servant money to maintain and aid him in the suit in all these cases it will not be said to be any maintenance in his person.[55]

Even Prysot CJCP, whose views on maintenance were strict, endorsed this view.[56] A variant on this view limited the legitimacy of the master's payment of money to those cases in which the action against the servant could result in his imprisonment and cause the loss of the servant's services. Fineux CJ endorsed this view, saying, "I may maintain my servant, and expend my own money to aid him, and this is for the loss of his services." He distinguished between a debt action against the servant, where paying money was permissible as the services would be lost, and *praecipe quod reddat* for land, where payment was not lawful because no loss of services was threatened.[57]

Another view was diametrically the opposite. Those taking that view said that it was illegal maintenance for the defendant to pay his own money, as it exceeded the bounds of legitimate support.[58] This was the

---

[55] "*Car il est loial [al'] mastre de maintenir le servant , come d'estre ove luy al' barre, et la estoir ove luy , et doner a luy counsel; et port son counsel demense ove luy a doner counsel a son servant; et si bien come il est loyal a luy pur counseller son servant et porter son counsel demense, ou counseller son servant, si bien poit il doner son propre argent a un apprentice pur doner a luy son counsel. Car il est loial al'apprentice de prendre pur son counselle. Auter est ou le mastre dona ascun argent pur son servant [doner] a un juror a dire son verdit: car en cele n'est loial al juror a prendre. Et tout soit que son counsel, et eux luy mesme paiere pur le servant lez fees al' court, ou discharge le servant de son counsel, et eux luy mesme paer pur le servant en l'advantage de son servant, ou autrerment doner ou aprester son servant argent pur luy maintenir et aid en le suit; en toutz ceux cases il ne sera dit en son person ascun maintenaunce.*" Pomeroy v. Abbot of Buckfast, Y.B., Mich., 21 Hen. VI, fol. 15, pl. 30 (1443), Seipp No. 1442.126; TNA: PRO CP 40/729, m. 301, AALT Img. No. 594 (tr.). Lawyers in later cases referred to this case in support of this view. Clement v. Mader, Y.B. Trin., 28 Hen. VI, fol. 12, pl. 28 (1450), Seipp No. 1450.038; TNA: PRO CP 40/756, m. 104, AALT Img. No. 209.

[56] He said, "*Et Sir, jeo di que l'ou jeo purrai jusitifier pur mon servant, jeo purrai doner a ses homes erudites en le ley deniers estre de son consele, auxibien come eux prier estre de son consele: mes uncore jeo ne purrai doner mes deniers a jurors pur lour verdit dire pur sa part ne auter home nient apris de le ley pur maintenir sa part.*" Clement v. Mader, Y.B. Trin., 28 Hen. VI, fol. 12, pl. 28 (1450), Seipp No. 1450.038, CP 40/756, m. 104 (Hil. 1450), AALT Img. No. 209.

[57] "*Jeo puis maintaine mon servant, et expend de mes propres deniers pur luy aider, et cest pur le perde de ses services.*" Y.B. Mich., 21 Hen. VII, fol. 40, pl. 62 (1505), Seipp No. 1505.062. Later actions drew this same distinction. Stone v. Walters, Moore 813, 72 Eng. Rep. 923 (Mich. 1610).

[58] Fitzherbert, La Grande Abridgement, Issue 83, fol. 40 (Trin., 29 Hen. VI 1451), Seipp No. 1451.013abr; Y.B. East., 28 Hen. VI, fol. 7, pl. 1 (1450), Seipp No. 1450.11 (Serjeant

view of Bryan CJCP.[59] One lawyer explained that although a master could intermeddle for his servant, he could not pay his own money, as the servant's loss was not his loss.[60] In a 1452 action, Fortescue CJ concluded it was maintenance for a master to pay for his servant's counsel, as it strengthened the servant's likelihood of prevailing in the action to the disadvantage of his opponent. He said:

> It needs to be seen whether a master can give his money to the counsel of his servant, whether it be lawful or not: and Sir, I say that [it is] not. For a man cannot do more for his servant in such a case than ask such a justice that the servant's matter can hastily be speeded, as the law wishes, for the deliverance of his servant, and likewise he can ask a man of law to be of counsel with his servant as the law wills, for the deliverance of his servant. For if he loses the service of his servant, he has his remedy against the servant; also he need not pay his salary if he withdraws his service. Thus the master can save himself harmless. And to prove the delivery of the money is maintenance; I will prove it. For by the money the servant's matter can be strengthened on his side, so it may be presumed that the other party is delayed for a longer time in his suit or barred where recovery was against him, therefore it is illegal maintenance.[61]

Moile); *Clement v. Mader*, Y.B. Mich., 31 Hen. VI, fol. 8, pl. 1 (1452), Seipp No. 1452.020 (Fortescue CJKB and Serjeant Moile) (writ of error); TNA: PRO KB 27/761, m. 24, AALT Img. Nos. 50–53, 226–28; Y.B. Hil., 32 Hen. VI, fol. 24, pl. 11 (1454), Seipp No. 1454.011 (Serjeant Wangford).

[59] He said, "*Si un del company de Lumbards veigne icy a London, et un de son company ala ove luy a un home sachant del ley, et il dit a luy que de eux est melior, cest ne poit estre dit ascun maintenaunce, mes s'il delivera ascun argent pur son compaignon al dit home del ley, adonques cest serra dit maintenaunce.*" Y.B. Mich., 19 Edw. IV, fol. 3, pl. 9 (1479), Seipp No. 1479.038.

[60] "*Issint il dit que le maister poit mesler pur le servan. et via versa, le servant pur son maister. Mes nul de eux poit doner argent, ne auter doner pur l'auter de ses biens: car le perte le maister n'est le perte le servant; nec converso, etc.*" Y.B. Hil., 32 Hen. VI, fol. 24, pl. 11 (1454), Seipp No. 1454.011 (Serjeant Wangford).

[61] "*Il est a voir le quel le maistre purroit doner deniers al' consel son servant, soit loyal ou nemy: et Sir jeo di que non: car home ne point plus faire pur son servant en tiel cas que prier un tiel justice, que le matter son servant poit hastivement estre spede, come la ley veut. Et issint poit prier un home de ley estre a consell ove son servant come le ley veut, pur le deliverance de son servant: car s'il perd le service de son servant, il ad son remedy vers le servant, et auxi il ne covient de paier son salary, s'il sustreit son service, et issint le maistre luy poit garder sans damage. Et de prover que le deliverance des deniers est maintenance, jeo proveray: car per les deniers le matter pur le servant poit estre enforce de sa party; issint que il poit entendre l'auter party est per le plus long temps delay en sa suit, ou barre, ou recovery ew envers luy per ceo, adonques il est maintenance, nient congeable, etc.*" Y.B. Mich., 31 Hen. VI, fol. 8, pl. 1 (1452), Seipp No. 1452.020; TNA: PRO KB 27/761, m. 24, Img. Nos. 50–53, 226–28 (writ of error) (tr.).

But Fortescue's rationale, strengthening one party that causes disadvantage to the other party, is different from and inconsistent with the justifications asserted by other justices. It is also puzzling because, on that theory, any support would seem to be maintenance.

A third view took a middle position, asserting that sometimes the master could pay his own money. Several actions took this view and said that payment of money by the master was not illegal if it were made from the wages that the master owed the servant.[62] Fortescue's discussion of the availability of a remedy for the master who lost the service of his servant by withholding his salary may indicate that he was actually espousing this view.[63] In sum, many of the justices supported at least a limited right for masters to spend their own money to support a servant's litigation. The leading case, *Pomeroy v. Abbot of Buckfast*, supported the right to do so. Several cases viewed the expenditure as lawful when the nature of the action would cause the loss of the servant's services or when the payment was from wages owed the servant. A few justices supported a total prohibition of such expenditures, although plaintiffs' lawyers voiced that view.

Other Justifications for Payment of Money

This issue also arose outside the master–servant context in cases in which the maintenance defendant had another type of relationship with the party in the principal action. For example, several justices opined that a feoffor could pay for counsel for his feoffee and perhaps the feoffee for the feoffor as well.[64] Moreover, in some actions feoffors sued in the name of their feoffees.[65] Prysot CJCP said that it was legal for them to do so and at their own cost.[66] These cases may suggest that paying for counsel

---

[62] *Horne's Case*, Hil., 34 Hen. VI, fol. 25, pl. 3 (1456), Seipp No. 1456.003 (Serjeants Choke and Laken); Y.B. Mich., 19 Edw. IV, fol. 3, pl. 9 (1479), Seipp No. 1479.038. Later actions also endorsed this position. *Petson v. Penygton et Hagas* 15 Hen. VIII (Trin. 1523); J.H. Baker, ed., *The Reports of Sir John Spelman*, 2 parts (London, 1976), part I, 93 Selden Soc., p. 163; *Roos v. Hurleston*, TNA: PRO CP 40/1042, m. 446 (1524); Anon., Moore 6, 72 Eng. Rep. 401 (Mich. 1549); *Saukell's Case*, Hetley 78, 124 Eng. Rep. 357 (Hil. 1628).

[63] Hawkins cited this speech for that proposition. Hawkins, *Pleas of the Crown*, Book I, c. 83, sec. 23, p. 253.

[64] Y.B. Mich., 35 Hen. VI, fol. 15, pl. 25 (1456), Seipp No. 1456.079 (Moile JCP); Y.B. Hil., 15 Hen. VII, fol. 2, pl. 3 (1500), Seipp No. 1500.003.

[65] *Wyndsore v. Frome*, TNA: PRO KB 27/848, m. 51 (1473), AALT Img. No. 110.

[66] He said, "*Come si un soit oblige a un auter a mon use et j'ay l'obligation, est loial pur moy a mesler et a suir cest suite a mon cost demesne, et en le nom de l'auter. Issint est si ascun*

may have been lawful whenever the defendant had a legitimate interest in the principal action.

Some justices thought that the legitimacy of paying for counsel was not limited to such cases and that it was also lawful to pay for counsel for kin in certain situations. Ayscough JCP said a son could pay for counsel for his father, whose heir he would be.[67] As the heir apparent, it might be argued that the son had the kind of interest in the subject matter of the litigation that permitted such intermeddling.[68] Moile JCP stated further that a father could do so for his son or any heir apparent, but not for other relatives.[69] But, as in the servant cases, some justices disagreed. Choke JCP said one could intermeddle for his brother or kinsmen, but that giving money would be illegal maintenance.[70] Further, there were other situations in which paying one's own money for another's counsel might be

---

soit enfeoffe de terre a mon use, est loial pur moy a suir ascun maner suite que touche cest terre, en le nom des feoffees, ou s'ils soient empledes a mesler." Horne v. Forster, Y.B. Hil., 34 Hen. VI, fol. 30, pl. 15 (1456), Seipp No. 1456.016; TNA: PRO CP 40/780, m. 124, AALT Img. No. 250.

[67] He said, "Si mon pere, que heir je suis, soit emplede de son terre, et jeo dona argent a sage counsel pur counseller mon pere en le suit, ceo est nul maintenance, et uncore il est estranger al' suit." Pomeroy v. Abbot of Buckfast, Y.B. Mich., 21 Hen. VI, fol. 15, pl. 30 (1443), Seipp No. 1442.126; TNA: PRO CP 40/729, m. 301 (1443), AALT Img. No. 594.

[68] Serjeant Markham replied to Ascough JCP arguing that the son, as the heir apparent, could pay for his father's counsel because he would have an interest and right in the land. He said that "en vostre case il est voier pur le interresse et le droit que le fits en le terre eit, etc." But Ascough disagreed because the son was only an heir apparent. He asserted that "le fitz eit nul droit n'interesse en le terre vivant le pere." Pomeroy v. Abbot of Buckfast, Y.B. Mich., 21 Hen. VI, fol. 15, pl. 30 (1443), Seipp No. 1442.126; TNA: PRO CP 40/729, m. 301, AALT Img. No. 594.

[69] He based his argument on the father's obligation to find necessaries for the son or the heir apparent. He said, "Et ils dient que le pere poit doner monnoie de ses propres costs pur son fitz ou heire apparent pur ceo que il est oblige de trover luy, et de cest il poit justifier, mes d'autre cosin nemy." Horne's Case, Y.B. Hil., 34 Hen. VI, fol. 25, pl. 3 (1456), Seipp No. 1456.003. Earlier in the opinion, Moile, in noting the right of the father to intermeddle for his son and vice versa, seemed to imply the opposite when contrasting the broader right of the master to maintain the servant. He said, "jeo ne suis oblige de trover mon fitz manger et boyer, ne auters de sez necessaries mes a mon volunte demesne: issint est de chescun cosin. Mes le maistre est oblige pur vray droit de trover son servant ses necessaries, ou auterment il fait tort a luy; purque il point aver bref de convenant envers luy, s'il avoit endentures de covenants." Ibid.

[70] "Car home poet en tiel manner medler pur son frere ou cosin, mes s'il done ascun argent, donque est especial maintenance." Y.B. Mich. 9 Edw. IV, fol. 31, pl. 4 (1469), Seipp No.1469.093. A note in an earlier case took the same position: "Nota si mon cosin que per possibilitie puit este heire a moy done de ces deniers propries a home appriser en ley d'estre mon conceil ou money a un d'este mon attorney cest maintenance agarde per bon avise." Fitzherbert, Le Grande Abridgement, Maintenaunce, 12, fol. 64 (Trin., 29 Hen. VI, 1451),

permissible. For example, Prysot CJCP noted that it was not maintenance for an attorney to give his own money to his client's counsel.[71]

Another situation that prompted discussion was whether one could pay for a poor man's counsel. Several justices thought it was permissible as an act of charity. In *Pomeroy v. Abbot of Buckfast,* Paston JCP said it was not maintenance to do so.[72] Martin JCP said, as with maintaining servants and kin, that poverty gave "cause or colour" to intermeddle. He opined that one can "give gold or silver to a man who is poor to maintain his plea, if he himself cannot because of his poverty; this is not maintenance against the law."[73]

If it was permissible to give money to a poor man to support his litigation, it would seem to follow that loaning money for similar reasons and purposes also was not illegal. Several lawyers, who were sued for maintenance because they gave money to their clients for litigation expenses, argued that the payment was a loan. In one action, two lawyers argued that they loaned their client money to prosecute a writ, as he was constrained by poverty (*paupertate compulsus*) and needed money.[74] Loans by a lawyer to his client raised an interesting issue regarding their

---

Seipp No. 1451.013abr. Plaintiffs also asserted that it was illegal. *Beauchamp v. Monyngton,* TNA: PRO KB 27/833, m. 113 (Trin. 1469), AALT Img. No. 295.

[71] "Nota par Prysot ... et tenus per tout le court que un attorney puit doner de ces deniers propries a un serjant ou apprentice pur son client, et cest nul maintenance." Fitzherbert, *Le Grande Abridgement, Maintenaunce,* 21, fol. 65 (Trin., 35 Hen VI, 1457), Seipp No. 1457.043abr.

[72] He said, "*Mettomus que jeo de mon almes dona un summe dargent a povre home, que ad un suit, pur luy aider en la suit, cest n'est ascun maintenance.*" *Pomeroy v. Abbot of Buckfast,* Y.B. Mich., 21 Hen. VI, fol. 15, pl. 30 (1443), Seipp No. 1442.126; TNA: PRO CP 40/729, m. 301, AALT Img. No. 594. Serjeant Prysot as counsel for a plaintiff also took this position and said that "it was lawful for anyone in the world to do so (*ceo est loial pur chescun d' mounde affaire*)." Y.B. Mich., 22 Hen. VI, fol. 35, pl. 54 (1443), Seipp No. 1443.113.

[73] He said, "*jeo di que jeo puis doner or ou argent a un home que est pauvre pur maintenir son plee, s'il mesme ne puit pur pauvrete, et ceo n'est maintenance encontre ley.*" Y.B. Hil., 9 Hen. VI, fol. 64, pl. 17 (1431), Seipp No. 1431.017.

[74] *Tewe v. Catesby,* TNA: PRO KB 27/750, m. 105 (1448), AALT Img. No. 210. In a 1391 champerty action, an apprentice loaned money to his client, who was also his servant. *Martell v. Sallowe,* TNA: PRO KB 27/522, m. 50 (Mich. 1391), AALT Img. No. 116. *Tewe v. Catesby* is particularly noteworthy, as it provided clear evidence that for a period of time the Exterior Temple was an Inn of Court. J.H. Baker, "Note: The Inn of the Outer Temple," *Law Quarterly Review* 124 (2008), p. 384. Baker noted further that in the case of 1448, a lesser inn was accorded the same status as an "inn of men of court and of counsellors of the law," which was the formula used by lawyers to describe their membership in the inns of court. Baker also noted that this action was the earliest one in which a lawyer pleaded membership of an inn of court. Ibid., pp. 385–86.

legality. That lawyers did so may suggest that they thought it was not improper.[75] On other hand, if a concern about maintenance was that it prompted excessive litigation, then perhaps loans by lawyers to facilitate litigation by their clients should have been treated more harshly than loans by others.[76]

Such loans may have been permissible in certain other situations. In a champerty action, the defendant said that "having been moved by pity and inspired by charity," he loaned his poor villein money to prosecute a writ of *de homine replegiando* against a knight who had claimed and imprisoned him and sued the lord.[77] Newton CJCP and Paston JCP said that a master could loan his servant money to support his litigation.[78] In another case, the court seemed to reject the plaintiff's claim that the defendant's payment for a party's counsel with his own money was illegal. The defendant alleged that the payment was made by the party out of money loaned by the defendant to the party. As result, it was the court's opinion that money was not that of the defendant, even though the party was obligated to repay it.[79] Although there was always a risk that a loan would not be repaid, the defendants in one action alleged that they had loaned the money to the party, who was bound to pay the loan.[80] Thus, making loans to parties for counsel and other litigation expenses might be permissible in some instances, although the authority for this is unclear and sparse.

---

[75] Ibid., p. 386.

[76] The current ethical rules of the United States and the United Kingdom say that loans to clients by lawyers present conflict of interest problems and may be unethical. *Am. Bar Assoc. Model Rules of Professional Conduct*, Rule 1.8 (ed) (1983); *Solicitors Regulation Authority, Code of Conduct* 2011, chap. 3, O (3.2), IB (3.8).

[77] "*Pietate motus, pro eo quod idem Adam pauper fuit, non habens unde sibimet in hac parte auxiliaret, caritatis intuitu accommodavit eidem Ade certam pecunie summam.*" The defendant said that he was the lord of a third part of a manor. The jury asked whether the lord's profit from the covenant would exceed 40s and found that he undertook to maintain in return for a portion of the villein's recovery and was, therefore, guilty of champerty. The defendant obtained a writ of error, which was sent to the King's Bench. *Courtenay v. Bryt*, TNA: PRO CP 40/560, m. 385d (1401), AALT Img. Nos. 1998–99.

[78] *Pomeroy v. Abbot of Buckfast*, Y.B. Mich., 21 Hen. VI, fol. 15, pl. 30 (1443), Seipp No. 1442.126; CP 40/729, m. 301 (East. 1443), AALT Img. No. 594.

[79] "*Et opinio Curiae que ceo n'est my plee, car quant le defendant dona al plaintiff en le primer action, etc. Et donques il delivera les xx. d. a dit J. at S. adonques cest ne fuit my l'argent le defendant nient obstant que il fuit tenus en ley de render les deniers al defendant et issint fuit adjudge, etc.*" Y.B. Mich., 19 Edw. IV, pl. 16, fol. 5 (1494), Seipp No. 1479.045.

[80] *Payn v. Van Bleken*, TNA: PRO KB 27/739, m. 94d (1446), AALT Img. No. 462.

Conclusion

Despite the claims and fears by modern scholars of extensive illegal maintenance, the types of support and assistance that were illegal were quite limited. The conduct that was most clearly illegal maintenance was also often in violation of statutes other than those directed against maintenance. In addition, there was neither a clear prohibition nor a broad license permitting one person to pay his own money for another person's counsel or litigation expenses. The law regarding this conduct was unclear, as the justices were divided on whether it violated the statute prohibiting maintenance. Nevertheless, it was not an uncommon practice and a number of justices found it to be lawful in certain situations. In sum, medieval justices construed the legislation narrowly and took a restricted view of illegal maintenance.

11

Livery

The wearing of a lord's livery was a symbolic way of attesting his man's attachment to him.[1] It had very ancient antecedents.[2] Bean said that it existed before 1200 and was likely a well-known practice in the middle of the twelfth century.[3] Livery had its origins in the household, but extended outside it as well.[4] Saul noted that during the fourteenth century, the nobility made widespread use of images denoting identity to embellish

---

[1] Lords had several ways of formally retaining men, such as a retainer for life, an annuity, or fee for services, all of which required a written document. J.M.W. Bean, *From Lord to Patron* (Manchester, 1989), pp. 10–17, 143–46; Gerald Harriss, *Shaping the Nation: England 1360–1461* (Oxford, 2005), pp. 189–90. McFarlane described the nature of the written indentures and their early use. K.B. McFarlane, "Lords and Retainers," unpublished manuscript in the Magdalen College Archives, University of Oxford, Lecture III, pp. 5–11.

[2] Harriss, *Shaping the Nation*, pp. 189–90. Hicks concurred. Michael Hicks, *Bastard Feudalism* (London, 1995), pp. 63–65. One commentator suggested that livery existed in Anglo-Saxon England and in other civilizations. Frederique Lachaud, "Liveries of Robes in England, c. 1200–c. 1330," *English Historical Review* 111 (1996), p. 281.

[3] He provided several examples. Bean, *From Lord to Patron*, pp. 143–45. He explored its origins and said that because of the lack of records "the beginnings lie shrouded in mystery." Ibid., pp. 143–46. Lachaud argued that the earlier livery was different from that in the late medieval period. In the earlier period, it identified the hierarchy of the household and was "essential for aristocratic image" and establishing the lord's power and dignity. But it lacked the emblematic quality that it had for retainers in the later period. Later, in the thirteenth century, livery increasingly signified the relationship between and lord and his retainers. Like other medieval social realities, it presented "numerous difficulties of interpretation." Lachaud, "Liveries of Robes in England," pp. 280–96.

[4] Bean said the medieval contemporaries' notion of the household was not confined to those persons providing daily necessities to the lord and his family, but was viewed "in a much looser way," consisting of "a group of dependents, which spread outward from the lord's nearest kin." He said that livery "was a visible sign that a man belonged to his lord's affinity ... a means of extending a lord's influence beyond the circles of his household members, the administrative staff of his estates, his indentured retainers and annuitants ... It was a public indication that the recipients enjoyed his support and protections." Thus, there was an incentive for a beneficiary, who hoped for protection and the ability "to impress his neighbors with his powerful connections." Lords were

valued items. But he noted that in a process that "is exceptionally ill charted," they were transformed from decorative use and "embark[ed] on a life of their own."[5]

Robes were a traditional form of livery and may have served as a method of compensation as well.[6] Over time, the types of livery increased to include badges, chaperons, distinctively colored cloth, and wrought metalwork collars.[7] By the end of the fourteenth century, chaperons[8] and badges became a very common form of livery.[9] Bean said that livery was

tempted, as their only cost was that of the cloth. Bean, *From Lord to Patron*, pp. 18–19, 21–22, 145–46.

[5] He suggested that the Lancastrian use of the SS collar in the 1370s and 1380s may have been the turning point. Nigel Saul, "The Commons and the Abolition of Badges," *Parliamentary History* 9 (1990), p. 308. A 1388 Commons' petition said that 1327 was the critical date. L.C. Hector and Barbara Harvey, eds., *The Westminster Chronicle 1381–1394* (Oxford, 1982), p. 457, reprinted in part in "Introduction," Parliaments of Richard II: September 1388, appendix, item 1, *PROME*.

[6] In the fourteenth century, it was common for lords to give their men fees and robes, which indicated that the latter were the lord's men and which were "the outward sign of dependence." G.A. Holmes, *The Estates of the Higher Nobility in Late Medieval England* (Manchester, 1917), p. 59.

[7] Collars were a special type of livery whose use was confined primarily to kings. In the reign of Henry IV, it became the exclusive preserve of kings and was used by successive kings from Henry IV to Henry VIII. The most famous collar was the Lancastrian SS. The Yorkist collar was one of alternating suns and white roses. Its use as a sign of rank and prestige had ancient precedents. The livery collar was a significant symbol of royal power and dignity and reflected the recipients' status. Matthew Ward, "The Livery Collar: Politics and Identity during the Fifteenth Century," in Linda Clark, ed., *The Fifteenth Century XIII: Exploring the Evidence: Commemoration, Administration, and the Economy* (Woodbridge, 2014), pp. 41–61.

[8] "Chaperon" originally meant "hood." In the early fifteenth or late fourteenth century, as fashion changed, it also acquired an alternative meaning. The new form of chaperon consisted of a round headpiece or hat, attached to a long tail (derived from the liripipe of the hood), which was worn over one shoulder so that the headpiece was suspended at the back. This would have been a different color from the gown, sometimes parti-colored, and could thus serve as a distinctive livery. It was still used in early modern times to distinguish members of the London livery companies. See Herbert Druitt, *A Manual of Costume as Illustrated by Monumental Brasses* (London, 1906; 1970 facsimile), pp. 209–10. Gratitude is expressed to Prof. John Baker for explaining this and sharing several sources, including his own unpublished work and hand-drawn images, with me.

[9] These types of livery generally replaced the giving of robes, which was the most expensive form of livery. Bean, *From Lord to Patron*, p. 146. The first badge used was the Swan, which was embroidered on the Bohun's luxury items in the fourteenth century. Badges were cheap and easy to produce quickly, which made them "the favored device of magnates." Saul, "Abolition of Badges," *Parliamentary History* 9 (1990), pp. 307–9. Given-Wilson has described the different types of livery. Chris Given-Wilson, *The Royal Household and the King's Affinity* (New Haven, 1986), pp. 236–37.

"at once the most well known and most amorphous of the links between lord and man in late medieval England."[10] In its legitimate form, it was a "traditional symbol of patriarchal authority … a status symbol which legitimized aspirations of respectability … it gave visible expression to the bond between lord and man" and signified the protection and support of the latter "in all causes and disputes" and the latter's reciprocal loyalty.[11]

Over time the distribution of livery increased as retinues expanded.[12] In the later fourteenth century, livery became a matter of concern.[13] This concern was a function of the association of livery with a powerful person retaining numerous individuals in an affinity or support group and the

---

[10] Bean, *From Lord to Patron*, p. 17. He explored its nature and form and its use in connection with retaining as one source of manpower in times of crisis and civil war. Ibid., pp. 17–22, 174–78.

[11] Saul, "Abolition of Badges," pp. 306–7. Davies said that, by distributing livery, the aristocracy "could manifest visibly its capacity to command dependence, particularly from members of gentle society," and it also was a public measure of a lord's wealth and standing. R.R. Davies, *Lords and Lordship in the British Isles in the Late Middle Ages* (Oxford, 2009), pp. 32–33, 63–66, 111–12, 208. Stubbs viewed it as signifying the vanity and power of great men. He said that the protection they afforded their clients was "sometimes by force of arms, but generally in the courts of law." Moreover, he asserted that "the livery of a great lord was as effective security to a malefactor as was the benefit of clergy to the criminous clerk." William Stubbs, *Constitutional History of England*, 3 vols. (Oxford, 1897; reprint, 1967), vol. III, pp. 549–50, 352.

[12] McFarlane studied the composition of *meinie*, the contemporary word for these groups, and the resulting wearing of livery. He found that retinues were drawn from a wide variety of sources, including knights and near-knightly families, the group below them who became known as gentlemen, and the growing class of literate laymen. He identified three main groups: kinsmen, frequently the poorer ones, tenants by knight service, and neighbors. But membership fluctuated as the benefits of the various lords rose and fell, and waiting lists existed for the more desirable lords. He provided numerous examples. McFarlane, "Lords and Retainers," Lecture I, pp. 2, 4–5; ibid., IV, pp. 1–15. Bellamy said that those men retained and those receiving advice and protection were a larger and less permanent group, which could produce overlaps with neighboring magnates. J.G. Bellamy, *Crime and Public Order in England in the Later Middle Ages* (Toronto, 1973), p. 23.

[13] Given-Wilson, *The King's Affinity*, pp. 236–43; Saul, "Abolition of Badges," pp. 302–15; R.L. Storey, "Liveries and Commissions of the Peace, 1388–90," in F.R.H. Du Boulay and Caroline Barron, *The Reign of Richard II* (London, 1971), pp. 131–52. McFarlane documented several medieval livery rolls to determine the type of livery that retainers wore to clarify the extent of the danger posed by this practice. In his inquiry, he identified those instances in which livery may have been given solely for maintenance as well as its influence on sheriffs, justices of the peace, *oyer et terminer* commissions, and parliamentary elections. McFarlane, "Lords and Retainers," Lectures V–VI, pp. 1–16; K.B. McFarlane, *The Nobility of Later Medieval England* (Oxford, 1973), pp. 102–12.

connection between livery and maintenance.[14] "These symbols of a lord's protection could embolden the wearers to intimidate and oppress with impunity."[15] Griffiths said that livery was "a provocation and incitement to others."[16] Badges became "associated with the twin evils of maintenance and disorder."[17] According to Davies, livery and maintenance were the two terms "in the lexicon of the late medieval period" that became "shorthand for the malaise of aristocratic lordship."[18]

In addition, there was a renewed concern about a related issue, the magnates' retainer of royal justices and giving them fees and robes.[19] Concern about this practice had emerged in the mid-fourteenth century.[20] By the later part of the century, it became a major political issue for the first time, and "the retaining of justices had become part of a much broader dispute over maintenance and retaining in general."[21] "As part of a general parliamentary protest against corrupt and inefficient government,"[22] the Commons petitioned about the retainer of

---

[14] Bean said that "our knowledge of the practice is anchored in the phrase 'livery and maintenance.'" Bean, *From Lord to Patron*, p. 17. Griffiths said that "for those of gentle or noble rank, maintenance took the form of offering livery to men who might engage in crime with or without the knowledge of their lord or maintainer." Ralph Griffiths, *The Reign of King Henry VI* (Stroud, 1998), p. 134. McFarlane found it simple to understand the advantages of livery and obvious how liveried retinues were "lump[ed] together under the heading of maintenance." McFarlane, "Lords and Retainers," Lecture II, pp. 1–6.

[15] Harriss, *Shaping the Nation*, p. 190. Keen said that the wearing of livery by groups of men embarking on forcibly entering another's land signaled that resistance would be difficult and violence could ensue. He noted that Lord Moleyn's men were wearing his livery when they attacked the Paston's manor of Gresham, Norfolk. Maurice Keen, *English Society in the Later Middle Ages* (Middlesex, 1990), pp. 204–08.

[16] Griffiths, *Henry VI*, p. 592.

[17] Saul, "Abolition of Badges," p. 310. "Symptomatic of the general decay was the magnates' distribution of badges, or 'signs' as they were known, to those on the fringes of their affinities. Bestowal of these marks of favour emboldened the wearers and encouraged them in their misdeeds." Nigel Saul, *Richard II* (New Haven, 1997), p. 200.

[18] Davies, *Lords and Lordship*, p. 211.

[19] This practice had begun by middle of the thirteenth century. By the fourteenth century, the relationship between the justices and magnates deepened as a result of broader changes in society. It reflected the justices' need for greater income and the magnates' need for favor and advice. J.R. Maddicott, *Law and Lordship: Royal Justices as Retainers in Thirteenth- and Fourteenth-Century England*, Past & Present, Supp. (1978), pp. 4–10, 24–25.

[20] The result was the enactment of the 1346 Ordinance of Justices, which included a prohibition on taking fees and robes from anyone other than the king, and a corresponding oath to that effect. Maddicott said that it was largely ignored and generally ineffective. Ibid., pp. 40–59.

[21] Ibid., pp. 59–81.   [22] Ibid., p. 69.

justices,[23] which produced a statute prohibiting the taking of robes, fees, and gifts from lords.[24] But the justices' substantial influence undermined this effort.[25] The Commons petitioned again, but without success, as the statute was invalidated.[26]

Saul said that "the debate about liveries burst upon the late fourteenth-century scene with surprising suddenness."[27] It generated a great deal of parliamentary action in the late medieval period.[28] The Commons frequently petitioned Parliament, complaining about its adverse effects.[29] There were twenty-three petitions regarding livery, half of them during

---

[23] They complained that justices and barons were in the retinues of lords appearing before them, from whom they received fees and large gifts, and they requested that the justices not takes "robes, fees, pension, or gift from anyone except the king." The king willed it, on pain of loss of office and paying a fine and ransom, and said that a statute should be enacted. Parliaments of Richard II: November 1384, no. 18, *PROME*.

[24] The statute affirmed the 1346 Ordinance of the Justices and also prohibited giving counsel in any action where the king was a party or in any plea before them. 8 Rich. II, c. 3 (1384), *Statutes of the Realm*, vol. 2, p. 37.

[25] In 1385, the justices petitioned parliament "to repeal and wholly annul the heinous statutes made in the last parliament" concerning the justices and barons, which were detrimental to the justices and other ministers, and they said further that the ancient laws and statutes provided sufficient authority to punish them if they did wrong. *Rotuli Parliamentorum*, 7 vols. (London, 1767), vol. 3, p. 176, no. 6; Parliaments of Rich. II, October 1385, no. 18, appendix no. 15 (1385). Thus, in that parliament, the king confirmed all prior statutes except the 1384 statute regarding the justices and barons "which, because it is very hard, and needs declaration, the King wills that it be of no force until it be declared by Parliament." 9 Rich. II c. 1 (1385), *Statutes of the Realm*, vol. 2, p. 38; Parliaments of Richard II, October 1385, no. 18, *PROME*. Maddicott said it "was not implausible to see this as a victory for the justices and magnates." Maddicott, *Law and Lordship*, p. 66.

[26] The next year the Commons reiterated their request that the 1346 Ordinance of the Justices, barring their taking of taking of gifts, rewards, fees, and robes, "be firmly upheld in all respects, notwithstanding any repeal made thereof." The king responded that he ordered the justices to "do impartial justice" and would "chastise" them if they erred. As a result, he willed that the statutes concerning the justices and barons "be annulled and invalidated." Parliaments of Richard II: October 1386, no. 24, *PROME*. Nevertheless, the retaining of justices continued to be a political issue that was connected with the potential for public disorder. But, by 1390, this practice seemed to have ceased. Maddicott, *Law and Lordship*, pp. 67, 78–81.

[27] Saul, "Abolition of Badges," p. 305. But the debate about maintenance was longstanding, as was the one about conspiracies and alliances, and livery was connected to both of these concerns.

[28] Hicks, *Bastard Feudalism*, pp. 124–33.

[29] Walker noted that recent historians evinced some skepticism toward these petitions, believing them to be oversimplified. Simon Walker, "Lordship and Lawlessness in the Palatinate of Lancaster 1370-1400," in *Political Culture in Later Medieval England* (Manchester, 2006), p. 18.

the reign of Richard II (1377–99). As a result of these petitions, parliament enacted thirteen statutes. Most of the remaining petitioning and legislative actions in this period occurred during the reign of Henry IV (1399–1413). In sum, the concern about liveried retainers and their wrongful conduct produced substantial political and legal activity in the first twenty-five years of the late medieval period.

The Initial Petitions and Statutes Regarding Livery, 1377–1411

Among the many petitions in Richard II's first parliament was one concerning livery. The complaint singled out those "with small holdings of land or rent" who kept retinues of men, squires, and others "to perform great maintenance in lawsuits" and gave them livery "to support them in disputes."[30] The king responded that there were existing statutes as well as the common law, which should be enforced. But he added more specifically that neither the "livery of chaperons, nor any other" shall be given for maintenance of lawsuits or any other confederacy.[31] As a result, parliament enacted the first regulation of livery. The preamble explained the statute's objective. It said that "many people of small income (*plusours gentz de petit garison*)" formed great retinues of people that included esquires and annually gave them "chaperons and other livery of uniform color and material (*chaperons et autre livery d'une suyte*)" in return for their agreement and assurance that they would maintain each other in all quarrels.[32] After stating that existing statutes should be enforced,[33] this statute provided that "no such livery [shall] be given to any man for maintenance of quarrels, nor other confederacies."[34] The

---

[30] The Commons complained further that "because of the alliances and affinities made by such people to give their livery, they are bound to support both reasonable and unreasonable suits." Parliaments of Richard II: October 1377, no. 92, *PROME*.

[31] Ibid.

[32] The preamble also noted that the recipients paid for the cost of the livery and perhaps in some cases twice the cost. Gratitude is expressed to Prof. John Baker for clarifying the meaning of "suit," as used in this context. He explained that it meant uniformity of material and color, which made them distinctive and tied them visually to the giver. The cloth would have been made into a single garment, such as a gown or a jacket, and not into a suit as now understood.

[33] These are presumably the numerous maintenance and perhaps conspiracy statutes and ordinances.

[34] The statute also provided, as had the king in his response to the petition, that the justices of assize should inquire of "all those who gather them together in fraternities by livery to effect maintenance." 1 Rich. II, c. 7 (1377), *Statutes of the Realm*, vol. 2, p. 3.

preamble's language, "chaperons and other livery of uniform color and material," seemed to explain that "such livery" meant all or most livery. The reference in the petition and statute to lesser landowners may have limited the prohibition to the gentry or perhaps the lesser gentry.[35] Thus, the first statute was not a broad prohibition on giving livery. Although it applied to all livery, it did not extend to the nobility and other great magnates and may have applied only when it was given for the specifically expressed purposes. But the Commons' petition was similarly limited.[36]

What occurred next was an extended debate among the Commons, the Lords, and the king that began in 1384 and culminated in the enactment of an ordinance in 1390.[37] The Commons now took a more aggressive approach than it had in 1377. In the April 1384 parliament, the Commons

> complained bitterly about the tyranny of certain locally powerful persons who, furnished with badges ("*signis*") ... by the lords of realm and sheltered by their favour, and having in natural consequence an exaggerated conceit of themselves, unjustly oppressed and dismayed the poor and helpless of their neighborhoods, trying to overthrow laws passed and published for the common weal of the realm, and, in full reliance on their own smartness and friendship of their lords, refusing to allow those laws to hold to their straight course.[38]

They asked for a "general statute to prevent their deceit and chicanery." Their efforts met with a "firm rebuff" and "firm opposition" from the Lords.[39] John of Gaunt, duke of Lancaster and after the king the most powerful person in the realm, responded that the complaint was "too general" and should be made with "full particulars." He said further that

---

[35] Given-Wilson argued that the reference to small landowners, "men of lesser estate," may have meant only knights and not lords and that the prohibition was limited to the giving of chaperons. Given-Wilson, *The King's Affinity*, p. 237. But the king's response to the petition was not so limited. It said "livery of chaperons nor otherwise (*autrement*)."

[36] Three years later, in one of the items in a petition dealing with several subjects, the Commons requested that the earlier statute "concerning those who give chaperons and liveries to do maintenance shall be duly executed in accordance with the tenor of the same." The king's response was to include violations of this statute among several forms of misconduct in the commissions of justices of the peace, to which he gave *oyer et terminer* power. Parliaments of Richard II: January 1380, XIII, no. 38, *PROME*.

[37] Saul, *Richard II*, pp. 199–200; Storey, "Liveries and Commissions," pp. 131–35; Saul, "Abolition of Badges," pp. 302, 310; J.A. Tuck, "The Cambridge Parliament 1388," *English Historical Review* 84 (1968), pp. 227–29, 234–35; Given-Wilson, *The King's Affinity*, pp. 238–39.

[38] Hector and Harvey, *The Westminster Chronicle*, pp. 82–83; Keen, *English Society*, pp. 16–23.

[39] Saul, *Richard II*, pp. 81–82.

"every lord was competent and well able to correct and punish his own dependents for such outrages."[40] The Commons, realizing that no remedy was forthcoming, were "reduced to silence."[41]

But the Commons did not give up and persisted in their aggressive manner, boldly confronting the Lords in the Cambridge Parliament of September 1388.[42] In the first petition, they requested that "all the liveries called 'badges,' as well of our lord the king as of other lords ... and all other lesser liveries, such as chaperons, shall henceforward not be given or worn but shall be abolished."[43] Repeating sentiments similar to those expressed in 1384, they said that those who wore badges issued by lords were "by reason of the power of their masters, flown with such insolent arrogance that they do not shrink from practising with reckless effrontery various forms of extortion." After describing the negative effects of this conduct, they concluded that "it is certainly the boldness inspired by their badges that makes them unafraid to do these things and more besides."[44] Again, the Lords wanted more specific cases and offenders. The king, in an attempt to mediate, offered to give up his own badges. But the Lords refused to agree "after launching a great deal of abuse and vituperation at the [C]ommons."[45] Thus, the king, "anxious to avoid a

---

[40]   Gaunt said that if one of his dependents acted in this fashion, he would be punished in such a manner that it would "strike into the hearts of the rest a terror of committing similar misdeeds." Ibid., p. 83. Saul said that by lecturing John of Gaunt on the evils of maintenance, they risked incurring his wrath. Saul, "Abolition of Badges," p. 310.

[41]   Hector and Harvey, *The Westminster Chronicle*, p. 83.

[42]   Storey pointed out that many of the members of this parliament had been members of the February 1388 Merciless Parliament, which was dominated by the Lords Appellant who controlled government then, and that "a fair proportion of the [Cambridge Parliament] were retained by or connected to the Appellants." Storey, "Liveries and Commissions," pp. 132–33. Saul said that in the Cambridge Parliament, the Commons "provoked a confrontation with the Lords Appellant" by requesting the abolition of badges. Saul, "Abolition of Badges," p. 310.

[43]   Hector and Harvey, *The Westminster Chronicle*, pp. 356–57; Parliaments of Richard II: September 1388, appendix no. 1, *PROME*. In his discussion of Chaucer's poem regarding Richard, *Lak of Stedfastnesse*, Strohm noted the importance of the "common environment of ideas about collusion and maintenance, extortion and representation, and princely redress" in understanding the petition, Richard's response, and Chaucer's poem. Paul Strohm, *Hochon's Arrow: The Social Imagination of Fourteenth Century Texts* (Princeton, 1992), pp. 55–74.

[44]   Hector and Harvey, *The Westminster Chronicle*, pp. 354–55. Storey said that the Commons' willingness to be in "open discord with the Lords" was that their primary concern was the "public order in the country." He provided numerous examples of the unpunished crime that troubled them. Storey, "Liveries and Commissions," pp. 132–35.

[45]   Hector and Harvey, *The Westminster Chronicle*, pp. 355–57.

general split" and hoping for "domestic tranquility," postponed the matter until the next parliament, which permitted lords to continue using their badges.[46] He also promised that he and the Lords would ordain a provision in the meantime, a promise that he seems to have kept.[47]

The Commons, still determined, persisted in their effort, petitioning again in the next parliament.[48] In first of two petitions on livery, they noted their complaint at the Cambridge Parliament about lords giving badges and the harmful effects and reminded the king that the existing provision was only temporary and that they still awaited the "final judgment of parliament." The king's response was noncommittal.[49] In their other petition, they requested a comprehensive ban on "liveries of

---

[46] In responding to the petition the king said it was his will, assented to by the Lords, "that the matter touching this article shall be continued in its present state until the next parliament in the hope that in the meantime amendment will be effected by him and the lords of his council, without prejudice to the dignity of the king and of the lords and of all other estates of the parliament." Ibid., pp. 356–57; Parliaments of Richard II: September 1388, appendix no. 1, *PROME*. Tuck called this postponement a compromise. Tuck, "Cambridge Parliament," p. 235. But Storey said it hardly merited that description. Storey, "Liveries and Commissions," p. 135.

[47] Saul, *Richard II*, pp. 199–201; Given-Wilson, *The King's Affinity*, p. 239. A Commons' petition in the January 1290 parliament described the details of this provisional remedy. It provided that "no one, of whatever estate or condition he may be, shall wear any lord's badge unless he stays with the same lord for the term of his life, both in peace and war, and that by indentures sealed under their seals without fraud or ill intent. And concerning valets and archers, that throughout the whole realm of England none of them shall wear any lord's badge unless he be a menial dwelling with him in his household for a whole year. Saving always, if the aforesaid ordinance does not provide a suitable remedy that the said Commons may remain with their ancient stay of judgment until the next parliament." Parliaments of Richard II: January 1390, no. 27, *PROME*.

[48] Perhaps they were more hopeful since the king had resumed control of the government in May 1389. Scholars have viewed his actions regarding law and order in this period as indicating a desire to win favor with the gentry. Given-Wilson, "Introduction." Parliaments of Richard II: January 1390, *PROME*; Saul, *Richard II*, pp. 162–65; Given-Wilson, *The King's Affinity*, pp. 238–39; Anthony Tuck, *Richard II and the English Nobility* (London, 1973), pp. 145–48. At that time, Richard issued a proclamation stating his desire for "greater order and tranquillity" and proclaiming a prohibition on "congregations, oppressions, maintenances, or illegal assemblies." *Rotuli Parliamentorum*, vol. III, p. 404, no. 31. Storey described how the king diligently pursued these objectives. Story, "Liveries and Commissions," pp. 135–43. Thus, he may have been more sympathetic to the Commons' objectives regarding livery and their view of its critical connection to law and order.

[49] He said that he would "consider it further with his council, and ordain such a remedy as shall seem best to him for the peace and quiet of his people." Parliaments of Richard II: January 1390, no. 27, *PROME*. This petition engendered a long and bitter debate, given the Lords' resistance to eliminating their badges. But they finally agreed to give them only to those who were retained by life indenture and only to archers and yeoman who

cloth." Their view was that Lords or anyone else should be barred from giving it except to their household servants ("*familiers*"), kin and allies, steward, councils, and bailiffs. The king was again noncommital.[50] Nevertheless, the Ordinance of 1390 regulating livery was promulgated.

This ordinance, which resembled both the provisional remedy and the Commons' petition, took the form of a writ to the sheriff of Kent.[51] It contained a preamble recounting "the outrageous oppressions and main-tenances" of the many wrongdoers who "are the most embolded and encouraged in their maintenance and evil deeds because they are in the retinue of the lords and others ... with fees, robes and other liveries called liveries of company."[52] The ordinance began with a general pro-hibition on giving of livery of company by any prelate, bachelor (perhaps meaning knight bachelor),[53] esquire, or other of lesser estate. It then provided that no duke, earl, baron, or banneret[54] shall give livery of

regularly were domiciled with their lords. Not surprisingly, the Commons was not satisfied. Storey, "Liveries and Commissions," p. 143.

[50] The Commons also requested that "no livery be given by color of gild, fraternity, or other association, as well of nobles and valets as of the Commons." They recommended penalties of a year's imprisonment, a fine of £100, and loss of the franchise of the various groups. In response, the king said that he would consider it further with his council. Parliaments of Richard II: January 1390, no. 29, *PROME*.

[51] It also stated that like writs were directed to other sheriffs throughout England. 13 Rich. II, st. 3 (1390), *Statutes of the Realm*, vol. 2, pp. 74–75; A.R. Myers, ed., *English Historical Documents 1327–1485*, 10 vols. (New York, 1969), vol. IV, pp. 1116–17. Although this provision has often been called a statute, it is not one, as Storey correctly pointed out. Storey, "Liveries and Commissions," p. 147.

[52] Livery of company probably meant livery that was given to a distinct group of recipients, which would distinguish them from outsiders and could include cloth, chaperons, or badges. But one of the later statutes directed at livery of company dealt only with badges. 1 Hen. IV c. 7 (1399), *Statutes of the Realm*, vol. 2, pp. 113–14; Parliaments of Henry IV: October 1399, no. 84, *PROME*. McFarlane said it meant livery worn outside the house-hold. McFarlane, *Nobility*, p. 123.

[53] "Bachelor" was a term that was used in several contexts and was often associated with youth. Bean explored its use in the context of the lord and man relationships. He determined that it was used frequently in that context and referred to a person whose functions were an integral part of the relationship. He concluded that a bachelor was a knight, but not necessarily a youthful one and that the terms were not interchangeable. He also believed that it was a knight associated with the household and "a person of superior knightly status who occupied a position of special trust within the immediate entourage of his lord." Bean, *From Lord to Patron*, pp. 22–32. Given this definition, the absence of knights in this list of prohibited givers of badges seems odd.

[54] Banneret was "a superior military rank" of a knight, whose primary duties were military ones and whose retinue was larger than that of a simple knight. Given-Wilson, *The King's Affinity*, pp. 21, 204–5, 294 n. 70; Peter Coss, *The Origins of the English Gentry* (Cam-bridge, 2003), pp. 240–41. "Baron" referred to great land holders and was the lowest rank

company unless the recipients were retained for life by indenture or were domestic or household servants living in his household.[55] Further it prohibited giving such livery to any valet, "called a yeoman archer," or to anyone of lesser estate than esquire unless he was a household servant living in his household.[56] The ordinance also required all spiritual and temporal lords as well as all others completely to remove their fees, robes, and other livery from all "maintainers, instigators, barretors, procurers, and embraceors of quarrels and inquests" and eject them from their "service, company or retinue." It also reiterated the prohibition of maintenance contained in the 1377 statute.[57]

The Commons had failed to obtain the complete ban on the giving of livery that they desired. Although they were likely disappointed, it may have been a limited victory, given the persistent, strong opposition of the Lords, who had stymied them for six years. But it also was a limited victory for the Lords. They had forestalled legislation requiring them to abandon all their livery, and the statute reflected clear concessions to them. In that sense, it may have been the kind of compromise that the king sought at the Cambridge parliament. Moreover, in the political world, it was all that the Commons could obtain at that time.[58] But from a substantive standpoint, its effectiveness depended on its impact in

---

of the nobility. It could mean those who held baronies or who were the greater tenants-in-chief. Its meaning may have varied over time. S.H. Rigby, *English Society in the Later Middle Ages* (London, 1995), pp. 195–97. Coss, *English Gentry*, pp. 239–41. But it was also used to denote all the nobility. Davies, *Lords and Lordship*, p. 22.

[55] Lewis found the exceptions for household servants justified and indispensable, but thought the exception for indentured retainers less clear. But after substantial analysis, he found it acceptable based on their working relationship and cooperation with the contract army and baronial household as well as on the "constitutional mouthpiece of contemporary opinion." N.B. Lewis, "The Organisation of Indentured Retinues in Fourteenth Century England," *Transactions of the Royal Historical Society* 27, 4th series (1945), pp. 29–39.

[56] 13 Rich. II, st. 3 (1390), *Statutes of the Realm*, vol. 2, p. 75. Strohm drew on the 1390 statute's provision permitting livery to be given to domestic servants (*mesnal*) to describe Geoffrey Chaucer's relation with Edward III and Richard II. He said that Chaucer's receipt of an annuity qualified him as a "*mesnal gentil*," which obligated him to render good service and provided him with status and security. Further, it evidenced a royal interest in Chaucer's career. Paul Strohm, *Social Chaucer* (Cambridge, MA, 1989), pp. 18–23.

[57] The penalty was appropriate imprisonment, fine, ransom, or other punishment as well as the giving up of all livery prohibited by the statute within ten days of the proclamation of the Ordinance by the sheriffs.

[58] Saul said the ordinance "had the merit of accommodating to the social realities of the time." Saul, "Abolition of Badges," p. 303.

restricting retaining and stopping maintenance and other wrongful conduct by liveried retainers. There is little evidence that it had such an impact.

Although McFarlane said that the 1390 Ordinance was the "first thorough-going statute against liveries,"[59] most commentators have taken a skeptical view of its effectiveness. Saul said it "was unenforced and unenforceable."[60] Some may have seen it as a victory for the Lords.[61] Storey was the harshest critic, arguing that it was unimportant, insignificant, and ineffective as an "instrument against 'livery and maintenance' ... It ended the hopes of those commoners who had so vigorously pressed for the abolition of all liveries."[62]

Nevertheless, despite this extended saga, the Commons persisted. They petitioned three more times during the remainder of the Richard's reign, and parliament enacted two more statutes dealing with livery. In 1393, they complained that, notwithstanding the 1390 Ordinance, livery had been given to the members of various trades and occupations, who were wearing livery to engage in maintenance. They requested that the justices of the peace have the power to inquire into the wearing of livery and badges by such artificers and victualers and for a remedy.[63] The king agreed and a statute was enacted incorporating the king's response. The

---

[59] McFarlane, *Nobility*, p. 111. Lewis said it dealt "in greater detail" than any prior legislation dealing with retinues. Lewis, "Indentured Retinues," p. 29. Dunham said that it was "the first major attempt to regulate retaining." William Dunham, *Lord Hastings' Indentured Retainers 1461–1483* (New Haven, 1955), p. 12.

[60] Saul, "Abolition of Badges," p. 303; Tuck said it was "never enforced strictly." Tuck, "Cambridge Parliament," p. 235; Given-Wilson said that the ordinance "was by no means entirely effective." Given-Wilson, *The King's Affinity*, p. 239.

[61] Tuck said that the ordinance "did not greatly restrict the freedom of the great magnates." Tuck, "Cambridge Parliament," p. 235. Dunham said it "gave a monopoly on retaining companies of knights and esquires to lords temporal" and created an "aristocratic monopoly." He seemed, however, to exhibit hope in the peers' ability to keep retaining within lawful boundaries. Dunham, *Lord Hastings*, pp. 12, 69–71. Saul thought that king had given in to magnate influence and had backed away from his earlier commitment to reform. Saul, *Richard II*, pp. 263–64.

[62] He also denied that it created a baronial monopoly on retaining. He saw the ordinance important, however, in marking the end of the king's "efforts to woo the Commons." He also acknowledged that it was "the most realistic solution for the problem of liveries, granted the social conditions of the time." He said that the king lacked the desire and ability to prohibit all livery by lords and that only lords could discipline their retainers, as legislation was useless since lords could manipulate it. Storey, "Liveries and Commissions," pp. 145–50.

[63] They said that notwithstanding the ordinance "many tailors, drapers, cobblers, tanners, fishmongers, butchers and other artificers, and also serving men like squires and valets

statute prohibited yeoman and anyone else below the estate of esquire from wearing livery of company of any lord unless they were domestic servants or family living continuously in the household, and it empowered the justices of the peace to inquire and punish offenders.[64] But the 1393 statute added no further prohibitions on livery as the 1390 Ordinance had made giving livery to these persons illegal. Several years later the Commons submitted two petitions on the same subject. One complained that the 1393 statute, among others, was not being enforced and requested that a specific penalty be ordained.[65] The other complained that "valets called yeomen and others of lesser estate than squire," who were not household servants or a continual officer, were wearing livery of company of lords.[66] Parliament confirmed the 1377 livery statute and enacted a statute almost identical to that of 1393.[67] During the latter years of the reign, the king's aggressive retaining, the substantial growth of his affinity, and the distribution of his White Hart livery[68] had intensified the concern with livery.[69] As the reign of Richard II came to its violent end, it had endured substantial debate and controversy regarding livery and concluded with no broad prohibition on giving livery, but with some limitations and exceptions for

who have small livelihood, wear liveries and signs." Parliaments of Richard II: January 1393, no. 31, *PROME*.

[64] 16 Rich. II c. 4 (1393), *Statutes of the Realm*, vol. 2, p. 84. It is likely that the justices of the peace were already authorized in these matters. Parliaments of Richard II: January 1380, XIII, no. 38, *PROME*.

[65] Parliaments of Richard II: January 1397, no. 13, *PROME*.

[66] Parliaments of Richard II: January 1397, no. 38, *PROME*.

[67] The only difference was the addition of "continual officer" to the exception. 20 Rich. II, cc. 1–2 (1397), *Statutes of the Realm*, vol. 2, p. 93.

[68] Although Richard had worn the Lancastrian SS collar during his reign, he began to distribute his badge of the White Hart after the crisis of 1386–89 as the rivalry between him and his uncle, John of Gaunt and John's son, the future Henry IV intensified. Their competing distribution of livery badges was a visible manifestation of their arms race and induced a gang culture, for which both sides were criticized. Chris Given-Wilson, *Henry IV* (New Haven, 2016), pp. 93–94.

[69] After Richard regained control of government, he embarked on these efforts. By the end of his reign, his affinity numbered 2,000 men of varying social status, including some below the rank of esquire, which was illegal. Nor was it clear that all these men were formally retained by the king. The size of this affinity increased substantially by the inclusion of 760 Cheshire men, the "Chester chyders (brawlers)" who were targeted in the poem *Richard the Redeless*. Given-Wilson, *The King's Affinity*, pp. 222–23, 239, 251, 311 n. 88; Harriss, *Shaping the Nation*, p. 28; Saul, *Richard II*, pp. 369–70, 393–94, 440, 444–45. Richard's retaining had begun much earlier and increased over the years. Given-Wilson, *The King's Affinity*, pp. 213–17.

servants living in the household and those retained for life by indenture.[70]

Livery was also a source of active complaints during the reign of Henry IV (1399–1414). But the new king imposed more severe restrictions on the giving of livery than his predecessor.[71] "To eliminate maintenance and nourish love, peace and quietude," Henry IV's first parliament enacted a broad, detailed prohibition on livery.[72] It forbade all lords of whatever estate or condition from giving "livery of sign of company to any knight, esquire, or yeoman."[73] Except for yeomen, the prohibition did not apply to the king.[74] But this special treatment for the Lancastrian affinity caused unease.[75] Unlike the prior legislation, this statute also punished knights, esquires, and yeomen who took illegal livery.[76] Finally, the statute prohibited archbishops, bishops, abbots, priors, other clerics, and any other temporal person of any estate from giving livery of cloth to anyone except "menial servants (*menialx*)" and officers, those "that be of his council," and those "spiritual [or] temporal, learned in one law or the other."[77]

---

[70] Ostrom asserted that Richard II used livery to indicate his power, gain support, and assert his prominence. She explored its connection with the use of signs in the poem *Sir Gawain and the Green Knight*. Theresa Ostrom, "'And He Honoured Þat Hit Hade Euermore After': The Influence of Richard II's Livery System on Sir Gawain and the Green Knight," unpublished Master's thesis, University of Florida (May, 2003).

[71] Harris, *Shaping the Nation*, p. 190.

[72] 1 Hen. IV c. 7 (1399), *Statutes of the Realm*, vol. 2, pp. 113–14; Parliaments of Henry IV: October 1399, no. 84, *PROME*; *Calendar of Close Rolls, Henry IV 1399–1402*, p. 182 (April 23, 1400) ("any livery as a mark of fellowship"). It made no reference to any of the earlier statutes, as was common, which Storey thought was evidence of the 1390 Ordinance's insignificance. Storey, "Liveries and Commissions," p. 147.

[73] The penalty for lords who violated the statute was a fine and ransom at the king's will.

[74] It said that the king could give livery to his lords temporal and to his household (*"menialx"*) knights and esquires who were in his retinue and received an annual fee for life, but that they could not wear their livery in the countries or counties where they resided or elsewhere "out of the king's presence." There was a related exception for the constable and marshal, who could use the king's livery in their retinues on the frontier and in the marches. Also those who went "abroad to seek honor" could use that same livery.

[75] Given-Wilson said that Henry IV was insensitive to this concern and that after 1399 England was flooded with Lancastrian SS collars. He estimated a thousand persons may have been entitled to wear them. Given-Wilson, *Henry IV*, pp. 93–95.

[76] Knights and yeoman lost their livery and permanently forfeited their fees. The king could not give livery to yeoman.

[77] Although the lawyers were commonly retained by fees and robes, this statute was the first specifically to authorize giving livery to lawyers. Earlier livery statutes had not distinguished the retainer of lawyers from that of nonlawyers. Eric Ives, *The Common Lawyers of Pre-Reformation England: Thomas Kebell: A Case Study* (Cambridge, 1983), p. 132.

The Commons had now achieved the victory, at least at a political level, that had eluded them in the prior reign. Given-Wilson said that this statute "was the high water mark of anti-livery legislation." He called it "a drastic step" and a "reaction to the political events" of the prior years. He said that the abusive lordship of several noble followers of Richard II was the primary motivation for its enactment.[78] Saul said that in the early years of Henry IV's reign, "the Commons were at their most truculent and were in no mood to be fobbed off."[79]

Another petition in 1401 reflected further evidence of that mood.[80] The Commons again called for the abolition of all livery of badges and cloth, subject to several exceptions for nobles, lords, and others.[81] The treatment requested for the king was similar to that in the 1399 statute.[82] But this petition introduced a new notion regarding enforcement and penalties. It said that enforcement of the statute should be at the suit of the king or any subject by indictment, inquiry, bill, or writ. In addition, it provided monetary penalties for violations depending on the status of the offender, with half of the penalty for the king and the other half for the

---

[78] He singled out the earls of Rutland, Kent, Huntingdon, and Somerset, who had been accused in the same parliament of various oppressions. Given-Wilson, *The King's Affinity*, p. 240. In this parliament, these individuals were named as supporters of Richard II who had engaged in wrongdoing and the records of their misdeeds were read in parliament. After they responded to the charges, William Thirning CJCP gave judgment, which included that none of them "should give any livery of badges, or create a retinue of men, except of the necessary officers within and outside of their households" and except as was necessary for governance and counsel for their lands and possessions. As result of their lordships and their "great position," some of their men had engaged in "extortion and oppression ... and maintenance of quarrels." Parliaments of Henry IV: October 1399, nos. 1–10, *PROME*.

[79] Saul, "Abolition of Badges," p. 303.

[80] Harriss said that there was "a growing reaction against the partisan character of his rule and the accumulation of rewards by his retainers. There were vivid and recent memories of the oppressions committed by the wearers of Richard's livery of the white hart." Harriss, *Shaping the Nation*, p. 496.

[81] Lords and others of lesser estate could give livery of cloth to their household servants, officers, and counselors learned in one law or the other. The king's sons, dukes, earls, barons, and bannerets could wear the livery collar of the king, but only in his presence, and no one else should wear livery of the king, another lord, or any person of lesser estate in the presence or absence of the king. The "presence of the king" meant within a twelve-mile radius of his household. Parliaments of Henry IV: January 1401, no. 110, *PROME*.

[82] The king could give livery of cloth to his household servants, officers, counselors, justices of both benches, chancery clerks, barons of the Exchequer, and those of his council learned in one law or the other. The petition also stated that king had "granted that his livery for yeomen or valets, of the crescent with the star, should be completely abolished." Ibid.

person suing.[83] But there was another petition, which Saul discovered in the Ancient Petitions in which a more combative and defiant Commons demanded the abolition of all livery, including that of the king, with no exceptions. Moreover, it stressed the notion of the commonalty, "the whole commons" ("*un comyn entier*") and how the giving of livery divided the "unity of people, enforcement and good regard of the law of the land and the common right of the realm" and caused the "maintaining of most evil quarrels."[84] But in a later parliament, the speaker of the Commons, concerned that the king had been misinformed, and other members denied making such a request.[85] Given-Wilson doubted the veracity of the denial and believed that the petition was likely submitted in the January 1401 parliament.[86] Although this petition was never enrolled, Saul's discovery seems to eliminate any doubt of its existence.[87]

As result of the enrolled petition, to which the king had assented except for the requests regarding enforcement and penalties, parliament enacted a statute.[88] After reciting and confirming the 1399 statute, the statute provided that dukes, earls, barons, and bannerets could use the king's livery and that knights and esquires could use it in going to and from the king's house,

---

[83] The penalty was £40 for a knight below the status of a duke, earl, or baron; £20 for a squire; and £10 for a yeoman or valet for each violation. The petition also requested that enforcement should be before justices of both benches in the counties where they sat and by the justices of peace, who should have *oyer et terminer* power. Ibid.

[84] TNA: PRO SC 8/100/4985 (1401); Saul, "Abolition of Badges," pp. 303–5, 314–15; Harriss, *Shaping the Nation*, p. 496.

[85] The speaker, Sir Arnold Savage, was concerned that the king had been informed that Savage, on his own and "of his own authority," had filed a petition demanding that all livery, including that of king, be abolished. Savage said that he never made such a request and that the request was "in accordance with the tenor of the statute" made in the reign of Henry IV and that it requested that that statute and the others "should be kept." His fellow members "publicly testified before the king and Lords" that that was what they had agreed. Parliaments of Henry IV: January 1404, no. 9, *PROME*.

[86] Given-Wilson, *The King's Affinity*, p. 240; Given-Wilson, *Henry IV*, p. 393; Saul, "Abolition of Badges," pp. 303–5.

[87] He said that "the fact that it passed quickly into oblivion was a mark of the embarrassment that it caused. Its survival among the public records proves that it was handed in and received by the clerk of Parliament." He said further that it was likely that the council deemed it too sensitive for royal consideration. He said that the petition may have been authored by a group of individuals who hoped the Commons would adopt it. He opined that the king, because of his identification with the magnates and his own desire to retain supporters among the gentry, "would not have taken kindly to a petition so sweeping in its criticism." Ibid., pp. 304–05.

[88] 2 Hen IV, c. 21 (1401), *Statutes of the Realm*, vol. 2, pp. 129–30. Given-Wilson said that this statute and the 1399 one targeted the "noble and gentry gang-masters." Given-Wilson, *Henry IV*, p. 212.

but not where they resided. It also provided that the prince could give livery
to his lords and his household ("*meignalx*") gentlemen and that lords could
use it in the same manner as the king's livery. This statute was a modifica-
tion of the 1399 statute, permitting a more liberal use of royal livery.[89] It also
empowered the justices of both benches as well as the justices of assize and
of the peace to inquire, hear, and determine these matters.[90]

   After the January 1404 Parliament,[91] Given-Wilson asserted that the
parliamentary controversy regarding livery diminished.[92] Nevertheless,
in the remaining years of Henry IV's reign, the Commons submitted two
more petitions and two further statutes were enacted, one of which was
significant from a legal standpoint. In 1406 petition, the Commons
complained that the 1399 statute was not being enforced and that "many
bannerets, knights and esquires ... jointly and individually give liveries
of cloth, sometimes to as many as 300 valets, and sometimes to 200
men ... in support of their wrongful quarrels and for maintenance."
They also complained of the "numerous homicides, thefts, murders,
felonies, rapes of women, extortions" and other wrongdoing by those
wearing livery, "against whom no help can be had because of the
confederacy, alliance and support of the multitude of their companions
with the aforesaid livery of the cloth." They repeated their request for
specific monetary penalties for offenders and the authority for individuals to sue and collect half of the penalty.[93] The king was receptive to the

---

[89] Given-Wilson considered the statute something of a victory for king, because of the
   provision permitting his knights and esquires to wear his livery in coming and going to
   his house and not just in his presence and because of those regarding the prince. Given-
   Wilson, *The King's Affinity*, p. 240.

[90] It said that they should proceed "by record made in their presence, or by inquiry to be
   made from time to time." 2 Hen IV, c. 21(1401), *Statutes of the Realm*, vol., 2, p. 130.

[91] Two other matters regarding livery had arisen in the January 1404 Parliament. First, the
   Commons petitioned to have aliens removed from the king's household. The king agreed
   and the Lords promulgated an article to that effect, which included a prohibition on
   giving livery to the aliens in question. Parliaments of Henry IV: January 1404, nos. 26–31.
   In the other matter, the earl of Northumberland petitioned for a pardon. The Lords,
   claiming judgment belonged to them and not to the justices, considered the treason and
   livery statutes and determined that the earl had not committed treason or felony but a
   trespass for which he ought to pay a fine and redemption. The earl took an oath of fidelity
   and loyalty and received a pardon for the trespass and fine and redemption. Ibid., nos.
   11–14; Given-Wilson, *The King's Affinity*, p. 242.

[92] His rationale was that the subsequent statutes concerned livery of robes and chaperons
   and not of badges. Ibid., p. 241.

[93] They also requested that justices of the assize and of the peace be authorized to inquire and
   determine these matters. Parliaments of Henry IV: March 1406, no. 147, *PROME*. Walker
   said that the 1399 and 1406 livery legislation reflected the Commons' longstanding concern

request for enforcement and supported the suggested penalties. As a result, parliament enacted another statute, which began by reciting the 1377 and 1399 statutes' prohibition on livery of cloth and chaperons and that they should be "firmly kept and put in due execution."[94] It provided that any knight or person of lesser estate, who gave livery of cloth or chaperons, be fined 100s. It also said, as the Commons had proposed, that anyone who received such livery be fined 40s for each violation and further that private parties could sue on behalf of the king and receive half the penalty. The statute also prohibited the giving of such livery by any "congregation or company" with a fine of 40s, with an exception permitting guilds, fraternities, and trade associations "founded or ordained to a good intent or purpose" to give such livery.[95]

This statute was significant because it was the first livery statute to provide specific penalties for its violation and a mechanism for private enforcement, remedies that the Commons had previously requested without success. Five years later, the Commons petitioned again, requesting that the 1377, 1399, and 1406 statutes be enforced.[96] The king agreed and a statute followed, which confirmed those statutes and provided that they should be enforced, as "they were very profitable for the ease and quietude of him and all his realm."[97]

The Later Petitions and Statutes Regarding Livery, 1413–1485

During the remainder of the late medieval period, parliamentary activity dealing with livery declined substantially. There were, however, several petitions and statutes during the reigns of Henry VI (1422–61) and Edward IV (1461–83).[98] In 1429, the Commons complained that the 1399 and 1406 livery statutes were not being observed. They explained that it was "because those who act contrary to the said

---

with the presence of magnates on the commissions of peace. He said that "it was the maintenance and protections of evil-doers practised by the magnates which lay behind many contemporary breakdowns in public order." Simon Walker, "Yorkshire Justices of the Peace, 1389–1413," in *Political Culture in Later Medieval England* (Mancester, 2006), p. 83.

[94] 7 Hen. IV, c. 14 (1406), *Statutes of the Realm*, vol. 2, pp. 155–56.

[95] The statute also permitted lords, knights, and esquires to give livery of cloth or chaperons in connection with war. It granted power to inquire, but not to determine, to assize justices and to certify their findings to the King's Bench, but granted no authority to justices of the peace, contrary to the Commons' request.

[96] Parliaments of Henry IV: November 1411, no. XIII, 38, *PROME*.

[97] 13 Hen IV, c. 3 (1411), *Statutes of the Realm*, vol. 2, p. 167.

[98] None occurred during the reigns of Henry V (1413–22) or Richard III (1483–85).

ordinances are unable to be indicted before the said justices on account of the great maintenance had in this matter."[99] To eliminate this problem, they proposed a summary procedure for enforcing these statutes.[100] Although an earlier identical petition had been unsuccessful,[101] this one produced a statute incorporating their request.[102] It provided that for the purpose of enforcing the 1399 and 1406 statutes, the justices of assize and justices of the peace were empowered to issue writs of attachment and distraint to the sheriff, returnable before them, in actions at the suit of the king or a party. If the sheriff returned that the accused had nothing, the statute authorized issuing a *capias* and exigent that should be awarded in the same way as against those indicted for trespass before the justices of the peace. If the accused appeared, those justices were authorized to examine them and, if they had violated the statute, to impose the specified penalties as if they had been convicted by inquest before the justices.[103] The statute also extended the prohibition on giving livery of cloth and chaperons by knights and those of lesser status to those who received it from any spiritual or temporal lord or any lady. Finally, it prohibited any person

[99] A particular problem was the forcible expulsion of men from their lands, prompting a desire to authorize justices of the peace to restore possession. R.L. Storey, *The End of the House of Lancaster*, 2nd ed. (Gloucester, 1986), p. 26.

[100] Parliaments of Henry IV: September 1429, no. IIII, 35, *PROME*. In the same parliament, in an item dealing with avoidance of riots and other wrongdoing, the Lords ordained that no lord of the council should maintain felons and other wrongdoers, support or maintain another man's suit orally or in writing to any officer, judge, jury, or party, or "by gift of his clothing or livery or taking the party into his service." They were also obligated to insure that their neighbors and servants and all others of lesser estate under their authority observed this ordinance. Ibid., no. 27, XVI, *PROME*.

[101] The response was general and said only that the previous statutes should be enforced. Parliaments of Henry VI: October 1427, VII, no. 34, *PROME*.

[102] 8 Hen. VI, c. 4 (1429), *Statutes of the Realm*, vol. 2, pp. 240–41. McKelvie thought that the numerous indictments of many men in 1428 and the political and military context of 1429 influenced the concern about livery and the receptiveness to the 1429 petition, unlike in 1427. Gordon McKelvie, "The Livery Statute of 1429," in Linda Clark, ed., *The Fifteenth Century* (Woodbridge, 2015), vol. XIV, pp. 57–60. Griffith noted several instances of livery associated with maintenance and other wrongdoing that also may have influenced the adoption of this statute. He also noted the 1429 and 1433 oaths, which required of the council and lords to abstain, *inter alia*, from livery and maintenance. Griffiths, *Henry VI*, pp. 133–36, 144–47.

[103] As also previously requested, the statute extended the earlier statutes to the counties of Chester and Lancaster, with comparable procedures. Although the statute was ambiguous, it seemed to exempt certain officials and their recipients from these statutes. It also reiterated the exception in connection with war. Ibid., p. 241.

from buying and wearing the livery of any lord, lady, knight, esquire, or other person in order to have "support, help, or maintenance in any quarrel or other matter."[104]

The parliamentary activity concerning livery during the reign of Edward IV was somewhat different, as it reflected a sharper focus on retainers. In Edward's first parliament, the chancellor announced that, because illegal "gifts of livery and other badges," maintenance of quarrels, and violent wrongdoing had multiplied, the king had ordained certain articles that the Lords in parliament had promised to uphold and to cause others to do the same. The king said that the articles should be publicly proclaimed and observed.[105] Among the several articles were two dealing with livery. One article ordained a new prohibition on retainers, and the other repeated the prior prohibitions and exceptions on giving livery of cloth.[106] The new prohibition provided that "no lord or person of lower estate or degree shall henceforth give any livery of badge, mark or token of retainer" except as "specially commanded by the king" for the defense of the realm against enemies or riots.[107] There was a comparable prohibition regarding wearing of livery by recipients, which preserved existing exceptions.[108] A decade later, Edward IV denounced livery and maintenance. In a letter to the mayor of Coventry and the sheriffs, he made comments similar to those made in the above article, reciting the negative impact of livery,

---

[104] The penalty for violating this last provision was imprisonment for a year without bail or mainprise "for their falsity and subtle plotting." Ibid. McKelvie believed that this was a significant and novel provision in the context of the livery legislation. McKelvie, "The Livery Act of 1429," pp. 58, 62.

[105] He also said that king wished to be more fully informed on this maintenance and other wrongdoings and would, therefore, travel throughout the realm to hear those aggrieved, who should have their bills of complaint ready for presentation. Parliaments of Edward IV: November 1461, no. 38, *PROME*.

[106] Ibid., no. 39, *PROME*. In ordaining the article, the king said that because the illegal "giving of liveries and badges, maintenance of quarrels, extortions, robberies and murders have multiplied," he "wish[ed] to remedy such troubles and for there to be due process of law." In 1457, the king had granted virtual military powers to certain magnates and sheriffs to deal with illegal giving of livery and badges associated with wrongdoing by York's retainers, and in 1469 he authorized an "extraordinarily powerful" *oyer et terminer* Commission containing some of the same men regarding other livery-based wrongdoing. Griffiths, *Henry VI*, pp. 801, 829.

[107] There was an exception for wardens of the Scottish marches. Violators of the article would suffer the penalties of the existing statutes.

[108] It would seem that those who gave livery for retaining to those who were permitted to wear it under prior statutes would be also excepted, although the article does not explicitly say that.

maintenance, embracery, corruption, and other wrongdoing and his desire for order and equal administration of justice. He urged them to uphold the law and insure that "no retainers, liveries, signs, or tokens of clothing be taken, had or used" in Coventry, to expel violators from city, and to certify to the king the names of the givers, takers, and their supporters.[109]

But the most important development during this reign was the Statute of Livery 1468.[110] Its significance was the broad ban that it enacted on the giving of livery and retainers.[111] After reciting that there were diverse earlier statutes that were not being observed and that they should be upheld, it provided that no person, whatever his estate, degree, or condition, or any other for him, "shall give any such livery or badge or retain any person other than his household servant, officer, or man learned in one law or the other." The statute mandated penalties of 100s for each livery or badge given and 100s for both the giver and recipient for each month of the retainer.[112] It provided further that all retainers in violation of the statute were void, but it did not prohibit fees, annuities, pensions, or compensation in kind for giving counsel or other lawful service.[113] Certain types of ceremonial

---

[109] Myers, *English Historical Documents,* vol. IV, no. 666, p. 1132 (1472).

[110] 8 Edw. IV, c. 2 (1468), *Statutes of the Realm,* vol. 2, pp. 426–29. Both Ross and Bellamy believed that the Grey–Vernon dispute in Derbyshire had prompted the statute. Charles Ross, *Edward IV* (Berkeley, CA, 1974), p. 412; J.G. Bellamy, "Justice under the Yorkist Kings," *American Journal of Legal History* 9 (1965), pp. 151–54. Hicks said that it was the most obvious fruit of Edward IV's commitment to justice made in parliament on May 17, 1468 (Parliaments of Edward IV: June 1467, nos. 24–27, *PROME*). M.A. Hicks, "The 1468 Statute of Livery," *Historical Research* 64 (1991), pp. 16–20.

[111] Although there is an item on liveries included in the Commons' petitions in parliament, it recited the statute and did not specifically state what the Commons requested. Its substance was identical to the statute and the language was nearly so. Parliaments of Edward IV: June 1467, no. 41, *PROME*.

[112] The statute then authorized a very large number and types of courts in which suit could be brought for violations of this statute and for individuals to give such information for the king. It provided further that such informers could sue for themselves or the king against numerous offenders in one bill or information without individual bills or original writs with the same process as was available in a writ of trespass against the king's peace. The complainant would receive half of the forfeiture with the other half to the king unless it occurred in a court of a franchise or liberty, in which case the holder of that would receive the other half. 8 Edw. IV, c. 2 (1468), *Statutes of the Realm,* vol. 2, pp. 426–28.

[113] It specifically provided that the person providing counsel or service did not have to be learned in one law or the other. Ibid., p. 428.

livery were also permitted.[114] The statute also provided a summary procedure for its enforcement.[115]

Significantly, retainers by indenture, contract, fee, oath, promise, or other means of any person not within the exceptions were now prohibited. McFarlane said that not until this statute was enacted "was the attack mounted against all retainers as such."[116] Interestingly, there is no evidence that the Lords resisted as they had done earlier. But retainers, especially by magnates and peers who would seem to have been covered by the statute, did not end.[117] Harriss thought that the act had little effect.[118]

Understanding the Livery Statutes

Understanding the livery statutes enacted in the late medieval period has two dimensions. The first dimension requires an analysis of the legal rules applied to livery, since the rules were derived from multiple

---

[114] These included royal coronations, installations of archbishops and bishops, magnate marriages, creation of university clerks, and as to liveries given by serjeants at their creations. There were also exceptions for wardens of the Scottish marches, the constable and marshal, and certain other officials, and in defense of the realm or the king. Ibid., pp. 428–29.

[115] It authorized the judges of the various courts to convict violators without the necessity of an indictment or jury verdict or do so by trial. There were a number of other procedures that facilitated enforcement and made it easier to convict defendants. It also gave mayors and other city officials the authority to hear and determine pleas by summary procedure or trial. But the justices of the courts of counties palatine of Lancaster and Chester and the bishopric of Durham were not authorized to award exigent. Ibid., pp. 427–28. Bellamy thought that this procedure for informations created a precedent for Tudor penal law. J.G. Bellamy, *Criminal Law and Society in Late Medieval and Tudor England* (Gloucester, 1984), pp. 17, 19, 95–96, 110.

[116] McFarlane, *Nobility*, pp. 106–07. Dunham made similar comments. Dunham, *Lord Hastings*, p. 12.

[117] McFarlane, *Nobility*, pp. 107–13; Dunham, *Lord Hastings*, pp. 12–13, 47–89. Rowney viewed Lord Hasting's affinity and retaining in positive terms. He said that this "impressive affinity ... was moulded to the contours of gentry society, which represented and fostered stability rather than factional rivalry or social unrest." Ian Rowney, "Resources and Retaining in Yorkist England: William, Lord Hastings and the Honour of Tutbury," in Tony Pollard, ed., *Property and Politics: Essays in Later Medieval History* (New York, 1984), pp. 151–52.

[118] He said that there was no enforcement against peers and suggested that the statute might have been evaded by changing the language of indentures. G.L. Harriss, "Introduction," in K.B. McFarlane, *England in the Fifteenth Century: Collected Essays* (London, 1981), p. xxii. McFarlane said that the disorder of the last quarter of the fifteenth century caused "a partial relaxation of the statutes against retaining and liveries." McFarlane, "Lords and Retainers," Lecture VIII (VII), pp. 1–2.

statutes. The second aspect involves their evaluation in a broader social, political, and legal context.

The Legal Rules

In the period 1377–1468, there were twelve measures directed at livery.[119] These regulations all varied according to the type of livery involved, the persons to whom the prohibition applied, the exceptions of permitted livery, and the procedures for enforcement. Furthermore, none of these measures was ever repealed and many of the later statutes confirmed the earlier ones. McFarlane said that what was produced was less clear than desirable and "nothing but confusion and misunderstanding."[120] Perhaps the best way to fit them all together is to analyze them according to the type of livery prohibited. There were three types of livery: badges (*signes, signa*), chaperons (*chaperons, capitia*), and cloth (*suyte, drap, pannus*). Contemporaries distinguished them, and, to some extent, they were given for different purposes.[121]

Badges or other signs were frequently linked with wrongful and harmful conduct. They were cheap to make and could be quickly given to large numbers of people. There were six prohibitions directed at badges, with the first one in the 1390 Ordinance.[122] This ordinance initiated a regulatory pattern based on social stratification and distinctions in status for both givers and recipients.[123] All clerics, "bachelors," esquires, and those of lower status were prohibited from giving livery, but peers, barons, and bannerets were permitted to give it to knights or esquires retained by indenture or to servants, family, yeoman archers, or those of lesser estate living in the household. But these distinctions are not completely clear. Bannerets and bachelors would both seem to be high-ranking knights at the top of the gentry status, yet one was a

---

[119] Nine were statutes, two ordinances, and one article. This does not include the enactments dealing with judges. Appendix B is a table comparing these statutes.

[120] He reviewed the statutes enacted in the period 1377–1411. He called it "legislation by reference." He explained that the subsequent statutes cited the earlier ones, as "they did not see the need to re-enact their prohibitions; they merely added supplementary clauses, which were not intended to supercede what had been enacted previously." K.B. McFarlane, "Lords and Retainers," Lectures V–VI, pp. 16–19.

[121] Given-Wilson, *The King's Affinity*, pp. 236–37. Several statutes also prohibited livery of company, but that term related more to the type of giver or recipient or the purpose of giving than to a type of livery.

[122] 13 Rich. II, st. 3 (1390), *Statutes of the Realm*, vol. 2, pp. 74–75.

[123] McFarlane, *Nobility*, pp. 122–25.

permitted giver and the other a prohibited one. Perhaps the military status of the former was the explanation.[124] Moreover, the absence of knights among the prohibited givers seems odd, as their status would seem to be similar to that of bachelors.[125] Finally, the phrase "living in the household" presented interpretative problems.

The next three statutes built on the status structure of the earlier one. The 1393 statute explicitly extended the prohibition on receiving badges to yeoman or those of lesser rank than esquire unless they were servants or family dwelling continually in the household, which made that exception clearer.[126] The 1397 statute seemed to repeat that statute, only clarifying that varlets, known as yeomen, could not use or wear badges.[127] But the 1399 statute made an important change in this structure. It prohibited all lords of whatever estate from giving badges to any knight, esquire, or yeoman. This prohibition would include peers, but there was an exception for the king.

Livery of cloth was the giving of robes and cloth of uniform color and material for making robes or garments. The cloth was not necessarily of only one color and could be of several colors ("parti-colored"). Livery of cloth was more expensive and time consuming to produce than badges.[128] This type of livery received considerable legislative attention, with five statutes regulating its distribution, although during a somewhat later period than those dealing with badges. The initial regulation of it in 1377 was quite limited, prohibiting only livery that was given by the gentry for maintenance of confederacies.[129] It remained the only regulation of this type of livery for more than twenty years. But in 1399, all spiritual and temporal persons of whatever estate were prohibited from giving livery of cloth to anyone except a domestic servant ("*menial*"), officers, and spiritual and temporal counsel learned in one law or another.[130]

---

[124] Coss recognized the distinction between bannerets and bachelors, but said it was one of degree, not of kind, although one "of considerable social significance." Coss, *English Gentry*, p. 241.

[125] It may be possible that all knights were intended by the term "bachelor," but that seems unlikely, given that knights are listed in the provision dealing with dukes, earls, and barons.

[126] 16 Rich. II c. 4 (1393), *Statutes of the Realm*, vol. 2, p. 84.

[127] 20 Rich. II, cc. 1–2 (1397), *Statutes of the Realm*, vol. 2 p. 93.

[128] Davies, *Lords and Lordship*, pp. 104, 204.

[129] 1 Rich. II, c. 7 (1377), *Statutes of the Realm*, vol. 2, p. 3.

[130] 1 Hen. IV c. 7 (1399), *Statutes of the Realm*, vol. 2, pp. 113–14.

Livery of chaperons received less legislative attention. Only three statutes were directed at this form of livery, and all of these statutes applied to livery of cloth as well. The regulation of giving chaperons was basically the same as that applied to livery of cloth.

Thus, as of 1399, the law governing giving of all types of livery seemed relatively clear. These prohibitions constituted the basic regulation of the distribution of livery for the next eight decades, although there were some minor modifications that broadened it.[131] Moreover, retainers, life indentures, and payment of fees were still lawful. But in 1468,[132] the law made all retainers and the giving of any livery or badges by anyone illegal unless it was to a menial servant, officer, man learned in one law or another, or any person, whether or not a lawyer for counsel or for lawful service.[133] Although the 1468 statute did not change the basic prohibitions regarding livery, its novelty was the broad ban on retainers.

It is also important to understand the mechanisms prescribed for enforcing these statutes. The enforcement procedures of the six statutes enacted between 1377 and 1399 were the standard criminal ones, indictment and penalties of imprisonment and fines.[134] But starting in 1401, the statutes created additional and more complicated enforcement methods. First, the 1406, 1429, and 1468 statutes set specific monetary penalties for violations and authorized *qui tam* actions, in which a person could sue to enforce the statute and collect half of the penalty.[135] Second,

---

[131] In 1406, the prohibition was extended to giving by congregations and companies other than guilds, fraternities, and the mysteries of city and borough people founded for beneficial purposes. 7 Hen. IV, c. 14 (1406), *Statutes of the Realm*, vol. 2, pp. 155–56. The 1429 statute made taking livery of cloth from any spiritual or temporal lord or great lady explicitly illegal, made wearing it by one's own authority and cost illegal, and extended the prohibition to the counties of Lancaster and Chester. 8 Hen. VI, c. 4 (1429), *Statutes of the Realm*, vol. 2, pp. 240–41.

[132] An article ordained in parliament in 1461 seemed to repeat the status quo, prohibiting all lords from giving badges to retainers, except those previously excepted, and retainers from wearing any badges. But it did create an exception if specially ordered by the king in connection with defending against revolts and riots. It also restated the 1399 prohibition of the giving, taking, or wearing of livery of cloth by anyone other than those excepted by that statute. Parliaments of Edward IV: November 1461, no. 39, *PROME*.

[133] These exceptions were described above in the discussion of badges. 8 Edw. IV, c. 2 (1468), *Statutes of the Realm*, vol. 2, pp. 426–29. There also some special exceptions for coronations, marriages, and other giving as described above. Ibid. See p. 289.

[134] The justices of assize and the peace were empowered to enforce most of these statutes.

[135] 7 Hen. IV, c. 14 (1406), *Statutes of the Realm*, vol. 2, pp. 155–56; 8 Hen. VI, c. 4 (1429), *Statutes of the Realm*, vol. 2, pp. 240–41; 8 Edw. IV, c. 2 (1468), *Statutes of the Realm*, vol. 2, pp. 426–29.

the 1401, 1406, 1429, and 1468 statutes created enhanced enforcement procedures. The 1401 statute, which applied to livery of company, authorized the justices of both benches and the justices of assize and of the peace to hear and determine these matters "by record made in their presence or by inquiry made from time to time."[136] The first process seems to contemplate a summary procedure by which these justices could produce sufficient evidence for determining violations, which they could view in court without the need of an indictment or jury inquest, but the second process seems to be based on a traditional indictment and jury verdict. The 1406 statute created a different procedure for determining illegal giving of cloth and chaperons. It authorized the justices of assize to inquire from time to time in their sessions of these matters and certify them to the King's Bench.[137] But the 1429 statute expanded the use of summary procedure to the giving of livery of cloth and chaperons by knights or those of lesser estate. It authorized the justices of assize and peace to compel appearance of alleged offenders at the suit of the king or party, using writs of attachment and distraint and *capias* and exigent, if they did not appear, in the same manner as in indictment for trespass *vi et armis*. But if they did appear, the justices were authorized to compel such persons to answer a sworn complaint by an informer and to examine the defendants and to convict them, presumably without an indictment or jury inquisition.[138] The 1468 statute created a similar summary process applicable to all retainers and livery, which was somewhat broader and expanded the power to many more justices and courts.[139]

Qui tam procedures were used for enforcement of other statutes, although they were not that common. But the summary procedures for convicting violators without an indictment or jury inquisition or verdict seem more unusual. The rationale is clear in light of the Commons complaint that maintenance precluded indictment of offenders. But interference with criminal enforcement occurred with other statutes, for which no summary procedures were adopted. Perhaps their use with livery was an indication of the actual or apparent strength of

---

[136] 2 Hen IV, c. 21, *Statutes of the Realm*, vol. 2, p. 130 (1401).

[137] 7 Hen. IV, c. 14, *Statutes of the Realm*, vol. 2, pp. 155–56 (1406);

[138] 8 Hen. VI, c. 4, *Statutes of the Realm*, vol. 2, pp. 240–41 (1429). Brand believes that "at the king's suit" did not require a formal action by the crown and included the justices acting on their own initiative based on an oral complaint or suggestion of a knowledgeable local official or person. Gratitude is expressed to Prof. Paul Brand for this explanation.

[139] 8 Edw. IV, c. 2, *Statutes of the Realm*, vol. 2, pp. 426–28 (1468).

parliamentary sentiment. No evidence has been found, however, regarding the actual use of these procedures in the late medieval period.

The Broader Context

Livery should be understood in a broader context as another manifestation of the persistent medieval problem of conduct that undermined law and order.[140] The giving of livery to large numbers of retainers was a means by which the justice system was disrupted by wrongful conduct. As earlier chapters have shown, the problem of preserving law and order and the creation of legal remedies to control illegal activities started primarily in the reign of Edward I. These livery statutes were just another legislative effort in a long list of legal measures directed at this same longstanding problem. Moreover, as was true with other statutes, there were repeated complaints about the failure of enforcement.[141]

Several factors illustrated the connection between livery and illegality and disorder. First, as the petitions and statutes amply illustrated, livery was often associated with maintenance as a mechanism to facilitate and effectuate it. Also as previously discussed, it was a persistent problem, and efforts to eradicate this form of legal corruption began in 1275. Livery was also a form of collective misconduct. In the early fourteenth century, it had been linked to conspiracy, as the 1305 Ordinance defining conspirators included those who "retain men in the country with liveries."[142] The 1377 statute specifically associated livery and confederacy. Conspiracy was perhaps the earliest remedy directed at perversion of the justice system. Further, the late medieval creation of affinities, the expansion of retainers, and the widespread distribution of livery were reminiscent of the earlier formation of conspiracies, confederations, and covins, which had prompted similar concerns and litigation.

In addition to the dynamics of these contemporary social and political institutions, contemporary events such as the disorder during the reign of

---

[140] Davies said that "by the mid-late fourteenth century the indiscriminate distribution of livery had come to be seen, among the new aristocratic gentle classes, as the unacceptable and oppressive face of irresponsible lordship and as a root cause of disorder." Davies, *Lords and Lordship*, p. 212.

[141] Griffiths pointed out that enforcement was hampered because "such restrictions ran counter to the social and political need and also because their enforcement depended on the very men who gained the most from their breach as employers or retainers." Griffiths, *Henry VI*, pp. 592–93.

[142] 33 Edw. I (1305), *Statutes of the Realm*, vol. 1, p. 145.

Richard II and the 1381 Peasants' Revolt were catalysts that provoked and intensified the concern about the giving of livery.[143] Saul viewed the Peasant's Revolt as an important factor in the Commons' repeated attacks on livery. He said they saw maintenance and livery as producing a breakdown in the social hierarchy and that they feared that such lawlessness and misrule would prompt discontent again.[144] Moreover, as the disputed 1401 petition illustrated, the Commons was concerned that the manner in which livery was distributed divided the community of the realm and created inequality.[145] Saul said that they were concerned about the "increasing stress to which the social fabric was being subjected" and the need for "recalling the estates to a sense of the former responsibilities."[146] Lordship had "to operate both within a framework of (changing) conventions of behaviour" and in a "sophisticated and multi-textured and far more complex" society.[147] Thus, as is true with most legal issues, the livery statutes must be understood in their social, political, and historical context.

Criminal and Civil Livery Litigation

To use a modern phrase, all this livery legislation was the "law in the books." But it revealed nothing about the "law in action," the actual enforcement of these statutes and their effect in curbing livery and maintenance. Although most scholars have been skeptical about the enforcement and effect of these statutes, there has not been significant

---

[143] A related concern was with riots and unlawful assembly. Starting in the late fourteenth century and continuing into the fifteenth century, several statutes were enacted to deal with them. 17 Rich. II, c. 8 (1393–94), *Statutes of the Realm*, vol. 2, p. 89; 13 Hen. IV, c. 7 (1411), *Statutes of the Realm*, vol. 2, p. 169; 2 Hen. V, st. 1, c. 8 (1414), *Statutes of the Realm*, vol. 2, pp. 184–86; "The Late Medieval World of Riot," in Bellamy, *Criminal Law and Society*, pp. 54–89.

[144] He said that "symptomatic of the general decay was the magnates' distribution of badges" and that "bestowal of these marks of favor emboldened the wearers and encouraged them in their misdeeds." Saul, *Richard II*, pp. 81–82, 200.

[145] Given-Wilson pointed out that the perspectives of the Commons and the king were likely different. The Commons feared the petty tyrannies that magnate power created, while the king feared the threat of revolt posed by magnate power, taking a more political view of the livery legislation. Given-Wilson, *The King's Affinity*, pp. 241–42, 256–57.

[146] He also said that the gentry were concerned about the "threat to their status represented by the growing aspirations of their inferiors." Saul, "Abolition of Badges," pp. 311–12. Given-Wilson also noted the importance of livery on social distinctions. Given-Wilson, *The King's Affinity*, p. 238.

[147] Davies, *Lords and Lordship*, p. 213.

inquiry into their actual enforcement by examination of the plea rolls for the late medieval period. Those records contain a number of cases and actions involving violations of the livery statutes. The livery litigation, however, differed substantially from that involving maintenance. First, it was much less extensive.[148] Second, it was almost entirely crown enforcement. There were virtually no private civil actions, which constituted the bulk of the maintenance litigation in this period. No evidence was found of writs authorizing civil actions, as existed for maintenance actions. Moreover, the crown was much less aggressive in enforcing the livery statutes than it was with the maintenance statutes.[149]

There were no livery cases before 1410. This was more than three decades after the enactment of the first statute and after the period of the greatest legislative and political activity. Perhaps the tumult and aftermath of the reign of Richard II and lack of interest by the crown account for the delay in this activity. The great majority of the livery cases were criminal prosecutions (88%).[150] The first presentment was in 1410, with a substantial increase in criminal enforcement during the reign of Henry V (1413–22),[151] decreasing during the reigns of Henry VI (1422–61), and jumping substantially during the remainder of the period, with the majority (53%) occurring in the period 1461–85. No civil actions appeared until 1428 and they remained at about the same low level

---

[148] In the plea rolls, Some 162 actions and cases were found. During the late medieval period, there were more than four times more maintenance actions and cases than livery ones.

[149] Even though the number of private maintenance actions in this period was substantially greater than crown livery actions and criminal maintenance cases, the number of those crown maintenance cases was substantially greater than the crown livery actions and criminal livery cases.

[150] The remainder was crown livery actions. Mesne process entries constituted 40% of the records in the criminal cases. Also all but one of the crown livery actions were mesne process entries, and, similar to crown maintenance actions, several defendants appeared and asked the king to count against them. Since no complainant ever appeared in response to the proclamation, the defendants went without day, as was the case with the crown maintenance actions. TNA: PRO KB 27/698, m. 1 rex (1435), AALT Img. No. 232.

[151] All but one of the cases in the period 1399–1422 occurred during the reign of Henry V and 75% of them were in 1414 and from two counties, Staffordshire and Shropshire, especially the former. The unusually high number may have been a product of the feud between Hugh de Erdwick and his brothers and Edmund Ferrers, Baron Chartley, and others in Staffordshire and of similar disorders in Shropshire. Many of these livery cases relating to Hugh and his supporters and their antagonists as well as those in Shropshire involved other wrongdoing. Edward Powell, *Kingship, Law and Society: Criminal Justice in the Reign of Henry V* (Oxford, 1989), pp. 53, 123, 139, 169–70, 208–24, 241–42. Powell found substantial livery litigation in these two counties, but none in Leicestershire, Nottinghamshire, or Derbyshire. Ibid., p. 278.

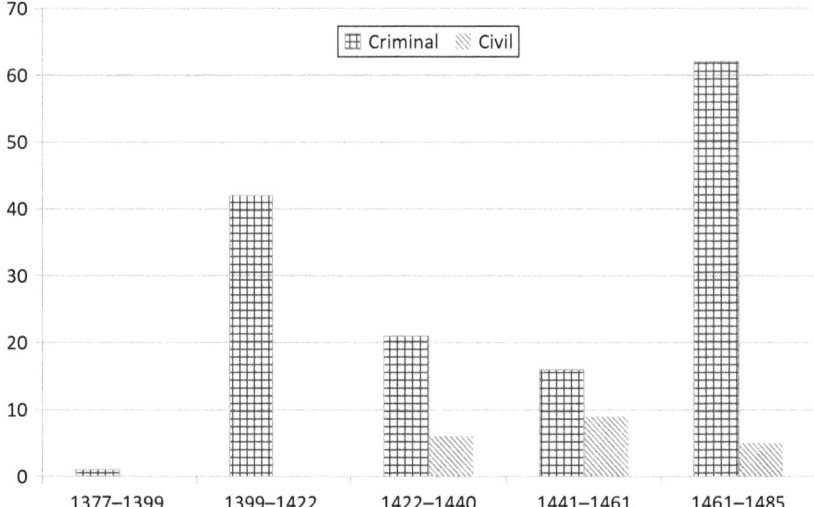

Figure 11.1. Livery litigation, 1399–1485.

throughout the period. The only non-crown-based actions were *qui tam* actions pursuant to the 1406 and later statutes.[152] Figure 11.1 shows the frequency and distribution of criminal and civil livery litigation.

Most of the criminal presentments (70%) as well as the crown livery actions (91%) alleged violations of the statutes regarding livery without identifying any particular statute.[153] Similarly, many criminal cases (66%) and civil actions (90%) only alleged that the defendants had given or received livery of cloth without any further details.[154] But some did identify the type of livery given or received. Robes (*togas*) were the most commonly

---

[152] There were only seven such cases. They have been classified as criminal cases because they were an aspect of the enforcement of the statute. The plaintiffs sued for half of the statutory penalty and did not allege person harm nor seek compensatory damages. One of these cases was actually after 1485, but only by a few years. It was included as it was the only case found that specifically alleged a violation of the 1468 statute. TNA: PRO KB 27/916, m. 74 (1489), AALT Img. Nos. 166–67, 402.

[153] Many just alleged violation of the "statutes" or the "statutes and ordinances." Several (18%) referred to the specific statutes. The most common statutory references were to 1 Hen. IV, c. 7, 7 Hen. IV, c. 14, and several presentments quoted these statutes. A few cases also mentioned 1 Rich. II, c. 7. There was only one reference to the controversial 1390 Ordinance, 13 Rich. II, st. 3, and one to the 1468 Statute, 8 Edw. IV, c. 2.

[154] This calculation includes the mesne process entries that alleged a violation of the statutes regarding livery of cloth, as presumably it is reasonable, without further information, to treat them as involving the giving and receiving of cloth.

specified (22%), and those presentments frequently involved multiple recipients, who were alleged to have been given one robe each. Several cases (23%) gave further details regarding the quantity of cloth or the color of the livery.[155] Although the giving of badges apparently caused the greatest concern in parliament, only one case alleged such an offense.[156]

The nature of the defendants and the breakdown between givers of livery and the recipients is generally what would be expected given the statutory prohibitions and exceptions as well as the contemporary social stratification.[157] By and large, the primary givers were of high social status and the recipients of lower status.[158] Contrary to the assertions of some scholars, peers, such as dukes, earls, and barons, were among those indicted, and in these cases, such nobility were only givers and never recipients.[159]

---

[155] The quantity was usually three yards or three ells of colored or wool cloth; in some cases it was said that the recipient was to fashion the appropriate livery. For example, one presentment said that seven men received three yards of wool cloth from a knight and that three other men received three yards of green and white cloth from the same knight. TNA: PRO KB 27/619, m. 10 rex (1416), AALT Img. No. 23. Some cases specified the color of the robes, jackets, and chaperons. One said that Henry Grey, lord of Codnor, gave each of twelve men a tawny-colored jacket of his livery, and another said that Walter Blount, lord of Mountjoy, gave ten men a russet robe of his livery, and another that nineteen conspirators undertook to maintain each other's pleas and that each acquired a rayed (striped) hood of various colors, in violation of the livery ordinance. TNA: PRO KB 9/13, m. 20 (1468), AALT Img. No. 39; TNA: PRO KB 9/13, m. 22 (1468), AALT Img. No. 43; TNA: PRO KB 9/11, m. 17 (1434), AALT Img. No. 34.

[156] In that case, the jurors presented that John Talbot, earl of Shrewsbury, gave silver talbots to an esquire, a gentleman, and twenty yeoman. TNA: PRO KB 9/13, m. 23 (1468), AALT Img. No. 45. Gratitude is expressed to Prof. John Baker for indicating that silver talbots were uncommon (only one has been found). Pewter ones were more common. Three other cases alleged that John Talbot gave and others received a jacket in one case, cloth and hood in two cases, and a hood in another case.

[157] The records identified 1,164 defendants in the criminal cases and 142 defendants in the civil cases. In the former, it was not possible to identify whether the defendant was a giver or recipients in 275 cases because they were named in mesne process entries, although their social status or occupation was identified. That was true in almost all the civil actions, with one exception, and also in all the crown livery actions, as they were mesne process entries. Also there were 59 criminal cases in which the social status was not identified because they occurred before the 1413 Statute of Additions, which required such information. 1 Hen. V, c. 5 (1413), *Statutes of the Realm*, vol. 2, p. 171. Finally, 31 individuals were named in presentments but were not charged as defendants, as was true with one individual in a civil action.

[158] In the criminal cases, the social status of 89 givers of livery and 741 recipients were identified. In civil actions, the status of only one giver and one recipient were identified.

[159] Two important men were indicted for giving livery of cloth for war, although it had been specifically permitted since 1406. 7 Hen. IV, c. 14 (1406), *Statutes of the Realm*, vol. 2, pp. 155–56. Sir Henry Grey, Baron Grey of Codnor, and Sir John Gresley, a

Table 11.1 *Defendants in criminal livery cases, 1377–1485*

Status	Give	Receive	Unknown	Total
Nobility	19 (21%)	0 (0%)	0	19
Knights	21 (24%)	19 (2%)	17	57
Esquires	37 (42%)	85 (11%)	29	151
Gentlemen	9 (10%)	43 (5%)	31	83
Yeomen	2 (2%)	422 (53%)	151	575
Husbandmen	0 (0)	22 (3%)	4	26
Trades-occupations	1 (1%)	150 (19%)	43	194
Not stated	0 (0%)	57 (7%)	2	59
Totals	89	798	277	1,164

Yeomen, husbandmen, and the members of various trades and occupations,[160] with very minor exceptions, were all recipients.[161] The gentry –
knights, esquires, and gentlemen – however, were mixed, being both givers
and recipients, with knights evenly divided and esquires and gentlemen
more likely to be recipients. Seventeen presentments involved twenty or
more recipients.[162] As Table 11.1 shows, esquires were the most common

member of parliament, retainer of William, Lord Hastings, and whose wife was a
descendant of Geoffrey, Count of Anjou, both gave livery of cloth for war in the north,
but both were pardoned. TNA: PRO KB 27/843, m. 25 rex (1472), AALT Img. No. 249;
TNA: PRO KB 27/844, m. 36d rex (1472), AALT Img. Nos. 669–70. In addition,
another important figure, Sir Walter Blount, Baron Mountjoy, former treasurer of
England, whose wife was the daughter of Ralph Neville, earl of Westmoreland and
widow of Humphrey Stafford, duke of Buckingham, was indicted for giving livery of
cloth for the 1461 coronation of Edward IV. Giving livery for royal coronations,
marriages, and other ceremonial events was not exempted until 1468. 8 Edw. IV, c. 2
(1468), *Statutes of the Realm*, vol. 2, p. 428.

[160] Members of 62 different trades and occupations were defendants in the criminal cases.
They were identified not by their social status but by their "mystery," as required by the
Statute of Additions. But presumably their status was below that of esquire, the general
line of demarcation for purposes of the livery statutes.

[161] Two yeomen and one courtholder were presented for giving livery. Both of them
received pardons. TNA: PRO KB 27/619, m. 9d rex (1416), AALT Img. No. 280;
TNA: PRO KB 27/829, mm. 13 rex, 4d rex (1468), AALT Img. Nos. 220, 446.

[162] The largest involved three indictments of John Mowbray, the duke of Norfolk, for giving
robes to a total 137 men in groups of 43, 28, and 67. TNA: PRO KB 27/839, m. 31 rex
(1471), AALT Img. Nos. 256–58, 495–96. In another case, John Talbot, the earl of
Shrewsbury, was indicted for giving livery of cloth to 61 recipients and another presentment listed 68 men, who were likely recipients. TNA: PRO KB 9/13, m. 11 (1468), AALT
Img. No. 23; TNA: PRO KB 27/778, m. 13d rex (1455), AALT Img. No. 565.

givers and yeomen the common recipients.[163] The distribution of defendants in the civil cases was similar.[164]

Although there were only seven *qui tam* actions, they merit some
discussion. The identified plaintiffs were all gentry, four knights and two
esquires.[165] All but one of these cases involved large groups of defendants.[166] The nature of the defendants in the *qui tam* cases was similar to
those in which the defendants had been indicted. In the seven cases, the
identified givers of livery were gentry, two knights and three esquires.[167]
The remaining 137 defendants consisted of fifty-four yeoman, thirty-six
members of trades and occupations, seventeen husbandmen, seven
gentlemen, and twenty-three whose status was not indicated.[168]

Several of these *qui tam* actions presented interesting legal questions. In
one action, a writ ordered the sheriff to have Sir Thomas Statham, a
retainer of Henry, Lord Grey of Codnor, William, Lord Hastings,[169] and
thirty-three yeomen in court to answer Thomas Vaughan, esquire[170] and
the king because Statham had given livery of cloth and chaperons in
violation of three livery statutes. But the king's attorney, pursuant to an
order of the king, appeared and waived and released the king's suit against
all the defendants.[171] Given the criminal nature of these *qui tam* actions, it
would seem that the waiver and release of king's action would have
negated the right of the esquire's action as he was not suing for damages

---

[163] The difference between "unknown" and "not stated" is that the former meant that their
names and status appeared in mesne process records, whereas in the latter the cases were
prior to the Statute of Additions. It is likely that all the "unknowns" among the yeomen,
husbandmen, and members of trades and occupations were recipients.

[164] There were 142 defendants in the civil actions. Since all but one were mesne process
entries, it was possible to identify their names and status, but not whether they gave or
received livery. None of the nobility was involved in the civil actions. The defendants in
civil cases included 1 knight, 2 esquires, 5 gentlemen, 93 yeoman, 10 husbandmen,
30 members of 16 different trades and occupations, and 1 rector. Only one of these
defendants was specifically identified as a recipient, but it is likely that they all were
recipients, with exception of one of the esquire defendants, who was a giver.

[165] One was not identified.

[166] There were a total of 143 defendants. The number of defendants in each case was 20, 10,
24, 25, 26, 34, and 3.

[167] In two cases, the givers were not identified.

[168] None of the records indicated whether these defendants were givers or recipients of
livery, but it seems likely that they were all recipients.

[169] Susan Wright, *The Derbyshire Gentry in the Fifteenth Century* (Chesterfield, 1983), p. 10.

[170] There were several persons named Thomas Vaughan who appeared as litigants during
this period. But one of them was an esquire to the body of Edward IV.

[171] TNA: PRO KB 29/97, m. 29 (1467), AALT Img. No. 85. The plaintiff would have
recovered £35 10s if he had been successful.

for personal harm, but to enforcement the statutory penalties.[172] Alleging a violation of the 1468 statute,[173] Peter Peckham, esquire, a Chancery clerk,[174] brought a *qui tam* action by his sworn bill of information.[175] He alleged that Sir Ralph Hastings, holder of several royal offices and brother of William, Lord Hastings, had retained two husbandmen and given each of them one and half yards of green medley and the same amount of wool cloth to make a robe of his faction and livery. He alleged further that the recipients had done that and had used the robes frequently.[176] Peter requested that process be issued against the defendants according to the form of the statute, which specifically provided that the process to be used was that which was used in an original writ of trespass against the king's peace. Although that was set out verbatim in the bill, the court was hesitant, perhaps because of the novelty of the procedure.[177] In the following term, Peter came again and obtained process.[178]

Overall, the livery litigation did not produce much pleading, which is not surprising given that it was largely criminal and most of the entries only recorded mesne process. But several cases did involve pleading.[179]

---

[172] Baker identified a later action that would seem to support that result. In that case, the attorney general's withdrawal of the crown's *praemunire* action nullified the informer's action. *Parret and Doctor Matthews Case*, 3 Leonard 139, 74 Eng. Reps. 592 (K.B. 1586). Gratitude is expressed to Prof. John Baker for sharing the case with me.

[173] 8 Edw. IV, c. 2 (1968), *Statutes of the Realm*, vol. 2, pp. 426–29.

[174] Ives, *The Common Lawyers of Pre-Reformation England*, pp. 106–07.

[175] The 1468 statute created a new procedure authorizing an informer to sue by a sworn bill of information and that "this information so given shall stand and be instead of a bill or original writ." 8 Edw. IV, c. 2 (1468), *Statutes of the Realm*, vol. 2, p. 427.

[176] The bill specified a number of dates and periods during the subsequent thirteen months on which the robes were used. TNA: PRO KB 27/916, m. 74 (1489), AALT Img. Nos. 166–67, 402.

[177] The court said that it wished to be advised as to the kind of process and what it wished to decide on that. Ibid.

[178] The court ordered the sheriff to put the defendants by gage and secure pledge to appear and answer the king and Peter. One *qui tam* action was notable because of the amount of pleading it generated. TNA: PRO KB 27/596, m. 76 (1410), AALT Img. Nos. 170–71, 158. One *qui tam* action produced a demurrer because the defendant's general denial was incomplete and insufficient. TNA: PRO CP 40/822, m. 288 (1466), AALT Img. Nos 535–36, 1467.

[179] There were 14 instances of pleading, 10 in presentments, 3 in *qui tam* actions, and 1 in a civil action. In 9 presentments, the pleading consisted of a general denial of giving and receiving of livery. In the 3 of those cases in which there were jury verdicts, the defendants were found not guilty. TNA: PRO KB 27/695, m. 7 rex (1435), AALT Img. Nos. 152–53, 348; TNA: PRO KB 27/696, m. 17 rex (1435), AALT Img. No. 189; TNA: PRO KB 27/861, m. 4d rex (1476), AALT Img. No. 1621. In one criminal case, the defendant denied the allegations and later received a pardon, and in a civil action, the

The most interesting pleaded cases were those that raised issues regarding the scope of the statute. In one case, Edmund Ferrers, Baron Chartley,[180] was charged in three separate presentments for giving livery to twenty-eight men.[181] Although he and six of the recipients denied the giving and receiving of livery,[182] he and the other twenty-two recipients said that the giving and receiving was permissible. Edmund as well as the recipients alleged that he was entitled to give livery because 7 Hen. IV, c. 14, which he recited, barred the giving of livery only by those who were knights or of lesser status and that "he and his all his ancestors since the time of the conquest were barons and called and acknowledged by the name of lord both in the king's presence and elsewhere," and therefore he was not restricted by the statute. The court then told Edmund and the recipients that they should certify fully to the court a record of what they alleged.[183] Neither of them did so. Edmund received a pardon from the king, but the recipients were found to have violated the statute for failing to certify and were each fined the statutory penalty of 40s.[184] Edmund's plea regarding barony is puzzling. The basis of the presentment was both 1 Hen IV, c. 7, and 7 Hen IV, c. 14. Although Ferrers might have had a defense under the latter statute if he had certified his peerage because that statute only prohibited giving of livery by knights and those of lesser estate, his giving of livery would still have violated 1 Hen IV, c. 7. His certification would not have been a defense under that statute since it prohibited giving of livery by anyone "of whatever estate" to anyone except household (menial)

---

defendant appeared and pleaded a pardon. TNA: PRO KB 27/829, mm. 13 rex, 4d rex (1468), AALT Img. Nos. 220, 446; TNA: PRO KB 27/778, m. 1 rex (1455), AALT Img. Nos. 635–36.

[180] TNA: PRO KB 27/613, m. 30 rex (1414), AALT Img. Nos. 131–32, 122–23v. Some sources treat him as the fifth Baron Chartley and others as the fourth. This presentment was likely connected to his dispute with Hugh de Erdwick.

[181] It was alleged that he gave 27 men 3 yards of green and red cloth on Christmas, 1413, 6 men 3 yards of green and white cloth on December 24, 1413, and 8 men in another 3 ells of cloth for their clothing annually, starting Christmas, 1413. Some of the recipients were in more than one of these groups. His father had died a few months earlier and he had recently thus become Baron Chartley.

[182] The king's attorney alleged the giving and receiving, and all the parties put themselves on the country.

[183] The king's attorney did not enter a responsive plea, but perhaps he felt it was premature until the defendants certified their allegations by a record.

[184] McFarlane said that the plea had been rejected. He pointed out that Edmund's ancestors had not received a summons to parliament since 1311 and that Chartley was not a "tenurial barony." McFarlane, Nobility, pp. 106–7, 123–24. Although McFarlane may be right as to those facts, the pardon precluded the need for a judgment on Edmond's plea.

servants, officers, and counsel spiritual or temporal learned in one law or the other, and the recipients were not in the excepted groups.[185]

Other cases raised issues regarding the interpretation of the exceptions, which permitted livery to be given to "household servants (*familiares*), officers, or counsel learned in one law or the other."[186] One case is particularly interesting because it involved a royal official. Sir John Etton, a royal forest steward,[187] was charged with giving livery of cloth to two men. John came and said that he was the forest steward, holding attachments in the king's forest court at and before the time of his indictment. He said further that he had retained one of the men as his clerk and counsel for holding the courts in his presence and absence, paying him 13s 4d annually and giving him livery of cloth for that reason. He said further that he was also the king's master forester and retained the other man to serve as his bow bearer and to be present at the attachments and other defaults as was the custom, paying him 13s 4d annually and giving him one livery of cloth. Both recipients repeated what John said. The king's attorney made the standard allegation that John gave the livery to men "who were not household servants (*familiares*), officers, or counsel learned in one law or the other."[188] In two other cases, defendants traversed the standard allegation in the presentment that giving and

---

[185] The pardon precluded reaching that issue as to Edmund and also as to the recipients because the court based their violation on the failure to certify. But that seems to be an odd reason. The correct legal reason was because they were permissible recipients of livery, as was correctly stated in the fine roll in the next term, which does not mention the failure to certify. TNA: PRO KB 27/614, m. 2 fine roll (1414), AALT Img. Nos. 230–31. Adding to the puzzlement, Edward Basset, esquire, one of the recipients, was presented again for receipt of the exact same livery, but received a pardon. TNA: PRO KB 27/614, m. 30 rex (1414), AALT Img. No. 285. It seems that the correct plea would have been *autrefois convict*, but perhaps a pardon was a quicker way to proceed. Unlike the prior presentment, he appeared by attorney in the second one.

[186] This exception appeared first in 1 Hen. IV, c. 7 (1399), *Statutes of the Realm*, vol. 2, pp. 113–14.

[187] The forest was Galtres, Yorkshire. He was also sheriff of Yorkshire on three earlier occasions and a member of parliament for Yorkshire on four occasions, including about the same time as his indictment. J.S. Roskell, Linda Clark, and Carole Rawcliffe, eds., *The History of Parliament: the House of Commons 1386–1421*, 4 vols. (Stroud, 1992), vol. 3, p. 36.

[188] The parties put themselves on the country and the sheriff failed twice to send the writ. TNA: PRO KB 27/642, m. 31 rex (1421), AALT Img. No. 304. Although most presentments regarding livery contained language that the recipients were not household servants or any other excepted persons, it did not appear in this one, which alleged that the giving violated various statutes of the king now and his ancestors for giving livery of cloth.

receiving did not fall within the statutory exceptions of permissible livery and alleged that the recipients were household servants retained in service by the giver of the livery. In both cases, the jury found the defendants not guilty.[189]

In this livery litigation, forty pardons were given to fifty-nine individuals, thirty-four to givers of livery and twenty-five to recipients.[190] Although pardons were generally quite common in medieval litigation, the 1406 statute, which established the monetary penalties and *qui tam* actions for livery of cloth and chaperons, expressly provided that these penalties could not be pardoned.[191] Although this prohibition was not expressly repeated in the subsequent statutes, those statutes commonly confirmed the earlier ones and presentments were usually based on multiple statutes without identifying a specific one. In these livery cases, all of the pardons were subsequent to 1406, the earliest being in 1414, and none of those defendants was prosecuted further in any fashion.[192] Thus, it seems that the prohibition was ignored. Many of peers indicted for giving livery were pardoned (58%).[193] John Mowbray duke of Norfolk,

---

[189] In one case, there was only one recipient, who received a robe and was alleged to have been a servant of John de la Pole, esquire, for food, drink, and money and continuously living in his house. The king's attorney rejected those allegations and alleged a violation as presented. TNA: PRO KB 27/695, m. 1 rex (1435), AALT Img. No. 140. In the second case, Sir Richard Vernon gave robes to 25 men, mostly yeomen. Both Richard and the recipients denied the giving and receiving of any livery to 8 of the men, and the king's attorney joined issue. Richard and the other 17 recipients said they were Richard's servants retained by him for a year. The king's attorney alleged that Richard gave and they received in violation of the statute. The jury seemed to ignore the special traverse that the 17 were servants and found that Richard gave no livery to any of the 25 men and that they received no livery. TNA: PRO KB 27/695, m. 7 rex (1435), AALT Img. Nos. 152–53, 348.

[190] All but one of the pardons involved criminal cases and all but one of the individuals involved criminal cases. There was one pardon to one individual in a crown livery action. In one case, Hugh Erdwick was indicted for several types of wrongdoing connected to his dispute with Edmund Ferrers, which involved force and violence including murder as well as his indictment for livery. He was pardoned for all his crimes except livery, on which the court wished to be advised further. TNA: PRO KB 27/614, m. 4 rex (1414), AALT Img. Nos. 235–36.

[191] 7 Hen. IV, c. 14, *Statutes of the Realm*, vol. 2, p. 155 (1406). Six pardons to 16 individuals were given in 1399–1422, none in 1422–40, 7 to 7 individuals in 1441–61, and 13 to 14 individuals in 1461–85.

[192] In most of the cases, the defendants went without day; in one, he was quit; and in a few the record was incomplete.

[193] Many of these peers may have been pardoned because they had backed Edward IV politically in 1469–71. Gratitude is expressed to Prof. Michael Hicks for this suggestion.

Table 11.2 *Pardons in livery litigation, 1377–1485*

Status	Giver	Receiver	Total	Indicted	Pardoned
Nobility	11	0	11	19	58%
Knights	6	2	8	57	14%
Esquires	13	3	16	151	11%
Gentlemen	1	0	1	83	1%
Yeomen	1	15	16	575	3%
Husbandmen	1	0	1	22	5%
Trades-occupations	1	5	6	150	4%
	34	25	59	1057	6%

indicted three times for giving robes to 137 men, was pardoned for all of them.[194] John de la Pole, duke of Suffolk was pardoned for giving robes to twenty-five men.[195] Other peers who were pardoned included Henry Grey, Baron Grey of Codnor; James Tuchet, Baron Audley; Walter Blount, Baron Mountjoy; and Edmund Ferrers, Baron Chartley.[196] A number of knights (29%) and esquires (35%) who were indicted for giving livery were also pardoned. In a number of the cases, in which the givers of livery were indicted and pardoned, the recipients, who were charged with illegally receiving livery, were not pardoned. In one case, in which the giver was pardoned, twenty-two recipients were convicted and paid the fine.[197] The gentry (12%) were much more likely to be pardoned

[194] TNA: PRO KB 27/839, m. 31 rex (1471), AALT Img. Nos. 256–58, 495–96.

[195] TNA: PRO KB 27/839, m. 32 rex (1471), AALT Img. No. 259.

[196] TNA: PRO KB 27/843, m. 25 rex (1472), AALT Img. No. 248; TNA: PRO KB 27/785, m. 2d rex (1457), AALT Img. No. 450; TNA: PRO KB 27/830, m. 47 rex (1468), AALT Img. No. 393; TNA: PRO KB 27/613 (1414), m. 30 rex (1414), AALT Img. Nos. 131–32, 122–23v. McFarlane said that Edmund Ferrers was pardoned for his agreement to accompany the king's expedition to France, where he fought at Agincourt and in several other battles. McFarlane, *Nobility*, p. 122. John Talbot, earl of Shrewsbury, was indicted twice, one for giving robes to 61 men and another time for giving silver talbots to 22 men, some of whom also received the robes. TNA: PRO KB 9/13, m. 11 (1468), AALT Img. No. 23; TNA: PRO KB 9/13, m. 23 (1468), AALT Img. No. 45. He appeared and said that the king had pardoned him for both offenses. But the record does not contain the king's letters patent nor a judgment by the court that John go without day. Thus, he was not counted as having been pardoned. TNA: PRO KB 27/829, m. 19d rex (1468), AALT Img. No. 476.

[197] TNA: PRO KB 27/613 (1414), m. 30 rex (1414), AALT Img. Nos. 131–32, 122–23v; TNA: PRO KB 27/614, m. 2 fine roll (1414), AALT Img. Nos. 230–31.

than those of lower status (3%). As Table 11.2 shows, givers were by far more commonly pardoned (38%) than recipients (3%).[198]

Evaluating the Impact of the Livery Statutes and Their Enforcement

Evaluating the impact of the livery statutes and their enforcement depends on what one believes the parliamentary and royal objectives were with regard to the distribution of livery. If the purpose was to eliminate livery except for the stated exceptions, then it seems that the statutes had little impact. Although a number of individuals were indicted, convictions for violating any of the livery statutes occurred in only two cases.[199] Perhaps the statutes and their enforcement, especially during the reign of Edward IV, deterred some giving of livery.[200] But the gentry, a major target of the prohibitions on giving livery, constituted the majority of the givers indicted (76%), and giving to recipients not within the exceptions was common, which may suggest that any deterrent effect was slight. In addition, the relatively liberal pardon policy undercut any notion of aggressive enforcement and significant impact. Further, the crown's abandonment of its livery actions if no complainant appeared in court also casts doubt on energetic enforcement. Moreover, the Commons complained repeatedly of inadequate enforcement. Contemporary officials evinced a similar attitude. In 1485, William Hussey CJKB, and Edward IV's former Attorney General, told an after-dinner gathering of justices that the livery and other statutes intended to prevent wrongdoing

> [would] never be well executed until the lords spiritual & temporal are of one mind, for love and dread that they have of God, or of the King, or of both, to execute them effectively ... For he said that, when he was the king's attorney, all the lords swore to keep the statutes which they with others had then compiled together, by order of the same king, and

---

[198] Table 11.2 does not include those who were indicted and whose status was not identified because the indictments were prior to the enactment of the Statute of Additions 1413.

[199] In one case, 22 recipients were convicted and fined 40s each for receiving 3 yards of green and red cloth from Edmund Ferrers, Baron Chartley, who was pardoned. TNA: PRO KB 27/613 (1414), m. 30 rex (1414), AALT Img. Nos. 131–32, 122–23v; TNA: PRO KB 27/614, m. 2 fine roll (1414), AALT Img. Nos. 230–31. In the other case, an esquire was charged with giving 3 yards of green and blue cloth to 2 yeomen. He admitted the violation as to one recipient and paid the 100s penalty. He asserted that the other was a servant and, despite the disagreement of the king's attorney, received a pardon. TNA: PRO KB 27/613, m. 20 rex (1414), AALT Img. Nos. 113–14.

[200] Bean made such a suggestion and said that the livery legislation contributed to the maintenance of royal authority. Bean, *From Lord to Patron*, p. 208.

diligently to execute them, and he saw that within an hour, while they were in the Star Chamber, several of the lords made retainers by oath and swearing, and did other things that were directly contrary to their said sureties and oaths ... And he told this to the king.[201]

Over the years, commentators have reached a similar conclusion.[202] Although most prosecutions occurred during the reign of Edward IV, Ross said that "the crucial failure of Edward's government was its reluctance to make any serious attack on the system of livery and maintenance and that there was no evidence that the 1468 statute was ever enforced."[203] Dunham expressed a similar view. In his study of Lord Hastings's indentured retainers, he found that all but five (93%) indentures were after 1468 and only one of these sixty-four agreements involved an individual falling within the standard exceptions.[204] But noting the agreements' "meticulous regard for legal niceties," he thought that the statute could be evaded by careful drafting, which would bring the agreements within the loophole created by the clause in the statute that permitted retaining "for lawful service done or to be done."[205] Dunham asserted that Edward's government permitted peers to retain and likely

---

[201] Y.B Mich., 1 Hen. VII, f. 3, pl. 3 (1485), Seipp No. 1485.003. His comment was made with regard to the statutes regarding "robberies and other felonies, riots, routs, and forcible entries, labourers and vagabonds, liveries, maintenance, and embracery." Ibid. William Hussey was Attorney General from June 16, 1471, to July 7, 1478. John Sainty, *A List of English Law Officers, King's Counsel and Holders of Patents of Precedence* (London, 1987), p. 44.

[202] Bean said that livery legislation in the period 1390–1461 was not strictly observed. Bean, *From Lord to Patron*, pp. 201–08.

[203] Ross, *Edward IV*, pp. 412–13.

[204] He was described as "counsel learned." Dunham, *Lord Hastings*, p. 73.

[205] Ibid., pp. 74–79. The 1468 statute is long and complicated and the exceptions are somewhat confusing. The prohibition on retaining and livery, which appears at the beginning of the statute, preserved the standard exceptions, "menial servant, officer, or man learned in one law or the other." Later in the statute, it said that any retaining prior to the effective date of the statute was void unless it was of a menial servant, officer, council member, or for lawful service done or to be done. Shortly after that portion of the statute, it said that the act did not apply to any "gift, grant or confirmation made or to be made of any fee, annuity, pension, rent, lands, or tenements by the king or any other person or persons to any person or person for their counsel given or to be given and their lawful service done or to be done or to any other cause not unlawful nor any other intent not unlawful." The statute said further that the person giving counsel need not be learned in one law or the other. 8 Edw. IV, c. 2 (1468), *Statutes of the Realm*, vol. 2, pp. 426, 428. It is the law service provision that would seem to apply to Lord Hasting's agreements, and Dunham said that if it were given a broad construction, it would make those agreements lawful. But he regretted that neither the courts nor Edward's council clarified the meaning of this exception. Dunham, *Lord Hastings*, pp. 74–75.

drafted the law, particularly the lawful service exception to allow such retaining.[206] Griffiths also doubted the efficacy of the statutes and noted Henry VI's willingness to permit retainers through his use of pardons.[207]

Not all commentators took such a negative view. They asserted that the objectives of the statutes were narrower, aimed at limiting, but not eliminating, livery and retaining. Bean rejected Dunham's argument and view and said that the 1468 statute was a basis of the law in the future. He did not, however, suggest that it was significantly enforced but said that the statute "did not lie entirely unused."[208] Moreover, he took a positive view in his review of royal policies toward retainers and livery for the period 1390–1504, saying that it was "one of growing rigour."[209] McFarlane seemed also to take a limited view of the livery statutes, saying that they were directed at "the casual recruitment of idle and potentially lawless hangers-on to the fringes of households" and not to "regular members of a lord's service."[210] Similarly, Bellamy noted the indictment

[206] He said further that, absent positive evidence that parliament intended to deprive peers of the right to retain, the conclusion that the statute was not intended to apply to peers was unavoidable. Ibid., pp. 77–89. He said that no peer was indicted under the 1468 act until 1506. Ibid., p. 75. But that is not entirely clear. There were several peers indicted after the June 24, 1468, effective date of the statute, including the dukes of Norfolk and Suffolk. They were indicted for giving livery of cloth against the "form of the statute," without identifying any particular statute. No cases were found during the reign of Edward IV or Richard III specifically identifying the 1468 statute as the basis of the presentment.

[207] He said that statutory prohibitions on livery "ran counter to the social and political need and also because their enforcement depended on the very men who gained the most from their breach." More generally, he said that Henry's government's effort to deal with public order lacked conviction. Griffiths, *Henry VI*, pp. 592–97. McKelvie found that there was not much enforcement of the 1429 livery statute and that it had little short-term impact. More generally, he said that there was only sporadic enforcement of the various livery statutes after 1429, but that the primary significance of the 1429 legislation was "the light it sheds on the evolution of late medieval parliamentary statutes." McKelvie, "Livery Act of 1429," pp. 61–65.

[208] He viewed the several prosecutions that occurred in 1468 and the enactment of the statute as responses "to the political ambitions of Richard, earl of Warwick." He said that the statute created royal authority, but enforcement depended on the "king's will at any given time." He said that Edward "turned a blind eye to retaining after his restoration to the throne in 1471." Bean, *From Lord to Patron*, pp. 211–19.

[209] He said that it "dealt effectively with the need to maintain a balance between the maintenance of the military resources of the kingdom and the dangers inherent in uncontrolled retaining." Ibid., pp. 225.

[210] McFarlane, *Nobility*, p. 106. In his unpublished lectures, he reviewed the statutes enacted from 1377 to 1411 in more detail. He said enforcement against retaining "by lesser men" was successful since "little more is heard of this practice in legislation of the next period." He likely meant giving of livery by those below the nobility during the latter part of the reign of Richard II. But subsequent statutes do mention the gentry, and they were the

of peers and said that the king "may have wished to demonstrate to the nation the illegality of the giving of livery on a casual basis ... without risking the total alienation of the nobles," which was further effectuated by his use of pardons.[211] But later he found it difficult to evaluate enforcement, and the subsequent enactment of further statutes was evidence of its ineffectiveness.[212] Hicks also believed that the statute had narrower objectives. He said that it was directed at "more compact, more cohesive, and thus more effective retinues" and it prohibited "extraordinary retaining" by those of lesser status than peers and the "casual giving of livery" to menial servants and those not retained by lifetime indentures. He felt, however, that Edward had changed his mind and lost interest in prohibiting "extraordinary retaining" by the nobility.[213] Thus, parliament and the crown may have had the less ambitious objective of controlling and limiting the distribution of livery rather than eliminating it. If the standard exceptions were given a broad scope, significant giving of livery would be permissible. Moreover, prohibiting all retaining and livery may have been unrealistic, given the accepted social and political norms and the large affinities of the peers. Also, the crown itself depended on and engaged in extensive distribution of livery to its retainers.

most common of those indicted for giving. He also said that there was no abatement in the giving of livery collars, which may be true, although it is difficult to tell from the presentments, which are almost always for the giving of livery of cloth and collars that seem to be a sign or badge. He credited the zeal of Henry IV in his adoption of aggressive livery legislation, noting "the merit of a baronial usurper is that of a poacher-turned-gamekeeper." He largely just described the prohibitions of the Henry IV's legislation. He noted also that none of these statutes prohibited retainers or giving of fees. McFarlane, "Lords and Retainers," Lectures V–VI, pp. 19–25.

[211] Bellamy, "Justice under Yorkist Kings," pp. 152–54. Bean used Bellamy's view to criticize that of Dunham, but then criticized Bellamy for focusing on livery and ignoring the statute's prohibition of retainers. Bean, *From Lord to Patron*, pp. 215–16.

[212] He wrote this work twenty-five years later. Bellamy, *Bastard Feudalism and the Law* (Portland, OR, 1989), pp. 81–85.

[213] But he said further that it was directed at the peers' retaining of the non-household and non-officer gentry. He also argued more generally that the statute's enforcement should be understood in terms of "later political priorities rather than the intentions of the original legislators." Hicks, "The 1468 Statute of Livery," pp. 16, 20–22, 26–28. His use of the term "extraordinary retaining" is not always clear. He has explained this term further, saying that "extraordinary means those who don't fit into natural/automatic categories – household, feudal tenants, estate officers, possibly legal counsel. Extraordinary are indentured retainers, annuitants, liveried and their dependents who extend the retinue beyond the lord's household and estate." Gratitude is expressed to Prof. Michael Hicks for clarifying that.

It is also possible, however, to view the objectives of the livery statutes in a different fashion. It is not clear that there was a fundamental objection to livery as such, but only to its association with retainers and maintenance. Thus, perhaps the objective should be understood in the context of these three practices.[214] In that sense, the question is whether enforcement was directed at the distribution of livery as a facilitating device for maintenance or other wrongdoing. But only a few records indicated the association of livery with maintenance and other wrongdoing. Most of the records provide no evidence as to this question, except what one might infer from those cases where livery was distributed to a large number of recipients, suggesting the possibility of group wrongdoing.

The clearest examples of this association are the livery cases connected to personal conflicts and local disorder, in which the defendants, both givers and recipients, were also presented for wrongdoing involving force and violence. This was clearly true in the 1414 disorder in Staffordshire and Shropshire. The Staffordshire attacks on the Lancastrian forces by Hugh Erdwick, esquire, and his brothers[215] and his conflict with Edmund Ferrers, Baron Chartley, produced a significant amount of wrongdoing involving force and violence, including the murder of one of Ferrers's servants. These activities produced numerous presentments of these men and their associates for livery and violent wrongdoing.[216] In

---

[214] Dunham, *Lord Hastings*, pp. 67–72; J.G. Bellamy, *Bastard Feudalism and the Law*, pp. 80–91.

[215] "Erdeswyk and his three brothers are chiefly remembered for the protracted and vicious feuds in which they became involved during the early years of the fifteenth century, although the colourful language of contemporary legal records makes it easy to exaggerate their disruptive influence, and, indeed, to forget the overtly hostile nature of much of the evidence." "Erdeswyk, Hugh (c. 1386–1451), of Sandon, Staffs.," in Roskell, Clark, and Rawcliffe, eds., *The History of Parliament*, vol. 3, pp. 329–32.

[216] TNA: PRO KB 27/613, m. 24d (1414), AALT Img. No. 115; TNA: PRO KB 27/614, m. 4 rex (1414), AALT Img. Nos. 235–36; TNA: PRO KB 27/614, m. 4d rex (1414), AALT Img. Nos. 578–79; TNA: PRO KB 9/113, m. 40 (1414), AALT Img. No. 70; TNA: PRO KB 27/632, m. 17 rex (1419), AALT Img. No. 184; TNA: PRO KB 27/613, m. 30 rex (1419), AALT Img. Nos. 131–32, 122–23v; TNA: PRO KB 27/614, m. 16 rex (1414), AALT Img. No. 261; TNA: PRO KB 9/113, m. 2 (1414), AALT Img. No. 6; TNA: PRO KB 9/113, m. 11 (1414), AALT Img. No. 18 (two presentments); TNA: PRO KB 9/113, m. 28 (1414), AALT Img. No. 48 (two presentments); TNA: PRO KB 9/113, m. 41 (1414), AALT Img. No. 70; TNA: PRO KB 9/113, m. 41 (1414), AALT Img. No. 71; TNA: PRO KB 9/113, m. 42 (1414), AALT Img. No. 72 (two presentments); TNA: PRO KB 9/113, m. 42 (1414), AALT Img. No. 73; TNA: PRO KB 9/113, m. 43 (1414), AALT Img. No. 73; TNA: PRO KB 27/618, m. 28d rex (1415), AALT Img. No. 587; TNA: PRO KB 27/619, m. 19 rex (1416), AALT Img. No. 41; TNA: PRO KB 27/619, m. 9d rex

one case, Hugh was charged with gathering up to 1,000 wrongdoers to kill the Lancastrian knights, who had been ordered to arrest him and his followers.[217] William Newport, a Lancastrian retainer, was presented for giving three ells of cloth to nine men for their clothing annually, who were to come to him whenever he requested and stand with him against all adversaries, both in good and evil.[218] A similar situation occurred in Shropshire as a result of the disorder and conflict between the supporters of Thomas FitzAlan, earl of Arundel and treasurer of England, and John Talbot, Lord Furnival and later the earl of Shrewsbury. Again those charged with giving and receiving livery were also presented for violent wrongdoing.[219] Roger Corbet, one of the earl's men who was indicted several times for livery, gave three ells of wool cloth to wrongdoers "for the purpose to oppress and destroy people and that each of them would be obligated to maintain and support such wrong-doing" and oppose by force all those who opposed them.[220] He was also presented for gathering a large number of wrongdoers from the "worst wrongdoers in Shropshire for the purpose that each of them would to maintain and support the other in their wrongdoing, espe-cially to oppress, maim, and beat people" to facilitate Roger's scheme to enrich himself by extortion.[221] Further, Roger and Roger Lacun, who was also indicted for giving livery, were also charged for arraying 400 men in the manner of war to assist the earl in a property dispute he

---

(1416), AALT Img. No. 280. Both Ferrers and Erdwick submitted petitions to parliament complaining about the other's violent wrongdoing. *Rotuli Parliamentorum*, vol. IV, pp. 32–33, nos. 12 and 13. Other parliamentary items also recounted this disorder. Parliaments of Henry V: January 1410, Nos. 37 and 38, *PROME*. Powell has discussed the Staffordshire disorder in detail. Powell, *Kingship, Law and Society*, pp. 53, 123, 139, 169–70, 208–16, 241–42.

[217] TNA: PRO KB 27/614, m. 4 rex (1414), AALT Img. Nos. 235–36.

[218] TNA: PRO KB 9/113, m. 28 (1414), AALT Img. No. 48.

[219] TNA: PRO KB 27/613, m. 20 rex (1414), AALT Img. Nos. 113–14; TNA: PRO KB 27/613, m. 38 rex (1414), AALT Img. No. 148; TNA: PRO KB 27/613, m. 38d rex (1414), AALT Img. No. 138; TNA: PRO KB 27/613, m. 38d rex (1414), AALT Img. Nos. 138, 151; TNA: PRO KB 27/613, m. 38 rex (1414), AALT Img. No. 151 (two presentments); TNA: PRO KB 27/613, m. 38d rex (1414), AALT Img. No. 140; TNA: PRO KB 27/613, m. 38d rex (1414), AALT Img. Nos. 140, 153; TNA: PRO KB 27/613, m. 38 rex (1414), AALT Img. No. 154; TNA: PRO KB 27/613, m. 38d rex (1414), AALT Img. No. 141. Powell has also discussed the Shropshire disorder in detail. Powell, *Kingship, Law and Society*, pp.124, 139, 174, 193–94, 216–24, 231, 233–34, 243.

[220] TNA: PRO KB 27/613, m. 38d rex (1414), AALT Img. No. 140.

[221] TNA: PRO KB 27/613, m. 38d rex (1414), AALT Img. Nos. 140, 153.

had with the prior of Wenlock, who had enlisted Talbot's men to protect him.[222]

Presentments revealing the connection between livery, maintenance, and group wrongdoing were not limited to these 1414 Staffordshire and Shropshire instances and appeared both earlier and later in other counties. In Derbyshire, this association occurred involving many of the county leaders such as Henry, Baron Grey of Codnor, Sir Richard Vernon, Sir John Cokayne, and Sir Roger Leech.[223] Perhaps the most significant Derbyshire disorder occurred in the mid-fifteenth century, producing numerous indictments for violent crimes, including murder.[224] There were also numerous presents for livery, including defendants who had also been indicted for violent crimes.[225] The animosity between Henry, Baron Grey of Codnor, and Sir Richard Vernon and their respective associates exacerbated this criminal and other wrongful activity.[226] One aspect of the Grey–Vernon conflict involved the 1433 shire elections, in which each of them pursued the election of their favorites.[227] On June 24, Grey showed at Derby with 200 men arrayed in the manner of war "to impede the free election of

---

[222] TNA: PRO KB 27/613, m. 38d rex (1414), AALT Img. No. 138.

[223] Wright has discussed the Derbyshire personal conflicts and disorder in substantial detail. Wright, *The Derbyshire Gentry*.

[224] Wright has recounted this violence and other disorders. Ibid., pp. 119–42.

[225] The 1434 *oyer et terminer* commission, which produced numerous indictments for violent felonies, also made 12 presentments for giving livery charging almost 100 men. Members of each faction served on the jury that indicted their adversaries. Ibid., pp. 130–31. Prior to this dispute, Grey had retained and given livery to both Vernon and Cokayn in 1432, for which Grey was indicted. TNA: PRO KB 27/696, m. 16 rex (1435), AALT Img. Nos. 401–2. Moreover, they had resolved their differences by 1437 when the two latter men were feoffees of Grey's land. "Vernon, Sir Richard," in Roskell, Clark, and Rawcliffe, eds., *The History of Parliament*, vol. 4, pp. 712–17.

[226] The feud between Sir Henry Pierrepont, retained by Grey, and Thomas Foljambe, retained by Vernon, further aggravated the situation. Moreover, Vernon also retained Hugh Erdwick and his brother, Sampson, leading troublemakers in Staffordshire, as discussed above. "Vernon, Sir Richard (1390–1451), of Harlaston, Staffs. and Haddon, Derbys," Roskell, Clark, and Rawcliffe, eds., *The History of Parliament*, vol. 4, pp. 712–17. Wright, *The Derbyshire Gentry*, pp. 128–33. Some of those involved in the Derbyshire disorder were also connected to Staffordshire politics and landowning, which is not surprising given the proximity of the two counties.

[227] Livery also seemed to have played a role in the 1449 Nottinghamshire elections. In 1451, Sir John Talbot, earl of Shrewsbury, brought a *qui tam* action against John Stanhope, esquire, and the 24 men, to whom he gave livery of cloth. TNA: PRO CP 40/763, m. 483d (1451), AALT Img. No. 2368; TNA: PRO CP 40/769, m. 138 (1452), AALT Img. Nos. 270–71, 1270–71v. Payling determined that seven of these men voted for Stanhope in the election. He also said it was common for one of the election contestants to bring a large

knights" for the county, for which he was indicted.[228] The next day Vernon and his associate Sir John Cokayne showed up with 300 men for the same purpose, for which he was indicted.[229] During this period, Vernon and his associates were indicted for giving livery to numerous men, presumably those involved with each of them in the election conflict.[230]

In the complicated and dynamic politics of Derbyshire, the Grey–Vernon conflict was continued by their descendants, heightened by the murder of Roger Vernon, and the Vernons also developed a new dispute with Sir John Gresley, member of another leading Derbyshire family.[231] In addition, another conflict involving disorder and livery had occurred at the end of the first decade of the fifteenth century between Sir Roger Leche (Leech), an important and influential royal official,[232] and William Vernon, esquire, a member of a leading Derbyshire gentry family, which involved potential violence and

number of armed men to the county court to prevent a lawful election. Payling, *Political Society in Lancastrian England* (Oxford, 1991), pp. 160–64, 163 n. 26.

[228] TNA: PRO KB 9/11, m. 17 (1434), AALT Img. No. 34; TNA: PRO KB 27/696, m. 16d rex (1435), AALT Img. Nos. 401–02.

[229] TNA: PRO KB 9/11, m. 17d (1434), AALT Img. No. 36; TNA: PRO KB 27/695, m. 7d rex (1435), AALT Img. Nos. 152–53, 349. Vernon and Cokayne were returned as the shire knights. "Vernon, Sir Richard," in Roskell, Clark, and Rawcliffe, eds., *The History of Parliament*, vol. 4, pp. 712–17.

[230] During this period, there were 15 indictments of 144 men for violations of the livery statutes. TNA: PRO KB 9/11, m. 15, 15d, 17d (1434), AALT Img. Nos. 27–29, 28, 36; TNA: PRO KB 27/695, mm. 1 rex, 7 rex (1435), AALT Img. Nos. 140, 152–53, 348; TNA: PRO KB 27/696, mm. 16d rex, 17 rex (1435), AALT Img. Nos. 189, 401–2; TNA: PRO KB 27/719, m. 20d rex (1435), AALT Img. No. 529. Numerous feuds in Cheshire in the 1420s, including that between the Egertons and Breretons, may have been linked to the large number of livery cases in Cheshire, which involved 14 indictments of 104 men. McKelvie, "The Livery Statute of 1429," pp. 57–58; Griffiths, *Henry VI*, p. 137.

[231] Wright, *The Derbyshire Gentry*, pp. 60–83, 95–102, 116–39. Although Henry, Baron Grey of Codnor, son of the prior Baron, and Sir John Gresley were indicted several times for giving livery to numerous men in the reign of Edward IV, it does not appear that those indictments were connected to these disputes, but were for the purpose of war. TNA: PRO KB 27/841, mm. 46 rex, 52 rex (1471), AALT Img. Nos. 349, 363; TNA: PRO KB 27/843, m. 25 rex (1471), AALT Img. No. 249; TNA: PRO KB 27/844, m. 36d rex (1472), AALT Img. Nos. 669–70.

[232] "Leche, Roger (d. 1416), of Chatsworth and Nether Haddon, Derbys," in Roskell, Clark, and Rawcliffe, eds., *The History of Parliament*, vol. 3, pp. 570–73. He was controller of the king's household and later its steward. One of his duties was to insure that no livery was given to any aliens in the household. J.L. Kirby, *Henry IV of England* (London, 1970), pp. 167, 237, 259.

maintenance.[233] As part of Roger's duty to protect threats to royal authority and the king's peace, he brought a *qui tam* action for violation of the livery statute against William for giving three yards of green cloth to twenty-three men.[234] Roger believed that William had recruited an armed group of men.[235] William alleged that six were his servants and were lawfully and continuously retained doing daily service.[236] Roger traversed that plea, alleging that the six men resided in their own and separate houses, attending to their own affairs "except when William sent for them or ordered them to ride with him to market towns and elsewhere to maintain him in his pleas under color of negotiating and holding love-days in the said pleas." The concern was that William's men would use intimidation to undermine arbitration.[237]

In addition to these instances, there were other indictments that linked livery with violence. In 1393, thirty-three wrongdoers, dressed and assembled in the livery of a single company, assaulted a man, and by corrupt allegiance and confederacy, they agreed to maintain each other in all pleas against anyone who complained against any of them.[238] During

---

[233] There is some confusion regarding William's identity. Several sources said he was the brother of Sir Richard Vernon, but the plea roll record said he was the son of Sir Richard Vernon. Since there were several Sir Richard Vernons, it was possible that he was the son of one and the brother of another one, but no William Vernon was identified who was either a brother or son and alive at the time of the giving of livery and the litigation. The Vernons, especially Richard, were involved in substantial litigation, violence, and disorder. Wright, *The Derbyshire Gentry.*

[234] TNA: PRO KB 27/596, m. 76 (1410), AALT Img. Nos. 170–71, 158v, reprinted in G.O. Sayles, ed., *Select Cases in the Court of the King's Bench*, 7 vols. (London, 1939), VII, 88 Selden Soc., pp. 193–94; TNA: PRO KB 27/600, m. 42d (1411), AALT Img. No. 351.

[235] "Leche, Roger (d. 1416), of Chatsworth and Nether Haddon, Derbys," in Roskell, Clark, and Rawcliffe, eds., *The History of Parliament*, 3, pp. 570–73. Wright, *The Derbyshire Gentry*, pp. 83–85.

[236] William, protesting, also denied giving any livery. Only two of the recipients were attached, and they denied receiving any livery and alleged that they were servants lawfully retained and doing service every day. William denied giving livery to the remaining 17 men and Roger joined issue.

[237] TNA: PRO KB 27/596, m. 76 (1410), AALT Img. Nos. 170–71; Wright, *The Derbyshire Gentry*, pp. 123–24.

[238] They had worn the livery for the previous six years and they were also accompanied by eighty unknown men of their covin. They recited a rhyme that said, *inter alia*, "And we too will maintain our neighbours through thick and thin with all our might." The 1390 Ordinance was the basis of the presentment. TNA: PRO KB 27/528, m. 37 rex (1393), AALT Img. No. 417, reprinted Sayles, ed., *Select Cases in the Court of the King's Bench*, VII, 88 Selden Soc., pp. 83–85.

the Wars of the Roses, Sir Walter Devereux, a prominent Yorkist, was indicted for his attacks in Hereford and on Carmarthen and Aberystwyth castles and for giving livery to sixty-seven of his men.[239] In the bitter mid-fifteenth century Percy-Neville conflict, the various incidents of violence involved men wearing their lord's livery, and there were some indictments for violation of the livery statutes.[240] In the 1381 Peasants' Revolt, the rebels, who were indicted for their violent conduct at Scarborough, wore the livery of chaperons.[241] In one action, in which livery was also linked with maintenance and conspiracy, Nicholas Maisham, a butcher, one of bailiffs of Derby, conspired and confederated with eighteen other men and each of them purchased a rayed (striped) hood of several colors, with the understanding that the pleas of one of them would be the plea of each of them.[242]

Although substantial evidence showed the connection between livery and maintenance, violence, and various forms of wrongdoing, these cases represented a small portion of the presentments for livery during the late medieval period. Thus, these types of circumstances were not a primary focus of the enforcement of the livery statutes. In sum, it seems fair to conclude that the livery statutes did not have a significant impact on eliminating livery and retainers, but limited it in a feasible and practical manner that reflected contemporary social and political realities.

---

[239] TNA: PRO KB 27/784, mm. 22 rex, 22d rex (1457), AALT Img. Nos. 240–41, 515–16. He instigated the uprising in Hereford. R.L. Storey, *The End of the House of Lancaster* (1986, Stroud), pp. 228–30; TNA: PRO KB 9/148/1, m. 10 (1454), AALT Img. No. 21; TNA: PRO KB 9/149, mm. 20, 21, 49, 53 (1454), AALT Img. Nos. 44, 46, 106, 114; Ralph Griffiths, *King and Country: England and Wales in the Fifteenth Century* (London, 1991), pp. 321–38.

[240] TNA: PRO KB 9/148/1, m. 10 (1454), AALT Img. No. 21; TNA: PRO KB 9/149, mm. 20, 21, 49, 53 (1454), AALT Img. Nos. 44, 46, 106, 114; Ralph Griffiths, *King and Country: England and Wales in the Fifteenth Century* (London, 1991), pp. 321–38.

[241] TNA: PRO KB 27/500, m. 12 rex (1386), AALT Img. Nos. 156–57, 298, 314v.

[242] They asserted in justification that the purpose of the livery was to found and sustain the priests of the Church of Blessed Mary, Derby, to say divine service there. TNA: PRO KB 9/11, m. 17 (1434), AALT Img. No. 34. They were also indicted for their conspiracy and covin made to annul and destroy the laws and customs of Derby. TNA: PRO KB 9/11, m. 17d (1434), AALT Img. Nos. 37–38.

12

Achieving the Legislative Objectives of the Maintenance Statutes

Ascertaining whether the medieval statutes directed at maintenance achieved their objectives is an important aspect of this study of maintenance. Determining the objectives of statutes is a common form of legal inquiry. Several sources are useful in evaluating the success of statutes. The most direct source is the statute itself and any accompanying preamble. Another source is any documented history that produced or influenced the enactment of the statute. Finally, statements of contemporary judges, lawyers, officials, and others may also be relevant. Although these medieval statutes were enacted many centuries ago, extensive and available legal records facilitate this task. These sources will be examined to determine the objectives of the maintenance statutes. This chapter argues that the primary statutory objective of these statutes was to control the abuse of power by influential individuals and officials in litigation, but that they did not significantly achieve that goal. Further, it is suggested that the statutes may actually have been misused to harass adversaries.

Controlling the Abuse of Power

Several of the statutes, as well as the theme of some petitions to the king, his council, and parliament, focused primarily on the use and abuse of social, economic, and political power by the nobility, gentry, and office holders to influence litigation. Many maintenance statutes were expressly directed at abuse by powerful individuals and officials. During the reign of Edward I (1272–1307), the initial maintenance statutes singled out abuse of power by officials. Officers of the king were the target of the Statute of Westminister I 1275, which prohibited champerty, and perhaps also maintenance.[1] Similarly, the next provision, which was in the

---

[1] Statute of Westminster I, c. 25, 3 Edw. I (1275), *Statutes of the Realm*, 11 vols, (London, 1810–28), vol. 1, p. 33.

same statute and dealt with pending pleas of advowson, was directed at the justices' and sheriffs' clerks.[2] A provision of the Statute of Westminster II 1285 again targeted royal officials, prohibiting champerty by the chancellor, treasurer, justices, other members of the king's Council, the clerks of the Chancery and Exchequer, justices and other officials, and the clerical and lay members of the king's household.[3] But powerful lords were not ignored. The 1305 Ordinance of Conspirators defined conspiracy and explicitly highlighted its use as a mechanism to facilitate maintenance by the "stewards and bailiffs of great lords who through lordship, office or power undertake to maintain or uphold pleas or disputes for parties, other than those which concern the estate of their lords or themselves."[4] In addition, as discussed in Chapter 3, virtually all of the petitions to the king and his council, including those enrolled in the parliamentary rolls, complained of legal corruption by powerful individuals and officials.[5] Nobles were significantly the largest group targeted by complainants, followed by officials, knights, and sheriffs. In general, petitioners complained that the power and influence of these persons hindered the exercise of their legal rights or seeking remedies for their violation.

Statutes enacted during the reign of Edward III (1327–77) reflected the same objectives. In the first year of the reign, a statute was directed at abuse by royal officials and powerful individuals. It specifically prohibited maintenance of quarrels by the king's counsellors, officers, and members of his household and by any magnate of the land.[6] The statute was a

---

[2] Ibid., c. 28, 3 Edw. I (1275), *Statutes of the Realm*, I, pp. 33–34. Another provision involved barretors, a related concern, and restricted the stewards and attorneys of great lords from giving or pronouncing judgments in the county courts. Ibid., c. 33, *Statutes of the Realm*, vol. 1, pp. p. 35.

[3] Statute of Westminster II, c. 49, 13 Edw. I (1285), *Statutes of Realm*, vol. 1, p. 95.

[4] "The Ordinance concerning conspirators," Edward I Parliaments: *Vetus Codex* 1305, *PROME*.

[5] See Chapter 3, pp. 106–10. In discussing the period 1322–1340, Ormrod noted the striking evidence of the antibaronial stance of the common petitions that revealed the Commons' political opposition. Petitions complained of oppressive lordship due to maintenance, biased commissions, bribery, and unreasonably high amercements. Edward III's legislative response was a product of two decades of political events. W.M. Ormrod, "Agenda for Legislation, 1322–c. 1340," *English Historical Review* 105 (1990), pp. 19–22.

[6] It also prohibited maintenance by any small or great person in the realm. The preamble said that the king desired that "the common right be administered to all people." I Edw. III, st. 2, c. 14 (1327), *Statutes of the Realm*, vol. 1, p. 256. Another provision of the same statute prohibited maintainors of evil or barretors from serving as keepers of the peace. Ibid., c. 16, vol. 1, pp. 256–57.

response to a Commons' petition in Edward III's first parliament requesting that no member of the King's Council or other magnate of the realm or anyone from the king's household or any royal official maintain parties or disputes by which the common law is disturbed.[7] Moreover, the preamble to a statute in the next parliament noted that great men as well as other several other persons "have made alliances, confederacies, and conspiracies, to maintain parties, pleas, and disputes."[8] A later statute reiterated this prohibition, singling out members of the royal household, prelates, earls, and barons.[9] In the same parliament, another statute commanded all great men to expel all maintainers of quarrels and parties from their retinues because the lords were maintaining and protecting them.[10] Finally, a 1377 statute, which was the basis for the substantial increase in private maintenance actions in the late medieval period, followed this same pattern of expressly targeting abuse by the king's counsellors, officers, and servants as well as prohibiting maintenance by any person.[11]

In addition, contemporaries viewed the maintenance statutes as directed at abuse of power. Royal justices voiced this opinion. In *Pomeroy v. Abbot v. Buckfast*, Newton CJCP said that it was maintenance for a person "who has great rule or great power in the county" to come to the bar with the party, even though he said nothing or did nothing, because it "will perhaps cause those who will be the jurors to favor the party and find for him," as the person would be "understood to wish well to that party."[12] Similarly, Prysot CJCP said that support from a "lord or powerful man" was maintenance "because the party is comforted in the suit and this is great maintenance from a worthy man."[13] Further, at the opening day of the 1329–30 Eyre of Northampton, Scrope CJKB explained the reason for holding the eyre. He

---

[7] Parliaments of Edward III: January 1327, C 65/1, no. 33, *PROME*.

[8] 4 Edw. III, c. 11 (1330), *Statutes of the Realm*, vol. 1, p. 264.

[9] Like the earlier statute, the prohibition also extended to other great and small men of the land. *Statutes of the Realm*, vol. 1, c. 4, p. 304.

[10] Ibid., c. 5, vol. 1, pp. 304–5.

[11] 1 Rich. II, c. 4 (1377), *Statutes of the Realm*, vol. 2, p. 2.

[12] "*Car mettomus que un que rien n'ad affaire ove le matter vient al' barre ove le pleintif ou defendant et estoit ove luy, et ryen dit, ne rien fait; uncore ceo ne serra adjuge un maintenance, et un continuel maintenance tout temps pendant le ple; et le cause est par ceo que paraventure il est tiel persone que ad grand rule ou grand poiar en le county et eux que vient al' barre ove l'un party entend que il veut bien a cele party, et que il est plus favorable a cele party que a l'autre, que paradventure causera ceux que serront jurours favourer le party et passer ove luy.*" Mich. 22 Hen. VI, fol. 6, pl. 7 (1443), Seipp No. 1443.066 (motion in arrest of judgment) (tr.).

[13] "*S'il ne soit apris de ley, mes seignior ou autre puissant home estre maintenance, pur ceo que le party est conforted en le suit et cest graund maintenance d'un proude home.*"

referred to the complaints at the 1328 Northampton parliament about the suffering caused by the "manifold oppressions of the magnates and from the extortions of the maintainers" and other wrongdoing and the failure to keep the peace. He ordered the gathered magnates, "the leading men of the country," to "support no maintainers of false suits and no persons of evil reputation."[14] Moreover, litigants were well aware of this abusive influence, as indicated by common fifteenth-century complaint that "law goeth as lordship biddeth"[15] and Sir John Fastolf's statement to his lawyer and advisor, John Paston, that "for now adays ye know well that law goeth as it is favored."[16] In addition, the poem, *Mum and the Sothsegger* complained that the "law lieth much in lordship."[17] In sum, these sources provide strong evidence that the primary objective of the maintenance statutes was to curtail the abuse of power by the nobility, gentry, and officials to influence litigation.

The Nature of the Maintenance Litigants

Examining the nature of the parties in both private and crown actions provides an insight into whether this purpose of these statutes was actually achieved. Given this objective, one would think that those sued for maintenance would have been powerful individuals and officials, those targeted by the statutes. But substantial research in the plea rolls identified the maintenance litigants and revealed a more complex and significantly different picture. The writs in civil actions provided most of

Anthony Fitzherbert, *La Grande Abridgement* (London, 1577), *Maintenance*, 22, fol. 65 ((1458), Seipp No. 1458.066abr.

[14] "The Eyre of Northamptonshire, Opened by Geoffrey Scrope C.J. on Monday, 6 November 1329," in Donald Sutherland, ed., *Eyre of Northampshire, 3–4 Edward III*, 2 vols. (London, 1983), vol. I, 97 Selden Soc., pp. 2, 5–6.

[15] Gerald Harriss, *Shaping the Nation* (Oxford, 2005), p. 135; Edward Powell, "Law and Justice," in *Fifteenth-Century Attitudes*, ed. Rosemary Horrox (Cambridge, 1994), p. 38.

[16] Norman Davis, Richard Beadle, and Colin Richmond, eds., *Paston Letters and Papers of the Fifteenth Century*, 3 parts (Early English Text Society, Supplementary Series 20–22) (Oxford, 2004–5), part II, no. 520, p. 115. Jolliffe said that "in the suits of the land, great lords maintain each other, so that opposing parties dare not proceed." J.E.A. Jolliffe, *The Constitutional History of Medieval England from the English Settlement to 1485*, 4th ed. (London, 1961), pp. 410–11. In discussing the origins and history of maintenance, Bodkin said that the crown failed to curb the power of the great barons, who formed confederacies, and seized the land of less powerful neighbors and forcibly maintained their possesson of it. Edmond Bodkin, *The Law of Maintenance and Champerty and the Lawful Financing of Actions by Solicitors, Legal Aid and Trade Protection Societies and Others* (London, 1934), pp. 1–4.

[17] *Mum and the Sothsegger*, ll. 1582–84.

information on the parties' status and occupations. The Statute of Additions 1413 required plaintiffs to provide this information as to defendants, and they did so voluntarily for themselves as well in a limited number of actions.[18] The basis for the following analysis is the traditional classifications of persons in the stratification of English medieval society as nobility, gentry, and sub-gentry.[19]

Defining these groups is not free from doubt and disagreement.[20] "Gentry" was not a contemporary term, but one constructed by and commonly used by historians for historiographic purposes.[21] There is agreement, however, that the term "gentry" should be used for the middle group, consisting of the lesser landowners below the peers, who were knights, esquires, and gentlemen, in that order.[22] Although knighthood was a long recognized status with a ceremonial creation, the status of esquire (*armiger*) and that of gentleman were later developments. Esquire was well established as a specific status by the second half of the fourteenth century.[23] It had military origins, and the status entitled its holders to use a

---

[18] 1 Hen. V, c. 5 (1413), *Statutes of the Realm*, vol. 2, p. 171. No actions were found in which the defendant challenged the accuracy of the status or occupation stated in the writ except in situations of mistaken identity, in which the defendant alleged that the plaintiff had sued the wrong person.

[19] The stratification of medieval English society, especially the origins and development of the gentry, has prompted substantial scholarship. E.g., Harriss, *Shaping the Nation*, pp. 136–49; Peter Coss, *The Origins of the English Gentry* (Cambridge, 2003); Eric Acheson, *A Gentry Community: Leicestershire in the Fifteenth Century* (Cambridge, 2003); Chris Given-Wilson, *The English Nobility in the Late Middle Ages* (London, 1996); Simon Payling, *Political Society in Lancastrian England* (Oxford, 1991); Susan Wright, *The Derbyshire Gentry in the Fifteenth Century* (Chesterfield, 1983); Peter Coss, "Hilton, Lordship and the Culture of the Gentry," in Christopher Dyer, Peter Coss, and Chris Wickham, eds., *Rodney Hilton's Middle Ages: An Exploration of Historical Theories, Past & Present* Supplement 2 (Oxford, 2007), pp. 34–52.

[20] Coss, *Origins*, pp. 1–19; Michael Johnston, *Romance and Gentry in Late Medieval England* (Oxford, 2014), pp. 21–27. Dyer created a chart depicting the social hierarchy in late medieval England. Christopher Dyer, *Standards of Living in the Later Middle Ages: Social Change in England, c. 1200–1520* (Cambridge, 1998), p. 20.

[21] Coss, *Origins*, pp. 1–19; Scott Waugh, "Book Review of Coss, *Origins*," *American Historical Review* 109 (2004), pp. 1623–24.

[22] Coss has provided the most detailed identification of the gentry's characteristics, a lesser nobility, which derived its wealth primarily from land and whose power was territorial. Coss, *Origins*, p. 11; Peter Coss, *Lordship, Knighthood and Locality* (Cambridge, 1991), p. 309. But Horrox also argued that there was an urban gentry. Rosemary Horrox, "The Urban Gentry in the Fifteenth Century," in J.A.F. Thomson, ed., *Towns and Townspeople in the Fifteenth Century* (Gloucester, 1988), pp. 22–44.

[23] Commentators have said that the 1363 sumptuary legislation (37 Edw. III, cc. 8–15 [1363], *Statutes of the Realm*, vol. 1, pp. 380–82) first identified it as a social status.

family coats of arms.[24] "Gentleman" was a status whose origins and qualifications are somewhat ambiguous. Its use in documents and as a legal status became common by the fifteenth century, influenced by the Statute of Additions 1413.[25] It was often used to describe a person of gentle birth and to characterize a person who did not live by manual labor.[26] But it was not a homogenous group. In some instances, "gentleman" denoted a man who had lordship over land and possessed a manor and a court,[27] but it was used in other contexts as well, especially with office holders and lawyers.[28] Below this group were the "middling sort" of people such as yeomen, husbandmen, and persons of various occupations, all of whom the commentators have treated as the sub-gentry. "Yeomen," "the peasant aristocracy," were at the top of this group.[29] Originally associated with a household and forest administration, "yeoman" came to describe a small landowner, whose holdings were not, however, insubstantial and who perhaps employed others to assist him.[30] A husbandman seemed also to have been a farmer with less land and less wealth, but generating sufficient income to support himself.[31] He was a person who "labour[ed] at the

Harriss, *Shaping the Nation*, pp. 136–37; Coss, *Origins*, pp. 3, 18, 216, 228, 251; Maurice Keen, *The Origins of the English Gentleman* (Stroud, 2002), p. 101.

[24] Harriss, *Shaping the Nation*, pp. 136–37; Keen, *English Gentleman*, pp. 71–86, 88 ("Esquires thus established their status in the armigerous and traditionally militarised upper echelons of English society . . .").

[25] Keen, *English Gentleman*, pp. 101–2; Harriss, *Shaping the Nation*, p. 137; Coss, *Origins*, pp. 4, 216, 237, 251; Christopher Brooks, *Lawyers, Litigation, and English Society since 1450* (London, 1998), p. 77, n. 60.

[26] Keen identified several criteria, starting with having an ancestor of "gentle blood," although it was not necessarily essential. He said that it was difficult to denote when its usage began. Keen, *English Gentleman*, pp. 101–20. A characteristic, perhaps common to all of them, is that they did not work with their hands. Pollard, *Late Medieval England*, pp. 186–87.

[27] Harriss, *Shaping the Nation*, p. 137.

[28] Many office holders in the royal and other great households as well as lawyers were styled as gentlemen. R.L. Storey, "Gentleman-Bureaucrats," in Cecil Clough, ed., *Profession, Vocation, and Culture in Later Medieval England* (Liverpool, 1982), pp. 90–129; Christine Carpenter, "England: The Nobility and the Gentry," in S.G. Rigby, ed., *A Companion to Britain in the Later Middle Ages* (Oxford, 2003), p. 265; J.H. Baker, *The Men of Court 1440-1550*, 2 vols. (London, 2012), vol. I, pp. 37–39.

[29] Harriss, *Shaping the Nation*, pp. 240–41.

[30] Dyer said extensive land and suggested 80 acres. Dyer, *Standards of Living*, pp. 15, 23. Pollard suggested a countryman owning 60 acres of land. A.J. Pollard, *Late Medieval England, 1399-1509* (Harlow, 2000), p. 189.

[31] He was distinguished from the laborer, who sold his labor to another. He may have employed live-in servants. P.J.P. Goldberg, *Medieval England: A Social History 1250-1500* (London, 2004), pp. 92–93; Pollard, *Late Medieval England*, p. 189; Dyer, *Standards of*

plough and cart," the ploughman.[32] Persons of occupation and trade were a diverse group. It included both merchants, who sold goods made by others; artisans, who were managers of small workshops who produced goods; and perhaps laborers.[33] The fundamental difference between the gentry and nongentry was that former lived by the land or their office and the latter by their labor.

Despite a general consensus on the primary notions underlying the stratification of medieval English society, these classifications have certain limitations. The boundaries that divided the different groups were not always bright lines. Harriss said that below knights and esquires, the "gradations of gentle society were fluid.[34] Moreover, the line between gentleman, the lowest gentry status, and yeoman, the highest sub-gentry status, was blurred.[35] In addition, there was probably significant variability within each group as to wealth, power, and influence.[36] Although social status was frequently a function of a person's relationship with land and wealth and perhaps power, they were not always exactly correlated.[37] For example, there were certain merchants who were quite wealthy and influential within urban areas, which perhaps indicated higher social status.[38] Finally, social status and occupation were dynamic.

Living, p. 15. But like yeomen, they participated in the legal system as officials, pledges, and presenting jurors. Harriss, *Shaping the Nation*, p. 252.

[32] 12 Rich. II, c. 5 (1388), *Statutes of the Realm*, vol. 2, p. 57; Goldberg, *Medieval England*, pp. 93–94; R.H. Hilton, *The English Peasantry in the Later Middle Ages* (Oxford, 1975), p. 21.

[33] Goldberg, *Medieval England*, pp. 100–113; Sylvia Thrupp, "The Grouping of the Population by Crafts and Occupations," in Sylvia Thrupp, *The Merchant Class of Medieval London, 1300–1500* (Chicago, 1964), pp. 1–14.

[34] Harriss, *Shaping the Nation*, p. 137.

[35] Coss, *Origins*, pp. 4, 7. Wright thought that the use of the terms "gentleman" and "yeoman" might have sometimes been interchangeable. She also said that "gentleman" depended on an individual's view and his neighbors' view of his position. Wright, *Derbyshire Gentry*, p. 2. In some cases, a man might be designated as a gentleman or by his "mystery" and considered as similar to a yeoman, who was a household servant. Storey, "Gentleman-Bureaucrats," pp. 90–93.

[36] Harriss, *Shaping the Nation*, pp. 137–40; Wright, *Derbyshire Gentry*, pp. 1–10; Pollard, *Late Medieval England*, pp. 185–86. Payling, *Political Society*, p. 2. Harriss suggested that "prospering yeoman and husbandman" might have overtaken some of the sons of the minor gentry in wealth. Ibid., p. 145. Given-Wilson distinguished the country gentry and parish gentry. Given-Wilson, *Nobility*, pp. 70–78. Dyer said an occupation could include wealthy wholesalers and relatively poor retailers. Dyer, *Standards of Living*, p. 16.

[37] Coss, *Origins*, pp. 1–19; Given-Wilson, *Nobility*, pp. 69–83; Carpenter, "England: The Nobility and the Gentry," pp. 264–82.

[38] Pollard, *Late Medieval England*, pp. 188–90; Dyer, *Standards of Living*, pp. 15–16.

A person's position might change as result of social mobility, particularly as a result of the acquisition of land, or changed conditions.[39] For example, "a successful merchant's ambition [was] to become a gentleman," and they shared certain cultural affinities.[40] These limitations do not, however, make the classifications meaningless or negate their utility. As the studies and scholarly literature show, medievalists regularly have used them. But recognizing the limitations is necessary to avoid oversimplification in drawing inferences from the data and to suggest using a more nuanced approach in interpreting the data.

The Defendants in Maintenance Actions

The records of the maintenance actions, as a result of the Statute of Additions, identified the status or occupation of more than 1,915 defendants. They can be classified in seven major groups, consisting of 143 different types of defendants: persons identified by their occupation (118 types),[41] clerks and religious persons (11 types),[42] officials (7 types), gentry (3 types), lawyers, yeomen, and husbandmen. Despite this overall diversity of the defendants, those who were not gentry predominated as parties in these actions. Husbandmen, yeoman, and persons of various occupations and trades accounted for the great majority of the defendants in the maintenance actions (77%). In contrast, gentry, those who were knights, esquires, and gentlemen, were only a small proportion (12%). No nobles were defendants. Thus, most of the actions were against ordinary persons and not against powerful individuals and officials.[43] Table 12.1 shows the frequency of each of these types of defendants.

These statistics do not, of course, eliminate the possibility that the nobility or gentry engaged in significant maintenance, but only show that they were not common targets of litigation. As Table 12.2 shows, when

---

[39] Harriss, *Shaping the Nation*, pp. 140–42; Pollard, *Late Medieval England*, pp. 185–86.

[40] Although such upward movement may have occurred, it was difficult to determine and may have occurred over two or more generations and have been influenced by other service or activity. "Trade and Gentility," in Thrupp, *The Merchant Class*, pp. 234–87.

[41] There were 887 of this type of defendant, but only a few were substantial in number: merchants (65), weavers (64), brewers (53), and tailors (50). The contemporary parlance used in the Statute of Additions was "mystery." 1 Hen. V, c. 5 (1413), *Statutes of the Realm*, vol. 2, p. 171.

[42] Of the 142 of this type of defendant, half were clerks (72) and a quarter were chaplains (35). No attempt was made to classify these defendants as gentry or sub-gentry.

[43] It is possible that the sub-gentry defendants may have been more dominant, as most of the clerks and chaplains were not likely to have been powerful or influential.

Table 12.1 *Maintenance defendants by type*

Persons of occupation and trade	46% (887)
Husbandmen and yeomen	31% (584)
Knights, esquires, and gentlemen	12% (224)
Clergy and religious	8% (142)
Officials	2% (34)
Women	1% (20)
Lawyers	1% (19)

Table 12.2 *Gentry as maintenance defendants*

Gentlemen	7.5% (141)
Esquires	3.5% (65)
Knights	1% (18)

the gentry were sued, it was most commonly gentlemen, the lower gentry, who made up almost two-thirds of the gentry defendants (141 of 224,) and not the knights and esquires. Although the number of gentlemen sued was not insignificant (7%), it was substantially less than the defendants who were husbandmen (17%) and yeomen (14%). When members of the gentry were defendants, they were most commonly sued by other gentry, as half of the identified plaintiffs (53 of 105) in such actions were other gentry.[44] A partial explanation may be that some sub-gentry were reluctant to sue the nobility and higher ranking gentry, although some of those types of persons did sue the gentry for maintenance (27%).[45] The crown brought the remaining actions against the gentry (23%). Prior to the fifteenth century, enforcement by the crown seems to have been minimal. Although the level of enforcement increased in the fifteenth century, it is unlikely that it contributed significantly to controlling corruption of the legal system by powerful individuals and officials. Most of the litigation was civil actions and not criminal prosecution. As was the case with private civil actions, most of the crown maintenance

---

[44] These 53 gentry plaintiffs were as follows: 22 gentlemen, 21 esquires, 7 knights, and 2 earls.

[45] The 28 sub-gentry plaintiffs were as follows: 12 persons of occupations, 9 religious persons, 3 officials, 2 widows, 1 husbandman, and 1 servant of the archbishop of Canterbury.

actions were also against the "middling" folk, and not against the nobility or the gentry.

The Plaintiffs in Maintenance Actions

Although the actions identified the status or occupation of fewer plaintiffs, the picture is consistent with that regarding defendants. The records reveal the status and occupation of 349 plaintiffs in maintenance actions. Husbandmen, yeoman, and persons of occupation and trade were again the most numerous, accounting for 40% of the plaintiffs. But there was a significant change regarding the gentry and nobility, who constituted 33% of the plaintiffs. The gentry and nobility, those influential persons who were the target of the maintenance statutes, were almost three times more likely to be a plaintiff in a maintenance action (33%) than to be a defendant in one (12%).[46] Tables 12.3 and 12.4 show the distribution of maintenance plaintiffs.

Moreover, when members of the nobility or gentry were plaintiffs, sub-gentry accounted for 66% of the defendants, including a number of yeomen and husbandmen, and the status of most of the gentry who were sued was that of gentleman (57%).[47]

When the analysis of maintenance defendants and plaintiffs is combined, a general pattern in the maintenance litigation seems to emerge. Ordinary persons were more likely to be sued than to sue others, and, conversely, higher status and likely more powerful persons were more likely to sue than to be sued. When these persons were sued, it was most commonly by other powerful persons. But when they were plaintiffs, they were more likely to sue ordinary persons. Finally, the most common parties in maintenance litigation, whether they were plaintiffs or defendants, were the "middling sort of people" and not the more powerful, higher status persons of medieval English society.[48] Thus, it is reasonable

---

[46] As was the case with religious defendants, half of the religious plaintiffs (49) were clerks (24), although the percentage of chaplains was less (14%). But also there were a number of priors (6), abbots (5), and bishops (2), whose status would seem equivalent to gentry or higher. Including them would increase the percentage of plaintiffs who were gentry or higher from 33% to 37%. The nature of the clerks is ambiguous, as it was in the case of the defendants.

[47] When nobles or gentry were plaintiffs, the status of 248 of the defendants was identified. The 164 sub-gentry sued by those plaintiffs were: yeomen (66), persons of occupation (49), religious persons (22), husbandmen (21), and officials (6). The 84 gentry sued by those plaintiffs were: gentlemen (48), esquires (29), knights (7), and nobles (0).

[48] Other studies have shown that it was not unusual for husbandmen, yeoman, and persons of occupation to be common defendants in medieval litigation, and the nobility and the

Table 12.3 *Maintenance plaintiffs by type*

Persons of occupation and trade	34% (119)
Knights, esquires, and gentlemen	32% (110)
Religious	14% (49)
Husbandmen and yeomen	6% (21)
Women	6% (20)
Officials	5% (17)
Lawyers	1% (5)
Nobility	1% (4)

Table 12.4 *Nobles and gentry as maintenance plaintiffs*

Gentlemen	15% (52)
Esquires	13% (44)
Knights	4% (15)
Nobility	1% (4)

to conclude that the maintenance statutes were not used to curb legal corruption and abuse by powerful individuals and officials and, therefore, did not achieve their statutory objective.[49]

gentry uncommon ones. Maddern studied East Anglian litigation in the King's Bench involving violence for the period 1422–42. Philippa Maddern, *Violence and the Social Order* (Oxford, 1992), pp. 27–74. Palmer did a study of the social status of the litigants in the Common Bench, Trinity Term, 1465. Robert Palmer, "England: Law, Society and the State," in S.G. Rigby, ed., *A Companion to Britain in the Later Middle Ages* (Oxford, 2003), p. 257; "The Social Status of Litigants in the Court of Common Pleas: 1465," http://aalt.law.uh.edu/ELHOv/Status.html. Brooks did a study of Michaelmas Term, 1441 Common Bench litigants. Brooks, *Lawyers, Litigation and English Society*, pp. 77–78. But it is difficult to compare these other studies because they involved different courts, different types of actions, and different time periods. Therefore, these other studies do not suggest that the types of maintenance defendants were simply another occurrence of an ordinary pattern of medieval litigants and not otherwise significant.

[49] Some might claim that using absolute numbers of the different types of litigants, as was done in the preceding analysis, is problematic, as the numbers of each type varied considerably. For example, perhaps more sub-gentry were defendants as there were more of them and fewer gentry as defendants because there were less of them. A more scientific statistical analysis would relate the numbers of the litigants to the percentage of society made up by the gentry and sub-gentry and their constituent groups. But that information is not available, and the studies of medieval litigants, as discussed above, use the numbers revealed by the records. Moreover, the limitations of only using numbers does not

Another Possible Statutory Objective: Reducing Litigation

Medieval England, like many societies, had an ambivalent attitude toward litigation. It was very popular, as the evidence demonstrates by the large and growing number of persons who made substantial use of it to secure their property and other legal rights. Moreover, it was important to the crown, which also engaged in substantial litigation to vindicate its interests and to enforce the law. Ives said that, during fifteenth century and afterward, law, "the ligaments of the body politic," had a fundamental and broad role. He noted a "frenzied preoccupation with the law" and an "intensely 'law-minded' society, obsessed with legal considerations, legal rights, and legal remedies." These attitudes produced a litigious society that relied heavily "upon the law as administered by the courts."[50]

But a contemporary criticism was that litigation was excessive and had a negative social impact. The legislative response focused on the abuses that impacted on the operation of the legal system and those that caused excessive and specious litigation. In particular, there were several provisions in the Statute of Westminister I 1275 prohibiting maintenance, champerty, barratry, and abusive litigation tactics.[51] Commentators contemporary with their adoption voiced these concerns with the conduct targeted by this legislation. In discussing these sections of the Statute of Westminister I, *Fleta* said that royal officials should take no rewards or bribes for exercising their office and should "be content with their fees" and that those who "foment or maintain suits ... [are] despisers of the law."[52] *Britton* complained of conduct "hindering justice" and causing "damage or grievance" to the people and referred to those "who through malice have procured suits to be stirred up," causing oppression and wrongful litigation.[53] Later, Coke noted the role of maintenance and champerty in causing excessive litigation. In his extensive discussion of the chapters of the Statute of Westminister I, he referred to "mischief," "vexation," and "delay" and said that champerty

---

undermine the significance of the substantial differences in the numbers of defendants between gentry and sub-gentry as defendants and as plaintiffs.

[50] He suggested that these attitudes were related to the structure of property ownership, the broader role of law as foundational to English pre-reformation society, and the importance and widespread diffusion of legal knowledge as a result of its universal relevance. Eric Ives, *The Common Lawyers of Pre-Reformation England* (Cambridge, 1983), pp. 7–10, 22.

[51] 3 Edw. I, cc. 24–30, 33 (1275), *Statutes of the Realm*, vol. 1, pp. 33–35.

[52] G.O. Sayles, ed. and trans., *Fleta*, 3 vols. (London, 1983), 99 Selden Society, vol. IV, book VI, pp. 138–40, 153, 225.

[53] F.M. Nichols, ed. and trans., *Britton*, 2 vols. (Oxford, 1865), vol. I, pp. 91–92, 94–95.

did substantial "mischief therein to the subverting of justice and truth" and that maintenance "stir[red] up and maintain[ed] quarrels" and "is punished with great severity."[54]

Contemporaries put part of the blame for excessive litigation on the legal profession. One obvious response to this complaint was the regulation of lawyers. A common refrain was that there were too many attorneys, which resulted in excessive and unmeritorious litigation. As a fourteenth-century poem complained, "Attorneys in country, they get silver for naught; They make men begin what they never had thought."[55] Three thirteenth-century enactments focused on controlling the number of lawyers and prohibiting and punishing their misconduct.[56] In commenting on the 1292 Ordinance, which controlled entry by attorneys to the Common Bench, Coke said that "it was thought good to decrease the number of attorneys, finding them to be the causes of the multiplication of suits ... to great inconvenience in the common-wealth and to the no small blemish and discredit of that ancient and necessary vocation."[57] Brand stated that "the underlying theory seemed to be that excessive numbers of attorneys led to unnecessary litigation, as attorneys tried to make a living not by serving a pre-existing demand for their services but by creating it themselves."[58] Similar sentiments continued into the late medieval period. Statutes in 1402 and 1455 that regulated the legal profession again linked lawyers to excessive litigation.[59] As to these

---

[54] He also said that barratry was not adequately remedied by the Statute of Merton and caused mischief that required further remedy. Edward Coke, *The Second Institute of the Laws of England*, 2 vols. (London, 1642; reprint, 1986), vol. I, pp. 205–18, 224–25.

[55] "Poem on the Evil Times of Edward II," in Thomas Wright, *Political Songs of England* (1839; Peter Coss ed., 1996 edition), pp. 323, 339.

[56] Statute of Westminster I, 3 Edw. I, c. 29 (1275), *Statutes of the Realm*, vol. 1, p. 34; London Ordinance of 1280, *Munimenta Gildhallae Londoniensis ii, part ii, Liber Custamarum*, pp. 280–82; "Ordinance of 1292, *De Attornatis et Apprenticiis*," Edward I Parliaments: Roll 5, Hilary 1292, no. 24 (22), *PROME*; Paul Brand, *The Origins of the English Legal Profession* (Oxford, 1992), pp. 106–42; Jonathan Rose, "The Legal Profession in Medieval England: A History of Regulation," *Syracuse Law Review* 48 (1998), pp. 49–105.

[57] Coke, *Second Institute*, vol. I, p. 250. Although Coke did not explicitly mention the ordinance, the marginalia indicated that it was included in his reference to the action taken "in divers parliaments." Ibid.

[58] He also stated that "excessive numbers meant that some attorneys could only survive by 'fraud and malice.'" He also noted the concern with the "unnecessary stirring up of litigation." Brand, *Origins*, pp. 115–16, 122, 209 n. 73.

[59] Both statutes were the product of Commons' petitions that voiced the same complaint. 4 Hen. IV, c. 18 (1402), *Statutes of the Realm*, vol. 2, p. 138; 33 Hen. VI, c. 29 (1455), ibid., pp. 377–78.

statutes, Coke commented that "the multitude of atturnies, more than is limited by law, is a great cause of increase of suits" and that these statutes were "made for avoiding and decreasing of vexatious suits."[60] The maintenance statutes were one of the products of this persistent climate of opinion concerned with excessive litigation.

Further evidence also suggests that reducing litigation may have been the objective of the maintenance statutes. Criminal enforcement was predominant, and many of the presentments charged the defendants with maintenance of false pleas and quarrels. This concern with the falsity of pleas was consistent with the conspiracy prosecutions and other cases involving the procurement of false appeals and indictments. An aspect of the complaint about excessive litigation was that it lacked legal merit.

Although this evidence of a contemporary perception reveals the view that maintenance caused excessive and specious litigation, the linkage in reality seems somewhat questionable in the late medieval period. In that period, it seems rather difficult to connect the legislative prohibition of maintenance with a reduction in litigation. As result of the 1377 statute and the availability of a writ from Chancery, numerous maintenance actions were instituted. Officials encouraged aggrieved parties to complain. Although the volume of maintenance actions that resulted was not comparable to those involving trespass, debt, or defamation, it was certainly not insubstantial. Thus, although it is difficult to know for certain, the maintenance statutes may have contributed to increasing litigation in the fifteenth century rather than reducing it.

The volume of the maintenance litigation raises the question of why so many actions were brought in this period. Several explanations seem plausible. First, some of the plaintiffs were victims of unlawful conduct, such as bribery, procuring inquisitions, and jury misconduct. Officials encouraged aggrieved parties to complain and a writ was made available. In addition, perhaps some maintenance plaintiffs may have felt that they would not have been sued but for the support received by their adversaries. It seems most likely, however, that those who brought maintenance actions usually were those who had lost or feared that they would lose the principal action. They may have believed that such a result was made more likely by the assistance or support given to their adversary. A less benign motive was the ability to bring an action as a means of retaliating against an adversary and burden him.

---

[60] Coke, *The Fourth Part of the Institutes of the Laws of England*, p. 76.

Maintenance Litigation as a Means of Harassment

The litigation records provide considerable evidence to show that some litigants in fact used maintenance actions as a weapon to harass an opponent. The plea rolls reveal numerous instances of extended disputes and litigation between the parties in the maintenance actions. When the maintenance litigation is linked to other actions involving the same parties, it suggests that the maintenance actions were being used to harass existing opponents and burden them with additional expense and difficulties.[61] To use a modern term, it became a form of satellite or ancillary litigation because it did not involve a substantive dispute between the parties, but an additional lawsuit provoked by the underlying substantive dispute, which was the subject of the principal litigation. About sixty instances in which the maintenance litigation and other abuses of legal procedure could be connected with other actions involving the same parties or their associates were found. In some instances, these broader disputes included other forms of satellite actions such as attaints, bribery, or other litigation misconduct. Several examples of these extended disputes and other evidence of the use of maintenance actions as harassment are worth examining in detail.[62]

The Widow and the Tailor

In 1448, Gertrude de Lunes, a London widow, appealed William Clement, a tailor, for robbery, and the jury found William not guilty.[63] Not satisfied, she then sued William for trespass, accusing him of breaking

---

[61] Arbitration was also used as a form of harassment. Stevens, "Failed Arbitrations," p. 24. More generally, the legal system through use of "malicious indictments and counter-accusations" was "turned into an instrument of revenge." Simon Walker, *The Lancastrian Affinity 1361–1399* (Oxford, 1990), pp. 156–57.

[62] In these examples, the proportion of gentry using maintenance and other actions as means of harassment is substantially higher (ca. 50%) than the proportion of gentry who were defendants in maintenance actions (12%). But the remainder of the 60 instances of this harassment were largely sub-gentry. These examples were chosen because they were more extensive, detailed, and interesting than the other instances. Perhaps the percentage of gentry engaging in harassment was higher because they were willing and able to spend the additional money required for multiple actions or felt that more was at stake in the conflicts with their adversaries.

[63] The appeal was by bill, as William was in the custody of the marshal of the Marshalsea. TNA: PRO KB 27/748, m. 23 (1448), AALT Img. Nos. 48–49.

into her home with others and assaulting her.[64] William then brought a maintenance action against Gertrude and three men for maintaining on John Rudby's behalf a trespass action brought against William by John, Gertrude's groom. Gertrude claimed all she did was help the groom find counsel in the trespass action, but William said she paid two men 100s to distribute to others in Surrey to maintain for the groom against William. Gertrude was found guilty of maintenance and William was awarded 200 marks' damages.[65] Gertrude then brought a *decies tantum* action[66] against eight jurors for taking bribes and food and drink in the maintenance action brought by William.[67] Next she brought a writ of error in William's maintenance action against her, which was unsuccessful.[68] Subsequently, Gertrude and her new husband brought an attaint against William and the jurors in William's maintenance action.[69] The original trespass action had prompted three further satellite actions.

The Norwich Villein

In about 1410–11, William Lynsted brought a trespass action against Richard Shurlock for assault and seizing him as Richard's villein. The jury found Richard guilty and awarded William damages of 100 marks.[70]

---

[64] William said the breaking was into a tavern to buy and drink wine, and as to the assault, he said that he asked permission to leave the tavern by kissing Gertrude, who then followed him home and took hold of his arm and he pushed her breasts and shoulders to remove her grip. Gertrude repeated her charge and the parties put themselves on the jury. TNA: PRO KB 27/748, m. 69 (1448), AALT Img. Nos. 140–41.

[65] William brought actions in both the King's Bench and Common Bench. He remitted 50 of the 200 marks' damages. The three other defendants denied the maintenance and the jury acquitted them. TNA: PRO KB 27/754, m. 109 (1449), AALT Img. No. 224; TNA: PRO CP 40/756, m. 104 (1450), AALT Img. Nos. 209–10, 1120–21. William had difficulty collecting damages from Gertrude and sued for execution of them. TNA: PRO KB 27/760, m. 55d (1451), AALT Img. No. 334. Gertrude paid a 20s fine to the king. TNA: PRO KB 27/766, fine roll m. 1 (1452), AALT Img. No. 237.

[66] Such an action was based on a statute that permitted an individual to sue to have half of ten times the amount of the bribe. See Chapter 5, pp. 104–06 and notes 52 and 53.

[67] The defendants denied taking anything and the matter was sent to a jury. TNA: PRO KB 27/760, m. 23d (1451), AALT Img. Nos. 271–72.

[68] TNA: PRO KB 27/761, m. 24 (1451), AALT Img. Nos. 50–53, 226–28. Gertrude finally paid the damages assessed against her in William's maintenance. Ibid. AALT Img. No. 228.

[69] TNA: PRO KB 27/766, m. 94 (1452), AALT Img. Nos. 203–05, 543–45.

[70] Although Richard claimed that he and his ancestors always had been seized of William and his ancestors, Richard satisfied William for the damage and paid a 20s fine to the king. TNA: PRO CP 40/597, m. 202 (1410), AALT Img. No. 421.

Richard responded by bringing an attaint action against William and eleven of the jurors in the trespass action.[71] William then brought a maintenance action against Sir John Heveningham for maintaining Richard's attaint on the side of Richard, alleging that John incited the trespass jurors against William and gave money to seven jurors.[72] William then brought another maintenance action against John, alleging that John incited three of the other trespass jurors against William and gave them money.[73] Richard then brought a *decies tantum* action against the eleven trespass jurors that he had sued in his attaint action, alleging that they took money from Roger Waverly, whom William had given £10 and food and drink.[74] As a result of the original trespass, four satellite actions were brought.

The Norfolk Neighbors

Sir Henry Grey and John Jenney were well-known members of the Norfolk gentry,[75] who had conflicts over the use of their neighboring

---

[71] He lost the attaint because he failed to appear and later paid a fine to the king. TNA: PRO KB 27/604, m. 23d (1412), AALT Img. No. 235; TNA: PRO KB 27/605, m. 30 (1412), AALT Img. Nos. 66–67.

[72] John denied and imparled. TNA: PRO KB 27/604, m. 36 (1412), AALT Img. No. 77. Sir John Heveningham was an important East Anglian knight. He had been a knight of the shire for Suffolk, serving twice, before and after the alleged maintenance, the sheriff for Norfolk and Suffolk, and later a justice of the peace for Suffolk. J.S. Roskell, Linda Clark, and Carole Rawcliffe, eds., "Heveningham, Sir John," in *The History of Parliament: the House of Commons 1386–1421*, 4 vols. (Stroud, 1992), vol. 3, pp. 368–69.

[73] Again John denied and imparled. TNA: PRO KB 27/604, m. 36d (1412), AALT Img. No. 263.

[74] The jurors denied taking anything and the parties put themselves on the country. TNA: PRO KB 27/604, m. 74 (1412), AALT Img. No. 155.

[75] Henry Grey was the son of Sir Henry Grey (d. 1463), the prominent Yorkist, who was a knight of shire for Norfolk. The younger Henry was the escheator for Norfolk and Suffolk (1469–70, 1478–79) and was knighted at Tewkesbury (1471). Colin Richmond, *The Paston Family in the Fifteenth Century: Endings* (Manchester, 2000), pp. 185–88. John Jenney was a lawyer and a member of Lincoln's Inn and part of a family of lawyers. Baker, *Men of Court*, vol. II, pp. 941–45. He and his family were associated with the Paston family and Sir John Fastolf. As a result of that association, they were adversaries of the East Anglian Suffolk faction, whose leaders Thomas Tuddenham, John Heydon, and others were indicted for conspiring to maintain each other and extorting money from John Jenney, senior, John Jenney, junior, and William Jenney, as well as threatening them, and they filed false actions against the Jenneys because of their legal representation of Suffolk opponents and their opposition to the Suffolk faction. TNA: PRO KB 27/767, m. 7 rex (1453), AALT Img. Nos. 173–74, 397; TNA: PRO KB 27/793, m. 6 rex (1459), AALT Img. Nos. 331–39, 740–47.

lands.[76] They were involved in a considerable amount of litigation, which started when Robert Martin successfully sued Grey in 1466 for trespass for taking and carrying away a box of his seals and charters and other muniments.[77] Jenney was Robert's counsel in the trespass action.[78] After losing the trespass action, Grey brought a successful attaint, an uncommon occurrence, against the twelve trespass jurors.[79] Sir John Scott then brought a *decies tantum* against the same jurors, alleging that they accepted varying amounts of money and food and drink from Robert in the trespass action.[80] Scott then brought a *decies tantum* action against Jenney and John Stevenson, who was attorney for the jurors in the prior *decies tantum* action, alleging that they were embracers of the trespass

[76] Jenney's recount of an accord in a maintenance action by Henry against him and a replevin action that Jenney filed against Grey and others suggest that they were neighbors and probably adjoining landowners. TNA: PRO KB 27/847, m. 35 (1473), AALT Img. Nos. 76–77, 336–37; TNA: PRO KB 27/861, m. 28 (1476), AALT Img. Nos. 197–98.

[77] Henry Grey alleged that his father was seised of the manor of Ketteringham and gave the box to Henry, as a result of which Henry was seised in fee tail of the manor with his wife Joan. Henry said that he gave the box for safe custody to another man, who gave it to Robert to deliver to Henry. Robert said that the box, which he claimed Henry's father had given him, contained charters and muniments regarding his manor of Costyns and not the manor of Keteringham. The jury found that Henry, the father, did not give the box to his son, and Robert recovered 200 marks. TNA: PRO KB 27/817, m. 32 (1465), AALT Img. Nos. 71–73, 392. This all seems to be part of a family dispute, as Robert's wife, Eleanor, was Henry's sister, and Robert had brought another action against Henry for abducting Eleanor and her father, Henry Grey, senior. Douglas Richardson, *Magna Carta Ancestry: A Study in Colonial and Medieval Families*, 2nd ed., 4 vols. (Salt Lake City, 2011), vol. II, p. 256.

[78] In a maintenance action that Grey filed against him, Jenney explained that Martin retained him as counsel in the trespass action. TNA: PRO KB 27/847, m. 35 (1473), AALT Img. Nos. 76–77, 336–37.

[79] The court, initially wishing to be advised further on an inquisition regarding Grey's damages, decided that Grey should be reimbursed for 210 marks assessed against him in the trespass, if it had been executed, and have all other loss restored. The draconian penalties for attaint were imposed on the jurors, although four were pardoned. TNA: PRO KB 27/820, m. 60 (1466), AALT Img. Nos. 132–35, 391–94.

[80] The defendants denied taking anything and the parties put themselves on the country. TNA: PRO KB 27/820, m. 61 (1466), AALT Img. Nos. 136–37. Scott brought another *decies tantum* action against one of the trespass jurors. TNA: PRO KB 27/821, m. 98d (1466), AALT Img. Nos. 494–95. There is no further information on the plaintiff, who under the statute was entitled to half of penalty, which was ten times the bribe. Sir John Scott may have been the prominent Kent Yorkist who held several royal offices, including controller of the household. He also had a familial relationship with Sir Henry Grey, who was married to Jane Scott, daughter of William Scott, esquire and likely sister of Sir John. Peter Fleming, "Scott Family," *Dictionary of National Biography Online*; Richardson, *Magna Carta Ancestry*, vol. II, p. 256.

inquisition. He accused Jenney of taking £20 and Stevenson £10 as well as both taking food and drink worth 30s from Martin to bring and procure the inquisition in the trespass.[81] In the same year, Grey accused Jenney and Stevenson of conspiring with Martin falsely and maliciously to procure his indictment for feloniously taking Martin's goods, for which he was subsequently acquitted.[82] By the end of this turmoil, Grey was in the King's Bench prison for surety of the peace toward the king and "especially toward John Jenney."[83]

But this was not the end of Grey–Jenney litigation growing out of Martin's trespass action against Grey.[84] In 1473, Grey sued Jenney for maintaining Martin's trespass action against Grey on behalf of Martin. Jenney responded that he had been retained by Martin as his counsel in the trespass action, who had asked Jenney whether his bill was sufficient in law, and Jenney opined that, based on his knowledge, it was sufficient and good according to the law of the land. Grey's replication asserted that Jenney gave 6s 8d to one of the jurors to say his verdict for Martin, which

---

[81] Jenney and Stevenson imparled several times. TNA: PRO KB 27/821, m. 96d (1466), AALT Img. Nos. 490–91. Walter Goldery, Grey's essoiner in the trespass action, also brought a *decies tantum* action against the jurors in the trespass action for taking money and food and drink from Martin. They denied the charge and put themselves on the jury. TNA: PRO KB 27/820, m. 61d (1466), AALT Img. Nos. 396–98.

[82] One of the jurors in the trespass and attaint was also a defendant. TNA: PRO KB 27/821, m. 89d (1466), AALT Img. Nos. 472–73. Grey also sued Martin and several other men for the same conspiracy. TNA: PRO KB 27/821, m. 89d (1466), AALT Img. No. 473; TNA: PRO KB 27/841, m. 70d (1471), AALT Img. Nos. 472–73; TNA: PRO KB 27/842, m. 52d (1472), AALT Img. No. 466.

[83] He found mainpernors and was released on bail. TNA: PRO KB 27/842, m. 9d rex (1472), AALT Img. No. 562.

[84] There was another land dispute in Norfolk involving several maintenance and other satellite actions, one of which was brought by Jenney. In 1447 Margaret Wetherby successfully sued Robert Slapper and Thomas Stalon, his servant, for a trespass to her land, which Margaret and Robert both claimed. TNA: PRO KB 27/744, m. 49 (1447), AALT Img. Nos. 100–101. Following their loss in trespass action, Slapper and Stalon filed an attaint. TNA: PRO KB 27/754, m. 1 (1449), AALT Img. Nos. 3–4, 319–20. Margaret brought a maintenance action against three men for maintaining Slapper and Stalon in the trespass action. TNA: PRO KB 27/756, m. 54 (1450), AALT Img. No. 120. She also successfully sued Slapper in a maintenance action, alleging that he had maintained Sir Miles Stapleton, John Heydon, John Paston, and several others, who had brought a successful assize of novel disseisin against Margaret regarding different land. TNA: PRO KB 27/744, m. 22d (1447), AALT Img. No. 296. John Jenney also brought a maintenance action against Slapper for the same conduct. TNA: PRO KB 27/753, m. 24d (1449), AALT Img. No. 265. Slapper was also sued for maintenance involving different litigation and parties. TNA: PRO KB 27/753, m. 20d (1449), AALT Img. No. 256.

Jenney denied.[85] Even this was not the end of the Grey–Jenney feud. In 1476, as further evidence of the ongoing feud, Jenney brought a replevin action against Grey and others for illegally taking and detaining 900 of Jenney's sheep. Grey denied taking some, but admitted taking most of them because they were on his land.[86] Overall, the initial trespass action had spawned eight ancillary actions, an attaint, four *decies tantum* actions, two conspiracy actions, and a maintenance action, as well as other litigation between Grey and Jenney.[87]

The King's Bench Justice

In 1448, Sir William Yelverton JKB brought an action for trespass against Richard Holdernes and Thomas Skepper for cutting down his gorse and heath and digging up his soil. The defendants said they were unable to deny the trespass, and the court assessed damages of 5 marks which the defendants paid.[88] In the same term, the justice brought a maintenance

---

[85] Jenney later withdrew his denial and asserted Grey's action should be precluded by an accord that the two had entered. The accord provided that Grey would give Jenney an acre of land, whose ownership seemed to be in dispute, and would restore the hedges and ditches on that land and that Jenney would not depasture any other land with his sheep and would permit Grey to use a certain road and have access to a particular meadow to make hay. Finally the accord provided that each provide 8s for a breakfast for the other and his friends. Grey denied being bound by the accord and both put themselves on the jury. TNA: PRO KB 27/847, m. 35 (1473), AALT Img. Nos. 76–77, 336–37.

[86] He said that the sheep had trampled his land and he impounded them as security for the damage to his land, although in the process of doing so they escaped onto Jenney's land and he detained them until Jenney broke into the enclosure and abducted the sheep and now possessed them. Jenney denied breaking into the enclosure and possessing the sheep as well as Grey's right to impound them. TNA: PRO KB 27/861, m. 28 (1476), AALT Img. Nos. 197–98.

[87] Jenney also seems to have brought a trespass action against Grey. TNA: PRO KB 27/848, m. 25 (1473), AALT Img. No. 51; TNA: PRO KB 27/863, m. 28d (1477), AALT Img. No. 316. In addition to his involvement in litigation as a lawyer for litigants, Jenney was an active litigant himself. In particular, he frequently filed maintenance actions, as illustrated by these six actions. TNA: PRO KB 27/753, m. 24d (1449), AALT Img. No. 265; TNA: PRO KB 27/755, m. 12 (1450), AALT Img. No. 25; TNA: PRO KB 27/776, m. 67d (1455), AALT Img. No. 428; TNA: PRO KB 27/785, m. 81d (1457), AALT Img. No. 413; TNA: PRO KB 27/793, m. 103 (1459), AALT Img. Nos. 263–64, 679; TNA: PRO KB 27/793, m. 105d (1459), AALT Img. Nos. 683–84.

[88] The defendants were two husbandmen living in Weasenham, Norfolk. The land was in Weasenham, which was where the defendants lived and was adjacent to Rougham, where Yelverton lived. TNA: PRO KB 27/750, m. 2d (1448), AALT Img. No. 350; TNA: PRO KB 27/752, m. 36d (1449), AALT Img. No. 319. Yelverton was appointed to the King's Bench on July 1, 1443, and served until April 6, 1471. He was associated with the Paston family

action against two men, one of them probably Thomas's relative, for maintaining the defendants in the trespass action for the defendants. One of the defendants said that he was unable to deny the charges, and Yelverton recovered 8 marks.[89] Then the Crown brought a maintenance action against that defendant, and he was convicted and paid a 10s fine.[90] Afterward, the justice brought another trespass action against one of the maintenance defendants.[91]

Although this episode was not as extensive or as detailed as the other disputes discussed above, it is an interesting and somewhat unusual illustration of the misuse of maintenance actions. In the first place, Justice Yelverton was successful in his trespass action and collected damages from the defendants. It was not common for someone who had already prevailed in the principal action to bring a maintenance action. Moreover, it was uncommon for both a private party and the crown to sue the same defendants for maintenance. Normally, an aggrieved party either brought their own action or complained to the crown, which sued but would not pursue the action if the complainant did not appear.[92] It seems likely, therefore, that the crown filed and pursued the action at the behest of Yelverton.[93] As a result of these maintenance actions, Yelverton, who had already collected 5 marks in his trespass action, was able to impose almost £6 in additional damages on a small farmer, not a small amount for him, as well as the burden of dealing with two additional lawsuits.

The East Anglian Wars

In the mid-fifteenth century, a substantial conflict, which included numerous legal actions, arose in East Anglia between the duke of Suffolk

---

and Sir John Fastolf. E.W. Ives, "Sir William Yelverton," *Oxford Dictionary of National Biograph Online*.

[89] TNA: PRO KB 27/750, m. 73d (1448), AALT Img. No. 490; TNA: PRO KB 27/752, m. 46 (1449), AALT Img. No. 95; TNA: PRO KB 27/754, m. 25 (1449), AALT Img. No. 53.

[90] TNA: PRO KB 27/753, m. 27 rex (1449), AALT Img. No. 205; TNA: PRO KB 27/766, fine roll m. 2d (1452), AALT Img. No. 576.

[91] The defendant was John Skepper, a Weasenham husbandman, who was likely a relative of Thomas Skepper, a defendant in the initial trespass action. TNA: PRO KB 27/757, m. 13 (1450), AALT Img. No. 30.

[92] As discussed in Chapter 8, defendants went without day in crown actions where they prayed that the king count against them and no one responded to the court's proclamation to complain. TNA: PRO KB 27/626, m. 12d (1417), AALT Img. No. 564.

[93] In addition, the maintenance defendants could have been assessed fines to the king in Yelverton's action, and, therefore, an additional action by the crown seemed unnecessary.

and his affinity and their adversaries, who included the Paston family and Sir John Fastolf.[94] One aspect of this conflict was eight legal actions, including four maintenance actions and two attaints, that were brought involving John Andrew, a lieutenant of the late duke of Suffolk and a member of the still dominant Suffolk forces in East Anglia, and Fastolf's servants, Thomas Howes and John Porter. In 1452, Andrew brought a conspiracy action against Howes and Porter, alleging that they had illegally procured his indictment.[95] The jury found for Andrew and awarded him 165 marks' damages.[96] As a result, Porter brought an attaint action against Andrew and the jury in the conspiracy action.[97] In the following year, Howes brought a maintenance action against

---

[94] Jonathan Rose, "Litigation and Political Conflict in Fifteenth-Century East Anglia: Conspiracy and Attaint Actions and Sir John Fastolf," *Journal of Legal History* 27 (2006), pp. 53–80.

[95] Andrew was indicted on September 22, 1450, at Norwich for combining with Thomas Tuddenham and John Heydon, leaders of the Suffolk faction, to extort money from Fastolf in 1438. Andrew also sued several of the jurors who had been members of the inquest that indicted him. Andrew's action was actually for violating a statute that prohibited indictments in a foreign county, as it was returned in Norfolk and Andrew lived in Suffolk. The statute provided an action on the case for the indicted person and for triple damages. 8 Hen. VI, c. 10 (1429), *Statutes of the Realm*, vol. 2, pp. 246–48. Many contemporary sources referred to Andrew's action as a conspiracy action. Tuttenham, Heydon, and others in the Suffolk faction were also indicted several times for maintenance, conspiracy, and other offenses at Norwich in 1452 and 1454. TNA: PRO KB 9/267, mm. 23–25 (1452), AALT Img. Nos. 46–51; TNA: PRO KB 9/272, mm. 2–5 (1454), AALT Img. Nos. 4–8, 15–19, 22–29. The jurors acquitted Tuddenham on one of the charges. TNA: PRO 27/762 m. 1d (1451), AALT Img. No. 539.

[96] The defendants pleaded different defenses. Porter denied the procuring and he and Andrew put themselves on the jury. Howes alleged a justification for his action, which Andrew traversed, and both put themselves on the country. The jurors demurred on the ground that they followed the justices' instructions and acted lawfully. The court delayed several times, saying it needed to be advised further, and ultimately Andrew dropped the action against them. TNA: PRO KB 27/767, m. 32 (1453), AALT Img. Nos. 64–66, 289–90.

[97] TNA: PRO KB 27/775, m. 40 (1455), AALT Img. Nos.82–83. Andrew successfully challenged the attaint jury on the ground that the sheriff had convened an array favorable to the plaintiff. TNA: PRO KB 27/776, m. 37 (1455), AALT Img. Nos. 79–83, 353–58. Fastolf asked his lawyers, John Paston and William Jenney, to get the advice of Sir William Yelverton JKB on whether to proceed with the attaint. Based on their advice, Fastolf agreed to give the sheriff a "reward" to hold him "content; wherfor that youre reward may be the largere so he woll there-vpon returne that panell for the seyd ateynte." Davis, Beadle, and Richmond, eds., *Paston Letters*, part II, no. 511, p. 107. Porter challenged the second attain jury successfully because the sheriff's wife was related to Andrew. On May 12, 1460, the action was still unresolved. TNA: PRO KB 27/776, m. 37 (1455), AALT Img. Nos. 79–83, 353–58.

various Suffolk adherents for maintaining Andrew's conspiracy action.[98] Andrew also brought a maintenance action against another Fastolf servant because of his efforts resisting the execution of Andrew's judgment in the conspiracy action.[99] In addition to these private actions, the crown brought two actions for maintaining the attaint, one against Thomas Deyvill, a Suffolk supporter, for maintaining Andrew,[100] and another against John Bokking and William Barker, two of Fastolf's servants, for maintaining Porter.[101]

In 1457, Andrew brought another similar conspiracy action against Howes for illegally procuring his indictment in another matter.[102] But this time his action was unsuccessful.[103] In 1458, Andrew brought an

[98] The defendants denied the charge and imparled numerous times. TNA: PRO KB 27/782, m. 97d (1456), AALT Img. No. 533; TNA: PRO KB 27/784, m. 60 (1457), AALT Img. Nos. 125–26, 403.

[99] Fastolf paid 5s 8d for his defense. The Fastolf Papers, in the archives of Magdalen College, University of Oxford, include an account of payments and expenses made in this litigation and four other major legal disputes from 1448 to 1458, Fastolf Paper 42. In the section *Custus in Attincta ac pro judicio querele conspiracionis Johannis Andrews*, there are sixteen entries concerning the conspiracy and attaint, which are in reproduced in Rose, "Litigation and Political Conflict," appendix 1, pp. 77–80.

[100] He imparled. TNA: PRO KB 27/782, m. 34 rex (1456), AALT Img. No. 653. John Paston and Howes had sued Deyvill and Sir Phillip Wentworth, sheriff of Norfolk and Suffolk (1447–48) and knight of the shire for Suffolk (1447 and 1449) and another member of Suffolk's affinity. TNA: PRO KB 27/KB 27/785, m. 80d (1457), AALT Img. Nos. 410–11. In addition, Andrew and Devyvill had sued Howes and William Jenney in the Common Bench in 1456. Davis, Beadle, and Richmond, eds., *Paston Letters*, part II, no. 552, p. 148; ibid., part III, p. 148.

[101] TNA: PRO KB 27/784, m. 33d rex (1457), AALT Img. No. 541. The *Paston Letters* contain several letters in which Fastolf discussed his personal involvement in several maintenance actions. Davis, Beadle, and Richmond, eds., *Paston Letters*, part II, no. 457, p. 44; ibid., part III, nos. 987, 991, 1005, 1007, 1019, pp. 93, 102–3, 124, 128, 149.

[102] Howes and Porter attempted to bring their own conspiracy action against Andrew, claiming he falsely accused them of conspiring to have him indicted at Norwich in September 1450. When the *oyer et terminer* commissioners refused to permit their bill of conspiracy to proceed, they petitioned the chancellor for a writ of *dedimus potestatem* "to call and examine [ms stained] theym or any other conspyred procured and made any unlawfull labour at the day of the cessions or before to theym or to any other." TNA: PRO C1/26/621, AALT Img. No. 831. The two indictments of Andrew are on the subsequent membrane. TNA: PRO C1/26/622, AALT Img. No. 832.

[103] The indictment was on the same day at Norwich as the other indictment. In this one, Andrew was indicted for trespass regarding Fastolf's manor at Beighton, Norfolk, in 1449. Howes alleged the same exonerating circumstances as he did in the first action, but this time he was successful and was found not guilty. TNA: PRO KB 27/783, m. 43 (1457), AALT Img. Nos. 89–90, 308. Andrew also sued several others, but not Porter. TNA: PRO KB 27/775, m. 63d (1455), AALT Img. Nos. 417–18; TNA: PRO KB 27/776, m. 78d (1455), AALT Img. Nos. 454–55. In addition, both the Fastolf and Suffolk allies

attaint against Howes and the jury in the second conspiracy action, which was dismissed because various dates alleged in the pleading were erroneous.[104] In the same year, Howes brought a maintenance action against twenty-one individuals for maintaining this conspiracy action on behalf of Andrew.[105]

Radford's Case

In 1438–39 Devon, a family property dispute between Thomas and William Tremayne, the sons of Nicholas Tremayne, spawned several lawsuits and involved several lawyers as litigants.[106] Thomas Tremayne brought an action in Chancery against William Tremayne and Roger Champernon[107] for forging title deeds to show that Nicholas Tremayne, his father, had granted a manor to William, the brother of the petitioner. John Bydelake, the father's steward, and Champeron supported William, who claimed his father had settled the manor on him. Nicholas Radford was William's lawyer and was alleged to have been complicit in the forgery.[108] Having been accused of criminal activity, Champernon and Radford brought a conspiracy action in 1438 against Thomas, William,

brought trespass actions against each other regarding this manor and other Fastolf manors. TNA: PRO KB 146/6/35/1 (1456), Mich., 35 Hen. VI (panella file); TNA: PRO KB 27/795, m. 44 (1459), AALT Img. No. 93 (Wentworth against Howes: Bradwell); TNA: PRO KB 27/785, m. 53, (1457), AALT Img. Nos. 111–12 (John Bokking and William Worcester against Wentworth, John Barnard, Thomas Deyvill: Bradwell); TNA: PRO KB 27/785, m. 80d (1457), AALT Img. Nos. 410–11 (Paston and Howes against Wentworth, Barnard, and Deyvill: Bradwell and numerous other manors); KB 27/791, m. 53 (1459), AALT Img. No. 116 (Fastolf against Wentworth, Henry Wentworth, Andrew, and Deyvill: Cotton).

[104] TNA: PRO KB 27/790, m. 58 (1458), AALT Img. No. 124; TNA: PRO KB 27/791, m. 33 (1458), AALT Img. Nos. 75–76, 293–94.

[105] TNA: PRO KB 27/790, m. 79d (1458), AALT Img. No. 544; British Library, MS Additional. 27444, fol. 57 (Thomas Howes's writ against John Wynham).

[106] Kleineke has chronicled the dispute and the legal actions in detail. Hannes Kleineke, "The Chancery Case between Nicholas Radford and Thomas Tremayne: The Exeter Depositions of 1439," *Devon and Cornwall Record Society* 55 New Series (Exeter 2013).

[107] Champernon was a member of a prominent Devon gentry family, former sheriff of Devon, and closely associated with Thomas Courtenay, earl of Devon. Ibid., pp. xlv–xlvi.

[108] TNA: PRO C 1/39/142 (c. 1438), AALT Img. No. 184; Kleineke, "Chancery Case," pp. xvi–xvii. Radford was an apprentice and a member of the Middle Temple. Sir Thomas Courtenay, son of the earl of Devon, and his gang of robbers murdered Radford. An appeal by his kinsman for his murder described him as "one of the most noteworthy and apprentices of the law in England." Baker, *Men of Court*, vol. II, pp. 1286–87.

and Bydelake.[109] An attempt to have William Courtenay, the earl of Devon, arbitrate this dispute failed, and it was moved into Chancery.[110] In the same year, Radford brought a maintenance action against Sir John Speke for maintaining the conspiracy action.[111] Speke claimed that his action was justified as he was a member of Lincoln's Inn, learned in law, and had been retained as counsel to the defendants.[112] Apparently, there was enmity and other litigation between Radford and Speke.[113]

These examples of extended litigation impacting the same parties illustrate the manner in which adversaries could engage in legal battles to burden and harass their opponents. In addition, Wright has documented a somewhat different series of countywide conflicts and rivalries in Derbyshire involving substantial violence, in which maintenance also played a role.[114] Some of this activity was a product of competitive

---

[109] William Tremayne and Bydelake were dropped from the action. Ibid., pp. xvii–xix. Thomas Tremayne sued Radford, William Tremayne, and nine other men for violation of the statute prohibiting the making and fabricating false deeds by conspiracy and covin. 1 Hen. V, c. 3 (1413), *Statutes of the Realm*, vol. 2, pp. 170–71. TNA: PRO CP 40/ 715, m. 247d (1439), AALT Img. No. 1962.

[110] Kleineke has explored the Chancery inquiry and the depositions taken there and provided biographies of the witnesses. Kleineke, *Chancery Proceeding*, pp. xviii–xxv, xlii–lxxxviii, 1–53.

[111] He also alleged that Speke procured Thomas Courtenay, earl of Devon, to support the defendants in Radford's conspiracy action and also that he procured a goldsmith to testify falsely that Radford had fraudulently counterfeited the signet of Nicholas Tremayne to seal a charter by which Nicholas enfeoffed William of a manor. Speke explained that Radford had engaged the earl to arbitrate the matter and that the conspiracy defendants had retained him to represent them in the arbitration. The parties put themselves on the jury. TNA: PRO CP 40/714, m. 320 (1439) (not in AALT), reprinted in Kleineke, *Chancery Case*, pp. 56–62.

[112] Speke was a member and former governor of Lincoln's Inn and former member of parliament for Devon. Baker, *Men of Court*, vol. I, p. 1437. He also claimed that he was a relative of Bydelake's wife. Radford said he was a layman and "little learned in law."

[113] Kleineke, *Chancery Case*, pp. 62–63.

[114] The conflicts in Derby were different in several respects from those discussed above. They involved numerous conflicts and persons throughout the county, which also had effects in other counties. In addition, the widespread lawlessness and resulting litigation involved murder, assaults, and other criminal conduct. These conflicts included the dispute between Henry, lord Grey of Codnor, and Sir Richard Vernon, discussed in Chapter 11. See Chapter 11, pp. 312–14. Wright, *Derbyshire Gentry*, pp. 119–42. There was also conflict between the Vernon and Gresley families, although Sir John Gresley and William Vernon were both Stafford retainers. Ibid., 72–74, 99–102, 125–26. Sir Richard Vernon also brought two related maintenance actions against John Gresley and others who may have been his associates. TNA: PRO KB 27/757, m. 31d (1450), AALT Img. No. 174.

maintenance, in which magnate rivalry produced active competition for support and influence.[115] The nature of the maintenance accusations was more varied and not limited to maintenance of pleas. For example, Richard Browne, a local lawyer, was indicted for using a fraudulent scheme to obtain the acquittal of Thomas Foljambe, who had been indicted with others, for riot, assaults, and murder. He was also indicted for maintaining Thomas Scot, who had been indicted for theft, by embracing and procuring the jury, who acquitted Scot, in exchange for Scot's enfeoffing Browne of a messuage and half a virgate of land. Because of these offenses and other fraudulent and deceptive conduct, the jury said that Browne was "a common embracer and procurer of juries and a maintainer and supporter of false pleas."[116] In a mid-fifteenth-century case involving an unethical lawyer, Sir Sampson Meverell complained to the chancellor that John Tunstead, an apprentice in law and a retainer of Sir Richard Vernon, was an ambidexter, taking money to be of counsel to both Sampson and his adversary and disclosing his counsel to his adversary. Sampson also complained that John had maintained Thomas Tunstead, his brother, who deceived Sampson by supporting his adversaries and threatening jurors to pass against Sampson. He complained further that John had maintained similar conduct by George Bagshaw, his brother-in-law and a bailiff.[117] In these Derby disputes, there were also actions for maintaining pleas and other satellite actions.[118]

---

[115] Wright, *Derbyshire Gentry*, pp. 127, 137.

[116] Both Browne and Foljambe were associated with Sir Richard Vernon. The jury acquitted Browne. TNA: PRO KB 27/692, m. 7 rex (1434), AALT Img. Nos. 170–71; Wright, *Derbyshire Gentry*, pp. 123–28. At the same *oyer et terminer* session, the jury indicted Vernon, Browne, Foljambe, and many others, including Ralph, Lord Cromwell, and Joan Beauchamp, Baroness Bergavenny, for violations of the livery statute. TNA: PRO KB 9/11, mm. 15–15d, AALT Img. Nos. 26–29.

[117] TNA: PRO C 1/72/112–13; Wright, *Derbyshire Gentry*, pp. 66, 98, 121, 248, 249; Baker, *Men of Court*, vol. II, p. 1564.

[118] Sir Richard Vernon and Sir William Trussel had several land disputes, including one involving land in Staffordshire, which Trussell claimed this land as his inheritance. But Vernon also claimed an inherited right. "Although he initially failed to establish his title, Vernon refused to accept defeat, and employed every tactic at his disposal, from champerty to blatant intimidation, in an attempt to evict his rival." "Vernon, Sir Richard," in Roskell, Clark, and Rawcliffe, eds., *The History of Parliament*, vol. 4, pp. 712–17. He also resorted to legal efforts and arraigned an assize of novel disseisin against Trussel. Vernon prevailed and was awarded £2,080 damages. As a result, Trussell brought an attaint against the assize jury, but as was often the case, there was difficulty in

Maintenance of Maintenance Actions and Reciprocal Maintenance Actions

In addition to these disputes, other litigation also showed that maintenance actions were used to harass opponents. For example, there are several maintenance actions for maintaining maintenance actions. A dispute between Essex men began when John Shank sued Henry Says and two men for lying in wait with many others to kill him and for threatening his life.[119] Says and several others then sued John Asshe, an associate of Shank,[120] for unlawful entry.[121] Says and the other unlawful entry plaintiffs then brought a maintenance action against Shank and several other yeoman for maintaining the unlawful entry action on behalf of Asshe.[122] To retaliate against them for suing him for maintaining Asshe, Shank brought a maintenance action against eight yeomen for maintaining the maintenance action of Says and the others against Shank on behalf of Says and the others.[123]

---

arraigning the attaint jury. TNA: PRO KB 27/756, m. 28 (1450), AALT Img. Nos. 58–68, 267–76. Soon afterward, Trussell brought a *decies tantum* action against the jury in the assize of novel disseisin, alleging that each of the jurors took 100s and food and drink worth 31s 4d from Vernon. The jurors denied taking anything and the parties put themselves on the jury. TNA: PRO KB 27/756, m. 34 (1450), AALT Img. Nos. 79–80. Trussell claimed that Vernon had forged title documents and ultimately secured possession of the land. "Trussell, Sir William," in Roskell, Clark, and Rawcliffe, eds., *The History of Parliament*, vol. 4, pp. 669–71.

[119] Shank said that it prevented him from collecting the debts owed him and supervising the repair of his tenements for three weeks. The defendants denied the wrongdoing and the parties put themselves on the jury. TNA: PRO KB 27/860, m. 33 (1476), AALT Img. No. 77.

[120] Asshe was mainpernor for Shank's surety of peace, as he was imprisoned for assault. TNA: PRO KB 27/862, m. 10 rex (1477), AALT Img. Nos. 221–22.

[121] Two groups of men, one including Henry Says and the other John Asshe, claimed the right to the land by virtue of past grants. Says claimed Asshe unlawfully entered the land and Asshe alleged that he and others had been unlawfully expelled by Says and his associates. There was no evidence that John Shank was involved in this dispute. TNA: PRO KB 27/844, m. 3 (1472), AALT Img. Nos. 14–15, 358–59.

[122] TNA: PRO KB 27/844, m. 70d (1472), AALT Img. No. 510; TNA: PRO KB 27/862, m. 1d (1477), AALT Img. No. 263.

[123] They denied the maintenance and imparled. TNA: PRO KB 27/864, m. 63d (1477), AALT Img. No. 385. In another instance of a maintenance action for maintaining a maintenance action, Thomas Baker brought a successful maintenance action against Thomas Hanwell, dean of the collegiate church of South Malling, Sussex, for maintaining Richard Broun in Baker's maintenance action against Broun. Baker recovered £200, which Hanwell paid. TNA: PRO KB 27/785, m. 22 (1457), AALT Img. Nos. 45–46.

Another example of harassment involved adverse parties filing maintenance actions against each other. John Lounde, a London leather seller and John Arnold, also a leather seller and a cleric,[124] both claimed seisin of several shops and houses in London. As a result of this conflict, Lounde brought two trespass actions, one in the King's Bench against Arnold and another in the Common Bench against Robert Winterburn, Arnold's tenant.[125] Lounde then brought a maintenance action against Arnold for maintaining Winterburn in the Common Bench trespass action. Although Arnold attempted to justify his action by saying he found counsel for his tenant at the latter's request, Lounde prevailed in the maintenance action.[126] The next year, Arnold sued Lounde by bill in the Chancery for maintaining Richard Burdon in his trespass action against Arnold.[127] There were also other instances of adverse parties bringing maintenance actions against each other.[128]

---

[124] Although Lounde described Arnold only as a leather seller, Arnold in both this action and another described himself as a leather seller and a cleric. John Baker thought that such a dual identification was unusual.

[125] Each party's claim to the property involved numerous grants reaching back to the reign of Edward II. Both actions alleged that the defendant had unlawfully entered the property and carried off a substantial quantity of goods. Lounde prevailed against Arnold in the King's Bench and was awarded £8 damages. TNA: PRO KB 27/750, m. 134 (1448), AALT Img. Nos. 263–64, 620–21. The Common Bench action was described in Lounde's maintenance action against Arnold. TNA: PRO KB 27/750, m. 131 (1448), AALT Img. Nos. 254–58, 611–15.

[126] Lounde recovered £24, three times as much as he had recovered in his trespass action against Arnold. Arnold's justification would only have been valid if he had a legitimate interest the property, in which he claimed Winterburn was his grantee. But the basis for his claim to the property in this action was the same claim that was rejected in Lounde's trespass action against him, which may explain why Lounde prevailed in the maintenance action. In both the maintenance and the trespass actions, there were multiple delays by the court in entering judgment, as it repeatedly said that it wanted to be advised further. TNA: PRO KB 27/750, m. 131 (1448), AALT Img. Nos. 254–58, 611–15.

[127] As a servant of the chancellor, Arnold could sue a bill of privilege in the Chancery rather than bringing his action by writ in the Common Bench or by writ or bill in the King's Bench. After the suit was initiated in Chancery, the chancellor transmitted the record to the King's Bench, which ordered the sheriff to convene a jury. Although the earlier trespass against him by Lounde stated he was a leather seller and parson of the church of St. Stephen, Colman Street, London, this action described Arnold as leather seller and a servant of the archbishop of Canterbury. TNA: PRO KB 27/752, m. 70 (1449), AALT Img. No. 144.

[128] Thomas White, merchant, sued John Fleming, gentleman, and another gentleman and a grocer for maintenance, and then Fleming sued White and a different grocer for maintenance. TNA: PRO KB 27/749, m. 56 (1448), AALT Img. No. 118; TNA: PRO KB 27/749, m. 76d (1448), AALT Img. No. 445. Also Hamo Sutton, esquire, brought a maintenance action against Robert Burton, clerk, and several other Lincoln men, and

Several disputes involved both maintenance of a maintenance action and reciprocal maintenance actions. A dispute among London drapers began with an action for trespass to land by John Hunt, draper, against John and Joan Marchal.[129] Then Hunt brought a maintenance action against William Stokdale, draper, and Thomas Otehill, cutler, for maintaining the trespass action on behalf of the Marchals. Fighting fire with fire, Stokdale and Otehill brought a maintenance action against Aumary Matenay, another draper, for maintaining Hunt's maintenance action against them on behalf of Hunt.[130] Shortly after, Joan brought a trespass action against Matenay and three others, two drapers and a gentleman. In return, those defendants brought a maintenance action against Stokdale and Otehill and another member of his family for maintaining Joan's action on her behalf.[131] Another dispute between Thomas Nicoll and Richard Fobell involved multiple maintenance actions. Afterward Thomas Hertwell sued John Mitchell and his wife, Matilda, servants of Thomas Nicholl, for trespass. Herwell brought a maintenance action against Thomas Nicholl for maintaining the Mitchells in the trespass action.[132] Then Nicholl brought a maintenance action against Richard Fobell for maintaining Herwell in his maintenance action against Nicholl.[133] But that was not the extent of the dispute. Contemporaneously, Nicholl brought two other maintenance actions against Fobell, one for maintaining Richard Walfrey in his trespass action against Nicholl[134] and another for maintaining Richard Walfrey, who sued Nicoll for not delivering timber that he had sold and undertaken to

---

Burton sued Sutton for maintenance. TNA: PRO KB 27/718, m. 100d (1440), AALT Img. No. 574; TNA: PRO KB 27/718, m. 122 (1440), AALT Img. No. 260.

[129] The action was by bill and the status or trade of the defendants not stated. The plaintiffs said that the defendants had broken the close and house of the plaintiff, but there was no indication that it was a title dispute. The defendants were found guilty and Hunt awarded 10 marks' damages. TNA: PRO KB 27/698, m. 14 (1435), AALT Img. No. 31.

[130] TNA: PRO KB 27/703, m. 78d (1437), AALT Img. No. 370.

[131] The defendants denied the maintenance and imparled. TNA: PRO KB 27/701, m. 57d (1436), AALT Img. No. 310.

[132] Nichol justified assisting the Mitchells on the ground that they were his servants. He said that he stood with them in the trespass action against them and provided assistance. Herwell alleged that the Mitchells were not Nichol's servants at the time of the maintenance. The parties put themselves on the jury. TNA: PRO KB 27/744, m. 80d (1447), AALT Img. No. 416.

[133] TNA: PRO KB 27/750, m. 117d (1448), AALT Img. No. 576.

[134] Fobell denied the maintenance and the action was sent to the jury. TNA: PRO KB 27/750, m. 105d (1448), AALT Img. No. 562.

deliver to Walfrey, a carpenter.[135] These instances of multiple maintenance actions between adverse parties and maintenance of maintenance
actions demonstrate further that maintenance actions were being used to
retaliate against those with whom there was some underlying personal or
commercial dispute.

In sum, all of these maintenance and other satellite actions illustrate
how they were employed to harass and burden opponents, which aug-
mented the parties' conflicts. The actions also exemplify the late medieval
tendency of individuals and their adversaries to use litigation to wage
their battles. Further, the use of these maintenance actions in this fashion
underscores the failure of the maintenance statutes to achieve their
objectives.

---

[135] Fobell again denied the maintenance and the action was sent to the jury. TNA: PRO KB
27/750, m. 123d (1448), AALT Img. No. 594. In the same term, Fobell brought a debt
action against Nicholl. There was extended pleading regarding an arbitration of land
dispute, which Nicholl claimed was a condition of the bond and which Fobell alleged did
not preclude his action and then a demurrer, in which Nicholl joined issue. The court
wished to be advised in rendering judgment, and the matter remained unresolved for an
extended period. TNA: PRO KB 27/750, m. 121 (1448), AALT Img. Nos. 234–35, 590.

13

Conclusion

Medieval Developments Summarized

The medieval prohibitions on maintenance and related forms of abuse of legal procedure were the initial attempts of the Common Law legal system to deal with those who misused litigation and abused legal procedure. As the legal institutions for dispute resolution developed and functioned in medieval England, they had an inherent potential for misuse and corruption. The review of criminal indictments and civil actions in the period 1272–1485 revealed that many individuals exploited this capacity for abuse. To respond to this social and legal problem and the numerous complaints about it, parliament enacted numerous statutes.

The initial mechanisms to deal with this abuse were prosecutions and actions directed at conspiracy, maintenance, and champerty. Conspiracy involved two or more persons confederated to engage in wrongful conduct. Initially, it focused on procuring false appeals and indictments. Most conspiracy cases were criminal, but those who had been falsely charged and then acquitted had a civil action for damages. Maintenance, in its legal sense, meant intermeddling in litigation by providing assistance or support to a party in a legal action or prosecution in which the maintainer was not a party. In addition, "maintenance" was a word well known in medieval English society, as evidenced by its use in petitions and in secular and religious literature. In those contexts, the word had a broader and less clearly defined meaning and denoted various forms of wrongdoing that interfered with litigation and the vindication of legal rights. Champerty was an aggravated form of maintenance in which a party agreed to give the maintainer all or part of the subject matter in dispute in exchange for his assistance.

Initially, conspiracy and maintenance were interrelated and overlapping concepts. Some presentments charged individuals with conspiracy to maintain each other, and other cases accused defendants with engaging in other types of abuse of legal procedure. As the fourteenth century progressed, conspiracy and maintenance became more distinct notions. Although litigation continued to be primarily criminal and not civil, a procedure that facilitated civil champerty actions developed by means of a writ of *audita querela* sent by the king to the justices. By the late medieval period, 1377–1485, civil maintenance actions became dominant by virtue of the 1377 statute proscribing maintenance and an original writ based on the statute for use by aggrieved parties in bringing maintenance actions for violations of the statute. By the fifteenth century, those actions had increased substantially.

Since the statutes did not define what types of conduct were illegal, the justices were required to distinguish lawful from unlawful conduct. In some actions, defendants alleged a justification for giving their support and assistance to a party in the principal action. The Year Books show that the justices favorably viewed several of these justifications. As a result, they created categories of lawful and unlawful maintenance. Five categories of conduct supporting and assisting litigants were generally considered permissible: acting as a lawyer; a master assisting a servant and vice versa; having an interest in the subject matter in the dispute; assisting family, friends, and the poor; and legitimate participation in the process of litigation. Providing monetary assistance divided the justices and it was neither broadly permissible nor impermissible. But a number of justices thought it was lawful in several types of situations. These forms of lawful conduct coincided closely with the preexisting social norms regarding assisting and supporting individuals that had emerged by the eleventh century. Thus, the fears of McFarlane and others that maintenance statutes had made venerated conduct illegal were unfounded. But the justifications asserted by defendants were only allegations, and plaintiffs often challenged their veracity or asserted that the defendants had engaged in other more grievous conduct, such as bribery or corruptly influencing jurors or officials, procuring false inquisitions, or other abuses of legal process. By the fifteenth century almost all of these forms of conduct that were unlawful maintenance also violated some other statute, but aggrieved parties chose to seek redress though maintenance actions.

Giving livery by powerful individuals to their clients was another form of conduct that caused concern. It was frequently linked to maintenance and retainers. Some contemporaries believed that the distribution of livery facilitated maintenance and other forms of abuse of legal procedure. In some instances, it accompanied additional violent and serious criminal conduct. Although numerous statutes were enacted to regulate livery, prohibiting it altogether proved impractical, as it was a longstanding practice deeply embedded in the social culture. In the end, only the most significant abuses were outlawed and it became permissible for lords to give livery only to their household retainers and officers.

Despite the extensive statutes and litigation, it seems questionable whether the maintenance statutes realized their objectives. Nevertheless, even though the gentry and nobility may have engaged in maintenance, they were not frequently indicted or sued for such conduct. Most maintenance actions were brought against the sub-gentry such as husbandmen, yeomen, and persons of trade and occupations. Reducing excessive and specious litigation was another possible objective of these statutes. But ascertaining whether that objective was realized is difficult. In fact, it is possible that private maintenance actions may have contributed to increasing rather than reducing litigation in the late medieval period. In addition, maintenance actions perversely became a form of abuse as some litigants used them to harass and burden their adversaries.

Later Developments

Concern about maintenance,[1] livery, and retainers persisted after 1485.[2] McFarlane said that the social atmosphere in which the law was administered in 1603 had changed very little since 1485. He said further that it was unlikely that maintenance was eradicated and that it through the sixteenth century. He said that maintenance, like livery and retainers, became the privilege of the king's friends. It was used "as one more way of preserving the dynasty and its supporters in power."[3]

The developments regarding maintenance and livery during the reign of Henry VII have attracted particular attention.[4] Large retinues existed

---

[1] The research for this book did not include examining the plea rolls and Year Books in this period.

[2] Dunham, *Lord Hastings*, pp. 90–116.

[3] He also said that the attitude of Henry VIII differed little from that of Edward I. The Tudor Council's "justice was not impartial where the king and his dependents were parties." He also said that in 1603, "maintenance was far from being a thing of the feudal past." K.B. McFarlane, "Lords and Retainers," unpublished manuscript in the Magdalen College Archives, University of Oxford, Lecture VIII (VII), pp. 1, 2b–3, 6.

[4] A. Cameron, "The Giving of Livery and Retaining in Henry VII's Reign," *Renaissance and Modern Studies* 18 (1974), pp. 17–35; Dominic Luckett, "Crown Office and Licensed Retinues in the Reign of Henry VII," in Rowena Archer and Simon Walker, eds., *Rulers and Ruled in Late Medieval England: Essays Presented to Gerald Harriss* (London, 1995), pp. 223–38; S.B. Chrimes, *Henry VII* (Berkeley, 1972), pp. 187–93; Sean Cunningham, *Henry VII* (London, 2007), pp. 209–15.

during the reign and there were numerous problems in controlling them.[5] Henry VII, like other kings, depended on nobles and their gentry affiliates to manage local affairs and protect royal interests. As result, the abuse of power through the exercise of lordship remained a problem. Lords created affinities to protect their power in exchange for supporting their servants' and affiliates' concerns, problems, and quarrels.[6] But "Henry could not tackle the independence of the nobles directly," and the key to doing so was an effective means of controlling the circumstances in which the king permitted giving livery.[7]

His efforts to achieve this objective began early in the reign and continued throughout it.[8] In Henry VII's first parliament, the Commons as well as the temporal and spiritual Lords took an oath not to retain any man by indenture or oath; illegally give any livery, badge, or token; or cause or assent to any maintenance.[9] But the judges expressed doubt in the effectiveness of the oaths.[10] Bean believed that these developments showed that retainers had spread to those below the gentry.[11] As a result, further statutes were enacted. The first was the famous 1487 "Star Chamber Act," which, *inter alia*, targeted maintenance and livery.[12]

---

[5] Cameron, "Giving and Retaining," pp. 22–25. Luckett described the manner in which the retinues were constituted, organized, and operated. Sir Thomas Lovell's retinue had more than 1,300 men. Luckett, "Licensed Retinues," pp. 230–34.

[6] Cunningham, *Henry VII*, pp. 164–65.   [7] Ibid., p. 210.

[8] Cameron asserted that assessing the achievements of Henry VII depended critically on an evaluation of his policy toward the giving of livery and retainers. Cameron, "Giving of Livery and Retaining," p. 17. Dunham said no policy toward retainers appeared in the first two decades of the reign, but when it emerged, it was "in principle ... one of repression; but in practice it amounted to connivance and control." He said it was driven by insuring royal loyalty, privilege, and military needs. Dunham, *Lord Hastings*, pp. 90–106. Cunningham said that Henry VII's legislation against illegal retainers "did little more than rearrange the problem." Cunningham, *Henry VII*, pp. 210–11.

[9] Parliaments of Henry VII: November 1485, Part I, no. 15 [20], PROME. The king personally received the oath. Cunningham, *Henry VII*, p. 145. In the following year, a commission was created to produce a similar oath. *Calendar of Patent Rolls, Henry VII 1485-1494* (London, 1914), pp. 39–40, 71 (September 25, 1485, January 4, 1486).

[10] It was at this gathering that Huse CJ made his statement, based on his experience as Edward IV's attorney general, about the failure to enforce the law and violations by the lords, which has been previously quoted. Y.B. Mich., 1 Hen. VII, fol. 3, pl. 3 (1485), Seipp No. 1485.003.

[11] Bean, *From Lord to Patron*, p. 219. Bellamy said that there was no evidence that the oaths were effective. He thought that both Edward IV and Henry VII put unrealistic faith in men's words. Bellamy, *Crime and Public Order in England in the Middle Ages* (London, 1973), p. 115.

[12] 3 Hen. VII, c. 1 (1487), *Statutes of the Realm*, vol. 2, pp. 509–10; Parliaments of Henry VII: November 1487, no. 17, PROME. Dunham, *Lord Hastings*, pp. 94–95; J.G.

The act consolidated the earlier legislation and identified "as cognate offences maintenance, livery, indentures, retainers, embracery, the impaneling of corrupt juries, the false returning of verdicts, and riot and unlawful assembly for overawing courts."[13] It authorized a committee of named officials, including one lord of the Council,[14] to proceed by bill or information against the designated offenses, which provided a quicker procedure for dealing with them.[15]

The creation of this authority to deal with perversion of justice was linked to the inability otherwise to police the abuses of powerful men.[16] Cunningham said that the act neglected to challenge abuse of lordship and "implied that the king and his officers were almost powerless to curtail maintenance, the giving of livery, embracery, [and] corruption by the sheriffs."[17] In his discussion of the Court of the Star Chamber in *De Republica Anglorum* (1583), Thomas Smith said that

> [the] effect of this court [was] to bridge such stout noble men and
> gentlemen ... [and] to repress the insolence of the noble men and

Bellamy, *Criminal Law and Society in Late Medieval and Tudor England* (Gloucester, 1984), pp. 75–76. Baker called the statute the "so-called act 'pro camera stellata.'" He suggested Huse's opinion may have prompted its enactment. The name was misleading, as it did not create the Star Chamber, which had functioned judicially since the mid-fourteenth century. J.H. Baker, *Oxford History*, vol. VI, pp. 70 and n. 101, 196.

[13] Nicholas Pronay, "The Chancellor, the Chancery, and the Council at the End of the Fifteenth Century," in H. Hearder and H.R. Loyn, *British Government and Administration* (Cardiff, 1974), p. 99.

[14] Baker explained that the Star Chamber could act under its authority because it usually contained the requisite people and more, but it was a larger and grander body and the statute did not actually require it to be involved. Gratitude is expressed to Prof. John Baker for this explanation.

[15] Luckett said that the statutory prohibition on the retainers of the king's tenants manifested the exclusive loyalty that Henry demanded of his office holders. Reflecting the same emphasis on royal authority, the king required an oath in 1505 from his tenants that they not be retained by anyone else. 3 Hen. VII, c. 12 [15] (1487), *Statutes of the Realm*, vol. 2, pp. 522–23; Luckett, "Licensed Retinues," p. 227; Bean, *From Lord to Patron*, pp. 219–21. Also a 1491/2 conciliar ordinance, which created a council of regency and was directed at preserving the peace and maintaining justice, prohibited lords of the Council from supporting or maintaining other men's causes or quarrels by various means, including the gift of clothing or livery to any officer, judge, jury, or party or by retaining the party in his service. M.M. Condon, "Anachronism with Intent? Henry VII's Council Ordinance of 1491/2," in Ralph Griffiths and James Sherborne, eds., *Kings and Nobles in the Later Middle Ages* (Gloucester, 1986), pp. 228–53, appendix, no. 16.

[16] Ryan Patrick Alford, "The Star Chamber and the Regulation of the Legal Profession," *American Journal of Legal History* 51 (2011), pp. 643–53.

[17] Cunningham, *Henry VII*, p. 157.

gentlemen, who ... made their force the law, banding themselves with their tenants and servants to do or revenge injury one against the other ...[18]

But the impact of the Star Chamber in attacking maintenance seems to have been negligible, at least initially.[19] Another statute in 1495 linked rioting to retainers.[20]

In 1504, a statute, *De Retentionibus Illicitis*, the first major enactment on livery and retainers since the 1468 Act, reaffirmed the earlier statutes and their penalties and procedures.[21] But it also provided that the act did not apply to persons licensed by the king to retain men and give them livery "to be in readiness to do the king service in war or otherwise at his commandment."[22] The license granted the recipient

> full power and authority ... to take, appoint and retain by indenture or covenant ... such persons, our subjects, as by your discretion shall be thought and semeth to you to be able men to do us service in the war in your company under you and at your leading at all such times and places and as often as it shall please us to command or assign you.[23]

---

[18] Thomas Smith, *De Republica Anglorum* (London, 1583; 1970 ed.), book 3, ch. 4, p. 96.

[19] In discussing the jurisdiction and activities of the Star Chamber, the Selden Society editors said that "although maintenance occupies a prominent place in the Act *pro Camera Stellata* and though the energy in suppressing it is one of the Star Chamber's titles to fame, the offence has left few traces on the records of Henry VII's court." C.G. Bayne and William Huse Dunham, eds., *Select Cases in the Council of Henry VII* (London, 1958), 75 Selden Society, p. cxi. Several maintenance cases appeared in the Star Chamber in the early seventeenth century. William Baildon, ed., *Les Reportes del Cases in Camera Stellata 1593-1609* (London, 1894), pp. 165, 242-43, 279-81, 331.

[20] The statute prohibited riots and unlawful assemblies, which it said were often engaged in by "receivers, stewards, bailiffs of lordships and other offices" and also by retainers. 11 Hen. VII, c. 7 (1495), *Statutes of the Realm*, vol. 2, pp. 573-74.

[21] 19 Hen. VII, c. 14 (1503-4), *Statutes of the Realm*, vol. 2, pp. 658-60. McFarlane said that the 1504 act strongly reinforced the 1468 statute's attack on retainers. McFarlane, *Nobility*, pp. 106-7. Chrimes said that the evidence of prosecutions was not abundant. Chrimes, *Henry VII*, p. 190.

[22] The licensing provision was in Part 10 of the statute. Part 11 also provided a number of exemptions for livery given for specific purposes or by named officials, including serjeants at law for their creation ceremony. Ibid., c. 14, parts 10-11, p. 660.

[23] To obtain a license, the man wishing to retain would submit a written request listing the names of the men retained to serve in his retinue for the permitted purpose. Cameron, "Giving of Livery and Retaining," p. 25. The license contained detailed conditions regarding its use. Dunham, *Lord Hastings*, pp. 148-50. Dunham also printed the specific licenses to six particular individuals. Ibid., pp. 151-57. In requiring prior licensing, this provision seemed to be a narrower version of the broader exemption in the 1468 statute for livery "given in the defense of the king and his realm." 8 Edw. IV, c. 2 (1468), *Statutes of the Realm*, vol. 2, p. 429.

Licensing employed a more flexible approach.[24] Luckett said that the licensing of retainers showed the impact of the importance of personal relationships with the king and revealed the change in the constitution of Henry's personal authority in the shires. It illustrated how royal office holders had replaced the king's household as chief representatives and mainstays of royal authority. He asserted that the various statutes dealing with livery and retainers "articulated with increasing clarity his claim to the sole allegiance of the subject.[25] The crown seemed finally to have recognized that it was more realistic to legitimate certain practices and neither politically practical nor possible to restrict livery and retainers more stringently.[26]

Some enforcement did continue. Indictments for illegal livery or retainers appeared in the early months of Henry VII's reign and continued throughout the reign and may have deterred the misuse of retainers in personal disputes.[27] The returns into King's Bench by justices of the peace described their organization and operation.[28] Although those giving or receiving livery, if it did not fall within the

---

[24] It also created a formal role for the Council that it had been performing informally and a more political approach to abuse of lordship. Cunningham, *Henry VII*, pp. 212–13.

[25] Luckett, "Licensed Retinues," pp. 223–29, 237–38.

[26] Elton said that the Tudors did not alter the social structure of a hierarchical age, but only prevented these practices as a means of facilitating the abuse of power. Legislation targeting the "delicate distinctions implicit in social usage" was unworkable. Geoffrey Elton, *The Tudor Constitution* (Cambridge, 1972), pp. 30–31. In addition to these practices being ingrained in the social and political culture, Henry VII was dependent on the great men and their private armies for his military needs. Cameron, "Giving of Livery and Retaining," p. 18. Cunningham said that Henry created a virtual standing army by permitting his local servants to retain on his behalf. By granting licenses, he could command 50,000 men from royal lands to serve both as a peacetime affinity to avoid civil war and as a potent force for war. Cunningham, *Henry VII*, pp. 211–12.

[27] Ibid., pp. 25–26, 30–34. Cameron explained how the process worked by removal of indictments from the quarter sessions to the King's Bench, certification by the attorney general, or reporting of violations by the justices of the peace to the King's Bench. He also noted that after 1504, the indictments often stated that the retainer was "without delivery of his license (*sine licencia sue deliberatione*). Ibid., pp. 25–27; Bean, *From Lord to Patron*, p. 219.

[28] The statute authorized the justices of peace to cause those suspected of illegal retainers and the giving of livery to appear before them and be examined. The justices were required to certify to the King's Bench the names of the suspects and those found to have violated the statute, with a £100 penalty for each justice who failed to comply. 19 Hen. VII, c. 14, part 5 (1503–4), *Statutes of the Realm*, vol. 2, p. 659. Bellamy said that this provision illustrated the desire of the crown to have the best procedural and judicial devices for operation of this statute, as livery and illicit retainer were critical to it. Bellamy, *Criminal Law and Society*, p. 36. He stressed the significance of the use of the justices of

permitted exceptions, were sometimes indicted, the preferred method for dealing with violations was by settlements imposing fines and recognizances and giving bonds for good behavior.[29] Moreover, enforcement against peers was minimal. Chrimes said only one peer was prosecuted[30] and McFarlane said prosecutions of the nobility were rare.[31]

Overall, Henry VII's approach to retainers was realistic and practical. Cunningham said that he was reluctant "to clamp down on a practice that he needed to maintain." "Loyalty and allegiance" were the basis of his policy regarding retainers.[32] Cameron concluded that Henry's policy was "geared to the social realities of his kingdom ... Within his more limited aims ... he was eminently successful. He tamed retainers by

the peace and summary procedures in enforcement of the livery laws. J.G. Bellamy, *Bastard Feudalism and the Law*, pp. 20–21.

[29] This approach was not limited to retainers, but was a general one. Cunningham, *Henry VII*, pp. 215–23. Those who falsely asserted membership in a retinue as a cover for their personal wrongdoing, apparently a common practice in some areas, were also indicted. Cameron, "Giving of Livery and Retaining," pp. 25–30. Dunham said that the prosecutions during Henry VII's reign showed that "the statutes against livery and retainers were by no means dead letters." Dunham, *Lord Hastings*, p. 102.

[30] He said the only peer prosecuted in the reign of Henry VII was George Neville, Lord Bergavenny. (See the following note.) He also mentioned an anecdote, likely apocryphal, noted by Francis Bacon in his biography of Henry VII regarding the indictment of John de Vere, the earl of Oxford, which he said lacked documentary support. Chrimes, *Henry VII*, p. 190 and n. 2. Cunningham said that although it was a plausible indication of the king's attitude, no evidence had been found to support it. Cunningham, *Henry VII*, p. 213. According to Bacon, the earl invited the king to his castle at Hedingham. On seeing the earl's servants in their livery, the king said that "these handsome gentlemen and yeomen, which I see on both sides of me are sure your menial servants." The earl responded that "most of them are my retainers," who had come on this occasion to serve the earl and see the king. "The king started a little, and said, 'by my faith, my lord, I thank you for my good cheer, but I may not endure to have my laws broken in my sight: my attorney must speak with you.'" Bacon then wrote that it was reported that the "earl compounded for no less than fifteen thousand marks." J. Rawson, ed., *Bacon's History of the Reign of King Henry VII* (Cambridge, 1885), pp. 192–93.

[31] McFarlane said that "the Tudors rarely tried – and can therefore not be held to have wished – to enforce the statutes against members of the nobility." But he considered the indictment of George Nevill, Lord Bergavenny, who had retained 471 Kent men, mostly yeomen, significant. Although he was found guilty and fined £70,000, Henry VIII pardoned him. McFarlane, Lecture VIII (VII), p. 2a. McFarlane recounted how Sir Richard Empson, "the great man E," and Edmund Dudley maintained actions against their adversaries. Although Sir Robert Plumpton, Empson's target, was found guilty by securing a panel of unfavorable jurors, Empson was indicted for coming to the York assize with 200 men and members of the king's body guard to maintain Plumpton's adversaries in the litigation. Ibid., p. 5.

[32] He said further there were numerous indictments, but "few offenders received serious punishment in the King's Bench." Cunningham, *Henry VII*, pp. 212–13.

rooting out its worst abuses."[33] Bean said that, unlike Edward IV, Henry VII's policy was more clearly "one of control rather than detection and prosecution of offenses."[34] Luckett seemed less enthusiastic, saying that the 1504 act "merely regularized existing practice rather than creating new possibilities for retainers." Overall, he felt that Henry demonstrated the same "royal ambivalence" as his predecessors toward livery and retainers and similarly permitted its use to the extent it advantaged the crown.[35] Baker said that although enforcement proceedings were instituted, they had little effect.[36] Nevertheless, as a result of the 1504 statute, one could conclude that, after almost 130 years of petitions, statutes, and litigation, a compromise in dealing with livery and retainers may have been achieved.[37]

Retainers continued to receive casual attention during the reign of Henry VIII.[38] In 1514, he issued a proclamation forbidding retainers

[33] He said further that Henry "managed to adapt an institution which had proved a severe problem to his predecessors into an instrument which on the whole served its purpose very well." Ibid., p. 34. But he did not agree with "the accepted point of view," which was critical, as he said it was based on insufficient enforcement evidence and "legalistic" statutory interpretation. He said that the problem of retainers was more complex than thought earlier and was never intended to be outlawed completely, which would have been viewed by "contemporaries as an intolerable attack on baronial rights." Cameron, "Giving of Livery and Retaining," pp. 17–22, 34.

[34] He viewed the 1504 act, a refurbishment and reenactment of the 1468 statute, as a more coherent and clearer expression and the culmination of Henry's policies directed at insuring royal authority. Further, it recognized the benefit of retainers to the king and his realm. Bean, *From Lord to Patron*, pp. 219–25.

[35] He pointed out that livery had been given on Henry's behalf for some time and that givers adapted their giving to conform to the new statute. Luckett, "Licensed Retinues," pp. 228–30. Bellamy said that although the 1504 statute "should have gone a long way toward eliminating the evils of illegal livery-giving and retaining," the evidence did not permit making a satisfactory assessment of its achievements. But he noted that no further statutes on these subjects were enacted. Bellamy, *Bastard Feudalism and the Law*, pp. 85–91.

[36] He said there were proceedings by indictment and common-informer actions, but they were mostly against recipients and not givers. He stated that the main stream of prosecution of livery apparently ended in 1516 although prosecutions continued. He opined that private retainers could be eliminated only by the creation of a public militia, which to some extent occurred in the middle of the sixteenth century, but that the records of the King's Bench and Star Chamber revealed that other forms of legal corruption still existed in the middle of the sixteenth century. Baker, *Oxford History*, vol. VI: *1483–1558* (Oxford, 2003), pp. 71–73.

[37] Baker said that indentured retainers had ended with Henry VII, but that "informal retainers … by giving uniform clothing … remained common." Baker, *Oxford History*, vol. VI, p. 70.

[38] Dunham, *Lord Hastings*, p. 99.

contrary to existing statutes, which also precluded pardons.[39] Like Henry VII, Henry VIII had to tolerate retainers.[40] The king as well as powerful individuals such as Cardinal Wolsey, the duke of Buckingham, Sir Thomas More, and other lords retained large numbers of men. In some instances, these retainers met important military needs and were useful in dealing with riots.[41] Dunham said that the indispensability of retainers continued through the reigns of Edward VI, Mary, and Elizabeth.[42] Large retinues and the distribution of livery continued to cause "provincial instability" until the end of the sixteenth century, and "'good lordship may have suffered transmutation and decline, but it had not yet ceased to matter."[43]

Maintenance was also the target of further statutes. In 1496, an act directed at "perjury, unlawful maintenance, and corruption in officers" reflected the interrelationship between various forms of legal corruption. It asserted that an increase in perjury was the product of "unlawful retainers, maintenance, embracing, champerty and corruption of good as well of the sheriffs and other officers," despite the earlier enactments for punishing such offenses.[44] In 1540, a new statute targeting maintenance and embracery was enacted.[45] The preamble recited that maintenance,

---

[39] It was issued to the sheriffs of Middlesex and London. Dunham, *Lord Hastings*, pp. 98–101.

[40] Ibid., p. 100. McFarlane cited a number of instances in which great lords retained and fed royal officers and others in the same manner as their ancestors and their friends and kin importuned them for protection in litigation and some instances in which bribery and violence were involved. McFarlane, "Lords and Retainers," Lecture VIII (VII), pp. 6–11.

[41] Ibid., pp. 100–2, 105–09.   [42] Ibid., pp. 109–16.

[43] Further, as late as the eve of the Civil War, "the patronage of great men could still determine appointments to local offices." J.R. Maddicott, "The County Community and the Making of Public Opinion in Fourteenth Century England," *Transactions of the Royal Historical Society*, 5th series, 28 (1978), pp. 27–28. But Holdsworth thought that the "vigilance and growing power of the Tudor Council" eliminated the need for further legislative regulation of retainers. W.S. Holdsworth, *A History of English Law*, 17 vols. (London, 1936–66), vol. IV, pp. 520–21.

[44] The statute authorized aggrieved parties who were victims of perjured judgment or perjury induced by unlawful maintenance, embracing, or corruption of officers to complain by bill. But the statute was temporary, effective only until the next parliament. 11 Hen. VII, c. 25 (1495), *Statutes of the Realm*, vol. 2, pp. 589–90. In 1497, parliament extended the statute for another year. 12 Hen. VII, c. 2 (1496), *Statutes of the Realm*, vol. 2, p. 636.

[45] Stephen said that statute showed that the nature of the crime had changed since the enactment of the 1487 Star Chamber Act. "Fraud, perjury, and chicanery" had replaced open force as the forms of breaking the law. James Fitzjames Stephen, *A History of the Criminal Law of England*, 3 vols. (London, 1883), vol. III, p. 239. Holdsworth generally agreed with Stephen and attributed the new nature of the offense to a change in social and political conditions and the "standard of efficiency demanded by the more exacting

champerty, and embracery had undermined the just administration of the law and facilitated perjury. It prohibited engaging in or procuring unlawful maintenance and retainers for the purpose of maintenance of pleas or embracing jurors or suborning witnesses for the purpose of maintenance as well as perjury.[46] These and other later statutes suggest that perjury had become a dominant concern in sixteenth century.[47]

Finally, the emergence of solicitors in the sixteenth century raised new maintenance issues.[48] Because solicitors, who were neither barristers nor attorneys, did not have any recognized qualification to practice, they ran afoul of the prohibition on maintenance. Judges and perhaps other members of the legal profession saw the prohibition as a way to curtail their activities.[49] A 1606 statute, motivated by a concern with the excessive number of solicitors, regulated their right to practice, but it "proved to be, ironically, the solicitors' charter."[50] There was no objection to soliciting by barristers, attorneys, or household servants, but antipathy continued toward solicitors because of their lack of qualification and of the control over their activities.[51] Eventually, solicitors became a recognized and established type of lawyer.

---

requirements of a modern state." He viewed the actions of the Star Chamber pursuant to the 1540 statute as marking "the transition between the mediaeval and the modern law." Holdsworth, *History of English Law*, vol. V, pp. 201–3. But other scholars have asserted, as discussed in Chapter 1, that such a change toward nonviolent lawbreaking occurred by the late fourteenth century. Moreover, although violence and force continued in the late medieval period, the maintenance and other litigation involving legal corruption exhibited substantial nonviolent lawbreaking by fraud, deceit, and other more subtle forms of conduct.

[46] The penalty was £10 for each offense. The act authorized private individuals to sue to enforce the prohibition and receive half the penalty. The act also contained a one-year statute of limitations. The act also prohibited buying or selling land unless the seller had been in possession or taken profits for one year. 32 Hen. VIII, c. 9 (1540), *Statutes of the Realm*, vol. 3, pp. 753–54.

[47] The role of the Star Chamber in development and broadening of the offense was also a factor. Holdsworth, *History of English Law*, vol. IV, pp. 515–20.

[48] J.H. Baker, "Solicitors and Law of Maintenance 1590–1640," reprinted in J.H. Baker, *The Legal Profession and the Common Law* (London, 1986), pp. 125–50.

[49] As a result of 1590 decision in a maintenance action against a member of the Inner Temple, who had pleaded his membership and that he was learned in the law, but had not pleaded his degree, lawyers considered it essential to plead specifically membership in an Inn and a degree, which was required to practice law and showed that he had been called to the bar. Ibid., pp. 129–43.

[50] Ibid., pp. 143–45.

[51] The activities of what were called "common solicitors" continued to be problematic. Ibid., pp. 145–49.

Later commentators said that, over time, the concern with maintenance diminished. Although Holdsworth said that various "methods of abuse of legal procedure were still rampant" in the sixteenth century, he believed that progress had been made in dealing with these forms of legal corruption.[52] He said further that by the seventeenth century, maintenance was no longer "so crying an evil" as it had been and that its nature had changed. "The modern law of maintenance came to be regarded as a tort rather than as a crime."[53] By this time, maintenance "had assumed substantially its modern form," as civil actions for damages replaced criminal penalties.[54]

A Retrospective

Concern with maintenance persisted into the modern era. In the early twentieth century, Percy Winfield discussed the existing law of maintenance and champerty.[55] His discussion of those types of legal corruption as torts resembled the law of the medieval period.[56] If there was a legitimate interest in the principal litigation, the intermeddling was not tortious and the justifications creating such an interest were

---

[52] He credited the "steady pressure exerted by the Council [that] effected an improvement which the long series of mediaeval statutes and the efforts of the common lawyers had been unable to effect." Holdsworth, *History of English Law*, vol. IV, p. 521. Stephen asserted erroneously that the Tudors had eliminated maintenance. He said that they had done not by new laws, "but by the vigorous, unflinching execution of the old ones by a severe court acting under the orders of a succession of kings of unusual force of character." Stephen, *History of Criminal Law*, vol. III, p. 238.

[53] He said that "a thin stream of actions from the seventeenth to the twentieth century" recognized and "defined its modern incidents." He recognized that damage actions for aggrieved parties were available in the medieval period. Ibid., vol. VIII, pp. 397–99. He recounted that Jeremy Bentham had condemned the laws against maintenance and champerty on the basis on his economic *laissez faire* views. Ibid., vol. XIII, pp. 110–11.

[54] Ibid., vol. VIII, p. 398. Perhaps Holdsworth exaggerated the difference between the medieval and modern law. The civil damage actions in the late medieval period were also torts (trespasses) and were a form of common law action, a private action based on a statute, which remains a recognized form of civil action.

[55] It is interesting that the discussion of maintenance constitutes almost half of Winfield, *The Present Law of Abuse of Legal Procedure* (Cambridge, 1921), pp. 1–116, although it was only 14% of his book, *The History of Conspiracy and Abuse of Legal Procedure*, written in the same year.

[56] He also discussed contractual agreements, which implicated maintenance and champerty. Several of these in which the maintained party agreed to give all or a portion of the subject matter of the litigation to the maintainer were similar to medieval champerty. Ibid., pp. 94–111.

quite similar to those that were acceptable in the medieval period.[57] Holdsworth expressed a similar opinion. He said that the main essential features of the tort of maintenance were the same elements that constituted the crime.[58] Two interrelated issues, which did not arise in medieval actions and which generated significant discussion by both Winfield and Holdsworth, involved damages. The questions were whether special damages needed to be proved and whether success in the principal action barred the loser from suing for negligence.[59] Civil actions were dominant in recent centuries, but the medieval statutes had not been repealed and maintenance and champerty were still crimes. Winfield said that the modern crime of maintenance was "interference in civil litigation not justifiable on the grounds recognizable by law" and that champerty was unlawful maintenance in exchange for some part of the subject matter in dispute or other profit.[60]

[57] The primary defenses that he identified were professional legal assistance by attorneys, solicitors, and counsel; kinship; contingent and reversionary interest in the subject of the litigation; master and servant; assistance to the poor; compulsion by the law; friendship and courtesy; assignment of choses in action; and several other legitimate interests. The only defense not having a clear medieval counterpart was the assignment of a chose in action, which will be discussed below. In his discussion, Winfield referred to several medieval statutes and actions. Bodkin's assessment of the modern law was similar. Edmund Bodkin, *The Law of Maintenance and Champerty and the Lawful Financing of Actions by Solicitors, Legal Aid and Trade Protection Societies and Others* (London, 1934), pp. 20–30.

[58] Holdsworth, *History of English Law*, vol. VIII, p. 399. The interest-based analysis had governed the common law of maintenance since the late eighteenth century. In an 1883 case, Lord Coleridge CJKB reviewed 23 cases decided during that period. *Bradlaugh v. Newdegate*, [1883] 11 Q.B.D. 1. Relying on those cases and referring to concurring views of the leading commentators, he stated that "as a general rule there is no doubt that such common interest, believed on reasonable grounds to exist, will make justifiable that which otherwise would be maintenance." Many of the same justifications were listed. He called maintenance "a living doctrine." Ibid., pp. 11, 14.

[59] Most of their discussion involved analysis and criticism of a 1919 House of Lords decision, *Neville v. London Express Newspaper, Ltd.*, [1919] A.C. 368. The case narrowly held that proof of special damages was required. Both Winfield and Holdsworth found the law on these matters unsettled, confused, and somewhat illogical. Winfield, *The Present Law*, pp. 84–89; Holdsworth, *History of English Law*, vol. VIII, pp. 399–402.

[60] Winfield, *The Present Law*, pp. 112–16. Some authorities have asserted that they were common law crimes, independent of medieval statutes. Ibid., p. 113. Winfield was critical of Stephen's definition, which required the absence of a "valuable interest" justifying assistance or the presence of an "improper motive" for acting. Ibid., pp. 13–15, 113–15. Holdsworth seemed to think that the crime of maintenance had become moribund after the reign of Henry VIII. Holdsworth, *A History of English Law*, vol. VIII, pp. 398–99.

In 1967, criminal and tort law regarding maintenance and champerty became a matter of history and relevant only to legal historians. The Law Commission recommended that parliament abolish the statutory misdemeanors of maintenance and champerty and that maintenance and champerty as actionable wrongs should cease to exist.[61] But the report recognized that champertous agreements, including contingent fee agreements, were contrary to public policy and should remain so.[62] Parliament adopted these recommendations in the Criminal Law Act 1967, abolishing the crimes of maintenance and champerty as obsolete crimes and eliminating common law tort liability for any conduct involving maintenance or champerty.[63] But the legislation provided that the elimination of criminal and civil liability for this conduct "shall not affect any rule of [the law of England and Wales] as to the cases to which a contract is to be treated as contrary to public policy or otherwise illegal."[64]

Almost three decades later, Lord Mustill said that "maintenance and champerty have become almost invisible in both their criminal and tortious manifestations," but he added that "they have maintained a

[61] The report said that the crimes of maintenance and champerty were "a dead letter in our law" and that there were "no records of prosecution for either for many years past." It also said that the interest-based approach applied to these torts had increased the number of justifications and that it was difficult to determine what was a lawful justification. Also the report said that it was almost impossible to prove damages and questioned whether these torts served any useful purpose in the law. Further, it stated that retention of these torts was inconsistent with other developments in the practice of litigation. The Law Commission, *Proposals for Reform of the Law Relating to Maintenance and Champerty* (London, 1966), pp. 4–5, 7.

[62] Ibid., pp. 5–6.

[63] The act also repealed many of the statutes discussed in the prior chapters of this book. Criminal Law Act of 1967, Part II, section 1(a), Part III, sections 1 and 2, Schedule 3, Part 1, and Schedule 4, Part 1. The National Archives, legislation.gov.uk.

[64] Since the seventeenth century, maintenance and champerty had existed side by side with malicious prosecution and malicious abuse of process in tort law. The latter tort actions arose in the sixteenth and seventeenth centuries as a product of the impact of the more liberal and expansive nature of the action on the case of conspiracy on the statutory writ of conspiracy. Holdsworth, *History of English Law*, vol. VIII, pp. 385–91; Winfield, *The Present Law*, pp. 174–204. Holdsworth said that the action on the case for conspiracy became the basis of new torts during the middle of the seventeenth century. "Thus the common law tort of conspiracy, founded on the statutory writ and action on the case, developed into the torts of malicious prosecution, and other malicious abuses of the process of the court." Ibid., pp. 390–91. Baker took a different view of the origins of malicious prosecution. He argued that it evolved in the sixteenth century from the plaintiff's replication of *de malicia* in defamation actions. Anticipating that the defendant would assert that a prosecution was lawful, plaintiffs began to allege malice and the absence of reasonable cause in their declarations. Baker, *Oxford History*, vol. VI, p. 797.

living presence in only two respects."[65] One of those areas involves assignment of choses in action. Although the common law had prohibited such assignments, influenced perhaps by maintenance and champerty,[66] the prohibition has been relaxed, and various types of assignments have become permissible.[67] In Winfield's view, the development of the law of assignment was "untrammelled by attempts to bring it within the law of champerty and maintenance." But he said that it was equally true that assignment of choses in action was not "outside of the law of champerty and maintenance if it be made with the improper purpose of stirring up litigation."[68] Courts have continued to find certain assignments to be illegal champerty and unenforceable.[69] Champertous agreements that involve "wanton or officious intermeddling with the disputes of others" are illegal.[70] Contract law provides the doctrinal basis for treating such agreements as contrary public policy and void.

Lawyer's fees and litigation funding are the second area in which maintenance and champerty have remained alive and relevant. These matters have produced substantial litigation and public comment. The

---

[65] *Giles v. Thompson* [1994] 1 A.C. 142, 153, [1993] 2 W.L.R. 908. But some conduct that is actionable as malicious prosecution, including abuse of civil process and vexatious use of process, seems to overlap with what had been tortious maintenance. Malicious prosecution may have narrowed over the years due to the advent of public prosecution, the concern with chilling legitimate litigation, and the availability of other methods to deal with bad faith litigation. However, it remains a tort and the courts continue to deal with the appropriate doctrinal and policy concerns. P. Giliker, "Malicious Prosecution," in *Clerk and Lindsell on Torts*, 21st ed. (London, 2014), sections 16-01 to 16-73, pp. 1175–223; B.S. Markesinis and S.F. Deakin, *Tort Law*, 4th ed. (Oxford, 1999), pp. 402–05.

[66] Guenter Treitel, *The Law of Contract*, 11th ed. (London, 2003), pp. 672, 695.

[67] Winfield discussed examples of assignments that no longer constituted maintenance or champerty as well as ones that were unlawful. He traced the history and development of law of assignment as regards maintenance and champerty. He found some of the early statements of the law confused and inaccurate. He was critical of the early commentators, especially Coke. Winfield, *The Present Law*, pp. 44–69.

[68] Ibid., pp. 51–52; J. Murphy, "Capacity of Parties," in *Clerk and Lindsell on Torts*, sections 5-66 to 5-67, pp. 350–51. In addition, champerty also may have influenced the general rule that tort claims are unassignable. Neil Andrews, *Contract Law* (Cambridge, 2011); Treitel, *Contracts*, p. 696; Winfield said that the assignment of a tort action "is contrary to public policy or savours maintenance." Winfield, *The Present Law*, pp. 67–69.

[69] *Trendtex Trading Co. v. Crédit-Suisse* [1982] A.C. 679, 3 All E. R. 721; *Laurent v. Sale & Co.* [1963] 1 W.L.R. 829, 2 All E.R. 63. In 2012, a Pennsylvania court held that the assignment of a legal malpractice claim was "champertous and therefore invalid." The court said that "under Pennsylvania law, champerty remains a valid defense." *Frank v. Terwinkle*, 45 A.3d 434, 441 (Pa. 2012).

[70] Treitel, *Contracts*, p. 431.

common law prohibited contingency fees as champerty. For some time, contract law treated them as illegal and enforceable as a matter of public policy.[71] The Criminal Law Act 1967 had exempted this prohibition from its abolition of the crimes and torts of maintenance and champerty and it survived until the end of the last century. But in the wake of the Woolf Reforms,[72] concern focused on the access to justice and the costs of litigation. As a result, the concern with impact of champerty and maintenance on the legality of lawyers' fee agreements diminished.[73]

Beginning in the late twentieth century, three significant developments occurred regarding lawyer's fees and litigation funding, which in the past "would have been viewed as unethical at best and illegal at worst."[74] The first change involved a new type of legal fee, Conditional Fee Agreements (CFAs). The Courts and Legal Services Act 1990 authorized such fees, which were implemented in 1995, and expanded in 1998. CFAs permitted "no-win, no fee" agreements and a percentage increase over the usual compensation by "success fees."[75] Although CFAs are not without problems,[76] their authorization turned out to be a revolution in the rules and policies toward funding legal services.[77] Even more surprising than the

---

[71] Andrews, *Contracts*, pp. 635–36; Treitel, *Contracts*, pp. 430–31.

[72] Neil Andrews, "The Main Pillars of the Woolf Reforms," in Neil Andrews, *English Civil Procedure: Fundamentals of the New Civil Justice System* (Oxford, 2003), pp. 29–48.

[73] A recent essay reviewed the developments regarding these matters that occurred after the Woolf Reforms. It discussed how traditional litigation funding had changed because of the decrease of state-funded legal aid and the excessive and unpredictable costs of litigation, which created a disincentive for many litigants to pursue their claims. John Sorabji and Robert Musgrove, "Litigation Cost, Funding, and the Future," in Déidre Dwyer, ed., *The Civil Procedure Rules: Ten Years On* (Oxford, 2010), pp. 229–46.

[74] Ibid., p. 232.

[75] The act exempted criminal proceedings and family proceedings. Courts and Legal Services Act 1990, sections 58 and 58A, The National Archives, www.legislation.gov.uk. Access to Justice Act 1999, Part II, section 27, www.legislation.gov.uk; Andrews, "Conditional Fees and Funding," in Andrews, *Civil Procedure*, pp. 795–822. The 1999 Act also created the Community Legal Service Fund to replace civil legal aid, expand the availability of legal services, and develop funding to support that objective. Ibid., sections 1–5; Andrews, "The Community Legal Service Fund," in Andrews, *Civil Procedure*, pp. 816–21.

[76] Andrews, "Conditional Fees and Funding," pp. 808–16; Sorabji and Musgrove, "Litigation Cost and Funding," p. 233.

[77] Zander predicted this impact. He reviewed the developments that had occurred from 1990 to 2000. Michael Zander, "Will the Revolution in the Funding of Civil Litigation in England Eventually Lead to Contingency Fees?," *De Paul Law Review* 52 (2002), pp. 259–97. A barrister reviewing recent decisions regarding CFAs and cost indemnity provisions concluded that during the second half of the twentieth century, the law of

institution of CFAs was the second development, the 2013 authorization of contingent fees, known as "Damages Based Agreements."[78] Although the United States had long permitted contingent fees, England had always banned them as champertous. Some lawyers and judges strongly opposed contingent fees,[79] but other members of the profession and public figures supported their adoption.[80] These changes prompted a reassessment of maintenance and champerty and the development of an appropriate public policy to guide the law on these matters.

Drawing on medieval antecedents, leading justices have skillfully articulated a public policy to implement the modern objectives of maintenance and champerty. Lord Mustill said that the need to protect the courts from "the oppression of private individuals through suits fomented and sustained by unscrupulous men of power" had changed since medieval times and that other methods existed to prevent abuse and injustice. He asserted further that these ancient notions had not disappeared from the general view but were "being ascribed a vigorous new life, in a context as far away from the local oppressions practiced by overweening magnates in the 15th century as one could imagine." What was needed was "a modern law of champerty," and "the law on maintenance and champerty can be best kept in forward motion by looking to its origins as a principle of public policy designed to protect the purity of justice and the interests of vulnerable

---

champerty had been attenuated and now "champerty at common law is virtually dead." "The End of Champerty?," *The New Law Journal* (April 15 and 22, 2011), pp. 547–48.

[78] The Damages-Based Agreements Regulations 2013, www.legislation.gov.uk; Courts and Tribunals Judiciary, "Damages-Based Agreements (DBAs): Publication of CJC Recommendations," *CJC News* (September 2, 2015), www.judiciary.gov.uk; Sidley, "U.S. Style Contingency Fees Added to the Menu in England and Wales and Other Key Changes," *News and Insights* (April 2, 2013), www.sidley.com. Lord Justice Jackson had recommended that contingency fees be permitted. *Review of Civil Litigation Costs: Final Report* (2009), pp. 125–33, www.judiciary.gov.uk. In predicting whether England would permit contingency fees in the foreseeable future, Zander said in 2002, "Two years ago, it would have been unthinkable. Today it is a possibility." Zander, "Funding of Civil Litigation in England," p. 297.

[79] *Re Trepca Mines Ltd.* [1963] Ch 199, 3 All E.R. 351 (Court of Appeal) (Lord Denning); *Trendtex Trading Co. v. Crédit-Suisse* [1982] A.C. 679, 3 All E.R. 721, 741 (Court of Appeal) (Lord Denning). The response of current litigation lawyers was cautious and lukewarm. The president of the Forum of Insurers Lawyers, a member of the Civil Justice Council, said that "whether they will be regarded as sufficiently financially attractive to the claimant market remains to be seen." "What Is the Future of DBAs?," *The New Law Journal* (September 11, 2015), p. 4.

[80] Moreover, they said that there was no real difference between permissible CFAs and prohibited contingency fees. Zander, "Funding Civil Litigation," pp. 293–97; Sorabji and Musgrove, "Litigation Cost and Funding," pp. 244–46.

litigants."[81] Lord Justice Steyn said that "protect[ing] the integrity of institutions of government in the broad sense [was] the public policy which renders champertous agreements illegal." He said that the critical question was "whether the agreement had a tendency to corrupt public justice."[82] Citing the views of Lords Mustill and Steyn and reviewing many past decisions regarding lawyers' fees and champerty, Lord Neuberger more recently refused to find an indemnity agreement in a CFA, which was not authorized by statute, champertous. He said that "it would be inappropriate in the 21st century to extend the law of champerty." Further "judicial observations strongly suggest that champerty should be curtailed, not expanded."[83]

These judicial views provided the foundation for consideration of the final development, third-party funding of litigation, which was even more novel and radical than the authorization of contingent fees.[84]

[81] *Giles v. Thompson* [1994] 1 A.C. 142, 153–54, 156, 164 (House of Lords); Andrews, "Abuse of Process," in Andrews, *Civil Procedure*, pp. 404–5.

[82] He stated this objective of this public policy of protection in several ways: "the integrity of public civil justice," "the integrity of the English judicial system," "the integrity of English public justice ... [and] the administration of justices," *Giles v. Thompson* [1993] 3 All E.R. 321, 1993 WL 963259 (Court of Appeal). Many years ago, Danckwerts J. said with regard to champerty and maintenance that public policy should not be "frozen into immutable respectability, so as to be no longer capable of alteration" in view of the changed times. *Martell v. Consett Iron Co., Ltd.* [1954] 3 W.L.R. 648, 658 (Chancery Division). Although he acknowledged the existence of maintenance as a common law misdemeanor and tort, his statement that the statutory tort was abolished in 1881 was inaccurate. Ibid., p. 652. Although 4 Edw. 3, c. 11(1331) was repealed by the Statute Law Revision and Civil Procedure Act 1881, that medieval statute is not the one on which the private actions were based, and that provision was not repealed until the enactment of the Criminal Law Act 1967.

[83] He emphasized that "access to justice is an essential ingredient of a modern civilised society." He quoted a judge in the Trendtex case, who said, "The trend of all recent authorities has been to foreshorten [champerty's] shadow." *Sibthorpe and Morris v. Southwark LBC* [2011] 1 W.L.R. 2111, 2 All E.R. 240 (Court of Appeal). In a 2013 lecture outlining his support for litigation funding, Lord Neuberger discussed the history and current relevance of maintenance and champerty, the public policy regarding litigation funding, and its importance as an effective mechanism for providing "genuine access to the courts" although remaining sensitive to the potentials risks involved. Lord Neuberger, President, Supreme Court, United Kingdom, "From Barretry, Maintenance, and Champerty to Litigation Funding," Harbour Litigation Funding First Annual Lecture (Gray's Inn, May 8, 2013), available at https://www.supremecourt.uk/docs/speech-130508.pdf

[84] Third-party litigation funding has become a major issue in the United States as well and has prompted substantial professional and public discussion. Carol Langford, "Betting on the Client: Alternative Litigation Financing Is an Ethically Risky Proposition for Attorneys and Clients," *University of San Francisco Law Review* 49 (2015), pp. 247–65; W. Bradley Wendel, "Alternative Litigation Finance and Anti-Commodification Norms," *DePaul Law Review* 62 (2014), pp. 655–95; Anthony Sebok, "The Inauthentic Claim," *Vanderbilt Law Review* 64 (2011), pp. 61–139; Ralph Lindeman, "Special Report: Third-Party Investors Offer New

Under such an arrangement, third parties would agree to provide funds to permit litigants to pursue their claims in return for some part of the recovery or other profit.[85] In fact, such a funding trade has emerged during the last decade. The Court of Appeal decision in the Arkin case[86] stimulated the growth of the market in third-party funding, with increased entry by litigation funders and brokers.[87] At first blush, it would seem that such agreements would be champertous and void for public policy. But some initial judicial decisions recognized their benefit in increasing access to justice and seemed to consider them acceptable.[88] Sir Anthony Clarke, Master of the Rolls and Chairman of the Civil Justice Council, said, "I am in principle a supporter of third-party funding, provided that appropriate regulation is put in place."[89]

Funding Source for Major Commercial Lawsuits," *ABA/BNA Lawyers Manual on Professional Conduct* 26 (March 31, 2010), pp. 207–14; "Should You Be Allowed to Invest in a Lawsuit?," *New York Times Magazine* (October 23, 2015), http://nyti.ms/1NVIdoN.

[85] Another motive for financing another person's litigation might be spite or malevolence toward the defendant in the principal case. One commentator reviewed the American law of maintenance and called this "malice maintenance," which he condemned and said was not primarily maintenance and likely actionable under other tort doctrines. Sebok, "The Inauthentic Claim," *Vanderbilt Law Review* 64 (2011), pp. 94–120. A recent American case, in which a billionaire financed another party's law suit against a media firm to retaliate against it for outing him as gay, received significant publicity and prompted discussions of maintenance. Walter Olson, "Champerty and Maintenance Explainer (Gawker/Hogan/Thiel edition)," *Overlawyered*, May 25, 2016, http://overlawyered.com/2016/05/champerty-maintenance-explainer-gawkerhoganthiel-edition/; Eugene Kontorovich, "Peter Thiel's Funding of Hulk Hogan–Gawker Litigation Should Not Raise Concerns," *Volokh Conspiracy*, May 26, 2016, http://overlawyered.com/2016/05/champerty-maintenance-explainer-gawkerhoganthiel-edition/.

[86] *Arkin v. Borchard Lines Ltd* [2005] 1 W.L.R. 3054, 3 All ER 613 (Court of Appeal).

[87] Rachel Mulheron and Peter Cashman, "Third Party Funding: A Changing Landscape," *Civil Justice Quarterly* 27 (2008), p. 312. They described a typical funding agreement in some detail. Ibid., pp. 314–17. A recent study found that more than half of the top 200 United Kingdom law firms used litigation funders. Not all were impecunious claimants, but those who wanted to share the risk of litigation. In this study over 75% of the claims were for £3,000 or less and 8% were for £10,000 or more. "Client Funding Alternatives," *New Law Journal* (September 10, 2010), p. 1202.

[88] *Arkin v. Borchard Lines Ltd* [2005] 1 W.L.R. 3054, 3 All ER 613 (Court of Appeal); *R (Factortame Ltd.) v. Secretary of State for Transport, Local Government and the Regions (No. 8)* [2003] 3 Q.B. 381. The Privy Council expressed similar views in the early twentieth century, stating that "a fair agreement to supply funds in consideration of having a share of the property, if recovered, ought not to be regarded as *per se* opposed to public policy." Bodkin, *The Law of Maintenance and Champerty*, p. 6.

[89] Quoted in Neil Rose, "Drive for Transparency on Third-Party Funding," *Law Gazette* (February 15, 2008), www.law.gazette.co.uk. A royal court on the Channel Island of Jersey held in 2013 that a third-party funding agreement did not violate the Jersey Code of 1771, which said "no person may contract for thing or matters in litigation. The Code had incorporated a 1635 Star Chamber Ordinance that stated, "For avoiding maintenance and champerty, it is thought fit that no man should buy or contract for any debt or other

This "new judicial mood in an era in which access to justice is judicially regarded as being a fundamental right which ought to be readily available to all litigants"[90] has enhanced support for third-party funding of litigation. One proposal recommended that there be "a clear and principled reformulation of [the] rules" on third-party funding, with a "clear demarcation" between what was permissible and what was not. It advocated encouraging third-party funding to the extent that it "advance[d] access to justice without having a detrimental effect on the proper administration of justice" and with a continued role for a "reformulated ... law of maintenance and champerty."[91] As to the latter, it said that the appropriate public policy to guide the law was "the protection of the proper administration of justice."[92] Relying on the increased need for access to justice expressed by the Woolf Reforms and other sources, the writings of Jeremy Bentham, and the European Convention on Human Rights, Article 6, this proposal recommended "an etiolated role for champerty and maintenance."[93] It stated that reformulating the law of maintenance and champerty would permit "the development of alternative methods to finance litigation." Thus, certain agreements directed to achieve this goal would not be void for public policy, although the possibility that other arrangements would be champertous and unenforceable remained. Another study developed a more detailed approach, suggesting the possibility of both self-regulation and externalized regulation through legislative enactment or administrative regulation. It reviewed the existing judicial decisions relevant to champerty and third-party funding as well other applicable legal rules. It concluded that litigation funding was "now an entrenched part of litigation and that a new era ha[d] well and truly dawned." The study found that third-party funding was desirable and recommended that "at the very minimum a code of practice should be introduced" to regulate it. To that end, the authors provided a "draft content" of relevant factors drawn from existing case law.[94] But the law remains unsettled and such agreements still could be challenged and struck down as champertous.

---

things in action. In view of the changes in public policy over time and the court's power to develop customary law, the agreement "would not harm the purity of justice" and would "facilitate the important objective of access to justice" and was not abuse of justice that should preclude the continuation of the litigation. *Barclays Wealth Trustee (Jersey) Ltd and Barclays Wealth Fund Managers (Jersey) v. Equity Trust (Jersey) Ltd. and Equity Trust Services Ltd.* [2013 JRC094, www.jerseylaw.je/judgments/unreportedjudgments/documents/display.aspx?url=2013/13-05-16_Barclays_Wealth-v-Equity_Trust_094.htm. Gratitude is expressed to Nicholas Le Poidevin, QC for sharing this case with me.

[90] Mulheron and Cashman, "Third Party Funding," p. 313.
[91] Sorabji and Musgrove, "Litigation Cost and Funding," pp. 242–43.
[92] Ibid., pp. 237–242.   [93] Ibid., pp. 240–42.
[94] Mulheron and Cashman, "Third Party Funding," pp. 320–41.

It is interesting, and perhaps ironic, that maintenance and champerty, originally the legal remedies for dealing with legal corruption and abuse of legal procedure, became eight centuries later impediments to insuring access to justice by litigants. Given the passage of time and the changes in the legal, social, and economic context, perhaps this modern negative impact should not be surprising. But despite the changes, abusive litigation has not disappeared. It endures and is an international as well as a persistent problem. Current legislators, judges, lawyers, and academics continue to grapple with it. They conceive of and devise new approaches and weapons to deal with these problems.[95] But given the lack of success over many centuries, one wonders whether any society can eliminate the potential for abuse inherent in any litigation system as means to resolve disputes. In the words of the great legal historian Sir William Holdsworth, maintenance "is an offence which in any political society is as ineradicable as larceny and homicide."[96]

---

[95] Michele Tartufffo, ed., *Abuse of Procedural Rights: Comparative Standards of Procedural Fairness* (The Hague, London, and Boston, 1999). This work is the product of the International Association of Procedural Law, International Colloquium.

[96] Holdsworth, *History of English Law*, vol. VIII, p. 398.

Appendix A

Summary of the Research

I. Plea Rolls 1272–1485: Maintenance and Other Abuse of Legal Procedure Cases and Actions

A. 1272–1327

1. Criminal Indictments

a. Conspiracy to maintain	65
b. Other conspiracy and false indict/appeal	81
c. Maintenance	32
d. Ambidexterity	20
e. Champerty	5
f. Other criminal actions	27
Total	230

2. Civil and Other Actions

a. Private conspiracy	68
b. Private champerty	19
c. Private maintenance	0
d. Crown maintenance actions	0
e. Aid/abet false indict/appeal:	0
f. Procure false indict/appeal, civil action	0
g. Other	0
Total	87

Total Cases and Actions, 1272–1327   317

B.   1327–77

1.   Criminal Indictments

a. Conspiracy to maintain	71
b. Other conspiracy and false indict/appeal	241
c. Maintenance	82
d. Ambidexterity	41
f. Champerty	19
g. Other criminal actions	9
Total	463

2.   Civil and Other Actions

a. Private conspiracy	91
b. Aid/abet false indict/appeal	44
c. Private champerty	10
d. Private maintenance	0
e. Crown maintenance actions	0
f. Procure false indict/appeal, civil action	0
g. Other	4
Total	149

Total Cases and Actions, 1327–77   **612**

Total Cases and Actions, 1272–1377   **929**

C.   1377–1485

1.   Criminal Indictments

a. Conspiracy to maintain	13
b. Livery	142
c. Other conspiracy and false indict/appeal	73
d. Maintenance	24
Total	252

2.   Civil Actions

a. Private maintenance	420
c. Private conspiracy	45
d. Private champerty	38
e. Livery	20
Total	523

3.   Other Actions

Crown Maintenance Actions	253
Total Cases and Actions, 1377–1485	**1028**
Total Cases and Actions, 1272–1485	**1957**

Plea Rolls Examined, 1272–1485

Completely	289
Partially	149

Plea Roll Entries

1272–1327	328
1327–1377	561
1377–1485	2304
Total Entries, 1272–1485	3,193

II.   Year Book Cases, 1327–1485

A. Maintenance and champerty	148
B. Conspiracy	104
Total	252

III.   Petitions Regarding Maintenance and Other Abuse of Legal Procedure, 1270-1485

A. Ancient Petitions, TNA: PRO SC 8	245
B. Enrolled Rolls of Parliament, PROME	138
C. Chancery, TNA: PRO C 1	89
Total	472

Appendix B

Livery Statutes, 1377–1485

Statute	Persons	Prohibited Livery	Exceptions: Lawful Livery	Enforcement Procedure	Penalty
1 Rich. II, c. 7 (1377), 2 S.R. pp. 2–3	"People of small income," Lesser landowners, gentry	Chaperons and cloth of one color to any man for maintenance or confederacies	None	Criminal	Imprison, forfeiture to king
Ordinance 3 Rich. II, Jan. 1380 Parliament, XIII, No. 38	NA	NA	NA	Justices of Peace power to enforce 1377 statute	
Ordinance 13 Rich. II, st. 3 (Jan. 1390), 2 S.R. pp. 74–75	(1) Prelates and other men of the holy church, bachelors, esquires, and those of lesser estate; (2) Dukes, earls, barons, and bannerets	(1) Livery of company to anyone; (2) Livery of company to knights, esquires; exceptions; (3) Valets called yeoman archers; exceptions	Bannerets and higher status to knights or esquires retained by life indenture or domestic or household servants, or yeoman archers or of lesser estate, household servants living in household	Criminal	Spiritual and temporal lords expel all maintainers, etc., from fees, robes, all manner of livery and service, company or retinue. All who wear livery of company stop wearing within 10 days. Imprison, fine, ransom as advised by king and his council
16 Rich. II, c. 4 (1393), 2 S.R. p. 84	Yeomen or others of lesser estate than esquires	Use of livery of company of any lord; there are exceptions	If they are domestic or household servants continually dwelling in household	Criminal; Justices of Peace are authorized to inquire and punish	According to discretion of the Justices of the Peace

20 Rich. II, cc. 1–2 (1397), 2 S.R. p. 93	(1) Varlets called yeomen or others of lesser estate than esquires; (2) Uphold Statute 1 Rich. II, c. 7	Use or wearing of sign or livery called livery of company; there are exceptions	If domestic or household servants, or continual officer of his lord	(1) Criminal; authorize Justices of Peace to inquire and punish; (2) Criminal	(1) According to discretion of the Justices of the Peace; (2) Imprison, fine, and ransom to king
1 Hen. IV, c. 7 (1399), 2 S.R. pp. 113–14	(1) Lords of whatever estate; (2) Knights and esquires; (3) Yeomen; (4) Archbishops, bishops, abbots, priors or other men of the holy church, or temporal of whatever estate	(1) Livery of sign of company to knights, esquires, or yeomen; there is an exception for the king; (2) Not wear their liveries in countries or counties where they reside or dwell and in no other place in realm out of the king's presence; (3) Not wear king's or any lord's livery; (4) Livery of cloth to any man; there are exceptions	(1) King to temporal lords who please him, household knights and esquires, knights and esquires retained by annual fee for life; (2) Constable and Marshall may wear the king's livery in their retinues of knights and esquires on the borders and in the marches in time of war; (3) All those who travel beyond sea to seek honor may wear king's livery in those parts; (4) Household; servants, officers, counsel spiritual or temporal learned in one law or the other	Criminal; applicable starting next Candlemas (Feb. 2, 1400)	(1) Fine and ransom at king's will; (2) Lose livery and forfeit fee forever; (3) Imprisonment, fine, and ransom at king's will; (4) Fine and ransom at king's will

(cont.)

Statute	Persons	Prohibited Livery	Exceptions: Lawful Livery	Enforcement Procedure	Penalty
2 Hen. IV, c. 21 (1401), 2 S.R. pp. 129–30	Uphold, confirm, and amend Statute 1 Hen. IV, c. 7 (1399)	Livery of company; Knights and esquires may not use king's livery in counties or country where they reside or dwell	(1) Dukes, earls, barons, and bannerets may use king's livery in their country and elsewhere; knights and esquires may use king's livery in going from and returning to king's house; (2) Prince may give his livery of the swan to his lords and household gentlemen, and lords and household servants of the prince may use the same in the same manner as king's household servants	Criminal; justices of both benches, Justices of Peace and Assize have the power and authority to inquire, hear, and determine by record in their presence or by inquiry from time to time	Fine and ransom at the king's will

7 Hen. IV, c. 14 (1406), 2 S.R. pp. 155–56	(1) Knights or persons of lesser estate; (2) Congregation or company; Statute 1 Hen. IV, c. 7, and Statute 1 Rich. II, c. 7, confirmed and put into execution	(1) Livery of cloth and chaperons by a knight or persons of lesser estate given against the form of those statutes; there are exceptions; (2) Livery of cloth or chaperons may not be made at their cost; there are exceptions	(1) Lords, knights, and esquires may give livery of cloth and chaperons to those who travel in time of war in ways that seem best to them for time such war; (2) Guilds, fraternities, people of crafts of cities and boroughs found or ordained to good intent or purpose	Criminal; *qui tam* actions authorized and half the penalty to person who sues; Justices of assizes given the power to inquire from time to time in their sessions and to certify to King's Bench	(1) Givers pay 100s to king for each livery of cloth or chaperons, recipients pay 40s; no pardon of penalty; (2) Each member congregation or company pays 40s to king
13 Hen. IV, c. 3 (1411), 2 S.R. pp. 167	(1) Statute 1 Hen. IV, c. 7, Statute 7 Hen. IV, c. 14, and Statute 1 Rich. II, c. 7 confirmed	Previous statutes	Previous statutes	Enforce and uphold previous statutes at the special request of Commons	Previous statutes

Statute	Persons	Prohibited Livery	Exceptions: Lawful Livery	Enforcement Procedure	Penalty
8 Hen. VI, c. 4 (1429), 2 S.R. pp. 240–41	(1) Knights or others of lesser estate (2) Statutes extended to counties of Chester and Lancaster; (3) Those who take from spiritual and temporal lords or great ladies; (4) Those who by own authority and cost buy or wear; Enforcement of Statutes 1 Hen. IV, c. 7 (1399), and 7 Hen. IV, c. 14 (1406)	(1) Livery of cloth and chaperons; there are exceptions; (2) Same; (3) Same; (4) Same of any lords, great ladies, knights, esquires, or any other persons for support, aid, maintenance in any quarrel	(1) Knights or others of lesser estate to household servants, officers, men learned in one law or another (1 Hen. IV, c. 7, 1401); the statute does not apply to giving by London mayors and sheriffs, serjeants at law at the time of their creation, entrants to the universities or those who take from them Lords, knights, and esquires give livery cloth and chaperons to soldiers in time of war as seen best and lawful; (2) Same	(1) Criminal, *qui tam* actions, half of the penalty to person suing on behalf of king and half to king; Justices of Assize and Justices of the Peace at the suit of king or a party shall have the power to issue writs of attachment and distress directed to the sheriffs returnable before same justices and a *capias* and exigent against them, if sheriff returns that they have nothing, as in indictments for trespass force and arms, and if they appear, justices have the power to examine and impose penalties on violators found by examination to have acted contrary to the statutes;	(1) Givers pay 100s, recipients pay 40s; (2) Same; (3) Same; (4) Same as (1) and imprison, no bail or mainprise

Article						
Article 1 Edw. IV, Nov. 1461 Parliament, No. 39	(1) Lords or persons of lower estate spiritual or temporal; (2) No man; (3) Lords or persons of lower estate; (4) No man	(1) Any livery of badge, mark, or token of company; exceptions; (2) Wear any badge, mark, or token, any lords or persons of lower estate; (3) Livery of clothing of any lord or person of other estate spiritual or temporal; (4) Take it on himself to wear any livery of clothing of any lords or persons of other estate spiritual or temporal	(1) If specially commanded by king for defense of revolts or riots; wardens of the Scottish marches may give north of Trent if necessary for the defense marches; (2) Those previously excepted; (3) Household and household men, officers, and learned counsellors spiritual and temporal; 4) Those mentioned above	(2) Examination and process, as above, by the justices in those counties; (3) Examined and punished as those who take livery from knights or others of lesser estate, given against the form of prior statutes;(4) Same as (1)	(1) Criminal (2) Same; (3) Same; (4) Same	(1) Contained in statute made on that matter and incur king's great displeasure; (2) Same; (3) Same; (4) Same

Statute	Persons	Prohibited Livery	Exceptions: Lawful Livery	Enforcement Procedure	Penalty
8 Edw. IV, c. 2 (1468), 2 S.R. pp. 426–29	No person whatever estate shall give by himself or any other for him; All prior statutes and ordinances fully observed and kept	Give any livery or badge or retain any person by oath, writing, or promise; exceptions; All prior retaining by indenture or other writing, oath, or promise	Household servant, officer, or man learned in one law or the other; Act not extended to any gift, grant, or confirmation of any fee, annuity, pension, land, etc. by king or any person for counsel and lawful service, and person need not be learned in one law or another; Ordinance not extended to livery given royal coronations, installation of archbishop or bishop, marriages of lord and lady of estate, knights of Bath, commencement, university clerk, creation serjeants at law or by guild, fraternity, mystery corporate, mayor or sheriff of London or chief officer of another city, etc. for executing their office nor to badge for defense king or realm, or given to Constable or Marshal or anyone for giving badge,	Criminal. Any person who sues or complains shall be admitted before king in his Bench and Justices of Common Pleas, Justices of Peace, Justices *Oyer et Terminer*, and Gaol Delivery, justices of palatine courts Lancaster and Durham, justices court Archbishop York and Bishop Durham at justices' discretion to give information for king of any of the foregoing giving and taking of livery against the statute; and every informer shall be admitted to sue for king and himself and against many offenders in one bill or information instead of bill or original writ; the process is to be as in writ trespass against king's peace; if the offender is present, he shall be brought to answer informer's sworn bill or information before justices by oath without	Givers pay 100s for each livery or badge given and 100s for every month the person is retained by him; every person retained by writing, indenture, oath, or promise pays 100s for every month retained; all prior retaining other than permitted exceptions is void

378

livery, or token for feat of arms in realm or to wardens Scottish marches from Trent northward as necessary to levy people for defense of marches

further process; all of the above judges have power to examine defendants on information and convict him on examination or by trial as case requires in their discretion and compensate the complainant for all costs at the discretion of the judges and the complainant have half penalty and king other half and have execution as in debt or trespass; the mayors and chief officers of a city, borough, town, and port have power to hear and determine personal pleas and have power to receive information and hear and determine by examination or trial; the king shall have half the penalty and informer or complainant and city, etc., half; cities, etc. where there is a franchise, liberty, etc. it have king's half; no power to issue exigent by justices palatine Lancaster and Chester, bishop of Durham

BIBLIOGRAPHY

Manuscript Sources

The National Archives: Public Record Office

C 1   Court of Chancery: Six Clerks Office: Early Proceedings, Richard II to Philip and Mary

C 66   Chancery and Supreme Court of Judicature

CP 40   Court of Common Pleas: Plea Rolls

JUST 1 Justices in Eyre, of Assize, of *Oyer et Terminer*, and of the Peace, etc.; Rolls

KB 9   Court of King's Bench: Crown Side: Indictment Files, *Oyer et Terminer* Files and Information Files

KB 27   Court of Kings' Bench: Plea and Crown Sides: *Coram Rege* Rolls

KB 29   Court of King's Bench: Crown Side: Controllment Rolls

KB 146 Court of King's Bench: Plea Side: Panella Files

SC 8   Special Collections: Ancient Petitions

British Library

MS Additional 20,059

MS Additional 31,826

MS Harley 445

MS Harley 748

MS Harley 961

MS Harley 1118

MS Harley 4021

MS Harley 4701

MS Lansdowne 466

Cambridge University Library

MS Additional 3469

MS Additional 3505

MS Additional 6854

MS Ee. 5.22
MS Ff. 5.19
MS Gg. 5.19
MS Hh. 2.11

Bodleian Library, University of Oxford

MS Additional A 107
MS Hatton 28

Harvard Law School

MS 177

Printed Primary Sources

Am. Bar Assoc. Model Rules of Professional Conduct (1983).
Ancient Charters Royal and Private Prior to A.D. 1200, J.H. Round, ed., 10 *Pipe Roll Society* (London, 1888).
Anglo-Norman Political Songs, Isabel Aspin, ed. (Oxford, 1953).
The Anonimalle Chronicle 1333 to 1381, V.H. Galbraith ed., (New York, 1970).
Bacon's History of the Reign of King Henry VII, J. Rawson, ed., (Cambridge, 1885).
Bede, *The Ecclesiastical History of England* (Oxford, 1994).
Blackstone, William, 4 vols., *Commentaries on the Laws of England* (London, 1765–69; facsimile of the first edition, Chicago, 1979).
Bracton de Legibus et Conseutudinibus Angliae, G. Woodbine, ed., and Samuel Thorne, trans., 4 vols. (Cambridge, MA, 1968).
Britton, F. M. Nichols, ed., 2 vols. (Oxford, 1865).*Calendar of Chancery Warrants, A.D. 1244–1326* (London, 1927).
Calendar of Close Rolls, Edward I 1279–1288 (London, 1902).
Calendar of Close Rolls, Edward I, 1302–07 (London, 1908).
Calendar of Close Rolls, Edward II 1318–1323 (London, 1895).
Calendar of Close Rolls, Edward III 1354–1360 (London, 1908).
Calendar of Close Rolls, Henry IV 1399–1402 (London, 1927).
Calendar of Fine Rolls, Edward I. A.D. 1272–1307 (London, 1911).
Calendar of Patent Rolls, Edward I, A.D. 1272–81 (London, 1901).
Calendar of Patent Rolls, Edward I, A.D. 1301–07 (London, 1898).
Calendar of Patent Rolls, Edward III, A.D. 1330–1334 (London, 1893).
Calendar of Patent Rolls, Edward III, A.D. 1343–45 (London, 1902).
Calendar of Patent Rolls, Edward III, A.D. 1345–48 (London, 1902).
Calendar of Patent Rolls, Henry VII 1485–1494 (London, 1914).

Calendars of the Proceedings in Chancery in the Reign of Queen Elizabeth, 2 vols. (London, 1827).

"The Carpenters: The Resurrection" in Richard Beadle, ed., *The York Plays. A Critical Edition of the York Corpus Christi Play as Recorded in British Library*, MS Additional 35290, 2 vols. (Early English Text Society, Supplementary Series 23, Oxford, 2009).

The Charters of the Honour of Mowbray, D.E. Greenway, ed. (London, 1972).

Chrimes, S.B., and Brown, A.L., eds., *Select Documents of English Constitutional History 1307–1485* (London, 1961).

The Complete Works of John Gower, G.C. Macaulay, ed., 4 vols. (Oxford, 1899).

Conventum inter Guillelmum Acquitanorum comitem et Hugonem Chiliarchum, reprinted and translated in Jane Martindale, ed., *Status Authority and Regional Power: Acquitaine and France, 9th to 12th Centuries* (Aldershot, 1997).

Cowell, John, *The Interpreter* (Cambridge, 1637).

Coke, Edward, *The First Part of the Institutes of the Laws of England or a Commentary on Littleton*, 2 vols. (London, 1832).

    The Second Part of the Institutes of the Laws of England (London, 2 vols. (1797; reprint, 1986).

    The Fourth Part of the Institutes of the Laws of England, 2 vols. (London, 1797; reprint, 1986).

Crown Pleas of the Wiltshire Eyre 1249, C.A.F. Meekings, ed. (Devizes, 1961).

De Pace Regis et Regni (London, 1609; reprint, 2007).

Digest of Justinian, Alan Watson, ed., 4 vols. (Philadelphia, 1998).

Dugdale, William, *Monasticon Anglicanum*, 6 vols. (London, 1847).

Early Yorkshire Charters, William Farrer, ed., 12 vols. (Edinburgh, 1914).

English Historical Documents, David Douglas, ed., 3 vols. (London, 1953).

English Historical Documents, David Douglas, ed., 10 vols. (New York, 1969).

The Eyre of Northamptonshire, 3–4 Edward III, A.D. 1329–1330, Donald Sutherland, ed., 2 vols. (London, 1983), Selden Society, vols. 97 and 98.

Fitzhberbert, Anthony, *La Graunde Abridgement* (London, 1577).

    The New Natura Brevium, 9th ed. (Dublin, 1793).

Fleta, G.O. Sayles, ed. and trans., 3 vols. (London, 1953, 1972, 1983), Selden Society, vols. 72, 89,

Foulke Le Fitz Waryn, E.J. Hathaway, P.T. Ricketts, C.A. Robson, and A.D. Wilshere, eds. (Oxford: Anglo-Norman Text Society, 1975).

Hawkins, William, *A Treatise of the Pleas of the Crown*, 5th ed. (London, 1771).

Hoccleve, Thomas, *The Regiment of Princes*, Charles Blythe, ed., METS TEXTS, Teams, Middle English Texts Series, http://d.lib.rochester.edu/teams/text/blyth-hoccleve-regiment-of-princes.

Jacob, Giles, *A New Law Dictionary*, 9th ed. (London, 1772).

Langland, William, *The Vision of Piers Plowman*, A.V.C. Schmidt, ed. (New York, 1978).

Piers Plowman: A Parallel-Text Edition of the A, B, C, and Z Versions, 2nd ed., A.V.C. Schmidt, ed., 3 vols. (Kalamazoo, 2011).

The Law Commission, Proposals for Reform of the Law Relating to Maintenance and Champerty (London, 1966).

Leges Henri Primi, L.J. Downer, ed. (Oxford: Clarendon Press, 1972).

Liber de Antiquis Legibus: Cronica Maiorum et Vicecomitum Londonarium, Thomas Stapleton, ed. Camden Society, original series, 34 (1846; reprint, New York 1968).

The Macro Plays, Mark Eccles, ed. (London, 1969).

Ministry of Justice, *Review of Civil Litigation Costs: Final Report* (2009), pp. 125–33, www.judiciary.gov.uk (Jackson Proposals).

"Mum and the Sothsegger," James Dean, ed., METS TEXTS, Teams, Middle English Texts Series, www.lib.rochester.edu/camelot/teams/richtext.htm.

Munimenta Gildhallae Londoniensis, Henry Riley, ed., 4 vols. (Rolls Series, London, 1860–62).

The National Archives, legislation.gov.uk.

Novae Narrationes, Elsie Shanks and S.F.C. Milsom, eds., Selden Society, vol. 80 (London, 1963).

Parliament Rolls of Medieval England, C. Given-Wilson, Paul Brand, Seymour Phillips, Mark Ormrod, Geoffrey Martin, Anne Curry, and Rosemary Horrox, eds. (online version).

Paston Letters and Papers of the Fifteenth Century, Norman Davis, Richard Beadle, and Colin Richmond, eds., 3 vols. Early English Text Society, Supplementary Series 20–22 (Oxford, 2004–05).

The Poems of William of Shoreham, M. Konrath, ed. Early English Text Society, Extra Series, LXXXVI (London, 1902).

Private Indentures for Life Service in Peace and War 1278–1476, in XXII *Camden Misc.* (5th ser.), Michael Jones and Simon Walker, eds. (London, 1994).

Rastell, William, *A Collection of Entrees* (London, 1670).

Les Termes de la Ley (London, 1721).

Register of Early Writs, Elsa de Haas and G.D.G. Hall, eds. (London, 1970), Selden Society, vol. 87.

Registrum Omnium Brevium tam Originalium quam Judicialium, William Rastell, ed., 3 vols. (London, 1531).

"Richard the Redeless," James Dean, ed., METS TEXTS, Teams, Middle English Texts Series, www.lib.rochester.edu/camelot/teams/richtext.htm.

The Riverside Chaucer, 3rd ed., Larry Benson, ed. (Dallas, 1987).

Rotuli Parliamentorum, 6 vols. (London, 1767).

"Second Shepherd's Play," in A.C. Cawley, ed., in *The Wakefield Pageants in the Towneley Cycle* (Manchester, 1958), pp. 43–63.

Select Cases in Chancery, William Baildon, ed. (London, 1896), Selden Society, vol. 10.

Select Cases in the Council of Henry VII, C.G. Bayne and William Huse Dunham, eds. (London, 1958), Selden Society, vol. 75.

Select Cases in the Court of the King's Bench, G.O. Sayles, ed., 7 vols. (London, 1939), Selden Society, vols. 55, 57, 58, 74, 76, 82, 88.

Selected English Works of John Wyclif, Thomas Arnold, ed., 3 vols. (Oxford, 1871) (republished in Liberty Fund Online).

Smith, Thomas, *De Republica Anglorum* (London, 1583; 1970 ed.).

Solicitors Regulation Authority, *Code of Conduct 2011*.

Statutes of the Realm, A. Luders, T. Tomlins, J. France, W. Tauton, and J. Raithby, eds., 11 vols. (London, 1810–28).

Staunford, William, *Les Plees del Coron* (London, 1567; 1971 ed.).

Surveys of the Estates of Glastonbury Abbey c. 1135–1201, N.E. Stacy, ed. (Oxford, 2001).

The Treatise on the Laws and Customs of the Realm of England Commonly Called Glanvill, G.D.G. Hall, ed. and trans., (Oxford, 1993).

Viner, Charles, *Abridgement*, 2nd ed. (London, 1793).

Secondary Sources

Acheson, Eric, *A Gentry Community: Leicestershire in the Fifteenth Century* (Cambridge, 2003).

Alford, John, "Literature and Law in Medieval England," *PMLA* 92 (1977), pp. 941–51.

  Piers Plowman: A Glossary of Legal Diction (Cambridge, 1988).

  A Companion to Piers Plowman (Berkeley, 1988).

Alford, John, and Seniff, Dennis, *Literature and Law in the Middle Ages* (New York, 1984).

Alford, Ryan Patrick, "The Star Chamber and the Regulation of the Legal Profession," *American Journal of Legal History* 51 (2011), pp. 639–726.

Andrews, Neil, *English Civil Procedure: Fundamentals of the New Civil Justice System* (Oxford, 2003).

  Contract Law (Cambridge, 2011).

Anglo-Norman Dictionary Online.

Avery, Margaret, "The History of the Equitable Jurisdiction of Chancery before 1460," *Bulletin of the Institute of Historical Research* 42 (1969), pp. 129–44.

Baker, J.H., *The Order of Serjeants at Law* (London, 1984).

  "Counsellors and Barristers" in *The Legal Profession and the Common Law* (London, 1986), pp. 99–124.

  "Solicitors and the Law of Maintenance 1590–1640," in *The Legal Profession and the Common Law* (London, 1986), pp. 125–50.

  Introduction to English Legal History, 4th ed. (London, 2002).

  The Oxford History of the Laws of England, vol. VI: *1483–1558* (Oxford, 2003).

"Note: The Inn of the Outer Temple," *Law Quarterly Review* 124 (2008), pp. 384–87.

The Men of Court 1440–1550 2 vols. (London, 2012).

Baldwin, J.F., *The King's Council in England during the Middle Ages* (Gloucester, MA, 1913; reprint, 1965).

Baldwin, William Edward, ed., *Bouvier's Law Dictionary, Baldwin's Edition* (Cleveland, 1934).

Barlow, Frank, *The Feudal Kingdom of England 1042–1216*, 5th ed. (London, 1999).

Barton, J.L., "Equity in Medieval Common Law," in Ralph Newman, ed., *Equity in the World's Legal Systems* (Brussels, 1973), pp. 139–59.

Baxter, Stephen, Karkov, Catherine, Nelson, Janet L., and Pelteret, David, eds., *Early Medieval Studies in Memory of Patrick Wormald* (Farnham, 2009).

"Lordship and Justice in Late Anglo-Saxon England: The Judicial Functions of Soke and Commendation Revisited," in Baxter, Karkov, Nelson, and Pelteret, eds., *Early Medieval Studies*, pp. 389–407.

Bean, J.M.W., *From Lord to Patron* (Pittsburgh, 1989).

Beardwood, Alice, "The Trial of Walter Langton, Bishop of Lichfield, 1307–1313," *Transactions of the American Philosophical Society* 54 (1964), pp. 1–45.

Bellamy, J.G., "The Coterel Gang: An Anatomy of a Band of Fourteenth-Century Criminals," *The English Historical Review*, 79 (1964), pp. 698–717.

"Justice under the Yorkist Kings," *American Journal of Legal History* 9 (1965), pp. 135–55.

Crime and Public Order in England in the Middle Ages (London, 1973).

Criminal Law and Society in Late Medieval and Tudor England (New York, 1984).

Bastard Feudalism and the Law (Portland, 1989), pp. 79–101.

Bennett, Michael, *Richard II and the Revolution of 1399* (Gloucester, 1999).

Black's Law Dictionary, 6th ed. (St. Paul, 1990).

Bodkin, Edmund, *The Law of Maintenance and Champerty and the Lawful Financing of Actions by Solicitors, Legal Aid and Trade Protection Societies and Others* (London, 1934).

Booth, Paul, "The Last Week of the Life of Edward the Black Prince," in Hannah Skoda, Patrick Lantschner, and R.J. Shaw, *Contract and Exchange in Later Medieval Europe: Essays in Honor of Malcolm Vale* (Woodbridge, 2012), pp. 221–45.

"Taxation and Public Order: Cheshire in 1353," *Northern History* 12 (1976), pp. 16–25.

Brand, Paul, "Oldcotes v. d'Arcy," in R.F. Hunnisett and J.B. Post, eds., *Medieval Legal Records Edited in Memory of C. A. F. Meekings* (London, 1978), pp. 64–113.

The Making of the Common Law (London, 1992).

The Origins of the English Legal Profession (Oxford, 1992).

"Ethical Standards for Royal Justices in England, c. 1175–1307," *The University of Chicago Law School Roundtable*, 8 (2001), pp. 250–74.

"Stewards, Bailiffs, and the Emerging Legal Profession," in Ralph Evans, ed., *Lordship and Learning: Studies in Memory of Trevor Austin* (Woodbridge, 2004), pp. 139–53.

Brooks, Christopher, *Pettyfoggers and Vipers of the Commonwealth* (Cambridge, 1986).

Lawyers, Litigation, and English Society since 1450 (London, 1998).

Brundage, James, "Vultures, Whores, and Hypocrites: Images of Lawyers in Medieval Literature," *Roman Legal Tradition* 1 (2002), pp. 56–103.

Bryan, James, *The Development of the English Law of Conspiracy* (Baltimore, 1909).

Burrow, J.A. "Lady Meed and the Power of Money," *Medium Aevum* 74.1 (2005), pp. 113–18.

Cam, Helen, "Studies in the Hundred Rolls: Some Aspects of Thirteenth-Century Administration," in Paul Vinogradoff, ed., *Oxford Studies in Social and Legal History* (1921; reprint, New York, 1974), pp. 1–198.

The Hundred and the Hundred Rolls (London, 1930).

Cameron, A., "The Giving of Livery and Retaining in Henry VII's Reign," *Renaissance and Modern Studies* 18 (1974), pp. 17–35.

Carpenter, Christine, "Law, Justice, and Landowners in Late Medieval England," *Law and History Review* 1 (1983), pp. 205–237.

Locality and Polity: A Study of Warwickshire Landed Society, 1401–1499 (Cambridge, 1992).

The Wars of the Roses: Politics and the Constitution in England, c. 1437–1509 (Cambridge, 1997).

"England: The Nobility and the Gentry," in S.G. Rigby, ed., *A Companion to Britain in the Later Middle Ages* (Oxford, 2003), pp. 261–82.

Carpenter, D.A. "The Second Century of English Feudalism," *Past & Present* 168 (2000), pp. 30–71.

Castor, Helen, *The King, the Crown, and the Duchy of Lancaster* (Oxford, 2000).

Chrimes, S.B., *Henry VII* (Berkeley, 1972).

Clanchy, Michael, "Law and Love in the Middle Ages," in John Bossy, ed., *Disputes and Settlememts: Law and Human Relations in the West* (Cambridge, 1983), pp. 47–67.

Clark, Elaine, "Some Aspects of Social Security in Medieval England, *Journal of Family Law* 7 (1982), pp. 307–20.

Clark, Linda, ed., *Parchment and People: Parliament in the Middle Ages* (Edinburgh, 2004).

Cohen, Herman, *A History of the English Bar and Attornatus to 1450* (London, 1929).

Condon, M.M., "Anachronism with Intent? Henry VII's Council Ordinance of 1491/2," in Ralph Griffiths and James Sherborne, eds., *Kings and Nobles in the Later Middle Ages* (Gloucester, 1986), pp. 228–53.

Coss, Peter, "Bastard Feudalism Revised," *Past & Present,* 125 (1989), pp. 27–64.

Lordship, Knighthood and Locality (Cambridge, 1991).

The Origins of the English Gentry (Cambridge, 2003).

"Hilton, Lordship and the Culture of the Gentry," in Christopher Dyer, Peter Coss, and Chris Wickham, eds., *Rodney Hilton's Middle Ages: An Exploration of Historical Theories,* Past & Present Supplement 2 (Oxford, 2007), pp. 34–52.

Crook, David, "The Later Eyres," *The English Historical Review* 97 (1982), pp. 241–68.

Records of the General Eyre (London, 1982).

"Triers and the Origin of the Grand Jury," *Journal of Legal History* 12 (1991), pp. 103–16.

Crouch, David, "Bastard Feudalism Revised," *Past & Present* 131 (1991), pp. 170–77.

Cunningham, Sean, *Henry VII* (London, 2007).

Davies, R.R., *Lords and Lordship in the British Isles in the Late Middle Ages* (Oxford, 2009).

DeWindt, Edwin, The *Liber Gersumarum* of Ramsey Abbey: A Calendar and Index of B.L. Harley MS 445 (Toronto, 1976).

Dictionary of National Biography (online version).

Dodd, Gwilym, "The Hidden Presence: Parliament and the Private Petition in the Fourteenth Century," in Anthony Musson, ed., *Expectations of Law in the Middle Ages* (Rochester, 2001), pp. 135–49.

"Henry IV's Council, 1399–1406," in Gwilym Dodd and Donald Biggs, eds., *Henry IV: The Establishment of the Regime, 1399–1406* (York, 2003), pp. 95–115.

Justice and Grace: Private Petitioning and English Parliament in the Late Middle Ages (Oxford, 2007).

Dunham, William, *Lord Hastings' Indentured Retainers 1461–1483* (New Haven, 1955).

Dyer, Christopher, *Standards of Living in the Later Middle Ages: Social Change in England, c. 1200–1520* (Cambridge, 1998).

"The Ineffectiveness of Lordship in England, 1200–1400," in Christopher Dyer, Peter Coss, and Chris Wickham, eds., *Rodney Hilton's Middle Ages* (Oxford, 2007).

Elton, Geoffrey, *The Tudor Constitution* (Cambridge, 1972).

Fisher, John, *John Gower, Moral Philosopher and Friend of Chaucer* (New York, 1964).

Fletcher, George, *Loyalty: An Essay on the Morality of Relationships* (Oxford, 1993).

Frye, N.M., "Edward III's Removal of His Ministers and Justices, 1340–1," *Bulletin of the Institute of Historical Research* 48 (1975), pp. 149–61.

Galloway, Andrew, "Piers Plowman and the Subject of the Law," *Yearbook of Langland Studies* 15 (2001), pp. 117–28.

Ganshof, F.L., *Feudalism*, 3rd ed. (Northampton, 1964).

Giancarlo, Matthew, *Parliament and Literature* (Cambridge, 2007).

Gibson, Gail, "Doodles and Dragons," in Folger Shakespeare Library, *The Collation: Research and Exploration at the Folger* (November 12, 2015), http://collation.folger.edu/2015/11/doodles-and-dragons/.

Given-Wilson, Chris, *The Royal Household and the King's Affinity* (New Haven, 1986).

The English Nobility in the Late Middle Ages (London, 1996).

Henry IV (New Haven, 2016).

Goldberg, P.J.P., *Medieval England: A Social History 1250–1500* (London, 2004).

Gorski, Richard, *The Fourteenth-Century Sheriff* (Woodbridge, 2003)

Green, Richard Firth, *A Crisis of Truth: Literature and Law in Ricardian England* (Philadelphia, 1998).

"Medieval Literature and Law," in David Wallace, ed., *The Cambridge History of Medieval Literature* (Cambridge, 2002), pp. 410–31.

Griffiths, Ralph, *The Reign of King Henry VI* (Gloucester, 1981; 1998 ed.).

King and Country: England and Wales in the Fifteenth Century (London, 1991).

The Reign of King Henry VI, 2nd ed. (Stroud, 1998).

Guy, J.A., "The Development of Equitable Jurisdiction," in E.W. Ives and A.H. Manchester, eds., *Law, Litigants, and the Legal Profession* (London, 1979), pp. 80–86.

Hanawalt, Barbara, *The Ties That Bound* (New York, 1986).

Hanna, Ralph, *London Literature, 1300–1380* (Cambridge, 2005).

Happe, Peter, *Cyclic Form and the English Mystery Plays: A Comparative Study of the English Biblical Cycles and Their Continental and Iconographic Counterparts* (New York, 2004).

Harriss, Gerald, The Dimensions of Politics," in R.H. Britnell and A.J. Pollard, eds., *The McFarlane Legacy: Studies in Late Medieval Politics and Society* (New York, 1995), pp. 1–20.

Shaping the Nation (Oxford, 2005).

ed., *K.B. McFarlane: Letters to Friends 1940–1966* (Oxford, 1997).

Harding, Alan, *The Law Courts of Medieval England* (London, 1973).

"Plaints and Bills," in Daffyd Jenkins, ed., *Legal History Studies 1972* (Cardiff, 1975), pp. 65–86.

"The Origins of the Crime of Conspiracy," *Transactions of the Royal Historical Society* (5th Ser.), 33 (1983), pp. 89–108.

England in the Thirteenth Century (Cambridge, 1993).

Medieval Law and the Foundations of the State (Oxford, 2002).

Hector, L.C., and Harvey, Barbara, eds., *The Westminster Chronicle 1381–1394* (Oxford, 1982).

Heffernan, Thomas, "A Middle English Poem on Lovedays," *Chaucer Review* 10 (1975), pp. 172–85.

Helmholz, Richard, *The Oxford History of the Laws of England*, vol. I: *The Canon Law and Ecclesiastical Jurisdiction from 597 to the 1640s* (Oxford, 2004).

Hicks, Michael, *Bastard Feudalism* (London, 1995).

"The 1468 Statute of Livery," *Historical Research* 64 (1991), pp. 15–28.

Hilton, R.H. *The English Peasantry in the Later Middle Ages* (Oxford, 1975).

Holdsworth, W.S., *A History of English Law*, 17 vols. (London, 1936–66).

Holmes, G.A., *The Estates of the Higher Nobility in Late Medieval England* (Manchester, 1917).

"Judgement of the Younger Despenser, 1326," *English Historical Review* 70 (1955), pp. 261–67.

The Good Parliament (Oxford, 1975).

Horner, Olga, "'Us must make lies': Witness, Evidence and Proof in the York Resurrection," *Medieval English Theatre* 20 (1998), pp. 24–76.

Horrox, Rosemary, "Urban Patronage and Patrons in the Fifteenth Century," in Ralph Griffiths, ed., *Patronage, the Crown and the Provinces in Later Medieval England* (Gloucester, 1981), pp. 156–61.

Richard III: A Study in Service (Cambridge, 1986).

"The Urban Gentry in the Fifteenth Century," in J.A.F. Thomson, ed., *Towns and Townspeople in the Fifteenth Century* (Gloucester, 1988), pp. 22–44.

Fifteenth-Century Attitudes (Cambridge, 1994).

Hudson, John, *Land, Law, and Lordship in Anglo-Norman England* (Oxford, 1997).

The Oxford History of the Laws of England, vol. II: *871–1216* (Oxford, 2012).

Hunter, Linsey, "Charter Diplomatics and Norms of Landholding and Lordship between the Humber and Forth, c.1066-c.1250," unpublished PhD thesis, University of St. Andrews (2012).

Hyams, Paul, "Warranty and Good Lordship in Twelfth Century England," *Law and History Review* 5 (1987), pp. 437–503.

Rancor and Reconciliation (Ithaca, 2003).

"Thinking English Law in French: The Angevins and the Common Law," in Belle Tuten, ed., *Feud, Violence and Practise: Essays in Medieval Studies in Honor of Stephen D. White* (Burlington, VT, 2010).

Ives, Eric, *The Common Lawyers of Pre-Reformation England: Thomas Kebell: A Case Study* (Cambridge, 1983).

James, Mark, "The End of Champerty?," *The New Law Journal* (April 15 and 22, 2011), pp. 547–48.

John, Eric, *Orbis Britanniae and Other Studies* (Leicester, 1966).

Johnston, Michael, *Romance and Gentry in Late Medieval England* (Oxford, 2014).

Jolliffe, J.E.A., *The Constitutional History of Medieval England from the English Settlements to 1485* (London, 1961).

Kaeuper, Richard, "Law and Order in Fourteenth-Century England: The Evidence of Special Commissions of Oyer and Terminer," *Speculum* 54 (1979), pp. 734–84.

Kaye, J.M., *Medieval English Conveyances* (Cambridge, 2010).

Keen, Maurice, *English Society in the Later Middle Ages* (Middlesex, 1990).
   The Origins of the English Gentleman (Stroud, 2002).

Kendall, Elliot, *Lordship and Literature: John Gower and the Politics of the Great Household* (Oxford, 2008).

Kennedy, Kathleen, "Maintaining Injustice: Literary Representations of the Legal System c. 1400," unpublished PhD thesis, Ohio State University (2004).
   "Retaining Men (and a Retaining Woman) in Piers Plowman," *Yearbook of Langland Studies* 20 (2006), pp. 191–214.
   Maintenance, Meed, and Marriage (New York, 2009).

King, Pamela, "Morality Plays," in Richard Beadle and Alan Fletcher, eds., *The Cambridge Companion to Medieval English Theatre*, 2nd ed. (Cambridge, 2008), pp. 247–52.

Kirby, J.L., *Henry IV of England* (London, 1970).

Kleineke, Hannes, *The Chancery Case between Nicholas Radford and Thomas Tremayne: The Exeter Depositions of 1439*, 55 Devon and Cornwall Record Society, New Series (Exeter 2013).

Kontorovich, Eugene, "Peter Thiel's Funding of Hulk Hogan-Gawker Litigation Should Not Raise Concerns," *Volokh Conspiracy*, May 26, 2016, http://overlawyered .com/2016/05/champerty-maintenance-explainer-gawkerhoganthiel-edition/.

Lachaud, Frederique, "Liveries of Robes in England, c. 1200–c. 1330," *English Historical Review* 111 (1996), pp. 279–98.

Lambert, T.B., and Rollason, David, eds., *Peace and Protection in the Middle Ages* (Toronto: Pontifical Institute for Medieval Studies, 2009).

Lancaster, Lorraine, "Kinship in Anglo-Saxon Society (7th Century to Early 11th)," in Sylvia Thrupp, ed., *Early Medieval Society* (New York, 1967).

Lander, J.R., "Family, 'Friends' and Politics in Fifteenth-Century England," in Ralph Griffiths and James Sherborne, *Kings and Nobles in the Later Middle Ages: A Tribute to Charles Ross* (Gloucester, 1986), pp. 27–40.

Langbein, John, Lettow, Rene Lerner, and Smith, Bruce, *History of the Common Law: The Development of Anglo-American Legal Institutions* (New York, 2009).

Langford, Carol, "Betting on the Client: Alternative Litigation Financing Is an Ethically Risky Proposition for Attorneys and Clients," *University of San Francisco Law Review* 49 (2015), pp. 247–65.

Latham, R.E., *Revised Medieval Latin Word-List* (Oxford, 1980).

Lewis, N.B., "The Organisation of Indentured Retinues in Fourteenth-Century England," *Transactions of the Royal Historical Society* (4th Ser.), 27 (1945), pp. 29–39.

Leyser, Karl, "Kenneth Bruce McFarlane: A Memoir," in Gerald Harriss, ed., *K.B. McFarlane, Letters to Friends, 1940-1966* (Magdalen College, Oxford, 1997).

Lindeman, Ralph, "Special Report: Third-Party Investors Offer New Funding Source for Major Commercial Lawsuits," *ABA/BNA Lawyers Manual on Professional Conduct* 26 (March 31, 2010), pp. 207-14.

Luckett, Dominic, "Crown Office and Licensed Retinues in the Reign of Henry VII," in Rowena Archer and Simon Walker, eds., *Rulers and Ruled in Late Medieval England: Essays Presented to Gerald Harriss* (London, 1995), pp. 223-38.

McFarlane, K.B., Lectures, "Lords and Retainers," unpublished manuscript in the Magdalen College Archives, University of Oxford. These lectures were delivered in 1966 and are a revision of lectures given in a 1959 course.

The Nobility of Later Medieval England: The Ford Lectures for 1953 and Related Studies (Oxford, 1973).

England in the Fifteenth Century: Collected Essays (London, 1981).

McIntosh, Marjorie, *Autonomy and Community: The Royal Manor of Havering, 1200-1500* (Cambridge, 1986).

McKelvie, Gordon, "The Livery Statute of 1429," in Linda Clark, ed., *The Fifteenth Century* (Woodbridge, 2015), vol. XIV, pp. 55-65.

Maddern, Phillippa, "Honour among the Pastons: Gender and Integrity in Fifteenth-Century English Provincial Society," *Journal of Medieval History* 14 (1988), pp. 357-71.

Violence and Social Order: East Anglia 1422-1442 (Oxford, 1992).

Maddicott, J.R. "The County Community and the Making of Public Opinion in Fourteenth Century England," *Transactions of the Royal Historical Society* (5th Ser.), 28 (1978), pp. 27-43.

Law and Lordship: Royal Justices as Retainers in Thirteenth- and Fourteenth-Century England, Past & Present, Supp. (1978).

"Parliament and the Constituencies 1272-1377," in R.G. Davies and J.H. Denton, eds., *The English Parliament in the Middle Ages* (Manchester, 1981).

"Poems of Social Protest in Early Fourteenth-Century England," in W.M. Ormrod, ed., *England in the Fourteenth Century: Proceedings of the 1985 Harlaxton Symposium* (Bury St. Edmunds, 1986), pp. 130-44.

Marshall, John, "'Fortune in the Worldys Worschyppe': The Satirising of the Suffolks in *Wisdom*," *Medieval English Theatre* 14 (1992), pp. 37-66.

Markesinis, B.S., and Deakin, S.F., *Tort Law*, 4th ed. (Oxford, 1999).

Martindale, Jane, "*Conventum inter Gullelmum Acquitanorum comitem et Hugonem Chiliarchum*," *The English Historical Review* 84 (1969), pp. 528-48.

Middleton, Anne, "The Audience and Public of 'Piers Plowman,'" in David Lawton, ed., *Middle English Alliterature Poetry and Its Literary Background* (Bury St. Edmunds, 1982), pp. 101-23.

Miller, William, *Bloodtaking and Peacemaking: Feud, Law and Society in Saga Iceland* (Chicago, 1990).

Milsom, S.F.C., *The Legal Framework of English Feudalism* (Cambridge, 1976).

Morgan, Gerald, "The Status and Meaning of Meed in the First Version of Piers Plowman," *Neophilologus* 72.3 (1988), pp. 449–63.

Mulheron, Rachel, and Cashman, Peter, "Third Party Funding: A Changing Landscape," *Civil Justice Quarterly* 27 (2008), pp. 312–41.

Murphy, J., "Capacity of Parties," in *Clerk and Lindsell on Torts*, 21st ed. (London, 2014), sections 5-66 to 5-67, pp. 350–51.

Musson, Anthony, *Public Order and Law Enforcement: The Local Administration of Criminal Justice, 1294–1350* (Woodbridge, 1996).

Musson, Anthony, and Ormrod, W. Mark, *The Evolution of English Justice* (Basingstoke, 1999).

Myers, Alec, "Parliamentary Petitions in the Fifteenth Century. Part I: Petitions from Individuals and Groups," *The English Historical Review* 52 (1937), pp. 385–404.
  "Parliamentary Petitions in the Fifteenth Century. Part II: Petitions of the Commons and Commons Petitions," *The English Historical Review* 52 (1937), pp. 590–613.

Neuberger, [David Edmond], Lord Neuberger, "Barretry, Maintenance, and Champerty to Litigation Funding," Harbour Litigation Funding, First Annual Lecture (Gray's Inn, May 8, 2013), available at https://www.supremecourt/uk/docs/speech-13058.pdf.

Nightingale, Pamela, "The Intervention of the Crown and the Effectiveness of the Sheriff in the Execution of Judicial Writs, c. 1355–1530," *English Historical Review*, 123 (2008), pp. 1–34.

Nisse, Ruth, *Defining Acts: Drama and the Politics of Interpretation in Late Medieval England* (Notre Dame, 2005).

O'Brien, Bruce, "Authority and Community," in Julia Crick and Elisabeth Van Houts, eds., *A Social History of England 900–1200* (Cambridge, 2011), pp. 76–97.

Olson, Walter, "Champerty and Maintenance Explainer" (Gawker/Hogan/Thiel edition)", *Overlawyered*, May 25, 2016, http://overlawyered.com/2016/05/champerty-maintenance-explainer-gawkerhoganthiel-edition/.

Ormrod, W.M., Dodd, Gwilym, and Musson, Anthony, "Agenda for Legislation, 1322–c. 1340," *The English Historical Review* 105 (1990), pp. 1–33.
  The Reign of Edward III: Crown and Political Society in England 1327–1377 (New Haven, 1990).
  eds., *Medieval Peititions: Grace and Grievance* (York, 2009).
  Edward III (New Haven, 2011).

Ostrom, Theresa, "'And He Honoured Þat Hit Hade Euermore After': The Influence of Richard II's Livery System on Sir Gawain and the Green Knight," unpublished Master's thesis, University of Florida (May, 2003).

Oxford English Dictionary Online.

Owst, G.R., *Preaching in Medieval England: An Introduction to Sermon Manu-scripts of the Period c. 1350-1450* (New York, 1965).

Literature and Pulpit in Medieval England (New York, 1966).

Palmer, Robert, "The Feudal Framework of English Law," *Michigan Law Review* 79 (1980–81), pp. 1130–64.

The County Courts of Medieval England 1150-1350 (Princeton, 1982).

"The Origins of Property," *Law and History Review* 3 (1985), pp. 1–50.

"England: Law, Society and the State," in S.G. Rigby, ed., *A Companion to Britain in the Later Middle Ages* (Oxford, 2003), pp. 242–60.

"The Social Status of Litigants in the Court of Common Pleas: 1465," http://aalt.law.uh.edu/ELHOv/Status.html.

"Volume of Litigation," *AALT, A Statistical Overview of English Legal History*, http://aalt.law.uh.edu/ELHOv/Enrollments.html.

Payling, Simon, *Political Society in Lancastrian England: The Greater Gentry of Nottinghamshire* (Oxford, 1991).

Perruso, Richard, "The *Iuramentum Perhorrescentiae* under Canon Law: An Influ-ence on the Development of Early Chancery Jurisdiction," *Comparative Legal History* 3 (2014), pp. 2–37.

Phelan, Amy, "A Study of the First Trailbaston Proceedings in England, 1304-7," unpublished PhD thesis, Cornell University (1997).

Pike, Luke, *History of Crime in England*, 2 vols. (London, 1873–76; reprint, 1983).

Plucknett, T.F.T., *Statutes and Their Interpretation in the First Half of the Four-teenth Century* (London, 1922).

Edward I and Criminal Law (Cambridge, 1960).

Pollard, A.J., *Late Medieval England 1399-1509* (Harlow, 2000).

Pollock, Frederick, and Maitland, Frederic William, *The History of English Law before the Time of Edward I*, 2 vols. (Cambridge, 1968).

Post, J.B. "Equitable Resorts before 1450," in E.W. Ives and A.H. Manchester, eds., *Law, Litigants, and the Legal Profession* (London, 1979), pp. 68–79.

Postles, David, "Gifts in Frankalmoign, Warranty of Land, and Feudal Society," *Cambridge Law Journal* 50 (1991), pp. 330–46.

"Seeking the Language of Warranty in Twelfth-Century England," *Journal of the Society of Archivists* 20 (1999), pp. 209–22.

Powell, Edward, *Kingship, Law and Society: Criminal Justice in the Reign of Henry V* (Oxford, 1989).

"Law and Justice," in *Fifteenth-Century Attitudes*, ed. Rosemary Horrox (Cambridge, 1994), pp. 29–41.

Prestwich, Michael, *Plantagenet England 1225-1360* (Oxford, 2005).

Pronay, Nicholas, "The Chancellor, the Chancery, and the Council at the End of the Fifteenth Century," in H. Hearder and H.R. Loyn, eds., *British Govern-ment and Administration, Studies Presented to S.B. Chrimes* (Cardiff, 1974), pp. 87–103.

Raftis, J., *Ambrose, Tenure and Mobility* (Toronto, 1964).

Reynolds, Susan, *Fiefs and Vassals* (Oxford, 1994).

Richardson, H.G., and Sayles, G.O., "Parliaments and Great Councils in Medieval England – I," *Law Quarterly Review* 77 (1961), pp. 1–49.

Richmond, Colin, "Elizabeth Clere: Friend of the Pastons," in Jocelyn Wogan-Browne, Rosalynn Voaden, Arlyn Diamond, Ann Hutchison, Carol Meale, and Leslie Johnson, eds., *Medieval Women: Texts and Contexts in Late Medieval Britain: Essays for Felicity Riddy* (Brepols, 2000), 259–73.

The Paston Family in the Fifteenth Century: Endings (Manchester, 2000).

Rigby, S.H., *English Society in the Later Middle Ages* (London, 1995).

Robbins, Rossell Hope, *Historical Poems of the XIVth and XVth Centuries* (New York, 1959).

Roskell, J.S., Clark, Linda, and Rawcliffe, Carole, eds., *The History of Parliament: the House of Commons 1386–1421*, 4 vols. (Stroud, 1992).

Rose, Jonathan, "The Legal Profession in Medieval England: A History of Regulation," *Syracuse Law Review* 48 (1998), pp. 1–137.

"Of Ambidexters and Daffidowndillies: Defamation of Lawyers, Legal Ethics and Professional Reputation," *The University of Chicago Law School Roundtable* 8 (2001), pp. 423–66.

"Litigation and Political Conflict in Fifteenth-Century East Anglia: Conspiracy and Attaint Actions and Sir John Fastolf," *Journal of Legal History* 27 (2006), pp. 53–80.

"The Law of Maintenance and The Obligations of Lordship: A Case Study," in Per Andersen, Kirsi Salonen, Helle Møller Sigh, and Helle Vogt, eds., *Law and Disputing in the Middle Ages. Proceedings of the Ninth Carlsberg Academy Conference on Medieval Legal History 2012* (Copenhagen, 2013), pp. 111–21.

Rose, Neil, "Drive for Transparency on Third-Party Funding," *Law Gazette* (February 15, 2008), www.law.gazette.co.uk.

Ross, Charles, *Edward IV* (Berkeley, CA, 1974).

Rowney, Ian, "Resources and Retaining in Yorkist England: William, Lord Hastings and the Honour of Tutbury," in Tony Pollard, ed., *Property and Politics: Essays in Later Medieval History* (New York, 1984), pp. 139–55.

Sainty, John, *A List of English Law Officers, King's Counsel and Holders of Patents of Precedence* (London, 1987).

The Judges of England 1272–1990 (London, 1993).

Saul, Nigel, "The Commons and the Abolition of Badges," *Parliamentary History* 9 (1990), pp. 302–15.

Richard II (New Haven, 1997).

Sayles, G.O., "Introduction, XI, Conspiracy and Allied Offenses," in *Select Cases in the Court of the King's Bench* (London, 1939), vol. III, 58 Selden Society.

The Dissolution of a Gild at York in 1306," *English Historical Review* 55 (1940), pp. 83–98.

The Medieval Foundations of England, 2nd ed. (London, 1950).

Scase, Wendy, *Literature and Complaint in England, 1272–1553* (Oxford, 2007).

Sebok, Anthony, "The Inauthentic Claim," *Vanderbilt Law Review* 64 (2011), pp. 61–139.

Seipp, David, "Jurors, Evidences and the Tempest of 1499," in John Cairns and Grant McLeod, eds., *The Dearest Birth Right of the People of England: The Jury in the History of the Common Law* (Oxford, 2002), pp. 75–92.

"Patterns and Problems in Fifteenth-Century Litigation: A View from the Year Books," paper presented at the American Society for Legal History Annual Conference, Austin, TX, 2004.

Sheehan, Michael, *The Will in Medieval England* (Toronto, 1963).

"Should You Be Allowed to Invest in a Lawsuit?," *New York Times Magazine* (October 23, 2015), http://nyti.ms/1NVIdoN.

Smith, D. Vance, "The Labors of Reward: Meed, Mercede, and the Beginning of Salvation," *Yearbook of Langland Studies* 8 (1995), pp. 127–54.

Smith, R.M., "The Manorial Court and the Elderly Tenant in Late Medieval England," in Margaret Pelling and Richard Smith, eds., *Life, Death, and the Elderly: Historical Perspectives* (London, 1991), pp. 33–61.

Sorabji, John, and Musgrove, Robert, "Litigation Cost, Funding, and the Future," in Déidre Dwyer, ed., *The Civil Procedure Rules: Ten Years On* (Oxford, 2010), pp. 229–46.

Spence, George, *The Equitable Jurisdiction of the Court of Chancery*, 2 vols. (London, 1846).

Stenton, Frank, *Documents Illustrative of the Social and Economic History of the Danelaw* (London, 1920).

The First Century of English Feudalism 1066–1166 (Oxford, 1932).

Anglo-Saxon England, 3rd ed. (Oxford, 1971).

Stephen, Henry John, *New Commentaries on the Laws of England*, 21st ed., 4 vols. (1841–45) (London, 1950).

Stephen, James Fitzjames, *A History of the Criminal Law of England*, 3 vols. (London, 1883).

Stevens, Matthew, "Failed Arbitrations before the Court of Common Pleas: Cases Relating to London and Londoners, 1400–1468," *Journal of Legal History* 31 (2010), pp. 21–44.

Stones, E.L.G., "The Folvilles of Ashby-Folville, Leicestershire and Their Associates in Crime, 1326–1347," *Transactions of the Royal Historical Society*, Fifth Series, 7 (1957), pp. 117–36.

Storey, R.L., *The End of the House of Lancaster* (Guildford, 1966).

"Liveries and Commissions of the Peace, 1388–90," in Caroline Barron and F.R.H. Du Boulay, *The Reign of Richard II* (London, 1971), pp. 131–52.

"Gentleman-Bureaucrats," in Cecil Clough, ed., *Profession, Vocation, and Culture in Later Medieval England* (Liverpool, 1982), pp. 90–129.

Strohm, Paul, *Social Chaucer* (Cambridge, MA, 1989).

Hochon's Arrow: The Social Imagination of Fourteenth-Century Texts (Princeton, 1992).

Stubbs, William, *Constitutional History of England*, 3 vols. (Oxford, 1897; reprint, 1967).

Tartufffo, Michele, ed., *Abuse of Procedural Rights: Comparative Standards of Procedural Fairness* (The Hague, London, and Boston, 1999).

Tatlock, John, and Kennedy, Arthur, *A Concordance to the Complete Works of Geoffrey Chaucer* (Gloucester, MA, 1963).

Thrupp, Sylvia, *The Merchant Class of Medieval London, 1300–1500* (Chicago, 1964).

Tierney, Brian, *Medieval Poor Law: A Sketch of Canonical Theory and Its Application in England* (Berkeley, 1959).

Tout, T.F., and Johnstone, Hilda, *State Trials of the Reign of Edward the First 1289–1293* (London, 1906).

Treitel, Guenter, *The Law of Contract*, 11th ed. (London, 2003).

Tuck, J.A., "The Cambridge Parliament 1388," *The English Historical Review*, 84 (1968), pp. 225–43.

Richard II and the English Nobility (London, 1973).

Tucker, P. "The Early History of the Court of Chancery: A Comparative Study," *The English Historical Review* 115 (2000), pp. 791–811.

van Dijk, Conrad, *John Gower and the Limits of Law* (Woodbridge, 2013).

Virgoe, Roger, "The Crown, Magnates, and Local Government in Fifteenth-Century East Anglia," in J.R.L. Highfield and Robin Jeffs, eds., *The Crown and Local Communities in England and France in the Fifteenth Century* (Gloucester, 1981), pp. 72–87.

Walker, Simon, *The Lancastrian Affinity 1361–1399* (Oxford, 1990).

Political Culture in Later Medieval England (Manchester, 2006).

Ward, Matthew, "The Livery Collar: Politics and Identity during the Fifteenth Century," in Linda Clark, ed., *The Fifteenth Century XIII: Exploring the Evidence: Commemoration, Administration, and the Economy* (Woodbridge, 2014), pp. 41–61.

Watts, John, *Henry VI and the Politics of Kingship* (Cambridge, 1996).

Waugh, Scott, "Tenure to Contract: Lordship and Clientage in Thirteenth-Century England," *The English Historical Review* 101 (1986), pp. 811–39.

England in the Reign of Edward III (Cambridge, 1991).

"The Third Century of English Feudalism," in Michael Prestwich, Richard Britnell, and Robin Frame, eds., *Thirteenth Century England VII* (Woodbridge, 1999), pp. 47–60.

"Book Review of Coss, Origins," *American Historical Review* 109 (2004), pp. 1623–24.

Wendel, W. Bradley, "Alternative Litigation Finance and Anti-Commodification Norms," *DePaul Law Review* 62 (2014), pp. 655–95.

Wenzel, Siegfried, *Latin Sermon Collections from Later Medieval England: Orthodox Preaching in the Age of Wyclif* (Cambridge, 2009), pp. 66–73.

Wetherbee, Winthrop, "John Gower," in David Wallace, ed., *The Cambridge History of Medieval Literature* (Cambridge, 2002), pp. 589–609.

"What Is the Future of DBAs?," *The New Law Journal* (September 11, 2015), p. 4.

White, Stephen D., "'*Pactum ... Legem Vincit et Amor Judicium*': The Settlement of Disputes by Compromise in Eleventh-Century Western France," *American Journal of Legal History* 22 (1979), pp. 291–309.

"Kinship and Lordship in Early Medieval England: The Story of Sigeberht, Cynewulf, and Cyneheard," *Viator* 20 (1989), pp. 1–18.

"Maitland on Family and Kinship," in John Hudson, ed., *The History of English Law: Centenary Essays on Pollock and Maitland*' (Oxford, 1996).

Re-thinking Kinship and Feudalism in Early Modern Europe (Aldershot, 2005).

"Protection, Warranty, and Vengeance in La Chanson de Roland," in Lambert and Rollason, *Peace and Protection* (2009), pp. 155–67.

Whittick, Christopher, "The Role of the Criminal Appeal in the Fifteenth Century," in J.A. Guy and H.G. Neale, *Law and Social Change in British History* (London, 1981), pp. 55–72.

Wickert, Maria, *Studies in John Gower*, trans. Robert Meindl (Washingon, DC, 1981).

Winfield, P.H., *The History of Conspiracy and Abuse of Legal Procedure* (Cambridge, 1921).

The Present Law of Abuse of Legal Procedure (Cambridge, 1921).

Wood-Legh, K.L., "Sheriffs, Lawyers, and Belted Knights in the Parliaments of Edward III," *English Historical Review* 46 (1931), pp. 372–88.

Worby, Sam, *Law and Kinship in Thirteenth Century England* (Woodbridge, 2010).

Wright, R.S., *Law of Criminal Conspiracies and Agreements* (London, 1873).

Wright, Susan, *The Derbyshire Gentry in the Fifteenth Century* (Chesterfield, 1983).

Wright, Thomas, *Political Songs of England* (London: Camden Society, 1839).

Political Poems and Songs Relating to English History, Composed during the Period from the Accession of Edw. III. to That of Ric. III., 2 vols. (London, 1861).

Yunck, John, *The Lineage of Lady Meed: The Development of Medieval Venality Satire* (Notre Dame, 1963).

Zander, Michael, "Will the Revolution in the Funding of Civil Litigation in England Eventually Lead to Contingency Fees?," *De Paul Law Review* 52 (2002), pp. 259–97.

INDEX

abuse of legal procedure
  bribery as a form of, 30, 104–06
  champerty, as a form of, 33
  conspiracy, as a form of, 43–44, 49,
    147
  development of legal norms
    regarding, 30, 33
  maintenance as a form of, 4
  medieval forms summarized, 346–47
  other forms of, 103–06
  petitioning for remedies for, 53–64,
    70, 106–10
  statutes directed at, 30–52, 95–105,
    195–204
abuse of power
  as objective of maintenance statutes,
    12, 30, 316–19
  petitions directed at, 11–12, 53–64,
    106–10, 195–206
advowson, 37, 40, 110, 123, 231, 317
allegory, in medieval literature,
    179–80
ambidexterity
  lawyers and, 68–71, 75–76, 78, 91,
    133, 134–35, 341
  in litigation, 65–66, 68–69, 70–79,
    82, 91, 94, 104, 111–14, 116,
    129, 133–39, 219
Andrew, John, 337–39
Anglo-Saxon period
  conspiracy roots during, 43
  kinship during, 14
  livery during, 268
  lordship during, 17–19, 209
  maintenance during, 7
Arbitration, 82, 137, 214, 216, 219, 224,
    314, 330, 340, 345

Articles of the Eyre, 32–34, 44–46, 52,
    65, 75, 92–93
Articuli super Cartas, 9, 42–43, 47–48, 60
  civil litigation under, 65, 80, 86–91,
    145–46, 147, 185
assignment of choses in action, 358, 360
Athenian law, maintenance in, 4–5
audita querela, writ of, 42, 87–91,
    145–47, 347

Babington, William (CJCB), 184, 186,
    233, 236, 246
badges as livery, 161, 192–93, 269, 271,
    274–77, 279–80, 282, 287,
    290–92, 295, 298
Baldock, Robert (chancellor), 96, 107–08
barratry and barrators, 10, 101, 154,
    159, 327–28
bastard feudalism, 6, 128, 207–13
Beauchamp, Cecily de, 41, 60, 63
Beauchamp, Joan, 249–50
Bentham, Jeremy, 357, 365
Bereford, Sir William (CJCP), 39, 84
Blackstone, William, 2, 3, 4, 10–11,
    236
Blount, Walter, 298–99, 305
bribery, 30, 31, 40, 151, 154, 157,
    166–67, 173, 194, 219
  Edward III statutes, 104–06, 317–19
  as illegal maintenance, 249–53
  of jurors, 3, 104–05, 137, 186,
    249–52
  of sheriffs, 252–53
  writ of *decies tantum*, 105, 251, 331,
    332, 333, 334, 335, 342
Brompton, William of (JCP), 36–37
Bromyard, John, 169–74

52
in forma pagins

Lightning Source UK Ltd.
Milton Keynes UK
UKHW021105111218
333796UK00009B/140/P

9 781107 619791